Politics, Democracy, and E-Government:
Participation and Service Delivery

Christopher G. Reddick
The University of Texas at San Antonio, USA

INFORMATION SCIENCE REFERENCE

Hershey · New York

Director of Editorial Content: Kristin Klinger
Director of Book Publications: Julia Mosemann
Acquisitions Editor: Lindsay Johnson
Development Editor: Elizabeth Arder
Typesetter: Gregory Snader
Quality control: Jamie Snavely
Cover Design: Lisa Tosheff
Printed at: Yurchak Printing Inc.

Published in the United States of America by
    Information Science Reference (an imprint of IGI Global)
    701 E. Chocolate Avenue
    Hershey PA 17033
    Tel: 717-533-8845
    Fax: 717-533-8661
    E-mail: cust@igi-global.com
    Web site: http://www.igi-global.com/reference

Library of Congress Cataloging-in-Publication Data

Politics, democracy, and e-government : participation and service delivery / Christopher G. Reddick, editor.
    p. cm.
 Includes bibliographical references and index.
 Summary: "This book examines how e-government impacts politics and democracy in both developed and developing countries"--Provided by publisher.
 ISBN 978-1-61520-933-0 (hardcover) -- ISBN 978-1-61520-934-7 (ebook) 1. Internet in public administration. 2. Political participation--Technological innovations. 3. Democratization--Technological innovations. I. Reddick, Christopher G.
 JF1525.A8P63 2010
 352.3'802854678--dc22
                         2009039788

British Cataloguing in Publication Data
A Cataloguing in Publication record for this book is available from the British Library.

All work contributed to this book is new, previously-unpublished material. The views expressed in this book are those of the authors, but not necessarily of the publisher.

Josep Lluis de la Rosa, *University of Girona, Spain*
Mercè Rovira, *Ajuntament de Girona, Spain, EU*
Panos Fitsilis, *TEI Larissa, Greece*
Leonidas Anthopoulos, *Hellenic Ministry of Foreign Affairs, Greece*
Hee Jung Cho, *Sogang University, Seoul, Korea*
Willem Pieterson, *University of Twente, The Netherlands*
Hyunjin Seo, *Syracuse University, USA*
Stuart Thorson, *Syracuse University, USA*
Pieter Verdegem, *Ghent University, Belgium*
Laurence Hauttekeete, *Ghent University, Belgium*
Shang-Ching Yeh, *National Science and Technology Museum, Taiwan*
Pin-Yu Chu, *National Chengchi University, Taiwan*
Xia Li Lollar, *University of Wisconsin-Whitewater, USA*
Maniam Kaliannan, *Universiti Teknologi MARA, Malaysia*
Magiswary Dorasamy, *Multimedia University, Malaysia*
Stephen Fariñas, *Florida International University, USA*
Rebecca Moody, *Erasmus University Rotterdam, The Netherlands*
Dennis de Kool, *Center for Public Innovation, The Netherlands*
Jody C Baumgartner, *East Carolina University, USA*
Ailsa Kolsaker, *University of Surrey, UK*
Mark Liptrott, *Edge Hill University, UK*
Anne Powell, *Southern Illinois University Edwardsville, USA*
Douglas B. Bock, *Southern Illinois University Edwardsville, USA*
Catalin Vrabie, *National School of Political Studies and Public Administration, Romania*
Mark Deakin, *Edinburgh Napier University, UK*
T. Ramayah, *Universiti Sains Malaysia, Malaysia*
Mitch Miller, *The University of Texas at San Antonio, USA*
José Rodrigues Filho, *Universidade Federal da Paraíba, Brazil*
Ari-Veikko Anttiroiko, *University of Tampere, Finland*
George E. Higgins, *University of Louisville, USA*
Sudha Arlikatti, *University of North Texas, USA*
Tong-yi Huang, *National Chengchi University, Taiwan*
Maria del Carmen Caba Pérez, *University of Almería, Spain*
Antonio Manuel López Hernández, *University of Granada, Spain*
Peter Shackleton, *Victoria University, Australia*
Erin L. Borry, *University of Kansas, USA*
Sungsoo Hwang, *Yeungnam University, Korea*
Howard Frank, *Florida International University, USA*
Jason Wilson, *University of Wollongong, Australia*
Brian Lake, *University of Limerick, Ireland*
Jason G. Caudill, *Carson-Newman College, USA*
Ruth Halperin, *London School of Economics, UK*
James Backhouse, *London School of Economics, UK*
Ronnie Korosec, *University of Central Florida, USA*

Table of Contents

Section 1
E-Participation

Chapter 1

> *Patrizia Lombardi, Politecnico di Torino,Italy*
> *Pekka Huovila, VTT Technical Research Centre of Finland, Finland*
> *Minna Sunikka-Blank, University of Cambridge, UK*

Chapter 2

> *Jennifer A. Kurtz, Conundrum Creek Consulting, USA*
> *Roland J. Cole, Sagamore Institute for Policy Research, USA*
> *Isabel A. Cole, Independent Librarian, USA*

Chapter 3

> *Eduardo Araya Moreno, University of Valparaíso, Chile*
> *Diego Barría Traverso, Leiden University, The Netherlands*

Chapter 4

> *J. Ramón Gil-García, Centro de Investigación y Docencia Económicas, Mexico*
> *Fernando González Miranda, Universidad Autónoma del Estado de México, Mexico*

Section 3
E-Governance

Detailed Table of Contents

Section 1
E-Participation

Section 1 examines the concept of electronic participation of e-participation in government. In this section, there are chapters that discuss e-participation in many different countries. One notable finding is that there are efforts to create e-participation, but the results of these chapters show that progress is slow, at best, in most countries.

Chapter 1

  Patrizia Lombardi, Politecnico di Torino,Italy
  Pekka Huovila, VTT Technical Research Centre of Finland, Finland
  Minna Sunikka-Blank, University of Cambridge, UK

Lombardi, Huovila, and Sunikka-Blank discuss the issue of e-participation in decision making and sustainable development evaluation. They examine the types of policies currently adopted by cities to engage their citizens in public participation in the European Union (EU). E-government has the potential to play an important role in accelerating the transition to a more sustainable way of life; revolutionizing business and how citizens use cities. The case studies presented in this chapter provide awareness that e-participation and empowerment processes in policy making being an important aspect of more sustainable communities in the EU.

Chapter 2

  Jennifer A. Kurtz, Conundrum Creek Consulting, USA
  Roland J. Cole, Sagamore Institute for Policy Research, USA
  Isabel A. Cole, Independent Librarian, USA

Kurtz, Cole, and Cole examine successful techniques for increasing citizen use of electronic applications for two common activities – vehicle registration renewal and income tax filing – in four Midwestern states (Illinois, Indiana, Kentucky, Ohio) in the United States. Usage patterns depend in part on an individual citizen's technological sophistication. This chapter examines the impact of marketing efforts made by state government agencies to expand citizen use of e-government service options. In general, the experiences of these four states indicate a direct relationship between a state government's level of effort in promoting e-government services for individual income tax filing and vehicle registration renewal and citizen participation rates.

Chapter 3

Eduardo Araya Moreno, University of Valparaíso, Chile
Diego Barría Traverso, Leiden University, The Netherlands

Moreno and Traverso analyze the participation opportunities for citizens that use websites of Chilean government ministries. Their conclusion is that there is a wide range of available information regarding ministerial management but, websites lack participatory mechanisms. The evaluation of the Chilean ministries websites revealed the lack of open channels throughout these websites. Essentially, these authors argue for the potential of citizen participation in e-government, but their evidence does not support this in Chile.

Chapter 4

J. Ramón Gil-García, Centro de Investigación y Docencia Económicas, Mexico
Fernando González Miranda, Universidad Autónoma del Estado de México, Mexico

Gil-Garcia and Miranda did an analysis of 32 government web portals in Mexico. This chapter proposes an index of citizen participation opportunities, ranking the portals according to this index, and explores some of the determinants of the availability of these participation opportunities through a case study of the Mexican State of Michoacán. In Mexico, implementations of e-government have made some significant progress. More and more government processes are becoming available through Web sites and other Internet technologies, including opportunities for citizen participation, but the progress is very modest.

Chapter 5

Bekir Parlak, Uludag University, Turkey
Zahid Sobaci, Uludag University, Turkey

Parlak and Sobaci examine Local Agenda 21 (LA 21) which is a democracy project aiming at enhancing the public's participation in the processes of political and administrative decision-making. Through an analysis of websites, this study found that e-participation services offered by the LA 21s in Turkey on their websites are insufficient. According to the authors, despite progress in the recent years, the efforts of e-government in Turkey are still unsatisfactory.

Cho and Hwang examine the various e-participation tools and services of e-government in South Korea. Although South Korea's e-government seems to be heading in the right direction, more information sharing across the agencies and jurisdictions is still needed. South Korea is still at the very early stages of Government 2.0, but scholars need to engage in assessing the effectiveness of these e-participation services, particularly the impact of certain policy proposals put into practice through e-participation.

Baumgartner examines the relationship between the use of the Internet for campaign information and two dimensions of the political engagement of young adults during the 2008 United States presidential campaign. In spite of the promise the Internet holds for increasing political interest and participation among this disengaged age group, those who rely on the Internet as their main source of news do not seem any more inclined to participate in politics.

Aikins believes that a well designed participatory e-planning system can serve as an enabler for collaborative decision-making and help reduce conflict and mistrust between planning officials and the local community. E-planning has a great potential to improve public participatory processes, and consultative features of many existing systems, helping to bridge the gap between participatory e-planning theory and practice. This author believes that the future for e-planning systems to be effective as enablers, the features of existing software will have to move beyond mere documented feedback and allow more real-time consultation.

Section 2
E-Democracy

The second section of this book examines electronic democracy or e-democracy and its influence on citizens and government. The chapters in this section cover electronic voting or e-voting and efforts by governments to enhance and support e-democracy. These chapters delve into e-democracy in the United States, United Kingdom, European Union, and Korea. Many of the perspectives from authors have one common theme, that there is not as much e-democracy in governments.

Powell, Bock, Doellman, and Allen analyze public opinion data using subjects from two different age groups (18-to-25 and 60+ years) in the United States through a survey to determine the factors affecting their intent to use online voting systems. The results indicate that performance expectancy, social influence, and computer anxiety are factors affecting the intent to use online voting. Significant differences were found between the young adults and seniors study groups on all four independent variables as well as on intent to use online voting. The results of their chapter indicate that government should consider using different approaches for different age groups with regard to online voting systems.

Williams describes the evolution of Massachusetts Governor Deval Patrick's website through a content analysis of its features, functionality, and interviews with key officials in his election campaign. This website provides an interested case study of how to encourage citizen participation in an election. There was high voter turnout from online supporters in large part from this innovative website. This case study shows the idea of the permanent campaign, or the blurring of the lines between campaigning and governing.

Liptrott discusses electronic voting or e-voting in the United Kingdom through a review of the literature and uses semi-structured interviews with key officials to determine the benefits and challenges in the implementation of this program. The results of this chapter indicate that the UK has adopted an incrementalist approach towards the introduction of e-voting as a strategy to address falling voter turnout at the polls. The author notes that the literature argues that voting methods will not enhance voter turnout due to public disengagement with conventional political activity.

Chapter 12

Romano examines digital democracy and this author notes that the Internet had not fulfilled any democratic promise, but instead has become a forum for "new elites." Romano argues that the Internet has created a "Long Tail" effect; this is where single websites see a disproportionate amount of web traffic in comparison to other sites, thereby, reducing the level of participation in a democracy.

Chapter 13

Deakin examines what is called the fourth phase of digital government; the development of digital technologies as socially inclusive platforms through an examination of city government web portals. At this stage, e-government is open, transparent, and accountable with the increased adoption of democratic principles to include citizens in the process of governance. Deakin believes City Web portals are gateways to services and should increase the democratization of government.

Chapter 14

Lake believes that in the European Union (EU) the ability of e-government initiatives to increase citizen awareness does not necessarily correspond to an increase in democratic legitimacy. This chapter discusses the EUs e-government initiative called the Information Society, which is anticipated to have a positive impact on institutional transparency and democratic legitimacy. This Information Society initiative is expected to increase awareness of EU democratic institutions and provide more legitimacy of the system of governance.

Chapter 15

Seo and Thorson examine Café USA, which is an initiative by the U.S. Embassy in South Korean capital, Seoul, to reach out to that country's citizens. Café USA is part of the Embassy's efforts to interact with the younger generation of South Koreans, a substantial proportion of which are regarded as having anti-U.S. sentiments. Social networking tools have begun to transform the practice of public diplomacy by permitting governments to build and maintain direct relationships with citizens of other countries.

Chapter 16

Fariñas examines radical activists who now can use the Internet as a significant source to mobilize support and disseminate information to other activists'. This author argues that activism online is alive and well. The Internet has enabled symbolic relationships with offline and real world activism. Not everyone is amenable to the idea of "taking it to the streets" as the author mentions; therefore online activism has served as a complimentary rather than a substitute for real world activism.

Section 3
E-Governance

The final section of this book examines electronic governance or e-governance. The focus of this section is on ways that governments are promoting governance in their respective counties. The chapters in this section cover e-governance from many different countries, therefore, the experiences that the authors present are varied and nuanced.

Chapter 17

Anthopoulos and Fitsilis focus on describing the latest digital city architecture and experiences for the City of Trikala in Greece, examining how digital cities impact e-government. A digital city has all information systems linked virtually through technologies such as wireless. The author found that no one stop portal of a digital city exists so far, but there has been much progress in the development of digital cities.

Chapter 18

Gulati, Yates, and Tawileh did an analysis of the global digital divide using data from over 170 counties. There is little research, as the authors' note, that examines the global digital divide through a large country empirical dataset. When controlling for economic, social, and political developments, there is a greater capacity for e-governance in countries that have a regulatory authority for telecommunications, competition in telecommunications industries, and higher financial investment in technological development. One key, and important policy finding, is that enabling competition in telecommunications industries had the greatest impact on the capacity of a country for e-governance diffusion.

Chapter 19

Jason G. Caudill, Carson-Newman College, USA

Caudill believes to bridge the digital divide technical solutions will have to be part of the solution. The digital divide is the difference between the haves of technology and have-nots in society. Even knowing there is availability of technology in many developed countries, such as the United States, there are still many people who do not have regular access to this technology. Open source software and freeware and other alternative solutions can be beneficial to helping citizens get access to new media.

Chapter 20

Axel Bruns, Queensland University of Technology, Australia
Jason Wilson, University of Wollongong, Australia

Burns and Wilson examine citizen engagement through e-government in Australia. They advocate for implementing e-government using a bottom up approach from citizen participation. This is where individuals and nonprofit organizations debate current policy challenges among themselves. They present the idea of political informatics, or customizing parliamentary information as a tool for political engagement to allow community dialogue on issues rather than have this information just presented from the top-down.

Chapter 21

José Rodrigues Filho, Universidade Federal da Paraíba, Brazil

Filho examines the e-government from the view of Brazilian citizens. This chapter analyzes the impact of e-voting and e-health on promoting citizenship in Brazil. This author found that e-government in Brazil, as in many other countries, is following a service first and democracy later approach. Filho believes that currently in Brazil e-voting and an e-health initiatives only reinforce dominant forms of power and do not promote democracy giving citizens more say in these decisions.

Chapter 22

Marvine Hamner, George Washington University, USA
Doaa Taha, Independent Consultant, USA
Salah Brahimi, Grey Matter International Ltd, USA

Hamner, Taha, and Brahimi examine the potential barriers to implementing e-government in developing countries. These barriers include infrastructure, privacy and security, sustainability, culture, knowledge, skills and abilities of citizens. These authors argue that the that developing countries can overcome these barriers more so than developed countries since they are more amenable to change, since they do not have as rigid institutions in place to inhibit change.

Chapter 23

Peter Salhofer, FH Joanneum, Austria
Bernd Stadlhofer, FH Joanneum, Austria
Gerald Tretter, FH Joanneum, Austria

Salhofer, Stadlhofer, and Tretter examine ontology and e-government. Ontology is an explicit specification or a conceptualization of a problem. According to their model there is an interaction split between citizens and public administration into two major parts: planning/informative and execution/performance. Planning is the activities that need to be taken to provide citizens with information necessary to find administrative services. The execution is essentially providing the output and communicating the results to citizens. This chapter provides another way of conceptualizing the relations between citizens and their government through the field of software engineering.

Chapter 24

Rebecca Moody, Erasmus University Rotterdam, The Netherlands
Dennis de Kool, Center for Public Innovation, The Netherlands
Victor Bekkers, Erasmus University Rotterdam, The Netherlands

Moody, de Kool, and Bekkers examine the degree in which Geographic Information Systems (GIS) oriented neighbors websites improve service delivery by government to citizens. GIS has the potential to improve relations between citizens and government to provide new ways of service delivery and citizens' participation. Their results of a comparative case study indicate that when citizens have a large impact on the problem and solution to the problem, they have a strong influence on creating virtual neighborhoods.

Preface

Much of the scholarly research on e-government argues that this technology will have a positive influence on politics and democracy. The book bolsters the claims that e-government has enabled increased citizen participation, but there is much more that can be done. E-government will ultimately improve service delivery and accountability of government to its citizens, according to many authors of this book.

This book examines how e-government impacts politics and democracy in both developed and developing countries. This is accomplished through an examination of participation of citizens in government service delivery. There is growing body of research that examines participation and service delivery, but there is no book, that I am aware, that examines how e-government influences this important function of governing.

I believe that the audience for this book is both academics and practitioners that need to know leading edge research and theories on e-government and its influence on politics and democracy. Another secondary audience is students of political science where they want to know about how e-government impacts governance. This book, I believe, provides a comprehensive discussion of the role of e-government on politics and democracy. There are chapters from leading e-government scholars and practitioners from around the world explaining how e-government influences democratic institutions and processes.

There are twenty four chapters in this book, which are divided into three sections, with each of the sections examining an important area of e-government influencing politics and democracy. The first section examines the role of electronic participation, or e-participation, on government. E-participation is the influence of Information and Communication Technologies (ICT) on the citizens' ability to participate in the governance of their country. E-government is said to enhance participation since citizens have access, more readily, to governing institutions through various electronic means. In this section e-participation is examined in both developed and developing countries such as South Korea, Mexico, European Union, United States, Chile, Mexico, and Turkey. After reading this section, readers will have a very solid grasp of e-participation and its impact on governments throughout the world.

The second section of this book examines electronic democracy, or e-democracy, and its influence on citizens and government. In this section there is a demonstration of the role that ICT has had on democratic institutions of government. The e-democracy theory argues that e-government will enable citizens more opportunities to participate in their government because of information technologies like electronic voting, internet and democracy, online public diplomacy, and online social activism. Many of these chapters in this section support the importance of ICT to enhance democracy, but there are chapters more skeptical of its actual impact on democracy.

The third section of this book examines e-governance or the role that ICT has on political institutions and public administration. In this section, there are chapters that examine the digital city, the digital divide, and e-governance in developed countries such as Australia and developing countries such as Brazil. After reading this section, readers should understand that e-government has a very broad impact on the governance and its development varies from country to country. The following sections will provide a summary of the key contributions of each of the chapters in this book.

E-Participation

In Chapter 1 Lombardi, Huovila, and Sunikka-Blank deal with the issue of e-participation in decision making and sustainable development evaluation. They examined the types of policies currently adopted by cities to engage their citizens in public participation in the European Union (EU). According to the authors, e-government has the potential to play an important role in accelerating the transition to a more sustainable way of life, revolutionizing business and how citizens use cities. The case studies presented in this chapter provided awareness that e-participation and empowerment processes in policy making are an important aspect of more sustainable communities in the EU.

In Chapter 2 Kurtz, Cole, and Cole examined successful techniques for increasing citizen use of electronic applications for two common activities – vehicle registration renewal and income tax filing – in four Midwestern states (Illinois, Indiana, Kentucky, Ohio) in the United States. Usage patterns depend, in part, on an individual citizen's technological sophistication. This chapter examines the impact of marketing efforts made by state government agencies to expand citizen use of e-government service options. In general, the experiences of these four states indicated a direct relationship between a state government's level of effort in promoting e-government services for individual income tax filing and vehicle registration renewal and citizen participation rates.

In Chapter 3 Moreno and Traverso analyzed the participation opportunities for citizens that use websites in Chilean government ministries. Their conclusion is that there is a wide range of available information regarding ministerial management but, websites lack of participatory mechanisms. The evaluation of the Chilean ministries websites revealed the lack of open channels throughout these websites. Essentially, these authors argued for the potential of citizen participation in e-government, but their evidence does not support this in Chile.

Chapter 4 Gil-Garcia and Miranda conducted an analysis of the 32 government web portals in Mexico. This chapter proposed an index of citizen participation opportunities, ranking the portals according to this index, and explored some of the determinants of the availability of these participation opportunities through the case of the Mexican state of Michoacán. In Mexico, implementations of e-government have made significant progress. More and more government processes are becoming available through Web sites and other Internet technologies, including opportunities for citizen participation, but the progress is very modest at best.

In Chapter 5 Parlak and Sobaci examine Local Agenda 21 (LA 21) which is a democracy project aiming at enhancing the public's participation in the processes of political and administrative decision-making in Turkey. Through an analysis of websites, this study found that e-participation services offered by LA 21s in Turkey on their websites were insufficient. According to these authors, despite the progress in the recent years, the efforts of e-government in Turkey are still unsatisfactory.

Cho and Hwang in Chapter 6 examine the various e-participation tools and services of e-government in South Korea. Although South Korea's e-government seems to be heading in the right direction, more information sharing across the agencies and jurisdictions is needed. South Korea is still at the very early stages of Government 2.0, but scholars need to engage in assessing the effectiveness of these e-participation services, particularly the impact of certain policy proposals put into practice through e-participation.

Baumgartner in Chapter 7 examined the relationship between the use of the Internet for campaign information and dimensions of the political engagement of young adults during the 2008 United States presidential campaign. In spite of the promise the Internet holds for increasing political interest and participation among this disengaged age group, those who rely on the Internet as their main source of news do not seem to be any more inclined to participate in politics.

In Chapter 8 Aikins indicates that a well designed participatory e-planning system can serve as an enabler for collaborative decision-making and help reduce conflict and mistrust between planning officials and the local community. E-planning has a great potential to improve public participatory processes, the geographical capabilities as well as interactivity and consultative features of many existing systems, helping to bridge the gap between participatory e-planning theory and practice. This author believes that for future e-planning systems to be effective as enablers, the features of existing software will have to move beyond mere documented feedback and allow more real-time dynamic consultation. The following section presents chapters on the impact of e-government on democracy.

E–Democracy

In Chapter 9 Powell, Bock, Doellman, and Allen analyze public opinion data using subjects from two different age groups of young adult voters and seniors in the United States through a survey to determine the factors affecting their intent to use online voting systems. The results indicate that performance expectancy, social influence, and computer anxiety are factors affecting the intent to use online voting. Significant differences were found between the young adults and seniors study groups on all four independent variables as well as on intent to use online voting. The results of their study indicated that government should consider using different approaches for different age groups with regard to online voting systems.

In Chapter 10 Williams describes the evolution of Massachusetts Governor Deval Patrick's website through a content analysis of its features and functionality and interviews with key officials in his election campaign. This website provides an interested case study of how to encourage citizen participation in an election. There was a high turnout from online supporters in large part from this innovative website. This case study shows the idea of the permanent campaign, or the blurring of the lines between campaigning and governing.

Liptrott in Chapter 11 discusses electronic voting or e-voting in the United Kingdom, through a review of the literature and using semi-structured interviews with key officials in the implementation of this program. The results of this chapter indicated that the UK has adopted an incrementalist approach towards the introduction of e-voting as a strategy to address falling voter turnout at the polls. Liptrott concludes that that voting methods will not enhance voter turnout primarily due to public disengagement with conventional political activity.

In Chapter 12 Romano examines digital democracy and this author notes that the Internet had not fulfilled any democratic promise, but instead has become a forum for "new elites." Romano believes the Internet has created a "Long Tail" effect; this is where single websites witness a disproportionate amount of web traffic in comparison to other sites, thereby, reducing the level of citizen participation in a democracy.

In Chapter 13 Deakin examines what is called the fourth phase of digital government; the development of digital technologies as socially inclusive platforms through city government web portals. At this stage e-government is open, transparent, and accountable with the increased adoption of democratic principles to include citizens in the process of governance. Deakin believes City Web portals are gateways to services and should increase the democratization of government.

Lake in Chapter 14 argues that in the European Union (EU) the ability of e-government initiatives to increase citizen awareness does not necessarily correspond to an increase in democratic legitimacy. This chapter discusses the EUs e-government initiative called the Information Society, which is anticipated to have a positive impact institutional transparency and democratic legitimacy. This Information Society initiative was expected to increase awareness of EU democratic institutions and provide more legitimacy of the system of governance.

In Chapter 15 Seo and Thorson examined Café USA, which is an initiative by the United States Embassy in South Korean capital, Seoul, to reach out to its country's citizens. Café USA is part of the Embassy's efforts to interact with the younger generation of South Koreans, a substantial proportion of which are regarded as having anti-U.S. sentiments. These authors believe that social networking tools have begun to transform the practice of public diplomacy by permitting governments to build and maintain direct relationships with citizens of other countries.

In Chapter 16 Farinas examines radical activists who now can use the Internet as a significant source to mobilize support and disseminate information to other activists'. This author believes that activism online is alive and well. The Internet has enabled symbolic relationships with offline and real world activism. However, not everyone is amenable to the idea of "taking it to the streets" as the author notes; therefore online activism has served as a complimentary tool to real world activism. The following section provides examples of e-government impacting the governance of nations, focusing on government performance and accountability.

E-Governance

In Chapter 17 Anthopoulos and Fitsilis focus on describing the latest digital city architecture and experiences for the City of Trikala in Greece to examine how digital cities impact e-government. A digital city has all information systems linked virtually through technologies such as wireless. The author found that no one stop portal of a digital city exists so far, but there has been much progress in the development of digital cities in Greece among other countries.

In Chapter 18 Gulati, Yates, and Tawileh performed an analysis of the global digital divide using data from over 170 counties. There is little research, as the authors' note, that examines the global digital divide through a large country data set. When controlling for economic, social, and political developments, there is a greater capacity for e-governance in countries that have a regulatory authority for telecommunications, competition in telecommunications industries, and higher financial investment in technological development. One key finding of this chapter is that enabling competition in telecommunications industries had the greatest impact on the capacity of a country for e-governance diffusion.

In Chapter 19 Caudill believes to bridge the digital divide technical solutions will have to be solution. The digital divide is the difference between the haves of technology and have-nots in society. Even knowing there is availability of technology in many developed countries, such as the United States, there are still many citizens who do not have regular access to this technology. Open source software and freeware and other alternative solutions can be beneficial to helping citizens get access to new media.

In Chapter 20 Burns and Wilson examined citizen engagement through e-government in Australia. They advocate for implementing e-government using a bottom up approach from citizen participation, rather than the traditional method of top down. The bottom up approach is where individuals and non-profit organizations debate current policy changes among themselves. They present the idea of political informatics, or customizing parliamentary information as a tool for political engagement to allow community dialogue on issues rather than have this information just presented from the top-down.

Filho in Chapter 21 examines the e-government from the view of Brazilian citizens examining two topical issues. In particular, this chapter analyzes the impact of e-voting and e-health on promoting citizenship in Brazil. This author found that e-government in Brazil, as in many other countries, is following a service first and democracy later approach. Filho believes that currently in Brazil, e-voting and e-health initiatives merely reinforce dominant forms of power, and do not promote democracy giving citizens more say in these decisions.

In Chapter 22 Hamner, Taha, and Brahimi examine the potential barriers to implementing e-government in developing countries. These barriers include infrastructure, privacy and security, sustainability, culture, knowledge, skills and the abilities of citizens. These authors believe that developing countries can overcome these barriers more so than developed countries since they are more amenable to change because they do not have as rigid institutions in place to inhibit change.

In Chapter 23 Salhofer, Stadlhofer, and Tretter examine ontology and e-government. Ontology is an explicit specification or a conceptualization of a problem. According to their model there is an interaction split between citizens and public administration into two major parts: planning/informative and execution/performance. Planning is the activities that need to be taken to provide citizens with information necessary to find administrative services. The execution is essentially providing the output and communicating the results to citizens. The important contribution of this chapter is that it provides another way of conceptualizing the relations between citizens and their government through the field of software engineering.

In Chapter 24 Moody, de Kool, and Bekkers examined the degree in which Geographic Information Systems (GIS) neighbors websites improved service delivery by government to citizens. GIS has the potential to improve relations between citizens and government to promote new ways of service delivery and citizens' participation possibilities. The results of a comparative case study indicated that when citizens have a large impact on the problem and solution to the problem, there is a higher degree of success in the e-government solution.

Acknowledgment

I would like to thank the authors of this book who have made tireless efforts to get me, on time, their first drafts and revised chapters. I am also especially grateful to the peer reviewers of this book and their thorough comments on the draft chapters. I am very thankful for the editorial advisory board of the book; they were a good source of advice and inspiration. I am very much appreciative of the help that the staff at IGI Global provided to me for the development of this book; special thanks goes to Ms. Elizabeth Ardner. On a personal note, I would like to thank my wife Cathy and my two daughters Rachel Olivia and Abigail Sophia for their support during this book project.

Section 1
E-Participation

Chapter 1

The Potential of E-Participation in Sustainable Development Evaluation:
Evidence from Case Studies

Patrizia Lombardi
Politecnico di Torino, Italy

Pekka Huovila
VTT Technical Research Centre of Finland, Finland

Minna Sunikka-Blank
University of Cambridge, UK

ABSTRACT

If sustainable development is really to be based on substantive community participation, a change in attitudes, beliefs and values is required. Even these changes will not be sufficient to reach the ambitious goals set across Europe through the Local Agenda 21 and other policy documents. The rigorous adaptation of decision-making processes to include community participation is necessary. Development and specification of indicators play an important role in bridging this gap. The indicators should not only form a technical input in the latter type of assessment tools but act as media to communicate the progress towards sustainable development to the local communities and other stakeholders. This chapter deals with the issue of e-participation in decision making and sustainable development evaluation. It presents first a critical overview of sustainable development and knowledge society indicators, metrics and assessment tools currently in use. Then, it introduces the role of Civil Society Organizations (CSOs) in urban regeneration processes by using a number of European case studies. Finally, it states the need for a more systematic approach to integrate CSOs earlier in the decision-making process and to ensure a more effective use of sustainable development indicators – with the help of the Information and Communication Technologies (ICTs).

DOI: 10.4018/978-1-61520-933-0.ch001

Figure 1. Summary of the roadmap diagram developed by Intelcity (Curwell, 2003)

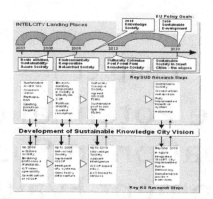

INTRODUCTION

The Lisbon European Council (CEC, 2000) sought to make Europe "the most competitive and dynamic knowledge-based economy in the world capable of sustainable economic growth with more and better jobs and greater social cohesion". Given the importance of Information and Communication Technology (ICT) for today's economy, the i2010 strategy is a key element of the Lisbon strategy for growth and employment. It promotes the positive contribution that ICT can make to the economy, society and personal quality of life (http://ec.europa.eu/information_society/eeurope/i2010). The Knowledge Society (KS) is seen as a key factor by the European Union (EU) for achieving Sustainable urban development (SUD) in Europe, following the so-called "*eAgora*" model. Ancient Greeks went to the Agora, a civic square used for public assembly or commerce, to do business or discuss plans for their community. The Intelcity (2003) roadmap, developed under the EU's 5th Framework Programme, envisaged modern Europeans acting similarly in the context of eAgora that could support the improved management of cities and help to achieve long-term physical, social and economic sustainability – by bringing together previously unconnected information sources and making it digitally available to planners, developers, policy makers and individual citizens.

The eAgora vision is based on the active participation of citizens (supported by ICTs) in decision-making. It encourages collaboration between different stakeholders in policy-making processes. The trajectory to achieve the eAgora vision is shown in Figure 1. The timeline raises a question: *How are we progressing towards achieving the eAgora and the knowledge society aimed by the EU?*

IntelCities (2004), a research project in EU's 6th Framework programme, looked at the types of policies currently adopted by cities to engage their citizens in public participation. It suggests that until both sides of the equation – policy makers in cities and the citizens – engage with and exploit digital technologies more fully, the eAgora will remain an unrealized vision (Lombardi & Cooper, 2007; Lombardi et al., 2009).

It remains uncertain whether the eAgora can be an effective vehicle to enable citizen engagement that can contribute to sustainable development by 2030 (Cooper et al., 2005; Lombardi & Cooper, 2007). The answer to this question requires quantitative evidence that is acceptable to all parties involved, turning the question into: *What aspects of civic behavior do we need to evaluate and how? Is the eAgora an effective space for displaying this kind of information?*

The current lists of indicators, indices and assessment tools which have been developed to measure and display performance in the eAgora at different spatial levels (global, national, city, community, building and material) show that progress has been made (Deakin et al., 2002; OECD, 2008; Eurostat, 2007). There are, however, a large number of indicators, mainly relating to social and political issues that are difficult to capture and represent in a meaningful way (Therivel, 2004). Furthermore, if only quantitative measures are used, there is a risk of losing a significant parameter in creating sustainable communities. Inter-generational equity, aesthetics and especially governance are examples of this category. How is it possible to capture and measure them, and represent this back in a meaningful way to disparate groups of stakeholders in a society?

This paper presents a critical overview of the current sustainable development indicators and their role in public participation processes in the EU. It argues for a more systematic approach to integrate Civil Society Organizations (CSOs) earlier in the decision-making by using a number of European case studies. It finally concludes with a discussion on e-participation tools and how they could contribute to sustainable development indicators and policy-making. The data is based on the previous work by the authors and analyzed in the context of e-participation.

BACKGROUND

Potential synergy between policy-making and public participation lies in the evaluation of policy impact. The current lists of indicators, however, are little connected to policy-making. Many European countries are facing the challenge of urban renewal and pressure to reduce carbon emissions, and there is recognition of the limitations of traditional policy instruments (Sunikka, 2006). Actually, most of the reasons why people did not save energy in buildings in the 1980s are still familiar today (Van Raaij & Verhallen, 1983). This raises the question whether the top-down government policy has been disoriented since the eighties. New approaches and

combinations of policy instruments are needed to achieve the government policy targets – but how to determine the effectiveness of a policy and what role could SD indicators play in it?

Critical Overview of Current Sustainable Development Indicators

Indicators are presentations of measurements to suit a particular need. They are pieces of information that summarize the characteristics of systems or highlight what is happening in a system (Brandon & Lombardi, 2005). As such, they are indispensable for measuring progress towards achieving set goals and thus constitute a key tool for evaluating the effectiveness of policies and their implementation actions. Secondly, indicators simplify the communication of positive and negative developments to politicians, administrators, the public and others (OECD, 2003). Both functions rely on the main feature of indicators: summarizing the complexity into indicators can provide crucial guidance for policy-making processes, in particular regarding a better integration of policies horizontally across different sectors, and vertically between the different levels of governance (United Nations, 2001).

The modern Sustainable Development Indicator process started at the Rio Earth Summit in 1992. Recent surveys estimate that there are now over 600 formal or recognized full sustainable development indicator sets in use, many more that have been formally developed, or have been created as a subset of a wider agenda. Most present indicators have been developed by governments and intergovernmental bodies in response to their needs. This ensures policy relevance, but often fails to capture what is going on at the grass roots of society. Other indicators have been created by CSOs or academics to draw attention to policy issues. Few indicators have been devised by or are designed for the real agents of change – businesses and individuals operating at a decentralized level in all societies. The most effective indicators

Figure 2. INTELCITY countries and regions mapped in relation to progress in SUD and ICT (Curwell, 2003)

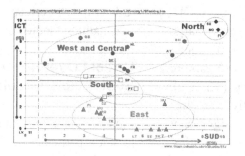

and feedback loops are those created and managed directly by users for their own purposes. The issue of how to reconcile the centralized approaches needed to produce standard comparable indicators and the decentralized nature of most decision making affecting sustainability has not been sufficiently explored, yet.

Benchmarking adds context to indicators, for instance by ranking countries. In Intelcity roadmap (Curwell, 2003), the "sustainable knowledge society" position of different countries was mapped using environmental sustainability indicator (ESI) as one dimension and information society indicator (ISI) as the other dimension (see Figure 2). Positioning the countries in such a map showed that geographical clustering did not fully support the original objective that aimed to have four homogenous regions in Europe validating the roadmap.

Another IST roadmap: New Partnerships for Sustainable Development in the Knowledge Economy (Neskey, 2003) stated that new economic feedback system should use a core set of measures, indexes, and methods commonly used by businesses, cities and regions, civil society, and governing bodies where global networks and practice communities collaboratively improve measures and methods. The roadmap advised research to focus on intangible reporting for cities and regions

and identified city and regional metrics as drivers for corporate and government scorecards linking measures to local and regional quality of life. The Neskey roadmap suggests that in the knowledge society (unlike in our industrial society dominated by big corporations) small business, civil society, government and education are the real drivers of the economy and offer higher leverage (Ahlskog, 2003; Allee, 2009).

Sustainability indicators are generally intended to target on-going political processes. Because such indicators are at the interface of science and politics, framing the issues in a policy-relevant way is particularly important and generally entails a participatory process. To be effective, indicators must be credible (and/or scientifically valid), legitimate in the eyes of users and stakeholders, and salient or relevant to decision-makers.

Indicators must meet different information needs at various stages of a policy life cycle. One function would be early warning, raising awareness of an unfavorable trend that may be evidence of a new and emerging issue or signaling a policy gap for an existing issue. Other indicators are used in impact assessments or outlooks, when new policy proposals are being developed, and still others contribute to the mid-term to long-term monitoring of policy implementation.

Governments tend do not monitor the impact of their sustainable building policies and when data exists it is not analyzed (Klinckenberg & Sunikka, 2006; Meijer et al., 2009). Compared to metrics that address the themes of sustainable development, there are few indicators to evaluate effectiveness, cost-efficiency and legitimacy of policy instruments and the related decision-making processes – especially regarding social sustainability instead of resource efficiency. Consequently, policy making is based on images and (often un-built) reference projects, feelings and politics – not numbers. The input for these policy-related metrics should also come from the field – the residents. The CSOs could contribute to the measurement of potential behavioral change resulting from the knowledge exchange between local community groups and different policy levels, including minority and disadvantaged groups.

It should be stated, however, that indicators do not replace other policy instruments like building regulations or economic instruments – they have a strong supporting role. In the context of policy analysis indicators are recognized as communication instruments with the related weaknesses (unpredictable impact resulting from their voluntary nature, they do not address the economic barriers) and strengths (low-cost instrument for the government, essential in information dissemination and changing of values).

According to the European Environment Agency (EEA) indicators can be described as communication tools that: a) simplify complex issues making them accessible to a wider audience (i.e. non-experts); b) can encourage decision-making by pointing to clear steps in the causal chain where it can be broken; c) inform and empower policymakers and laypeople by creating a means for the measurement of progress in tackling environmental progress (EEA, 2007). It is the capacity of the indicator to reach its target audience that determines its success. Failure to communicate makes the indicator worthless. However, because sustainable development is a multi-stakeholder process, indicators must communicate to a variety of different actors.

The business community is an essential actor for sustainability that is not well represented by current indicators. Indicators of sustainable business behavior would complement indicators at the government level. Although many corporate reports now include information on environmental and social performance that could be used for indicators, it is still difficult to get businesses to share the information they collect. Some information is seen as confidential because it provides a commercial advantage, and businesses are not motivated to share negative information that might damage their reputation or profitability. Yet much of the effort to move toward sustainability involves identifying and reducing problems such as pollution. This is an important gap that must be filled, particularly for small and medium enterprises that are responsible for the bulk of business activity.

User involvement is important to indicator design and acceptance. Stakeholders may have local knowledge that can contribute to more effective indicators. Participation also ensures relevance to the decision-making process, political commitment, and ownership of the results. Participatory processes can reveal conflicting social interests, values, and preferences that must be taken into account. The quality of the process is important.

Acceptance and use of indicators are a continuing challenge. Indicators that reflect badly on politicians, corporate executives, and senior officials will be rejected or suppressed, and most indicators of sustainable development show negative trends. Careful indicator development processes, outside pressure, and objectivity will be necessary to overcome this obstacle.

In addition, metrics could be connected to other policy instruments like regulations, for example when achieving a certain environmental assessment level is used as a prerequisite for a building permission, or economic incentives, for example when a certain assessment level qualifies for a subsidy. Rather than suggesting new policy instruments like household carbon trading it would make sense to build on the existing ones.

In the field of energy efficiency for example, the EC Energy Performance of Buildings Directive (EPBD) is one of the key instruments of the EU to address energy savings in the existing housing (Beerepoot & Sunikka, 2005; Sunikka, 2006). Metrics like the EPBD could be used to collect an European database that would enable an extensive comparison between different projects and their sustainability strategies – one of the weakness of the existing indicators is a lack of references where citizens could compare results to other similar projects and with these concrete examples participate in a more active way in setting sustainable development targets for a project.

Metrics for eAgora can be constituted using different approaches. One dimension is the built environment, where the present rating schemes focus on environmental impacts in the use of buildings, namely the energy use. Other dimension is the corporate aspect, where triple bottom line reporting emphasizes also environmental and social issues, but the discursive civic square environment risks to be dominated by economic sustainability of the production and growth-oriented business environment. The third dimension is the city itself with its social networks, concerned on the indicators for employment and crime, for example. The fourth dimension aims to measure the quality of life of individual citizens which is not easy to define. At the present, all four approaches are separately used without interoperability between the systems. Each of them measures just one aspect of the eAgora.

What conclusions can be drawn from the state of the art in indicator development for sustainability? There has been useful progress since the Rio Earth Summit in 1992 adopted Agenda 21 and launched an international indicator process. Many indicator sets have been assembled; countries have started their own indicator programs at the national level, as called for by the Commission on Sustainable Development (CSD), and many aspects of sustainability have been given a more precise definition or measure through indicators. However, we are still far from fully integrated sets of indicators or indices to support self-regulating sustainability and policy decisions.

THE CHALLENGE OF E-PARTICIPATION IN POLICY-MAKING

ICTs have the potential to play an important role in accelerating the transition to a more sustainable way of life, revolutionizing business and how citizens use cities (Castells, 1996). According to Pratchett (1999), ICT have the potential to fulfill three complementary roles of local authorities: local democracy; public policy making; and direct services delivery. However, as Pratchett claims, there is a systematic bias, which favors service delivery applications and overlooks applications regarding the other two roles. The reason for the bias, according to Pratchett, is that the decision-makers who initiate the ICT policy are not active in the other policy areas.

If sustainable development is to be based on substantive community participation and the use of indicators, the participation of CSOs needs to be ensured in decision-making processes. On the other hand, the CSOs could support policy targets by mobilizing citizens to achieve the goals set by the government. At this moment, however, policy-making in the field of sustainable built environment tends to happen top-down (Sunikka, 2006). Apart from (professional) stakeholder consultations input from the field is limited. This can be especially problematic in the existing housing stock that has become an important area in sustainable building policies (Meijer et al., 2009).

The potential role that ICT can have in developing new forms of public participation in decision-making is quite clear, as the concept of e-governance itself reveals. But to what extent these new forms of interaction between stakeholders can influence evaluation procedures, and impact the enhancement of policy goals still needs to be object of further discussion.

This section aims to explore these issues by introducing the role of Civil Society Organizations (CSOs) in policy-making at the neighborhood level. Case studies demonstrate the potential of e-participation for environmental, economic and social sustainability of urban areas.

The Case Study of Western Garden Cities in Amsterdam

Urban regeneration projects are recognized as good intervention points to improve environmental sustainability of urban areas but if these improvements are to be implemented the process needs to be supported by the inhabitants and the CSOs. The need for public participation is emphasized by the fact that regeneration projects tend to happen in increasingly free market – also in the areas that have traditionally been covered by local governments. The following example from the Netherlands illustrates the current situation of public participation in sustainable urban regeneration, in this project improving energy efficiency in the context of urban regeneration of a post-war neighborhood. The aim is not to generalize this situation but to highlight the need for a more systematic approach to integrate CSOs in the decision-making process earlier and to ensure a more effective use of sustainable development indicators.

The case study of Western Garden Cities in Amsterdam consists of post-war neighborhoods that have around 130,000 people living in 54,000 dwellings, 10,000 of which are to be demolished as part of the regeneration of the area and replaced by 17,500 new homes by 2015. The case study was analyzed as a part of a wider Corpovenista project where Dutch housing associations developed their practice of sustainable urban restructuring. The analysis is based on the key policy documents and expert interviews of actors working in the project. The observations are limited to this case study only but the discussions on the results of the project with housing associations within the wider project indicate the identified barriers are applicable to similar restructuring projects of large-scale post-war housing areas in the Netherlands. The inhabitant structure in the case study has a large proportion of social rental housing and rather low-income households that may affect the results. There is also a relatively high proportion of immigrants and elderly people. As a positive factor, the case study is located rather close to the city of Amsterdam so there are incentives for renovation and a potential to attract higher income households. Policy documents estimated that a 34-49% carbon dioxide reduction is feasible as part of the sustainable regeneration of the Western Garden Cities (Ligthart et al., 2000). The case of the Western Garden Cities demonstrates barriers that were encountered when replacing gas-fired heating with district heating provided by industrial waste heat, a project that could contribute an annual CO_2 reduction of 34 million kilos a year to the city of Amsterdam. If a new energy infrastructure is implemented only in new build in the regeneration project, the carbon reduction is very limited. Due to the economic and social barriers met in the process, this option, however, is the one that will be adopted.

The case study showed that careful consideration should be given to the preferences of residents in the existing housing when choosing a new energy source for a fuel switch. When the plans for the district heating system in the Western Garden Cities were far enough advanced to be really open to discussion and presented to the inhabitants, the policy faced resistance from the residents, who feared higher energy bills and increased rents and disliked the idea of switching from gas to electricity for cooking. Most residents felt that having their own boiler was something far more tangible than district heating, and since many were against demolition, assumed that housing associations would use implementing the new energy infrastructure an argument for demolishing even more homes in the area. The policy documents and interviews indicate that further uncertainties in the process were created by use of temporary boilers until the energy infrastructure will be completed, the final cost of the new energy infrastructure, the number of dwellings to be connected to the network and responsibilities divided to too many parties in the regeneration process. The residents were regarded as being 'not interested in energy efficiency' at the beginning of the renewal process, but the monitoring of the process shows that they were not given much information on the various different options either – or it did not reach them. The lack of knowledge led to a negative response of environmental improvements that the residents did not want to commit themselves to.

In the Netherlands, large urban regeneration projects are increasingly administered by policy networks, rather than local government. Not only the role of housing associations has become more commercial; the liberalization of the energy market has produced commercial energy companies that are more interested in market factors and less in the environment. In the Western Garden Cities, the analysis shows that less governance led to divided responsibilities: in the case study the energy supplier (the plant), the energy distributor, several departments of the municipal authority, four neighborhoods, 10-12 housing associations which play an important role in regeneration, and the residents, each with their own interests and economic position, and importantly, their own concepts of sustainable development. Policy documents illustrate that different perceptions of sustainability exists even within the local government. Traditionally, environmental aspects in spatial planning have focused on green and water, in the Netherlands these objectives are initiated by

the Environmental Departments in municipalities. The Environment Department is a specialist on environmental matters but it is not particularly interested in the costs or the residents – this is the area of the Housing Departments, which has not been a traditional target group of an environmental policy. In the case study, indicators embedded in the policy-making process and a more active participation of the CSOs in the field of the environment could have been helpful in enabling an open discussion on sustainable development based on a more coherent public participation. A comprehensive sustainability strategy would have prioritized sustainability themes in the context of this project and lead to alternative suggestions to district heating – or its acceptance if consulted earlier in the process.

The analysis and interviews in the case study demonstrate that the assessment of social sustainability remains problematic in urban restructuring and related policy-making. There is a variety of established tools available in a building scale, related to specific environmental measures like energy, but indicators that could be used to set and to monitor targets for more qualitative aspects of sustainable development like equity or social sustainability – factors essential for sustainable neighborhoods – are less available, neither are they available electronically to support e-participation that may reach a wider sample of inhabitants. Most existing environmental impact assessment tools like BREEAM or LEED focus on resource efficiency rather than on sustainable development in general. The CSOs could help to bridge this gap by mobilizing citizens to contribute to the development and enhancement of indicators on social and cultural sustainability, possibly with the support of ICT tools. Policy is usually assessed not only according to effectiveness and cost-efficiency about also legitimacy (Sunikka, 2006) and public acceptance is in a key role of legitimacy. Local governments who despite the trend towards the free market still hold the power of regulatory measures like the control building permits should make sure that the outcome of this participation has to be considered by housing associations and other market parties. Indicators like the Agenda 21 support public participation, in principle, but contrasted with economic priorities and time pressure the power of these voluntary and vague documents is very limited.

IntelCities Case Studies in Finland, Iceland and Germany

A number of case studies demonstrate the variety of methods that have been tried and which are available to engage inhabitants in participation towards sustainable urban development.

Different approaches towards integration of e-participation with successful sustainable urban development were tried in case studies in Helsinki and Tampere in Finland, in Garðabær in Iceland and in Frankfurt in Germany in IntelCities (Intelligent Cities) project (Lahti et al., 2006). These cases represent diverse applications for citizen participation that are digitally accessible using wired or wireless devices. The case studies have been evaluated regarding their capability to enhance participatory behavior to improve public service relevance and thus lead into sustainable urban development.

Arabianranta (2004) is an old neighborhood in Helsinki that contains new urban development on a brownfield of an earlier major porcelain and glassware industry. New development is scaled for around 10,000 inhabitants, 7,000 jobs and 6,000 students by 2020. The area is provided with a fiber optic cable network for all houses. The local service portal (Helsinki Virtual Village) connects residents and other actors in the area to a virtual community. Each housing company (typically one building) has its own website and extranet discussion forum accessible through the portal, managed by a volunteer called "e-moderator" who lives in the building. Two new participation applications were tested in Arabianranta.

Residents were also asked about their participation needs, use of tools and interest towards new electronic services. The survey was made in the form of an e-questionnaire accessible through the local portal. Printed version of the questionnaire was distributed to all of the approximately 500 households in the area. 150 filled questionnaires were received by the deadline. 87 of the responses were submitted through Internet and 63 were returned by mail. 113 of the respondents were living in Arabianranta proper, 36 elsewhere and 1 person did not mention her area of residence. In the results, only people living in the Arabianranta area have been included. 56% of the respondents were female. Most of the respondents were between 25 and 50 years old. That survey showed that the residents were willing and capable to participate and act more interactively, especially in trusted networks and when the benefits are visible.

A Neighborhood profiling concept was developed into "Arkkikone" community web application in Tampere Vuores and, as a follow up, as "In the Hood" neighborhood profiling service in Helsinki Arabianranta. "Arkkikone", later called as "Sulevi" in Tampere, aims at enhancing a participative and inclusive role for citizens in sustainable urban development. In the case study it focused on urban plan evaluation in Vuores neighborhood in Tampere. The users profiled themselves and compared that to six architectural competition candidates that had got through from around 30 entries. The city of Tampere got as a result the best matching project, and also the prioritization of the statements the city had offered.

"In the Hood" neighborhood profiling service provides the inhabitants and other actors a set of questions relating with different aspects of quality of life in Arabianranta. The issues reflecting the current state were followed by questions indicating to which directions it should be developed in the future and what kinds of services are needed. This was done, similarly to "Arkkikone", by placing a set of pre-defined sentences into an order of preference. While reflecting on issues that the par-

Figure 3. E-participation in Helsinki Arabianranta with "In the Hood". Huovila (2005). (© [2004], [University of Art and Design, Helsinki]. Used with permission.)

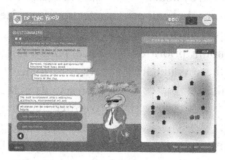

ticipating people personally find important, they also tell to others which kind of a neighborhood Arabianranta is and wishes to become. The answers produce a dynamic profile that is positioned on a four-dimensional character gallery consisting of the focus areas of citizens-workers-consumers-inhabitants (see Figure 3). The answers can also be compared in a more general profile of each housing company in accordance with the Helsinki Virtual Village portal.

Both Vuores and Arabianranta cases highlight the importance of understanding the interrelationships of the enabling and constraining structures within which the development of e-participation takes place: the policy context, the concrete technological structures and solutions, and the organizational and social structures sustaining e-participation on the municipal and at the local level.

The town of Garðabær in Iceland with 9,000 inhabitants and 95% internet access established a comprehensive e-governance internet platform (My Community) for its inhabitants, councilors and employees. The system uses the Stakeholder Profiling Registry, which is a module providing a gateway to active, on-line participation and policy-making processes. The system controls the access of participants to on-going policy-related processes such as e-consultation, surveys, polls, discussion groups, and petitions. Additionally it enables the stakeholders to start cases and follow up on case processes. The Registry holds an account of all

named users based on data transferred from a local or national registry. All users are issued with a user name and password. Upon log-in they select areas of special interest, define their profile and establish various communities of interest. The main actors and stakeholders that are involved in the use of the service are the City policy makers and the citizens and/or other registered stakeholders. It provides policy-makers such as administrations, planners, designers and politicians with a simple tool to select target groups for participation in their policy proposal and data gathering processes (e.g. by age, gender and postcode).

These three e-participation applications received positive feedback by the city authorities through obtaining a true communication channel with the end users. On the other hand the end users welcomed a new way of participation that could be used in addition to (not necessarily instead of) the traditional ones.

The IntelCities project made two more case studies of electronic and mobile participation.

The first one related with a web-based discussion forum in Frankfurt. A newly developed system for spatial discourse in the Frankfurt e-participation process was extended through integration of an open source webGIS. That was tested in a simulation, relating it thematically with the regional planning process of the former Frankfurt e-participation. The first evaluation led to a positive assessment concerning the quality of the discussion and the discussion results. The

Figure 4. The stakeholder profiler in "My Community" in Garðabær, Iceland. (Huovila, 2005)

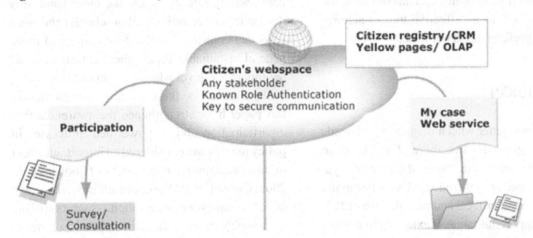

discussion was more precise, informed, focused and transparent than online discussions without the georeferencing feature.

The second case approached mobile participation using an electronic bulleting board in Arabianranta. That service utilized MMS technology and the Nokia Image Frame device was placed in the staircase of an apartment block to get some immediate feedback from its use by mobile phones. This kind of new local information channel showed to be in a difficult market situation between traditional physical notice boards and existing popular electronic bulletin boards in internet. To be successful, such new media should have some exceptionally appealing features in order to become competitive, or even to be noticed. The Arabianranta development company ADC got from the case study an idea of wireless larger screens that have since been taken into use with locally produced content mainly by the media and art schools.

FUTURE RESEARCH DIRECTIONS

The most difficult challenge facing policymakers is deciding the future directions of society and the economy in the face of conflicting demands of short-term political favor, economic growth, social progress, and environmental sustainability. Wrong decisions can have severe consequences, increase human suffering, and even precipitate crises. Improving the basis for sound decision-making by integrating many complex issues (while providing simple indicators for busy decision-makers) is a high priority. At a time when modern information technologies increase the flow of information we need information tools that condense and digest information for rapid assimilation while making it possible to explore issues further as needed.

As concluded in the overview of this paper, a number of sustainability indicator systems exist that can be used at a global, national, regional, city, community, organization, building or material levels. Many of them are applied to assess the state of the art or to monitor the trend from a selected perspective. Proper metrics for eAgora, however, as introduced in this paper seem to be lacking. Indicators at a neighborhood level that measure the quality of life of individual citizens which could be used in corporate and government scorecards and in building rating schemes would be needed as metrics for the eAgora in the knowledge society. As the impact of most government policies are not monitored in a systemic way, CSOs could also play a role in collecting information of the situation in the field and feed it back to policy-makers with the help of ICT tools fitted in to suitable indicators. At this moment, the potential of ICT as an effective tool to achieve the citizen preferences is not used.

CONCLUSION

No one knows better what a neighborhood needs than the people who live there. The European case studies demonstrate the need for a more systematic approach to integrate CSOs earlier in the decision-making process and how the use of ICT tools can support this target, if extended to support environmental targets in particular. In the case of Western Garden Cities in Amsterdam, a considerable CO_2 reduction could have been achieved if more mechanisms had existed for the inhabitants to participate in setting the environmental targets – either in local policy-making processes or in the form of ICT tools provided by commercial actors as in the case studies in Arabianranta in Helsinki, Vuores in Tampere or Frankfurt in Germany. The latter ICT case studies did not collect the feedback from the inhabitants for an environmental policy in particular but by committing inhabitants to the development they contribute to social sustainability and participation in the area. These kinds of ICT tools could be an effective and cost-efficient measure to support the environmental program and SD indicators. If response data from the inhabitants is collected in a digital form, it is easier for the market actors like housing associations or developers to gather, process, analyze and store the information.

Traditionally the organization of public participation has been led by local authorities and supported by CSOs. However, as seen in the case study in Amsterdam, urban restructuring processes are now often led by networks, focused on commercial targets and market demand, instead of local governments. Rather than policy guidelines only, these market oriented networks need e-participation tools that are easy to use and attractive for the inhabitants – the case studies present a variety of user-friendly interfaces. On the other hand, this data collected per individual households or housing units can contribute to the development of more general sustainable development indicators in the neighborhood level where less metrics exists.

In conclusion, the case studies presented in this paper have strengthened the awareness that e-participation and empowerment processes in policy making are considered an important aspect of more sustainable communities (Cooper et al., 2005; Curwell et al., 2005). In addition, they have called into question one implicit assumption of the Lisbon objectives. That is the implied 'soft transformation' from resource-intensive traditional industry towards much more resource efficient knowledge and service industries of a dynamic information society, and that this will contribute to achieving more sustainable development. Urban planning and urban redevelopment professionals are well placed to integrate policy in both these areas in cities. To do this effectively, new metrics are needed to measure progress: to establish the contribution that the e-services and e-business are making to overall economic and social progress as well as to environmental improvements in cities. This needs to be much more fine-grained than the current metrics on Sustainable Urban Development and the eEurope Action Plan (Cap Gemini, 2004).

REFERENCES

Allee, V., & Schwabe, O. (2009). Measuring the Impact of Research Networks in the EU: Value Networks and Intellectual Capital Formation. Online version of Paper for *European Conference on Intellectual Capital Haarlem*, The Netherlands. Retrieved April 28, 2009, from http://www.vernaallee.com/value_networks/AlleeSchwabe-ResearchNetworks.pdf.

Arabianranta (2004). *Arabianranta* Retrieved April 28, 2009, from http://www.helsinkivirtual-village.fi/Resource.phx/adc/inenglish.htx

Beerepoot, M., & Sunikka, M. (2005). The contribution of the EC energy certificate in improving sustainability of the housing stock. *Environment and Planning B*, *32*(1), 21–31. doi:10.1068/b3118

Brandon, P., & Lombardi, P. (2005). *Evaluation of sustainable development in the built environment*. Oxford, UK: Blackwell.

Cap Gemini. (2004). *Online Availability of Public Services: How is Europe Progressing*. Retrieved April 28, 2009, from http://www.capgemini.com/news/2003/0206egov.shtml

Castells, M. (1996). *The Rise of the Network Society, The Information Age: Economy, Society and Culture* (*Vol. I*). Oxford, UK: Blackwell.

(2000). *Communication from the Commission to the Council, the European Parliament, the Economic and Social Committee and the Committee of the regions - Social Policy Agenda. In 28.6.2000, COM(2000) 379 final, Commission of the European Community*. Brussels: CEC.

Cooper, I., Hamilton, A., & Bentivegna, V. (2005). Sustainable Urban Development: Networked Communities, Virtual Communities and the Production of Knowledge. In Curwell, S., Deakin, M., & Symes, M. (Eds.), *Sustainable Urban Development: the Framework, Protocols and Environmental Assessment Methods* (*Vol. 1*, pp. 211–231). London: Routledge.

Curwell, S., Deakin, M., Cooper, I., Paskaleva-Shapira, K., Ravetz, J., & Babicki, D. (2005). Citizens' expectations of information cities: implications for urban planning and design. *Building Research and Information*, *33*(1), 55–66. doi:10.1080/0961321042000329422

Deakin, M., Huovila, P., Rao, S., Sunikka, M., & Vreeker, R. (2002). The assessment of sustainable urban development. *Building Research and Information*, *30*(2), 95–108. doi:10.1080/096132102753436477

EEA. (2007). *European Environment Agency. Halting the loss of biodiversity by 2010: proposal for a first set of indicators to monitor progress in Europe (Technical Report, 11)*. Copenhagen, Denmark: European Environment Agency.

Eurostat. (2007). *Measuring progress towards a more sustainable Europe. 2007 monitoring report of the EU sustainable development strategy*. Luxembourg: Office for Official Publications of the European Communities. Retrieved April 12, 2008, from http://epp.eurostat.ec.europa.eu/cache/ITY_OFFPUB/KS-77-07-115/EN/KS-77-07-115-EN.PDF

Huovila, P. (2005, September) *e-Inclusion and e/m-Participation in IntelCities*. Presented at the IntelCities Conference, Rome. IntelCities – *Intelligent Cities project* (N°: IST.2002-507860) EU VI Framework, Information Society Technologies. Retrieved October 12, 2007, from http://www.intelcitiesproject.com

Intelcity (2003) - *Towards Intelligent Sustainable Cities Roadmap*, (N°: IST-2001-37373) EU V Framework, Information Society Technologies. Retrieved January 12, 2009, from http://www.scri.salford.ac.uk/intelcity/

Klinckenberg, F., & Sunikka, M. (2006). *Better buildings through energy efficiency: A roadmap for Europe*. Brussels, Belgium: Eurima.

Lahti, P., Kangasoja, J., & Huovila, P. (2006). *Electronic and Mobile Participation in City Planning and Management. Experiences from IntelCities – an Integrated Project of the Sixth Framework Programme of the European Union. Cases Helsinki, Tampere, Garðabær/Reykjavik and Frankfurt.* Picaset Oy, Helsinki, Finland. Retrieved July 29, 2009, fromhttp://www.hel2.fi/tietokeskus/julkaisut/pdf/Intelcity.pdf.

Ligthart, F. A. T. M., Verhoog, S. M., & Gilijamse, W. (2000). Lange termijn energievisie op Parkstad, Amsterdam: Petten (ECN)

Linster, M. (2003). *Environment Indicators. Development, Measurement and Use.* Paris: OECD.

Lombardi, P., & Cooper, I. (2007). eDomus vs eAgora: the Italian case and implications for the EU 2010 strategy. In P. Cunningham, & M. Cunningham (eds), Expanding the Knowledge Economy: Issues, Applications, Case Studies vol. 1 (pp. 344-351). Amsterdam: IOS Press

Lombardi, P., Cooper, I., Paskaleva, K., & Deakin, M. (2009). The Challenge of Designing User-Centric e-Services: European Dimensions. In: C. Reddick (ed.) Strategies for Local E-Government Adoption and Implementation: Comparative Studies (pp. 460-477).Hershey, PA: IGI Global books.

Lorentsen, L. G. (2008). *Key environmental indicators.* Paris: OECD.

Meijer, F., Itard, L., & Sunikka-Blank, M. (2009). Comparing European residential building stocks: performance, renovation and policy opportunities. *Building Research and Information, 37*(5), 533–551. doi:10.1080/09613210903189376

Neskey Roadmap. (2003). *New partnerships for Sustainable development in the Knowledge Economy.* Retrieved April 22, 2009, from www.vernaallee.com/value_networks/Neskey_Exec_Summary.pdf

Pratchett, L. (1999). New technologies and the modernization of local government: An analysis of biases and constraints. *Public Administration, 7*(4), 731–750. doi:10.1111/1467-9299.00177

Sunikka, M. (2006). *Policies for improving energy efficiency if the European Housing Stock.* Amsterdam: IOS Press.

Therivel, R. (2004). *Sustainable Urban Environment – Metrics, Models and Toolkits: Analysis of sustainability/social tools,* Oxford, North Hinksey Lane. Retrieved (n.d.), from http://download.suemot.org/soctooleval.pdf

United Nation. (2007). *Indicators of Sustainable Development: Guidelines and Methodologies.* New York: United Nations publications. Retrieved July 28, 2009, from http://www.un.org/esa/sustdev/natlinfo/indicators/guidelines.pdf

Van Raaij, F., & Verhallen, T. (1983). A behavioral model of residential energy use. *Journal of Economic Psychology, 3*(1), 39–63. doi:10.1016/0167-4870(83)90057-0

ADDITIONAL READING

Affairs Review, 34(3), 372-96.

Amoretti, F. (2007). International organizations ICTs policies: e-democracy and e-government for political development. *Review of Policy Research, 24*(4), 331–344. doi:10.1111/j.1541-1338.2007.00286.x

Barber, W. F., & Bartlett, R. V. (2007). Problematic Participants in Deliberative Democracy: Experts, Social Movements, and Environmental Justice. *International Journal of Public Administration, 30*, 5–22. doi:10.1080/01900690601050021

Bentivegna, V., Curwell, S., Deakin, M., Lombardi, P., & Nijkamp, P. (2002). A vision and methodology for integrated sustainable urban development: BE-QUEST. *Building Research International, 30*(2), 83–94. doi:10.1080/096132102753436468

Deakin, M., & Allwinkle, S. (2006). The IntelCities Community of Practice. *International Journal of Knowledge. Culture and Change Management, 6*(2), 155–162.

European Commission (2005). – A European Information Society for growth and employment. Presented at *i2010.* COM(2005) 229

Ho, T.-K. A. (2002). Reinventing local governments and the e-government initiative. *Public Administration Review, 62*(4), 434–444. doi:10.1111/0033-3352.00197

Hollands, R. (2008). Will the real smart city please stand up? *City, 12*(3), 303–320. doi:10.1080/13604810802479126

In Castells, M., & Hall, P. (Eds.). (1994). *Technopolies of the world.* London: Routledge.

Kolsaker, A. (2007). Understanding e-government (G2C) in the knowledge society. *International Journal of Information Technology and Management, 6*(2-4), 138–147. doi:10.1504/IJITM.2007.013997

Lee, L., Tan, X., & Trimmi, S. (2006). Current practices of leading e-government countries. *Communications of the ACM, 48*(10), 100–104.

Lombardi, P. (1997). Decision making problems concerning urban regeneration plans. *Engineering, Construction, and Architectural Management, 4*(2), 127–142. doi:10.1108/eb021044

Lombardi, P. (1998). Sustainability indicators in urban planning evaluation. In Lichfield, N., Barbanente, A., Borri, D., Kakee, A., & Prat, A. (Eds.), *Evaluation in Planning* (pp. 177–192). Dordrecht, The Netherlands: Kluwer Academic Publishers.

Lombardi, P., & Curwell, S. (2005). Analysis of the INTELCITY Scenarios for the City of the future from a South-Mediterranean perspective. In Miller, D., & Patassini, D. (Eds.), *Beyond Benefit Cost Analysis -- Accounting for Non-Market Values in Planning Evaluation* (pp. 207–224). Aldershot Hampshire, UK: Ashgate.

Nath, B., Heans, L., & Devuyst, D. (1996). *Sustainable Development.* Brussels, Belgium: VUB Press.

Organisation for Cooperation and Economic Development. (2001). *Understanding the digital divide.* Paris: OECD.

Organisation for Cooperation And Economic Development. (2003). *Engaging citizens online for better policy-making,* Paris: OECD. Retrieved February 27, 2008, from http://www.oecd.org/dataoecd/62/23/2501856.pdf

Paskaleva-Shapira, K. (2007). Urban sustainability and governance: Challenges of the Knowledge Society. In Vreeker, R., Deakin, M., & Curwell, S. (Eds.), *Sustainable Urban Development.* London: Routledge.

Paskaleva-Shapira, K. (2008). Assessing local e-governance in Europe. *International Journal of Electronic Government Research, 4*(4), 17–36.

Pierre, J. (1999). *Models of urban governance: The institutional dimensions of urban politics.* Urban.

Rhodes, R. (1996). The new governance: Governing without government. *Political Studies, 44*(4), 652–667. doi:10.1111/j.1467-9248.1996.tb01747.x

Riley, T. B. (2007). Strategies for the effective implementation of E-Government projects. *Journal of Business and Public Policy, 1*(1), 1–11.

Torres, L., Pina, V., & Acerete, B. (2006). e-Governance development in European Union cities: reshaping government's relationship with citizens. *Governance: an International Journal of Policy. Administration and Institutions, 19*(2), 277–302.

United Nations. (2004) "Sustainable cities programme", United Nations. Retrieved January 02, 2009, from http://www.unhabitat.org/content.a sp?cid=116&catid=369&typeid=24&subMenu Id=0.

Verdegem, P., & Verleye, G. (2009). User-centered e-government in practice: a comprehensive model for measuring user satisfaction. *Government Information Quarterly, 26*(3), 487–497. doi:10.1016/j. giq.2009.03.005

KEY TERMS AND DEFINITIONS

Civil Society Organizations (CSOs): These are considered to be any legal entity that is non-governmental, not-for-profit, not representing commercial interests, and pursuing a common purpose in the public interest (Work Programme 2009, Cooperation Theme 6, Environment (Including Climate Change), European Commission C(2008)4598 of 28 August 2008).

eAgora Vvision: Aims to support improved management of cities and to achieve long-term physical, social and economic sustainability by bringing together unconnected sources of information in one place, and making that place available in digital space to everyone, from city planners, building developers, politicians, to individual citizens.

E-Participation: Consists of three main components (OCED, 2001): information provision; transactions (delivery of on-line services), and deliberation (citizen engagement in civic decision-making). Achieving this vision puts citizens at the centre of attention in the design of such on-line developments in terms of accessibility including, for example, the visually disabled, different age and language groups.

Information & Communication Technologies (ICTs): It is a general term that describes any technology that helps to produce, manipulate, store, communicate, and/or disseminate information.

Metric: It is a standard unit of measure, such as meter or mile for length, or more generally, part of a system of parameters, or systems of measurement, or a set of ways of quantitatively and periodically measuring, assessing, controlling or selecting a person, process, event, or institution, along with the procedures to carry out measurements and the procedures for the interpretation of the assessment in the light of previous or comparable assessments (Retrieved 30 April, 2009 from http://en.wikipedia.org/wiki/Metrics).

Policy: Typically, it is a deliberate plan of action to guide decisions and achieve rational outcome(s). It also refers to the process of making important organizational decisions, including the identification of different alternatives such as programs or spending priorities, and choosing among them on the basis of the impact they will have.

Sustainable (urban) Development: It is a pattern of resource use that aims to meet human needs while preserving the environment so that these needs can be met not only in the present, but also for future generations to come. It ties together concern for the carrying capacity of natural systems with the social challenges facing humanity.

Chapter 2
Citizens and E-Government Service Delivery:
Techniques to Increase Citizen Participation

Jennifer A. Kurtz
Conundrum Creek Consulting, USA

Roland J. Cole
Sagamore Institute for Policy Research, USA

Isabel A. Cole
Independent Librarian, USA

ABSTRACT

Without a plan for marketing the convenience, ease, and safety of online services, the goal of achieving an 80 percent adoption rate by citizens for certain e-government services (e.g., tax filing and vehicle registration) will remain a dream. Although states realize benefits from implementing online applications that reduce processing time and costs, the rate of growth in citizen e-government adoption rates seems to have leveled off. This chapter examines, from the state's perspective, successful techniques for increasing citizen use of electronic applications for two common activities – vehicle registration renewal and income tax filing – in four Midwestern states (Illinois, Indiana, Kentucky, Ohio). Usage patterns depend in part on an individual citizen's technological sophistication, whether digital naïf, digital immigrant, or digital native. Usage can be influenced, however, by state government investments to market electronic services (through awareness campaigns or financial incentives), establish alternative access points, and incorporate human use factors in applications.

INTRODUCTION

The IRS restructuring and reform act of 1998 (also known as the taxpayer bill of rights – pub. L. 105-206 112 stat. 685) declared congressional policy "that it should be the goal of the service to have at least 80 percent of all federal tax and information returns filed electronically by 2007." The target date for this achievement has now been pushed to 2012 and incentives implemented to make electronic

DOI: 10.4018/978-1-61520-933-0.ch002

filing a more attractive choice for taxpayers. The federal government is very clear about the importance of e-government adoption. A recent study about IRS efforts to promote e-government [IRS (2008)] describes "lessons learned" that may be applicable to state agencies.

States have not generally been as clear about their objectives and differ with respect to incentive programs. Better understanding about how to maximize return on investments made in e-government by identifying the most cost-effective marketing approach for promoting the use of online applications is needed. Existing studies have tended to focus on inherent characteristics of the service offerings, governmental structure, or population demographics to explain variations in citizen adoption of e-government services. This chapter examines the impact of marketing efforts made by state government agencies to expand citizen use of e-government service options. Successful results realized by the four case study states are then cross-referenced to the "lessons learned" from the IRS study.

Because of their scalability, e-government applications become more cost-effective with increased usage. A 2007 study, in fact, indicates that cost savings accrue from online service provisioning when citizen adoption rates exceed 30 percent: "while e-government is often implemented as a measure to provide efficiencies and to save costs (e.g., reducing the need for employees to perform some routine tasks such as customer service), actual dollar savings are not always realized by the states. However, e-government presents management challenges, and costs savings typically do not occur until the later phases of e-government implementation when at least a 30% adoption rate is realized. [Seifert 2007, 4] it is important that states actively promote the use of online services.

Our intention in performing this study was to address the question: how have citizens responded to e-government service options when state governments have encouraged their use? We used behavioral data gathered by state agencies – citi-

zen usage numbers for a particular e-government service – as evidence for favorable response from citizens. We also interviewed key state government officials about their respective agencies' marketing programs. Where available, we have included details about the actual marketing investment made by state agencies to promote the use of e-government services. Finally, we chose two citizen applications for scrutiny – vehicle registration and income tax filing – that are relevant to a broader citizen population than more specialized or intermittent interests (such as, hunting/fishing licenses and vital records).

BACKGROUND

Literature Overview

A solid body of knowledge exists to describe the various stages of development that characterizes e-government activities at all levels of government (local, county, state, national). [see, for example, Accenture (al-Hashmi and Daren (2008), Damodaran et al. (2005), Irani et al. (2006), Layne and Lee (2001), Reddick (2003), Siau and Long (2005), Seifert (2003 and 2007), West (2004, 2004, 2005, 2008)] although scholars and analysts may differ on minor details and combine certain utilities differently, the following four stages are most frequently identified:

- **Presence:** Government entity establishes an online presence to present relatively static information (often described as brochureware).
- **Interaction:** Government entity allows additional communication links (e.g., email) and downloadable forms, in addition to dynamic information.
- **Transaction:** Government entity uses online applications to accept and transmit fillable forms, payments, permits and licenses, and bid proposals.

- **Transformation:** Government entity uses computer techniques create new citizen-centric processes that transcend conventional agency boundaries.

Excellent work has also been done with the support of the European commission to examine social and cultural barriers and incentives for e-government, especially among certain economically disadvantaged groups through the e-lost project. [Lina van Aerschot et al. (2007)] many of its findings are similar to those from surveys of us municipalities with populations under 100,000. [Schwester (2009)] in their recommendations, however, these studies did not consider financial incentives. This chapter focuses on examples of techniques used to encourage e-government activities in the third stage, transaction. [Seifert (2003)]

E-government research is enriched by comprehensive surveys about citizen attitudes toward e-government. [Accenture's annual e-government survey, pew internet & American life project survey] the pew internet & American life project has performed telephone surveys of Americans since 2000 to understand their attitudes toward using the internet for a variety of purposes, including seeking information from, and interacting with, state agencies. [Horrigan, 2008] the pew surveys included questions about visiting government sites online through august 2003. At that time, 66% of the respondents who used the internet had visited a government site. [Trend spreadsheet accessed online at http://www.pewinternet.org/trend-data.aspx on 22 July 2009]

Other studies examine the supply side of e-government and record extensively the kinds of applications available, applicable fees, the degree of user-friendliness, and online payment mechanisms. [See, for example: annual state new economy index reports and west (2008)] these latter mechanisms are noteworthy because their deployment is essential at the transactional stage of e-government and their development is often outsourced. Outsourcing electronic payment sources can help states manage the start-up and maintenance cost for e-governments. Using electronic payment service providers has also allowed states in which fee schedules are established by legislation to provide e-government payment services without having to absorb the additional charge for credit card transactions. [Seifert 2007, 16]

As of April 30, 2009, agencies of 29 states plus the district of Columbia have contracted with the official payments corporation (OPC) for at least some electronic payment processing services. States not listed as having contracts with OPC are: Alaska, Arizona, Colorado, Florida, Hawaii, Idaho, Maine, Massachusetts, Michigan, Missouri, Montana, Nevada, New Hampshire, North Carolina, North Dakota, Oklahoma, South Carolina, South Dakota, Utah, Vermont, Wyoming.

A study of the efforts by the IRS to increase e-filing concluded with five major lessons for those managing a transition to online government transactions. The fIRSt lesson was to create a focus within the managing organization on increasing use of online processes. The second lesson was to develop collaborative partnerships with stakeholders (in tax cases, those who help citizens prepare tax forms). The third lesson was to invest in innovation, in both the transaction (new and better web forms) and the management techniques (work with stakeholders, lower costs). The fourth lesson, and the focus of this chapter, was to become proactive in encouraging online use instead of expecting citizens to flock to it just because it was there (a "field of dreams"). The fifth lesson was to use program performance data, such as the percentage filing online, to drive decisions about the management techniques. [IRS, 2008, p.5]

The study noted that the challenges to increasing online use are likely to vary over time, as those most likely to e-file are doing so and what are left have substantial resistance in motivation or capability to do so. As of 2008, the study noted that the current challenges were psychological and behavioral, not technological. [ibid.]The study also suggested that the techniques used by the IRS were "well described" and "prescribed" in the academic literature. [ibid. P.6] for instance, an urban institute study of nonprofit executives suggested that those considering e-filing were very apt to be swayed by financial incentives, such as free or low-cost filing options and the ability to pay via credit card. [Urban Institute, 2002, p. 10] since the IRS was successful in dramatically increasing the percentages of taxpayers filing online, such a result should gladden the hearts of all those who hope that academic recommendations are followed and are successful. The rest of the chapter describes what techniques each of the four states used, and then presents some conclusions and recommendations that constitute the "lessons" of these state experiences.

Methodology

Rather than submit surveys to state e-government officials to identify supply side characteristics, the basic data in this study come from interviews with state officials directly involved in planning and executing the required processes and support activities for enabling online citizen transactions. In this chapter, information about actual citizen usage is used as an indicator of demand for specific e-government services (vehicle registration and tax filing) in the four case study states: Illinois, Indiana, Kentucky, and Ohio. These data indicate actual citizen behavior with respect to acceptance of e-government, rather than attitude and intention, as with some of the surveys previously mentioned.

Agency officials were selected to participate based upon their familiarity with e-government processes in their respective agencies over a several year period. Given the behavioral nature of our inquiry, insights from those with practical experience in transaction activities was sought rather than policy-makers' statements. This quali-

tative research was balanced by the quantitative data on citizen activity received from the state agencies.

The selection of Illinois, Indiana, Kentucky, and Ohio for a case study approach was, in part, opportunistic – the authors are familiar with the states and have worked with officials there. Their demographic profiles are also similar, so similar civilian behavior with respect to e-government activities could be anticipated, thus underscoring effects from state-specific government incentive and other marketing programs. With the possible exception of areas within the Chicago metropolitan area, these states are commonly considered part of the "old" economy, characterized by heavy industry – especially vehicle manufacturing – in urbanized areas and grain agriculture in rural areas. The employee pool easily crosses state lines: all share at least two borders. None of the states is ranked in the top quartile in the US for broadband telecommunications infrastructure; however, three of the states rank within the top quartile for e-government services, according to the 2008 state new economy index. [Atkinson and Andes, 2008] the fourth state in our group is ranked in the second quartile. (See Table 1)

Conditions Affecting Citizen Adoption Rates

A 2008 study by the Brookings institution used content analysis techniques to examine 1,537 state and federal websites. [West, 2008] the researchers designed a ranking system for state websites that was based on 18 different features as well the number of online services that could be executed through the websites. The features noted in the study that can create impediments to using e-government services were: user fees, premium fees, credit card options, PDA or hand-held device compatibility, and foreign language accessibility.

Two of the states that scored among the top ten in the Brookings study are highlighted here

Table 1. State rankings from 2008 state new economy index (Atkinson & Andes, 2008)

State	Online population	Technology in schools	E-Government services	Broadband telecommunications
Illinois	22	31	25	16
Indiana	37	18	8	38
Kentucky	43	31	2	43
Ohio	34	19	10	24

– Kentucky (ranked sixth) and Indiana (ranked ninth). They also ranked among the top 10 in the 2008 new state economy index. Ohio, however, ranked in the second quartile for the Brookings study. Illinois ranked in the third quartile in both studies. (See Table 2)

Process Complexity

The 2003 congressional research services report "a primer on e-government: sectors, stages, opportunities, and challenges of online governance," observed that government to citizen (g2c) initiatives are generally designed to make government more accessible to citizens and to redirect attention toward citizen needs, rather than agency-centric processes. [Seifert, 2003] states are organized in different ways to perform common citizen processes, such as vehicle registration. The sophistication of their online vehicle systems may reflect the ease with which various departments work together to share information needed to complete the process, as well as the complexity of state laws. Kentucky, for example, imposes a per-

sonal property tax on motor vehicles. [Kentucky state website, 2009] property taxes owed on all vehicles must be current before online registration is allowed. Likewise, vehicle insurance must be obtained 45 days before renewing registration to ensure that the transportation database records are updated. Ohio, on the other hand, simply requires that the vehicle registrant "sign" an affidavit online that he or she has valid insurance.

State Government Culture

Not all states promote e-government as an objective, but rather, promote citizen self-service as just one among a range of options for interaction. Ohio, for example, uses a network of deputy registrar offices located in each county to deliver certain citizen services. These offices are small businesses that work under contract to the state and depend on transaction fees for their survival. The state of Ohio does not promote online services in a manner that would compete with these offices for business.

Table 2. State and federal website features (West, 2008)

	2001	2002	2003	2004	2005	2006	2007	2008
Ads	2%	2%	1%	9%	3%	1%	1%	2%
User fees	2	2	3	19	2	12	17	7
Premium fees	--	1	0.4	4	0	4	8	1
W3c[4] disability accessibility (state only)	--	--	33	37	40	43	46	19
Foreign language accessibility	6	7	13	21	18	30	22	40
PDA compatibility	--	--	1	1	1	1	1	3

Payment Options

States also vary in terms of payment method allowed for online transactions. Approximately 33 percent of government websites accept credit cards. [West (2008)] all four states examined for this chapter allow some form of e-check or electronic funds transfer for payment. They also allow credit card payment, but vary according to which cards are accepted and what additional charges are imposed for using a credit card, from a simple service fee to a service fee plus percentage of the associated transaction charge. Illinois allows the use of several different credit cards for online transactions, but only discover card for in-person transactions. This limitation on the use of cards for in-person transactions may serve indirectly as an incentive to use the online renewal process. States also may impose an additional "convenience fee" for using their online system. Kentucky, for example, charges a $5 convenience fee for each vehicle registered online. Indiana, on the other hand, gives a $5 discount to those who register their vehicle online (nb: this was true for 2008 and 2009).

Convenience and Other Premium Charges

In the early years of g2c, some state agencies recouped the cost of redesigning databases and creating appealing, easily navigable websites by charging a premium for electronic service delivery even though the resulting process was more cost-effective for the state agency. According to a 2008 Brookings institution study [west] that takes a longitudinal look at trends in premium fees for online services, however, only a small percentage of online applications – between 1 percent and 3 percent – were subject to such fees. One of the case study states for this chapter, Indiana, actually reversed its policy over time from imposing a surcharge to giving a discount for using an e-government application. Indiana initially charged a

$3 convenience fee for online vehicle registration. In 2008, Indiana reduced by $5 the online vehicle registration fee for those who renewed online, a difference of $8 to a citizen vehicle owner.

This study shows an irregular pattern for e-government services user fees between 2001 and 2008. According to Darrell M. West, principal investigator for the project and vice president and director of governance studies at the Brookings institution, there is a lot of variance across the states with respect to the use of fees; "for fee" models appear less frequently than convenience fees (typically, for credit card payment processing), although states that subscribe to a self-funding model for their web portals tend to have user fees. User fees reflect the general condition of a state's finances and not a geographical pattern. [West (2008)]

Trust Factors

In 2003, the state of Indiana released "Indiana interconnect," a study of Indiana's broadband capacity and usage. [Indiana department of commerce et al., 2003] as part of the study, more than 1500 citizens were interviewed to explore their internet usage patterns. Several questions pertained to e-government adoption. At that time, the majority of those who used internet at home had also visited the Indiana state government website. Only some 17 percent of them, however, had actually performed an e-government transaction through the website. The most frequently mentioned reasons for not using online applications for government transactions were related to trust: the majority of those who used the internet for commercial and other transactions said they trusted commercial websites more than government ones.

The survey questions did not explore how those interviewed perceived trust, that is, whether they were concerned about the integrity of the data transmitted and received, its confidentiality in transit, the forthrightness of those who had access to the information, or the assurance of privacy.

This is an interesting area for further research. The results from the Indiana survey may have indicated a lingering concern about "big brother" interference by government – or simply that the perceived value of performing government transactions online had not yet achieved a certain threshold that would allow greater risk taking.

The citizens have concerns, but will use online payment if risk/benefit calculation is better than for offline. Government can affect both the actual numbers involved, and the perception of those numbers. We posit that how much it does so is based on its calculation of both the benefit to the government and the benefit to the citizen. In areas where the government is the main employer, reducing government employment via closing payment stations and/or cutting back hours is not necessarily a good thing. Reducing errors, however, is almost always considered a good thing, as is confirmation on both sides that a payment has been made.

Access to Technology

Internet connectivity may not be as much a barrier to e-government adoption as it was in 2003. Public access points – libraries, coffee shops, transportation facilities, hotels – offer broadband, often at no charge (other than the anxiety that might arise from using public WiFi connections). And those who by habit, choice, or technophobia prefer to use in-line or mail-in channels for performing government transactions benefit from reduced waiting time and more rapid processing time.

In addition to usage fees, administrative barriers, and trust concerns, other factors impinge on an individual's decision about whether to use an online application to perform government business. In particular, access, habit, and awareness may help determine that selection.

State Agency Incentives

Citizens in Ohio, at least, appeared to respond to a vigorous marketing campaign for renewing vehicles online. Indiana also experienced a sharp increase in online renewals with its financial incentive program. Indiana has used a variety of channels to increase online renewals, by building partnerships with automobile dealerships, financial institutions, AAA, and others to make it easier for citizens to connect with government electronically. In a similar way, Indiana has also engaged a network of faith-based and other not-for-profit organizations to assist those more likely to be digitally disenfranchised, especially those who are currently unemployed.

Three of the four states examined promoted quicker tax refund processing in their appeals to citizens to file electronically. Illinois focused on electronic filing as being more environmentally advantageous generally, rather than more economically advantageous individually.

State Mandates

Of course, the ultimate incentive for using e-government services is the absence of alternatives. For certain classes of transactions, mandatory electronic filing seems to be the direction in which Indiana and Ohio are going. In Indiana, for example, applicants for unemployment benefits must register online to make claims. And in Ohio, electronic sales tax filing was mandated in 2008 and large quarterly business taxpayers have been required to file a commercial activity tax (a gross receipts tax applicable to most businesses) electronically since 2005. While it does make budgetary sense for state governments to mandate the use of electronic applications – by helping them leverage investments already made in technology, accelerate implementation breakeven point, and increase return on investment – it is important that citizens not lose recourse to the personal interaction that may be necessary to resolve more complex cases or simply explain a process.

The results of the state new economy index reports and other studies (for example, [West, 2008]) examine the supply side of e-government. As of April 30, 2009, agencies of 29 states plus the District of Columbia have contracted with the official payments corporation for at least some electronic payment processing services. The OPC website's drop-down menu lists all states; however, the following do not have contracts at this time: Alaska, Arizona, Colorado, Florida, Hawaii, Idaho, Maine, Massachusetts, Michigan, Missouri, Montana, Nevada, New Hampshire, North Carolina, North Dakota, Oklahoma, South Carolina, South Dakota, Utah, Vermont, Wyoming.

Although the supply side of e-government services has been fairly well documented, considerably less work has been done to understand the demand side. The pew internet & American life project has performed telephone surveys of Americans since 2000 to understand their attitudes toward using the internet for a variety of purposes, including seeking information from, and interacting with, state agencies.[Horrigan, 2008]

Internet connectivity may not be as much a barrier to e-government adoption as it was in 2003. Public access points – libraries, coffee shops, transportation facilities, hotels – offer broadband, often at no charge (other than the anxiety that might arise from using public WiFi connections). And those who by habit, choice, or technophobia prefer to use in-line or mail-in channels for performing government transactions benefit from reduced waiting time and more rapid processing time.

Vehicle Registration

Each of the four states studied organizes the vehicle registration function differently.

Illinois

Vehicle registration falls under the Illinois secretary of state's vehicle services department. For those eligible to renew their registration online, a renewal code and pin are sent with the renewal notice. Online payments may be made with major credit cards (visa, master card, American Express, Discover, Diner's Club) or by electronic check. A $1.75 convenience fee is charged for credit card use. The same charges apply for renewals using touch tone phones. The convenience fee charged for in-person registration renewals, $2, is slightly higher. The more significant benefit to renewing registrations online may be that more credit card companies are accepted. Only discover cards are accepted in-person (as are cash, personal check, traveler's check). According to the data processing division's online records, 10.4 million vehicles are registered in Illinois, including 7.1 million passenger and 66,000 disabilities registrations.

Indiana

The Indiana bureau of motor vehicles (BMV) requires annual vehicle registration renewal. It offers the widest range of in-person customer service options among the four states studied, including 24-hour self-service terminals (co-located at some BMV branches), five old national bank branches, seven AAA license branches, and clean air car check testing sites (for residents of lake or porter counties). New vehicle registration and title services may also be performed at 323 automobile dealerships in Indiana that have a partnership agreement with the state that covers newly purchased vehicles. Indiana also offers the most significant financial incentive for filing on-line. In 2008, Governor Daniels announced a $5 discount to those who renewed their vehicle registrations electronically. The success of that incentive program prompted the governor to announce the same discount for 2009. According to BMV official Dennis Rosebrough, use of the on-line registration system increased 224% between 2007 and 2008 (as can be seen in Table 3) and that increase has continued into 2009. Electronic renewal requests are processed seven days a week

Table 3. Indiana vehicle registration post-cash incentive (personal interview, Dennis Rosebrough, communications director, Indiana BMV, 24 April 2009)

	Number of online registrations	Online registrations as percent of total registrations
2007	399,235	5.5%
2008	1,293,254	17.8%
2009 (partial year)	631,624	23.5%

and require up to 11 business days for complete processing time.

As an additional administrative policy change to improve vehicle registration processing, the Indiana BMV also increased the number of registration expiration dates from 19 to 45, thus smoothing out the number of renewals throughout the year. In 2008, 1.3 million citizens renewed their vehicle registrations on-line, with a direct savings to taxpayers of $6.5 million. In addition, fewer citizen transactions in the branches have led to improved customer services delivery throughout the organization and quicker resolution of complicated transactions that require higher-level problem-solving. Other services, previously available only in-person or through postal mail, were added at the end of 2008 for citizens who register through the myBMV program. The BMV also announced the adoption of facial recognition technology in November 2008.

Other types of vehicle registration services – such as transferring ownership and sales – must be completed in-person at BMV branch locations.

Kentucky

Online registration for individual passenger vehicles (that is, neither commercial, fleet, motorcycle, nor marine) was first rolled out by the Kentucky transportation cabinet in 2000-2001. A $5 convenience fee is charged for each vehicle being renewed online. Only master card and visa are accepted for payment. The online registration process is supported by back-end coordination among agencies: the department of insurance veri-

fies that a registrant's listed insurance company is registered to do business in Kentucky. Insurance obtained within 45 days of vehicle registration might not be in the transportation database, thus necessitating an in-person visit to the county clerk and preventing online registration. Unlike Indiana and Ohio, Kentucky levies a property tax on personal as well as real property. This includes a property tax on motor vehicles that must be remitted to the county clerk on or before the last day of the month in which registration renewal is required for a vehicle. The owner of a vehicle cannot have overdue property taxes on any other vehicles. Address changes cannot be done online at this time either.

The state is in the process of implementing a new computer system -- the Kentucky automated vehicle information system -- that will allow the vehicle registration data to be provided easily and is also a key upgrade for the state's system. According to state officials, "the online system is a valuable tool for many Kentuckians. Kentucky is working to improve the online experience for our web customers and is continually exploring ways to enhance the services available electronically. The development of Kentucky's new vehicle information system will ultimately help improve the services offered online." Security features are already in place to protect the internet connection (encryption) and the server. Typically, marketing online registration to citizens is restricted to notices on the state website.

Figure 1. Ohio online vehicle registration increase post-marketing campaign (personal interview, Lindsay Komlanc, media relations director, Ohio DPS, 27 April 2009)

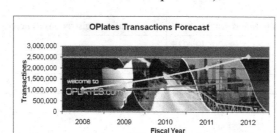

Ohio

Prior to 2000, the Ohio department of public safety explored different ways of making vehicle registration more convenient for citizens and started offering electronic services in 2000. Ohio contracts with small business owners to act as deputy registrars in each county. Some title services are provided by the county clerks of course, a fairly new added benefit. Although every county has at least one deputy registrar, citizens can go to any county for services regardless of their home residence. Delivering customer services is one of the main goals.

Self-funded business models are frequently used by states that have contracted with NIC USA to create their state web portals. As of April 30, 2009, NIC USA website indicates support contracts with 22 states for their e-government web portals: Alabama, Arizona, Arkansas, Colorado, Hawaii, Idaho, Indiana, Iowa, Kansas, Kentucky, Maine, Montana, Oklahoma, Nebraska, Rhode Island, South Carolina, Tennessee, Utah, Vermont, Virginia, and West Virginia. Rather than use a self-funded model, DPS set aside funds from its budget for development of the online vehicle registration system before releasing its RFP to the vendor community. Included in the contract was an ongoing per-transaction fee for deputy registrars. When a citizen goes in-person to renew

vehicle registration, he or she pays a $3.50 fee to the deputy registrar. In advertising its online services, the DPS focuses on citizen convenience, rather than agency cost reduction. Links to the online site are included on different websites and o-plate information is included on renewal notice envelopes. There was a billboard campaign during the first couple of years to raise awareness. Now, however, all options are discussed.

Approximately 26 percent of all registered vehicles are renewed online, out of some 12.5 million vehicle registrations. Citizen adoption of online renewals grew slowly. According to DPS officials, only two to three percent of renewals were done online for the first few years – it took awhile to reach the 15 percent level. Word-of-mouth and the previously mentioned billboard campaign helped promote online use, however. Citizen adoption of online registration appears to have been spurred by an ad campaign approved in late 2005, as shown in Figure 1.

According to the officials at the state department of motor vehicles, "beginning in early FY 2006 (fall of calendar year 2005), marketing funds were approved to promote o-plates. Since that time, customer awareness has increased at an amazing rate. Transactions have increased up to 39 percent, based on monthly comparisons for transactions between FY 2005 and FY 2006. In addition, the collection of transaction fees ($3.50

Table 4. Ohio online vehicle registration - forecast with ad campaign (personal interview, Komlanc, 2009)

Fiscal year	Forecast no ads	In-house gain	Npv
2008	1,054,330	$643,141	$355,007.46
2009	1,314,539	$801,869	$442,623.30
2010	1,638,597	$999,770	$551,862.73
2011	2,043,464	$1,246,513	$688,062.45
2012	2,547,791	$1,554,153	$857,876.27

per transaction) has *(sic)* increased up to $124,000 between FY 2005 and FY 2007. The total increase in fees equals more than $1.185 million, resulting in roughly $185,000 return on our $1 million marketing investment."

Based on past experience, Ohio DPS officials have projected a 24.68% increase in online vehicle registration if marketing campaigns continue and only a 10.77% increase if they do not, as seen in Tables 4 and 5.

Although Ohio does not validate insurance information as a condition of registration renewal, renewal submissions include an affidavit signed by the requestor. DPS does perform random verification checks and those submitting false information can be prosecuted. Motorcycle registration renewal follows the same process, but boats cannot be registered online. Commercial fleets are subject to a bulk renewal process. Fleets benefit from the annual requirement to validate state information about what vehicles are in their fleets.

Ongoing projects include the addition of commercial vehicles and heavy trucks and driver's license reinstatement to online processing. The latter can now only be accomplished in-person at one of five regional sites around the state. Moving the process online will offer citizens a convenient alternative to the existing mail-in option. DPS is also developing online licensing capabilities and has recently added interactive voice response (IVR) and Spanish language features. The IVR systems allow direct human-to-human customer service contact while citizens are online. According to DPS officials, "for the BMV, the real impetus is trying to offer as many options as possible for good customer service. We are one of the first states to go online. And we even offer more in terms of vehicle plate design and live help for citizens because our operators can communicate with up to five customers at the same." The FAQ site contains hundreds of responses to questions asked by Ohio citizens. Another DPS technology professional said, "I would sit and monitor ques-

Table 5. Ohio online vehicle registration - forecast without ad campaign (personal interview, Komlanc, 2009)

Fiscal year	Forecast no ads	In-house gain	Npv
2008	936,703	$571,389	$315,400.84
2009	1,037,586	$632,928	$349,369.51
2010	1,149,334	$701,094	$386,996.60
2011	1,273,118	$776,602	$428,676.14
2012	1,410,232	$860,242	$474,844.56

Table 6. Indiana department of revenue individual tax filing report (source: in.gov, "filing statistics," 2009)

Filing method	Total number returns posted	Total number of "amount due" returns	Total number of "overpaid" returns	Total number of " in balance" returns
2d barcode	169,426 (260,431)	35,165 (72,758)	127,359 (178,604)	6,902 (9,069)
Fed/state electronic	1,787,095 (1,729,845)	463,133 (471,202)	1,268,806 (1,215,619)	55,156 (43,024)
In internet	149,213 (115,527)	29,222 (24,628)	116,280 (88,117)	3,711 (2,782)
Paper	298,536 (486,145)	64,429 (101,736)	187,494 (327,432)	46,613 (56,977)
Total	2,404,270 (2,591,948)	591,949 (670,324)	1,699,939 (1,809,772)	112,382 (111,852)

tions coming in and incorporate recommendations to the system. For example, if citizens could not find a button, i would change the screen layout to make it easier to use."

Income Tax Filing

Illinois

The state of Illinois website encourages citizens to "save a tree, file electronically." Taxpayers must have an IL-pin (Illinois personal identification number) to file electronically. The IL department of revenue funds free tax counseling options statewide through the tax counseling project and the tax assistance program, and through teaming relationships with local governments and not-for-profits like the center for economic progress. As of march 24, 2009, more than 2.2 million individual tax returns had been filed electronically. This represents an increase of about 8 percent over 2008 when 52% of returns were filed electronically (more than 3.1 million). Officials anticipate that 60 percent of individual taxpayers will file electronically through the end of the 2009 tax season. According to department director Brian Hamer, "Illinois offers a free web file program for all taxpayers, regardless of income, that provides fast refunds that can be deposited directly into a family's bank account in about a week." [Illinois Department of Revenue, 2009.] There are no fees for filing electronically.

Indiana

The state of Indiana includes information about citizen tax filing methods on its website and cross-references filing method to refund status. The comparison for 2007 and 2008 (through April 13, 2008) are contained in Table 6, with the figures for 2007 (through April 14, 2007) in parentheses.

Indiana's e-pay system allows payment via major credit cards (visa, master card, discover) and electronic checks. Individuals can pay their annual tax, estimated or installment payments, and review their payments to date. The cost for tax payment online is $1 for an e-check and $1 plus 2 percent of the total for a credit card payment. There is no discount for paying taxes online.

Kentucky

According to Bruce Nix, director of the division of individual tax collection for the department of revenue, the state of Kentucky would like to see everyone file electronically. One key benefit to the state is that electronic processing has freed

Table 7. Kentucky individual income tax filing 1998-2007 (source: personal interview, Bruce Nix, director/division of individual income tax, Kentucky department of revenue, 30 April 2009)

	Tax year 1998	Tax year 1999	Tax year 2000	Tax year 2001	Tax year 2002	Tax year 2003	Tax year 2004	Tax year 2005	Tax year 2006	Tax year 2007
Elf	274,985	332,736	404,913	484,878	567,003	623,432	673,732	726,177	796,271	877,671
Telefile	40,825	54,713	47,588	50,615	47,307	45,355	40,929	0	0	0
Online	0	29,543	46,191	74,745	99,595	124,876	147,397	187,871	217,041	253,105
Total non-paper returns	315,810	416,992	498,692	610,238	713,905	793,663	862,058	914,048	1,013,312	1,130,776
Percentage increase of non-paper returns	46%	32%	20%	22%	15%	10%	8%	6%	10%	10%
Filing available	Elf and telefile	Elf, telefile, and online	Elf, telefile, and online	Elf, telefile, and online	Elf, telefile, and online	Elf, telefile, and online	Elf, telefile, and online	Elf and online	Elf and online	Elf and online
Total returns filed	1,700,202	1,716,834	1,743,866	1,750,093	1,733,707	1,741,110	1,754,303	1,784,587	1,816,293	1,899,371
Percent of non-paper returns	18.6%	24.3%	24.3%	34.9%	41.2%	45.6%	49.1%	51.2%	55.8%	59.5%

personnel from routine processing so that they can concentrate on exceptions. Paper returns are digitized to make their processing more electronic and to reduce the potential for keying errors. Kentucky first started offering e-government services for filing taxes for the 1994 tax year (1995 processing season). Nix said that citizens were initially reluctant to file electronically, explaining, "I think the problem at the start of this was that people believed it [electronic filing] would make them more likely to be audited. Now they understand that they can get their refunds as fast as possible by filing electronically." In reality, the chance of being audited is the same for all returns, whether filed electronically or manually. He also expressed concern that lack of access to appropriate technical resources may impede some citizens from filing electronically. From 2000 through 2009, the average increase per year for e-file versus paper filing was approximately 11 percent. That rate of increase was sharper earlier in the decade and is beginning to level out, as can

be seen Table 7. Almost 1.2 million citizens now file electronically. Those filing with non-resident or part-year resident status, or filing a reciprocal return, cannot file electronically at present.

From the administrative point of view, the perception of the online filing system is very positive. According to nix, "department of revenue employees appreciate the system and what it is capable of helping us achieve. The staff that actually processes the returns is minimal. It is considered one of our most effective processing systems in the department." Less staff is required to process electronic returns and the overall cost of processing returns has decreased significantly. The efficiency of processing returns electronically has also benefited those filing paper returns: the turnaround time for them is also shorter because of the decrease in volume. Nix continued, "in the early stages of e-file, it could take up to eight weeks for a return to make it through the processing system, from mail opening to completion. An electronic return with no errors can be processed

[now] in three to five business days – a paper return can take up to three weeks depending on the type of return being filed."

The Kentucky department of revenue does not charge a fee for filing electronically and has partnered with several tax preparation software companies to create the Kentucky free file alliance. The majority of the population falls into the "free" category. Individual filers can pay using direct debit when e-filing the return if they pay the full amount due on the return. The payment can be warehoused until April 15th in the e-pay system. After April 15th, the payment is processed once the return is filed. There is no charge when paying with this method. The taxpayer can also use the department of revenue e-pay system to pay via credit card. If the payment is made up to April 15th, no fee is charged. After April 15th, the surcharge imposed by the credit card companies, a percentage of the amount paid, is paid by the taxpayer.

The department of revenue advertised e-filing prominently on the state website and in hard-copy tax booklets. It is also mentioned in press conferences at the start of each tax season as well as in any training seminars the department holds for practitioners. Unlike Indiana and other states, Kentucky does not mandate electronic filing by practitioners. Although no demographic is targeted for e-filing, department officials have observed that younger taxpayers are more likely to embrace online filing as an option, perhaps because of their web-based banking practices and lower fear of transmitting data electronically.

Property taxes cannot be filed electronically in Kentucky. Most personal property tax returns are filed with the local property valuation administrator (PVA). Some are filed with the state valuation section and then forwarded to the local PVA. There are no incentives in place to encourage electronic filing.

Ohio

Electronic filing speeds processing – and refunds to citizens – enormously. In Ohio, refunds are received within two weeks of electronic filing as the April 15 deadline approaches. Returns filed early in the process are received within four to five days. Refunds for returns filed manually, by contrast, take weeks to process. A state official estimated that processing a paper returns costs the state $3, whereas processing an electronic return costs $1.15. With approximately 63 percent of the 5.4 million Ohio tax returns filed electronically in 2008 (as of April 30), the state avoided $6,193,800 in processing costs – and delivered refunds to taxpayers more rapidly. It is the latter benefit that is touted most frequently by the state to promote electronic filing. According to department of taxation representative Michael McKinney, "we anticipate that when all processing from this tax season is complete, about 65 percent of all returns will have been electronically filed, whether individually by taxpayers or through practitioners."

The initial implementation of i-file in 2003 was accompanied by a widespread marketing campaign. Now, its promotion is more intermittent, although reminders are included in all tax return booklets. Since 2003, growth in online filing has averaged about 4 percent per year. McKinney summarized the chronology for online filing as, "paperless filing of state income tax returns began in 1998 (for the 1997 tax year) with the tele-file telephone filing system. More than 232,000 taxpayers utilized it that first year; usage grew to a peak of nearly 622,000 in 2001, but this has since declined to about 142,000 in 2007. This system is limited to taxpayers with less complicated returns. In 1999, Ohio began accepting state income tax forms electronically filed through the IRS e-file system for the 1998 tax year. In 2003, Ohio i-file, an online 'wizard' application that builds a return for taxpayers by asking a series of questions about w-2s, dependents and other information, debuted for the 2002 tax year. In 2008 (for the 2007 tax year), we rolled out e-forms, income tax forms that look like the regular paper forms but can be filled out directly on a computer and then submitted online. Both applications are free to use."

Ohio is planning for increased online filing. Two measures have recently been authorized under Ohio law that will mandate online filing, similar to measures in place in Indiana. In 2010, for the 2009 tax filing season, any tax practitioner who prepares more than 75 returns is required to file electronically. On the business side, as of February of 2009, the monthly and semi-annual filing of sales tax returns must be done electronically.

Marketing initiatives are also credited with increasing the number of online individual (non-business) filers. The major draw for electronic filing is consistent emphasis in news releases, on the state web site, and in taxpayer and media contacts that by filing electronically, a taxpayer can expect to receive a refund in their bank account in five to seven days. There is no special incentive for filing online. Taxpayers can pay by credit card through the OPC, which does charge a handling fee (although the state does not receive any portion of it) or by electronic check.

The department of taxation examined the demographics of who filed electronically following the 2005 income tax filing season and found that "traditional" age categories held true. Taxpayers 22-30 were most likely to e-file (70.4 percent within this age group) and those over 65 least likely (33.4 percent). The study also showed that 66.6 percent of taxpayers in the 30-50 age group also filed electronically. The study did not look at income or ethnicity, but did look at counties and school districts. Most of the paper filers were concentrated in the northeast Ohio area, particularly in suburban Cleveland.

State officials attribute significant savings in taxpayer dollars and improvement in taxpayer services to the electronic filing system. A paper return costs $1.50 more to process than an electronic return. There are also fewer errors in electronic returns – and errors are identified more quickly, thus leading to their more rapid resolution. Fewer intermittent employees are hired by the department of taxation now. In 2003, the first year of Ohio i-file, the department employed 225 intermittents, mostly in the income tax area. That number declined to 175 in 2007 and is down about 30 percent from that this year. McKinney anticipates another 20 percent decline in intermittent hires next year, after the mandatory practitioner filing takes effect. The legislative and administrative branches of Ohio state government have been very supportive of the electronic filing programs, especially because of the cost savings. These accomplishments were achieved without special earmarks – electronic filing has been funded internally within the department's information system.

Tax filing is more complex for businesses than for individuals. Because of the lack of information received from other states, the authors have not included a detailed discussion of business tax filing in this chapter. Approximately nine percent of employers filed state withholding tax electronically in 2007. Large quarterly business taxpayers are required to file a commercial activity tax (a gross receipts tax applicable to most businesses) electronically through the Ohio business gateway as of 2005. Approximately 11 percent of sales tax filings were made electronically in 2008. Electronic sales tax filing was mandated in 2008. In Ohio, property tax payments are made at the county level. Online payments are not available. According to McKinney, the majority of property tax payments are accommodated through mortgage payments to financial institutions.

State Incentives: Mandatory Requirements

Of course, one way to ensure the success of any e-government program is to make its use mandatory. Often, the electronic delivery of government services is just one option for citizens – others are not eliminated. In 2001, the CIO for Indiana anticipated that savings would accrue from closing vehicle licensing branches, for example, as a consequence of implementing an electronic vehicle registration process. What occurred, however, was that routine cases were taken out of the in-person or in-paper process. Exceptional cases were still being handled in-person. Although staff hours were perhaps reduced overall, branch offices largely remained open to accommodate citizen needs that could not be handled electronically, whether because of administrative or legislative policy, or of citizen preference.

SOLUTIONS AND RECOMMENDATIONS

With 80 percent of its citizens filing electronically as of 30 April 2009, Indiana showed the highest participation rate among the four states studies. Indiana has thus already met the target participation rate set by congress for federal taxes, three years ahead of the revised schedule (2012). The authors have no single explanation for that program success in Indiana, but it is notable, especially given the online filing numbers recorded by the comparison states: Ohio (63 percent), Illinois (60 percent), and Kentucky (60 percent).

It is possible that Indiana's multi-faceted programs to create awareness and provide personal support to taxpayers encouraged taxpayers to "go electronic." The state's approach aligns well with recommendations made by both us and European scholars and analysts. There may be a kind of "halo" effect when citizens engage successfully with government electronically for one service that leads to greater willingness to use – and trust in the value – of e-government applications. The combination of human and online support, as well as financial incentives, may be behind Indiana's dramatic success in increasing the number of online vehicle registrations. Ohio's experience

with online vehicle registration indicates that its awareness campaign return desired results.

The disadvantages of making payments offline – fewer pay stations, inconvenient hours, travel time, fewer payment options (e.g. no or limited credit card use), postmark requirements – may become more apparent to citizens if convenience fees for online payments are eliminated. From the citizens' perspective, the risk/benefit calculation is improved, especially if the online applications are user-friendly and inspire trust. And of course, moving more standard processing online gives government personnel the opportunity to respond more effectively to those will not or cannot use online services. Where the government is the main employer, reducing government employment by closing payment stations and/or cutting back hours is not necessarily a good thing. Reducing errors, however, is almost always considered a good thing, as is confirmation on both sides that a payment has been made.

Again, confirmation about payment and reduced errors enhance trust in online services. One area in which states seem to be retreating is the posting of contact information for individuals within the government. It is not as accessible as it was just a few years ago. One must work through more layers of web pages to find the names of individual staff members and phone numbers that are staffed by humans and not sophisticated voice response units. Also, it would be helpful if agencies tracked and posted the actual usage of e-government applications so that citizens, researchers, and policy-makers could understand what and how work is accomplished. It's important to promote understanding and trust – for government, the less opaque the better. A further refinement to data collection would be useful for understanding demographic patterns in online use, as is being done in Europe. A focus on nonparticipating populations would help bridge technology and awareness gaps. By understanding citizen online activity, additional opportunities for delivering on the promise of greater efficiency, effectiveness, and participation may be targeted.

We did identify the following, points, similar to the "lessons" from the IRS e-filing study:

1. If accepting online payments is a real advantage to state governments, then more effort should be invested to encourage them. Ohio invested in a $1 million marketing campaign in 2006 that helped push current online renewals to 26 percent of total individual vehicle registration renewals. Explicit marketing, in other words, does work. Note the parallel to the "field of dreams" lesson from the IRS study.

2. Encouragement need not be restricted to financial incentives or promotional campaigns. Indiana's strategy of partnering with automobile dealerships, financial institutions, AAA, and automotive service provider may serve to put a human face on electronic transactions – and help digital naives through their first e-government encounter. Other third parties, such as charitable groups, can be engaged to market e-government services and work to make computers and internet connectivity more widespread (such as more terminals in public libraries and community centers). They could even join the call for more widespread residential broadband, especially in poor or rural areas that are unserved or underserved now. Note the parallels to the IRS lessons of collaborative relations with stakeholders.

3. Financial incentives – the $5 discount for online vehicle registration – certainly contributed to the 224 percent increase in electronic transactions experienced by Indiana. A dramatic intervention was apparently needed, however, since only 5.5 percent of registrations were processed electronically in the year before the incentive program. Since this was a recent change, note the parallel to the IRS lesson about investing in innovation.

4. These agencies collected performance data and appeared to adjust management techniques and user experience based on that data. Note the parallel to IRS lesson five and its recommendation about using program performance data.

FUTURE RESEARCH DIRECTIONS

We have the following suggestions for future research directions:

1. Extend the data collection about citizen behavior across the US and even to other countries. Incorporate data collection approaches used by the European commission (e-lost project).

2. Develop statistical models based on longitudinal data collected by states about online payments. Compare online participation rates across states and demographic groups to develop hypotheses about behavior across groups (digital divide). Identify best practices at the state level. (Ss a caveat, statistical modeling will be limited by the data collection policies and practices of state governments; states do not uniformly track the demographic information related to filing transactions.)

3. A very useful study would be a cost/benefit analysis based on the average cost of processing returns electronically as opposed to other means to develop benchmarks for ROI calculations. Combine this analysis with an examination of other states and the management techniques they have used to increase either online percentage or value to government or citizens. The resulting study would serve to guide government officials about how to align campaigns and incentives to increase citizen adoption of e-government services with a particular agency's budgetary objectives and mission goals.

4. Expand research to include other countries to give insight into economic and cultural factors that affect e-government participation rates. Again, the e-lost wp5 report from the European commission is a good example.

CONCLUSION

In general, the experiences of these four states seem to indicate a direct relationship between a state government's level of effort in promoting e-government services for individual income tax filing and vehicle registration renewal and citizen participation rates. The influence of different promotional efforts varies, however. Both awareness campaigns and financial incentives work, but the latter seems to have a more significant and immediate effect on citizen behavior. More research is needed to determine what incentive mix is the most efficient in terms of citizen response and cost to government agencies. The lessons articulated in the IRS study could form a useful set of hypotheses.

Using a third-party payment processing service provider (in particular, OPC) that charges a transaction fee does not seem to present a disincentive to citizens' use of online services. All four of the states studied in this chapter have contracts with OPC for some of their citizen applications. Kentucky, however, only uses OPC for its Kentucky children's health insurance program and not for tax filing, unlike Illinois, Indiana, and Ohio. Developing alliances with charitable, community, and even commercial organizations to deliver and/or facilitate the use of e-government services is an innovative approach that expands the number of channels for awareness and technical support, in addition to humanizing the electronic process. It should be considered as a strategy option by state governments.

It is possible that for states with smaller populations – and thus fewer citizen transactions for renewing vehicle registrations or filing income taxes – promoting e-government services through financial incentives may not be as cost-effective as for states with larger populations. On the other hand, for large but sparsely populated states, the inconvenience factor of driving longer distances to in-person government offices might influence citizen behavior and encourage the use of online transactions. Again, more research is needed.

REFERENCES

Activegovernment. *Government Online Payments*. Retrieved April 30, 2009, from http://www.activegovernment.com/government-online-payments.htm

Ahituv, N., & Raban, Y. (2008). *Policy Recommendations for Improving E-Government use among low Socio-Economic Status Groups*. E-Government For Low Socio-Economic Status Groups (Elost). Retrieved July 25, 2009, from http://www.elost.org/ahituv.pdf

Atkinson, R. D., & Andes, S. (2008). *2008 State New Economy*. Information technology and innovation foundation. Retrieved April 30, 2009, from http://www.itif.org/files/2008_state_new_economy_index.pdf

Federation of Tax Administrators. *States with* .Retrieved April 30, 2009, from http://www.taxadmin.org/fta/link/internet.html

Forman, C., Ghose, A., & Goldfarb, A. (2007, September).*Competition Between Local and Electronic Markets: How the Benefit of Buying Online Depends on Where You Live*. Net institute working paper no. 06-15.Retreived (n.d.), from http://ssrn.com/abstract=941175

Holden, S. H. (2007). *A model for Adaptation: from the IRS e-file*. IBM center for the business of government. Retrieved June 26, 2009, from http://www.businessofgovernment.org/pdfs/management07.pdf

Horrigan, J. B. (2008). *Home broadband 2008*. Pew internet & American life project. Retrieved May 4, 2009 from http://www.pewinternet.org/~/media//files/reports/2008/pip_broadband_2008.pdf

H&R Block Online. *H&R Block*. Retrieved April 29, 2009, from http://www.hrblock.com/taxes/products/product.jsp?productid=31

Illinois Department of Revenue. *Illinois Department of Revenue*. Retrieved April 29, 2009, from http://tax.illinois.gov/

Illinois Secretary of State. *Cyberdriveillinois*. Retrieved April 29, 2009, from http://www.cyberdriveillinois.com/

Indiana Department of Commerce and Indiana Economic Council (2003). *Connections in an information age: indiana at work and home*. Retrieved January 27, 2008, from www.in.gov/legislative/igareports/agency/reports/econdev01.pdf

In.gov. (n.d.). *BMV: home*. retrieved April 29, 2009, from http://www.in.gov/bmv/

In.gov. (n.d.). *Indiana Department of Revenue i-file*. Retrieved April 29, 2009, from https://secure.in.gov/apps/dor/ifile/2008/

In.gov. (n.d.). *Indiana department of revenue: filing statistics*. Retrieved May 5, 2009, from http://www.in.gov/dor/3648.htm

Internal Revenue Service. *Online Services*. Retrieved April 29, 2009, from http://www.irs.gov/efile/article/0,id=151880,00.html?portlet=4

Internal revenue service (2008). *Advancing e-file study phase 1 report -- executive summary: achieving the 80% e-file goal requires partnering with stakeholders on new approaches to motivate paper filers*. Case number 08-1063, document number 0206.0209. Retrieved June 23, 2009, from http://www.irs.gov/pub/irs-utl/irs_advancing_e-file_study_phase_1_executive_summary_v1_3.pdf

Kentucky: Department of Revenue. *Individual Information*. Retrieved April 29, 2009, from http://revenue.ky.gov/individual/

Kentucky.gov. *Home*. Retrieved April 29, 2009, from http://kentucky.gov/pages/home.aspx

mvl.ky.gov. *Registration renewal requirements*. Retrieved April 29, 2009 from http://mvl.ky.gov/mvlweb/requirementpage.jsp

(n.d.). *Efile Express*. Retrieved April 29, 2009, from http://www.efile-express.com/

Nic incorporated. *Nic incorporated*. Retrieved April 30, 2009, from http://www.nicusa.com/html/index.html

Official payments corporation. *Official payments corporation*. Retrieved April 30, 2009, from https://www.officialpayments.com/index.jsp

Ohio Bureau of Motor Vehicles. *BMV*. Retrieved April 29, 2009, from https://www.oplates.com/

Ohio.gov. *Department of Taxation*. Retrieved April 29, 2009 from http://www.tax.ohio.gov/index.stm

Online Taxes. *Olt* Retrieved April 29, 2009 from http://www.olt.com/main/home/default.asp

Schwester, R. (2009). Examining the barriers to e-government adoption. *Electronic Journal of e-government, 7*(1), 113-122. Retrieved July 25, 2009, from http://www.ejeg.com/volume-7/vol7-iss1/schwester.pdf

Seifert, J. W. (2003). *A primer on e-government: sectors, stages, opportunities and challenges of online governance. Congressional research service*. Retrieved April 24, 2009, from http://www.fas.org/sgp/crs/rl31057.pdf

Som - State of Michigan. (n.d.). *Som*. Retrieved April 29, 2009, from http://www.michigan.gov/

State of Michigan Department of Treasury. (n.d.). *Michigan taxes*. Retrieved April 29, 2009, from http://www.michigan.gov/taxes

State of Michigan Secretary of State. (n.d.). *License plate registration renewals*. Retrieved April 29, 2009 from http://www.michigan.gov/sos/0,1607,7-127-1640_14837-133039--,00.html. (n.d.). *Taxact*. Retrieved April 29, 2009, from https://www.taxactonline.com/

Taxslayer.com. (n.d.). *Taxslayer*. Retrieved April 29, 2009, from http://www.taxslayer.com/

Turbotax online. (n.d.). *Turbotax*. Retrieved April 29, 2009, from http://turbotax.intuit.com/

Van Aerschot, L., Kunz, J., Haglund, E., et al. (2007). *Cross-cultural analysis on barriers and incentives for lsgs' use of e-government*. e-government for low socio-economic status groups (elost). Retrieved July 25, 2009 from http://www.elost.org/d5-2.pdf

West, D. M. (2008). *State and federal electronic government in the united states*. Washingtong, DC: The Brookings Institution.

ADDITIONAL READING

Al-Hashmi, A., & Darem, A. B. (2008). *Understanding phases of e-government project*. Retrieved April, 24 2009 from http://www.iceg.net/2008/books/2/17_152-157.pdf

Antiroikko, A. (2007). Encyclopedia of digital government. Hershey, PA: Information science reference

As-Saber, S. N. Srivastava, A., &Hossain, K. (2006). Information technology law and e-government: a developing country perspective. *Journal of administration & governance, 1*. Retrieved April 24 2009 from http://www.joaag.com/uploads/6-_as-sabersrivastava_hossain.pdf

Boynton, C., Lisowsky, P., & Trautman, W. B. (2008). *e-file, enterprise structures, and tax compliance risk assessment*. tax notes, 120. Retrieved April 24, 2009, from http://ssrn.com/abstract=1267024

Chellappa, K. Sin, R. G.; Siddarth, S. (2007). *Price-formats as a source of price dispersion: a study of online and offline prices in the domestic us airline markets*. retrieved 24 april 2009 from http://ssrn.com/abstract=991156

Dawes, S. S., Helbig, N., & Gil-Garcia, J. R. (2004). *Center for technology and government, University at Albany, State University of New York*. Retrieved April 24, 2009, from http://www.ctg.albany.edu/projects/journal

Duncan, H., & Burrus, R. (2005). *Electronic filing takes hold in state and federal tax agencies*. State Tax Notes, 36. Retrieved April 24, 2009, from http://ssrn.com/abstract=713722

Fletcher, D. (2009). *Digital Government Controversy*. Dave Fletcher's government and technology weblog, v. 2.0. Retrieved 24 april, 2009 from http://davidfletcher.blogspot.com/2009/02/digital-government-controversy.html

Fletcher, G. L. (2003). *Utah [report on permanent public access to electronic government information*. State-by-state Report on permanent public access to electronic government information, pp. 247-251. Retrieved April 24, 2009, from http://ssrn.com/abstract=1154220 Galbi, D. A. (2001). *e-government: developing state communications in a free media environment*. Washington, DC: FCC

Hansford, A., Lymer, A., & Pilkington, C. (2006). IT adoption strategies and their application to e-filing self-assessment tax returns: the case of the uk. *ejournal of tax research, 4*, 80-96. Retrieved April 24, 2009, from http://ssrn.com/abstract=938023

Irani, Z., Al-Sebie, M., & Elliman, T. (2006). Transaction stage of e-government systems: identification of its location and importance. *Systems Sciences*, *4*, 82c–82c.

Joseph, R. C., & Kitlan, D. P. (2005). *Key issues in e-government and public administration*. Retrieved April 24, 2009, from http://www. igi-global.com/downloads/excerpts/reference/ igr5202_1yprpc8bau.pdf

Koh, C. E., Prybutok, V. R., & Zhang, X. (2008). Measuring e-government readiness. *Information & Management*, *45*, 540–546. doi:10.1016/j. im.2008.08.005

Layne, K., & Lee, J. (2001). Developing fully functional e-government: a four stage model. *Government Information Quarterly*, *18*, 122–136. doi:10.1016/S0740-624X(01)00066-1

Litan, R. E., Eisenach, J. A., & Caves, K. (2008). The benefits and costs of i-file. Retrieved April 24, 2009, from http://ssrn.com/abstract=1159844

Lymer, A. (2000). Taxation in an electronic world: the international debate and a role for tax research. Atax discussion paper no. 3.University of New South Wales.

Minnesota department of revenue. (n.d.). *Minnesota department of revenue*. Retrieved April 29, 2009, from http://www.taxes.state.mn.us/

Minnesota driver and vehicle services: renewal. (n.d.). *Minnesota driver and vehicle services*. Retrieved April 29, 2009, from https://www. mvrenewal.state.mn.us/

Moon, M. J. (2002). The evolution of e-government among municipalities: rhetoric or reality? *Public Administration Review*, *62*, 424–433. doi:10.1111/0033-3352.00196

Ozgen, F. B., & Turan, H. A. (2007, September 27-28). *Usage and adoption of online tax filing and payment system in tax management: an empirical assessment with technology acceptance (tam) model in turkey*. 9th international scientific conference, management horizons: visions and challenges, Vytautas Magnus University, Kaunas. Retrieved April 24, 2009, from http://ssrn.com/ abstract=1012660

Reddick, C. G. (2003). A two-stage model of e-government growth: theories and empirical evidence for U.S. Cities. *Government Information Quarterly*, *21*, 51–64. doi:10.1016/j. giq.2003.11.004

Reitz, J. C. (2006). e-government. *american journal of comparative law,54*. Retrieved April 24, 2009, from http://ssrn.com/abstract=887664

Satyanarayana, J. (2004). *E-government: the science of the possible*. India: Prentice hall.

Siau, K., & Long, Y. (2005). Synthesizing e-government stage models a meta-synthesis based on meta-ethnography approach. *Industrial Management & Data Systems*, *105*, 443–458. doi:10.1108/02635570510592352

Thomas, D. W., Manly, T., & Ritsema, C. (2004). *Initiatives for increasing e-filing: taxpayer attitudes reveal what works*. Tax Notes, 104. Retrieved April 24, 2009, from http://ssrn.com/ abstract=565562

United Nations Global E-Government Readiness Report. (2005). *Web measure model: stages of e-government evolution*. Retrieved April 24, 2009, from http://www.access2democracy.org/papers/ web-measure-model-stages-e-government- evolution.

West, D. M. (2004). E-government and the transformation of service delivery and citizen attitudes. Public Administration Review, 64, 15-27. West, D. M. (2005). *Digital government: technology and public sector performance*. Princeton, NJ: Princeton university press.

Wisconsin Department of Revenue. *E-services*. Retrieved April 29, 2009, from http://www.revenue.wi.gov/eserv/index.html

Wisconsin Department of Transportation. *Online registration renewal*. Retrieved April 29, 2009, from http://www.dot.wisconsin.gov/drivers/vehicles/renew/online.htm

Zhe Jin, G., & Kato, A. (2006). *Dividing online and offline: a case study*. Retrieved April 24, 2009, from http://ssrn.com/abstract=917317

KEY TERMS AND DEFINITIONS

Convenience Fee or Online Payment Fee: Sometimes the government or the 3rd-party in a "3rd-party payment" actually charges more if the payment is made online, to cover "merchant fees" and "setup and operation costs." Payment via a 3rd-party almost always involves paying such a fee.

Online Discount: Sometimes, the government seeks to encourage online payment and share the savings it receives by offering an actual discount from the amount due if the payment is made online. This discount is the opposite of the "convenience fee" that other governments charge to cover merchant fees and online payment operation costs.

G2c: The form of e-government involving a government agency and individual citizens of that government -- e.g. The state of Ohio and residents of Ohio. Most authors also distinguish "g2g," one government agency to another, whether in the same state or not; "g2b," where the non-government is an organized entity, usually for-profit; and some authors add "g2e," which is internal to the government, but involves government employees.

Merchant Fee: When paying via credit card, the bank issuing the credit card usually charges the merchant (or in this case the government agency) receiving the money a fee. The fee is usually a set amount per transaction, plus a percentage (two to 4 percent – 2% to 4%) of the amount being charged. The bank may also levy fees if the payer reverses the transaction, if the merchant wants more than a minimum set of reports, etc. Because state agencies are usually very large "merchants," and because they rarely have citizens reverse transactions, they sometimes can negotiate relatively low fees.

Online Payment: Paying an amount via a computer connected to the internet; can be either an electronic funds transfer from a checking or savings account or a charge to a credit card or a debit card. For our purposes, using the telephone to call in the appropriate numbers from one human to another is not "online payment".

Setup and Operation Costs: Often, an agency moving to add online payment to traditional payment methods will incur costs to set up the system and operate it. Eventually, these costs may be outweighed by lower costs incurred as more traditional methods are used less, but they are often a net addition in the early stages, and governments sometimes set an "online payment fee" to help cover these costs.

Transaction Stage: One of the stages of e-government; usually the 3rd of 4 (presence, one-way interaction, transaction, transformation), but some authors add stages prior to or after this one.

3rd-Party Payment: Every online transaction involves a bank as well as the person paying and the person receiving the payment, but some systems add yet another party that receives the payment, deducts its costs, and then sends the balance to the ultimate recipient. In some states, a state will deal directly with its citizens; in other states, it will deal directly with a few categories of citizens, but requires the rest to deal with one of the non-bank parties, such as onlinepayments.com. Many small non-government entities do the same thing -- they use a 3rd-party to process payments.

Chapter 3
E–Government and Citizen Participation in Chile:
The Case of Ministries Websites

Eduardo Araya Moreno
University of Valparaíso, Chile

Diego Barría Traverso
Leiden University, The Netherlands

ABSTRACT

Various international assessments have drawn attention to the level of development e-government has reached in Chile during the early 2000s. Despite this, even official reports recognize that there is an e-government deficit in opening spaces for citizen participation. These results coincide with several works which have shown the limits the State of Chile put to citizen participation. This chapter analyzes the participation supply that the websites of Chilean ministries offer the citizenry. We describe the existing interactive applications offered by the websites, and the possibilities they make available for citizens to participate in public policy discussions. Our conclusion is that there is a wide range of available information regarding ministerial management but, on the other; the lack of participatory mechanisms is confirmed. These results can be understood if considering that within the Chilean public administration a managerial predisposition exists, which makes open participation spaces subordinated to prevailing managerial logics.

INTRODUCTION

Various international assessments have drawn attention to the level of development e-government has reached in Chile during the early 2000s (UN, 2003, 2005). It is noticeable that, towards 2003, Chile ranked second in the world in the level of development of their websites and third in e-partic-

ipation, particularly when considering the fact that it is a South American country that is not part of the developed world (US11.100 per capita income for the year 2005, according to the World Bank). Nevertheless, these results are understandable when taking into account that, after the return to democracy in 1990, successive governments have attempted to modernize public administration, where new information technologies (NICTs) have played an important role (Araya & Barría, 2008).

DOI: 10.4018/978-1-61520-933-0.ch003

Despite of these improvements, even official reports recognize that there is an e-government deficit in opening spaces for citizen participation (SEGPRES, 2006b). A number of United Nations reports have stated that Chile has experienced a downturn in e-participation rankings (UN, 2003, 2005, 2008). These results, as we will show, coincide with several works which have shown the limits he State of Chile put to citizen participation. Participation is a big issue in Chile, not only in the political arena but also in academia, for the reason that there is a disagreement feeling within the citizenry, and the citizens are increasingly disinterested in politics in general, and in electoral processes in particular.

This chapter analyzes the participation supply that the websites of Chilean ministries offer the citizenry (because these are the bodies in charge of formulating public policies). We describe the existing interactive applications offered by the websites, and the possibilities they make available for citizens to participate in public policy discussions.

Based on these results, the conception of citizen participation on which each one of these e-participation project is analyzed. This exercise allows us to enter a greater discussion, on the degree of participation availability with which Chilean public administration meets its citizens.

E-GOVERNMENT, MANAGEMENT AND PARTICIPATION

Different approaches have been raised to understand the incorporation of NICTs to public administration. Margetts (2007, pp. 234-236) identifies three currents; Hyper-, Anti- and Postmodernism. Each one focuses on issues that are beginning to become the focus of attention in public organizations.

Hyper-modernists have an idealistic view of the role that technology might play within organizations, especially in relation to the potential of rationalization and organizational transformation they deliver. In contrast, while recognizing the transformation potential, Anti-modernists focus on the dangers technologies bring, particularly in regard to the social control that can be exerted through them. On the other hand, Postmodernist views are idealistic, just like modernists and, starting from the transformation potential, they show their enthusiasm for the liberation from bureaucratic control and the greater organizational flexibility and fluidity.

The incorporation of information technologies (IT) to public administration dates back to the second half of the twentieth century. At first, they were used to improve administrative efficiency. Later, the concern for the quality of services produced was incorporated (Snellen, 2005, p. 399).

With the rise of the internet, the use of ITs was no longer focused as an internal organizational issue, but started to centre outside of themselves, especially in relation to society, companies and other kinds of organizations (Margetts, 2007, p. 234). The possibilities are not limited to this new form of contact, but have more profound implications. Thus, the concepts of virtual States and virtual agencies have emerged, which not only refer to the presence of pre-existing agencies on the Internet, but also to the creation of new organizations, which only exist online (Fountain, 2001). Moreover, the idea of virtuality crosses different intra- and interorganizational areas. On the one hand, there is a virtual face, based on the websites through which the organizations present themselves to the public. On the other hand, there is an internal virtuality, where the organization is reduced to a small core, dedicated to manage the contracts with the suppliers. Finally, there are virtual networks, which coordinate joint actions between different agencies (Margetts, 2005).

Nevertheless, these changes are not mechanical, as believed by those who endorse that technologies, by themselves, generate change (technological determinism), and by those who claim that the success of these technologies is related to the willingness of the actors (voluntarists) (Snellen, 2005, p. 403). Although leadership is important (Takao, 2004; Fountain, 2009), technologies are finally only instruments which require organizational and institutional support.

Institutional literature has been incorporated into the study of e-government. Following the premises of historical determinism, Margetts (2007) has suggested that, in order to understand the usage of technologies in the public sector, one must take into account the history of computing in public agencies.

With the 'enacted technology framework', Fountain (2001) also integrates the institutional dimension to the debate on the incorporation of new technologies to public organizations. According to it, both objective technologies and institutional - cognitive, cultural, socio-structural, as well as legal and formal - arrangements influence the organizational characteristics of public agencies, thus indirectly affecting the enacted technology.

As she has pointed out, the enactment of technology is related to dominant societal values, as well as to political, technological, rational, and social logics. If we also consider that the technology used in policy arenas is related to their particular culture, history, mental models and practices (Fountain, 2001, pp. 32-33, 98-103), we can understand why ITs are used in different ways by governments. Luna-Reyes, Hernández and Gil-García (2009) have adapted Fountain's approach, incorporating contextual factors (demographic characteristics, size of the economies and political orientation of the governments). According to them, political orientation affects the organizational characteristics, the institutional framework and the success of e-government.

Starting from the fact that technologies are used in different ways by different governments, Amoretti (2006) poses the need of definitions on e-government regimes. He presents a typology based on both the network architecture and existing governance practices. What is interesting

about this typology for the subject approached in this chapter is that the participation possibilities delivered by e-government are mediated by governance practices.

The first type is the oriented reform regime. It is characterized by the modernization of administrative structures, and by a minimal participation potential, due to the inability of the government to collect citizen demands. A similar situation occurs in the authoritarian regime, with a State that uses technologies to control the population while, at the same time, modernizing the administration. The network, instead of being used as a bidirectional meeting point with society, is understood as a space to promote the state agenda. The third type is the managerial regime, influenced by e-commerce logics, and which main objective is reducing administration costs and improving the efficiency of the administration. Here, a vision of the citizen as a consumer emerges, where his needs must be fulfilled. The final type is the open regime, where citizen participation plays an essential role, improving the functioning of democracy, and improving the transparency and accountability levels (Amoretti, 2006).

Given that three out of four categories are preferably focused on administrative improvement, in order to understand the existing e-government type in a country, it is necessary to pay attention to the administrative improvement programme types that have been performed. Here, the fact that literature has focused primarily on the discussion on e-government and new public management (NPM), is an issue that affects the type of developed regimes.

In the beginning, the incorporation of NICTs was functional to the debate on NPM and it was believed that, with the incorporation of technologies, the government would become smaller (Margetts, 2009). Nevertheless, evidence has shown that NICTs have increased features inherent to bureaucracy, such as rationalization and regulation systems (although the latter are now less visible, since they are in the software and hardware) (Fountain, 2001).

In the same line, recent studies have shown that the e-government experience tends to alter some of the ideas characteristic of NPM, such as the separation of public agencies, competition as criteria for the rendering of services, as well as incentivizing public officials. The incorporation of NICTs in public administration has lead to the creation of a new administrative reform paradigm, the digital-era governance (DEG). The DEG has three components (reintegration, needs-based holism, and digital processes). The one that most clearly disregards NPM is reintegration. In a number of countries, some studies have warned on the setbacks of atomization and function duplication generated by NPM. At the same time, holistic logics have been incorporated (needs-based holism), where services are rendered under the one-stop-shop modality. Here, the private management logic is left for another, focused on the needs of the citizen. Finally, digitalization processes are no longer conceived as just another mechanism, but as a transformation, where the agency 'becomes its web site' (Dunleay et. al., 2006; Margetts, 2009).

In any case, DEG is a theoretical proposal that, although introduced as a new option on the reform type menu, does not entail that e-government is not influenced by NPM (Dunleay et. al., 2006). Moreover, the resulting e-government type depends on the expansion level of NPM in the countries (Margetts, 2007), and on their relation with **DEG**. Thus, there are four possible outcomes:

1. A Digital NPM State, where e-government is promoted under the NPM logic;
2. The transition to a Digital State, with the abandonment of the NPM logic;
3. A Policy Mess, where some of the NPM characteristics, such as fragmentation, are cut out; and
4. A State Residualization, where e-government is partially accepted, within a NPM scheme, while fighting reintegration (Margetts, 2005, p. 322).

Until now, we have only approached e-government in relation to regime types and their characteristics. Only two of the dimensions that Snellen (2005) uses to define e-government (supporting the economy of implementation, and the public service provision) are incorporated in this discussion. Nevertheless, the third dimension (democracy) is not approached, despite of the fact that the implications of NICTs on citizen participation have been a topic of interest that has opened a new field of study (Medaglia, 2007).

Although citizens and governments have the option of connecting via the Internet to public debates (Rose, Grönlund & Andersen, 2007; Macintosh, 2004), due to the online diffusion of policy proposals (Snellen, 2005), for instance, the participation dimension is probably the most problematic one of the e-government, because of the power redistribution it may generate. This sums to the fact that opening participation spaces does not generate easily noticeable profit to public organizations, as could be obtained through technological innovation in management.

This might be the reason why democracy is the e-government dimension where fewer regulations have been written. So far, there are doubts regarding the final impact of online citizen participation, especially when considering the different democracy theories which enlighten contact mechanisms (Harto de Vera, 2006), and the absence of clear regulations on how e-participation will affect policy-making processes.

Another point that deserves special attention is the way in which e-participation coexists with other areas of e-government. As shown by Amoretti's (2006) typology, the concern for administrative improvement is prevailing in the majority of e-government regimes. Only in the open regime is it possible to find efforts to incorporate participation. Although only in the authoritarian regime there exists an open intention to limit participation, in the rest of the regimes the issue has no options to enter an agenda dominated by the pursuit of modernization and administrative efficiency.

Although the absence of e-participation can be explained by the managerial predisposition with which the incorporation of technologies to the public organizations is generally met, we should not lose sight of the fact that it could respond to other sorts of issues. As previously stated, the way in which technology is proclaimed is enacted responds to prevailing social values (Fountain, 2001), which sums to the fact that the political orientation of governments is framed within the cultural schemes and characteristics of the political systems, which affect the way in which technology is conceived and used (Castells, 2001).

E-PARTICIPATION APPROACHES AND METHODOLOGY

There are a number of approaches on e-participation developed by international agencies. The Organization for Economic Co-operation and Development (OECD) approach understands that e-participation depends on critical dimensions, which are not connected by the mere availability of technologies. In particular, it is suggested that, among other things, it is fundamental to identify in which stages of the public policy cycle participation spaces are opened (Macintosh, 2004).

Regarding participation, this approach identifies different degrees of involvement, ranging from information to queries and active participation, which entails becoming part of the construction of policies and their contents, which nevertheless still is of government responsibility. Macintosh identifies types of initiatives. The most basic one, *e-enabling*, is focused on the delivery of understandable information to the widest possible audience. The second type of initiative, *e-engaging*, searches, for instance, through (top-down) queries on political topics. Finally, we find *e-empowering* projects, where citizens can suggest ideas, in a bottom-up perspective, which make them producers rather than consumers of policies (Macintosh, 2004, p. 3).

Another analysis framework, used to perform worldwide comparative investigations, is the one developed by the United Nations. This e-participation indicator has no political activity transforming purposes; on the contrary, it seeks to assess how they perform as a new information channel between government and citizens. Although not explicitly suggested, within the definition of the indicator lies a conceptualization of participation, where it is seen as a phenomenon where citizens, necessarily informed, participate in consultation spaces on public topics. The consultations will result in a number of suggestions on the discussed topics, which will in turn be considered by the government when making decisions.

The United Nations e-participation Index is a complex indicator, which comprises three different components: e-information, e-consultation and e-decision-making. The first component refers to the information that the government makes available for the citizenry, such as budgetary, legal or public policy related information, together with the existence of applications, such as forum or chat rooms, or e-mail listings. E-consultation, on the other hand, refers to the existence of consultation mechanisms, which are explained and promoted by the government. Finally, e-decision-making entails an explicit commitment by the government to incorporate the outcomes of the consultations as input for the decision making processes (UN, 2003, p. 19).

The United Nations Index presents a reduced vision of participation, since it ignores if the consultations to the citizens generate results when making decisions. Moreover, unlike Macintosh (2004), it does not identify at which moment these citizen proposals will be incorporated into the public policy cycles, a crucial issue when assessing the results of participation. Kingdon (2003) has suggested that it is not the same to influence when putting topics on the agenda than in the selection of political alternatives. Consequently, the moment in which participation occurs does matter. On the other hand, the e-participation

Table 1. Diagram used to analyze government agencies websites

Dimension		Indicators
Relevant information for participating		Structure of the Government Agency
		Authorities
		Relevant laws on the Agency and the sector of intervention
		Budget
		Annual Reports
		Ministerial Functions and their Policies
		Documents and assessments on policies, programmes or policy drafts
		Statistics
		FAQs
Contact mechanisms between Citizen and Government	Top-down Mechanisms	Surveys on Construction of Agenda
		Surveys on Management Priorities
		Surveys or consultations on laws and/or policies
		Chats or forums on specific topics
	Bottom-up Mechanisms	Available e-mails of authorities
		Contact forms
		Forms for suggestions on laws or policies
		Open topic chats or discussion forums
Rules on citizen participation processing		Policy on e-participation that specifies how information will be processed and whether consultation results will be binding
		Definition of e-participation areas
		Reply obligation of authorities
		Issuing of citizen input reception certificate

Source: Own elaboration based on Macintosh (2004), and UN (2003, 2005, 2008).

Index is not either capable of assessing in which extent the citizenry can control the topics to be discussed, seeing that it is the government who opens the discussion spaces in its portals.

In spite of the United Nations Index showing problems when analyzing the results of citizen participation, at the least it allows to analyze two issues of interest for this work:

1. The availability of quality information for the citizens to participate; and
2. The signal of the government's will to give spaces for the citizens to participate, i.e. it is an indicator of the e-disposition of governments towards participation.

3. Based on these frameworks, we constructed an analysis instrument that comprises 21 indicators, which revives Macintosh's (2004) e-enabling, e-engaging and e-empowering approaches, as well as the United Nations' (2003, 2005, 2008) e-information, e-consultation and e-decision-making. In the same way, it incorporates some participation indicators used by the United Nations (2003, 2005, 2008) when analyzing e-participation on State websites.

Three dimensions have been identified. The first one starts from the premise that, in order to participate, it is necessary to understand what will be discussed; hence, citizens require basic information on institutions, policies and management results (Macintosh, 2004; Setälä & Grönlund, 2006; UN, 2003, 2005, 2008).

The second dimension refers to existing consultation mechanisms. Here, it has been preferred to divide it into two sub dimensions: (a) one focused on top-down consultation mechanisms designed by the public agencies, and (b) another one, related to bottom-up mechanisms, by which citizens can deliver inputs openly, without restricting to predefined spaces by closed surveys, or topic chats.

The third dimension goes further into what we have called the e-disposition of governments towards participation. Here, emphasis is put on the existence of explicit rules on how citizen suggestions should be processed and incorporated into subsequent decision making processes. In this way, it can be more precisely measured to which extent governments are willing to allow citizens to participate through NICTs and have the ability to directly affect the policy-making process.

E-GOVERNMENT AND STATE REFORM IN CHILE

The modernization of the State has been a focus of attention of the *Concertación de Partidos por la Democracia* governments (1990-2010), the political coalition that governs Chile since the return to Democracy in 1990. Although the government of Patricio Aylwin (1990-1994) focused primarily on the consolidation of the transition process, during the mandates of Eduardo Frei Ruiz-Tagle (1994-2000) and Ricardo Lagos (2000-2006), projects on public management improvement were carried out (Armijo, 2002; Ramírez, 2001).

The public management improvement effort was based on several approaches, *in vogue* during the last decades, such as NPM and new economic institutionalism. During the government of Frei, in accordance with the core ideas of NPM, a number of management instruments - unused to that mo-

ment - were incorporated, such as management indicators (to carry out performance evaluations), as well as monetary incentives for results, conditioned to the accomplishment of management goals defined by public services and approved by the Budget Office of the Ministry of Finance (DIPRES). During the government of Lagos, the same path was followed, but adding the improvement of public institutionalism as an area of concern, particularly regarding State structure.

During the government of Michelle Bachelet (2006-2010), the previously promoted administrative reforms have been upheld, and it has been discussed on the need to expand the assessment on public policies and programmes, as well as resuming a State reform agenda. Nevertheless, further from the creation of a few working groups to approach these issues and the writing of a modernization agenda, no reform projects have appeared.

Since the creation of the *Interministerial Committee for the Modernization of Public Management*, in 1994, NICTs have been considered an essential instrument for the development of efforts to improve public management. Some important actors within the Government made the incorporation of NICTs become thoughtfully considered (e.g. the Ministry of Economy). In 1998, the *Interministerial Committee* summoned a working group on Information Society, formed by members of universities and both the public and private sectors. In January 1999, this team delivered a report where a programmatic issue was settled regarding e-government: NICTs are powerful tools for increasing the efficiency of public administration, diminishing its costs, improving the quality of its services and the transparency level in its acting. The report also encouraged the use of NICTs to improve coordination among public agencies, the creation of a State Intranet and website, and the use of e-signature in the public sector (Rivera, 2003, pp. 145-147).

The government of Ricardo Lagos continued putting NICTs in the centre of administrative

Table 2. Administrative improvement projects between 1990 and 2010

Government	Projects
Patricio Aylwin (1990-1994)	Creation of Ministries of Planning (MIDEPLAN) and General Secretary of the Presidency (SEGPRES) Creation of public national services dedicated to specific groups, such as National Corporation for Indigenous Development (CONADI) and the National Service for Women (SERNAM) *Pilot Modernization Project* in five public agencies (1993)
Eduardo Frei Ruiz-Tagle (1994-2000)	Creation of the *Interministerial Committee of Public Management Modernization* as administrative improvement process coordinator (1994) Dictation of a *Strategic Plan for Public Management Modernization*, focused on the following areas: strategic management; transparency and probity; quality of service and citizen participation; human resources; State institutionalism and; communication and extension (1997) Incorporation of performance evaluation instruments and incentives for achievement of goals (Management Improvement Programmes, PMG)
Ricardo Lagos (2000-2006)	Creation of the *State Modernization and Reform Project*, unit responsible for promoting State reform (2000) Signing of *Political-Legislative Agreement for the Modernization of the State, Transparency and Promotion of Knowledge*, document containing 49 compromises between the Government and the Opposition, including the creation of a *High Public Management System* as well as one of public purchasing (2003)
Michelle Bachelet (2006-2010)	Writing of the document *Modernization Agenda*, focused on seven areas (Human Resources and Public Management; Excellence in Service; Decentralization; Institutional Improvement; Transparency and Probity; Participation; Political Reforms)

Source: Armijo (2002), Ramírez (2001), SEGPRES (2006a), and Interior Ministry (2008).

reform efforts. During May 2001, a *Digital Offensive Plan* was announced, which included projects such as the use of NICTs in micro enterprises and the massification of computer use (Orrego & Araya, 2002), as well as a *Presidential Instruction for e-government Development*. This document defined the following areas of concern: citizen service, good government and the development of democracy. It settled the following schedule: in the first phase, public services should be present on the Internet, delivering information. Secondly, they should develop certain forms of e-interaction with the citizens. Thirdly, they should be able to perform online transactions, as an alternative to in-person procedures and, lastly, they should reach a transformation phase, where services would be rendered electronically (SEGPRES, 2006a, pp. 112-114).

During the following years, progress was made in the institutionalization of a number of support tools and organizations for e-government promotion. Among the main decisions we can find:

- The creation of a *Standards Committee*, in charge of suggesting strategies to promote the interoperability process between services.
- The enactment of an *E-government Agenda* for the period 2002-2005.
- The appointment of a Government Coordinator of NICTs in 2003.
- The creation of a *IT Community*, which enables the contact and experience exchange between the heads of the IT units of Chilean public agencies
- The creation of a public agency website contest
- The creation of the e-government PMG, which established a general guideline to public agencies on NICT incorporation (SEGPRES, 2006b).

The development of e-government has also paid attention to the improvement of information on the procedures citizens have to carry out in public agencies, as well as the improvement of related processes. This has occurred given the administrative simplification, as well as the creation of one-stop-shop websites, such as www.tramitefacil.cl.

Table 3. Principal e-government projects and experiences in Chile

Level	Experiences
General	Creation of the State Intranet (1999) Creation of a single window, which works as a guide for the citizens (Tramite Fácil) Creation of an e-market for the purchasing of consumables by the public agencies (Chilecompra)
Sectorial	Creation of a single window for enterprises (Sitio Empresa) Creation of the *Foreign Trade Window* Launching of an *E-health Agenda* Creation of a Social Subsidies portal
Public Agencies	The Internal Revenue Service enables citizens, every year, to declare their taxes through the Internet or mobile phones (*Operación Renta*)

Source: Araya & Barría (2008).

The conception that the government of Lagos has given e-government does not limit itself to management improvement, but it has also implications on economic growth and the insertion of Chile to the Information Society. E-government has been considered as a core of action within a **Digital Agenda**, a national policy regarding the promotion of NICTs as an important element for the productive development of the country. A first version was presented in 2003 and another was presented later, for the period 2007-2012 (SEGPRES, 2006b, p. 33).

During the period of Bachelet, apart from the new version of the *Digital Agenda*, a *Digital Action Plan* was dictated for the period 2008-2010, which seeks to create a digital window for municipal services, to create a Technology Project Control Office, to use technologies for the improvement of services delivered to enterprises, to make progress in the rendering of services through mobile phones, and to advance in the procedures in the public health area (Estrategia Digital Executive Secretary, 2008). This sums to the recent creation of virtual platforms for the application for funds (for the promotion of culture, scholarships, among others). Special attention has been given to the application for social benefits, with the creation of a portal for the application for assistance delivered by different public agencies.

As it has been seen, the development of online rendering of services holds a preferential focus.

An official evaluation (SEGPRES, 2006b, p. 84) has shown that, in the areas defined by the *Presidential Instruction*, projects have primarily been centred on citizen service and good government. On the contrary, the development of democracy has received less attention.

PARTICIPATION IN CHILE

The expansion of citizen participation is not trouble free. A series of issues limit or, at least, inhibit, the development of these initiatives, which makes them require special attention. On the one hand, citizen participation projects in public service management organs, under the *consumer democracy* viewpoint (Harto de Vera, 2006) focus citizen incorporation into the discussions in a technical way, resulting in professionals having control of those spaces (Cunill, 1997). In Chile, ever since 2006, this situation has become recurrent through the creation of a number of presidential advisory commissions (see Aguilera, 2007).

This sums to the fact that the opening of citizen participation spaces collides with the bureaucratic logic. At this point, a conflict arises between the participative logic –ideally, horizontal - and the hierarchy of bureaucratic organization. Even the radical democracy discourse presents limitations. As inequalities exist within societies, in terms of political resources, open spaces will possibly end

Table 4. UN evaluations on e-government in Chile

Year	Web Measure Index (Place)	E-participation Index (Place)
2003	0,838 (2)	0,828 (3)
2005	0,9115 (6)	0,5873 (12)
2008	0,5635 (35)	0,1818 (71)

Source: UN (2003, pp. 17-19; 2005, pp. 72, 94; 2008, pp. 44, 213).

up being controlled by those who are in better conditions to get hold of them. This entails the need that these projects to some extent incorporate empowering measures for participation, promoted by the State, to correct existing asymmetries (Cunill, 1997).

To the above mentioned problems, we must add the openness degree of the political system towards participation, and whether the political culture of a system is participative or not. The Chilean case shows a political system that is not eager to incorporate the citizenry and social movements into decision making processes. At the same time, since the 1990s, an increasing depoliticization of the citizenry can be appreciated (Silva, 2004), which becomes more apparent within the youth (González et. al., 2005).

Critical visions have suggested that, since 1990, governments have carried out a demobilization strategy of social organizations, in order to consolidate democracy (e.g. Toledo Llancaqueo, 2007). Thus, a logic has settled by which the State consults, but does not discuss with, the citizenry.

Furthermore, the State opens spaces for community participation in sectorial areas of focalized public policies, but without giving room for deliberation (Delamaza, 2009), and making social organizations compete against each other to attain financial funds to develop projects of their interest, as well as subordinating their objectives to the technical requirements that the terms and conditions of those funds impose (Espinoza, 2009).

Limits to participation can also be found in the municipal area. Although the State modernization

process has put emphasis on citizen participation, even establishing instruments for the citizen to participate in local administration, the institutionalism itself does not provide incentives to support community involvement. This way, mayors prefer to develop managerial approaches, rather than using the participation instruments that the Municipality Law defines (Montecinos, 2008).

E-PARTICIPATION IN MINISTRIES

Regarding e-government, a managerial lean can also be noticed. This is the reason behind successful experiences, such as the ones mentioned in the previous section. Nevertheless, only 27% of the total experiences have focused on the expansion of democracy. This is the least developed area of those created by the *Presidential Instruction* dictated by Lagos (SEGPRES, 2006b, p. 84). United Nations reports, on the other hand, show an increasing deterioration of e-participation in Chile. With almost identical measurement methodologies, Chile fell from the third place in the world, in 2003, to place 12, in 2005, and to place 71, in 2008 (UN, 2003, 2008). This evolution may lead us to concern about the United Nations' methodology itself, but it should also lead us to think that the 2003 results possibly over dimensioned the Chilean public administration's opening towards participation.

The absence of a State modernization plan during the government of Michelle Bachelet may also have incidence on these results, particularly if considering that the last United Nations' report

Table 5. Presentation of relevant information about ministries on their websites

Dimension	Indicators	Int.	RR.EE.	Def.	Hac.	SGP	SGG	Eco.	Pla.	Edu.	Jus.	Tra.	OO.PP.	Sal.	Viv.	Agr.	Min.	Tran.	BB.NN.
	Structure of the Government Agency	X	X	X	X	X	X	X	X	X	X	X	X	X	X	X	X	X	X
	Authorities	X	X	X	X	X	X	X	X	X	X	X	X	X	X	X	X	X	X
	Relevant laws on the Agency and the sector of intervention	X	X	X	X	X	X	X	X	X	X	X	X	X	X	X	X		X
Relevant information for participating	Budget						X				X	X	X	X	X	X	X	X	X
	Annual Reports		X			X						X	X	X	X	X	X	X	X
	Ministerial Functions and their Policies	X	X	X	X	X	X	X	X	X	X	X	X	X	X	X	X		X
	Documents and assessments on policies, programmes or policy drafts	X			X	X		X	X	X	X	X	X	X	X	X	X	X	X
	Statistics				X			X	X	X		X		X	X	X	X		
	FAQs		X		X		X	X	X			X		X	X	X			X

Acronyms: *Int.* (Ministry of the Interior); *RR.EE.* (Ministry of Foreign Affairs); *Def.* (Ministry of National Defence); *Hac.* (Ministry of Finance); *SGP* (Ministry General Secretary of the Presidency); *SGG* (Ministry General Secretary of Government); *Eco.* (Ministry of Economy); *Pla.* (Ministry of Planning and Cooperation); *Edu.* (Ministry of Education); *Jus.* (Ministry of Justice); *Tra.* (Ministry of Labour and Social Welfare); *OO.PP.* (Ministry of Public Works); *Sal.* (Ministry of Health); *Viv.* (Ministry of Housing and Urban Planning); *Agr.* (Ministry of Agriculture); *Min.* (Ministry of Mining); *Tran.* (Ministry of Transportation and Telecommunications); *BB.NN.* (Ministry of National Assets).

Source: Own elaboration. The inspection was made between April 13 and 24, 2009. The existence of some feature of the websites of each Ministry was confirmed, without discriminating the development level of each one of these applications.

on e-government (UN, 2008) let us hypothesize on the deterioration in the development of state websites, particularly when considering that just in 2008, i.e. halfway through the presidential term, an *E-Government Action Plan* was prepared, which considered to re-launch www.tramitefacil. cl (which had been abandoned for a while).

Table 5 shows that, on an information level, Chilean ministries comply with delivering relevant information for the citizens to be informed. All portals provide information regarding legislation applicable to the ministries, the names and payroll of the personnel, and even information on the purchases of each agency can be found. Moreover, it is possible to obtain documents on the government policies. Policy evaluation reports are not very common; this is due to the fact that in Chile, programme evaluation is a topic with little development. Although ministerial sites do not present annual management reports nor budgetary information, citizens can access this information at the Budget Office website (www. dipres.cl).

The drop of Chile in the e-participation ranking may be understood by the lack of contact mechanisms, via Internet, between the citizen and the ministries. There are surveys in few websites, and almost the only way of contact is through existing forms in most of the pages. The latter rather responds to the digitalization of the Information, Complaints and Suggestions Offices, created in Chilean public agencies in 1990. These offices, rather than responding to citizen participation logics, were conceived as a service initiative for the citizen/customer. There is not either a developed certificate issuing to backup the performed consultations – less than half of them have any registration mechanism at all - and the response obligation is only available in the Ministry of Defence website.

Currently, only four ministries hold any mechanisms by which citizens can deliver input in the discussion of public policies. On the Ministry of Foreign Affairs website, a survey can be found on whether Chileans living abroad should be entitled to vote on presidential elections (a topic that has taken a relatively important place in the public agenda). Likewise, the websites of the ministries of Justice, Health and Agriculture (in this case, the website of the Livestock and Agriculture Service, which depends on the Ministry) have made law drafts available for the citizenry, which are encouraged to contact ministerial employees to deliver their opinions and suggestions to them.

Summing up, citizens have scarce possibilities to deliver input to Chilean ministries, and they do not either have the certainty that their contacts are received or processed. Due to the absence of contact mechanisms, both in top-down and bottom-up logics, it is not surprising that there are no e-participation policies that specify how to process the consultations of the citizens.

The shortage of e-participation mechanisms and policies coexist with a context in which the current government has promoted – at least, in words – its desire to increase citizen participation. When coming to power, Bachelet stated that hers would be a 'citizen government', and she announced a *Presidential Instruction on Citizen Participation in Public Management* in August 27, 2006. That document encouraged each State administration organ to announce general measures in the topic. In accordance with it, they should:

- Give an annual public report to the citizenry on the management of the State administration, comprising plans, programmes, actions and their budgetary implementation.
- Establish civil society councils, of a consulting nature, obeying the principles of diversity, representativity, and pluralism.
- Put relevant information on plans, programmes, actions and budgets into public knowledge in a timely, complete and accessible manner for the citizenry.
- Develop participative Citizen Dialogues.

Table 6. Contact mechanisms between government and citizens on the ministry websites

Dimension		Indicators	Int.	RR. EE.	Def.	Hac.	SGP	SGG	Eco.	Pla.	Edu.	Jus.	Trn.	OO. PP.	Sal.	Viv.	Agr.	Min.	Tran.	BB. NN.
Contact mechanisms between Citizen and Government	Top-down Mechanisms	Surveys on Construction of Agenda																		
		Surveys on Management Priorities																		
		Surveys or consultations on laws and/or policies		X									X		X		X			
		Chats or forums on specific topics																		
		Available e-mails of authorities		X					X				X	X	X	X	X	X		
	Bottom-up Mechanisms	Contact forms	X	X	X		X	X	X	X	X	X	X	X	X	X	X	X	X	X
		Forms for suggestions on laws or policies		X	X							X								
		Open topic chats or discussion forums																		

Source: Own elaboration.

Table 7. Processing rules of citizen participation through the ministry websites

Dimension	Indicators	Int.	RR. EE.	Def.	Hac.	SGP	SGG	Eco.	Edu.	Jus.	Trn.	OO. PP.	Sal.	Viv.	Agr.	Min.	Tran.	BB. NN.
Rules on citizen participation processing	Policy on e-participation that specifies how information will be processed and whether consultation results will be binding																	
	Definition of e-participation areas			X														
	Reply obligation of authorities		X	X			X	X	X			X	X					
	Issuing of citizen input reception certificate		X	X								X	X					X

Source: Own elaboration.

As the key areas defined by this document show, the existing conception of participation is one by which citizens may have knowledge on the performance of public management, and have the opportunity to ask some questions on some topics.

This document does not refer to using government websites as tools for promoting citizen participation. What has happened is that websites have been marginally incorporated into the general rules of the ministries, as instruments to inform the citizenry on the performance of ministerial management.

Notwithstanding, the current setback situation of e-government regarding participation, could respond to the fact that only recently there are general rules implemented in the ministries. Some organisms, such as the Ministry of Foreign Affairs, have decided to carry out the consultation process through annual reports on their websites and are working on its implementation (Godoy, Planning Office, Ministry of Foreign Affairs, e-mail query, 21/04/2009).

The lack of development in e-participation mechanisms may be explained by the fact that the government has given priority to other modalities. What Bachelet has called 'citizen government', has materialized in the creation of a series of advisory commissions, in charge of suggesting public policies to the government in different areas (Aguilera, 2007). The *Presidential Instruction on Citizen Participation in Public Management* incorporated the council formula to the public agency management. This way, consultation mechanisms external to this formula, such as those searched for in this paper, have been ruled out.

DISCUSSION AND CONCLUSION

The previous analysis presents two characteristics of ministry websites concerning the participation potential. On the one hand, there is a wide range of available information regarding ministerial management but, on the other; the lack of participatory mechanisms is confirmed.

These results can be understood if considering, just as previously suggested, that within the Chilean public administration a managerial predisposition exists, which makes open participation spaces subordinated to prevailing managerial logics.

Taking this into account allows understanding why the development of e-government in Chile adapts to characteristics of what Amoretti (2006) has identified as the oriented reform regime and the managerial regime. Both regimes respond to the NPM governance logic, based on marketization and managerialism (Bevir, Rhodes & Weller, 2003, p. 203).

Since 1998, in Chile the use of technologies has been conceived as a tool for improving the efficiency of public administration, especially in cost reduction, quality of services and transparency (managerial regime). Accordingly, some of the main characteristics of the development of e-government in Chile are the incorporation of e-procurement, the progressive emergence of online services and platforms for applying for State assistance, as well as the delivery of information on the management of public agencies.

Another element concurrent with the reform oriented regime is the lack of citizen participation potential. The evaluation of the websites revealed on this paper, shows the lack of open channels throughout the websites. The only widespread mechanism is the contact form, which does not differ from the ones existing on enterprise websites. The remaining channels, just as the availability of public policy drafts, are isolated cases.

While transparency - associated with the open regime - is present on the websites, it can also be understood in a citizen-centric logic, characteristic of the managerial regime, where information is available to increase the knowledge of the citizen-customers on the received services.

The previous results can be understood from the governance practices with which Amoretti (2006) constructs his typology. They are based on beliefs, traditions and how different dilemmas are met (Bevir, Rhodes & Weller, 2003). As some authors have asserted (Silva & Cleuren, 2009; Navia, 2009), in Chile there is a fear of participation since the collective memory associates it with the era prior to the coup of 1973 (where Salvador Allende, constitutional President, was overthrown by a military dictatorship which governed until the early 1990s). Hence, since 1990, the transition to democracy was performed under the trade-off logic between order and participation. This, added to the fact that the Chilean political system only opens State-controlled participation spaces (Delamaza, 2009; Espinoza, 2009), serves as an explanation on why the democratic and participatory dimensions of e-government does not draw attention, as does the improvement in management and delivery of services.

Several causes can be alleged to explain the setback of e-participation noticed by the UN (2008). Although a first reason may be the transfer of the e-government responsibility from the PRYME to the executive Secretary of the Digital Agenda - which only halfway through the mandate of Bachelet developed an action programme – the most powerful explanation is that the Bachelet government has conceived participation to be carried out in person, in councils where experts on different matters, as well as public officials, meet with representatives of certain groups to consult them on policy issues (Aguilera, 2007). This logic collides with e-participation mechanisms for two reasons: (1) because virtual participation is not tangible, as are the government-created councils; and, (2) because through websites, participation is not carried out by representatives nominated by any controlling entity, but by individuals who do not report to their voters or those who nominated them.

That is, the problem does not lie in what Macintosh (2004) has called e-enabling. The success in this point can be explained by the fact that it is the only e-participation aspect that coincides with the public management participation scheme promoted by the government. however, e-engaging, e-empowerment and the existence of clear rules on how to process citizen input are dimensions that do not coincide with the currently prevailing participation scheme; therefore, these aspects show a scarce level of development among Chilean ministries.

REFERENCES

Aguilera, C. (2007). Participación Ciudadana en el Gobierno de Bachelet: Consejos Asesores Presidenciales. *América Latina Hoy, 46,* 119–143.

Amoretti, F. (2006). E-Government Regimes. In Anttiroiko, A., & Malkia, M. (Eds.), *Encyclopedia of Digital Government* (pp. 580–587). Hershey, PA: IGI Global.

Araya, E., & Barría, D. (2008). Modernización del Estado y Gobierno Electrónico en Chile, 1994-2006. *Buen Gobierno, 5,* 80–103.

Armijo, M. (2002). Modernización Administrativa y de la Gestión Pública en Chile. In Tomassini, L., & Armijo, M. (Eds.), *Reforma y Modernización del Estado. Experiencias y Desafíos* (pp. 267–297). Santiago: LOM.

Bevir, M., Rhodes, R. A. W., & Weller, P. (2003). Comparative Governance; Prospects and Lessons. *Public Administration, 81*(1), 191–210. doi:10.1111/1467-9299.00342

Castells, M. (2001). *La Galaxia Internet.* Madrid: Plaza y Janés.

Cunill, N. (1997). *Repensando lo Público a Través de la Sociedad. Nuevas Formas de Gestión Pública y Representación Social.* Caracas: Nueva Sociedad.

Delamaza, G. (2009in press). Participation and Mestizaje of State-Civil Society in Chile. In Silva, P., & Cleuren, H. (Eds.), *Widening Democracy. Citizens and Participatory Schemes in Brazil and Chile*. Leiden: Brill.

Dunleay, P. (2006). New Public Management is Dead–Long Live Digital-Era Governance. *Journal of Public Administration: Research and Theory, 16*(3), 467–494. doi:10.1093/jopart/mui057

Espinoza, V. (2009in press). Citizens' Involvement and Social Policies in Chile: Patronage or Participation? In Silva, P., & Cleuren, H. (Eds.), *Widening Democracy. Citizens and Participatory Schemes in Brazil and Chile*. Leiden: Brill.

Estrategia Digital Executive Secretary. (2008). *Plan de Desarrollo Digital, 2008-2010*. Retrieved (n.d.), from http://www.estrategiadigital.gob.cl/files/Plan%20de%20Acci%C3%B3n%20Digital%202008-2010.pdf

Fountain, J. E. (2001). *Building the Virtual State. Information Technology and Institutional Change*. Washington, DC: Brookings Institution Press.

Fountain, J. E. (2009). Bureaucratic Reform and E-Government in the United Status: An Institutional Perspective. In Chadwick, A., & Howard, P. N. (Eds.), *Routledge Handbook of Internet Politics* (pp. 99–113). New York: Routledge.

González, R. (2005). Identidad y Actitudes Políticas en Jóvenes Universitarios: El Desencanto de los que no se Identifican Políticamente. *Revista de Ciencia Política, XXV*(2), 65–90.

Harto de Vera, F. (2006). Tipologías y Modelos de Democracia Electrónica. *Revista de Internet. Derecho y Política, 2*, 32–44.

Interior Ministry (Chile). (2008). *Agenda de Modernización del Estado*. Retreived July 31, 2009, from http://www.modernizacion.gov.cl/filesapp/Presentacion%20Agenda%20Modernizacion.pdf

Kingdon, J. (2003). *Agendas, Alternatives and Public Policies*. New York: Logman.

Luna-Reyes, L., Hernández García, J. M., & Gil-García, J. R. (2009). Hacia un Modelo de los Determinantes de Éxito de los Portales de Gobierno Estatal en México. *Gestión y Política Pública, XVIII*(2), 307–340.

Macintosh, A. (2004, January 4-5). Characterizing E-Participation in Policy-Making. Paper presented at the *37th Hawaii International Conference on System Science 2004*, University of Hawai'i at Manoa, Manoa, HI.

Margetts, H. (2005). Virtual Organizations. In Ferlie, E., Lynn, L. E. Jr, & Pollitt, C. (Eds.), *The Oxford Handbook of Public Management* (pp. 305–325). Oxford, UK: Oxford University Press.

Margetts, H. (2007). Electronic Government. A Revolution in Public Administration? In B. G., Peters. & J. Pierre (Eds.) The Handbook of Public Administration (pp. 234-244). London: Sage.

Margetts, H. (2009). Public Management Change and E-Government: The Emergence of Digital-Era-Governance. In Chadwick, A., & Howard, P. N. (Eds.), *Routledge Handbook of Internet Politics* (pp. 114–127). New York: Routledge.

Medaglia, R. (2007). The Challenged Identity of a Field: The State of the Art of eParticipation Research. *Information Polity, 12*(3), 169–181.

Montecinos, E. (2008). Los Incentivos de la Descentralización en la Gestión Municipal Chilena. Gestión Política sin Participación Democrática. *Estado, Gobierno, Gestión Pública. Revista Chilena de Administración Pública, 12*, 105–123.

Navia, P. (2009in press). Top-Down and Bottom-Up Democracy in Chile under Bachelet. In Silva, P., & Cleuren, H. (Eds.), *Widening Democracy. Citizens and Participatory Schemes in Brazil and Chile*. Leiden, The Netherlands: Brill.

Orrego, C., & Araya, R. (2002). *Internet en Chile: Oportunidad para la Participación Ciudadana. Temas de Desarrollo Humano Sustentable Documento 7*. Santiago, Chile: PNUD.

Ramírez, A. (2001). *Modernización de la Gestión Pública. El caso Chileno (1994-2000). Estudio de Caso 58*. Santiago: Departamento de Ingeniería Industrial, Universidad de Chile.

Rivera, E. (2003). *Nueva Economía, Gobierno Electrónico y Reforma del Estado*. Santiago, Chile: Universitaria.

Rose, J., Grönlund, A., & Andersen, K. (2007). Introduction. In Advic, Anders et al (Eds.) Understanding eParticipation. Contemporary PhD eParticipation Research in Europe (pp. 1-15). Without city: Demo-Net.

SEGPRES (Secretaría General de la Presidencia). (2006a). *Reforma del Estado en Chile: 2000-2006*. Santiago, Chile: SEGPRES.

SEGPRES (Secretaría General de la Presidencia). (2006b). *Gobierno Electrónico en Chile. El Estado del Arte II*. Santiago, Chile: SEGPRES.

Setälä, M., & Grönlund, K. (2006). Parliamentary Websites: Theoretical and Comparative Perspectives. *Information Polity, 11*(2), 149–162.

Silva, P. (2004). Doing Politics in a Depoliticised Society: Social Change and Political Deactivation in Chile. *Bulletin of Latin American Research, 23*(1), 63–78. doi:10.1111/j.1470-9856.2004.00096.x

Silva, P., & Cleuren, H. (2009in press). Assessing Participatory Democracy in Brazil and Chile: An Introduction. In Silva, P., & Cleuren, H. (Eds.), *Widening Democracy. Citizens and Participatory Schemes in Brazil and Chile*. Leiden, The Netherlands: Brill.

Snellen, I. (2005). E-Government: A Challenge for Public Management. In Ferlie, E., Lynn, L. E. Jr, & Pollitt, C. (Eds.), *The Oxford Handbook of Public Management* (pp. 398–421). Oxford, UK: Oxford University Press.

Takao, Y. (2004). Democratic Renewal by 'Digital' Local Government in Japan. *Pacific Affairs, 77*(2), 237–262.

Toledo Llancaqueo, V. (2007). Prima Ratio. Movilización Mapuche y Política Penal. Los Marcos de la Política Indígena en Chile 1990-2007. *OSAL, VIII*(22), 253–293.

UN (United Nations). (2003). *World Public Sector Report 2003. E-Government at the Crossroads*. New York: United Nations.

UN (United Nations). (2005). *Global E-Government Readiness Report 2005. From E-Government to E-Inclusion*. New York: United Nations.

UN (United Nations). (2008). *2008 Global E-government Readiness Report. From E-Government to Connected Governance*. New York: United Nations.

Chapter 4
E–Government and Opportunities for Participation:
The Case of the Mexican State Web Portals

J. Ramon Gil-Garcia
Centro de Investigación y Docencia Económicas, Mexico

Fernando González Miranda
Universidad Autónoma del Estado de México, Mexico

ABSTRACT

Electronic government has been considered a powerful strategy for administrative reform. Identified benefits from e-government are numerous and range from efficiency and effectiveness to transparency and democratic participation. However, only a few studies focus on the potential of information technologies (IT) to promote citizen participation in government affairs. This participation could be conceptualized in many different ways, from the possibility of submitting a request or question to actively participating in decision-making and voting online. In some developing countries, opportunities for citizen participation are still very limited and information technologies have the potential to expand these communication channels. Based on an analysis of the 32 state portals in Mexico, this chapter proposes an index of citizen participation opportunities, ranks the portals according to this index, and explores some of the determinants of the availability of these participation opportunities through the case of the Mexican state of Michoacán. We argue that assessing the different channels for citizen participation available through e-government Web sites is an important first step for understanding the relationships between government and citizens. Citizen initiated contacts and participation cannot exist if communication channels are limited or nonexistent.

INTRODUCTION

Government reform through the use of information technology (IT) is an ongoing process. Few changes in government procedures are as visible as those promoted by IT applications. Some of the main benefits attributed to electronic government are related to greater citizen involvement, improved efficiency in public administration operations, better delivery of public services, and the development of better intergovernmental coordination, all of which contribute to achieving successful results

DOI: 10.4018/978-1-61520-933-0.ch004

from public policies (Kakabadse et al., 2003; OECD, 2003a; Netchaeva, 2002; OECD, 2005c). However, introducing technology into public administration or into the relationships between government and citizens does not guarantee that the potential benefits are attained or that participation will increase.

Given that representative democracy refers to the citizenry's right to vote and elect its representatives, some authors have reduced their analysis of e-Democracy to electoral issues, such as forms of e-Voting, remote voting, or preventing media bias from those interested in a particular outcome (Alvarez & Hall, 2004). However, e-Democracy does not only refer to elections through electronic means, but also to the exchange of information between citizens and elected officials (Murray, 2005). It also includes providing services over the Internet "that facilitate interaction between voters, candidates, and opinion leaders" (Chappelet & Kilchenmann, 2005), among other concepts. In fact, e-democracy should include any form of democratic participation by citizens using any form of IT. This participative aspect of the use of IT has also been considered an important element of a more comprehensive concept of e-government (Gil-Garcia & Luna-Reyes, 2006).

This chapter focuses on the opportunities for citizen participation in state Web sites. The inclusion of democratic concepts, such as transparency, accountability, and civic education may help to improve the relationships between government and citizens (Wong & Welch, 2004). Some of these concepts related to democracy are already reflected in the applications and tools currently used in e-government portals. Based on the analysis of the 32 state portals in Mexico, this chapter proposes an index of citizen participation opportunities, ranks the portals according to this index, and explores some of the determinants of the availability of these participation opportunities through the case of the Mexican state of Michoacán.

The chapter is organized into five sections, including the foregoing introduction. The second

section provides definitions of the main theoretical foundations and describes the variables used in this study. It also presents the construction of an index, which measures the opportunities for participation available in state Web portals. The third section presents the research design and methods used in this study. The fourth section contains the main findings from the evaluation and interviews. Overall, there is great diversity in the participation mechanisms available in each state, thereby providing differentiated opportunities to citizens. Finally, the fifth section provides some conclusions and suggests areas for future research.

ELECTRONIC GOVERNMENT AND E-DEMOCRACY

Theoretically and practically, electronic government and electronic democracy are interrelated phenomena. Both are related to the use of information and communication technologies, but have important differences (Alvarez & Hall, 2004; Amoretti, 2007; Birch and Watt, 2004; Grönlund, 2004; Macintosh et al, 2005a; Margain, 2001). Recent academic literature suggests several approaches that are useful in gaining a better understanding of these two concepts and identifying their differences and similarities, as well as their interrelations.

Electronic Government: A Broad Concept

There are many definitions of electronic government. One of them refers simply to "the delivery of government services and information electronically, 24 hours a day, 7 days a week" (Norris et al., 2001; Holden et al., 2003). The definition of electronic government that will be used in this study, although it condenses and synthesizes a number of definitions provided by various authors, is directly cited from Gil-Garcia and Luna-Reyes

Figure 1. Area of influence of an e-Government strategy (OECD, 2005c)

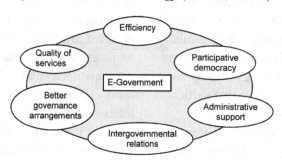

(2006). They establish that electronic government refers to "the selection, implementation and use of information and communication technologies by government to provide public services, improve managerial effectiveness, and promote democratic values and mechanisms, as well as the development of a regulatory framework which facilitates information intensive initiatives and fosters the knowledge society" (pp. 642).

According to the Organization for Economic Co-operation and Development (OECD) (2003), the main reasons for designing and implementing e-Government strategies as a means of achieving administrative reform and meeting public policy objectives are efficiency, participative democracy, administrative support, intergovernmental relations, better governance arrangements, and improved service quality (see Figure 1).

Gil-Garcia and Luna-Reyes (2006) describe four approaches to understanding electronic gov-

ernment: a definitional approach, a stakeholder-oriented approach, an evolutionary approach, and an integrative approach. For this last approach, the authors present a map, which contains some elements of e-government as they relate to public administration theory (see Table 1). This paper focuses on the political approach to public administration and emphasizes the e-democracy category, which the authors suggest is one of the main components of broader concept of e-government.

Murray (2005) describes e-democracy as the use of information and communication technologies (ICTs) by governments, international government organizations, elected officials, the media, political parties, nongovernmental organizations, and citizen or other interest groups in the political processes of local, regional, state, and national communities, up to the global level. We propose that the use of ICTs for citizen participation is

Table 1. Elements of e-government and public administration theory (Gil-Garcia & Luna, 2006)

Elements of e-Government and Public Administration Theory		
Approaches to P. A.	**Categories of e-Government**	**Elements of e-Government**
Administrative	e-Services	e-Services, e-Commerce
	e-Management	e-Management, e-Personal, e-Procurement
Political	e-Democracy	e-Democracy, e-Participation, e-Voting, e-Transparency
Legal	e-Policy	e-Policy, e-Governance

reflected in some tools and applications that are already available through e-government portals. Following, we briefly describe some fundamentals of democracy, which aid in identifying important concepts related to participation and IT tools and applications. This set of tools and applications will be the basis for the participation opportunity index that we propose in this chapter.

Democracy, Citizen Participation, and E-Democracy

The relevance of e-Democracy to public political processes is that, in order for a democratic government to function, citizens must have the opportunity to participate in the public arena. In order to arrive at a point where the state improves its interaction with society, it is necessary to first improve spaces for participation, in addition to the involvement and commitment of citizens to its government. The notion of representative democracy (or the popular election of representatives through a voting process) is associated with certain criteria that a society must comply with when governing. These criteria ensure that members of a society may participate, under conditions of equality, in decisions concerning government policies. According to Dahl (1998:37), these criteria include (1) effective participation, (2) vote equality, (3) illustrated understanding, (4) control of the agenda, and (5) inclusion.

There are a number of ways to promote active participation in public policy processes. Participation can be individual as well as collective. In addition, participation must stem from a well-defined, common identity among citizens within a community. In other words, participation can have a territorial (starting with neighborhood committees, for example), demographic (women, youth, the elderly, the disabled, etc.), or topical (environmental, cultural, educational, security, etc.) base. There are also certain prerequisites in order for participation to take place, which may include the following: (1) the existence of

information concerning the specific topic to be dealt with; (2) dissemination of information, requirements, obligations, and the process behind participation; (3) clear objectives behind the formulation of participation strategies; (4) personnel trained to handle the information gathered through participation; and (5) infrastructure that supports the logistics of participation (Ziccardi, 2004b). E-democracy is an instrument that can be used to fulfill some of these requirements.

According to Smith (2000), the mere existence of forums for citizen participation does not ensure the development of a deliberative and participative democracy; however, there are certain criteria that can be applied to evaluate the contribution of those forums. These criteria are (1) inclusion, which means the existence of an equal right to be heard in these forums, without exclusion; (2) deliberation, insofar as the dialog is guided by equality, liberty, and competence and is free from disillusion, deception, power, and strategies that undermine interactions; (3) citizenry, in which the experiences and judgments of citizens are brought into the public domain, and where citizens are motivated to develop mutual respect and understanding toward other citizens; and (4) legitimacy, where decisions are made through participation after a period of public deliberation. The democratic concepts mentioned above are the basis for assessing to what extent state Web portals promote citizen participation through the use of certain tools and applications. When combined, these tools and applications create a participation opportunity index, which will be applied to all 32 Mexican government Web portals (representing 31 states and the Federal District). Following, we briefly explain each of the proposed variables: (1) offline principles, (2) online involvement, (3) information for users, (4) discussion forums, (5) online contributions, (6) real time conversations, (7) petitions, (8) surveys, (9) voting, and (10) feedback and results of involvement.

Offline principles not only involve education, but also policies and legislation aimed at providing the basis for democracy and citizen participation (Masters et al., 2004). This variable can be observed in notices posted on state portals concerning workshops, meetings, courses, and committees, among others, which are then conducted face to face in public places and coordinated and conducted by authorities who are competent on democratic topics (Andersson, 2004; Macintosh et al., 2005a). One can also see whether laws or regulations that encourage citizen participation in state projects are posted on the portal (Scott, 2006).

Online involvement includes tools used to promote and motivate citizen participation through Web sites (OECD, 2007). They provide key potential advantages for active participation given that they can transcend certain limitations such as time and location (Masters et al., 2004). This variable includes online courses and tutorials that teach citizens how they can participate in the decision making process or at least influence it (Chappelet & Kilchemann, 2005). Tools for e-Learning (online learning), such as games (e-Participate, 2006) or Webcasts (online transmissions) that inform citizens on certain specific issues, can also be used (Parycek et al., 2004).

Information for users, at a minimum, includes names of officials, street addresses, electronic addresses, telephone numbers, and business hours (OECD, 2005b). However, there are a number of other components that are useful for democratic access and confidence when using these tools, such as availability and content of security and privacy policies, tools to facilitate use by the disabled, and translation or use of other languages (Netchaeva, 2002). Mailing lists are another technical component that users may take advantage of in order to subscribe to news groups or informative bulletins relevant to particular sectors, territories, or topics (Browning, 1996).

Discussion forums are areas that allow for debate on specific topics and expression of deliberative comments. The main advantages of these tools are that they support interaction, deliberation and debate, and allow for broad discussion. For this interaction to take place, it requires a team with sufficient time and abilities to moderate, support, and facilitate discussion, as well as to analyze the contributions (Masters et al., 2004; Macintosh et al., 2005b; Chappelet & Kilchenmann, 2005). In online discussion forums, site administrators post a specific topic for discussion over a long period of time (Roeder et al., 2005; Sæbo & Nilsen, 2004; OECD, 2007). The task of the forum moderator is to direct the discussion and remove comments that are out of place or do not contribute to previously defined objectives for the forum (Mahrer & Krimmer, 2005; Bonney, 2004).

Online contributions are known as Weblogs or simply blogs. They are a form of active participation used to increase awareness about general topics (Chappelet & Kilchenmann, 2005; Scott, 2006), as well as to record opinions, reports, stories, and other types of articles related to a particular community topic, sector, or territory (OECD, 2007; Macintosh et al., 2005b; Roeder et al., 2005). This tool also requires time and moderating in order to assure continuity of contributions and to prevent discussions that do not contribute to the development of the community (Bonney, 2004).

Real time conversations are similar to discussion tables, except that they are held virtually at specific and limited times (Chappelet & Kilchenmann, 2005). The conversations can provide opportunities for interested individuals to talk with government officials who have decision making powers at predefined times (Masters et al., 2004). Despite their highly ephemeral nature, they promote a high level of interaction between government and citizens; they also promote transparency and accountability because participants' questions are answered directly (Roeder et al., 2005). These types of conversations or "chats" are very easy tools to use and are widely accepted among today's younger citizens. Not unlike discussion tables, they require technical ability and sufficient funding to support moderation, synchronization, and analysis of data (OECD, 2007; Mahrer & Krimmer, 2005).

Petitions can be used to express opinions and build policies from the bottom-up (Masters et al., 2004). Petitions can be made through complaint and suggestion boxes, but also through Web pages specifically designed to gather petitions from citizens. The advantage of using these tools is that moderators are not necessarily required and petitions can be collected and compiled into more meaningful reports (Macintosh et al., 2005a; Mahrer & Krimmer, 2005; Browning, 1996; Scott, 2006). The purpose of these petitions is different from the specific political connotation of gathering signatures to support or prevent a policy action, but it is related.

Surveys can be used to gauge different perceptions related to implemented policies. The advantage of surveys is that they collect quantifiable data that is easy to analyze and understand, and they require minimal equipment or skill (Masters et al., 2004). The disadvantage is that surveys are easy instruments to manipulate, and it is also easy to obtain biased results or interpretations (Grönlund, 2004).

E-voting implies the introduction of technological components at some or all stages of the voting process, which makes it more difficult to implement than traditional voting methods (Masters et al., 2004; Birch & Watt, 2004). There are several forms of voting, which can range from innovations at the voting site, such as electronic ballots, multiple delivery channels (through SMS messages, the Internet and over the telephone, for example), and the use of electronic voter rolls, to unsupervised voting, such as automated booths that validate identity and record votes, among others (Xenakis & Macintosh, 2004; Moynihan, 2004). However, the main disadvantage of this type of voting is that it limits involvement and the development of deliberative thought and understanding of the topics (Chappelet & Kilchenmann, 2005).

Feedback and results of involvement are the results of consultations and discussions, which must be published after an event or decision in order to provide participants with feedback and to strengthen confidence in the decision making process (Masters et al., 2004). This feedback can be shared on portals in the form of reports from meetings, minutes, and surveys. (OECD, 2005b; Chappelet & Kilchenmann, 2005). In the case of voting in real time, one can also observe whether voting results are posted online and in real time (Macintosh et al., 2005a; Mahrer & Krimmer, 2005).

We argue that opportunities for participation in state government portals could be represented by these components and the following equation will be used as the basis for the opportunities for participation index:

$$PO = offP + onI + usI + disF + onC + Chat + eP$$

Where:

- PO = Opportunities for participation
- $offP$ = Offline principles
- onI = Online involvement
- usI = Information for users
- $disF$ = Discussion forums
- onC = Online contributions
- $Chat$ = Real time conversations
- $ePet$ = Petitions
- Sur = Surveys
- $eVot$ = Voting
- FB = Feedback and results

In order to assess each of these variables, we observed specific elements, tools, and applications. Table 2 shows the relationships between these variables and the specific elements, tools, and applications that were evaluated.

E-government encompasses a wide variety of tools and applications, which are used to improve many aspects of government activity, including the relationships between government and citizens. In

Table 2. Participation variables and components

Variable	Elements, tools, and applications
1. Offline principles	Agenda, Announcements, Institutions
2. Online involvement	Teaching, Games, Transmission, Access
3. Information for users	About, Addresses, Telephone numbers, e-Mail, Positions, Cabinet, Mailing lists
4. Discussion forums	e-Forums
5. Online contributions	Blogs
6. Real time conversations	Chat rooms
7. Petitions	e-Petitions, Comments
8. Surveys	Surveys
9. Voting	Official voting, Nonofficial voting
10. Feedback and results involvement	Publications, Statistics

contrast, e-democracy is generally understood as a more specific term related to the use of ITs in the political arena, including participation and voting. Based on these ideas, theoretically, e-government could be seen as the more comprehensive concept, which includes e-democracy as one of its fundamental components. Similarly, e-democracy includes several elements and mechanisms for citizens' participation using ITs. Figure 2 shows these relationships graphically.

In other words, providing opportunities for participation through the use of ITs is a way to establish e-democracy and strengthen citizen participation in democracy. It is not a question of simply inserting technology into government activities and processes, but of building opportunities for democratic participation institutionally, and reinforcing them by implementing suitable technology to support it. Technology is a tool that, if available for use in a convenient and efficient way, can make participation more visible and feasible for citizens and ultimately more useful for government and the society as a whole.

RESEARCH DESIGN AND METHODS

This section of the chapter is divided into two parts. The first part describes the methodology used to analyze the opportunities for participation

Figure 2. e-government, e-democracy, and opportunities for participation

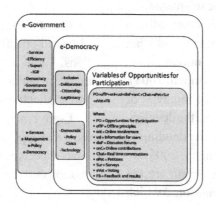

in the Mexican state portals. These types of indices have been used before to evaluate electronic government initiatives, both in Mexico (Sandoval, Gil-Garcia & Luna, 2007) and internationally (United Nations, 2005; Ramadan-Mamata et al., 2005). The second part of this section looks at the processes that state agencies are currently undertaking in relation to the management of information provided by users of these portals, the technologies they employ, and the resources (human, material, and financial) used to support their activities, as well as the work agenda they intend to follow. For this section, analysis will be based on documents and semi-structured interviews with public managers from the state of Michoacán. Several authors recommend this type of mixed method research design to better understand social phenomena (Fontana and Frey, 2000; Morgan, 1997; Kröll, 2000; Gil-Garcia, 2005). We think this is useful to untangle the complex relationships between the design of government Web portals, particularly the applications related to citizen participation, and several organizational, institutional, and contextual factors, which affect the capabilities of a state to introduce this type of application.

Evaluation of State Portals

This sub-section describes the assessment of the opportunities for participation in the Mexican state portals. The weight given to each variable is the same, since each one provides different opportunities for citizen participation through the Web portals. Each variable will be evaluated on a scale of one to ten in relation to the number of components with which the portal complies. For example, a component with two indicators will be 0 if none of them is present, 5 if one of them is present, and 10 if both of them are present. Similarly, a component with four indicators will be 0 if none of them is present, 2.5 if one of them is present, 5 if two of them are present, 7.5 if three of them are present, and 10 if four of them are present.

The items were applied to each state portal, including Mexico City's portal (the Federal District). Once the survey was complete, we were able to assess the status of each portal in relation to the opportunities it provides for citizen participation. We were also able to detect which variables and criteria are most developed or represented in a more comprehensive fashion in the Mexican Web portals, as well as those that still require greater attention from the public managers and chief information officers (CIOs) in the states.

Interviews

Semi-structured interviews were conducted with public managers from different levels and agencies within the government of the state of Michoacán. The interviewees were selected from both the current government and the previous administration. Although some of these individuals have changed position recently, they were and continue to be responsible for implementing ITs in the state government.

The state of Michoacán was selected for two main reasons. First, it was interesting to select a portal that did not perform well in the evaluation process, given that the study was attempting to understand the reasons why they were not providing participation opportunities for their citizens. Second, the evolution of Michoacán's portal over previous years is recorded by the *ranking of state portals* (Sandoval & Gil, 2006; Sandoval, Gil & Luna, 2007), which showed that during the 2006 evaluation the state portal was listed at 5th place, but later fell to 15th during the 2007 evaluation. This shift indicates that something changed in the state government and affected the quality or functionality of the state Web portal. Therefore, the main purpose in studying this particular state was to identify the most important managerial, organizational, and institutional factors that affected its capacity to provide participation opportunities to citizens. The interviews provided important information about the relationships between the opportunities for participation in the portals and the back office processes that support them.

ANALYSIS AND RESULTS

This section includes the main findings from the review of state portals and the interviews with public managers of the Michoacán state. First, we present the results of applying the index of opportunities for participation to the 32 state Web portals in Mexico. Then we describe our analysis of the case of Michoacán and organize the presentation of the results according to five categories of challenges identified in previous research.

Opportunities for Participation on State Portals

Table 3 shows the results of the evaluations of the 32 state Web portals based on the variables previously identified (the variables are represented by their respective initials). Only five of the state portals scored above 50 points on a scale from zero to one hundred. The variables most often present in the state portals in Mexico are *offline principles, online involvement, information for users, petitions,* and *feedback.* However, almost all of the scores across the variables are just above the average.

In the case of *offline principles* the variable reached a maximum of 7.78 points and a minimum of 1.11, with a mode of 5.56, an average of 5, and 17 states coming in over the average. *Online involvement* reached a maximum of 7.65 points and a minimum of 2.35, with a mode of 4.71, an average of 5.24, and 17 states also coming in over the average. *Information for users* reached a maximum of 9.3 points and a minimum of 3.57, with a mode of 6.43, an average of 5.98, and 22 states over the average. The variable referring to *petitions* reached a maximum of 10 points and a minimum of 0, with a mode of 3.33, an average of 5.52, and 16 states over the average. *Feedback,*

the last variable in this group, reached a maximum of 10 points and a minimum of 0, with a mode of 6, an average of 5.9, and 24 states coming in over the average.

The remaining variables, however, were seldom present on the portals, indicating that they require more attention. In the case of *discussion forums,* this variable is only present in 5 of the 32 states, with 2 over the average, reaching a maximum of 7.5 points. *Online contributions* are present on only one portal, whereas *online conversations* are present in 10 of the 32 portals. As for *surveys,* this variable is present on 10 portals, 6 appearing complete and the other 4 only partially. The last variable in this group, which involves variants of online *voting* such as *polls,* is also present in 10 of the 32 portals. When added together, the total sum of the grades/scores reached a maximum of 73.45 points for the state of Nuevo León and a minimum of 18.95 points for the state of Chiapas. The state of Michoacán fell into the bottom three states with a score of 22.71.

E-Government and Citizen Participation: The Case of Michoacán

On a theoretical level, Gil-Garcia and Pardo (2005) have drawn a map of the challenges for electronic government initiatives in general, which they group into five categories: (1) information and data, (2) information technology, (3) organization and managerial, (4) legal and regulatory, and (5) institutional and environmental. The following sections present the results from the interviews with public managers from the state of Michoacán, organized according to the categories proposed by these authors.

Information and Data

In the case of Michoacán, there is a planning process that underlies how information is handled and the type of technology that should be used to optimize its storage and collection. However, they lacked a well-designed catalog of services that could be provided over the Web and the information that would support that catalog, particularly in the case of participation opportunities. There

is no provision for structuring data to ensure quality, other than those provided through normal procedures used by government departments during day-to-day tasks. In other words, because electronic government is poorly planned from the

Table 3. Evaluation of state portals by variable

Evaluation of Portals by Variable												
Ranking	State	PO	OI	UI	DF	OC	CH	P	S	V	FB	Tot.Var.
1	Nuevo León	7.78	7.65	7.86	7.5	0	10	10.00	10	6.67	6	73.45
2	State of Mexico	6.67	5.29	4.29	7.5	10	10	6.67	5	6.67	4	66.08
3	Baja California Norte	6.67	6.47	7.14	0.0	0	10	10.00	5	3.33	8	56.61
4	Sonora	7.78	4.71	5.00	0.0	0	10	10.00	5	0.00	8	50.48
5	Distrito Federal	5.56	6.47	7.14	0.0	0	10	3.33	5	6.67	6	50.17
6	San Luis Potosí	4.44	7.06	5.00	0.0	0	0	10.00	10	6.67	6	49.17
7	Guerrero	4.44	4.71	6.43	5.0	0	10	10.00	0	0.00	8	48.58
8	Quintana Roo	4.44	4.71	5.00	0.0	0	0	6.67	10	3.33	6	40.15
9	Aguascalientes	7.78	7.65	6.43	0.0	0	0	6.67	0	3.33	8	39.85
10	Hidalgo	1.11	4.71	5.71	0.0	0	0	6.67	10	3.33	8	39.53
11	Durango	4.44	5.88	6.43	0.0	0	10	3.33	0	3.33	6	39.42
12	Coahuila	3.33	5.29	6.43	0.0	0	0	3.33	10	3.33	6	37.72
13	Chihuahua	5.56	5.29	4.29	0.0	0	10	3.33	0	0.00	8	36.47
14	Jalisco	5.56	5.29	7.14	0.0	0	0	10.00	0	0.00	8	35.99
15	Morelos	5.56	4.71	7.14	5.0	0	0	6.67	0	0.00	6	35.07
16	Tamaulipas	6.67	5.88	3.57	0.0	0	10	3.33	0	0.00	4	33.45
17	Yucatán	6.67	3.53	5.00	2.5	0	0	3.33	10	0.00	0	31.03
18	Tlaxcala	4.44	7.06	5.71	0.0	0	0	6.67	0	0.00	6	29.88
19	Veracruz	6.67	4.71	6.43	0.0	0	0	3.33	0	0.00	8	29.13
20	Zacatecas	5.56	5.29	6.43	0.0	0	0	3.33	0	0.00	8	28.61
21	Guanajuato	6.67	4.12	7.14	0.0	0	0	6.67	0	0.00	4	28.59
22	Nayarit	3.33	4.71	6.43	0.0	0	0	10.00	0	0.00	4	28.47
23	Colima	5.56	2.94	4.29	0.0	0	10	3.33	0	0.00	2	28.12
24	Tabasco	5.56	4.12	5.71	0.0	0	0	6.67	0	0.00	6	28.05
25	Oaxaca	2.22	6.47	9.29	0.0	0	0	3.33	0	0.00	6	27.31
26	Querétaro	3.33	5.29	6.43	0.0	0	0	3.33	0	0.00	6	24.39
27	Campeche	2.22	4.12	6.43	0.0	0	0	3.33	0	0.00	8	24.10
28	Sinaloa	3.33	4.71	6.43	0.0	0	0	6.67	0	0.00	2	23.13
29	Puebla	4.44	3.53	5.71	0.0	0	0	3.33	0	0.00	6	23.02
30	Michoacán	3.33	6.47	3.57	0.0	0	0	3.33	0	0.00	6	22.71
31	Baja California Sur	5.56	2.35	4.29	0.0	0	0	0.00	0	0.00	10	22.19
32	Chiapas	3.33	6.47	7.14	0.0	0	0	0.00	0	0.00	2	18.95

outset in the majority of cases, technology between agencies is very different. This disparity is often a source of difficulty when agencies attempt to collaborate, especially between agencies with similar goals and objectives. Due to the nature of the projects that were designed and awaiting implementation in Michoacán, it was also necessary to design processes and structures that support the collection and quality of data, as well as characteristics such as portability and transmission, which were also very useful and necessary for certain applications, including opportunities for citizen participation.

Information Technologies

The use of different programming languages, development platforms, and operating systems results in tremendous difficulties when it is necessary to share information. There are no clear rules that guide information managers toward accomplishing their goals in a collaborative environment; each one of them works in isolation from the others. A middle level manager said that "it's necessary that only one agency take control of the technological development in the state government and set short, medium and long term plans to develop the projects each agency has." In this case, the technology adopted by each government department follows the negotiations of those responsible for governmental purchasing and system designers, reducing the burden of exhaustive planning and consideration of all the possibilities on the market. The opinion of a high level manager was that "information processes have to be separated from the political matters; they should follow a more autonomous development." For this reason, in the future the Michoacán government needs to consider bringing in experts who can provide technical aspects and help select the best technological options for each specific application.

Organization and Administration

The goals and objectives government departments put forward in their annual programs are clear and realistic. However, communication channels between IT areas and other departments are non-existent, which leads to organizational inefficiencies and difficulties related to administration and control. A restructuring of the IT responsibilities is necessary so that the parties responsible for collection of information, intergovernmental collaboration, communication management, and systems development are not dependent on the government agencies to whom they provide their services. Due to the fact that electronic government initiatives permeate almost all activities undertaken by government agencies, the resources used to implement them become vague. On occasion, budget calculations made by agencies fail to take into account the needs of certain medium and long-term electronic government projects. A middle level manager said that "until now we don't have a definite budget, sometimes we only have enough money for the payroll, and that's it." Given the difficulty in measuring the results of electronic government initiatives, it is necessary to define clear objectives for each initiative in order to facilitate budgeting. In the majority of cases, budgets are allocated by agency, by program, or by project, but they do not always take into account the shared responsibility of electronic government initiatives, such as the Web portal and some opportunities for participation.

Legal and Regulatory Framework

The current legal framework for state public administration, which controls procedures and attributes of each and every government agency, limits the adoption of electronic government tools that promote citizen participation. The success of an electronic government initiative depends largely on whether the government secures a legal and regulatory framework suitable enough to implement it. There is currently no legal framework aimed at establishing collaboration between different government agencies for sharing information that may help to achieve policy objectives and provide more opportunities for participation to citizens. Equally important is the widespread lack of awareness of the necessity for collaboration and capacity in order to use the information of government agencies; as the size between agencies differ, so too do their resources available for implementing IT applications and tools. What is missing are legal frameworks that support the use of information and communication technologies, such as the use of information banks instead of paper for government electronic transactions. The government also needs to guarantee the safety and privacy of information, which circulates around agencies and over communication networks, including the Internet. This guarantee is particularly important for some forms of citizen participation.

Institutional and Environmental Context

The change with respect to this aspect is significant under the current administration. Government administrators are now paying much more attention to the importance and role of technological innovation. For example, a high level manager described the process: "In the previous administration there was this *sub-ministry of informatics* as a technology ruler inside the *Planning Ministry* [which is a normative instance], an informatics committee in the treasury ministry, and the Technology Center as an executive instance. Furthermore, there was an *informatics sub-committee* that would serve as an internal informatics development forum, but that only worked for budgetary competition between agencies. So, there was a lot of functions duplicity." While no allowance has been made for external companies to provide technical services, this circumstance is not true for providing equipment. The institutional environment had mixed reactions to these changes, and there are high

expectations surrounding the potential effects of outsourcing and similar strategies on the state government capacity to provide more services and opportunities for participation. As a result, mechanisms must also be established for evaluating results that will allow these initiatives to be evaluated over both the medium and long term.

CONCLUSION

This study provides evidence for the fact that information technologies are tools that can potentially help to promote citizen participation. Providing these opportunities and more general government services through state portals has become increasingly important and governments are allocating resources for this purpose. In Mexico, implementations of electronic government have made significant progress. More and more government processes are becoming available through Web sites and other Internet technologies, including opportunities for citizen participation. The global context and international competition exert influence and pressure on the macroeconomic conditions of the country. These pressures sometimes translate into establishing public policies that do not necessarily correspond to the Mexican reality and culture; therefore, some governments may have information and services that are not the most adequate for the needs of their citizens.

Despite the fact that Mexican portals have made significant advances at the functional level, there still remain many gaps that need to be filled. For instance, citizen participation must play a more prominent role. It is undesirable that decision-making should lie in the hands of a few politicians and public managers. It is also very difficult for a few government agencies to understand and take into consideration all dimensions of complex social problems. Informed citizens should participate and shape the direction taken by their government. It is therefore essential for governments to make more opportunities available for citizen participation. Information and communication technologies could help to significantly increase the number and variety of these participation opportunities. This chapter shows that this is already happening, although the progress is very modest.

From the evaluation of Mexican state portals in this study, we have observed that certain elements of participation have been considered and adopted by state governments. However, other elements are absent in the majority of them. In addition, there is a systematic lack of planning, design, implementation, and evaluation of the electronic government strategies applied in each state. The participation opportunities that state governments provide to their citizens are still limited. This lack of opportunity, however, cannot be attributed solely to a lack of vision by those who implement information technologies in the states. There are other important factors that exercise significant influence on the resulting availability of participation opportunities. Barriers related to legislation, regulations, technological change, and Internet access must be addressed if there is any hope of electronic government fulfilling the promise of improving government in general and promoting participation in particular.

There is still a long way to go in the realm of electronic government and opportunities for participation at the state level. Some states, like Michoacán, clearly show limitations at the organizational and regulatory framework level. All too often, changes in political leadership mean a long period of uncertainty, which is reflected in the creation of public policies, including opportunities for citizen participation. The lack of clarity when defining institutional roles, as well as the lack of collaboration between different government agencies, can also slow the development of good electronic government strategies. Another factor that can limit citizen participation is lack of interest, from decision-makers who define government policy through to the apathy of the citizens themselves. In addition, it does not seem clear that wealthier states have a better chance of placing higher in the rankings. In Mexico, five out of thirty two states contribute more than fifty percent of the country's Gross National Product, and from those five states, only three are in the top ten places in our index. It seems that there are many other factors, probably related to their management practices or their willingness to invest in participation channels for citizens, which allow states to have good opportunities for participation in their Web sites.

From a practical perspective, if the managers responsible for IT innovation in state governments could take into consideration the variables explained in this paper, they could better understand and probably increase citizen participation. This paper has identified a broad range of potential tools and applications that could be included in e-government portals to promote citizen-initiated contacts and participation. Public managers responsible for IT and citizen participation now have a list of options, some of which have not been used in state portals before, but all of which have the potential to increase the opportunities for citizens to participate in government. This paper also uncovers an initial set of factors that have an impact on the capacity of government to offer these opportunities. More research is needed in order to provide better guidance to public managers, but these preliminary results are an important first step in that direction. Citizen participation is an important element of good governance and IT could help to improve and increase the channels and opportunities and, therefore, to promote better democratic governments.

ACKNOWLEDGMENT

The authors want to thank Anna Raup-Kounovsky for her valuable assistance in the final stages of the development of this chapter. This work was partially supported by the National Science Foundation under Grant No. 0131923 and Grant No. 0630239. Any opinions, findings, conclusions, or recommendations expressed in this material are those of the authors and do not necessarily reflect the views of the National Science Foundation.

REFERENCES

Aguilar, L. F. (2003). *La hechura de las políticas*. México: Porrúa.

Aguilar, L. F. (2003). *Problemas públicos y agenda de gobierno*. México: Porrúa.

Alvarez, R., & Hall, T. (2004). *Point, Clic, and Vote: The future of Internet voting*. Washington, DC: Brookings Institution Press.

Amoretti, F. (2007). International Organizations ICTs Policies: E-Democracy and E-Government for Political Development. *Review of Policy Research, 24*(4). doi:10.1111/j.1541-1338.2007.00286.x

Arendt, H. (2003). *La condición humana*. Barcelona, Spain: Paidós.

Bajjaly, S. T. (1999). Managing Emerging Information Systems in the Public Sector. *Public Productivity & Management Review, 23*(1).

Berntzen, L., & Winsvold, M. (2005). Web-based tools for policy evaluation en M. Böhlen, J. Gamper, W. Polasek & M. A. Wimmer (Eds.) *E-Government: Towards Electronic Democracy*. Italia: International Conference, TCGOV2005.

Birch, S., & Watt, B. (2004). *Remote Electronic Voting: Free, Fair and Secret? The Political Quarterly Publishing Co. Ltd*. London: Sage Publications.

Bolgherini, S. (2007). The Technology Trap and the Role of Political and Cultural Variables: A Critical Analysis of the E-Government Policies. *Review of Policy Research. 24*(3). The Policy Studies Organization.

Bonney, N. (2004). Local democracy renewed? *The Political Quarterly Publishing., 75*(1), 43–51.

Booth, W., Colomb, G., & Williams, J. (2003). *The craft of research*. Chicago: The University of Chicago Press.

Bretschneider, S. (2003). Information Technology, E-Government, and Institutional Change. *Public Administration Review, 63*(6). doi:10.1111/1540-6210.00337

Brown, M. M. (2001). The Benefits and Costs of Information Technology Innovations: An Empirical Assessment of a Local Government Agency. *Public Performance & Management Review, 24*, No. (4). Sage Publications.

Browning, G. (1996). *Electronic Democracy: using the Internet to influence American Politics*. Wilton, CT: Pemberton Press.

Calderón, E., & Cazés, D. (1994). *Tecnología ciudadana para la democracia*. México: UNAM.

Chappelet, J., & Kilchenmann, P. (2005). Interactive Tools for e-Democracy: Examples from Switzerland en Böhlen, M., Gamper, J., Polasek, W., & Wimmer, M. A. (Eds.) *E-Government: Towards Electronic Democracy*. Italia: International Conference, TCGOV2005.

Chutimaskul, W., & Funilkul, S. (2004). The Framework of e-Democracy Development en Traunmüller, Roland, *Electronic Government: Third International Conference, EGOV2004*. España: Springer.

Cooper, P. J. (1998). *Public Administration for the twenty-first century*. New York: Harcourt Brace & Company.

Cunill, N. (2004). *Balance de la participación ciudadana en las políticas sociales. Propuesta de un marco analítico en Ziccardi, A. (Coord.) Participación ciudadana y políticas sociales en el ámbito local*. México: UNAM-IIS.

E-Participate. (2006). *The eParticipation Trans-European Network for Democratic Renewal & Citizen Engagement.* Retrieved March 23, 2008, from www.eparticipate.eu

Eifert, M., & Püschel, J. O. (2004). *National Electronic Government: Comparing governance structures in multi-layer administrations.* London: Routledge.

Fernandez, R., Fernández-Collado, F., & Baptista, P. (2006). *Metodología de la investigación.* México: McGraw-Hill.

Ferro, E., Helbig, N., & Gil-García, J. R. (2006). The Digital Divide Metaphor: Understanding Paths to IT Literacy. *NCDG Working Paper* No. 07-001. Cambridge MA: MIT Press.

Fontana, A., & Frey, J. (2000). The interview: from neutral stance to political involvement en Denzin, Norman y Lincoln, Yvonna S. (Eds.) Handbook of Qualitative Research. Thousand Oaks, CA: Sage Publications.

Fountain, J. (2006). Challenges to Organizational Change: Multi-Level Integrated Information Structures (MIIS). *NCDG Working Paper* No. 06-001 Cambridge, MA: MIT Press.

Gil-García, J. R. (2005). *Enacting State Websites: A Mixed Method Study Exploring E-Government Success in Multi-Organizational Settings.* Nelson A. Rockefeller College of Public Affairs and Policy. University at Albany.

Gil-García, J. R. & Martínez-Moyano. (2007). Understanding the evolution of e-government: The evolution of systems of rues on public sector dynamics. *Government Information Quarterly, 24,* 266–290. doi:10.1016/j.giq.2006.04.005

Gil-García, J. R., & Helbig, N. (2007). *Exploring E-Government Benefits and Success Factors. Encyclopedia of Digital Government (Vol. 2).* Hershey, PA: Idea Group Reference.

Gil-García, J. R., & Luna-Reyes, L. (2006). *Encyclopedia of E-Commerce, E-Government, and Mobile Commerce.* Hershey, PA: IDEA Group Reference.

Gil-García, J. R., & Luna-Reyes, L. (2007). *Modelo Multi-Dimensional de Medición del Gobierno Electrónico para América Latina y el Caribe. CEPAL-Colección Documentos de Proyectos.* Publicación de las Naciones Unidas.

Gil-García, J. R., & Pardo, T. (2005). E-Government Success Factors: Mapping Practical Tools to Theoretical Foundations. *Government Information Quarterly, 22*(2), 187–216. doi:10.1016/j.giq.2005.02.001

Grönlund, A. (2004). State of the art in e-Gov research: A survey, en Traunmüller, R. (Ed.) *Electronic Government: Third International Conference,* EGOV2004. España: Springer.

Heeks, R. (1999). *Reinventing government in the information age: international practice in IT-enabled public sector reform.* London: Routledge.

Holden, S., Norris, D. & Fletcher, P. (2003). Electronic Government at the Local Level: progress to date and future issues. *Public Performance and Management Review. 26*(4).

Huang, W., Siau, K., & Wei, K. K. (2005). *Electronic government strategies and implementation.* Hershey, PA: Idea Group Publishing.

Kröll, H. (2000). El método de los estudios de caso, en Tarrés, Ma. Luisa (ed.) Escuchar, observar y comprender: sobre la investigación cualitativa en la investigación social. México: Porrúa: COLMEX/FLACSO.

Macintosh, A., McKay-Hubbard, A., & Shell, D. (2005b). Using Weblogs to Support Local Democracy, en Böhlen, Gamper, Polasek & Wimmer (Eds.) *E-Government: Towards Electronic Democracy.* Italia: International Conference, TCGOV2005.

Macintosh, A., Whyte, A., & Renton, A. (2005a). *From the Top Down: An evaluation of e-Democracy Activities Initiated by Councils and Government. Local e-Democracy National Project.* Bristol, UK: Bristol City Council.

Mahrer, H., & Krimmer, R. (2005). Towards the enhancement of e-democracy: identifying the notion of the 'middle man paradox'. *Information Systems Journal, 15*, 27–42. doi:10.1111/j.1365-2575.2005.00184.x

Margain, J. (2001). e-México: la estrategia del gobierno. *Política Digital, 1*, 48–51.

Márquez, M. (2006). Una gran oportunidad para la democracia. *Política Digital., 27*, 56–57.

Masters, Z., Macintosh, A., & Smith, E. (2004). Young People and e-Democracy: Creating a culture of participation, en Traunmüller, R. *Electronic Government: Third International Conference, EGOV2004.* España: Springer.

Meijer, A. (2006). ICTs and Political Accountability: An assessment of the impact digitization in government on political accountability in Connecticut, Massachusetts and New York State. *National Center for Digital Government Working Paper* No. 06-002. USA.

Morgan, D. (1997). *Focus Groups as Qualitative Research.* New York: Sage Publications.

Moynihan, D. (2004). Building Secure Elections: E-Voting, Security and Systems Theory. *Public Administration Review, 64*(5). doi:10.1111/j.1540-6210.2004.00400.x

Murray, G. (2005). Democracy in the Information Age. *Australian Journal of Public Administration, 65*(2).

Naciones Unidas. (2005). *Global e-government readiness report 200: from e-government to e-inclusion.* Retreived (n.d.), from www.unpan.org/egovernment5.asp

Netchaeva, I. (2002). E-Government and E-Democracy: A comparison of the opportunities in the North and South. *The International Journal for Communication Studies, 64*, 467–477.

Norris, D., Fletcher, P., & Holden, S. (2001). *Is your local government plugged in? Highlights of the 2000 electronic government survey.* Washington, DC: International City/Council Management Association.

Nugent, S. (2002). *Digital Democracy in Ireland.* Dublin, Ireland: Seminar Presentation on Trinity College.

OECD. (2003a). *Promise and Problems of E-democracy: Challenges of Online Citizen Engagement.* Washington, DC: OECD Publishing.

OECD. (2003b). *The e-Government Imperative. OECD e-Government Studies.* Washington, DC: OECD Publishing.

OECD. (2005a). *Evaluating public participation in policy making.* Washington, DC: OECD Publishing.

OECD. (2005b). *OECD Government Studies: México.* Washington, DC: OECD Publishing.

OECD. (2005c). e-Government for Better Government. OECD e-Government Studies. Washington DC: OECD Publishing.

OECD. (2005d). Governance of Innovation Systems.: *Vol. 3. Case Studies in Cross-Sectorial Policies.* Washington, DC: OECD Publishing.

OECD. (2007). *Participative Web and User-created Content*. Washington, DC: OECD Publishing.

Olsson, A. (2004). Electronic Democracy and Power, en Traunmüller, R. (Ed) *Electronic Government: Third International Conference, EGOV2004*. España: Springer.

Oseguera, J. (2003). Democracia y tecnología. *Política Digital, 10*, 58–59.

Pardo, T., & Kumar, T. (2007). Interorganizational Information Integration: A Key Enabler for Digital Government. *Government Information Quarterly, 24*(4), 691–715. doi:10.1016/j.giq.2007.08.004

Rabotnikof, N. (2005). *En busca de un lugar común*. México: UNAM.

Ramadan-Mamata, M., Lerberghe, F., & Best. (2005). *European eDemocracy Award Report*. Brussels, Belgium: POLITECH Institute.

Ranerup, A. (1999). Internet-enabled applications for local government democratization: Contradictions of the Swedish experience, en Heeks, R. (Ed.) Reinventing Government in the Information Age. London: Rutledge.

Rech, A. (2005). E-Citizen: Why Waiting for e-Governments? en Böhlen, Gamper, Polasek & Wimmer (Eds.) *E-Government: Towards Electronic Democracy*. International Conference, TCGOV2005. Italia: Springer.

Rivera, E. (2006). Un problema de innovación institucional. *Política Digital, 27*, 60–61.

Rivera, J. (2001). e-gobierno: ¿estrategia política o tecnológica? *Política Digital, 1*, 24–29.

Rocheleau, B. (2003). Politics, Accountability and Governmental Information Systems en Garson, D. (ed.), Public Information Technology: Policy and Management Issues. Hershey, PA: Idea Group Publishing.

Roeder, S. Poppenborg, Michaelis, Märker, & Salz. (2005). Public Budget Dialogue: An innovative approach to e-Participation, en Böhlen, Gamper, Polasek & Wimmer (Eds.) *E-Government: Towards Electronic Democracy*. International Conference, TCGOV2005. Italia: Springer.

Sæbo, Ø., & Nilsen, H. (2004). The support for different democracy models by the use of a web-based discussion board, en Traunmüller, R. (ed.) *Electronic Government: Third International Conference, EGOV2004*. España: Springer.

Saward, M. (2000). *Democratic Innovation: Deliberation, representation and association*. London: Routledge.

Scott, J. (2006). "E" the people: Do U.S. Municipal Government Web Sites Support Public Involvement? *Public Administration Review, 66*(3), 341–353. doi:10.1111/j.1540-6210.2006.00593.x

Scully, D. (2004). (Manuscript submitted for publication). E-democracy [Institute of Technology Tallaght. Irlanda.]. *Evolution; International Journal of Organic Evolution*.

Smith, G. (2000). Toward deliberative Institutions, en Saward, M. (ed.) Democratic Innovation. London: Routledge.

Sotelo, A. (2006). *México: un gobierno digital en expansión*. México: Abraham Sotelo.

Thomas, J. (1995). *Public Participation in public decisions*. San Francisco: Jossey-Bass Publishers.

Warschauer, M. (2003). *Technology and social inclusión: Rethinking the digital divide*. Cambridge, MA: MIT Press.

Wong, W., & Welch, E. (2004). Does E-Government promote accountability? A Comparative analysis of website openness and government accountability, en *Governance: An International Journal of Policy, Administrations and Institutions, 17*, No. (2).

Xenakis, A., & Macintosh, A. (2004). Levels of Difficulty in Introducing e-Voting, en Traunmüller, R. (Ed.) *Electronic Government: Third International Conference, EGOV2004.* España: Springer.

Ziccardi, A. (2004a). *Claves para el análisis de la participación ciudadana y las políticas sociales en el espacio local, en Ziccardi, A. (Coord.) Participación ciudadana y políticas sociales en el ámbito local.* México: UNAM-IIS.

Ziccardi, A. (2004b). *Espacios e instrumentos de participación ciudadana para las políticas sociales del ámbito local, en Ziccardi, A. (Coord.) Participación ciudadana y políticas sociales en el ámbito local.* México: UNAM-IIS.

ADDITIONAL READING

Cresswell, A. M., & Pardo, T. A. (2001). Implications of legal and organizational issues for urban digital government development. *Government Information Quarterly, 18,* 269–278. doi:10.1016/S0740-624X(01)00086-7

Cushing, J., & Pardo, T. A. (2005). Research in the digital government realm. *IEEE Computer, 38*(12), 26–32.

Dawes, S. S., Gregg, V., & Agouris, P. (2004). Digital government research: Investigations at the crossroads of social and information science. *Social Science Computer Review, 22*(1), 5–10. doi:10.1177/0894439303259863

Dawes, S. S., Pardo, T., & DiCaterino, A. (1999). Crossing the threshold: Practical foundations for government services on the world wide web. *Journal of the American Society for Information Science American Society for Information Science, 50*(4), 346–353. doi:10.1002/(SICI)1097-4571(1999)50:4<346::AID-ASI12>3.0.CO;2-I

Dawes, S. S., Pardo, T. A., Simon, S., Cresswell, A. M., LaVigne, M. F., Andersen, D. F., & Bloniarz, P. A. (2004). Making Smart IT Choices: Understanding Value and Risk in Government IT Investments. Retreived (n.d.), from http://www.ctg.albany.edu/publications/guides/smartit2.

Gil-Garcia, J. R., Chengalur-Smith, I., & Duchessi, P. (2007). Collaborative E-Government: Impediments and Benefits of Information Sharing Projects in the Public Sector. *European Journal of Information Systems, 16*(2), 121–133. doi:10.1057/palgrave.ejis.3000673

Gil-Garcia, J. R., & Helbig, N. (2006). Exploring e-government benefits and success factors. In Anttiroiko, A.-V., & Malkia, M. (Eds.), *Encyclopedia of Digital Government.* Hershey, PA: Idea Group Inc.

Gil-Garcia, J. R., & Martinez-Moyano, I. (2007). Understanding the Evolution of E-Government: The Influence of Systems of Rules on Public Sector Dynamics. *Government Information Quarterly, 24*(2), 266–290. doi:10.1016/j.giq.2006.04.005

Hall, R. H. (2002). *Organizations. Structures, Processes, and Outcomes.* Upper Saddle River, NJ: Prentice Hall.

Harrison, T., Pardo, T. A., Gil-Garcia, J. R., Thompson, F., & Juraga, D. (2007). Geographic Information Technologies, Structuration Theory, and the World Trade Center Crisis. *Journal of the American Society for Information Science and Technology, 58*(14), 2240–2254. doi:10.1002/asi.20695

Luna-Reyes, L., Gil-Garcia, J. R., & Cruz, C. B. (2006). E-Mexico: Collaborative Structures in Mexican Public Administration. *International Journal of Cases on Electronic Commerce, 3*(2), 54–70.

Luna-Reyes, L., Gil-Garcia, J. R., & Cruz, C. B. (2007). Collaborative Digital Government in Mexico: Some Lessons from Federal Web-Based Interorganizational Information Integration Initiatives. *Government Information Quarterly, 24*(4), 808–826. doi:10.1016/j.giq.2007.04.003

Luna-Reyes, L., Gil-Garcia, J. R., & Estrada-Marroquín, M. (2008). The Impact of Institutions on Interorganizational IT Projects in the Mexican Federal Government. *International Journal of Electronic Government Research, 4*(2), 26–42.

Luna-Reyes, L. F., Zhang, J., Gil-Garcia, J. R., & Cresswell, A. M. (2005). Information systems development as emergent socio-technical change: A practice approach. *European Journal of Information Systems, 14*(1), 93–105. doi:10.1057/palgrave.ejis.3000524

Natalie, H., Gil-Garcia, J. R., & Ferro, E. (2009). Understanding the Complexity of Electronic Government: Implications from the Digital Divide Literature. *Government Information Quarterly, 26*(1), 89–97. doi:10.1016/j.giq.2008.05.004

Pardo, T. A., Cresswell, A. M., Thompson, F., & Zhang, J. (2006). Knowledge sharing in cross-boundary information system development in the public sector. *Information Technology and Management, 7*(4), 293–313. doi:10.1007/s10799-006-0278-6

Rocheleau, B. (2000). Prescriptions for public-sector information management: A review, analysis, and critique. *American Review of Public Administration, 30*(4), 414–435. doi:10.1177/02750740022064759

Zhang, J., Cresswell, A. M., & Thompson, F. (2002). *Participant's expectations and the success of knowledge networking in the public sector*. Paper presented at the AMCIS Conference, Texas

KEY TERMS AND DEFINITIONS

Citizenry: It is defined here as the creation of identity for a community or country, where citizens are motivated to develop mutual respect and understanding toward other citizens (Smith, 2000).

Deliberation: It is a public dialog which is guided by equality, liberty, and competence (Smith, 2000).

E-Democracy: It refers to the participation of governments, international government organizations, elected officials, the media, political parties, and nongovernmental organizations, as well as citizens and interest groups, in the political processes of local, regional or state, and national communities, up to the global level through the use of the information and communication technologies (Murray, 2005).

E-Government Portals: They are multi-functional information systems, which provide a single point of access to governments' relevant information and services via the Internet.

Electronic Government: It is the design, implementation, and use of information and communication technologies (ICTs) in government settings. Electronic government can also be understood as the selection, implementation, and use of ICTs in government to provide public services, improve managerial effectiveness, and promote democratic values and mechanisms; e-government also creates a regulatory framework that facilitates information-intensive initiatives and fosters a knowledge society (Gil-Garcia & Luna-Reyes, 2006, p. 642).

Inclusion: It is the existence of an equal right for citizens to be heard and participate in public forums or to influence public decisions (Smith, 2000).

Opportunities for Citizen Participation: They are the channels provided by governments or any societal organization for citizens to be heard and participate in the decision-making process and the development of their own communities.

Chapter 5
A Comparative Analysis of Local Agenda 21 Websites in Turkey in Terms of E-Participation

Bekir Parlak
Uludag University, Turkey

Zahid Sobaci
Uludag University, Turkey

ABSTRACT

Local Agenda 21 (LA 21) is a democracy project aiming to enhance the public's participation in the processes of political and administrative decision-making. E-government, in its own right as a facilitator of participation, is a functional instrument for LA 21s in terms of ensuring the public participation and implementing governance model. In this context, this study aims to examine whether the LA 21s benefit from the e-participation opportunities over the websites in Turkey. According to the findings of empirical research, the LA 21s in Turkey do not offer a wide of number of e-participation services on their websites. LA 21s do not provide real e-participation practices allowing an interaction among the citizens, partners and the officials, elevating the citizens to the position of partners, enhancing their participation and improving the notion of democracy in Turkey.

INTRODUCTION

Local Agenda 21 (LA 21) is a democracy project aiming to enhance the public's participation in the processes of political and administrative decision-making. The method of operation of LA 21 that entails participation and partnership is all regarded as their basis of existence. In order for these kinds of programs to materialize participation and co-operation more efficiently and comprehensively,

e-government facilities offer golden opportunities. E-government, in its own right as a facilitator of participation, is a functional instrument for LA 21s in terms of ensuring the public participation and implementing governance model.

E-government should not only be perceived as a concept associated with the field of administration. Apart from the improvement of the way public services are offered, simplification and unification of administrative processes, e-government should also be considered as a tool that gets the public involved in the processes of administrative and

DOI: 10.4018/978-1-61520-933-0.ch005

political decision-making. In other words, the concept of e-government includes, in addition to e-service and e-administration, the dimension of e-democracy within itself. As far as the level reached today is concerned, the contributions to be made by e-government to the concepts of participation and democracy attract ever more attention and the literature on this field is growing day by day (Becker, 2007; Barrati Esteve et al., 2007; Chadwick, 2003; Gibson et al., 2004; Kampen & Snijkers, 2003; Kinder, 2002; Moynihan, 2007; O'Toole, 2009; Wei Phang & Kankanhalli, 2007; Taylor & Burt, 2002; Yao & Murphy, 2007).

The contributions to be made by e-government to the consensus-building and cooperation can be analyzed within the framework of LA 21. The significant part of the literature formed on LA 21 either analyzes the implementation of LA 21 practices in one or more than one municipality in a geographical area or explicates the general analysis of implementation level in a country (Adolfsson Jörby, 2000, 2002; Barrett & Usui, 2002; Etxebarria et al., 2004; Feichtinger & Pregernig, 2005; Gan, 1999; Grochowalska, 1998; Lindstrom & Gronholm, 2002; Wild & Marshall, 1999). Some studies even focus on determining the factors effective on the level of implementation of LA 21. However, it is not very easy to encounter a study that associates LA 21 with the information and communication technologies (ICTs). In other words, there does not exist a study in the relevant literature that has analyzed whether LA 21, which itself is a participatory platform has benefited from advantages offered by the concept of e-government.

The onset point by which LA 21 can commence to benefit from the advantages brought by e-government in facilitating and enhancing participation can be constituted by setting up a website. In this context, this study aims to examine the websites of LA 21 programs in terms of e-participation in Turkey.

In this context, first of all, the conceptual framework of public participation will be made and the

effects of the ICTs on the concept of participation (e-participation) will be explicated. Subsequently, the participatory and cooperative nature of LA 21 and the significance of e-participation from the perspective of this platform will be dealt with. Finally, within the context of a list of criterion genuinely established, whether the websites of LA 21 in Turkey, which itself is a participatory platform, benefits from opportunities offered by e-government will be examined.

PUBLIC PARTICIPATION: CONCEPTUAL FRAMEWORK

The participation of the citizens to economical, political, social and cultural processes has not been a new fact. However, it has been one of the leading rising values especially in the literature of political theory and public administration. As far as the point reached today is concerned, the public participation to decision-making processes is expressed as an intrinsic right of citizenship and is encountered as one of the basic characteristics of contemporary democratic societies. While countries, on the one hand, seek for new methods and approaches that will move the concept of participation beyond the tradition of casting vote in elections and pave the way for more participation, they, on the other hand, exert some efforts to implement the participatory mechanisms in their political and administrative systems by means of administrative reforms.

Public participation is a process by which public concerns, needs and values are incorporated into governmental decision-making process. Public participation is a bilateral communication and interaction with the aim of better decisions supported by the public (Creighton, 2005). The motive behind public participation is the need for the public to take part in the decision-making processes that will have an impact on their own everyday lives. In fact, it is asserted that the citizens to be affected by the decisions of the government have the right of participation in this process of decision-making process (Box et. al., 2001; Crosby et al., 1986).

There are various reasons for including public in decision-making process. The first of those reasons that are very well documented in the literature of public administration is to understand the demands of the public, to determine their priorities and preferences and to ensure that these values are included in the decision-making process. Making it possible may lessen the conflicts and help build confidence. The other reason is to improve the quality of the decision made by incorporating the local knowledge, which can lead to better results. Another rationale behind public participation is its capacity to be able to enhance transparency and accountability, and improve fairness and justice (Callahan, 2007).

One of the basic debates related to the concept of participation is the question of what level participation. The interaction between the citizens and decision makers can take place at different levels. The most common typology regarding participation level is that of Arnstein. Arnstein (1969), who used the ladder pattern in order to explain his typology, determined eight levels at each of which the influence and power of citizens are different. These levels range from manipulation and therapy in which there is no participation to citizen control.

Another functional classification regarding the level of public participation is the one prepared by International Association for Public Participation (see for detail, www.ipa2.org). This association (2007) considers participation as a spectrum. There are five points on this spectrum, which are inform, consult, involve, collaborate and empower. As one moves from the point of inform to empower, the influence of the public increases. The purpose of the point of 'inform' is to provide balanced and objective information to the public to assist them in understanding the problems, alternatives and the decisions taken. The purpose of the point of 'consult' is to listen to the public and obtain public

feedback on analyses, alternatives and decisions. The point of 'involve' aims to work directly with the public throughout the process in order to ensure that their concerns and expectations are understood. The purpose of the point of 'collaborate' is to partner with the public in each aspect of the decision including development of alternatives and identification of preferred solutions. The point of 'empower' aims to final decision-making in the hands of the public.

Another basic question that springs to mind regarding public participation is the type of participation needed. Is it to be a direct one or an indirect public participation? The response to this question was discussed in the literature and the arguments regarding the types of participation were explicated (Callahan, 2007; Irvin & Stansbury, 2004; Roberts, 2004; Robins et al., 2008). Those who advocate the direct participation express that direct participation determines the priorities, improves the quality of the decisions taken, builds up confidence, encourages the democracy, enhances transparency, contributes to accountability, minimizes the conflicts and reinforces legitimacy. Those who are skeptical of direct participation, on the other hand, state that it is inefficient, costly, time consuming, politically naive and unrealistic (Callahan, 2007).

However, in an environment in which there is a transition from representative democracy to participatory democracy, there is an increasing interest in direct public participation. Moynihan (2003) puts this increasing interest in direct citizen participation down to the change in values, bureaucratic disappointment and the pursuit of a democratic ideal. Additionally, today many people are losing confidence and credit for the way countries are governed (Panopoulou et al., 2009). In this context, citizens' demands for transparency, accountability, openness and participation to decision-making process that will have an impact on them increase (OECD, 2001). There has been a shift in the public's demand from quantity to quality. This chance in public demand directly triggers public participation.

The fact that the participation is a "direct" one and that the citizens are directly involved in the formation of decisions and policies is expected to mature the democracy. Especially as a result of the developments experienced in the last quarter of the twentieth century, representative-natured democratic operation has been replaced by pluralistic democracy. Briefly, the idea that the direct democracy, commencing from the most local level possible in a country, is to be implemented in all decision-making processes of a government has started to be gradually accepted. In this context, the new administrative structures are being formed with this perspective in mind and the existing structures move into the process of transformation.

THE IMPACT OF ICTS ON PARTICIPATION: E-PARTICIPATION

There has been an increasing awareness regarding the likely contribution of the innovative ICT applications to participation and to democratic debates and processes. In this context, different countries have been implementing various e-democracy and e-participation projects and applications (OECD, 2003). The growing literature on the democratic significance of the new ICTs focuses on the contributions that it can make to the direct public participation (Kakabadse et al, 2003).

The democratic decision-making processes to be implemented through ICT can be divided into two basic interrelated categories: electoral process including e-voting and citizen e-participation in democratic decision-making (HM Government, 2002). E-participation refers the citizens' and other agents' participation to the formation process of decisions and policies that affect them by means of ICTs. ICTs both help to transfer the traditional participation procedures to the electronic environment and provide new participation channels. In fact, Snellen (2002) stated that in addition to the policy implementation processes, ICTs can be benefited from in the policy formation and policy evaluation processes and, in this context, can affect the relationships among citizens, politicians and administrators.

Within the context of participation, ICTs have the capacity to form policies interactively and make it possible to generate polices together by means of bringing the parties likely to be affected by a decision and incorporating their ideas and thoughts into the formulation of policies. Moreover, some of the ICT applications, after the policy has taken effect, have the mechanisms in order to facilitate feedback by conveying the results of these policies, their effects on the public and the ideas of citizens to decision makers.

In this context, the aims of e-participation can be explicated as in the following (Macintosh, 2004): It is expected to reach a wider audience to enable broader participation, support participation through a range of technologies to cater for the diverse technical and communicative skills of citizens, provide relevant information in a format that is both more accessible and more understandable to the target audience to enable more informed contributions, and finally engage with a wider audience to enable deeper contributions and support deliberative debate.

The benefits mentioned with regards to the participation of the agents in the decision-making process that will have an impact on them, are also true for e-participation. However, the benefits of e-participation according to the agents involved in decision-making process (Millard et al., 2008):

For participants, it is to increase convenience, satisfaction, feelings of involvement, greater engagement and commitment in community and society, also noting that e-participation is not only a rational but also an emotional experience. For organizations, it is to improve the efficiency, effectiveness and legitimacy of organizations, for example successful participation can increase the economic viability of private and civil sector organizations, and probably also public institutions as well, by reducing costs. For organizations, it is to increase the efficiency and quality of their own policy-making. For governments, it is to support social cohesion and other society-wide policies. For all, e-participation can increase overall participation rates and the intensity and quality of participation if undertaken in the right way.

While ICTs may contribute to the increase of participation to the processes of decision making and improvement of democracy, it is also possible to talk about its aspects, depending on certain variables, that restrict participation. Within the context of the concept of participation, ICTs may not be used with the same prevalence and functionality in every country and in every region and locality even within the same country. This may lead some sections of the community to attach their ideas and opinions to the process of decision making and some others unable to affect those decisions. It is possible to talk about some factors leading to this outcome.

The first factor is the fact that the cost of ICTs is very high. Every region or locality across a country may unable to afford the cost required by technological infrastructure. Therefore, the fact that ICTs in less developed regions are more difficult to access when compared to those in developed ones, can be regarded as a serious problem affecting participation. Therefore, the fact that the cost of e-participation services is relatively higher may confront us as a factor restricting participation. Moreover, the costs of internet access and internet use still constitute an important expenditure for the users in undeveloped and developing countries. Therefore, the socio-economic factor may be specified as a variable affecting e-participation.

Another factor is that the fact that the citizens do not have enough level of knowledge and experience in using the ICTs also negatively affects participation. Especially, from the point of view of the citizens who are either illiterate or have insufficient level of education and unable to use them, the ICTs are far from facilitating and encouraging participation.

Moreover, the level of awareness of the actors regarding participation and their tendencies towards using the ICTs regarding decision making processes may have either a negative or positive impact on the participation of citizens. When the politicians, bureaucrats or the citizens are negative about participation and about improving participation using the ICTs, all these opportunities cease to exist and lose their value.

Finally, unless the improvement of participation and democracy by using the ICTs are adopted as a basic policy and strategy both at the level of central administration and local governments, the expected benefits of ICTs regarding participation will not come out. Under these circumstances, due to temporal applications and populist policies, only few examples of the best e-participation applications across the country will emerge and e-participation applications will not be widespread and limited to these applications only. Therefore, depending on certain conditions and variables, ICTs are to contribute to the improvement of participation and democracy. Within this framework, in this study, ICTs, under certain circumstances, are regarded as instruments serving for the improvement of participation and democracy.

The first phase required for the public institutions to implement e-participation and for the benefits mentioned above to take effect, is to set up a website and allow for some participatory mechanisms in the website. In fact, Chadwick and May (2003) argue that e-government projects enables three different types of interaction model of managerial, consultative and participatory among the government, business and the public. The e-government sites allow for new means for communication between the governing and the governed, through e-mails, online meetings and forums, online transactions and online voting (Jaeger, 2005). In this context, e-government projects, in addition to enabling efficient and productive service provision, can be regarded as means that will inform the public about the laws and regulations, get them involved in the processes of decision-making and make them a part of a more comprehensive democratic debate, facilitate participation and strengthen democracy.

E-government projects have the potential of making contributions to all the participation levels mentioned above and of facilitating the fulfillment of the objectives aimed at those levels. Moreover, e-government applications can make these contributions at all phases of policy making process from agenda setting to monitoring. Therefore, they mediate to achieve better decisions, more legitimate institutions and more reliable and democratic system.

LOCAL AGENDA 21 AS A PARTICIPATION PLATFORM AND THE CRITICAL SIGNIFICANCE OF E-PARTICIPATION

Agenda 21 is one of the important documents approved at the end of the United Nation Conference on Environment and Development held in 1992 in Rio de Janeiro. Agenda 21 is the product of an international summit that centered on environment and development, and the relationship between them. Therefore, it can be regarded as the reflection of a global consensus for sustainable development and of a politic commitment. Agenda 21 is long term action plan introduced in order to implement the sustainable development.

The successful implementation of Agenda 21 depends primarily on governments. However, international, regional, local cooperation is a crucial component in backing and complementing these national efforts (Garcia-Sanchez and Prado-Lorenzo, 2008). An important emphasis has been placed especially on local governments in the implementation of Agenda 21. Chapter 28 of Agenda 21 entitled "Local authorities' initiatives in support of Agenda 21" is one of the strongest evidence for it. In fact, Chapter 28 states that "because so many of the problems and solutions being addressed by Agenda 21 have their roots in local activities, the participation and cooperation of local authorities will be a determining factor in fulfilling its objectives".

Local authorities have been accepted as the most important agents in fulfilling the objectives of Agenda 21 at local level. At the background of this acceptance is placed the proposal of a need for the local authorities to set up a partnership together with local business representatives, voluntary organizations and local groups in an attempt to establish a consensus among themselves on sustainable development. This also implicates the acceptance of the fact that there is a need for active participation, support and cooperation among all the sectors of the society for the formulation and implementation of these efficient sustainable development strategies (Patton and Worthington, 1996).

In this connection, LA 21 is the result of Chapter 28 and assumptions and anticipations in its background. LA 21 is a program aiming to implement sustainable development at a local level. It lays the groundwork for a debate on sustainable development and awareness based on a strong partnership between local government and local groups. The main focus of LA 21 is to get all groups involved in sustainable development planning in the main areas of economic, social and environmental development. This emphasis on participation distinguishes LA 21 from other projects that focus more on achieving the results for sustainable development (Environs Australia, 1999).

LA 21, allowing for the participation of local groups and being based on the cooperation among public, private and civic sectors is a local democratic platform where urban problems are discussed and their solutions are worked out. LA21 is comprised of various cooperative and participatory mechanisms allowing for the participation of all groups across the society and for the formation of common mind at local level.

The most beneficial administration for the public is the one that is closest to them and the one that enables them to govern themselves. This requires a structure and operation in which everyone can participate in administration and is equipped with the supervision power. LA21s have characteristics that just fit these features. LA 21 programs, when implemented successfully, may function just like shadow councils, incorporate civil initiative into the local decision-making mechanisms and entitle more say to local groups. When the successful examples in this field in the world are examined, we witness that the functions aforementioned above have been achieved.

The structure of LA 21s that is participatory and based on cooperation simplifies the public participation to a great extent and functionalizes it. These structures also function as intermediate institutions in order to collect the local demands and convey them over to more competent public positions. The LA 21s which are local projections of the idea of global cooperation have the potential of making crucial contributions to the democratic society concept of the new century as the pioneer programs of the voluntary movement. In fact, it is stated that LA 21s, together with the characteristics they have displayed in the world and Turkey, represent the idea of democratic local governance in the 21st century (Emrealp, 2005).

In practice, given the fact that LA 21 programs have implemented many participation-based projects and have many submechanisms that encourage participation, it is very obvious that it offers contemporary examples in terms of public participation. The platforms formed through civic participation such as "The Voluntary Working Groups", "Children Council", "Women Council", "Disabled Platform", "The Youth Council", "The Public Forums", "City Council", "Urban Voluntary Houses", "The Project Groups" and the other groups and platforms give us an idea about what kind of contributions LA 21s can make to the concept of participation. In fact, it is stated that LA 21s are not simple local programs or projects; on the contrary, they are processes that horizontally and vertically embrace all the areas and agents of

governance and develop a new understanding in this entirety (Emrealp, 2005).

It is possible for the concept of participation to be implemented in a fast and comprehensive fashion in today's world in which ICTs have developed to a great extent and been in widespread use. In other words, while e-participation, on the one hand, is likely to facilitate the implementation of the concept of participation, it will, on the other hand, expand the types of participation and enable new participation channels. In the age of information society, the direct and effective participation of citizens to the administrative processes offers humanity great and unprecedented opportunities that have never been seen before. The LA 21 programs that are truly participation programs, by using the most of the opportunities offered by e-participation, will be able to offer more efficient and beneficial services in the field of participation in which those programs are already relatively successful.

In summary, LA 21s have captured a historical chance in terms of enabling the inherent participation and cooperation. They will of course be using this chance to the point at which they will benefit from the opportunities offered by e-participation. In other words, e-participation can significantly contribute towards participation, consensus and the capacity of cross-sectoral cooperation which are reasons of existence of LA 21s. In this way, it will help democracy, both at local level and at national level, to be institutionalized in a country, contribute towards gaining the habit of participation and benefit the process of improving the awareness of active citizenship.

AN ANALYSIS OF THE LOCAL AGENDA 21 WEBSITES IN TURKEY: AN EMPIRICAL RESEARCH

Framework of the Research

The LA 21s in Turkey operate under the institutional framework of metropolitan and normal municipalities. In this connection, they have been structured as affiliated with the deputy general secretary as branch office in metropolitan municipalities. Since they are structured as branch offices affiliated with metropolitan municipalities, they have been organized as a unit of the metropolitan municipality in terms of budget, staff appointment, directive and instructions, personal record and disciplinary action, inspection and monitoring.

This is also almost the case in normal municipalities. There are the deputies of mayor instead of general secretary of the municipality and their deputies in normal municipalities. In those municipalities, the LA 21s have been structured as a unit or a branch affiliated with one of the deputy mayor. Nevertheless, as it is the case all over the world, LA 21s are not classical public institutions in Turkey either. They are semi-civilian organizations based on partnerships and participation, with a dominant civilian characteristic, funded by international budgets, in flexible and less organic relationships with the municipalities.

This study has focused on an original and current topic in the field of participation to administration. This topic is the comparative examination of the LA 21 websites in terms of e-participation in Turkey. In other words, the aim of our study is to examine whether the LA 21 programs that are growing ever so popular and are governance-based participatory organizations, benefit from the e-participation opportunities over the websites in the case of a developing country, Turkey.

The primary purpose of this study, considering the findings and results to be obtained, is to answer the question of how LA 21s, within the framework of the concept of e-government in their activities directed towards participation, can benefit more from the opportunities especially offered on their websites.

This study has taken as a population the currently operative 70 LA 21s affiliated with municipalities in Turkey. The LA 21s in question have been subjected to an evaluation in terms of website ownership. However, it has to be noted here that only 7 of the total of 70 LA 21 in Turkey have their own websites. Therefore, the sampling of the study is consisted of 7 LA 21s of Bursa, Izmir, Karaburun, Malatya, Mardin, Nilufer and Yalova and their websites.

We started our study in September, 2008 and completed it in March, 2009. In our study that lasted for six months, firstly all the LA 21s in Turkey were examined. And then, the websites of LA 21s that had their own websites were monitored on a regular basis in line with the predetermined criterion and evaluated. After the completion of the examination period, the findings obtained from observation, examination and assessments were systemized and comparatively analyzed.

Criteria of the Research

It has not been an easy job to constitute a cluster of criteria to enable us to comparatively analyze the websites of LA 21s in Turkey from the perspective of e-participation. It is simply because it is not easy to come across in the literature a list of criteria composed to examine the websites of LA 21s that are the semi-civil organizations closely related to public institutions and local governments. Fundamentally, this has given us a chance to prepare an original cluster of research criteria and therefore contribute to the relevant literature. Within this framework, taking account of the nature of and operations of LA 21s and e-participation applications, an original list of criterion has been constituted for analyzing the website applications of LA 21s in terms of e-participation.

The criteria have been collected under three different groups of "the services of information

Table 1. Criteria of research

SERVICES OF INFORMATION DELIVERY	Institutional Information Transfer
	Functional Information Transfer
	Access to the Agendas, Decisions and Records of LA 21s
	Access to Legal Arrangements regarding LA 21s
COMMUNICATION SERVICES	E-mail to Administrators
	Question-Answer
	E-petition and E-complaint
	Interaction with the Civil Society
ONLINE PARTICIPATION SERVICES	Online Subscription System
	Discussion Forum
	Webcasting
	Chat with the Administrators and Partners
	Free Chair
	Questionnaire
	Online Adult Education
	Project Governance

delivery", "the services of communication" and "the services of online participation". This grouping has been made taking into account the classification related to e-government services made by the European Commission (1998). Instead of the "online transaction services" found in the classification made by the European Commission, "online participation services" in line with the aims of this study have been used.

There are totally 16 criteria in the study. Those criteria have been determined in considering the levels of participation established by the International Association for Public Participation. In other words, the list of criteria includes all sorts of criteria related to all levels of participation from the level of 'inform' to that of 'collaborate' or 'empower'. In this perspective, the list of criteria can be regarded as a spectrum. In this way, those criteria will help us examine whether the citizens have been both informed and given the cannels to enable them to become partners. The entire list of criteria constitutes a sample one that may inspire future studies. The criteria of the study have been clearly illustrated in Table 1.

Most of the criteria are self-explanatory anyway. However, it will be useful to briefly explain some of the criteria.

Interaction with the Civil Society: This criterion signifies LA21s's interactive communication with NGOs in an extensive and sustainable fashion over the websites.

Free Chair: This criterion signifies the citizens resident in the relevant locality to directly submit their views, expectations, demands and evaluations on the LA 21 activities, services and investments of the local institutions, their policies and objectives, inter-institutional cooperation, new service tendencies and projects without any mediator and hesitations.

Chat with the Administrators and Partners: This criterion includes the citizens' the written and verbal forms of communication with the officials in LA 21 and with the representatives of the institutions that are the partners cooperating with LA 21s.

Online Adult Education: This is a criterion that signifies online education and training that will help the citizens to act more actively and

Table 2. Processing rules of citizen participation through the ministry websites

Dimension	Indicators	Int.	RR. EE.	Def.	Hac.	SGP	SGG	Eco.	Pla.	Edu.	Jus.	Trn.	OO. PP.	Sal.	Viv.	Agr.	Min.	Tran.	BB. NN.
Rules on citizen participation processing	Policy on e-participation that specifies how information will be processed and whether consultation results will be binding																		X
	Definition of e-participation areas			X															
	Reply obligation of authorities		X	X			X	X	X				X	X					
	Issuing of citizen input reception certificate		X	X			X	X	X				X	X					

Source: Own elaboration.

efficiently in the areas of business, politics, administration and social life.

Project Governance: This is the interaction enabled over the website in an effort to determine, shape up and realize the national or international projects running or to be run, or participating or to be participated by LA 21s together with the local people and civil initiation.

Within the framework of these 16 criteria, the websites of LA21s in Turkey have been examined in terms of e-participation. The LA 21s have been given a (+) for every participation service they provide on their websites and a (-) for every participation service they do not provide on the websites.

Findings

The research findings illustrated on Table 2 below constitute the fundamental outcomes of this study. The findings have been obtained in a period of six months through a continuous and systematic monitoring and examinations. The e-participation-oriented activities of LA 21 websites in Turkey have been evaluated through the personal participation and assessments of the researchers in the activities offered by the LA 21 websites. Before going through the details of Table 2, it will be useful to remind that only 10% of the LA 21s in Turkey have their own websites.

When the Table 2 containing websites of the LA 21s in Turkey is closely examined, it is immediately noticeable that the LA 21s in Turkey do not offer a wide number of e-participation services on their websites. The LA 21s in Turkey with a websites is already very limited. Those LA 21s with a website do not provide real e-participation practices allowing an interaction among the citizens, partners and the officials, elevating the citizens to the position of partners, enhancing their participation and improving the notion of democracy. The opportunities offered by the LA 21s on the websites are mostly those related to provision of information which is base for citizen participation. In this connection, it is possible to note that the websites are just like virtual brochures where the LA 21s have organizational and functional presentation of themselves. In other words, the practices found at the heart of e-participation have not been made available on their websites.

There are various reasons which cause this situation. First of all, the e-government activities and practices in Turkey have not reached at a satisfactory level. Secondly, it is the fact that LA 21s are regarded as relatively insignificant and inefficient units within the municipalities. Particularly, the fact the local officials do not take a sufficient interest in this issue has either direct or indirect impact on the operations and success of these organizations. The fact that LA 21s in Turkey facilitate participation by making use of the ICTs and encourage governance-based problem-solving strategies is dependent upon the attention and support of the concerned elected and appointed authorities with the mayors leading the way. In the case of Turkey, for the LA 21s to become successful especially in this issue, it is very decisive and explanatory whether they have a support or not. The LA 21s that have a strong political support may turn themselves into the homes of local participation and democracy by using the ICTs. On the other hand, the fact that the LA 21s are not sufficiently recognized by the public has a direct effect on the participation on the activities offered by them and the outcomes obtained. Finally, the fact that there is insufficient amount of PC ownership and internet access in Turkey constitute an impediment to the realization of these activities. After this general evaluation, it is possible to illustrate the details of Table 2 as in the following:

From the perspective of LA 21s

- Among the LA 21s with a websites, the highest score was obtained by the Bursa LA 21. After all, the Bursa LA 21 that

fulfilled 6 of the total of 16 criteria (6/16) could only reach the level of 37.50% in terms of e-participation services offered on the website. As is clearly seen, even the Bursa LA 21 relatively the best one is well below the level of 50%.

- Mardin obtained the lowest score out of those LA 21s with their own websites. The Mardin LA 21 that could fulfill only one of the 16 criteria determined (1/16) could not offer any other e-participation service other than the service of "Transfer of Institutional Information".

- The four LA 21s examined have scored (31.25%) close to the success of Bursa. The websites of İzmir, Karaburun (a town of İzmir), Malatya and Nilüfer (a town of Bursa) offer 5 different e-participation services. It is quite noticeable that Bursa and İzmir, in terms of e-participation-oriented website services leading the way offered through LA 21 organizations both in city centers and in some of the towns, have been relatively more active.

- The Yalova LA 21 only offers two e-participation services and is stuck at the activity level of 12.50%.

- It needs to be particularly noted down that the fact that five of the LA 21s out of seven with a website in Turkey are located in the West part of the country and that they are in the lead in terms of offering web-based e-participation services. As is commonly known, the Western part of Turkey has regions that are economically and socially more developed.

From the Perspective of E-Participation Services

- When the websites of the LA 21s in Turkey are considered in terms of the participation-oriented services offered on their websites, it is clearly seen that the services of information delivery is the one offered the most. In other words, it was established that the four criteria under this service group was provided the more, in comparison to other criteria, by the LA 21s. What follows it is the "communication services". "Online participation services" are the ones poorest ones.

- The fact that the most important of the e-participation services to be offered on the websites is found among the "online participation services" and that the LA 21s in Turkey have scored the lowest points concerning these services is one of the most noticeable findings of this study.

- "Institutional information transfer", "Functional information transfer", "Access to the agendas, decisions and records of LA 21s" and "Access to legal arrangements regarding LA 21s", which are criteria of "Information delivery services", constitute the web-based participation services from which LA 21s in Turkey got the most (+). Out of these, the service of "Institutional information transfer" is offered by all the LA 21s examined. The service of "Functional information transfer" is offered by all other LA 21s apart from Mardin one.

- The service of "Access to the agenda, decision and records of LA 21" is offered by only two out of the seven LA 21s. In fact, this service is one of the primary steps of e-participation. The more what the LA 21s stand for, what they do and will do, and which decision they will take is commonly known and access to this information made available, the more the ordinary citizens will be more aware of what is going on and thus their participation will be made easier.

- The service of "Access to legal arrangements regarding LA 21s" is the weakest link in terms of the "information delivery service". This criterion is fulfilled only by

the Bursa LA 21 and it is again the criterion with a very low level of realization of 1/7 on the LA 21 websites.

- If the "information delivery service" is subjected to cross analysis with LA 21s, it is clearly seen that the Bursa LA 21 is the most successful one and it is active in all of the four criteria. After Bursa comes the İzmir LA 21 with success level of (3/4). What follow İzmir in terms of the level of activity with (2/4) is Karaburun, Malaya, Nilüfer and Yalova. The weakest LA 21 in terms of information delivery services is the Mardin one with the level of (1/4).

- In the list of criteria, there are four criteria in the framework of "communication services". These services are more important in comparison to information delivery service in terms of the characteristics of web-based e-participation services and their contribution to public participation. The criteria within the communication services are "e-mail to the administrators", "question-answer", "e-petition and e-complaint" and "interaction with the civil society".

The mostly used of those services on the websites of LA 21s are those of "question-answer" and "e-petition and e-complaint". Both services are actively used with a level of (3/7) on the LA 21 websites. The service of "e-mail to the administrators" is offered by two of the LA 21s. The service of "interaction with the civil society", on the other hand, is not offered by any of the LA 21s.

- When the "communication services" are subjected to cross analysis with LA 21s, there is no single leading LA 21. The LA 21s of Bursa, Karaburun and Malatya are the leading ones with the level of 2/4, followed by Nilüfer and İzmir (1/4). The LA 21s of Mardin and Yalova, on the other hand, do not offer any of the services found under the service group.

- The last service group that is comparatively more important in terms of e-participation is that of "online participation service". Unfortunately, on the websites of LA 21s, the online services are the weakest ones in comparison to the other two service groups. The online participation services are composed of "online subscription system", "discussion forum", "webcasting", "chat with the administrators and partners", "free chair", "questionnaire"," online adult education" and "project governance". When the totals of eight services in question are evaluated, the most actively used one is the "online subscription system". These services are offered by three of the seven LA 21s. The services of "discussion forum" and "free chair" are each offered by two different LA 21s. The service of "discussion forum" in Nilüfer and "free chair" in Karaburun are both active as e-participation-oriented website services (at the level of 1/8). The other online participation services are not offered by any of the seven LA 21s.

- When the "online participation services" are subjected to cross analysis, the Nilüfer LA 21 is relatively the most successful one in terms of online participation services. The Nilüfer LA 21 offers two of the eight services in this service group on its website. The Nilüfer LA 21 is followed by İzmir, Karaburun and Malatya LA 21s with only one service out of 8 services.
- These results clearly illustrate that only seven out of the 70 LA 21s in Turkey have their own websites and that they fall short in terms of running e-participation-oriented website services.

CONCLUSION AND SUGGESTIONS

The fact that the wide-ranging e-participation opportunities offered by the internet are not made use of by the LA 21s, one of the most feasible platforms in terms of public participation in Turkey

constitutes a serious handicap. In a country like Turkey where people fall short of participating in administration and politics, it is crucially important to benefit form ICT for LA 21s and other participation platforms in order to popularize participation, accomplish participatory democracy and fix the relationships between the governing and the governed on a more interactive ground.

The fact that the e-participation services offered by the LA 21s in Turkey on their websites are *insufficient*, in general, closely related to Turkey's efforts of e-government and to the level of awareness of the society. Despite the progress in the recent years, the efforts of e-government in Turkey are still unsatisfactory. All the public institutions have not yet obtained the opportunities of e-government. Moreover, the public institutions with e-government opportunities have some serious deficiencies in using those opportunities and making the most of them. The LA 21s also have their share of those deficiencies. The fact that only 7 out of the total of 70 LA 21s affiliated with the municipalities in Turkey have functioning websites is a very clear indication of it.

The fact that the PC ownership and internet subscription in Turkey is at an insufficient level is a crucial factor in the success of e-government activities. This factor that is critical in terms of access to the LA 21 websites and interaction has a negative impact on the website-based activities of LA 21s.

Besides, the insufficiency at the level of education and awareness of the public in general, on the one hand, prevent the public from becoming a part of an encouraging or coercive power in order for the LA 21s to improve e-participation; on the other hand, even if the e-participation services are offered by the LA 21s, the resulting outcome is that the services are not sufficiently made use of. Additionally, the fact that the local administrators relatively regard the LA 21as insignificant units, that they are not interested in and do not make the necessary efforts and allocate the necessary funds also negatively affect not only each and every activity of LA 21s in Turkey but also their capacities to benefit from the ICTs.

The LA 21 websites in Turkey apart from being virtual advertisement brochure, the following suggestions, based on the explanations made above, can be made in order for them to become a channel encouraging participation and serving for democracy:

The foundations of e-government should be strengthened by cutting down the price of internet subscription and improving the internet infrastructure. On the other hand, the taxes collected from the equipment of data processing should be minimized, local production and software enterprises should be encouraged and PC ownership should be popularized. Besides, the e-government opportunities of public institutions and their ease of use should be promoted to the public. The public should be made aware of the changes and innovations regarding the issue of e-government. The public should also be made aware of the mechanisms encouraging participation to administration through e-government. Schools should, based on the level of education, introduce new courses on computers, the internet, e-government and e-participation. The funding capacities of LA 21s in Turkey should be improved and their budgets should be supported. The website activities of the LA 21s should be provided free-of-charge consultancy service. Finally, the efforts of the LA 21s and the results coming out of all these efforts should be efficiently utilized in the decision-making and implementation process of the local governments. All these necessities require a new mindset regarding the ICTs and LA 21s in terms of both national policy makers and executives, and local decision-makers and executives. Therefore, before anything else, the more challenging job of having a new mindset has to be tackled.

Finally, based on the results obtained from this study, the future studies may focus on the following points: The LA 21s in Turkey show weaknesses in terms of using the ICTs in general and e-participation applications in specific. This

outcome may be questioned country-wide and the reasons for it may be revealed. The 7 LA 21s included in our study as subjects of analysis may be comparatively examined within themselves and a deep analysis of the factors determining their level of success may be carried out. Moreover, the LA 21s in Turkey may be compared with their counterparts in other countries in terms of e-participation. In addition, relationships between the LA 21s and municipalities may be examined in terms of their functional, political, economical and financial dimensions and the impact of these relationships on the e-participation services of the LA 21s may also be analyzed. Finally, the approaches of the LA 21s without a website in Turkey towards participation in general and e-participation in specific may be examined and a specific analysis may be carried out in determining the real reasons behind those LA 21s' staying away from e-participation.

REFERENCES

Adolfsson Jörby, S. (2000). Local agenda 21 in practice–A Swedish example. *Sustainable Development*, 8(4), 201–214. doi:10.1002/1099-1719(200011)8:4<201::AID-SD147>3.0.CO;2-0

Adolfsson Jörby, S. (2002). Local agenda 21 in four Swedish municipalities: A tool towards sustainability. *Journal of Environmental Planning and Management*, 45(2), 219–229. doi:10.1080/09640560220116314

Arnstein, S. R. (1969). A ladder of citizen participation. *Journal of the American Planning Association. American Planning Association*, 35(4), 216–224. doi:10.1080/01944366908977225

Barrati Esteve, J., Castella-Roca, J., Domingo-Ferrer, J., & Reniui Vilamala, J. (2007). Internet voting. In Anttiroiko, A., & Malkia, M. (Eds.), *Encyclopedia of Digital Government* (pp. 1125–1129). Hershey, PA: Idea Group Inc.

Barrett, B., & Usui, M. (2002). Local agenda 21 in Japan: Transforming local environmental governance. *Local Environment, 7*(1), 49–67. doi:10.1080/13549830220115411

Becker, T. (2007). Teledemocracy. In Anttiroiko, A., & Malkia, M. (Eds.), *Encyclopedia of Digital Government* (pp. 1519–1523). Hershey, PA: Idea Group Inc.

Box, R. C., Marshall, G. S., Reed, B. J., & Reed, C. M. (2001). New public management and substantive democracy. *Public Administration Review, 61*(5), 608–615. doi:10.1111/0033-3352.00131

Callahan, K. (2007). *Elements of effective governance: Measurement, accountability and participation.* Boca Raton, FL: CRC Press.

Chadwick, A. (2003). Bringing e-democracy back in: Why it matters for future research on e-governance. *Social Science Computer Review, 21*(11), 443–455. doi:10.1177/0894439303256372

Chadwick, A., & May, C. (2003). Interaction between states and citizens in the age of internet: E-government in the United States, Britain and European Union. *Governance, 16*(2), 271–300. doi:10.1111/1468-0491.00216

Creighton, J. L. (2005). *The public participation handbook: Making better decisions through citizen involvement.* San Francisco: Jossey-Bass.

Crosby, N., Kelly, J. M., & Schaefer, P. (1986). Citizen panels: A new approach to citizen participation. *Public Administration Review, 46*(2), 170–178. doi:10.2307/976169

Emrealp, S. (2005). *Yerel gündem 21 uygulamalarına yönelik kolaylaştırıcı bilgiler el kitabı.* İstanbul, Turkey: IULA-EMME.

Environs Australia. (1999). *Our community our future: A guide to local agenda 21.* Canberra: Commonwealth of Australia.

Etxebarria, C., Barrutia, J. M., & Aguado, I. (2004). Local agenda 21: progress in Spain. *European Urban and Regional Studies, 11*(3), 273–281. doi:10.1177/0969776404041490

European Commission. (1998). Public sector information: A key resource for Europe. *Green Paper on Public Sector Information in the Information Society,* COM 585.

Feichtinger, J., & Pregernig, M. (2005). Imagined citizens and participation: Local agenda 21 in two communities in Sweden and Austria. *Local Environment, 10*(3), 229–242. doi:10.1080/13549830500075503

Gan, L. (1999). Implementation of agenda 21 in China: Institutions and obstacles. *Environmental Politics, 8*(1), 318–327.

Garcia-Sanchez, I. M., & Prado-Lorenzo, J. M. (2008). Determinant factors in the degree of implementation of local agenda 21 in the European Union. *Sustainable Development, 16*(1), 17–34. doi:10.1002/sd.334

Gibson, R. K., Römmele, A., & Ward, S. J. (2004). *Electronic democracy: Mobilisation, organisation and participation via new ICTs.* London: Routledge.

Government, H. M. (2002). *In the service of democracy: A consultation paper on a policy for electronic democracy.* London: Office of the e-Envoy.

Grochowalska, J. (1998). The implementation of agenda 21 in Poland. *European Environment, 8*(3), 79–85. doi:10.1002/(SICI)1099-0976(199805/06)8:3<79::AID-EET156>3.0.CO;2-F

International Association for Public Participation. (2007). *IPA2 spectrum of public participation*. Retrieved March 10, 2009, from http://www.iap2.org/associations/4748/files/spectrum.pdf

Irvin, R. A., & Stansbury, J. (2004). Citizen participation in decision making: Is it worth the effort? *Public Administration Review, 64*(1), 55–65. doi:10.1111/j.1540-6210.2004.00346.x

Jaeger, P. T. (2005). Deliberative democracy and the conceptual foundations of electronic government. *Government Information Quarterly, 22*(4), 702–719. doi:10.1016/j.giq.2006.01.012

Kakabadse, A., Kakabadse, N., & Kouzmin, A. (2003). Reinventing the democratic governance project through information technology? A growing agenda for debate. *Public Administration Review, 63*(1), 44–60. doi:10.1111/1540-6210.00263

Kampen, J., & Snijkers, K. (2003). E-democracy: A critical evaluation of the ultimate e-dream. *Social Science Computer Review, 21*(11), 491–496. doi:10.1177/0894439303256095

Kinder, T. (2002). Vote early, vote often? Teledemocracy in European cities. *Public Administration, 83*(3), 557–582. doi:10.1111/1467-9299.00318

Lindstrom, A., & Gronholm, B. (2002). *Progress and trends in local agenda 21 work within UBC Cities: Union of the Baltic Cities local agenda 21 survey 2001*. Turku: Abo University and Union of the Baltic Cities.

Macintosh, A. (2004). *Characterizing e-participation in policy-making*. Retrieved March 5, 2009, from csdl2.computer.org/comp/proceedings/hicss/2004/2056/05/205650117a.pdf

Millard, J. (2008). *E-participation recommendations: first version*. Retrieved March 5, 2009, from www.european-eparticipation.eu

Moynihan, D. P. (2003). Normative and instrumental perspectives on public participation. *American Review of Public Administration, 33*(2), 164–188. doi:10.1177/0275074003251379

Moynihan, D. P. (2007). E-voting in United States. In Anttiroiko, A., & Malkia, M. (Eds.), *Encyclopedia of digital government* (pp. 797–802). Hershey, PA: Idea Group Inc.

O'Toole, K. (2009). Australia local government and e-governance: from administration to citizen participation? In *M. Khesrow-Pour, E-government diffusion, policy and impact: Advanced issues and practices* (pp. 174–184). Hershey, PA: IGI Global.

OECD (Organisation for Economic Cooperation and Development). (2001). *Citizens as partners: OECD handbook on information, consultation and public participation in policy making*. Paris: OECD.

OECD (Organisation for Economic Cooperation and Development). (2003). *Promise and problems of e-democracy: Challenges of online citizen engagement*. Paris: OCED.

Panopoluou, E., Tambouris, E., & Tarabanis, K. (2009). Eparticipation initiatives: How is Europe progressing? European Journal of ePractice, 7(March), 1-12.

Patton, D., & Worthington, I. (1996). Developing local agenda 21: A case study of five local authorities in the UK. *Sustainable Development, 4*(1), 36–41. doi:10.1002/(SICI)1099-1719(199603)4:1<36::AID-SD32>3.0.CO;2-C

Roberts, N. (2004). Public deliberation in an age of direct citizen participation. *American Review of Public Administration, 34*(1), 315–353. doi:10.1177/0275074004269288

Robins, M. D., Simonsen, B., & Feldman, B. (2008). Citizens and resource allocation: Improving decision making with interactive web-based citizen participation. *Public Administration Review*, *68*(3), 564–575. doi:10.1111/j.1540-6210.2008.00891.x

Snellen, I. (2002). Electronic governance: Implications for citizens, politicians and public servants. *International Review of Administrative Sciences*, *68*(2), 183–198. doi:10.1177/0020852302682002

Taylor, A. J., & Burt, T. E. (2001). Pluralising tele-democracy: Not-for profits in the democratic polity. In Prins, J. E. J. (Ed.), *Designing e-government* (pp. 29–39). Hague, The Netherlands: Kluwer Law International.

Wei Phang, C., & Kankanhalli, A. (2007). Promoting citizen participation via digital government. In Anttiroiko, A., & Malkia, M. (Eds.), *Encyclopedia of Digital Government* (pp. 1352–1357). Hershey, PA: Idea Group Inc.

Wild, A., & Marshall, R. (1999). Participatory practice in the context of local agenda 21: A case study evaluation of experience in three English local authorities. *Sustainable Development*, *7*(3), 151–162. doi:10.1002/(SICI)1099-1719(199908)7:3<151::AID-SD111>3.0.CO;2-0

Yao, Y., & Murphy, L. (2007). Remote electronic voting systems: An exploration of voters' perceptions and intention to use. *European Journal of Information Systems*, *16*(2), 106–120. doi:10.1057/palgrave.ejis.3000672

ADDITIONAL READING

Anttiroiko, A. (2005). Democratic e-governance. In Khosrow-Pour, M. (Ed.), *Encyclopedia of information science and technology* (pp. 791–796). Hershey: Idea Group Reference.

Clift, S. C. (2004). E-government and democracy: Representation and citizen engagement in information age", Retrieved June 17, 2009, from http://www.publicus.net/articles/cliftegovdemocracy.pdf.

Dahl, R. (1998). *On democracy*. New Haven, CT: Yale University Press.

Fuchs, C. (2006). *eParticipation research: A case study on political online debate in Austria*. ICT&S Center, Research Paper No. 1, Salzburg.

Fung, A. (2006). Varieties of participation in complex governance. *Public Administration Review*, *66*(1), 66–75. doi:10.1111/j.1540-6210.2006.00667.x

Gaster, L. (1999). Participation and local government. In Lewis, D., & Campbell, D. (Eds.), *Promoting participation: Law or politics?* (pp. 113–135). London: Cavendish Publishing.

Gibson, R., Römmele, A., & Ward, S. (2004). *Electronic democracy: Mobilisation, organisation and participation via new ICTs*. London: Routledge.

Harvold, K. A. (2003). Consensus or conflict? Experiences with local agenda 21 forums in Norway. *Local Government Studies*, *29*(4), 117–135. doi:10.1080/03003930308559392

Held, D. (2006). *Models of democracy* (3rd ed.). Palo Alto, CA: Stanford University Press.

Jaeger, B. (2005). E-government, e-democracy and politicians. In Khosrow-Pour, M. (Ed.), *Encyclopedia of information science and technology* (pp. 990–994). Hershey: Idea Group Reference.

Kathlene, L., & Martin, J. A. (1991). Enhancing citizen participation: Panel designs, perspectives, and policy formation. *Journal of Policy Analysis and Management*, *10*(1), 46–63. doi:10.2307/3325512

Lowndes, V., Pratchett, L., & Stoker, G. (2001). Trends in public participation: Part 1 – local government perspectives. *Public Administration, 79*(1), 205–222. doi:10.1111/1467-9299.00253

Lowndes, V., Pratchett, L., & Stoker, G. (2001). Trends in public participation: Part 2 – citizens' perspectives. *Public Administration, 79*(2), 445–455. doi:10.1111/1467-9299.00264

Norris, D. (2006, July). *E-democracy and e-participation among local governments in the U.S.* A research paper presented at the Symposium on E-participation and Local Democracy. Budapest.

ODPM (Office of the Deputy Prime Minister). (2002). *Public participation in local government: A survey of local authorites.* London: ODPM.

Pratchett, L. (1999). New fashions in public participation: Towards greater democracy? *Parliamentary Affairs, 52*(4), 616–633. doi:10.1093/pa/52.4.616

Sanford, C., & Rose, J. (2007). Characterizing eparticipation. *International Journal of Information Management, 27*, 406–421. doi:10.1016/j.ijinfomgt.2007.08.002

Scott, J. K. (2006). "E" the people: Do U.S. municipal government web sites support public involvement? *Public Administration Review, 66*(3), 341–353. doi:10.1111/j.1540-6210.2006.00593.x

Sharp, L. (2002). Public participation and policy: Unpacking connections in one UK local agenda 21. *Local Environment, 7*(1), 7–22. doi:10.1080/13549830220115385

Smith, P. (2007). E-democracy and local government – dashed expectations. In Anttiroiko, A., & Malkia, M. (Eds.), *Encyclopedia of digital government* (pp. 448–454). Hershey: Idea Group Reference.

Smith, S., & Dalakiouridou, E. (2009). Contextualising public (e)participation in the governance of the European Union. *European Journal of ePractice, 7*, 1-11.

United Nations Department of Economic and Social Affairs. (2002). *Second local agenda 21 survey*, Background Paper No. 15.

Wei Phang, C. W., & Kankanhalli, A. (2007). Promoting citizen participation via digital government. In Anttiroiko, A., & Malkia, M. (Eds.), *Encyclopedia of digital government* (pp. 1352–1357). Hershey: Idea Group Reference.

Yang, K., & Callahan, K. (2007). Citizen involvement efforts and bureaucratic responsiveness: Participatory values, stakeholder pressures and administrative practicality. *Public Administration Review, 67*(2), 249–264. doi:10.1111/j.1540-6210.2007.00711.x

Young, S. C. (1996). Stepping stones to empowerment? Participation in the context of local agenda 21. *Local Government Policy Making, 22*(4), 25–31.

KEY TERMS AND DEFINITIONS

Participation: Participation is citizens' taking initiative in order to have effect on political and administrative decision-making processes.

E-Participation: E-Participation is realization of participation phenomenon in electronic environment by making the best use of ICTs.

Local Agenda 21: Local Agenda 21 is a governance platform which enables the participation of local communities and is based on cooperation between public, private and civil sectors.

Information and Communication Technology: Information and communication technology is information and technology related opportunities and means which, in the age of information society, enables the interaction of individuals, groups and societies with an extraordinary speed and efficiency.

Services of Information Delivery: Services of information delivery are the transfer of a set of structural and functional information to related citizens by using e-government means.

Communication Services: Communication services are website based services which enable one institution to interact with other actors.

Online Participation Services: Online participation services are website based services which enable citizens to incorporate their ideas and thoughts directly into decision-making processes.

Chapter 6
Government 2.0 in Korea:
Focusing on E-Participation Services

Hee Jung Cho
Sogang University, Korea

Sungsoo Hwang
Yeungnam University, Korea

ABSTRACT

This chapter looks at the various e-participation tools and services of e-government in South Korea. Korea has recently become a test bed for many information technology tools, particularly in the e-government and e-democracy domains. Many of the e-government evaluation indexes, including those of the UN and Brown University, rank the municipal and national e-government sites of Korea very high on the list. First, this chapter highlights a variety of e-government services available in Korea such as e-ombudsman (Shin-moon-go), the Korean Public Information Disclosure System (Open Government), Civil proposal services in e-rulemaking processes, and Call & Change (110 Service), which can be compared to those of other countries. The second part of this chapter focuses on citizen participation or e-participation, which is termed 'Gov 2.0', reflecting the concept of web 2.0. Characteristics of Gov 2.0 will be illustrated and then dimensions of possible evaluation measures will be discussed. Some illuminating cases will be introduced to investigate how policy recommendations and proposals from the people transform into actual policy changes. This chapter, thus, will discuss the challenges to implementing and evaluating Gov 2.0 services as well as present recommendations.

INTRODUCTION

Information Communication Technology (ICT) has been widely adopted by and diffused to both public and civil sectors in many countries. South Korea has become an exemplary country for a high level of Information Technology (IT) penetration. In the 1990's, there was an astonishing growth in dot com companies, distance education, e-commerce, and e-government. The Korean government's slogan, "Let us be at the front of the information revolution in the world, unlike with the industrial revolution" sums up their feelings well, stressing their strong desire to excel in building Korea's IT infrastructure

DOI: 10.4018/978-1-61520-933-0.ch006

and overall e-government services. Korea's central government (equivalent to the federal government of the U.S.) was a strong driver of this initiative, implementing many policies to promote IT infrastructure and e-government. Many evaluations of e-government indexes, including those of the UN and Brown University, rank the municipal and national e-government sites of Korea very high on the list.[1]

Since the establishment of the E-government Act in 2001, Korea has built a wide range of e-government websites for most public agencies. For example, the number of websites for the 43 ministries and agencies of Korea's central government was estimated at 1,643 in 2007 (MPAS, 2008). This number is a good indicator of the growth of IT infrastructure and e-government in Korea, although the quality of the websites and citizen satisfaction with the sites are different questions to probe. In fact, President Lee's administration announced in 2008 it plans to update the national information technology development plan (including e-Korea and ubiquitous-Korea) to catalyze more usage and participation from the public.

At the local district level, Kangnam-gu in Seoul, Korea prides itself on its advanced e-government site with its innovative technology applications and services to the residents. They have won numerous awards, including top seven communities in the world award by Intelligent Community Forum (ICF), and it stands as an example of a leading local government site. Kangnam-gu's e-government services include internet kiosks in shopping malls and bus stops so that residents can download and print out necessary permits and other documents. Given its nature as a local district government, Kangnam-gu aims to embed its services in community matters more and more (H.-J. Kim, Lee, & Kim, 2008).

Two broad goals of e-government can be to bring out *good management* and *good democracy* (Musso, Weare, & Hale, 2000). In other words, the e-government movement aims to increase efficiency for the management of the *back office* and

enhance service delivery to citizens to promote more democratic discourse and participation. It is believed that the current stage of e-government in both Korea and the U.S. has achieved good management but not good democracy. Particularly, e-participation is becoming an increasingly important research topic today in public administration, public policy, and political science. For instance, we have seen ample practices and research on the increased service delivery and civil appeals in Korea's e-government development in the last decade. Yet, citizen participation and consultation in the rule-making process and democratic deliberation are still rare. This is not only true in Korea but also in other countries in general.

Currently, we are witnessing a shift toward governance and e-governance in public administration. New governance, a term coined by Lester Salamon (Salamon & Elliott, 2002), has gained attention in recent public administration scholarship. Scholars currently discuss the shift from a government paradigm to a governance paradigm. A recent issue of *Public Administration Review*, a special issue on collaborative public management (2006 December, supplement to Volume 66), epitomizes the trend of studying collaboration and governance in public administration scholarship[2]. Other related terms are networked governance, third party government, and collaborative governance. In the information technology domain, scholars suggest that there is a shift from e-government to e-governance as well, stressing the engagement of civic groups and citizens (Brown, 2005; Coe, Paquet, & Roy, 2001; P. Kim, 2004; Riley, 2003; Snellen, 2002).

We are also witnessing a paradigm shift in information society in general, described as web 2.0, convergence or networked society. Web 2.0[3] technologies are being diffused to the government sector. Some public agencies use blogs, wikis, user-generated video sharing, and social networking tools to share information and communicate with citizens. Although the term web 2.0 is disputable, this term points out that new tools in Internet technology and web design are moving in the direction of creating more interaction, information sharing, collaboration and socializing on the web. There seems to be a consensus that many new tools have a potential to lower technology entry barriers, thereby encouraging technology novices to participate online more. It is anticipated that the newer generations, who are accustomed to these tools, have a higher expectation of a government which is interactive and transparent. We have already witnessed a huge landscape change in journalism. For example, online blogs, online journalism and citizen journalism such as the Huffington Post and Korea's ohmynews, are thriving today. It is, therefore, high time to add empirical research, scholarly discussion, and practical recommendations to enhance citizen participation in governance processes and to increase their satisfaction of e-participation.

This chapter evaluates Korea's e-government initiatives, focusing on e-participation aspects. Specifically, this chapter introduces notable Korean e-government projects that affect citizens' trust in and satisfaction with the government. Since 2005, five major citizen participation endeavors have been implemented. They are e-ombudsman (Shin-moon-go), the Korean Information Disclosure System (Open Government), e-rulemaking of the e-Assembly, Call & Change (110 Service), and e-voting. E-voting is excluded from our discussion as it is not being widely implemented yet. This chapter evaluates the current status of the remaining four services using the criteria of management efficiency and citizen engagement.

In the following section, we provide a brief review of existing scholarship while introducing an alternative framework to look at the components of citizen participation. This section also describes the trends and characteristics of Gov 2.0, and examines the future direction of e-government. Section 3 describes four major services encouraging citizen participation and evaluates the current status of how these services are utilized. The implications for e-participation services today in Korea are

discussed in section 4, and how to set up guidelines for tools to enrich e-participation is explored. In the last section, we conclude the discussion with possible future directions e-participation research may take, not only in the Korean context, but also in other countries.

EXISTING SCHOLARSHIP

Overlapping Studies on Information Technology, Government, and Politics and E-Participation

Why should we treat e-participation as an important feature of government practice and research? In looking at normative theory, stakeholders in society (citizens of the country, residents of locality, etc) are entitled to participate in the decision making process, consultation process, and rule-making process of public policy, public administration and politics. As a governance tool, citizen participation can lead to effective and good governance. Given these, there is an assumption that ICT, particularly the notion of Web 2.0 can improve citizen participation in the political and governance process.

Innovation and citizen satisfaction can be two key concepts of e-participation aspect of e-government initiatives. The advancement of technology triggered innovation, reinvention, and reform in the government sector to enhance the responsiveness and efficiency of government services. Governments today make an effort to utilize the advancement of technology well to promote interaction and communication between the government and citizens to increase the citizen's trust and satisfaction.

Technology alone does not automatically enable innovation and citizen satisfaction. As a matter of fact, many e-government scholars stress the complex interplay among social, technical, and human factors. Heeks and his associate (Heeks & Bailur, 2007, p. 249) did a meta-analysis of 84 papers on e-government research and found that most of them were written from a socio technical perspective rather than social determinism perspective or technological determinism perspective, stating the majority of e-government researchers reject crude technological determinism in favor of a recognition that human or social factors have at least some role to play. However, we have not reached the full potential of e-government services, particularly to spur citizen participation and trust.

There are a few notable scholarly works that studied e-government and its interaction with the public, although e-participation studies are still at an early stage. As introduced earlier, Musso et al (2000) found that a city government website works well as a management enhancement tool but does not contribute to democratic values. Fountain (2001) argued that agencies should consider customers and constituency in adopting IT. She asserts that organizational factors shape IT design and utilization. She classified three groups of variables as influences on institutional change with IT: technological variables, managerial variables, and political variables (Fountain & Osorio-Urzua, 2001). Scott (2006) investigated 100 municipal websites and learned that they provide a variety of information to citizens, but it can be interpreted differently according to the theoretical lens through which it is viewed, whether the expectation comes from a simple representative theory or direct-democracy theory. His work is useful in that he points out that there are different expectations and thus definitions of participation online. Danziger and Anderson (2002) did a meta- analysis on the impact of IT on public administration out of more than 200 articles published from 1987 to 2000 and found that almost half of the findings identify changes in capabilities of the public sector, categorized into 'information quality,' 'efficiency,' and 'effectiveness.' About one fourth of the findings looked at the IT impact on interactions of governments with citizens or other sectors. The majority (65%)

reported a positive impact of IT on interactions. Thomas and Streib (2003) cautioned, however, that most citizen contact through government web sites was only to obtain information and lacked a true interactive potential.

Some scholars in Europe also have looked at e-participation and e-consultation, stressing the point of citizen's involvement through IT. This is a part of or a big overlap with e-governance scholarship, but with more of a focus on citizen participation. Macintosh (2006, p. 365) defined e-participation as "the use of information and communication technologies to broaden and deepen political participation by enabling citizens to connect with one another and with their elected representatives." E-consultation can be defined as "the use of electronic computing and communication technologies in consultation processes and is complimentary to existing practices," according to this e-consultation research project.[4]

In a study to understand how IT is reshaping governance, Chadwick (2003) argued that new forms of digital technology have a democratization effect on e-government and e-democracy,. He outlined how IT practices are converging in four principal areas: "online consultations integrating civil societal groups with bureaucracies and legislatures, the internal democratization of the public sector itself, the involvement of users in the design and delivery of public services, and the diffusion of open-source collaboration in public organizations."

Macintosh and her associates examined how current e-participation tools work as a way for local authorities to engage with citizens (Macintosh, 2002, 2006; Macintosh, Malina, & Whyte, 2002; Macintosh & Whyte, 2006). Coleman investigated how IT can enhance higher levels of citizen participation and democratic deliberation, including alternative voting methods (Blumler & Coleman, 2001; Coleman, 2001; Coleman & Gøtze, 2001).

Research of IT has shifted to the interaction of the government with its outer environment. With the exception of discussion of a few topics such as the intranet between government agencies (Welch & Pandey, 2007), many IT issues with respect to the inside operation and management of governments have already been examined considerably, if not sufficiently. Currently, we are seeing a shift in research, looking more at the government's relationship to citizens and other sectors (Calista & Melitski, 2007; Evans & Yen, 2006; Parent, Vandebeek, & Gemino, 2005). Thus, there is increasing awareness of e-participation which this chapter aims to contribute to.

One group of scholars has engaged in the discussion of public participation via e-rule-making[5]. Internet technology is changing the rule-making process. For instance, regulations.gov, a federal web portal in the U.S. is an attempt to encourage public participation in the rule making process (Coglianese, 2004; Shulman, 2005). This group of scholars[6] is addressing questions such as: Are e-rule making tools increasing the dialogue between the public and lawmakers? Does the increased dialogue matter, if it is? Although research is still developing, e-rule making has come into existence as a legal mandate, and it is believed to be a positive endeavor towards increasing the dialogue between the public and lawmakers. It also seems to affect the rule making process in a positive way so as to enhance the value of democracy.

Overview of Existing Participation Models

In this section, we try to provide a short taxonomy of participation models. We illustrate five participation models in existing scholarship and also introduce a complementary and synthesizing model.

The first model is socio-economic participation model suggested by Nie and his colleagues (Nie & Verba, 1972; Nie, Verba, & Kim, 1978) in the 1970s. This theoretical model revolves around transactional cost. It a nut shell, they argue that the lower the transaction cost, the higher partici-

pation will be. One of things we can study under this model is the relationship of socio-economic status of the public and their participation. For example, a proposition under this model could be: e-participation has a low transaction cost, thus socio-economic variables will not influence e-participation levels.

The second model is a rational choice participation model. This model discusses incentives to participate, mostly regarding monetary or material incentives, although sometimes these expand to psychological or socio-political incentives. This model focuses more on individual incentives and behaviors to participate rather than a collective incentive for groups and parties (Barry, 1970; Downs, 1957). For example, a proposition under this model could be: the greater the number of incentives, the greater the amount of participation. In practice, some of Korea's e-government services offer monetary incentives to encourage citizen participation.

A third model is the social capital participation model, which focuses on social relationships. Putnam (2000; Putnam, 2002), Lin (Lin, 2001; Lin, Cook, & Burt, 2001) and others have stressed the importance of social capital. The term social capital refers to the benefits social actors derive from their membership in social networks (Putnam 2000). This model focuses on collective behavior and outcomes for citizens. For example, a proposition under this model could be: higher social capital can lead to more participation - organized groups (advocacy, citizen groups, etc), then, would participate more than isolated individuals.

The fourth is information communication technology and participation model. This model argues that ICT increases access, connectivity and communality, which in turn increases participation by lowering the entrance barrier to participating (Bell, 1976; Toffler, 1980). A current debate under this model is whether new ICT tools help to enable more participation from traditionally marginalized groups or whether new ICT tools merely reinforce the existing status quo.

Table 1. Overview of participation models and their applicability to e-participation research

	Socio-Economic Participation Model	Rational Choice Participation Model	Social Capital Participation Model	ICT Participation Model	Active Citizen Participation Model
Focus:	Transaction cost	Incentive	Social capital (Relationship)	Information Communication Technology	Active Netizen[7]
Key Argument:	The lower the transaction cost, the greater the participation	Incentives (mostly monetary but others) increase participation.	The higher the social capital, the more a person will participate	ICT increases access and connectivity, which in turn increases participation.	*Active* citizens participate more.
Propositions applied to e-participation:	E-participation has lower transaction costs; thus, it will bring higher participation.	Setting up monetary (material) incentives will increase e-participation.	Higher online (and offline) social capital will increase e-participation.	More affluent ICT users will participate more online.	One who does more activity will engage more in e-participation.

The fifth model is the active citizen participation model. Its simple assumption is that the more active (online or offline) a person is, the more that person will participate online. Under this model, we should measure activity level (how active) of citizens (either online or offline) and the level of participation online (Dulio, Goff, & Thurber, 1999; Margolis & Resnick, 2000; Negroponte, 1995).

We introduce a sixth model, a self-learning and political efficacy model, as an alternative but synthesizing model. Visiting websites of e-government services does not bear much cost to the citizen most of the times. This model argues that the feedback that citizens get after trying out an e-government service dictates future participation. That is, citizens' initial participation will be reinforced by positive feedback or discouraged by negative feedback, which is a process of learning of political efficacy that will shape their e-participation. The sixth model is still developing and we propose this view as a call for synthesizing some of models described above.

These competing models overlap or are complementary to one another in places. In the following section, we will briefly illustrate how these models have been utilized in evaluating e-government services in Korea.

A Brief History of Public Participation Scholarship with a Focus on Public Administration

Now, we would like to give another brief overview of public participation scholarship, particularly that with a focus on public administration. While these studies are not directly related to e-participation, they do explore issues in the context of public participation, particularly some landmark legal mandates.

A classic work by Arnstein (1969) is considered the origin of scholarly work on public participation. She (1969, p. 216) describes participation as "the redistribution of power that enables the have-not-citizens, presently excluded from the political and economic process, to be deliberately included in the future" and offers a typology of participation, 'a ladder of citizen participation', which can serve as a guide to measure degrees of public participation and empowerment. In this model, eight types of participation are arranged into three categories: citizen power, tokenism, and nonparticipation[8]. The model suggests that providing better access to data and knowledge helps citizens move up the ladder of participation.

Many public participation programs are implemented by the government because a requirement regarding such is specified in the by-laws of the state or federal government. Public participation has become a mandate or requirement particularly in land use planning and environmental policy makings. Public hearings and other mechanisms are often required before elected officials can approve a final plan for a locality. Roberts (2000, p. 309) points out that laws give citizens the right of access to government information, widely known as freedom of information (FOI) laws. The US adopted its first Freedom of Information Act (FOIA) [9] in 1966, and all 50 state governments had similar laws by 1984. These FOI laws stemmed from public demand based on the idea that American citizens have constitutional rights which make it necessary that government information be available to the public. Many mandated public participation programs are considered to meet the notion of democracy.

In generic public administration literature, the Tennessee Valley Authority (TVA) can be discussed as a starting point of public participation as its purpose was to provide information to the public to sell public projects by gaining local support (Selznick, 1949). This was called a cooptation approach, which was to involve supportive members of the public in the public agency operations.

Succeeding these earlier milestone works, two notable groups of scholars in public administration have advanced public participation discussion. One group of scholars approached public participation as involving the public in the decision making process of the bureaucracy and the deliberation of democracy. Thomas (1993; 1995; Thomas & Streib, 2003) applied a theory of decision-making to examine appropriate levels of public participation. He (1990) also tested the idea that public decisions with greater managerial and technical elements yielded less public involvement and public decisions with greater legitimacy need yielded greater public involvement. Some other scholars (King, Feltey, & Susel, 1998; Webler & O'Renn, 1995; Weeks, 2000) studied ways that public participation can

be better delivered in a deliberative democracy context in public administration.

Another group of scholars studied 'citizen participation' as civic engagement, which calls for building a stronger civil society by fostering collaboration between neighborhood groups with city agencies in order to build a more democratic governance. This body of work is best highlighted in the recent public administration volume 65 no 5 in 2005, from the Civic Engagement Initiative Conference[10] in 2004 led by Terry Cooper (Berry, 2005; Bingham, Nabatchi, & O'Leary, 2005; Boyte, 2005; Cooper, 2005; Kathi & Cooper, 2005; Portney, 2005). They are promoting and studying initiatives from the grassroots for the collaboration and deliberation in the public policy process.

Gov 2.0 and the Evolution of E-Government

The United Nation's global e-government readiness ratings rank Korea and the US in the top five both for the e-government readiness index and the e-participation index[11]. The UN's e-government readiness ratings take into account five stages of e-government evolution. These stages move from emerging governance to enhanced, interactive, transactional, and finally connected governance[12]. The UN urges e-governments to strive to reach the final stage of connected and networked governance. They stress the importance of utilizing ICT to actualize socially inclusive governance. This call to connect citizens via the internet for networked and inclusive governance can be labeled the Gov 2.0 movement. In connected governance, or the Gov 2.0 paradigm, there should be openness and transparency, convergence, two way communication and information sharing, and active citizen participation. As a result of the UN's urging and others' efforts, we see an increasing volume of studies on e-participation, e-rulemaking, e-governance, and so on.

The core competencies of Web 2.0[13] according to O'Reilly are openness, sharing and harnessing

Table 2. Core concepts and activities of Gov 2.0

Core concepts	Activities
Participation	Personalized and customized service, customer oriented service Citizen participation, e-rulemaking, e-town hall meetings (using tools such as blog, and wiki)
Information Sharing/Convergence	One-stop portals (Information sharing across departments, jurisdictions, etc), sharing a knowledge base
Openness/Transparency	Open source, enhanced citizen access to government information (more than just FOIA)

collective intelligence, trust and participation. Although Web 2.0 is a relatively well-diffused term, Gov 2.0 is a fairly new term. As Gov 2.0 is not yet well established, we would like to lay out some activities which represent core competencies and concepts of Gov 2.0.

A recent report by Gartner's group (2007) suggests there are four types of web 2.0 applications for government services. They are to provide better online services (case management, RSS feed), better integration (spatial analysis and online mapping for traditional services such as land/building permits, taxation, traffic management, etc), re-intermediation (convergence and information sharing, mashup), and constituent participation (e-participation using blog, wiki, tagging). A recent report by IBM (Wyld, 2007) suggests that citizens are willing to interact with government agencies online in today's web 2.0 environment and recommend governments reaching out to meet citizens where they congregate online with today's social computing trends, rather than sitting and waiting for them to come to their sites.

Although there is awareness on the part of governments for a need to take advantage of web 2.0, Gov 2.0 is not yet fully realized but is suggested as a future direction. Because at present we are still in the early development stages of Gov 2.0, it is critical to assess the current status of Gov 2.0 development now and propose sets of guidelines and recommendation.

E-GOVERNMENT SERVICES IN KOREA FOR E-PARTICIPATION

E-Ombudsman Service (Shin-moon-go)

Shin-moon-go is an ombudsman service online. Shin-moon-go literally is a type of big drum, but the term originated from a system[14] which handled complaints of people against government during the Jo-seon dynasty (1400's) to give the people one way to have a say in government affairs. It is intended to be a venue for governments to have closer communication with the people in areas such as administrative judgment, corruption reporting, petitioning, policy discussion and proposals.

In essence, there are two things citizens can do as the ombudsman service is intended to serve as a one-stop portal for civil petition and proposals. First, they can submit a civil application/petition and submit a policy proposal idea. To be more specific, they can submit a civil petition to resolve issues related to various kinds of administrative services either at the local, municipal, or national government level. Citizens can request information disclosure on any legal action (ordinance, etc), or street level implementation. Citizens can directly request that a government explain or interpret administrative affairs, including policy, administrative law, or implementation procedures. Secondly, citizens can also propose ideas to enhance existing services or devise new services (see Figure 1). They can further make an appeal to

Figure 1. Shin-moon-go: Korea's e-Ombudsman service (Source: www.e-people.go.kr)

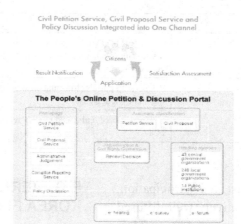

solve problems relating to government agencies' unlawful acts, unfair (unreasonable) measures or procedures. The Korean government has stated that they expect to achieve improved efficiency in administration, systematic reform through civil proposal services, and better policy discussion by providing shin-moon-go to the people[15].

The typical process for submitting an application is: (1) Fill out an application online (name, national ID number or foreign person ID number, contacts, option to make your petition public or not, contents). (2) Choose a responsible agency or department to distribute it to the appropriate party (otherwise the Anti-Corruption & Civil Rights Commission (ACRC)). Then the application is looked at by the appropriate party; usually it takes only 7 days for the investigation to be finished and the applicant to be notified of the result.

One of the greatest conveniences of this service is that Shin-moon-go since 2006 has acted as a one-stop portal; thus, citizens do not have to determine to which agency they should assign their applications. In most cases, citizens do not have the knowledge or resources to study who the agency responsible for their particular request would be, so this works positively to provide convenience to citizens, thereby lowering the transaction cost, and to increase the efficiency of administration. Furthermore, repeated applications concerning the

same issue go to a people's rights committee and this committee delves into how those issues can be addressed by making fundamental changes to the administrative service procedures or law.

Assessment and Evaluation of Shin-moon-go

Shin-moon-go boasts usage on and development/ maintenance costs on a massive scale. In 2009, the cost is estimated to be approximately 150 million dollars and the number of average monthly users 50,000. In 2008, it took 9.2 days on average to handle complicated petitions requiring multiple agencies' involvement from 36.1 days in average in 2005. General petitions took 6.9 days in average in 2008, down from 2005's 12 days in average. The entire process of handling a petition can be tracked in Shin-moon-go and the citizen is notified by email or SMS (short messaging service/text message) of the progress. This has contributed to citizen satisfaction and trust toward governments, demonstrated by the results of a 2009 ACRC survey evaluation which demonstrated that satisfaction of users was up to 51.2% in 2008 from 30% in 2005 (see Figure 2) (ACRC, 2009).

Shin-moon-go's success is evident from the fact that it was awarded a best practice award by

Figure 2. Assessment of Shin-moon-go's petition process (Source: ACRC 2009, P174)

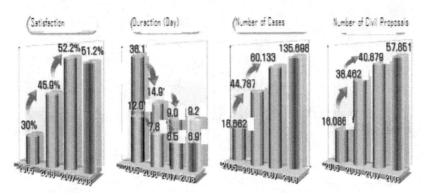

e-challenge 2008[16] (an ICT and e-government conference in Europe). Shin-moon-go and ACRC plan to enhance the search petition case database and provide more useful frequently asked questions (FAQs) and online guides. They also plan to deploy some of their reports into private online portals as an attempt to get closer to citizens (ACRC, 2009, p. 177). More discussion on civil proposals through Shin-moon-go follows in the civil proposal services section.

Korea Government's Public Information Disclosure System (PDIS: Open Government)

The Public Information Disclosure System (http://www.open.go.kr/pa/html/eng_main.htm), also known as Open Government, enables citizens to request that governments disclose information to public. Although there was a legal mandate, the Information Disclosure Act (similar to Freedom of Information Act in the U.S.), for open access to public information, it has made a tremendous difference now that requests and view government information online. For example, since PDIS was launched in 2006, requests for information disclosure have dramatically increased, with 150,000 requests in 2008, up from 26,000 in 1998 (see figure 3). Moreover, as of December 2008, PDIS had one hundred eighty million cases of

public information stored that could be disclosed to public. The goal of this system is to ensure the people's rights to know thereby promoting citizen participation and increasing transparency of government affairs.

PDIS provides reports and contents of public information in various formats including printed material, digital files, photos, and micro film. Requests made using this system are generally answered within 10 days. As of December 2008, 70,000 people per month on average requested information disclosure through this site.

Assessment and Evaluation of PDIS/Open Government

Among requests made using this service, information from local and regional governments is most often requested. Out of a total of 235,230 requests in 2007, 80.976 (34%) were for central government agencies, 140,846 (60%) were for regional and local government agencies, 13,174 (6%) were for city and province offices of education, and 234 (less than 1%) were for other public agencies (Central Bank, Public Broadcasting company, etc). Of the numerous central government agencies, the Ministry of Labor, Ministry of Justice, and National Police Agency receive the most information disclosure requests, most likely because these three central government agencies deal with

Figure 3. Requests of information disclosure, year by year (Source: MPAS 2008:8)

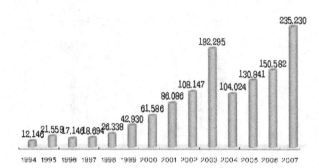

the public most closely. Construction and traffic related information (Ministry of Construction and Transportation) was requested next most often, followed by property/real estate related information. Two features, popular information disclosure and search database function are most useful.

The overall satisfaction of users has increased, but the Ministry of Public Administration and Security, which runs PDIS, aims to achieve even higher levels of user/citizen satisfaction.

Civil Proposal Services

In a broad definition of e-rulemaking process, governments open up and encourage the public to suggest proposals and participate in rulemaking process. Although as previously mentioned, Shin-moon-go acts as a centralized, one-stop portal to suggest policy proposals and such, there are two other notable civil proposal service sites. One is "People's Proposal (www.reco.or.kr)" run jointly by the MPAS and Mae-Il Business Newspaper, and the other is "Seoul Oasis" run by the Seoul Metropolitan government. Seoul Oasis won the

Table 3. Information disclosure requests breakdown (Source: MPAS 2008:13)

Year	# of cases	Breakdown of Decisions				Undecided	Withdrawn
		subtotal	disclosed	Partially disclosed	Not disclosed		
2007	235,230	197,617	157,958	21,479	18,180	401	37,212
	(%)	(100)	(80)	(11)	(9)	N/A	
2006	150,582	132,964	106,423	13,970	12,571	286	17,332
	(%)	(100)	(80)	(11)	(9)	N/A	

Table 4. Satisfaction level scores of PDIS users (Source: MPAS 2008:494)

Year	Central Government Agencies	City and Province	Offices of Education (City and Province)	Other Localities
2006	61.8	66.0	64.0	60.5
2007	64.9	65.6	65.3	61.5

Note: Satisfaction score was measured for 9 dimensions such as courtesy, responsiveness, diligence, validity in closed decisions, etc.

Table 5. Awarded civil proposals through Shin-moon-go (2006-2009)

Year	Category	Proposal	Reward
2006	1st place	[Rental property law] To revise a government operated rental property application process to better accommodate divorced woman.	Award (Prime Minister) & $3,000 reward
	2nd place	[Patent fee payment method] To revise the patent fee payment process (from mail to bank account wiring)	Award & $2,000 reward
	3rd place	[Welfare/healthcare] To reduce the national healthcare premium for families with more than 3 children.	Award & $1,000 reward
2007	1st place	[Property registration] To simplify the property registration process	Award (Prime Minister) & $3,000 reward
	2nd place	[Welfare] To mandate/encourage attaching fluorescent reflectors to mobile wheelchairs	Award & $2,000 reward
	3rd place	[Loan] To make it easier for people to borrow money from the government's housing fund	Award & $1,000 reward
2008	1st place	[Art/Culture] To support movie theaters' having English subtitles for Korean movies	Award (President) & $5,000 reward
	2nd place	[Welfare] To build/support 'experiencing disabled programs' to promote higher acceptance of the disabled population in society	Award (Prime Minister) & $3,000 reward

2009 United Nations Public Service Award for its innovation and best practices.

Civil Proposals through Shin-moon-go

Shin-moon-go provides multilingual petition services (English, Chinese, and Japanese). In promoting petitions, Shin-moon-go evaluates petitions using the criteria of feasibility, creativity, efficacy, cost-saving and rewards good petitions. Rewards are awards, or prize money.

These civil proposals are simple but creative ideas drawn from citizen's daily lives (see Table 5). These proposals are easy for the general public to understand and shared through Shin-moon-go. As governments accept some of the proposals and put them into practice, civil proposal services through Shin-moon-go are believed to be very effective both in participation and administration.

Civil Proposals through People's Proposal

"People's Proposal (www.reco.or.kr)" is unique in the sense that it is jointly run by a government agency and a newspaper company. This can be labeled new governance. It is also distinctive in that they set up panels specifically for citizens and for companies, respectively. These panels focus on economics and business. As of 2008, the people's panel had 10,000 registered users and the business enterprise panel had 500 registered users. They engage in a peer evaluation of proposals submitted through People's Proposal and award best ideas. The awarded ideas are then linked to Shin-moon-go. The peer evaluation process is similar to Web 2.0 in that, as with websites on Web 2.0, users/readers rate each proposal. Panel members can cast only one vote per proposal, giving a score between 1 and 10. Highly rated proposals get icons stating either "accepted", "being considered", or "not accepted", which acts as the government's a feedback mechanism. As of March 2009, the categories under which a citizen can submit a proposal are: domestic economy, politics/society, health/medical, agriculture/fishery, environment, culture/tourism, construction/distribution, finance/property, education/job, welfare, transportation/natural resources.

Table 6. Awarded proposals through People's Proposal (2009 March)

Category	Proposal
Domestic economy	Tax relief on purchasing fuel-efficient cars Building database of temporary workers of public programs
Politics/society	Including women in military draft Changing current policies toward North Korea
Health care/medical	Starting health screening/check ups earlier - from middle school Giving more rewards for donating blood
Culture/tourism	Developing Korean tourism brand items Giving financial assistance to tour companies run by foreigners
Construction/distribution	Changing the due date for the land development tax
Finance/property	Having ATMs accept tax/fee payments after bank business hours Leasing government owned properties more long-term (20 years)
Welfare	Expanding government run day care Assisting day care places at one's work Expanding benefits of the disabled

Some of the awarded proposals are listed in the following table as examples (see Table 6). Two recent best proposals won both an award and a monetary reward (for example, the Minister of Strategy and Finance Award and $1,000).

In October 2008, 7,320 proposals were uploaded. Some won the Presidential Award with a $3,000 reward for suggesting, for example, fuel-efficient taxis, women-only taxis, and automatic mail forwarding after moving. Some won the Prime Minister award along with a $1,000 reward for suggesting, for example, reducing plastic bag use at grocery stores, simplifying the customs process for foreign nationals married to Koreans, giving priority to the disabled for government-run rental properties. A total of 77 proposals were awarded. Some were instantly accepted by the governments for implementation, including one proposal for filling only 70% of fuel for government owned vehicles, and one for green building advantage.

Call and Change: Government Call Center (110 Service)

The call center 110 service (http://www.110. go.kr) is similar conceptually to the 311 call center service in New York City and other cities in the U.S. First developed by the Ministry of Public Administration and Security in 2003, it was actually put into service in 2007 and is now run by the Anti-corruption and Civil Rights Commission. This service serves as one-stop portal to ask any question about any governmental affair or administrative issue. It serves as a first point of contact, provides easy access over the phone rather than over the internet or face to face. Simple questions are answered by the call center while petitions, proposals and other concerns are directed to Shinmoon-go or other appropriate agencies.

For the Seoul metropolitan area, there is also the Seoul 120 call center (http://120.seoul.go.kr) to serve Seoul metropolitan's residents specifically. It is mostly used to get information about traffic, transportation, and general city affairs. Additionally, they provide a text messaging service and sign language through an online video chat feature.

The call center 110 service has contributed in bridging the digital divide to a certain degree, reaching out to older age groups and rural area residents. Interview data with call service center staff revealed that the majority of callers are in the older age groups. Call centers do not uti-

Table 7. Frequently asked questions of 110 call center (Source: FAQ, www.110.go.kr)

Some frequently asked questions
How can one register as a disabled person?
What is the homeless aid program? What does it do?
What after-school-programs are available in my neighborhood?
How does the domestic violence protection service work?
I would like to know about LPG car options for the disabled or veterans.
What is the aged person care voucher program?
What are social security benefits for the aged?

lize automated machine answering (automated response system) but rather provide a personal touch with a real person answering the calls. They also have a call-back service to keep the callers updated and report on the matter they discussed. It is believed that this effort has increased the satisfaction of citizens and perceived responsiveness of governments.

Other Notable Online Services

There are a few other notable online services. Public Affairs-pedia (www.gkmc.go.kr) started its service in December 2008 and is a part of an existing knowledge management system. It has the ambitious goal of accumulating knowledge and experience from the many civil servants in all of the government branches and jurisdictions. It is built on the wikipedia platform; thus civil servants and officers directly participate in sharing their knowledge and experience. It is not open to the pubic yet, but the plan is to do so in late 2009. This service is not related to e-participation yet, but it is a good example of a Gov 2.0 endeavor. Once it opens to the public, it is expected to build more information and knowledge sharing between the public and government, which should trigger a more inclusive information flow to encourage e-participation.

Many ministries and agencies of central governments have used the blogsphere to communicate with the public since 2008. One dis-

tinctive characteristic is that the blogs of about 20 ministries and agencies are placed inside of existing web portals operated by web companies rather than creating new one in government domain. For example, 'Daum' is arguably the most popular web blog sphere in Korea, where many clubs and forums exist, and the Department of Labor has built a blog space within the Daum service (www.blog.daum.net/nosanuri). This is in line with Coleman (Coleman & Gøtze, 2001)'s argument and a recent IMB report (Wyld, 2007)'s recommendation that the government should not expect to attract visitors to a newly created blog sphere of the government's but rather should go to where people gather online organically. However, as the blog has not existed for very long, it is not yet drawing a significant amount of visitors or experiencing large amounts of communication.

One exception, as a positive example using a blog is the 'hello-policy' moderated by the Ministry of Culture, Sports, and Tourism. After its debut in September 2008, this blog (http://blog. naver.com/hellopolicy) attracted one million visitors in its first four months. Most of its contents are closely related to daily life issues such as tax refunds, free children's health check-ups, and youth job creation. The most discussed item was "getting close to having one's driver's license suspended with penalties", with 60 related postings and 48,000 views. This showcases a potential for governments using a blog to increase interactions with the citizens. Another instance of a govern-

Table 8. Evaluation of e-participation services (achieving either good management or democracy effectively)

	Core concepts/ dimensions	Civil Application/ Petition (Shin-moon-go)	Open Government/ PIDS	Civil Proposal (Shin-moon-go & People's proposal)	Call Center
Good Management	Responsiveness	More effective	Effective	More effective	More effective
	Openness/Transparency	Effective	More effective		
Good Democracy	Information/Knowledge Sharing & Inclusive information flow	Effective	Effective	Effective	More effective
	Political Efficacy	Effective	Effective	More effective	More effective

ment agency pairing with a web business is The Department of Labor has made a MOU (memo of understanding) with NHN, the most popular search portal in Korea, to build a blogsphere within their web portal. .

Mobile service (also called M-Gov service) was launched in April 2006 and is run by the National Computing and Information Agency. Primarily, it sends text messages and pictures to cell phones to assist with emergency management (works with the National Emergency Management Agency), to alert the public of missing children (works with the National Police Agency), and to send school information to parents of students (works with the National Education Information System).

CHALLENGES AND FUTURE DIRECTIONS OF GOV 2.0

Four e-participation efforts were introduced in this chapter. Now, this section discusses which service affects good management and good democracy as scholars discuss. As Table 8 illustrates, there is not a single service that does it all. However, some services are partially contributing to the enhancement of elements of good management and good democracy. Ideally, we would hope to see a one-stop portal to meet the all dimensions of Web 2.0 and encompass all the services that can satisfy good management and good democracy.

However, the endeavors which presently exist appear to enhance participation of the public through the web sphere. It is positive in a sense that a service realizes certain dimensions of Gov 2.0 only after 4-5 years of web 2.0 tools became available.

There are some challenges to overcome and improvements to be made. Although Korea's e-government seems to be heading in the right direction, more information sharing across the agencies and jurisdictions is needed. Governments still need to open up more in revealing what kinds of civil petitions and applications were submitted and how they were handled. Proposals from the public are increasing, but they currently focus mainly on the domestic economy; they need to expand many other areas. Governments should continue to actively pursue putting in suggested proposals into their legislation or administration.

One of the bigger challenges is to assess policy outcomes of accepted proposals after they get implemented. It is also a challenge to give feedback to the public in reporting the outcomes, not to mention of implementing good ideas from proposals suggested by citizens to actual policy implementation. Tracking the feedback process of proposal's implementation and outcomes is one area for scholars to explore. We are still at the very early stages of Gov. 2.0, but scholars need to engage in assessing the effectiveness of these e-participation services, particularly the impact of certain policy proposals put into practice through e-participation.

Though we are still working to explore and test the models described earlier, it should be noted that more in-depth analysis of usage and satisfaction of these e-services with the dimensions such as socio-economic groups, IT proficiency, etc. For Shin-moon-go service, our initial findings suggest that there is no statistically significant relationship of usage of this service for education level and gender. We found that there is a statistically significant relationship of usage for income level and occupation. We are working to report more detailed analysis on this.

There also should be an effort to address certain fundamental issues using a holistic approach. For example, answering and solving daily transportation issues using a call center is useful, but policy makers and civil servants should be able to see beyond the surface requests to the root cause of these questions – problems with transportation policies and infrastructure which need to be addressed.

From the traditional political science perspective, there is an unanswered question about how future expansion of civil proposals will influence the existing landscape of representative democracy. We should proceed with a caution before undermining existing constructive functions of political parties and parliament. After all, e-participation services have been created to promote good democracy.

In essence, Gov. 2.0 requires technical and policy advancements. From a technical angle, user-friendliness and usability need to be constantly pursued and upgraded. Security in networked settings is also still a big concern. Novice users also have difficulties in downloading various plug-ins such as Active X as well as security patches and certificates. Many of these websites are designed to be optimal to view on Microsoft's Internet Explorer. This dependency on one private company's technology is problematic. Certainly, there is a cost issue to designing a website to be multi-browser optimal, but this is something to consider as well.

Policy-related issues are even more important to deal with than technical issues in general. So far, Korea's e-government services have successfully attracted users to participate, for instance, by providing monetary rewards. Yet, the public will want to see more proposals implemented and legislated in reality. Keeping up with the expectations of the public to adopt many proposals and successfully assessing the effectiveness as a feedback process, as discussed earlier, will be a great challenge.

Gov 2.0, particularly e-participation is still in the early stages. However, both practitioners and scholars see its great importance and potential to improve not only management but democracy. Gov 2.0 has the potential to catalyze good governance. We would like to conclude by calling for further research discussing guidelines and future directions of Gov 2.0 services as well as empirical research on them.

ACKNOWLEDGMENT

This chapter is in part based on the work supported by the Presidential Committee on Government Innovation and Decentralization. We thank Young-Min Yoon, Ph.D. and Dong-Wook Kim, Ph.D. for their contributions to the work.

REFERENCES

ACRC. (2009). *A report on civil petition operation assessment of 2008* [in Korean]. Seoul, Korea: Anti-Corruption & Civil Rights Commission.

Arnstein, S. R. (1969). A Ladder of Citizen Participation. *Journal of the American Planning Association. American Planning Association, 35*(4), 216–224. doi:10.1080/01944366908977225

Barry, B. (1970). *Sociologists, Economists and Democracy*. Chicago: University of Chicago.

Bell, D. (1976). *The coming of post-industrial society: a venture in social forecasting*. New York: Basic Books.

Berry, J. M. (2005). Nonprofits and Civic Engagement. *Public Administration Review, 65*(5), 568–578. doi:10.1111/j.1540-6210.2005.00484.x

Bingham, L. B., Nabatchi, T., & O'Leary, R. (2005). The New Governance: Practices and Processes for Stakeholder and Citizen Participation in the Work of Government. *Public Administration Review, 65*(5), 547–558. doi:10.1111/j.1540-6210.2005.00482.x

Blumler, J. G., & Coleman, S. (2001). *Realising Democracy Online: A Civic Commons in Cyberspace*. IPPR/Citizens Online.

Boyte, H. C. (2005). Reframing Democracy: Governance, Civic Agency, and Politics. *Public Administration Review, 65*(5), 536–546. doi:10.1111/j.1540-6210.2005.00481.x

Brown, D. (2005). Electronic government and public administration. *International Review of Administrative Sciences, 71*(2), 241–254. doi:10.1177/0020852305053883

Calista, D. J., & Melitski, J. (2007). *Digital Collaboration: Clarifying the Roles of E-Government and E-Governance*. Paper presented at the American Society of Public Administration.

Chadwick, A. (2003). Bringing E-Democracy Back In: Why it Matters for Future Research on E-Governance. 21(4), 443-455.

Coe, A., Paquet, G., & Roy, J. (2001). E-Governance and Smart Communities: A Social Learning Challenge. *Social Science Computer Review, 19*(1), 80–93. doi:10.1177/089443930101900107

Coglianese, C. (2004). E-Rulemaking: Information Technology and the Regulatory Process. *Administrative Law Review, 56*, 353–402.

Coleman, S. (2001). *2001: A Cyber Space Oddysey- the Internet in the UK Election*. London: Hansard Society.

Coleman, S., & Gøtze, J. (2001). *Bowling Together: Online Public Engagement in Policy Deliberation*. London: Hansard Society.

Cooper, T. L. (2005). Civic Engagement in the Twenty-First Century: Toward a Scholarly and Practical Agenda. *Public Administration Review, 65*(5), 534–535. doi:10.1111/j.1540-6210.2005.00480.x

Danziger, J. N., & Andersen, K. V. (2002). The Impacts of Information Technology on Public Administration: An Analysis of Empirical Research from the 'Golden Age' of Transformation. *International Journal of Public Administration, 25*(5), 591. doi:10.1081/PAD-120003292

Downs, A. (1957). *An economic theory of democracy*. New York: Harper.

Dulio, D. A., Goff, D. L., & Thurber, J. A. (1999). Untangled Web: Internet use during the 1998 election.(World Wide Web). *PS: Political Science & Politics, 32*(1).

Evans, D., & Yen, D. C. (2006). E-Government: Evolving relationship of citizens and government, domestic, and international development. *Government Information Quarterly, 23*(2), 207–235. doi:10.1016/j.giq.2005.11.004

Fountain, J. E. (2001). *Building the virtual state: Information technology and institutional change*. Washington, DC: Brookings Institution Press.

Fountain, J. E., & Osorio-Urzua, C. A. (2001). Public Sector: Early stage of a deep transformation. In R. E. Litan & A. M. Rivlin (Eds.), *The economic payoff from the internet revolution* (pp. 235-268). Washington, DC: Brookings Institution Press. Freedom of Information Act (United States). *Wikipedia, the free encyclopedia* Retrieved April 1, 2008, from http://en.wikipedia.org/wiki/ Freedom_of_Information_Act_%28United_ States%29

GartnerGroup. (2007). *What does Web 2.0 mean to Government?* Heeks, R., & Bailur, S. (2007). Analyzing e-government research: Perspectives, philosophies, theories, methods, and practice. *Government Information Quarterly, 24*(2), 243–265.

Kathi, P. C., & Cooper, T. L. (2005). Democratizing the Administrative State: Connecting Neighborhood Councils and City Agencies. *Public Administration Review, 65*(5), 559–567. doi:10.1111/j.1540-6210.2005.00483.x

Kim, H.-J., Lee, J., & Kim, S. (2008). Making the Connection between Local Electronic-Government Development Stages and Collaboration Strategy: A Case Study of Gangnam District, Seoul, Korea. *International Journal of Electronic Government Research, 4*(3), 36–56.

Kim, P. (2004, 14-18 July 2004). *Development of Democratic e-Governance in Cyberspace and Shaping e-governance for Quality of Life.* Paper presented at the 26th International Congress of Administrative Sciences, Seoul, Korea.

King, C. S., Feltey, K. M., & Susel, B. O. (1998). The question of participation: Toward authentic public participation in public administration. *Public Administration Review, 58*(4), 317–326. doi:10.2307/977561

Lin, N. (2001). *Social capital: A theory of social structure and action.* Cambridge, UK: Cambridge University Press.

Lin, N., Cook, K. S., & Burt, R. S. (2001). *Social capital: Theory and research.* New York: Aldine de Gruyter.

Macintosh, A. (2002). e-Democracy: Citizen engagement and evaluation. In S. Friedrichs, T. Hart & O. Schmidt (Eds.), *Balanced EGovernment:Connecting Efficient Administration and Responsive Democracy.* Germany: Bertlesman Foundation.

Macintosh, A. (2006). eParticipation in Policy-making: the research and the challenges. In P. Cunningham & M. Cunningham (Eds.), Exploiting the Knowledge Economy: Issues, Applications and Case Studies (pp. 364-369) Amsterdam, The Netherlands: IOS press.

Macintosh, A., Malina, A., & Whyte, A. (2002). Designing e-democracy for Scotland. *Communications: The European Journal of Communications, 27*, 261–278.

Macintosh, A., & Whyte, A. (2006). *Evaluating how eParticipation changes local democracy.* Paper presented at the eGovernment Workshop 2006, eGov06, London, UK.

Margolis, M., & Resnick, D. (2000). *Politics as usual: The cyberspace "revolution".* Thousand Oaks, CA: Sage Publications.

MPAS. (2008). *Annual Report on Information Disclosure in 2007* [in Korean]. Seoul, Korea: Ministry of Public Administration and Security.

Musso, J., Weare, C., & Hale, M. (2000). Designing Web Technologies for Local Governance Reform: Good Management or Good Democracy? *Political Communication, 17*(1), 1–19. doi:10.1080/105846000198486

Negroponte, N. (1995). *Being digital* (1st ed.). New York: Knopf.

Nie, N., & Verba, S. (1972). *Participation in America: Political Democracy and Social Equality.* New York: Harper and Row.

Nie, N., Verba, S., & Kim, J.-O. (1978). *Participation and Political Equality: A Cross-National Comparison*. Cambridge, MA: Cambridge University Press.

O'Leary, R., Gerald, C., & Bingham, L. B. (2006). Introduction to the Symposium on Collaborative Public Management. *Public Administration Review, Supplement to Volume 66*(6), 6-9.

Parent, M., Vandebeek, C. A., & Gemino, A. C. (2005). Building Citizen Trust Through E-government. *Government Information Quarterly, 22*(4), 720–736. doi:10.1016/j.giq.2005.10.001

Portney, K. (2005). Civic Engagement and Sustainable Cities in the United States. *Public Administration Review, 65*(5), 579–591. doi:10.1111/j.1540-6210.2005.00485.x

Putnam, R. D. (2000). *Bowling alone: The collapse and revival of American community*. New York: Simon & Schuster.

Putnam, R. D. (2002). *Democracies in flux: The evolution of social capital in contemporary society*. Oxford, UK: Oxford University Press.

Riley, T. B. (2003). *E-Government vs. E-Governance: Examining the Differences in a Changing Public Sector Climate (No. 4)*. Ottawa, Canada: Common Wealth Centre for E-Governance.

Roberts, A. S. (2000). Less Government, More Secrecy: Reinvention and the Weakening Law. *Public Administration Review, 60*(4), 308–320. doi:10.1111/0033-3352.00093

Salamon, L. M., & Elliott, O. V. (2002). *The tools of government: A guide to the new governance*. Oxford, UK: Oxford University Press.

Scott, J. K. (2006). "E" the People: Do U.S. Municipal Government Web Sites Support Public Involvement? *Public Administration Review, 66*(3), 341–353. doi:10.1111/j.1540-6210.2006.00593.x

Selznick, P. (1949). *TVA and the grass roots; a study in the sociology of formal organization*. Berkeley, CA: Univ. of California Press.

Shulman, S. W. (2005). eRulemaking: Issues in Current Research and Practice. *International Journal of Public Administration, 28*, 621–641. doi:10.1081/PAD-200064221

Snellen, I. T. M. (2002). Electronic governance: implications for citizens, politicians and public servants. *International Review of Administrative Sciences, 68*(2), 183–198. doi:10.1177/0020852302682002

Thomas, J. C. (1990). Public Involvement in Public Management: Adapting and Testing a Borrowed Theory. *Public Administration Review, 50*(4), 435–445. doi:10.2307/977079

Thomas, J. C. (1993). Public Involvement and Government Effectiveness: A Decision-Making Model for Public Managers. *Administration & Society, 24*(4), 444–469. doi:10.1177/009539979302400402

Thomas, J. C. (1995). *Public Participation in Public Decisions: New Skills and Strategies for Public Managers*. New York: Jossey-Bass.

Thomas, J. C., & Streib, G. (2003). The new face of government: citizen-initiated contacts in the era of e-government. *Journal of Public Administration Research & Theory: J-PART, 13*(1), 83 (19).

Toffler, A. (1980). *The third wave* (1st ed.). New York: Morrow.

Webler, T., & O'Renn, O. (1995). A Brief Primer on Public Participation: Philosophy and Practice. In *Fairness and competence in citizen participation: evaluating models for environmental discourse*. Boston: Kluwer Academic.

Weeks, E. C. (2000). The Practice of Deliberative Democracy: Results from Four Large-Scale Trials. *Public Administration Review, 60*(4), 360–372. doi:10.1111/0033-3352.00098

Welch, E. W., & Pandey, S. K. (2007). E-Government and Bureaucracy: Toward a Better Understanding of Intranet Implementation and Its Effect on Red Tape. *Journal of Public Administration: Research and Theory, 17*(3), 379–404. doi:10.1093/jopart/mul013

Wyld, D. C. (2007). *The Blogging Revolution: Government in the Age of Web 2.0*. Washington, DC: IBM Center for The Business of Government.

ENDNOTES

[1] Korea ranked 5th (2004 & 2005) and 6th (2007 & 2008) in the UN global e-government survey and ranked 1st in D. West's study, Brown University (2007).

[2] O'Leary and her associates (O'Leary, Gerald, & Bingham, 2006, p. 8) described the shift to governance and collaboration well, stating that *"the world of public administration has changed. Technological innovations such as the Internet, globalism (which permits us to outsource anywhere abroad), devolution (which may bring intergovernmental conflict), and new ideas from network theory have changed the business of government. Public managers now find themselves not as unitary leaders of unitary organizations. Instead, they find themselves convening, facilitating, negotiating, mediating, and collaborating across boundaries."*

[3] We use O'Reilly's definition of Web 2.0: "'Web 2.0' refers to a perceived second generation of web development and design that facilitates communication, secure information sharing, interoperability, and collaboration on the World Wide Web. Web 2.0 concepts have led to the development and evolution of web-based communities, hosted services, and applications such as social-networking sites, video-sharing sites, wikis, blogs, and folksonomies. Web 2.0 is a set of economic, social, and technology trends that collectively form the basis for the next generation of the Internet—a more mature, distinctive medium characterized by user participation, openness, and network effects." It should be noted that Tim Berners-Lee, inventor of the World Wide Web, has questioned whether web 2.0 is truly a new phenomenon, since many of the technological components of Web 2.0 have existed since the early days of the Web (In Wikipedia, the free encyclopedia).

[4] http://www.e-consultation.org/

[5] E-Rulemaking refers to the use of digital technologies by government agencies in the rulemaking process. Each year, regulatory agencies -- such as the U.S. Department of Agriculture, Environmental Protection Agency, Federal Aviation Administration, and Nuclear Regulatory Commission -- collectively issue thousands of new rules which have the binding effect of law on businesses, professionals, and citizens. How these agencies make and implement these regulations can have significant effects on the economy as well as on the advancement of important social goals. Appropriate use of information technology is thought to hold the potential for helping agencies manage the rulemaking process more effectively, enhance the legitimacy of their regulatory decisions, and promote more cost-effective compliance. http://www.law.upenn.edu/academics/institutes/regulation/erulemaking/index.html

[6] For an extensive list of publications on this topic can be found at http://www.law.upenn.edu/academics/institutes/regulation/erulemaking/papersandreports.html

[7] Michael Hauben (1973-2001) was a computer specialist and author, interested in the transformative social effects of online communities and the latent political power

of the Internet. In 1992 he coined the term Netizen to describe an Internet user who possesses a sense of civic responsibility for her/his virtual community in much the same way citizens would feel responsible for a physical community. [wiki]

[8] The eight types she offered were: Manipulation, Therapy (Non Participation), Informing, Consultation, Placation (Tokenism), Partnership, Delegated Power, and Citizen Control (Citizen Power).

[9] The Freedom of Information Act (FOIA) is the implementation of freedom of information legislation in the United States. It was signed into law by President Lyndon B. Johnson in July 1966 (Amended 2002), and went into effect the following year. This act allows for the full or partial disclosure of previously unreleased information and documents controlled by the U.S. Government. The Act defines agency records subject to disclosure, outlines mandatory disclosure procedures and grants nine exemptions to the statute. ("Freedom of Information Act (United States),")

[10] (http://www.usc-cei.org/?url=about.php, accessed March 19, 2008)

[11] http://www2.unpan.org/egovkb/global_reports/05report.htm (accessed April, 2009)

[12] http://unpan1.un.org/intradoc/groups/public/documents/UN/UNPAN028607.pdf

[13] Some regard the term web 2.0 as a meaningless marketing buzzword. See footnote 3 for more on this.

[14] Citizens could hit the drum and a designated agency would listen and handle their complaints or requests.

[15] http://www.epeople.go.kr/jsp/user/on/eng/intro01.jsp

[16] www.echallenges.org

Chapter 7
Internet Use and Political Participation of American Youth:
The Campaign of 2008

Jody C. Baumgartner
East Carolina University, USA

ABSTRACT

This chapter examines the relationship between the use of the Internet for campaign information and two dimensions of the political engagement of young adults. Drawing on data from a national survey of 18-24 year olds conducted online during the 2008 presidential campaign, it shows that the effect of Internet use for campaign information on political engagement among youth was marginal. While these young adults did take advantage of opportunities to participate on the Internet, reliance on the Internet for campaign information had no significant effect on knowledge about the campaign or more traditional types of political participation. Despite the promise the Internet holds for increasing political interest and participation, those youth who relied on the Internet as their primary source of campaign information did not seem any more inclined to participate in politics than others in their cohort.

INTRODUCTION

Research in political science has long noted the disparities in political participation between young adults and their older counterparts (Bauerlein, 2008; Mindich, 2005; Wattenberg, 2007). For example, while youth voter turnout increased in 2004 and 2008 (Curry, 2008), youth still consistently vote at lower rates than do other age groups (Baumgartner & Francia, 2008). Interestingly, during each election

cycle there are any number of stories claiming that the present election season will be the one in which youth will turn out in record numbers. In 2008 much of this speculation revolved around the role of the Internet in mobilizing youth to participate and vote (Lawrence, 2008; Malloy, 2008; Polantz, 2008; Simkins, 2008; Weisenmiller, 2008).

Is this too much to expect of a communications medium? Is the Internet a boon or bust for democracy? Historically, all advances in electronic communications technology have been accompanied by a fair amount of hyperbole regarding the

DOI: 10.4018/978-1-61520-933-0.ch007

effect, positive or negative, that they would have on democracy (Douglas, 1987). Having said this, the 2008 presidential campaign saw unprecedented amounts of Internet activity by citizens, organized groups, parties, and candidates alike.

In this paper I examine the relationship between the use of the Internet for campaign information and two dimensions of the political engagement of young adults during the 2008 presidential campaign. Employing a survey of 18-24 year olds, I show that the effects of reliance on the Internet as a primary source of campaign news and information on the political engagement of young adults was marginal. While youth did take advantage of the many opportunities the Internet affords to become involved in a presidential campaign, reliance on the Internet as the primary source of information about the campaign had no significant effect on their knowledge about the campaign or their participation in more traditional political activities. In other words, in spite of the promise the Internet holds for increasing political interest and participation among this chronically disengaged age group, those who rely on the Internet as their main source of news do not seem any more inclined to participate in politics than others in their cohort.

The research is important because the mass media is an important agent of political socialization (Chaffee, Ward, & Tipton, 1970) and has some effect on political mobilization (Newton, 1999; Eveland & Scheufele, 2000; Norris, 2000) and participation. However the present 18-24 age cohort has come of age in a media environment that is dramatically different than that of their elders. Simply put, unlike previous generations, these youth have array of convenient information choices to select from throughout the day. Understanding how they utilize these choices and the effects these choices have on their political engagement is critical, especially since political beliefs and habits formed in younger years tend to persist through adulthood (Sears, 1983).

In the following section I briefly review the literature on Internet use and political knowledge and participation. Following that I discuss the data and methodology of the study and present the findings. Finally, I discuss the implications of the results, suggesting fruitful avenues for future research.

REVIEW

There have been any number of studies in the past decade examining the relationship between various measures of Internet access and/or exposure and political engagement (political knowledge, political efficacy, and participation; for excellent reviews, see Norris, 2001; Dimaggio, Hargittai, Neuman, Robinson, 2001).

This research typically takes one of two approaches. The first focuses on the idea that the Internet constitutes a virtual community. Some research in this tradition suggests that belonging to online communities (social networking sites, chat rooms, blogs) not only helps people gain political knowledge, but that this sense of community may encourage participation (Pasek, Kenski, Romer, & Jamison, 2006; Coleman, Lieber, Mendelson, & Kurpius, 2008). The negative view of this approach is that Internet use, like television, isolates people from each other. This lack of conventional, face-to-face interpersonal contact leads to a loss of a sense of community, which in turn might lead to a decrease in political participation (Putnam, 2000). For example, Davis (2005) found that the impersonal nature of online contact led to hyper-partisan electronic talk on online blogs, chat rooms, and discussion groups, making these venues "problematic as a public discussion forum" (Davis, 2005, 119). By extension, this would suggest a decrease in engagement by all but the most politically interested.

Most researchers take a resource-based approach to studying the effects of Internet use on political engagement. Here, the focus is on the fact that the Internet lowers barriers to entry in information acquisition, as well as some forms of participation. With regard to information, the Internet reduces communication costs (for both citizens and political elites) by offering more information that is more conveniently accessible to users. No longer, in other words, are citizens bound by the timing and limited choices of information delivery associated with more traditional forms of news (e.g., network news broadcasts, newspapers). In addition, this approach highlights the idea that beyond chat rooms, there are now a number of online forms of political participation available to citizens (donating money online, forwarding emails, etc.). According to this logic, lower barriers to entry can serve to help mobilize citizens into greater political engagement (Krueger, 2002; Kenski & Stroud, 2006).

A consensus seems to have emerged in the past few years in scholarship that takes this resource-based approach to the effect of Internet use on political engagement that *if* the Internet is used for information seeking, it may have a minor, but positive effect on - or complement the use of other media in - promoting political engagement (Scheufele & Nisbet, 2002; Krueger, 2002, 2006; Jenning & Zeitner, 2003; Johnson & Kaye, 2003; Kaid, 2003; Weber, Loumakis, & Bergman, 2003; Shah, et al., 2005; Kenski & Stroud, 2006). This is because the mass media, including the Internet, are important sources of political knowledge (Delli Carpini & Keeter, 1996). Political knowledge, in turn, has a positive effect on political engagement (Sheufle & Nisbet, 2002; Shah, et al., 2005: 353; Pasek, Kenski, Romer, & Jamison, 2006).

There are, however, two problems with earlier resource-based analyses. The first deals with the fact that Internet access and use has historically been correlated with higher socio-economic status. This means that those already predisposed to be politically active would also be inclined to use the Internet for political purposes. Thus, many studies have shown that Internet access and use reinforces

or replicates preexisting political engagement patterns among citizens (Krueger 2002; Sheufle & Nisbet, 2002). A second problem deals with the fact that even those who have Internet access may not use it to seek out political information. This is consistent with what media scholars refer to as uses and gratification theory (Blumler & Katz, 1974; McQuail, 1997; Graber, 2001). In these cases, the effect of Internet use on political engagement would be negligible.

The present study departs in one very important way from previous research. This is because the Internet (access to, the technologies and content of) changes so rapidly. Previous research has been, in other words, attempts to "shoot at a moving target" (Jennings & Zeitner, 2003, 311). However, this project focuses on 18-24 year old youth in the year 2008. There is now very close to near-universal access to the Internet for this age group. A recent Pew Internet & American Life Project report suggests that 89 percent of youth are online (Jones & Fox, 2009). Moreover, this is a cohort that by and large never really knew a world without the Internet. Finding news and information online for this age group is as natural as watching broadcast network news was for most people 40 years ago. In other words, this cohort grew up in what one could argue is a completely different media environment (e.g., the Internet, cable television, text messageing and alerts, more) than that of previous generations. How they navigate this new media landscape and what effect their choices have on their political engagement is important to understand.

Because Internet access in now nearly universal for this age cohort one can make an important theoretical assumption in examining the effects of Internet use on their political life. This is where the present study begins. For this cohort the Internet is not an optional supplement to their media diet, it is a regular part of that diet. A full 59 percent of 18-29 year olds said that while they did not necessarily go online to get political news, they did "come across it," and 42 percent of this same age group claimed they regularly learned something about the 2008 campaign from the Internet (Pew Research Center, 2008). This fact alone sets this research apart from almost all previous attempts to examine Internet effects on political engagement. This is certainly true of resource-based approaches, and may well be true of the virtual community approach as well, especially given that conservative estimates suggest that three-quarters of this age group has a social networking profile (Lenhart, 2009).

My expectations, following the logic of resource—based studies of Internet use, are that the Internet, which offers more opportunities (in terms of volume of information as well as convenience of access) to access information, will a positive effect on the political engagement of youth. More specifically, exposure to political information on the Internet should lead to greater campaign knowledge and political participation (Tolbert,& McNeal, 2003; Drew & Weaver, 2006; Xenos and Moy, 2007). Based on this, I propose the following hypotheses:

H1: *Using the Internet as a primary source of news to follow the 2008 presidential campaign will have a positive effect on the political knowledge of youth.*

H2: *Using the Internet as a primary source of news to follow the 2008 presidential campaign will have a positive effect on the political participation of youth.*

In the following section I discuss the data and methodology of the research and present the findings.

DATA AND METHODS

Data for this research were collected from a six-wave online panel survey conducted during the 2008 presidential election campaign. In order to obtain the sample I contacted university registrars from ten public universities in each state and requested a directory of their institution's undergraduate student email addresses. With the request I included a brief description of my research, a copy of the initial survey instrument, as well as approval from my university's institutional review board. In all I received directories from 35 institutions in 20 states (AK, CA, CO, CT, FL, GA, ID, IL, MD, MI, MN, MO, NC, ND, NJ, NY, SC, TN, TX, WI), yielding a fairly representative geographic sample. Throughout 2007 I emailed these students, inviting them to participate in research about the political attitudes and behavior of college students. I informed them that the surveys would take approximately 10-20 minutes and that their participation was voluntary. A total of 10,343 students agreed to participate.

I pre-tested the instrument for the first wave of the panel in mid-December of 2007. Five hundred individuals were asked to take the survey and to note how long it took to complete, as well as any trouble they might have had in navigating the survey and understanding any questions. After making a few adjustments I emailed the link for the first survey to the entire sample on December 15, 2007. After sending reminders on December 19 and 21, I closed the survey on December 23, 2007. A total of 4,961 individuals completed this first wave, resulting in a response rate of 47.9 percent. While most of the variables used in this research came from this first wave, a few key dependent variables measuring political knowledge and participation were collected in wave four, conducted from September 15 through 23, 2008. Only those who completed the first three waves participated in this fourth wave, which resulted in an "n" of 1,754.

The main variable of interest in this research is the use of the Internet to follow the presidential campaign. As noted previously, by 2008, the Internet was one of the many media choices available to young adults. How does the political

Table 1. Sample demographic and political characteristics, by most campaign news source

Variable	*Percentage of sample*
Get most campaign news from: Internet Television Other (Newspaper, Radio, Other)	33.0% 44.8 22.2
Party identification Strong Republican Republican Independent Democrat Strong Democrat	5.1 27.9 28.9 30.7 7.5
Gender Female Male	68.1 31.9
Race White Non-white	88.5 11.5
Age (mean, St.D.)	20.18 (1.61)
Talk about politics (range 0-10; mean, St.D.)	5.48 (2.50)
Follow politics (range 0-10; mean, St.D.)	4.56 (2.50)
Civic knowledge (range 0-4; mean, St.D.)	2.84 (1.06)
N	1,754

engagement of those who relied mainly on the Internet for news about the campaign compare to those who relied mainly on other media? To get at this, I asked respondents, "how have you been getting most of your news about the current campaign for President of the United States? From television, from newspapers, from radio, or from the Internet?" This variable was recoded into three dummy variables, "most campaign news from Internet" (33% of the sample), "most campaign news from television" (44.8 percent), and "most campaign news from newspapers, radio, or other" (22.2 percent; see Table 1, below).

My approach is similar to that of Johnson and Kaye (2003), who focused on those who used the web for political purposes, controlling for other media use. Here, they found the Internet had a positive effect on political engagement in 2000, but their findings were restricted to a different breed of Internet user, since Internet access and use was not nearly as widespread as it is today. This approach also has the advantage of addressing

concerns posed by those who note that Internet use is not monolithic, and that many use the Internet for non-political purposes (see, for example, Kenski & Stroud, 2006, 177). While some may object that this approach ignores the fact that people get political information from a variety of disparate types (e.g., social network, candidate campaign, news organization) of websites, media research scholars are in agreement that the distinction between news and entertainment on television has become increasingly blurred in recent years as well. In other words, this approach focuses on what types of information citizens were seeking, not the types of websites where they sought it.

In order to determine the effect of gathering information about the campaign on the Internet on political engagement I controlled for a number of other factors as well. These included various demographic (age, race, gender) characteristics as well as partisan identification. I also included two measures of political interest in the model, asking respondents how often they talked about politics with family and friends as well as how closely they were following news about the 2008 presidential elections. Finally, I controlled for political knowledge by creating an index of correct responses from four questions that measured general civics knowledge (see Appendix for question wording and coding). Table 1 (below) shows the distribution of these variables within the sample.

The first test of the effect of using the Internet as a primary source of news about the campaign on political engagement of respondents examines their knowledge about the campaign. In the first wave of the survey (December, 2007) I asked respondents if they could identify six of the leading presidential candidates based on a description that had been widely discussed in the media. In particular, I asked respondents if they knew which candidate was: a practicing Mormon; formerly the mayor of New York City; a Senator from New York State; a first term U.S. Senator from Illinois; a prisoner of war during the Vietnam War; and, formerly a Baptist Minister. Responses were coded as "1" for each correct answer and "0" for an incorrect answer. Scores were then added to create an index, with values ranging from 0-6. I created a second campaign knowledge index based on responses to eight questions asked in wave four (September, 2008) about the campaign itself (range, 0-8; see Appendix for questions).

The results (see Appendix, Table A1), regressing these two measures (using ordinary least squares) against the predictors, suggest that using the Internet as a primary source of news and information about the campaign had a significant and positive effect, as hypothesized, on knowledge about the field of candidates. This was not the case as the campaign wore on. The effect on knowledge about the campaign was positive, but not significant. In each model Democratic Party affiliation was significant, perhaps because of the excitement generated by the Obama campaign, as was gender (male) and age (older). Interestingly, in neither case was relying on television for news

about the campaign significant. Finally, as one might expect, political interest (following politics and talking about politics) and civic knowledge were significantly associated with higher levels of campaign knowledge. However, the evidence here with regard to Hypothesis 1 is inconclusive. Using the Internet as the main source of campaign news may or may not have contributed to greater knowledge about the campaign.

The remaining tests deal with Hypothesis 2, or political participation. For this analysis I divided political participation into three separate categories: Internet political participation, conventional political participation, and campaign participation. The first, Internet political participation, includes various types of political participation that are carried out online. These include (1) posting a message on a blog to express a political opinion, (2) signing an email or web petition, and (3) forwarding a political email or link to another person. Respondents were presented with a list of these activities and asked, "Which of the following have you done in the past 12 months? Please check all that apply." Resulting variables were coded as "1" (did the activity in question) or "0" (did not do the activity in question) and were tested in a logistic regression model (using the predictors employed in the previous model).

The results of this test (Appendix, Table A2) show that using the Internet as the main source of campaign news had a positive and significant effect on all three Internet political participation measures. This finding is perhaps intuitive, given that individuals who rely on the Internet for most of their campaign news are likely online a fair amount of time. Nonetheless, the fact that their use of the Internet as a primary source of news and information about the campaign is positively associated with political activity on the Internet is an important empirical finding.

Following this, I conducted logistic regression of using the Internet as the main source of campaign information on six different measures of conventional political participation. These include (1) having written or called any politician at the state, local, or national level; (2) attended a political rally, speech, or organized protest; (3) attended a public meeting on town or school affairs; (4) written a letter to the editor of a newspaper or called a live radio or TV show to express an opinion; (5) signed a written petition; or (6) been an active member of a group that tries to influence public policy or government. As with the previous measures, respondents were asked if they had engaged in any of the activities in the previous 12 months.

The results (see Appendix, Table A3) suggest that Internet use may not be the panacea for political engagement that early proponents may have hoped. While it's effect was positive on four of the six measures included here, in no case was this effect significant. Moreover, in two cases (written a letter or called a live radio or TV show, and signed a written petition) the effect is negative, although here too it is not significant. In fact the only variable to consistently have a significant and positive effect on these measures was one of the two measures of political interest (talking about politics). It is also interesting to note that in all but one case (attended a public meeting on town or school affairs) the effect of relying on television as the main source of campaign news was negative, and, significant for three of the six measures.

The final test of Internet use as a primary source of campaign news examines its effect on campaign-specific participation. The first three of these questions were presented to respondents in the same manner as were the previous measures ("Which of the following have you done in the past 12 months?"): (1) personally tried to persuade another person to support particular political candidate or issue; (2) worn a campaign button, put a sticker on your car, or placed sign in front of your home; or, (3) worked for a political party or campaign. Other questions asked respondents "Did you, yourself, volunteer any of your time to help one of the presidential election campaigns

or not?" (1=Yes, 0=No), "Did you, yourself contribute money to a campaign in support of one of the presidential candidates this year, or not?" (1=Yes, 0=No), and "Did you vote in your state's presidential PRIMARY election, or caucus, earlier this year?" (1=Yes, 0=No, missing data= I was not old enough).

The analysis (Appendix, Table A4) shows that there is no significant association between Internet use as a primary source of campaign news and campaign participation. As in the previous models, there is a consistent positive and significant relationship between campaign activity and political interest. Party identification is also significant, and negative, meaning that Democratic Party identifiers were more likely to engage in these activities. This is a reflection of the fact that primaries and caucuses to decide the Democratic nomination for president were ongoing throughout the spring, and attracted a great deal of attention in the media. In only one case (volunteer to help presidential campaign) was television significant in the analysis, although in this case the relationship was negative.

To sum up the statistical portion of this analysis in a more accessible manner, I generated predicted probabilities for each of the models. Here, all variables except "most campaign news from Internet" were set at their mean values, and the resultant percentages reflect the probability of the respondent engaging in the activity based on the value of "most campaign news from Internet" (0 or 1). These are shown below, in Table 2.

As Table 2 clearly demonstrates, the effect of getting most news and information from the Internet on political participation is, by and large, underwhelming. With the exception of what I have referred to as Internet political participation, none of the differences in the probability of engaging in the activity in question by getting most campaign news from the Internet were significant. The relationship between Internet political participation and receiving most campaign information from the Internet was significant, but again, this finding is

Table 2. Predicted probabilities: political participation by most campaign news from internet

	Most Campaign News, Internet	Most Campaign News, Other Media
Internet Political Participation	17.8%	12.3%*
Post message on blog to express political opinion	35.1	24.9**
Sign an email or web petition	23.1	15.2**
Forward a political email or link to another person		
Conventional Political Participation	13.4%	12.9%
Written or call any politician at state, local, or national level	10.4	9.1
Attend political rally, speech, or organized protest	19.9	16.2
Attended a public meeting on town or school affairs	2.6	3.4
Written letter to editor or called live radio or TV show to express opinion	21.9	25.5
Signed a written petition	7.2	5.8
Been active member of group that tries to influence public policy or government		
Campaign Political Participation	52.9%	47.4%
Personally tried to persuade another person to support particular political candidate or	10.2	7.9
issue	2.9	1.7
Worn campaign button, put sticker on your car, or place sign in front of your home	4.1	5.2
Worked for a political party or campaign	5.2	5.7
Volunteer to help presidential campaign	37.6	37.9
Contribute money to presidential candidate		
Voted in 2008 presidential primary		

Differences significant at * p < .05 (two-tailed); ** p < .01 (two-tailed); *** p < .001 (two-tailed).

not terribly surprising. All other things being equal, an individual who spends more time on the Internet gathering news might be more likely to participate in other activities on the Internet, including those of a political nature. The differences between the effect of getting most news from the Internet and other sources on the likelihood of participating in conventional and campaign related activities is marginal, and, not significant.

In the final section I discuss the limitations of the study, its implications, and where future research might add to our understanding of the relationship between Internet use and political engagement.

DISCUSSION

The Internet continues to hold great promise for democratic citizenship. It is a communications medium that allows users to access extraordinary amounts of information whenever they choose to do so, enables individuals to join with others in virtual communities to promote collective action, and gives citizens a number of ways to become politically active online. This said, it's democratic promise remains largely unfulfilled. This research was designed to measure the independent effect of Internet use during a presidential campaign on 18-24 year olds, a group for whom Internet use is as normal as reading a daily newspaper or watching network news was for previous generations. The results suggests that by itself, Internet use has little effect (positive or negative) on the political engagement of this group.

While Internet use had a positive effect on knowledge of the field of presidential candidates in late 2007, it had no effect on their general campaign knowledge as the election season wore on. While Internet use did have a positive effect on the several activities that constitute Internet political participation, it had no effect on more traditional measures of political participation. Finally, and perhaps most disturbing, using the Internet as a primary source for news and information about the campaign had no effect on the six measures of campaign-related political participation, including whether the individual voted in a primary.

This study has certain limitations, especially having to do with its generalizability. Most obviously, the study is focused only on the political behavior of young people in the U.S. Even here, while national in scope, the survey relied on a convenience (non-random) sample of self-selected individuals. However a few points are in order in this regard. First, this 18-24 year old age group is increasingly difficult to contact by way of telephone, given the increased use of cell phone only users (Pew, 2006). Only one-quarter of the original sample reported that they had a traditional land line telephone in the residence where they live. In other words, a traditional random digit dialing telephone survey would not have reached a representative sample of youth either, making this online sampling strategy a more viable option. Second, the subjects of this research were all college students in the age range of the target population (18-24 year old youth). Third, the sample drew from a number of public universities from all major regions throughout the country and, as such, was fairly representative of the larger population of university students. In other words, in spite of the fact that the sample was not randomly selected, the research is more generalizable than many other surveys which employ convenience samples of college students (Sears, 1986).

Another limitation to this study may be the nature of some of the dependent variables. It may not, for example, be fair to use some of these measures of "conventional" political participation for today's youth. For example, questions that ask if the individual has attended a rally or written a letter to the editor may be an artifact of a different era in American politics. It may be the case that the Internet participation measures employed here are the wave of the future of political participation. This said, it must be acknowledged that many "traditional" measures like voting, donating money to a campaign, and working for a campaign, matter for democratic citizenship, and this is unlikely to change.

It might also be the case that my test was too strict, coding media use as either Internet, television, and other. However, it is probably the case that the factors that political scientists have identified through the years (partisan identification, age, education, political knowledge, political interest) as having an effect on political participation will continue to be more important than the medium or media one relies on for campaign information.

Future research should probably account not only for newer forms of electronic communications (e.g., text message news alerts and bulletins) as well as the changing nature of political participation as this generation matures and newer generations come of political age. In addition, research should pay special attention to the rapidly changing choices citizens have with respect to information gathering and account for the changing environment.

Expecting the Internet to transform democracy and democratic participation was probably too high of an expectation. Several decades of research in political science teach us that while a number of factors may facilitate political participation, some will simply not be interested. While the Internet by itself may not be a boom for democracy, it has certainly facilitated a number of new forms of political participation and is a conveniently accessible cornucopia of political information for those who seek it. This chapter has perhaps given us a glimpse into what democratic citizenship may look like in an Internet age, since the youth of today will carry these information gathering and participation habits with them throughout their lives.

REFERENCES

Bauerlein, M. (2008). *The dumbest generation.* New York: Tarcher Penguin.

Baumgartner, J., & Francia, P. L. (2008). *Conventional wisdom and American elections: Exploding myths, exploring misconceptions.* Lanham, MD: Rowman & Littlefield.

Blumler, J. G., & Katz, E. (1974). *The uses of mass communications: Current perspectives on gratifications research.* Beverly Hills, CA: Sage.

Chaffee, S. H., Ward, L. S., & Tipton, L. P. (1970). Mass communication and political socialization. *The Journalism Quarterly, 47,* 647–659.

Coleman, R., Lieber, P., Mendelson, A. L., & Kurpius, D. D. (2008). Public life and the internet: If you build a better website, will citizens become engaged? *New Media & Society, 10,* 179–201. doi:10.1177/1461444807086474

Curry, T. (2008, November 7). Young voters not essential to Obama win. *MSNBC.Com.* Retrieved January 9, 2009, from http://www.msnbc.msn.com/id/27582147/.

Davis, R. (2005). *Politics online: Blogs, chat rooms, and discussion groups in American democracy.* New York: Routledge.

Delli Carpini, M. X., & Keeter, S. (1996). *What Americans know about politics and why it matters.* New Haven, CT: Yale University.

Douglas, S. J. (1987). *Inventing American broadcasting, 1899-1922.* Baltimore: Johns Hopkins University.

Drew, D., & Weaver, D. (2006). Voter learning in the 2004 presidential election: did the media matter? *Journalism & Mass Communication Quarterly, 83,* 25–42.

Eveland, W. P. Jr, & Scheufele, D. A. (2000). Connecting news media use with gaps in knowledge and participation. *Political Communication, 17,* 215–237. doi:10.1080/105846000414250

Flanigan, W. H., & Zingale, N. H. (2006). *Political Behavior of the American Electorate* (11th ed.). Washington, DC: CQ Press.

Graber, D. A. (2001). *Processing politics.* Chicago, IL: University of Chicago.

Hargittai, E., Di Maggio, P., Neuman, W. R., & Robinson, J. P. (2001). The social implications of the Internet. *Annual Review of Sociology, 27,* 307–336. doi:10.1146/annurev.soc.27.1.307

Johnson, T. J., & Kaye, B. K. (2003). A boost or bust for democracy? How the web influenced political attitudes and behaviors in the 1996 and 2000 presidential elections. *The Harvard International Journal of Press/Politics, 8*(3), 9–34. doi:10.1177/1081180X03008003002

Jones, S., & Fox, S. (2009). Generations online in 2009. *Pew Internet & American Life Project,* January 28, 2009. Retrieved February 12, 2009, from http://www.pewinternet.org/PPF/r/275/report_display.asp

Kenski, K., & Stroud, N. J. (2006). Connections between internet use and political efficacy, knowledge, and participation. *Journal of Broadcasting & Electronic Media, 50,* 173–192. doi:10.1207/s15506878jobem5002_1

Krueger, B. S. (2002). Assessing the potential of Internet political participation in the United States: a resource approach. *American Politics Research, 30,* 476–498. doi:10.1177/1532673X02030005002

Lawrence, J. (2008). Young voters poised to flex voting muscle. *USA Today,* May 6, 2008. Retrieved January 23, 2009, from http://www.usatoday.com/news/ politics/election2008/2008-05-05-young-voters_N.htm

Lenhart, A. (2009). *Adults and social network websites*. January 14, 2009. Retrieved February 19, 2009, from http://www.pewinternet.org/PPF/r/527/press_coverageitem.asp

Malloy, D. (2008). Candidates facing up to youth on the Internet. *Pittsburgh Post Gazette*, February 1, 2008. Retrieved January 23, 2009, from http://www.post-gazette.com/pg/08032/853990-176.stm.

McQuail, D. (1997). *Audience analysis*. London: Sage.

Mindich, D. T. Z. (2005). *Tuned out*. Oxford, UK: Oxford University.

Newton, K. (1999). Mass media effects: Mobilization or media malaise? *British Journal of Political Science*, *29*, 577–599. doi:10.1017/S0007123499000289

Norris, P. (2000). *A virtuous circle: Political communications in post-industrial societies*. Cambridge, UK: Cambridge University.

Norris, P. (2001). *Digital divide: Civic engagement, information poverty, and the Internet worldwide*. Cambridge, UK: Cambridge University.

Pasek, J., Kenski, K., Romer, D., & Jamieson, K. Hall. (2006). America's youth and community engagement: how use of mass media is related to civic activity and political awareness in 14- to 22- year-olds. *Communication Research*, *33*, 115–135. doi:10.1177/0093650206287073

Pew Research Center. (2006). The cell phone challenge to survey research. Retrieved May 15, 2006, from http://people-press.org/reports/display.php3?ReportID=276

Pew Research Center. (2008). Internet's broader role in campaign 2008: Social networking and online videos take off. Retrieved May 11, 2008, from http://people-press.org/report/384/internets-broader-role-in-campaign-2008

Polantz, P. (2008, April 21). Digital campaigns attract young voters. *CBS News*. Retrieved January 23, 2009, from http://www.cbsnews.com/stories/2008/04/21/politics/uwire/main4033484.shtml

Putnam, R. D. (2000). *Bowling alone: The collapse and revival of American community*. New York: Simon & Schuster.

Sears, D. O. (1983). The persistence of early political predispositions: The roles of attitude object and life stage. In Wheeler, L., & Shaver, P. (Eds.), *Review of personality and social psychology* (*Vol. 4*, pp. 79–116). Beverly Hills, CA: Sage.

Sears, D. O. (1986). College sophomores in the laboratory: influence of a narrow data base on social psychologys view of human nature. *Journal of Personality and Social Psychology*, *51*, 515–530. doi:10.1037/0022-3514.51.3.515

Shah, D. V., Cho, J., Eveland, W. P. Jr, & Kwak, N. (2005). Information and expression in a digital age: modeling internet effects on civic participation. *Communication Research*, *32*, 531–565. doi:10.1177/0093650205279209

Simkins, C. (2008, September 18). Young voters divided over whether they will vote in U S presidential election. *Voice of America*. Retrieved January 23, 2009, from http://www.voanews.com/english/archive/2008-09/2008-09-18-voa27.cfm

Tolbert, C. J., & McNeal, R. S. (2003). Unraveling the effects of the Internet on political participation. *Political Research Quarterly*, *56*, 175–185.

Wattenberg, M. P. (2007). *Is voting for young people?* New York: Pearson Longman.

Weber, L. M., Loumakis, A., & Bergman, J. (2003). Who participates and why?: an analysis of citizens on the Internet and the mass public. *Social Science Computer Review*, *21*, 26–42. doi:10.1177/0894439302238969

Weisenmiller, M. (2008, February 13). Election outcome may hinge on youth vote. *IPS: Inter Press Service*. Retrieved January 23, 2009, from http://www.ipsnews.net/news.asp?idnews=41190

Xenos, M. A., & Moy, P. (2007). Direct and differential effects of the Internet on political and civic engagement. *The Journal of Communication*, *57*, 704–718.

ADDITIONAL READING

Delli Carpini, M. X., & Keeter, S. (1996). *What Americans know about politics and why it matters*. New Haven, CT: Yale University.

Eveland, W. P. Jr, & Scheufele, D. A. (2000). Connecting news media use with gaps in knowledge and participation. *Political Communication*, *17*, 215–237. doi:10.1080/105846000414250

Graber, D. A. (2001). *Processing politics*. Chicago, IL: University of Chicago.

Hargittai, E., Di Maggio, P., Neuman, W. R. & Robinson, J. P. (2001). The social implications of the Internet. *Annual Review of Sociology, 27*, 307_336.

Johnson, T. J., & Kaye, B. K. (2003). A boost or bust for democracy? How the web influenced political attitudes and behaviors in the 1996 and 2000 presidential elections. *The Harvard International Journal of Press/Politics*, *8*(3), 9–34. doi:10.1177/1081180X03008003002

Kenski, K., & Stroud, N. J. (2006). Connections between internet use and political efficacy, knowledge, and participation. *Journal of Broadcasting & Electronic Media*, *50*, 173–192. doi:10.1207/s15506878jobem5002_1

Krueger, B. S. (2002). Assessing the potential of Internet political participation in the United States: a resource approach. *American Politics Research*, *30*, 476–498. doi:10.1177/1532673X02030005002

Norris, P. (2001). *Digital divide: Civic engagement, information poverty, and the Internet worldwide*. Cambridge, UK: Cambridge University.

Pasek, J., Kenski, K., Romer, D., & Jamieson, K. H. (2006). America's youth and community engagement: how use of mass media is related to civic activity and political awareness in 14- to 22- year-olds. *Communication Research*, *33*, 115–135. doi:10.1177/0093650206287073

Wattenberg, M. P. (2007). *Is voting for young people?* New York: Pearson Longman.

KEY TERMS AND DEFINITIONS

Partisan Identification: the psychological attachment an individual feels toward a political party. Political engagement: the overall level of interest and involvement of an individual in public affairs.

Political Participation: activity (or activities) centered around public affairs.

Political Socialization: The process by which individuals acquire their political beliefs and values.

APPENDIX

Gender: What is your gender? (0=Female, 1=Male).

Age: How old are you? (Actual age recorded).

Race: What is your race? (1=White, 0=African-American, Non-white Hispanic, Asian, Other).

Partisan Identification: Generally speaking, do you consider yourself a Republican, a Democrat, an independent, or what? (1=Strong Democrat, 2=Democrat, 3=Independent, or neither, 4=Republican, 5=Strong Republican, missing data=I don't know, or I haven't given it much thought).

Political Interest ("Follow Politics"): On a scale of 1 to 10, with 1 being NOT AL ALL and 10 being VERY REGULARLY, how closely would you say you have been following news about the 2008 presidential elections?

Political Interest ("Talk Politics"): On a scale of 1 to 10, with 1 being NEVER and 10 being REGULARLY, how often would you say you talk about politics with family, friends, co-workers, fellow students, or others?

Most News: How have you been getting most of your news about the current campaign for President of the United States? From television, from newspapers, from radio, or from the Internet?

Civic Knowledge: Index of responses to the following four questions; each coded as, 1=correct answer; 0=incorrect or "don't know."

1. Who is the speaker of the U.S. House of Representatives? (Tom DeLay, George W. Bush, Dennis Hastert, Nancy Pelosi, None of these individuals, I don't know).
2. Do you know which party has a majority in the House and Senate of the U.S. Congress? (Republicans, Democrats, The Democrats control the House and the Republicans control the Senate, The Republicans control the House and the Democrats control the Senate, I don't know).
3. Which political party is more conservative? (Republicans, Democrats, I don't know).
4. How much of a majority is required for the U.S. Senate and House of Representatives to override a presidential veto? (One-third, One-half, Two-thirds, Three-fourths, I don't know).

Knowledge of Presidential Candidates: Index of responses to the following six questions; each coded as, 1=correct answer; 0=incorrect or "don't know."

Of the several candidates are seeking the nomination for president in 2008, do you happen to know which of the candidates:

1. Is a practicing Mormon? (Mitt Romney, Fred Thompson, Hillary Clinton, Newt Gingrich, None of these individuals, I don't know).

2. Was formerly the mayor of New York City? (Mike Huckabee, Barack Obama, Al Gore, Rudy Giuliani, None of these individuals, I don't know).

3. Is a Senator from New York State? (John McCain, Ron Paul, Hillary Clinton, Dick Cheney, None of these individuals, I don't know).

4. Is a first-term U.S. Senator from Illinois? (Barack Obama, Newt Gingrich, Nancy Pelosi, John Edwards, None of these individuals, I don't know).

5. Was a prisoner of war during the Vietnam War? (Fred Thompson, John McCain, Rudy Giuliani, Mike Gravel, None of these individuals, I don't know).

6. Was formerly a Baptist Minister? (Al Gore, Mike Huckabee, Mitt Romney, Barack Obama, None of these individuals, I don't know).

Knowledge about Campaign: Index of responses to the following eight questions; each coded as, 1=correct answer; 0=incorrect or "don't know."

1. Which of the candidates currently running for president favors making the Bush tax cuts permanent? (Barack Obama, John McCain, None of the above).

2. Which of the candidates currently running for president favors a health care plan in which the government provides coverage for most Americans? (Barack Obama, John McCain, None of the above).

3. Which of the candidates currently running for president did not vote in favor of the 2003 invasion of Iraq? (Barack Obama, John McCain, All of the above candidates voted in favor of the Iraq invasion).

4. True or False: The U.S. uncovered evidence of weapons of mass destruction in Iraq after the invasion of that country.

5. True or False: The U.S. has conclusive evidence that Saddam Hussein was involved in the planning of 9/11.

6. To the best of your knowledge, which party is in favor of drilling in the Arctic National Wildlife Refuge (ANWR) and off of the coast of the U.S. for oil? (Democrats, Republicans, Neither party).

7. In which of the following cities was the REPUBLICAN National Convention held this year? (Denver, Chicago, San Francisco, New York, Minneapolis-St. Paul).

8. In which of the following cities was the DEMOCRATIC National Convention held this year? (Denver, Chicago, San Francisco, New York, Minneapolis-St. Paul).

Table A1. Knowledge of the campaign by most campaign news from Internet

	Knowledge about candidates (Dec. 2007)		Knowledge about campaign (Sept. 2008)	
Most news Internet	.20	(.10)*	.17	(1.00)
Most news television	.03	(.10)	.02	(.09)
Partisan identification (1=Democrat)	.09	(03)**	-.18	(.03)***
Gender (1=Male)	.45	(.08)***	.44	(.08)***
Age	.13	(.02)***	.08	(.02)***
Race (1=White)	.12	(.12)	.12	(.11)
Talk about politics	.06	(.02)**	.07	(.02)***
Follow politics	.21	(.02)***	.11	(.02)***
Civic knowledge	.62	(.04)***	.37	(.04)***
Constant	-2.39	(.48)***	2.97	(.47)***
Adjusted R²	.422		.263	
N	1575		1575	

Table A2. Internet political participation by most campaign news from internet

	Post message on blog to express political opinion		Sign email or web petition		Forward political email or link to another person	
Most news Internet	.43	(.20)*	.49	(.19)**	.51	(.19)**
Most news television	-.34	(.20)	-.09	(.16)	.25	(.19)
Partisan ID (1=Dem.)	-.12	(.07)	-.23	(.06)***	.12	(.06)
Gender (1=Male)	.20	(.15)	-.16	(.13)	-.34	(.15)*
Age	.01	(.04)	.06	(.04)	.12	(.04)**
Race (1=White)	.31	(.25)	-.38	(.18)*	-.05	(.22)
Talk about politics	.19	(.04)***	.16	(.03)***	.28	(.04)***
Follow politics	.19	(.04)***	.07	(.03*)	.14	(.04)***
Civic knowledge	.13	(.09)	.10	(.07)	.13	(.08)
Constant	-4.36	(.98)***	-2.77	(.79)***	-7.01	(.93)***
LR X² (9)	214.13		155.57		238.49	
Log likelihood	-642.16		-886.44		-712.53	
N	1575		1575		1575	

Table A3. Conventional political participation by most campaign news from internet

	Written or called politician at state, local, or national level		Attend political rally, speech, or organized protest		Attended a public meeting on town or school affairs		Written letter to editor or called live radio or TV show to express opinion		Signed a written petition		Been an active member of any group that tries to influence public policy or government	
Most news Internet	.05	(.19)	.14	(.22)	.25	(.19)	-.30	(.31)	-.20	(.16)	.23	(.26)
Most news television	-.62	(.20)**	-.29	(.22)	.07	(.18)	-.68	(.32)*	-.38	(.16)*	-.10	(.26)
Partisan ID (1=Dem.)	-.18	(.07)*	-.16	(.07)*	.01	(.06)	-.13	(.11)	-.25	(.06)***	.04	(.08)
Gender (1=Male)	.04	(.16)	.00	(.17)	.03	(.15)	.32	(.26)	-.13	(.13)	.07	(.20)
Age	.05	(.04)	.01	(.05)	-.09	(.04)*	.01	(.07)	.04	(.04)	.04	(.06)
Race (1=White)	.09	(.09)	-.19	(.25)	-.17	(.21)	1.42	(.73)	-.14	(.19)	-.08	(.31)
Talk about politics	.21	(.04)***	.24	(.05)***	.17	(.03)***	.17	(.07)*	.16	(.03)***	.32	(.05)***
Follow politics	.06	(.04)	.13	(.04)**	.03	(.04)	.20	(.07)**	.02	(.03)	.07	(.05)
Civic knowledge	.07	(.09)	.30	(.10)**	.08	(.08)	.14	(.16)	.05	(.07)	.20	(.12)
Constant	-4.07	(.99)***	-4.67	(1.09)***	-1.03	(.92)	-6.47	(1.75)***	-1.87	(-2.32)*	-6.28	(1.28)***
LR X² (9)	114.29		164.34		66.68		68.98		85.88		111.53	

Table A3. continued on the following page

Table A3. continued.

	Written or called politician at state, local, or national level		Attend political rally, speech, or organized protest		Attended a public meeting on town or school affairs		Written letter to editor or called live radio or TV show to express opinion		Signed a written petition		Been an active member of any group that tries to influence public policy or government	
Log likelihood	-632.61		-536.29		-726.26		-272.00		-852.76		-423.62	
N	1575		1575				1575		1575		1575	

Table A4. *Campaign participation by most campaign news from internet*

	Personally tried to persuade another person to support particular political candidate or issue		Worn campaign button, put sticker on your car, or place sign in front of your home		Worked for a political party or campaign		Volunteer to help presidential campaign		Contribute money to presidential candidate		Voted in 2008 presidential primary	
Most news Internet	.21	(.16)	.27	(.24)	.54	(.41)	-.25	(.26)	-.08	(.26)	-.01	(.16)
Most news television	.04	(.15)	.16	(.24)	.02	(.43)	-.79	(.27)**	-.07	(.26)	.04	(.15)
Partisan ID (1=Dem.)	-.01	(.06)	-.16	(.08)*	-.15	(.12)	-.42	(.09)***	-.68	(.09)***	-.33	(.06)***
Gender (1=Male)	.12	(.13)	.08	(.18)	.02	(.28)	-.15	(.22)	.37	(.20)	.02	(.13)
Age	-.14	(.04)***	-.03	(.05)	-.08	(.08)	-.08	(.06)	.09	(.05)	.01	(.04)
Race (1=White)	.53	(.19)**	-.07	(.27)	-.20	(.43)	-.34	(.30)	-.24	(.28)	.41	(.19)*
Talk about politics	.23	(.03)***	.19	(.05)***	.15	(.08)	.21	(.06)***	.20	(.05)***	.08	(.03)*
Follow politics	.22	(.03)***	.17	(.04)***	.28	(.08)***	.22	(.05)***	.26	(.05)***	.19	(.03)***
Civic knowledge	.09	(.06)	.23	(.11)*	.40	(.20)*	.20	(.13)	.05	(.12)	.24	(.07)***
Constant	-.43	(.78)	-3.91	(1.14)**	-5.29	(1.87)**	-2.22	(1.34)	-5.17	(1.24)***	-2.11	(.78)**
LR X² (9)	357.52		133.83		80.70		142.55		216.45		228.80	
Log likelihood	-912.75		-504.99		-227.33		-375.07		-411.43		-914.91	
N	1575		1575		1575		1575		1575		1575	

Chapter 8
Participatory E-Planning:
Bridging Theory and Practice through Improvements in Technology

Stephen Kwamena Aikins
University of South Florida, USA

ABSTRACT

This chapter discusses the importance of leveraging information technology to link theory and practice of participatory planning. Citizen participation in urban planning and development processes is an important exercise that enriches community involvement in local planning decision-making. The advancement in Geographic Information Systems (GIS) and Planning Support Systems (PSS) technologies has provided the opportunity for planning agencies to adopt and facilitate participatory e-planning for improved decision-making. Despite this opportunity, studies show that a number of impediments to the widespread adoption these technologies exist. Drawing on the theoretical perspectives of planning, the literature on participatory planning and e-planning, as well as reviews of some existing technologies for supporting participatory planning practices, this chapter concludes that although a well designed participatory e-planning system could be an enabler for collaborative decision-making and help reduce tensions and conflicts that surround many urban development projects, the deliberative features of newer e-planning systems will have to be improved to move beyond general documented feedback, exploit the spatiality of the participatory environment, and allow more real-time dynamic consultation, if they are to be effective participatory tools.

INTRODUCTION AND BACKGROUND

This chapter discusses the importance of leveraging information technology (IT) to bridge the gap between theory and practice of participatory planning. The advancement in Geographic Information Systems (GIS) and Planning Support Systems (PSS) technologies has provided the opportunity for planning agencies to adopt innovative processes to aid and improve decision-making. Although studies show that a number of impediments to the widespread adoption these technologies exist, emerging

DOI: 10.4018/978-1-61520-933-0.ch008

trends point to opportunities for using GIS to facilitate participatory planning, as well as the integration of planning supporting systems with various models to help estimate urban growth, environmental, economic and social impact.

A potential value of e-planning is the use of GIS to assess the economic, fiscal, social, traffic and environmental impacts of urban development projects. A recent development, which has motivated the development of PSS, is the view of planning as "a process for articulation and negotiation among stakeholders, consensus building and dispute resolution" (Susskind and Cruikshank 1987; Leung 2003;, p. 22). Despite the potential of e-planning in enhancing citizen involvement, empirical studies appear to show mixed results. In a comparison of online and face-to-face citizens conference to determine the applicability of information and telecommunication technology in planning, Chen et al. (2009) concluded that the online mode does bring some improvement to such deliberation with online participants gaining more policy knowledge and greater opportunities than the participants in the face-to-face mode. However, in an initial evaluation, comparison and analysis of 12 participatory planning GIS applications on the basis of their usability, interactivity and visualization, Steinmann et al. (2004) concluded that a highly citizen information exchange platform is the exception rather than the rule. These results imply that in order to bridge the gap between the theoretical postulations and the practical benefits of e-planning tools from the standpoint of participatory planning, more has to be done to improve their interactive features.

While public participation in planning has a long history, the literature on e-planning is less well developed. As argued by Kingston (2006) much of the recent research in e-participation, e-democracy and what is now e-planning has attempted to map out the relationship between the citizens within a digital environment. Additionally, much of the research on e-planning has focused on specific aspects of the planning process and attempted to

mirror traditional participatory planning methods and investigate how information and telecommunication technology can enhance participatory processes. Although several studies have been conducted on the use of information technology to aid urban planning and development, (e.g. French &Skiles 1996, Warnecke et al. 1998, Yaakup et al. 2004), the role of web-based mapping in public participation in local policy decision-making (Kingston 2007), the role of citizen participation in e-planning (Kingston 2006) as well as the design of Internet tools for participatory planning (Seeger 2004, Howard & Gaborit 2007), few studies have attempted to bridge the theoretical and practical aspects of participatory e-planning. Drawing on the theoretical perspectives of planning, the literature on participatory planning and e-planning, as well as reviews of some existing technologies for supporting participatory planning practices, this chapter concludes that although a well designed participatory e-planning system could be an enabler for collaborative decision-making and help reduce tensions and conflicts that surround many urban development projects, the deliberative features of newer e-planning systems will have to be improved to move beyond general documented feedback, exploit the spatiality of the participatory environment, and allow more real-time dynamic consultation, if they are to be effective participatory tools.

THEORETICAL PERSPECTIVES OF PLANNING

The theoretical underpinnings of planning assume instrumental and communicative rationality as two key frames for planning. Instrumental (functional) rationality is based on a positivist ideal, which puts information gathering and scientific analysis at the core of planning. This approach to planning can be traced back to Auguste Comte (1798-1857) who sought to apply the methods of observation and experimentation to the study of societies and social phenomena. Theorists of rational comprehensive planning believe the more comprehensive the analyses of the planning problems, the better the plan. Instrumental rationality therefore assumes a direct relationship between the information available and the quality of decisions based on this information.

Communicative (substantive or procedural) rationality encompasses various sub-stances and focuses on an open and inclusive planning process, public participation, dialog, consensus building and conflict resolution (Innes 1996). Davidoff (1973) argues in a pluralist society, there cannot be any objective values scientifically or otherwise derived. He calls for advocate and pluralism planning whereby the planner aids democracy not only by permitting the citizen to be heard, but also to be able to become well informed about the underlying reasons for planning proposals, and be able to respond to them in the technical language of professional planners. Lindblom's (1965) incrementalist planning theory advances Davidoff's advocacy theory by focusing how agreement could be reached between diverse and conflicting interests in the planning process.

Lindblom (1965) argues the public sector planners are at the mercy of partial knowledge and future uncertainties in developing their plan due to inadequate time and material resources needed to engage in comprehensive analysis of the planning problem. As a result, planners have to concentrate only on short term planning, rely on the existing planning policy and experiences gained from former similar planning tasks, and broaden the knowledge base of planning by introducing various interest groups to the planning process. Although the incrementalist planning ideas became popular among urban planners in the 1970s due to the failures of the long-term master plans in the 1960s, it came under severe criticism by the communicative planning theorists in the 1980s and early 1990s. Other critics of incrementalist planning theory argue it builds on the existing policy by adding only small increments onto it

and by making small changes "at the margin", thereby building on the existing power relations. Therefore, incremental decisions tend to mirror the values of those already in power (Etzioni 1967, 387; Cates 1979, 528; Sager 1994, 160).

Forester (1993) argues both advocacy planning and incremental planning address the politics of planning through the dimension of uncertainty by reducing political pluralism into the coexistence of the mutually adversary interest groups that address each other strategically. He therefore distinguishes between uncertainty and ambiguity dimensions of planning problems. Uncertainty has to do with the technical dimension of planning, and is the lack of information of the planned object in its present and some future state, as well as the lack of time and resources for the rational programming of planning work. Ambiguity, on the other hand, has to do with the political dimension of planning that concerns the legitimacy of the ends and means of planning. Therefore, the planner facing uncertainty is more likely to be in search for more information while the planner facing ambiguity will likely be in search for practical judgement (Forester 1993). Parallel to the distinction between the technical (uncertainty) and political (ambiguity) dimensions of planning is Habermas' (1987) division of society into 'lifeworld' and its subsystems – the media of power and money. The Habermasian planning theory describes lifeworld as the domain of undominated communication where mutual understanding is sought. According to Habermas, the rationalization of the lifeworld makes possible the emergence and growth of subsystems whose independent imperatives turn back destructively upon the lifeworld itself (Harbermas 1987, 186).

Following Harbermas, Mantysalo (2000) argues the media of power and money are decisive in planning communication according to both advocacy and incremental planning. However, ambiguity would require lifeworldy communications, which is oriented towards mutual understanding instead of self-regarded success. Consequently, legitimate planning communication should aim at mutual understanding between the participants, instead of shallow bargaining and power plays between the self-regulated interest groups. Critics of the Habermasian planning theory (McGuirk 2001; Hillier 2000, 2002; Flyvbjerg 1998), who follow the power analytics of the French philosopher Michael Foucault, argue that although power is embedded in the mechanisms of bureaucratization and commodification society, it cannot be seen as an "outer distortion" to the lifeworld because it construes the social and cultural conditions under which people build up their self-conceptions and societal roles.

From the above perspectives, it can be determined that while instrumental and communicative theoretical stances are often viewed as competing (Mannheim 1940; Sager 1990, Yifachel 1999), the role of information is relevant to both instrumental and communicative rationality and not restricted to any one particular stance. Thus, participants in the planning process rely on many types of "information," including the formal analytic reports and quantitative measures, as well as the understanding and meaning attached to planning issues and activities (Innes 1998).). Additionally, since the output of planning efforts have impact on the planning community, the involvement of stakeholders in the planning process in the information age can be deemed beneficial. In this regard, information technology related planning tools like geographic information science and technology have begun to contribute to the planning practice, and in some areas as the developments transcend the "communicate" versus "calculate" dichotomy (Nedovic'-Budic' 2000). Central to the contribution of information technology to the practice of participatory planning is the need to conceptualize and operationalize the participatory mechanisms that will bridge the cap between theory and practice.

BRIDIGING THEORY AND PRACTICE OF PARTICIPATORY PLANNING

Citizen participation is a process which provides private individuals an opportunity to influence public decisions and has long been a component of the democratic decision-making process. The root of citizen participation can be traced to ancient Greece and Colonial New England. How best to involve citizens in government decision-making processes has been a concern since the creation of the nation. Urban scholars suggest that local government has the best opportunity to promote face-to-face interaction between the elected officials and the populace (Saltzstein 2003). Based on this, there is a strong tradition of fostering citizen involvement in local political decision-making. Cogan, Sharpe & Hertzberg (1986 .284) identify five benefits of citizen participation to the planning process. These are information and ideas on public issues; public support for planning decisions; avoidance of protracted conflicts and costly delays; reservoir of goodwill which can carry over to future decisions; and spirit of cooperation and trust between the agency and the public.

Before the 1960s, government processes and procedures were designed to facilitate "external" participation. Citizen participation was institutionalized in the mid-1960s with President Lyndon Johnson's Great Society programs (Cogan, Sharpe & Hertzberg 1986, p. 283). During that decade, the creation of Citizen Participation Organizations was a requirement for local governments to receive Community Development Block Grants. Allowing citizen boards to make resource allocation decisions is thought to foster high levels of social capital (Putnam 1993). Using social capital theory, the citizens represent key stakeholders for government programs and their input is solicited since they are the most likely to be impacted by the decision being made. In the area of planning, citizen involvement has grown in the United States with the advocacy planning movement during the 1960s (Howard & Gaborit

2007), and in other parts of the world. In recent decades, participatory planning has not only expanded, but has also been reshaped and redefined by politicians, planning professionals, developers, activists and citizens.

In discussing the theory of citizen participation, DeSario & Langton (1987) define and analyze two broad decision-making structures- the technocratic approach, and the democratic approach. Technocracy is defined as the application of technical knowledge, expertise, techniques and methods to problem solving. Democracy, as defined by DeSario & Langton (1987), refers to citizen involvement activities in relation to government planning and policy making. Technocratic approach to decision-making, which reflects instrumental rationality, has historically been applied to urban and regional planning decisions. A key argument in favour of this approach is that trained staff "experts" are best suited to make complex technical decisions. However, Nelkin & Pollack (1981 p. 274) concluded that scientific and technocratic approaches not only failed to solve social problems but often contributed to them. According to Nelkin and Pollack, the notion that the "cure is often worse than the disease" becomes increasingly important as the technology provides alternative solutions to public policy issues. It follows therefore that to avoid the "cure being worse than the disease" the inputs of citizens who can "provide practical insights into the causes of the disease and potential solutions" is essential.

The variety of practical techniques available to planners to solicit public input in the planning process to enhance democratic decision-making range from basic open meetings to more sophisticated techniques such as the Delphi and Nominal Group techniques. The Delphi working method support the participation of all stakeholders. In contrast to commonly used discussion techniques, the Delphi method visualizes the opinions of all people present in the meeting. Small cards with text up to ten words are clustered, discussed and then rewarded with points for quick insight in

priority. This ensures equal input from all stakeholders. Another group practical technique that has become common for developing regional land-use scenarios is visioning and scenario-building tools. Visioning is typically performed in cooperative, inclusive process among stakeholders – business owners, community residents, interest groups, and local officials, resulting in broad goals and principles which can guide future policies and plans (Lemp et al. 2008).

Visioning is a highly community oriented planning technique used to create regional land use and transportation goals (Federal Highway Administration (1996). Unlike land-use modelling, it is not a means to predict a community's future development based on historic trends and market forces. Instead, it offers stakeholders an opportunity provide input via media such as public meetings and community surveys to help determine development features most important to the community members and allow them to manage and create a regional feature that accommodates all stakeholders' interests (Federal Highway Administration (1996). Visioning projects typically result in a broad vision and associated strategies for a 20 to 30 year horizon, consistent with typical land-use and transportation endeavours (Lemp et al. 2008). The nature of participatory planning exercises like visioning embody value decisions and technical decisions based on the analysis and resolution of both scientific and normative social issues.

Kantrowitz (1975) identified three separate types of policy decisions; 1) technical decisions that are based solely on the application and extrapolation of scientific issues; (2) value decisions that are concerned with the resolution of important normative or societal issues; and (3) mixed decisions that have both technical and value components. The importance of participatory planning such as visioning lies in the fact that urban and regional planning decisions frequently affect social values. Additionally, although scientific information can provide guidance with respect to value decisions, it is rarely the sole determinant, and that technical approach to decision-making is difficult to apply successfully to social problems because social goals are often complex, conflicting and unclear (DeSario & Langton 1987). This implies democratic decision-making, which reflects communicative rationality and has a good blend of both technical and value components, could be beneficial in addressing social problems through collaboration and consensus building to help increase acceptance of complex decisions pertaining to social problems. Democratic decision-making, in contrast to bureaucratic or technical decision-making, is based on the assumption that all who are affected by a given decision have the right to participate in the making of that decision. Participation can be direct in the classical democratic sense, or can be through representatives for their point of view in a pluralist-republican model (Kweit & Kweit 1986, 22).

In the United States, community involvement planning projects that combine technical and value components have taken proactive and crucial roles nation-wide in ensuring community involvement in the process while cultivating regional support (Lemp et al. 2008). This was facilitated by the passage of the 1969 National Environmental Policy Act (NEPA) (42 U.S.C. 4332) and the 1991 Intermodal Surface Transportation Efficiency Act (ISTEA 1991). An example is the Baltimore Vision 2030 effort which included focus groups stakeholder interviews, regional workshops, and phone surveys to solicit community input on the preferred future vision of the region (Baltimore Regional Transportation Board [BRTB] 2003). Similarly, the leaders of Phoenix's Valley Vision 2025 (Maricopa Association of Governments [MAG] 2000) and Envision Utah (2003) emphasized community involvement by conducting interviews and holding workshops, meetings, and committees as part of the community oriented planning process.

Lang (1986) suggests that traditional comprehensive planning processes are insufficient and advocates more interactive approach to planning. He suggests conventional planning tends to be dominated by a technical/analytic style where the planner is a detached value-neutral expert advising decision-makers about the best way to accomplish their goals and serve the public interest. This implies as an instrumental rationality-based approach to planning, the emphasis is on data collection and analysis as the means to finding the best solutions to problems and developing a technically sound plan. The implicit assumption is that better information leads to better decisions. Therefore, success in conventional planning is measured by the extent to which the objective of the plan is achieved (Lang 1986). On the contrary, interactive planning, as a form of democratic decision-making, is based on the assumption that open, participative processes lead to better decisions. In an effort to bridge the gap between technical complexity and theory-based values, the planner engages directly with stakeholders to gain support, build consensus, identify acceptable solutions, and secure implementation. Success in interactive planning is measured by the extent to which balance can be achieved among competing interests and consensus is reached on appropriate actions (Lang 1986).

To successfully bridge the gap between theory and practice, outcome of community involvement in the planning process should meet anticipated goals. To accomplish this, guiding principles are developed to evaluate alternative future development scenarios and to shape policies and strategies to support the vision. This practice has been demonstrated by Southern California Association of Governments [SCAG] (2004), and the Sacramento Area Council of Governments [SACG] (2005). Such guiding principles are usually developed through public input and various outreach initiatives (MAG 2000). This is important because in participatory planning, the perception of stakeholders and planners should be seriously considered to ensure successful outcome. Well planned citizen involvement programs relate the expectations of both the planner and the citizen. Arnstein's (1969) "ladder of citizen participation" can assist the planner in aligning his or her perception of a program's purpose and those of citizen participants.

Participatory planning projects such as visioning normally end with the development of broad policies and implementation of strategies that are reflective of the unique nature of each region. The degree to which a vision is realized depends upon the quality of the public involvement and consensus building used in the process, as well as the feasibility of the preferred scenario (Lemp et al. 2008). Additionally, each region faces unique issues and challenges in making its community developed planning outcome relevant and realistic. In the case of Phoenix's Valley 2025, the process resulted in the development of four distinct scenarios. These included a base case or 'do nothing different' scenario, an urban revitalization scenario with significant infill development, a scenario development focused on city centers, and a fringe growth scenario. Thus in the end, the output of community developed planning process could be fully adopted, partially adopted or ignored depending on the quality of public involvement and realistic scenarios developed (Lemp et al. 2008). In this regard, the case can be made that the adoption of such output will depend on the improvements in information availability and accessibility, as well as the democratization of the planning process, which could be facilitated through interactive e-government.

E-GOVERNMENT AND DEMOCRATIZATION OF E-PLANNING

There has been a growing attention over the last decade on conceptualization of e-government (Bellamy & Taylor 1998, Garson 1999, Heeks 2001, Gronlund 2002). Some scholars argue the use of information and communication technologies to democratize government processes may be conceptualized on the basis of the idea that citizens need to be able to access information, to deliberate and discuss political issues, and to vote electronically or exert effective indirect influence on decision-making (Gross 2002, Barber 1984). Such information availability and accessibility could help to reduce the information asymmetry that plaques the participation process and ensure informed citizen participants in the policy process, including participatory planning. Others suggest one can apply the kind of conventional e-government development stage approach to the practices of e-democracy (Macintosh et al 2002 p. 235). Within the frame of e-government, the issue of participation and democratic governance have gradually become popular even to the extent that that the focus of the whole idea of e-government has ultimately been perceived by many as the means to improve interaction between government and citizens (Anttroiko 2004, Gronlund 2002).

The above reality implies that for policy makers and government officials to democratize government processes such as planning, they need to apply a citizen centered approach to fully utilize the local potential and to maintain their legitimacy in the eyes of the local community (Anttroiko 2004). The Internet has been advocated as one avenue by which apathy can be appreciably reduced to enable citizens to have increased access to information, provide substantial input into government decision-making and foster political community (Klotz 2004, Johnson & Kaye 2003, Trippi 2004). Despite scholarly interest in the Internet's potential to improve citizen participation, empirical studies show that although the Internet has great potential to improve government-citizen relations, many governments at all levels have not taken advantage of this potential to improve web site features to enhance web-enabled governance through online citizen participation in the policy process (West 2005, Needham 2004, Global e-Policy and e-Governance Institute and Rutgers University e-Governance Institute 2003, 2005, Jensen and Venkatesh 2007).

In a study of the websites of 582 cities with a population of 50,000 or more in the 2000 Census, (Conroy & Evans-Cowley 2004) found 35% provided an email address for citizens to contact the office, 74% offered the zoning ordinance, 55% had plans, and 37% minutes of planning meeting. In a comparative analysis of British and American executive and legislative branch websites, Needham (2004) argues that in practice, e-government "has primarily been conceived of as a way to expand the provision of services and information" and that from the standpoint of participatory objectives, "the experience of electronic government in the United Kingdom and United States is one of limited ambition and mixed achievement.

In an analysis of the most relevant issues driving e-government in 100 cities in the world, the Global e-Policy and e-Government Institute and Rutgers University e-Governance Institute (2003) found that 56.3% of the city web sites did not allow users to provide comments or feedback either to individual government departments / agencies through online forms, or to elected officials. In addition, 73.8% of the city web sites did not have online bulletin board or chat capabilities for gathering citizen input on public issues, and 78.8% did not have discussion forums on policy issues. In a subsequent study that replicated the study conducted in 2003, the Global e-Policy and e-Governance Institute and Rutgers e-Governance Institute (2005) found only 31% of municipality websites worldwide provide online forms for feedback to government departments or agencies. In addition, 68% did not have online bulletin boards or chat capabilities for gathering citizen input, and 75% did not have online discussion forum on policy issues.

Although most planning agencies have placed large amounts of information online, these are viewed as analogous to newspaper notices or the creation of official record for public view in person. Items posted online include planning board agendas, meeting minutes and a wide range of planning documents often in PDF format. Ad-

ditionally, many have adopted web GIS systems allowing visitors to view GIS data and create their own maps (Goodspeed 2008). Although posting documents online does provide access to citizens, and could facilitate participatory planning, it does not necessarily generate citizen involvement in the planning process. As argued by Tulloch and Shapiro (2003), while access and participation are related, they are clearly distinct issues and that different combinations of the presence or absence of access and participation do impact successful use of participation GIS systems. This implies that in addition to facilitating citizen access to planning information, government agencies need to put in place the necessary policies and procedures to enhance participatory planning.

In *Community Participation Methods in Design and Planning*, Sanoff (2000) states that there are three primary purposes for participation: (1) involve people in the decision-making process; (2) provide people with a voice in design and decision-making; and (3) promote a sense of community. Wulz (1986) suggests that there are five questions that need to be asked when planning a project that utilizes public participation. These are (a) who is to be involved? (b) what are the tasks to be performed? (c) where should the participation lead? (d) how should people be involved? and (e) when in the planning and design process is participation needed? The tasks to be performed may include generating ideas, identifying need, information dissemination, information gathering, conflict identification and resolution, opinion poll, design proposal review or simply as an outlet to vent emotions towards a project (Seeger 2004). Burns (1979) also argues the tasks and the goals of public participation can be grouped into four distinct categories: awareness, perception, decision-making and implementation. Indeed, the ability of planners to understand the primary purposes of participation, the necessary questions to ask and the tasks required could put them in a better position to design and implement appropriate policies and procedures as well as the specifications for planning websites that include features for real time dynamic consultation and access. Any effective implementation of policies and procedures can help to bridge the gap between theory and practice only if it builds on the democratization of the process and information availability by effectively leveraging information technology through enhancement of the consultative and interactive features of e-planning systems.

LEVERAGING TECHNOLOGY TO LINK THEORY AND PRACTICE

A well designed participatory e-planning system can help bridge the gap between theory and practice by serving as an enabler for collaborative decision-making, and reducing conflict and mistrust between planning officials and the local community. Research efforts over the past decade have mainly focused on the development of a range of technical tools to help support and implement e-planning than the use of technology to enhance participatory processes (Carver 2001, Craig 2002, Hudson-Smith 200, Kingston 2002). These tools have mainly been GIS focus though more recently a growing number of these have focused on 3 dimensional visualizations (Hudson-Smith 2003). Much of the e-planning research has focused on the technical development of e-planning systems such as participatory GIS (PGIS), virtual environments and back office integration, rather than democratic dimensions such as visioning. In the area of policy development, the literature focuses on the opportunity e-planning provides in terms of efficiency gains and the ability to receive applications online, cutting down on paperwork (PARSOL 2004, Kingston 2006).

The view of planning as "a process for articulation and negotiation among stakeholders, consensus building and dispute resolution" (Susskind and Cruikshank 1987; Leung 2003;, p. 22) is a recent development, which has motivated the development of PSS. Taking advantage of ubiq-uitous data, neighbourhoods and environmental groups have leveraged PGIS to support advocacy activities (Carver, Evans, Kingston & Thurston 2001; Sieber 2006). As argued by Forester (1989) and Innes (1996), the key to claiming validity of negotiated conclusions and planning actions are institutions and the personnel that facilitate inclusive and sincere conversations. As a key component of PSS, the simplest forms of PGIS can make data available to neighborhood groups, while the most sophisticated ones can solicit input from participation about conditions, plans, and proposals (Talen 2000), and link these comments to map locations when appropriate. In this regard, the use of tools and technology such as PSS help participants in the planning process to visualize alternative scenarios and their impacts, and to actively make and examine assumptions in real time.

PGIS provides the framework for collaborative decision making (Shiffer 1992). For example, the National Neighborhood Indicators Partnership (NNIP) aims to capture grassroots information on neighborhood conditions and make it available to neighborhood groups for use in community development activities. This democratization of information has empowered a number of non-traditional groups by providing them with GIS data analysis capabilities (Drummond & French 2008). In the area of land use planning, the United State Department of Interior's bureau of land management (BLM) has launched a new program that creates more efficient business practices and encourages an open and collaborative land use planning process through leveraging information technology. BLM administers 261 million acres of public lands in a manner that sustains the health, diversity, and productivity of these lands for the use and enjoyment of future generations. As part of the e-planning project, BLM has partnered with ESRI to build a common planning data model and core land management tools for the BLM enterprise. Powered by ESRI software programs ArcIMS and ArcSDE, the project is run from the

Planning, Assessment and Community Support Group in the BLM's Washington office, the BLM National Science and Technology Center in Denver, Colorado, and the BLM Alaska state office in Anchorage, Alaska (Zulick 2003).

Effective participatory e-planning depends on properly designed online participation tools that can be used in online design and planning situations, including community mapping, project visualization, land use planning and visual preference analysis (Seeger 2004). Table 1 details the capabilities/features of Internet-based participatory tools that may be customized for online design and planning. Besides the usual online participatory tools like chat rooms, HTML web content form, email/group mail, List serves, web forums, blogs, web conferencing, video chart and instant messaging, Geo-based web tools such as ESRI's ArchIMS provide access to spatial data. Others like the Web Mapping Server (WMS), Geo Tools, the University of Minnesota's MapServer, and Web Mapping Testbed (WMT) protocols all provide an open source (OpenGIS) development environment for building spatially enabled Internet application using JAVA or scripting languages like Perl and PHP. However, as argued by Seeger (2004) the usability of these tools is limited in the realm of design and planning where much of the information to be presented has visual and spatial qualities. Thus, although these GIS-based tools are rich in spatial interactivity, they lack some of the video and multi-path communication features that are desirable for online participation. Indeed, the missing features of these systems include participatory environments that can be leveraged to foster collaboration and allow real-time consultative engagement to help improve planning decisions. In a study of how web-based mapping tools improve local policy decision-making, Kingston (2007) concluded while the system is capable if increasing public access to decision-making process and improving the types of services offered, several issues including possible moderator roles in the discussions remained to be addressed.

Carver (2001) argues GIS-based decision tools should provide the means by which stakeholders can explore a decision problem using existing information, experiment possible solutions, view other people's ideas, formulate their own views, and share these with wider community. In response to transportation planning requirements and resources developed by the United States Department of Transportation (DOT) and the Environmental Protection Agency (EPA), community participatory planning processes frequently include the use of GIS-based scenario planning tools to generate and evaluate basic impact of alternative future land-use patterns. Commonly used scenario-planning models include GIS-based software programs such as the EPA's Smart Growth Index, CommunityViz, California's PLACE'S and Charlottesville's CorPlan. Each of these tools tend to support substantial community participation in generating and evaluating multiple scenarios (Lemp et al. 2008). The potential role of PGIS in bridging the gap between e-planning theory and practice should be to help minimize conflict and arrive at decisions that are acceptable to the majority of stakeholders through consensus building approaches based on awareness of the spatial implication of a decision problem. This implies the need to leverage technology to help provide better data and information for public consumption to assist them in forming a considered opinion (Carver 2001, Kingston 2006).

Although Craig et al. (2002) suggest that GIS is a powerful tool for empowering communities rather than an invasive technology that advantage some citizens and organizations while marginalizing others, a major criticism of GIS is the degree of technical expertise required to use the software, thereby depriving the less technically sophisticated communities of its use (Pickles 1995). Similarly, Vonk, Geertman & Schot (2005) identified a number of impediments to the widespread adoption of planning support systems, including lack of awareness of such systems, lack of experience with them, and lack of recognition of their value.

Table 1. Basic tools for potential support participatory e-planning

Online Tool	Full Capabilities/Features	Partial Capabilities/Limitations
Rich Internet Application (RIA)	One-way, two-way and multi-way communication, as well as videos, graphic interactivity, text-based interface, and static graphics.	Partially support geo-spatial data.
ArcIMS, Web Map Server, Geo Tools, U-MN Map Server	One-way communication, static graphics, graphic interactivity and geo-spatial data.	Partially supports text-based interface. Does not support two-way and multi-way communication. Requires technical expertise in using the software.
Video Conferencing	Two-way and multi-way communication, as well as video.	Does not support text-based interface, static graphics, graphic interactivity and geo-spatial data.
Text Graphic HTML Survey	One-way communication, text-base interface and static graphics.	Partially supports two-way and multi-way communication, graphic interactivity and video. Does not support geo-spatial data.
Instant Messaging	One-way and two-way communication and text-based interface.	Partially supports static interface and video. Does not support graphic interactivity and geo-spatial data. Additional tools required for multi-way communication capability.
Web Forums/BLOGS	One-way and multi-way communication. Partially supports two-way communication and static graphics.	Additional tools required for graphic interactivity and videos. Does not support geo-spatial data.
E-Mail/Group Mail	One-way and two-way communication and text-based interface.	Partially supports multi-way communication and static graphics. Does not support graphic interactivity.
HTML Web Comment Form	One-way communication, text-based interface and static graphics. Partially supports multi-way communication and graphic interactivity.	Additional tools required for video and geo-spatial data.

Source: Adapted from Seeger (2004), Customizable Internet Participatory Tools

The latest generation of online tools that can be used to create enhanced online public participation products are Rich Internet Applications (RIA). They combine the functionality of desktop software applications with the broad reach and low-cost deployment of web applications, resulting in significantly more intuitive, responsive, and effective user experiences (Seeger 2004). Open source platform allows for dynamic, data-driven visual and geo-spatial public participation solutions to be created with the combination of RIA and LAMP (Linux/Unix system, Apache web server, MySQL database and Perl/Python/PHP scripting language).

An example of an RIA that could enhance participatory planning, by creating application that supplements traditional face-to-face meetings, through kiosk or Internet browsers, is the Visual and Spatial Survey Builder (VaSS Builder). It utilizes Macromedia Flash MX 2004, MySQL databases and PHP to create customized participatory web application. Additionally, VaSS Builder uses dynamic building techniques similar to those used by websites such as www.flashhuilder.net and www.flashbannernow.com and allows the rapid building of websites, easy filling of online form and uploading of graphic content. It also allows the project administrator to create an online visual and spatial survey and customize it to fit their specific needs without having to write code or redesign the graphical interface (Seeger 2004). With the shortcomings of existing GIS-based participatory e-planning systems, improvements in interactive and consultative features is needed to help bridge the gap between theory and practice of participatory e-planning, and enhance community involvement in the urban planning and design process.

FUTURE TRENDS

To ensure a good and effective participatory planning system, there is the need to improve existing software by making virtual environment available to urban planning. By enhancing the way human beings can visualize, manipulate, and interact with computers and extremely complex data in urban planning setting, existing technology can be improved with more interactive features. Manoharan (2003) has worked on designing a prototype virtual environment to be used in the urban planning process. As Howard and Gaborit (2007) point out, although it is one of the most complete models regarding public participation, as it allows people to view information about the proposal itself, and it stores user comments, the public consultation features are basic. This implies that for future e-planning systems to be effective as enablers, the deliberative features will have to move beyond mere documented feedback, exploit the spatiality of the environment, and allow more real-time dynamic consultation.

Perhaps, one innovative way of improving the interactive features of e-planning systems is to integrate versions of e-participation platform such as - Gov2DemOSS with customized future versions of spatially enabled Internet tools such as ArcIMS, Web Mapping Server (WMS), Geo Tools, MapServer, and Web Mapping Testbed (WMT). Gov2DemOSS e-participation platform is an open source platform that provides user friendly channel for interaction between elected officials and citizens, and has the potential for extensive customization to suit the needs of planners in their quest to democratize the planning process, if modified and effectively integrated into e-planning systems. Considering the severe budgetary constraints affecting the investment capacity of most local governments and their planning agencies, adoption of more open source platforms for possible integration with geospatial tools is worth exploring.

The involvement of the public in urban planning and design processes helps to boost mutual trust and confidence between planning officials and citizens. The advent of the Internet provides tremendous opportunity for planning officials and designers to enhance existing GIS-based tools to facilitate online participation in the planning process. However, the challenge faced by planning officials in participatory e-planning is that, the characteristics of online interaction pose a significant challenge for the development of trust. This is because the effectiveness of planning in the information age depends partly on a critical mass of visible participants who actively engage in the planning process to help build respective communities. Therefore, policy makers, community leaders and designers of participatory planning tools should think of pragmatic ways of stimulating active online participation. By integrating e-government participatory platforms such as Gov2DemOSS into spatially enabled Internet tools, citizens who log on for consultative engagements in other government operations could be enticed to fully engage in the planning process given the appropriate access controls.

Some studies (Nonnecke & Preece 2000) suggest, lurkers, the invisible online participants who regularly read messages without responding, are reported to make up as much as 90% of the participants in some online communities. However, other studies show only a small percentage of people intend not to participate from the outset and that lurking varies depending on group context. Thus, trust in other group members can act a lubricant for active participation (Bargh & Mackenna 2004). As argued by Prieto-Martin (2005), an online participation system reaches its maximum potential when it is used continually, thereby helping to provide permanent "virtual web space for participation" and to enable government officials to incorporate citizens into decision-making processes. To help accomplish this, future participatory planning systems should be designed to include functions which serve to make users feel a bond with the participation system, thus inspiring them to want to continue using it.

An example is the possibility of personalizing the system's work environment in order to streamline the tasks that it carries out most frequently. This could lead to the fostering of greater and more frequent citizen involvement in issues affecting the locality. In order to adapt the system to the needs and capacities of all the different actors involved in the citizen participation processes, a a needs assessment of the local jurisdiction can be conducted prior to implementation. According to Prieto-Martin (2005), this will enable the system design to contemplate the interests, objectives, resources and interrelationships of all stakeholders. Additionally, it is important to continuously assess and improve the system's adaptation by engaging representatives of all stakeholders through dialogue and collaboration during the system design, development and trial phases.

In the design of participatory e-planning tools to help democratize the urban planning process, the planning agencies should consider and address the problem of digital divide to enhance inclusiveness. Although the United States has almost 70% Internet penetration rate (Internet Stats Report 2006), certain socioeconomic groups continue to lag behind, and may be excluded from the participatory planning process if appropriate steps are not taken. The PEW Internet American Life Project (2006) suggests that age, educational, and income backgrounds do have considerable influence on citizens' Internet usage. While 88% of 18-29 year olds, and 84% of 30-49 year olds go online, only 32% of 65 years or older go online. In addition, Just 54% of adults living in households with less than $30,000 annual income go online, versus 80% of those whose income is between $30,000-$50,000, and 86% of adults in households with annual income between $50,000 and $75,000. Furthermore, while 40% of adults who have less than a high school education use the Internet, 64% of adults with a high school diploma go online, and 91% of those with at least a college degree go online.

The potential exclusion of particular sectors of society from participating in web-based exercises due to the digital divide is a concern that has been expressed in many studies. As argued by Warschauer (2003), participation requires not only physical access to computers and connectivity, but also access to the requisite skills and knowledge, content and language, community and social support to be able to use ICT for meaningful ends. It follow therefore that in order to enhance participatory e-planning, agencies have to not only improve existing technologies and provide access but also explain the use of technical tools through online tutorials on their websites and provide training to needy users.

CONCLUSION

Citizen participation in urban planning and development processes is an important exercise that enriches community involvement in the planning and management of their locality. A well designed participatory e-planning system can serve as an enabler for collaborative decision-making and help reduce conflict and mistrust between planning officials and the local community. However, the view of planning as "a process for articulation and negotiation among stakeholders, consensus building and dispute resolution" is a recent development that calls for continual exploration. While e-planning has huge potential to improve public participatory processes, the geographical capabilities as well as interactivity and consultative features of many existing systems in the field are limited, and improvements are needed to help bridge the gap between participatory e-planning theory and practice. This implies that for future e-planning systems to be effective as enablers, the deliberative features of existing software will have to move beyond mere documented feedback, exploit the spatiality of the participatory environment, and allow more real-time dynamic consultation.

REFERENCES

Anttiroiko, A. (2004). Towards citizen-centered local e-government-The case of the city of Tempere. In Khosrow-Pour, M. (Ed.), *Annals of Cases on Information Technology* (*Vol. 6*, pp. 371–385). Hershey, PA: Idea Group Publishing.

Arnstein, S. (1969). A ladder of citizen participation. *American Institute of Planning Journal, 35*, 215–224.

Baltimore Regional Transportation Board (BRTB). (2003). Vision 2030. *Final Rep.* Baltimore Metropolitan Council. Retrieved September 27, 2008 from http://baltometro.org/vision2030.org.html

Barber, B. (1984). *Strong democracy: Participatory politics for a new age.* Berkeley, CA: University of California Press.

Bargh, J. A., & Mckeanna, K. Y. (2004). The Internet and social life. *Annual Review of Psychology, 55*, 573–590. doi:10.1146/annurev.psych.55.090902.141922

Bellamy, C., & Taylor, J. (1998). *Governing in the information age.* Buckingham, UK: Open University Press.

Burns, J. (1979). *Connections: Ways to discover and realize community potentials.* New York: McGraw Hill.

Carver, S., Evans, A., Kingston, R. & Thurston, R. (2001). Public participation, GIS and cyberdemocracy: Evaluating on-line spatial decision support systems. *Environment and Planning*, B, *28*(6) 907-921.

Cates, C. (1979). Beyond muddling: Creativity. *Public Administration Review, 39*(6), 527–532. doi:10.2307/976179

Chen, D., Lin, T., Huang, T., Lee, C., & Hiaso, N. (2009). Experimental e-deliberation in Taiwan: A comparison of online and face-to-face citizens' conferences in Beitou, Taipei. In Reddick, C. C. (Ed.), *Handbook of Research on Strategies for Local E-Government and Implementation: Comparative Studies* (pp. 323–347). Hershey, PA: IGI Global.

Cogan, A., Sharpe, S., & Hertzberg, J. (1986). Citizen participation. In So, F. S., Hand, I., & Madowell, B. D. (Eds.), *The Practice of State and Regional Planning. Municipal Management Series.* Chicago: American Planning Association.

Conroy, M. M., & Evans-Cowlery, J. (2004). Informing and interacting: The use of e-government for citizen participation in planning. *Journal of E-Government, 1*(3).

Craig, W., Weiner, H., & Harris, T. (2002). *Community empowerment, public participation and Geographic Information Science.* New York: Taylor & Frances.

Davidoff, P. (1973). Advocacy and pluralism in planning. In Faludi, A. (Ed.), *A reader in planning theory* (pp. 277–296). Oxford, UK: Pergamon.

DeSario, J., & Langton, S. (Eds.). (1987). *Citizen participation in public decision making.* New York: Greenwood Press.

Dorothy, N., & Pollak, M. (1981). *The Atom Besieged.* Cambridge, MA: MIT Press.

Drummond, W. J., & French, S. P. (2008). The future of GIS. *Journal of the American Planning Association. American Planning Association, 74*(2), 161–176. doi:10.1080/01944360801982146

Envision Utah. (2003). *The history of envision Utah.* Retrieved September 27, 2008 from http://content.lib.utah.edu/FHWA/image/1423.pdf

Etzioni, A. (1967). Mixed-scanning: A third approach to decision-making. *Public Administration Review, 27*(Dec), 385–392. doi:10.2307/973394

Federal Highway Administration and Federal Transit Administration (1996). Public involvement technique for transportation decision-making. *Publication No. FHWA-PD-96-031 HEP -30/9-96/(4M)QE,* USDoT. Washington, DC.

Flyvbjerg, B. (1998). Empowering civil society: Habermas, Foucault and the question of conflict. In Douglas, M., & Friedman, J. (Eds.), *Cities for citizens* (pp. 185–211). Sussex, UK: Wiley.

Forester, J. (1993). *Planning in the face of power.* Berkeley, CA: University of California Press.

French, S. P., & Skiles, A. E. (1996). Organizational structures for GIS Implementation. In M. J. Salling (Ed.). *URISA '96 Conference Proceedings* (pp.280-293). Salt Lake City,Utah.

Garson, G. D. (1999). *Information technology and computer applications in public administration: Issues and trends.* Hershey, PA: Idea Group Publishing.

Goodspeed, R. (2008). *The Internet as a participation tool.* Retrieved July 6, 2008 from http://goodspeedupdate.com/citizen-participation-and-the-internet-in-urban-planning

Gronlund, A. (Ed.). (2002). *Electronic government: Design, applications and management.* Hershey, PA: Idea Group Publishing.

Gross, T. (2002). E-democracy and community networks: Political visions, technological opportunities and social reality. In Gronlund, A. (Ed.), *Electronic government: Design, applications and management* (pp. 249–266). Hershey, PA: Idea Group Publishing.

Habermas, J. (1987). The theory of communicative action: *Vol. 2. Lifeworld and system.* Cambridge, UK: Polity Press.

Heeks, R. (2001). *Reinventing government in the information age: International practice in IT-enabled public sector reform.* London: Routledge.

Hillier, J. (2000). Going round the back? Complex networks and informal action in local planning processes. *Environment & Planning A, 32,* 33–54. doi:10.1068/a321

Hillier, J. (2002). *Shadows of power: An allegory of prudence in land-use planning.* London, UK: Routledge.

Howard, T. L. J., & Gaborit, N. (2007). Using virtual environment technology to improve public participation in urban planning process. *Journal of Urban Planning and Development, 133*(4), 233–241. doi:10.1061/(ASCE)0733-9488(2007)133:4(233)

Hudson-Smith, A., Batty, E. S., & Batty, S. (2003). Online participation: The Woodberry down experiment. *CASA Working Paper 60.* London: CASA.

Innes, J. E. (1996). Planning through consensus building: A new view of the comprehensive planning ideal. *Journal of the American Planning Association. American Planning Association, 62*(4), 460–472. doi:10.1080/01944369608975712

Innes, J. E. (1998). Information in communicative planning. *Journal of the American Planning Association. American Planning Association, 64*(11), 52–63. doi:10.1080/01944369808975956

Jensen, M., & Venkatesh, A. (2007). Government websites and political engagement: Facilitating Citizen entry into the policy process. In B. Thossen (Ed.). *Schriftenreihe Informatic*: Vol. 23. *Towards Electronic Democracy Conference Proceedings* (pp. 55-65). Linz, Austria: Trauner Verlag.

Johnson, T. J. & Kaye, B. K. (2003). A boost or bust for democracy: How the Web influenced

Kingston, R. (2006). *The role of participatory e-planning in the new English local planning system.* Retrieved May 13, 2009, from http://www.ppgis.manchester.ac.uk/downloads/e-Planning_LDFs.pdf

Kingston, R. (2007). Public participation in local policy decision-making: The role of web-based mapping. *The Cartographic Journal*, *44*(2), 138–144. doi:10.1179/000870407X213459

Klotz, R. (2004). *The politics of Interne communication*. Lanham, MD: Rowman & Littlefield.

Kurzman, J. S. (2000). The politics of representation: Social work lessons from the advocacy planning movement. Advocates Forum, *6*(1).

Kweit, M. G., & Kweit, R. W. (1981). *Implementing citizen participation in a bureaucratic Society*. New York: Praeger.

Lang, R. (1986). Achieving integration in resource planning. In Lang, R. (Ed.), *Integrated Approaches to Resource Planning and Management*. Calgary, Canada: The University of Calgary Press.

Lemp, J. D., Zhou, B., Kockelman, K. M., & Parmenter, B. M. (2008). Visioning versus Modeling: Analyzing the Land-Use-Transportation Futures of Urban Regions. *Journal of Urban Planning and Development*, *34*(9), 97–107. doi:10.1061/(ASCE)0733-9488(2008)134:3(97)

Leung, H. J. (2003). *Land use planning made plain* (2nd ed.). Toronto, Canada: University of Toronto Press.

Lindblom, C. E. (1965). *The intelligence of democracy*. New York: The Free Press of New York.

Macintosh, A., Davenport, E., Malina, A., & Whyte, A. (2002). Technology to support participatory democracy. In Gronlund, A. (Ed.), *Electronic government: Design, application and management* (pp. 226–248). Hershey, PA: Idea Publishing Group.

Mannheim, K. (1940). *Man and society in an age of reconstruction*. New York: Harcourt, Brace & World.

Manoharan, T. (2003). *Collaborative virtual environment for planning development control in cities*. PhD Thesis. Heriot-Watt University, UK.

Mantysalo, R. (2000). *Land-use planning as inter-organizational learning*. Acta Universitatis Ouluersis Technica, C 155, Oulu. Retrieved, August 25, 2003, from http://herkules.oulu.fi/isbn9514258444/

Maricopa Association of Government (MAG). (2000). *Valley vision 2025*. Retrieved, January 24 2008 from, http://www.mag.maricopa.gov/archive/vv2025/

McGuirk, P. M. (2001). Situating communicative planning theory: Context, power and knowledge. *Environment & Planning A*, *33*, 195–217. doi:10.1068/a3355

Nedovic'-Budic', Z., Kan, R. G., JohnsTon, D. M., Sparks, R. E. & White, D. C. (2006). CommunityViz-based prototype model for assessing development impacts in a naturalized floodplain-EmiquonViz. *Journal of Urban Planning and Development*, *132*(4), 201–210. doi:10.1061/(ASCE)0733-9488(2006)132:4(201)

Needham, C. (2004). The citizen as a consumer: E-government in the United Kingdom and United States. In Gibson, R. (Eds.), *Electronic democracy: Mobilization, organization, and participation via new ICTs* (pp. 43–69). New York: Routledge.

Nonnecke, B., & Preece, J. (2000). *Lurker demographics: Counting the silent*. Paper presented at the Proceedings of CHI 2000. Hague, TheNetherlands.

PARSOL. (2004). *E-Planning and e-regulation by local authorities for local authorities*. Retrieved May 15, 2009, from http://www.planningportal.gov.uk/wps/portal/search?scope=204&langid=0

PEW Internet & American Life Project. (2006) *Total Online Activities Report*. Retrieved October 23, 2007, from http://www.pewinternet.org/trend/asp.

Political attitudes in the 1996 and 2000 presidential elections. *Harvard Journal of Press/ Politics, 8*, 9-34.

Prieto-Martin, P. (2005). *Virtual environments for citizen participation*. Retrieved December 15, 2008, from, http://www.e-participa.org/en/files/e_Participa.VirtualEnvironmentsForCitizenParticipation.doc.

Putnam, R. (1993). *Making democracy work*. Princeton, NJ: Princeton University Press.

Sacramento Area Council of Governments (SACOG) and Valley Vision. (2005). *Sacramento region blue print: Preferred blueprint alternative*. Retrieved, March 17, 2008, from http://www.sacregionblueprint.org/sacregionblueprint/

Sager, T. (1990). *Communicate or calculate*. Stockholm: NORDPLAN.

Sager, T. (1994). Communicative planning theory. Avebury, UK: Aldershot.

Saltzstein, A. L. (2003). *Governing American urban areas*. Belmont, CA: Wadsworth Thomson Learning.

Sanoff, H. (2000). *Community participation methods in design and planning*. New York: John Wiley & Sons, Inc.

Seeger, C. J. (2004). *VaSS Builder: A customizable Internet tool for community planning and design participation*. Retrieved May 11, 2009, from http://www.kolleg.loel.hs-anhalt.de/studiengaenge/mla/mla_fl/conf/pdf/conf2004/41_seeger-c.pdf

Shiffer, M. J. (1992). Towards a collaborative planning system. *Environment and Planning B, 19*(6), 709–722. doi:10.1068/b190709

Sieber, R. (2006). Public participation geographic information systems: A literature review and framework. *Annals of the American Association of Geographers, 96*(3), 491–507. doi:10.1111/j.1467-8306.2006.00702.x

Southern California Association of Governments [SCAG]. (2004). *Southern California compass: Growth Vision Report*. Retrieved September 28, 2008, from http://www.socalcompass.org//about/index.html

Steinmann, R., Krek, A., & Blaschke, T. (2004). Analysis of online GIS participatory applications with respect to the differences between the U.S. and Europe. *Paper Published in the Proceedings of Urban Data Management Symposium*, Chioggia, Italy.

Susskind, L., & Cruikshank, J. (1987). *Breaking the impasse: Consensual approaches to resolving public disputes*. New York: Basic Books.

Talen, E. (2000). Bottom-up GIS: A new a tool for individual and group expression in participatory planning. *Journal of the American Planning Association. American Planning Association, 66*(3), 491–807.

The Global e-policy and e-governance institute & Rutgers University e-governance institute. (2003). *Assessing websites and measuring e-government index among 100 world cities*. Study sponsored by division of public administration and development, department of economic and social affairs, United Nations.

The Global e-policy and e-governance institute & Rutgers University e-governance institute. (2005). *Assessing websites and measuring e-government index among 100 world cities*. Study sponsored by division of public administration and development, department of economic and social affairs, United Nations.

Trippi, J. (2004). *The revolution will not be tele-vised: Democracy, the Internet, and the overthrow of everything.* New York: HaperCollins.

Tulloch, D. L., & Shapiro, T. (2003). The inter-section of data access and public participation: Impacting GIS users' success? *URISA Journal,* 15(2), 55–60.

Vonk, G., Geertman, S., & Schot, R. (2005). Bottlenecks blocking the widespread usage of planning support systems. *Environment & Plan-ning A, 37*(5), 909–924. doi:10.1068/a3712

Warnecke, L., Beattie, J., Cheryl, K., Lyday, W., & French, S. (1998). *Geographic information technology in cities and counties: A nationwide as-sessment.* Washington, DC: American Forests.

Warscheuer, M. (2003). *Technology and social inclusion: Rethinking the digital divide.* Cam-bridge, MA: MIT Press.

West, D. M. (2005) *State and Federal government in the United States, Providence, RI: Center for Public Policy, Brown University.* Retrieved Sep-tember 30, 2006, from http://www.insidepolitics.org/egovt05us.pdf

Wulz, F. (1986). The concept of participation. *Design Studies, 7*(3), 153–162. doi:10.1016/0142-694X(86)90052-9

Yaakup, A. B., Abu Bakar, Y., & Sulaiman, S. (2004, May 10-12). Web-based GIS for col-laborative planning and public participation toward better governance. In *Proceedings of the 7th International seminar on GIS for Developing Countries.* Johor Bahru

Yifachel, O. (1999). Planning theory at a crossroad: The third Oxford Conference. *Journal of Plan-ning Education and Research, 18*(3), 267–270. doi:10.1177/0739456X9901800308

KEY TERMS AND DEFINITIONS

E-Planning: The use of IT-based systems such as geographical information system (GIS), database management system (DBMS) and plan-ning support system (PSS) for managing urban planning and development processes.

Geographic Information System (GIS): A system enables data from a wide variety of sources and data formats to be integrated together in a common scheme of geographical referencing, thereby providing up-to-date information.

Planning Support System (PSS): A system that facilitates the process of planning via inte-grated developments usually based on multiple technologies and common interface. PSS con-tributes to data management, analysis, problem solving, and design, decision-making, and com-munication activities.

Citizen Participation: Citizen involvement in decision-making pertaining to the management of public affairs, including public policy delib-erations. Traditional citizen participation occurs through mechanisms such as hearing, citizen forums, community or neighborhood meetings, community outreaches, citizen advisory groups, individual citizen representation, etc.

E-Participation: The use of the Internet to support active citizen involvement in decision making pertaining to the management of public affairs, including public policy deliberations. This includes using government web sites to solicit citizens' opinion on policies and administrative services, to allow citizens to provide online feed-back to administrative agencies and the legislature, and to stimulate online public discussions on policy and the political process.

Internet Deliberative Features: Attributes that serve as democratic outreach by facilitat-ing communication, interaction and discussions between citizens and government. These include online discussion forums and feedback forms.

E-Government: Government's use of information and communication technology (ICT) to exchange information and services with citizens, businesses, and other arms of government. E-government may be applied by legislature, judiciary, or administration, in order to improve internal efficiency, the delivery of public services, or processes of democratic governance. Components are e-services, e-management, e-democracy and e-commerce.

Section 2
E–Democracy

Chapter 9
Perception Differences of Online Voting Between Young and Senior Voters

Anne Powell
Southern Illinois University Edwardsville, USA

Douglas B. Bock
Southern Illinois University Edwardsville, USA

Thomas Doellman
University of Florida, USA

Jason W. Allen
US Army, USA

ABSTRACT

This chapter presents a research study that examines the antecedents to voting intention with regard to the use of computer-based, online voting systems. The research is based on the Unified Theory of Acceptance and Use of Technology (UTAUT) model. Subjects from two different age groups (18-to-25 and 60+ years) in the United States are surveyed to determine the factors affecting their intent to use online voting systems. The results indicate that performance expectancy, social influence, and computer anxiety are factors affecting the intent to use online voting. Significant differences were found between the young adults (18-to-25) and seniors (60+ years) study groups on all four independent variables as well as on intent to use online voting. For young adults performance expectancy, social influence, and computer anxiety are significant factors affecting the intent to use online voting, while for senior citizens, performance expectancy and computer anxiety are significant factors. Ease of use was not a significant indicator of intent to use online voting for either group.

DOI: 10.4018/978-1-61520-933-0.ch009

Table 1. National voter turnout for U.S. federal elections – 1960 to 2008

Year	Eligible to Register	Registered Voters	Voter Turnout	Percentage Of Turnout
2008*	231,229,580	NA	132,618,580*	56.8%
2004	221,256,931	174,800,000	122,294,978	55.3
2000	205,815,000	156,421,311	105,586,274	51.3
1996	196,511,000	146,211,960	96,456,345	49.1
1992	189,529,000	133,821,178	104,405,155	55.1
1988	182,778,000	126,379,628	91,594,693	50.1
1984	174,466,000	124,150,614	92,652,680	53.1
1980	164,597,000	113,043,734	86,515,221	52.6
1976	152,309,190	105,037,986	81,555,789	53.6
1972	140,776,000	97,328,541	77,718,554	55.2
1968	120,328,186	81,658,180	73,211,875	60.8
1964	114,090,000	73,715,818	70,644,592	61.9
1960	109,159,000	64,833,096	68,838,204	63.1

*Source: 2008 election results: http://elections.gmu.edu/Turnout_2008G.html.

Source: Federal Election Commission. Data are drawn from Congressional Research Service reports, Election Data Services Inc., and State Election Offices. Information Please® Database, © 2008 Pearson Education, Inc. All rights reserved.

INTRODUCTION

Voting has always been viewed as a very special privilege accorded to United States citizens. This privilege applies to many other countries around the world. The early history of voting In the United States excluded suffrage for women. This changed in 1920 with the 19th amendment to the United States constitution. Also, the age at which voting privileges were extended to citizens varied among the states. The 26th amendment to the United States constitution standardized the voting age at 18 years in 1971, and this applies to all federal, state, and local elections.

Given the history of various suffrage efforts across the world, one might conclude that voting is a very important aspect of our lives. Unfortunately, while school systems teach youth about the importance of the privilege of voting, it is an obligation that is ignored by many of those eligible to vote. In countries where voter turnout is low this is viewed as a sort of social problem reflecting apathy on the part of many voters. Table

1 gives the turnout for presidential federal elections from 1960 to 2008 in the U.S. only. As you can see, the highest percentage of turnout was in 1960 with 63.1% of those eligible to vote actually casting ballots. The lowest percentage was the 1996 election with 49.1% casting a ballot, a turnout of less than 1 in every 2 voters.

In addition to the presidential elections held every four years in the United States, there are also federal elections every two years for various members of the Congress. While not shown in Table 1, voter turnout for non-presidential election years is considerably lower. Since 1974, voter turnout during these "off-year" elections ranged from low of 36.4% to a high of 39.8%, with fewer than two out of every five eligible voters casting ballots.

The failure of individuals to vote is often decried in the popular press. Whether the decision to not vote is driven by apathy or is a rational choice by the eligible voter, it is generally believed that if the costs associated with voting were reduced, turnout would increase (Rallings and Thrasher,

2007), The federal and state governments within the U.S. have responded with various efforts to increase voter turnout. Opportunities for citizens to register to vote have increased in a variety of ways: while purchasing vehicle licenses, while processing transactions at local banks, at registration booths for local and state fairs, and the like. Voters who know that they will be out of the country or away from their voting precincts can apply in advance for *in absentia* ballots. Recent efforts to get out the vote have also included provisions for setting up voting booths to enable early voting, thereby extending the voting period from the traditional one-day approach.

Interestingly, voter apathy is not homogeneous across the U.S. citizenry. Older citizens tend to turn out in larger numbers. In fact, about 70% of citizens over age 60 turnout while only about 35% of citizens in the 18-to-25 age group show up at the voting polls (Jameson, et al., 2002). This naturally raises questions about whether additional efforts and methods to make voting more convenient will improve voter turnout, particularly in younger voters.

With the increase in numerous technical innovations, the number of online services provided by government has increased. E-Democracy refers to the use of information and communication technologies in democratic processes in government (van der Graft and Svensson, 2006). One broad field of e-democracy include e-Participation and e-Voting (MacIntosh and Whyte, 2008). E-Participation is defined as "the use of ICTs to support information provision and 'top-down' engagement, i.e. government-led initiatives, or 'ground-up' efforts to empower citizens, civil society organisations and other democratically constituted groups to gain the support of their elected representatives" (MacIntosh and Whyte, 2008, p.16).

Examples include online grant application systems, Veterans Affairs information systems, job application systems, Social Security Administration assistance, electronic forums for discussing area issues, and the like.

A second broad area of e-Democracy is e-Voting. It is natural that attention has been given to the potential for adopting *online voting* via the Internet. The principal argument favoring online voting is that it may increase voter turnout by making the voting activity more convenient than that offered by traditional voting polls.

Online voting refers to the ability of a citizen to logon and access a secure government Internet site that supports voting in either (or all) local, state, and federal elections. Access that is available through both residential and non-residential Internet connections would best facilitate the goal of convenience – such a system should prove to be a quick, convenient alternative to conventional voting methods. Vote tallying through automated means can also enable a quicker turnaround of election results. Additionally, online voting provides absentee voters with better opportunities to vote, eliminating the need to procure an absentee ballot in advance of the established voting date.

Research has shown that individuals in the 18-to-25 age group are more likely to use computers on a daily basis, having used computers for much of their life. The convenience of online voting may improve voter turnout for these individuals. An important question is how will older citizens, particularly those in the 60+ age group respond to online voting? These older individuals (60+ age group) have been shown to have higher levels of computer anxiety than younger individuals. Older individuals may completely lack training in computer use (Martin et al., 2001). Would the 60+ crowd perceive online voting to be a hindrance to the voting patterns they have adopted throughout their life? Government would want to avoid the implementation of online voting if it increases participation in one sector of the citizenry only to affect adversely another sector.

This research provides evidence regarding the improved convenience argument and the effect that the availability of online voting may have on the intent of citizens to vote. Specifically, this research examines key differences between two age groups, 18-to-25 and 60+ with regard to online voter acceptance. Several interesting questions are examined: Would the availability of online voting increase voter turnout in the 18-to-25 age group? If older individuals have computer anxiety, would a change to online voting decrease voter turnout for the 60+ age group?

BACKGROUND

One notable online voting system project is the Secure Electronic Registration and Voting Experiment (SERVE). SERVE was funded by the Federal Voting Assistance Program of the United States Department of Defense, and was developed by Accenture Limited, a global management consulting, technology serves, and outsourcing company that is a Fortune Global 500 company (Jefferson et al., 2004). The intent of the SERVE system was to allow overseas military families to register and vote online. The major project concern was system security. Ultimately, security concerns were the primary reason that Accenture's final product was not used in the 2008 U.S. federal election. The long list of security concerns included insider attacks, lack of voter-verified audit trails, DOS attacks, spoofing, tampering, fabricated user accounts, and non-open source code, among others (Jefferson et al., 2004). Several articles have reported on the technical limitations of SERVE, and of online voting in general (Bishop and Wagner, 2007; Dill et al., 2003; Moynihan, 2004; Oravec, 2005).

In another online voting system project, a framework was developed to investigate risks of online voting versus traditional voting. In this case, a town in Canada using the framework implemented online voting as a supplement to traditional voting, with no reported problems (Kim and Nevo, 2008). While many studies have championed online voting for reducing impediments of traditional voting, costs associated with online voting must also be evaluated before implementing online voting (Dunlop, 2008).

Other research has reported on limitations for online voting that may arise from voter resistance. One study investigated online voting acceptance (Gefen et al., 2005). They found that socio-cultural similarity between the voter and government agency impacted both trust and perceived usefulness of online voting systems. In a study focusing on the intent to use e-government systems, the factors of trust, compatibility, and ease of use were found to relate significantly to the intent to use such systems (Carter and Belanger, 2005). While this latter study did not include online voting systems, one may theorize that these factors might also be important considerations when developing an online voting system. Similarly, several security gaps in technology and procedures were found in online voting pilots in the UK (Xenakis and Macintosh, 2008).

A study by Schaupp and Carter (2005) examined the intent of college students to vote online. They found perceived usefulness, compatibility, and trust to be significant factors affecting online voting intent. In related research by Lippert and Ojumu (2008), trust was again the central focus when those with a high level of trust of electronic voting were found to be more likely to be innovators or early adopters with regard to technology, and therefore, more likely to indicate an intention to vote online.

While the common reason favoring online voting is the potential to increase voter turnout, a study by Henry (2003) found only a slight increase in voter turnout in the United Kingdom when an online voting system was made available. Most of the online voters were already regular voters.

Some researchers have expressed concern about the possibility of legal challenges regarding the impingement of voting rights if online voting is adopted. Such challenges are a possibility since it has been found that the elderly, non-white, unemployed, and rural area residents are less likely to vote online (Alvarez and Nagler, 2001). Additional studies have also reported that the elderly are less likely to vote online (Yao and Murphy, 2007; Yao et al., 2006-07). These studies examine the antecedents for online voting intent for the elderly, but do not identify which antecedents influence voter intent for elderly versus young voters.

Adopting New Technology

This research examines the antecedents of online voting intent for two age groups: 18-to-25 and 60+. In order to provide a structure to guide the interested reader we present brief background information regarding the adoption and diffusion of technology.

The adoption and diffusion processes for various technologies have been studied in detail. Everett Rogers is considered the *guru* of adoption and diffusion research based on his original publication of *Diffusion of Innovations* in 1962 (now in its 5th edition). Literally thousands of research articles have referenced Rogers' seminal framework for adoption and diffusion processes.

A very nice, brief survey of technology adoption and diffusion as related to the Internet is provided by V. H. Carr Jr. His manuscript focuses on the social and other factors that have influenced the diffusion of Internet-based technology. Carr succinctly defines the terms adoption, innovation, diffusion, and integration – these are key terms to understand for individuals interested in the adoption and diffusion of technology as they define behavioral stages within the adoption/diffusion life cycle:

"...adoption refers to the stage in which a technology is selected for use by an individual or an organization. Innovation is similarly used with the nuance of a new or "innovative" technology being adopted. Diffusion refers to the stage in which the technology spreads to general use and application. Integration connotes a sense of acceptance, and perhaps transparency, within the user environment."

Within the information systems (IS) field, several different theoretical perspectives have been applied to the analysis of individual behavior regarding information technology (IT) adoption. Our research is based on the *Unified Theory of Acceptance and Use of Technology* (UTAUT) model attributed to Venkatesh et al. (2003). The UTAUT is a unified model that incorporates eight prominent models (theory of reasoned action, technology acceptance model, motivational model, theory of planned behavior, a combined theory of planned behavior/technology acceptance model, model of PC utilization, innovation diffusion theory, and social cognitive theory) from the technology acceptance literature.

The UTAUT purports to explain the intention of information system users with regard to IT use and subsequent behavior. Four key constructs (*performance expectancy, effort expectancy, social influence*, and *facilitating conditions*) determine *IT usage intention and behavior*. Additionally other factors (*gender, age, experience*, and *voluntariness of use*) are posited to mediate the impact of the four key constructs as shown in Figure 1. Validation of the UTAUT through a longitudinal study show that the model can explain up to 70% of the variance in usage intention (Venkatesh et al., 2003).

RESEARCH METHODOLOGY

Research Model and Hypotheses

In examining the antecedents of online voter intent, this research uses three of the UTAUT constructs (performance expectancy, effort expectancy, and social influence) and incorporates one other factor: level of computer anxiety. These factors are the basis for the development of four research hypotheses.

Performance expectancy is defined as "the degree to which an individual believes that using the system will help him or her attain gains in …

Figure 1. UTAUT (*Source: Venkatesh et al. (2003)*)

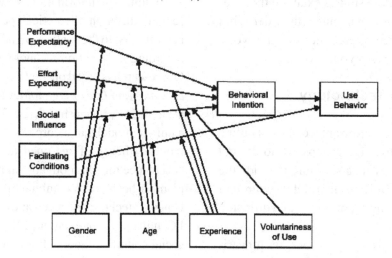

performance" (Venkatesh et al., 2003, pg 447). This is analogous to expected usefulness of the system and is related to the research question: Will citizens find online voting to be useful? Venkatesh et al., (2003) found performance expectancy to be positively related to the intent to use (adopt) new technology. Another study based on the UTAUT model found performance expectancy to be positively related to the adoption of business-to-business electronic marketplaces (Wang, et al., 2006) and to the acceptance of table personal computers (Anderson, et al., 2006).

Effort expectancy is defined as "the degree of ease associated with the use of the system" (Venkatesh et al., 2003, pg 450). This construct is comprised of items from other models' *ease-of-use* constructs. Venkatesh et al., (2003) found effort expectancy to be positively related to the intent to use a system. Wang et al., (2006) reported similar results. Hypothetically, if citizens believe that online voting will be easy to use or to learn, they will be more likely to indicate an intention to participate in online voting. Higher levels of effort expectancy relate directly to higher perceptions of ease-of-use.

Social influence is defined as "the degree to which an individual perceives that important others believe he or she should use the new system"

(Venkatesh et al., pg 451). This factor assumes that an individual is influenced by other individuals who are significant in their life. If a citizen knows that other important individuals are voting online, then they may feel an expectation to do likewise. Social influence is also positively related to the intent to use a system.

Computer anxiety is defined as "an individual's fear of incorrectly using computer technology." Voters are adamant that their vote be accurately counted; therefore, the fear of accidentally misusing an online voting system should correlate negatively with the intent to use the technology. Additionally, some older voters do not use computers on a daily basis while others do not use them at all. They may be expected to exhibit a higher level of computer anxiety. We posit that a higher level of computer anxiety will lead to a lower intent to use online voting.

The research model is depicted in Figure 2. The research hypotheses stated in the null form are:

$H1_0$: Higher levels of performance expectancy will not increase the intent to use an online voting system.

$H2_0$: Higher levels of effort expectancy will not increase the intent to use an online voting system.

Figure 2. Research model

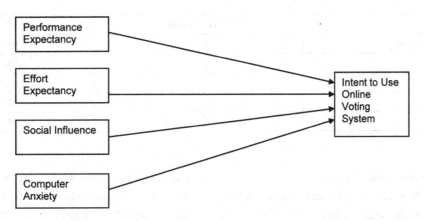

H3$_o$: Higher levels of social influence will not increase the intent to use an online voting system.

H4$_o$: Lower levels of computer anxiety will not increase the intent to use an online voting system.

Data Collection: Subjects and Sampling Plan

Data were collected by surveying two different subject groups: an 18-to-25 age group and a 60+ age group. These two groups are labeled *Young Adults* and *Seniors*, respectively in the analysis that follows. Young Adult subjects were surveyed from undergraduate college students in their 3rd

year of study at a mid-sized Midwestern United States university. Seniors comprised subjects at least 60 years of age who were resident at one of two retirement communities located in two small towns near the university. Both groups completed paper-based surveys.

Table 2 summarizes the demographic data for these two subject groups and for the overall sample. Although not shown in Table 2, the two groups exhibited comparable levels of education. All Young Adult subjects were currently enrolled in college while forty percent of Senior subjects had a college degree, and an additional 26% had attended college. Internet use varied considerably for the two groups. All of the Young Adults had used the Internet with routine internet usage at

Table 2. Subject demographics

	Young Adults	**Seniors**	**All Subjects**
Number surveyed	137	210	347
Number of usable responses	105 (76% Response)	85 (40% response)	55%
Age Range in years (average)	19-25 (21 years)	60-96 (79 years)	--
Gender	60% male	30% male	45% male
Percent Use of Computer	100%	69%	84%
Average Years Used Computer	11.4 years	6.9 years	8.8 years
Used Internet	100%	50%	74%
Internet Use weekly or better	97%	22%	58%
Access to Computer	99%	68%	83%

Table 3. Reliability analysis

Construct	Number of Items	Cronbach's Alpha
Performance Expectancy	4	.923
Effort Expectancy	4	.950
Social Influence	2	.959
Computer Anxiety	4	.889
Behavioral Intent	4	.943

97%. Fifty percent of Seniors had used the Internet, while 68% had convenient internet access (a higher percentage than those actually using the Internet) and 22% used the Internet at least weekly.

Instruments

Data were collected through the use of a survey instrument developed from construct questions previously validated through other research. Behavioral intent (dependent variable), performance expectancy, effort expectancy, social influence, and computer anxiety were measured with four survey items (Venkatesh et al., 2003). Items were modified to reflect the study. The instrument construct questions are given in Appendix A.

Table 4. Factor analysis

Item	1	2	3	4	5
PE1 Useful	*.811*	.243	.300	-.084	.124
PE2 Efficient	*.785*	.286	.314	-.153	.144
PE3 Participate	*.784*	.316	.211	-.201	.169
PE4 Likelihood	*.720*	.177	.378	-.137	.278
EE1 Clear	.489	*.600*	.280	-.207	.198
EE2 Skillful	.279	*.836*	.219	-.255	.116
EE3 Easy to Use	.301	*.801*	.260	-.283	.198
EE4 Learning	.264	*.829*	.182	-.335	.159
SI1 Influence	.259	.194	.204	-.039	*.903*
SI2 Important	.188	.129	.272	.004	*.910*
ANX1 Apprehensive	-.046	.057	-.322	*.742*	-.068
ANX2 Hesitate	-.176	-.431	-.013	*.738*	.065
ANX3 Intimidating	-.094	-.281	-.100	*.834*	-.091
ANX4 Scares	-.209	-.352	-.108	*.808*	.031
BI1 Would Use	.361	.187	*.821*	-.176	.205
BI2 See Myself	.366	.248	*.803*	-.195	.200
BI3 Would not hesitate	.311	.258	*.799*	-.222	.226
BI4 More Likely	.497	.194	*.582*	-.106	.262

Table 5. Regression analysis results—full sample

Hypothesis	Variable	Coefficient	t-value	Significance
1	Performance Expectancy	.499	6.685	**.000**
2	Effort Expectancy	.036	0.457	.649
3	Social Influence	.287	4.822	**.000**
4	Computer Anxiety	-.172	-2.820	**.005**

Table 6. Regression analysis results—young adults only

Hypothesis	Variable	Coefficient	t-value	Significance
1	Performance Expectancy	.540	5.802	**.000**
2	Effort Expectancy	-.017	-0.171	.864
3	Social Influence	.400	4.882	**.000**
4	Computer Anxiety	-.228	-2.652	**.010**

DATA ANALYSIS

Reliability Analysis

Reliability analysis results using Cronbach's alpha are given in Table 3. A factor analysis was used to assess construct validity with the results given in Table 4. Two items in the social influence construct did not load, and were dropped from further analyses.

Analysis of Hypotheses

All hypotheses were tested with multiple regression analysis. The level of significance selected this research is $\alpha = 0.05$. The model is significant with adjusted R^2 indicating that the four independent variables explain 64% of the variance for intent to use an online voting system. Table 5 provides results of the regression analysis for the entire sample for the four hypotheses. For the sample as a whole, performance expectancy, social influence, and computer anxiety are significant.

Tables 6 and 7 give regression results of the two sample groups: Young Adults and Seniors. The primary difference between the two groups is the effect of social influence. Both performance expectancy and computer anxiety are significantly related to intent to use an online voting system for both groups.

The last analysis examines the interest we have in whether there are differences regarding the intent to vote online between the two groups. Table 8 provides the regression results comparing the two different age groups. There are significant

Table 7. Regression analysis results—seniors only

Hypothesis	Variable	Coefficient	t-value	Significance
1	Performance Expectancy	.480	3.999	**.000**
2	Effort Expectancy	.098	0.910	.366
3	Social Influence	.179	1.680	.097
4	Computer Anxiety	-.198	-2.315	**.023**

Table 8. Regression analysis results—between groups

Variable	Young Adults Mean (Std Dev)	Seniors Mean (Std Dev)	Significance
Performance Expectancy	5.16 (1.48)	3.06 (1.87)	.000
Effort Expectancy	5.43 (1.30)	3.85 (1.90)	.000
Social Influence	3.13 (1.28)	2.71 (1.26)	.041
Computer Anxiety	2.71 (1.32)	4.02 (1.91)	.000
Intent to Use	4.42 (1.87)	3.01 (1.82)	.000

differences between Young Adults and Seniors on all dependent variables.

Discussion

While there is theoretical justification to expect all four independent variables to be significantly related to the dependent variable, in fact, effort expectancy was not significant for this data set. As predicted by theory, the intent to vote online was significantly higher for Young Adults than for Seniors. The discussion of results for each independent factor in the study follows.

Differences between New Voters and Seniors

Table 8 gives the results of our examination into the differences in intent to use an online voting system between the two groups. Young Adults are significantly more likely to indicate intent to use an online voting system.

No doubt, this has to do with their extensive experience in the use of information technology and its prevalence in their lives today. Additionally, there are differences between Young Adults and Seniors for the performance expectancy, effort expectancy, social influence, and computer anxiety factors. Young Adults are more likely to view online voting as useful and easy to use. Young Adults are also more likely to allow peer pressure to influence their intent to use online voting, although at an average of 3.13 this is still low. Young Adults are less likely to exhibit computer anxiety

with regard to online voting. It is also important to note that while Young Adults are significantly more likely to say they will vote online, the average factor score for this research is 4.42; a value between neutral and slightly agree.

Performance Expectancy

Hypothesis 1 is supported. If individuals perceive online voting systems to be useful, their intentions to use the system should increase. The significance of the performance expectancy variable is very important when considering the age of the subjects in the two samples. This finding supports the argument that the younger generation will find it much more convenient and useful to vote online over traditional voting methods. Consequently, government agencies should take this into consideration when making future voting systems available.

While Seniors do not have the same amount of computer experience as Young Adults, those that perceive online voting to be useful expressed an intent to use online systems. While performance expectancy is a significant indicator of intent to vote for both groups, Young Adults are significantly more likely than Seniors to view online voting as useful.

Effort Expectancy

Hypothesis 2 is not supported for the overall subject pool, but there is a significant difference between both groups. Effort expectancy measures the perceived ease of use of an online voting system. The Young Adults subject group consists of individuals who reported a background that included an extensive use of computers along with a high level of familiarity with the Internet. For this group, the survey results indicate that the ease-of-use factor is not a significant barrier to online voting. Their average score of 5.43 for this construct indicates Young Adults believe online voting is a task that will be easy or at least easy to learn.

In contrast, subjects in the Seniors group do not believe that online voting systems will be as easy to learn. The average score for the Seniors group for this construct is 3.85 – somewhat in between slightly disagree and neutral with regard to ease-of-use, and significantly lower than the score for Young Adults.

Social Influence

Hypothesis 3 is supported for the overall subject pool, and again there was a significant difference between both groups. Social influence is a significant factor in the intent to vote online. The possibility of seeing those who are influential and important to you voting with an online system is likely to influence you to vote online as well. However, when the sample was analyzed with the two groups separately, we found this construct is only significant for Young Adult subjects.

It may be that younger citizens feel more pressure to conform to social norms with regard to what their peers believe or do, especially with respect to information technology that pervades the society of educated young adults. Since the subject pool for Young Adults only included those in college, there is no evidence to extend this finding to those not attending college. Seniors, on the other hand, did not report social influence as a driving force in their intent to use online voting. This may indicate that with age comes maturity and reduction in the influence of peers on one's actions and decisions.

Computer Anxiety

Hypothesis 4 is supported for the total sample analysis. Somewhat surprisingly, it is also significant for both age groups.

Seniors expressed a fear that online voting systems may be based on computer technology that they may not use or understand. Further, online systems would require Seniors to change how they do voting from a manual system to an automated systems. Seniors are significantly more likely to exhibit computer anxiety than Young Adults (see Table 8 above) even though the subject group for this research included a number of well educated Seniors.

Many of the Young Adult subjects have been using technology since very early in their lives. Their anxiety factor is at a very low level (average = 2.71) so we would not expect computer anxiety to factor into their decision on whether or not to vote with online systems. However, anxiety is still significant for the Young Adult group. The rationale for this finding may be explained in the section below.

Qualitative Study Results

In addition to the survey questions for the four constructs, the survey also provided an opportunity for subjects to respond to two open-ended questions:

1. What would most influence your decision to use an online system (assuming it was available in your voting precinct)?
2. What would most influence your decision to NOT use an online system (assuming it was available in your voting precinct?

For the first question, Young Adult subjects primarily responded with answers focusing on the convenience, ease, and quickness of online voting. Typical responses include: "the convenience of voting from home", "I would not have to drive to a polling booth", "I would easily be able to access the online poll whereas a brick-and-mortar poll may be: (1) hard to locate, (2) inconvenient, (3) too busy", and "easy, convenient and quick."

Subjects also responded regarding the importance of online systems for voters who were living away from their registered voting precinct. Typical responses were: "As a college student I could vote without returning home. I would also not have to deal with absentee voting"). A comment that underscored a difference between inexperienced Young Adult voters and Senior voters was the response from one Young Adult: "People are more familiar with the Internet than with polling places".

Seniors often commented that nothing would stop them from voting, even if the only alternative was through online voting. They indicated that the major factor that would cause them to use an online voting system was if that was the only voting option. Typical comments were: "if I had no other alternative" and "I would exercise my right to vote no matter what system is used." Several Senior subjects also noted the convenience of online voting as a factor in their intent to use online voting. Typical comments include: "convenience" and "I wouldn't have to rely on someone getting me to the polling place." Seniors also mentioned the incidence of increasing physical ailments with age that could keep them from using traditional polls as a reason to use online voting. Comments included: "If I were physically unable to go to polling places" and "Increasing difficulty to get to the voting site, i.e., distance and/or disability and lack of mobility."

The question regarding the factors that would influence a decision not to use an online system resulted in fewer differences between the two groups. Most respondents, regardless of age, commented on security fears and a lack of trust in online voting. Comments included: "Possibility of votes being tampered with", "not secure", and "I don't trust the reliability."

For Young Adults, the majority of responses indicated a lack of trust in the security of votes cast online. Some of this fear may have been captured in the computer anxiety scale which resulted in computer anxiety as a significant construct for Young Adults. For Seniors, the second most common category of comments focused on not knowing how to use a computer. Comments included: "Computer ignorance would most influence my decision to not use an online voting system", "lack of knowledge" "I know nothing about how this would work", "At my age I choose not to learn a computer", and "Given the age of most poll workers (most poll workers are elderly), I don't think there would be sufficient help from them on computer questions." Another interesting set of comments focused on comparing online voting to the traditional approach to voting as a patriotic duty: "Voting in a Presidential election has always been a very moving experience for me. Somehow, I don't think I would have the same patriotic feeling if I were to vote on a computer" and "For my generation, 'going to the polls' is a patriotic, ingrained, habit."

Many Seniors indicated they do not want to vote online, while others noted that they believe it might be a good idea to have more than one voting option – noting that the younger generation might actually get out and vote if they could do it online: "If using a computer would encourage more young people to vote, I would be for it."

FUTURE RESEARCH DIRECTIONS

This research provides additional support for the UTAUT model of technology acceptance. Performance expectancy, effort expectancy, social influence, and computer anxiety explained 64% of the intent to vote online for Young Adults and Seniors. It is the first study that examines and compares two distinct groups of voters and their perceptions of online voting.

Given the responses in the open-ended questions and the overwhelming concern about the security of the Internet, future research examining citizens' intent to use online voting should concentrate on trust in the security of the Internet and the government itself. In addition, future research should consider all age groups rather than concentrating on just two distinct groups. This chapter has not examined the acceptance of online voting for those voters between the ages of 25 and 60 – a large portion of any country's population. To determine the level of online voting acceptance for any region, people from all age groups should be surveyed.

CONCLUSION

This research clearly indicates that government should consider using different approaches for different age groups with regard to voting. While the Young Adults subjects of this research are very comfortable with technology, they still worry about security issues. Because of the ubiquity of technology in their lives, they are very aware of the potential problems of online voting systems.

Seventy-five percent of the Young Adult respondents mentioned security/trust issues as a major factor influencing their decision to use online voting systems. These concerns will need to be addressed in order for an online system to succeed in the general goal of increasing voter turnout. The U.S. government can look to examples of online voting systems used in other countries, especially with regard to concern about the accuracy of voting results (Pieters and Kiniry, 2005; Tanner, 2005).

Seniors are also concerned with security issues, but believe that going to traditional polls is a patriotic duty, and worry about the learning curve, if not for themselves, then for other Seniors. A successful online voting system must be easy to use regardless of an individual's level of computer literacy. Additionally, because of resistance from both Young Adults and Seniors, governments should consider using online voting as an option

that supplements traditional polling precincts – this is more likely to maximize voter turnout.

Limitations

As with any research, there are limitations to this study. First and foremost, all respondents are U.S. citizens. We would be very hesitant to generalize these results to other societies, and we recommend the replication of this study in other countries in order to determine whether the significance of factors affecting the intent to use online voting is found to be consistent. Some countries are more advanced than the United States in providing e-government services to their citizens, including Estonia and the Netherlands (Pieters and Kiniry, 2005; Tanner, 2005), and it is quite possible that the study results will vary.

While our goal is to examine the intent to vote online, and to compare differences between two age groups, the subjects in both of our age groups are better educated than the average U.S. citizen. All of the 18-25 year respondents were currently enrolled in college. Since only 25% of U.S. citizens over the age of 25 have a college degree, the college junior subjects of this research may exhibit preferences that are representative of the general population of young adults. One may argue that these students are more technically savvy than the same age group in the general population. However, the increasing use of computers and computer training in primary and secondary education seems to indicate that in the future, those who do not attend college will still have a sufficiently high level of computer expertise to reduce computer anxiety.

There may also be a bias with the Seniors sample. Seniors living in retirement centers may not be representative of all Seniors. In addition, our sample of Seniors are not only very well-educated for that group, but with an average age of 79, they are also older than the average age of Seniors in the US.

Another issue is whether or not college students and college graduates exhibit a voter turnout tendency that is significantly different from the same age group of the general population. These questions that cannot be answered by this research and remain important issues to be addressed by further research.

REFERENCES

Alverez, R. M., & Nagler, J. (2001). The Likely Consequences of Internet Voting for Political Representation. *Loyola of Los Angeles Law Review, 34*, 1115–1152.

Anderson, J., Schwager, P., & Kerns, R. (2006). The Drivers for Acceptance of Tablet PCs by Faculty in a College of Business. *Journal of Information Systems Education, 17*, 429–440.

Bishop, M., & Wagner, D. (2007). Risks of E-Voting. *Communications of the ACM, 50*, 120. doi:10.1145/1297797.1297827

Carr, V. H., Jr. (n.d.). *Technology Adoption and Diffusion.* Retrieved March 15, 2009, http://tlc.nlm.nih.gov/resources/publications/sourcebook/adoptiondiffusion.html

Carter, L., & Belanger, F. (2005). The Utilization of E-government Services: Citizen Trust, Innovation and Acceptance Factors. *Information Systems Journal, 15*, 5–25. doi:10.1111/j.1365-2575.2005.00183.x

Dill, D., Schneier, B., & Simons, B. (2003). Voting and Technology: Who Gets to Count Your Vote? *Communications of the ACM, 46*, 29–31. doi:10.1145/859670.859692

Dunlop, T. (2008). Online Voting: Reducing Voter Impediments. *Policy Studies Journal: the Journal of the Policy Studies Organization, 36*, 685–686.

Gefen, D., Rose, G., Warkentin, M., & Pavlou, P. (2005). Cultural Diversity and Trust in IT Adoption. *Journal of Global Information Management, 13*, 54–79.

Henry, S. (2003). Can Remote Internet Voting Increase Turnout? *Aslib Proceedings, 55*, 193–203. doi:10.1108/00012530310486557

Jamieson, A., Shin, H., & Day, J. (2002). *Voting and Registration in the Election of November 2000.* Washington, DC: US Census Bureau.

Jefferson, D., Rubin, A., Simons, B., & Wagner, D. (2004). Analyzing Internet Voting Security. *Communications of the ACM, 47*, 59–64. doi:10.1145/1022594.1022624

Kim, H., & Nevo, S. (2008). Development and Application of a Framework for Evaluating Multi-mode Voting Risks. *Internet Research, 18*, 121–125. doi:10.1108/10662240810849621

Lippert, S., & Ojumu, E. (2008). Thinking Outside of the Ballot Box: Examining Public Trust in E-Voting Technology. *Journal of Organizational and End User Computing, 20*, 57–81.

Macintosh, A., & Whyte, A. (2008). Towards an Evaluation Framework for eParticipation, *Transforming Government People. Process and Policy, 2*, 16–26.

Martin, B., Stewart, D., & Hillison, J. (2001). Computer Anxiety Levels of Virginia Extension Personnel. *Journal of Extension, 39*.

Moynihan, D. (2004). Building Secure Elections: E-Voting, Security, and Systems Theory. *Public Administration Review, 64*, 515–529. doi:10.1111/j.1540-6210.2004.00400.x

Oravec, J. (2005). Preventing E-Voting Hazards: The Role of Information Professionals. *Journal of Organizational and End User Computing, 17*, 1–4.

Pieters, W., & Kiniry, J. (2005). Internet Voting Not Impossible. *Communications of the ACM, 48*, 12.

Rallings, C., & Thrasher, M. (2007). The Turnout "Gap" and the Costs of Voting. *Public Choice, 131*, 333–344. doi:10.1007/s11127-006-9118-9

Rogers, E. M. (2003). *Diffusion of Innovations* (5th ed.). New York: The Free Press.

Schaupp, L., & Carter, L. (2005). E-voting: From Apathy to Adoption. *Journal of Enterprise Information Management, 18*, 586–601. doi:10.1108/17410390510624025

Tanner, J. (2005). *Estonians Cast Online Ballots in World's First Nationwide Internet Election*, The Associated Press. Retreived (n.d.), fromhttp://www.abcnews.go.com/Technology/wireStory?id=1213426

Van der Graft, P., & Svensson, J. (2006). Explaining e-Democracy Development. *Information Policy, 11*, 123.

Venkatesh, V., Morris, M., Davis, G., & Davis, F. (2003). User Acceptance of Information Technology: Toward a Unified View. *Management Information Systems Quarterly, 27*, 425–478.

Wang, S., Archer, N., & Zheng, W. (2006). An Exploratory Study of Electronic Marketplace Adoption: A Multiple Perspective View. *Electronic Markets, 16*, 337. doi:10.1080/10196780600999775

Xenakis, A., & Macintosh, A. (2008). A Framework for the Analysis of Procedural Security of the e-Electoral Process. *International Journal of Public Administration, 31*, 711. doi:10.1080/01900690701690759

APPENDIX A. CONSTRUCT QUESTIONS

Behavioral Intent (dependent variable)

1. I would use an online voting site to vote in political elections.
2. I could see myself using an online voting system to participate in future elections.
3. I would not hesitate to use an online voting site to vote in future elections.
4. I would be more likely to vote in election if able to do it over the Internet.

Performance Expectancy

1. I would find an online voting site useful.
2. Using an online voting site would enhance my efficiency in voting in elections.
3. Using an online voting system would make it easier to participate in elections.
4. If I have access to an online voting system I will be more likely to vote.

Effort Expectancy

1. I believe interacting with an online voting site would be a clear and understandable process.
2. It would be easy for me to become skillful at using an online voting site.
3. I would find an online voting site easy to use.
4. Learning to use an online voting site would be easy for me.

Social Influence

1. People who influence my behavior think that I should use an online voting site.
2. People who are important to me think that I should use an online voting site.
3. I would use an online voting site because of the proportion of friends and coworkers who will use it.
4. In general, the federal government and its employees will support the use of an online voting system.

Computer Anxiety

1. I feel apprehensive about using an online voting system.
2. I would hesitate to use an online voting system for fear of making mistakes I cannot correct.
3. An online voting system would be somewhat intimidating to me.
4. It scares me to think that my vote could be lost using an online voting system by hitting the wrong key.

Chapter 10

24-7 Government, the Permanent Campaign, and e-Democracy:
Massachusetts Governor Deval Patrick's Interactive Website

Christine B. Williams
Bentley University, USA

ABSTRACT

This chapter traces the evolution of Massachusetts Governor Deval Patrick's website through content analysis of its features and functionality, participation rates and website traffic data, reactions of legislators, media and public, and interviews with the site's designer and director of the Governor's political committee. The chief attributes of the permanent campaign, polling, fundraising and public posturing, are all in evidence on the site. Devalpatrick.com provides informative resources on a variety of policy questions that are designed to promote his legislative agenda. It also supports features that allow visitors to interact with the Governor's team, such as posts and contributions, although visitors cannot contact the Governor, state or local officials, or other political entities directly from the site. Although devalpatrick.com is not able to deliver on high level e-participation goals, the level of citizen engagement it does offer is unique among U.S. elected officials.

INTRODUCTION

In 2006, a businessman, political newcomer, and long shot candidate for the governorship of Massachusetts, Deval Patrick ran a successful, innovative, technology savvy, grassroots campaign that secured his place in history as the second African American to be elected governor of an American state. Writing for the *Boston Globe*, Frank Phillips observed,

Patrick's willingness to shelve the advice of experienced political figures underscores his unconventional approach to politics. It also reveals a key part of the strategy that lifted him from obscurity... to enter the field for governor having never held,

DOI: 10.4018/978-1-61520-933-0.ch010

or even run for, public office, and win. (Phillips, 2006, p. B7)

His online campaign network helped generate enthusiasm and contributions, and created the infrastructure for 'meet Deval' events all over the state. Phillips attributes their high turnouts to the efforts of fervent online supporters who persuaded friends and neighbors to attend. The campaign's email list numbered over 40,000 who passed each blast onto at least 10 others, thereby reaching an estimated 400,000 field volunteers, supporters and potential supporters. A few months after the election, Deval Patrick's political committee made the campaign website permanent, turning it into a vehicle for facilitating dialog with constituents through tools that help them identify and organize around issues to which he will respond.

In an hour long interview conducted for this study, Charles SteelFisher, Director of New Media for the Governor's campaign and current website's designer, explained the transformation. "During the campaign we made the decision to invest heavily, not monetarily, but in terms of presentation and resources in the Deval Patrick concept, into online organizing, and empowering people" (C. SteelFisher, personal communication, May 11, 2007). The online tool for organizing caucuses on the ground evolved into the community tool, which allows people to identify common interests, talk to each other, and organize.

Why should a sitting Governor be so fearful of engaging his populace after he or she wins? So we started to play around with the idea...: creating structures that allowed people to feel connected with each other, with the administration, without having to have him on the campaign trail all the time. (C. SteelFisher, personal communication, May 11, 2007)

BACKGROUND

The Permanent Campaign

The 'permanent campaign' is a term coined by pollster and strategist Pat Caddell in 1977 and documented by Sidney Blumenthal (1982), to describe the blurring of the line between campaigning and governing. Its chief attributes, a preoccupation with polling, fund-raising, and public posturing, have been studied in both the U.S. (Ornstein and Mann, 2000) and UK (e.g., Franklin, 1994). Comparing communications strategies of Tony Blair and Bill Clinton, Needham (2005), however, sees a distinction between the role of office-seeker and incumbent. The latter one must provide 'post-purchase' reassurance and maintain his or her winning coalition of voters until the next election 'sale'. Politicians can preserve loyalty and create trust by highlighting a positive brand that is simple, unique, reassuring, aspirational, credible and value-based. The danger, warns Menefee-Libbey (2001), is that the permanent campaign systematically advantages a polarized, winner-take-all politics as well as people and interests that few would want controlling government. *An initial research question, then, is how does devalpatrick.com conform to, or depart from, these characterizations of the permanent campaign?*

Research Studies of Political Websites

Research studies of legislative, political party and candidate campaign websites in the U.S. and Europe show several trends. First, all actors have increased their web presence in recent years and second, content and functionality (tools) are becoming standardized. For example, nearly all sites include information about their producer: biographies, contact numbers and/or email addresses, speeches, press releases, and the like (Berntzen, et al., 2006; Gibson, et al., 2003; Williams and Gulati, 2006). Secure servers for credit card transactions have been available since 2000, and most campaigns now raise money online as well as collect information from visitors who wish to receive campaign emails or volunteer to work for the campaign (Benoit and Benoit, 2005; Conners, 2005). For all three types of websites, informational content (replication and transmission of content produced offline—'brochureware') remains dominant; two-way communication and interactive formats (aimed at relationship building or engagement, and mobilization) are less common ((Berntzen, et al., 2006; Bimber and Davis, 2003; Gulati, 2003; Karmack, 2002; Klotz, 2007; Williams, et al., 2002). There remain, however, significant differences in the quality of content and technological sophistication of these websites.

Researchers have proposed various developmental orderings of content and functionality (tools or activities). These generally distinguish between passive informational content and those features or tools that facilitate user manipulation of, or interaction with, the content, other users and/or the site's producer (Gibson and Ward, 2000; Lusoli, 2005; West, 2005). The lowest level or stage is the establishment of a web presence and posting of informational content that has been reproduced from other offline media sources, archived and transmitted to website viewers. The highest level or stage affords website users some degree of co-production of content (from personalization to blog entries or online chats and virtual town meetings), two-way communication, and follow-on offline or online activity.

For Foot and Schneider (2006), the informational level is foundational to all others, while involving and contacting are independent practices, but foundational to the highest level, mobilizing. Under their definitions, informing refers to the creation of website features that present information; involving refers to those that facilitate affiliation (relationship building) between the site's producer and visitors; connecting involves creating a bridge between site users and a third

actor; and mobilizing allows users to involve others in strategic goals and objectives, generally by employing online tools in the service of offline activities. *The second research question assesses the degree to which devalpatrick.com achieves higher level e-participation goals.*

Use of Technology by Elected Officials to Engage and Mobilize Constituents

While blogs and social networking tools are relatively new innovations in the political realm, other ICT tools have been around much longer: discussion forums, e-consultation, e-petitions, and the like. Indeed, the Hansard Society in the United Kingdom (http://parl4future.wordpress.com/about/) has been examining online participation as a vehicle for effective, manageable dialogue between representatives and the represented since 1997. Beginning in 2006, the European Commission funded DEMO-net, a four year Network of Excellence project, to strengthen scientific, technological and social research excellence in eParticipation (/). In November 2006, Dunne (2008) identified over 3000 online forums, some citizen initiated, others government hosted.

In the U.S., Kitchen Democracy (http://kitchendemocracy.org/), an Internet-based issues forum known as 'Web Augmented Democracy', provided a way for residents in the San Francisco, California area to interact with each other and their elected officials. Residents go to Kitchen Democracy to suggest, select and learn about issues, read what neighbors say, offer comments, and vote. Elected officials use Kitchen Democracy to suggest issues, increase community participation, get feedback, and make more informed decisions. However, the last article posted to this site was July 2007 and it shows no open forums thereafter.

Minnesota E-Democracy, established in 1994, created the first election oriented website. Its year round focus is on the use of the Internet to improve citizen participation and real world governance through online discussions and information and knowledge exchange. Its U.S. election information exchange and citizen-led forums have migrated to the UK, expanding the capacity and grass roots support of E-Democracy to additional areas. One report on the Minnesota e-democracy forum (http://www.e-democracy.org/research/minneapolisissues.html) boasts a membership of 13 City Council members, mayor, a nine member Park Board and seven member School board, not all of whom post regularly, although they seem well versed on list topics. Its blog posts are current through April 2009, but other content on the site has not been updated since 2007.

A new endeavor, DistrictIssues.com (http://districtissues.com), begun in April 2009, gives voters in the U.S. direct access to the politicians who represent them at the local, state, and federal levels of government. Its platform provides for video content posted by the representative, an interactive calendar of upcoming events, plus a Virtual Town Hall, and offers visitors opportunities to participate in a poll, chat with fellow constituents, read and post to the site blog and comment on legislation and views initiated by the representative. In its first month, the database includes only five entries from politicians in Colorado and two from Florida.

In the U.S., uses of technology by elected officials to engage and mobilize constituents are still relatively rare and difficult to locate. These examples illustrate a few, rather limited efforts. Like Deval Patrick, former New York Governor Spitzer maintained his campaign website allowing visitors to email the Governor, make contributions, and 'Join Eliot' to become a partner in reform, which simply meant signing up for his email list. He resigned from office, however, before fulfilling his promise to provide tools to facilitate citizen engagement or issue advocacy. California Governor Arnold Schwarzenegger also maintains a personal website (http://www.schwarzenegger.com) designed in 2007, that includes news about the Governor, links to his official state website

and to the Governor's Council on Physical Fitness and Sports. The remainder of the site highlights his Special Olympics Auction and features related to that charity and another, After-School-All-Stars. Interestingly, only 12.3% of visitors to this modestly ranked site (380,286 according to alexa.com on April 28, 2009) are from the United States. Michigan Governor Jennifer Granholm's personal website (http://www.jennifergranholm.com) is organized very much like a typical campaign website. Its menu has tabs across the top for her biography, news, making contributions, taking action, and posting comments to her blog. The site includes a photo album and links to the Governor's official state website as well as to Facebook, and notes that visitors can follow the Governor on Twitter for updates. Illustrative of a local elected official who maintains a personal web page is Mayor Tom Truex of Davie, Florida (http://davie.tv/DavTV/weblog.php), whose site supports his own blog, videocasts, and podcasts, and invites visitors to sign up for email updates and RSS feeds.

On February 17, 2009, President Obama launched http://www.recovery.gov, which claims to be the centerpiece of the President's commitment to transparency and accountability. It features information on how the Act is working, tools that will help citizens hold the government accountable, and up-to-date data on the expenditure of funds. The site is searchable and provides an email contact form; there are menu tabs for "Investments" (organized by category, state or federal agency), "Opportunities" (to obtain contracts or grants), "Impact" (a map with mouse-over data on job estimates and forecasts by state), News and FAQs. According to alex.com, its three month average traffic ranking on April 27, 2009 was 6,043 in the U.S. and 12,155 worldwide, but showing a steady decline to a seven day average rank of 31,591 worldwide. While 83.4% of visitors come from the U.S., other countries with the next highest percentages of visitors are China, India, Germany and Canada. The Recovery Act requires states to track their share of the federal economic stimulus package. Following the example set by the Obama Administration, states are creating similar stand alone websites or pages within the official site of their responsible government agency or office. The one created by Massachusetts Governor Deval Patrick is illustrative (http://www.mass.gov/?pageID=stimhomepage&L=1&L0=Home&sid=Fstim). Such a mandated, high profile, coordinated effort could represent a U.S. breakthrough in advancing the e-participation goals of strengthening citizen engagement and involvement in the processes of governance.

THE GOVERNOR'S WEBSITE ORIGINS, GOALS, AND CHALLENGES

This study relied on two key informants to understand how the websites' developers conceived its goals and challenges. By virtue of their positions, key informants have special knowledge and a unique perspective that, when combined with field observations and quantitative data, enrich the researcher's understanding of critical events (Gilchrist and Williams, 1999). The two interviews, lasting over an hour each, were recorded and professionally transcribed; both subjects signed consent forms authorizing their use.

Elizabeth (Liz) Morningstar, Executive Director of the Deval Patrick Committee identified four strategic goals for the website. First, it was a campaign commitment to open up governance to the people, captured in its recurring theme "together we can". A second and related goal was to use the technology as a tool for leveling an opening to government and allowing people to reach back in an equal way. In his interview, Charles SteelFisher, Director of New Media for the Governor's campaign and current website's designer, also saw the core campaign mission of engagement and empowerment as underlying the vision and theory for putting together the technol-

ogy. According to Mr. SteelFisher, "Deval is very forward thinking and web-thinking, he drives this forward. I think a lot of politicians just say 'let somebody else figure it out and I'll jump on it later'" (personal communication, May 9, 2007).

Ms. Morningstar characterized the website's political goals as the tricky piece: getting to know more about the people who are most interested, the ones who are willing to go the next step and activate. She acknowledges being warned that this could prove a dangerous strategy to get the Governor re-elected if it ends up undermining him instead. Finally, the website is recognized as a means to influence legislation and the legislature in a way that ultimately will change how governing is done. Mr. SteelFisher admits, "It's experimental and new, and it comes with all the hiccups of being that and all the great things of being that" (personal communication, May 9, 2007).

Both interviewees spoke at some length about the challenges they face, the inability to plan when things would pop up or down, and uncertainty about what constitutes success. For Ms. Morningstar, a key concern is that this website tool creates a possibility that is so large, it's almost impossible to keep up, to keep it fresh, and maintain the urgency around issues and people's desire to remain plugged in: "Inevitably the question is, 'You asked us all to check back in, what are you going to do with us?'" (Personal communication, May 11, 2007). The Governor's political committee faces the same dilemma experienced by candidates who opened their campaign blogs to visitor posts: What do you do when people start to feel they aren't being heard?

What information is accessible to the public on the website has generated its share of challenges, particularly in the early days. Initially, a visitor registered by entering his or her name and the website retrieved home addresses, and in some cases unlisted phone numbers, from the Massachusetts voter database to verify that the right person had been identified. Since this information could be obtained for any name entered, a chorus of complaints ensued, reaching all the way to the Secretary of State, prompting corrective action by the campaign committee. Another controversy surrounded the website's hosting of the issue postings for the coalition called 9/11 Truth, which maintains that attack "was scripted by a group within our government to create fear and allow for a doctrine of preemptive war against nations that are geostrategically important to our imperialistic desires". Although some believe the group is anti-Semitic, the campaign committee did not find such content in their posted comments, and after deliberating with advisors, decided not to suppress them.

A third challenge has been anticipating the reactions from state legislators. Liz Morningstar explained,

It's against the culture here.... It's not that they find technology threatening; they just don't see it as a tool that reaches their constituents.... For years, Democrats have controlled the legislature. They're not used to working with a Governor of the same political party. (E. Morningstar, personal communication, May 11, 2007)

She sees a huge paradigm shift from a Republican to Democratic Governor with everyone trying to figure out what that means to the relationship.

Finally, Mr. SteelFisher discussed criticisms of the Governor's use of a site hosted by his campaign committee to promote his own political agenda, facilitate issue advocacy and generate campaign contributions. He cited the ability to move faster than in the administration without having to go through the budget process and worry about whether it is the government's role to pay for creating a space for political action. Over there the Governor can be in communication and contact or not. "We'll take the heat if it doesn't work as well as we want. And if it succeeds, then we get the credit for it, and that's great. This particular entity can't go onto Mass.gov, I don't think it

fits" (C. SteelFisher, personal communication, May 9, 2007).

As for positives, Ms. Morningstar likes the site because it captures what being political means.

Going back to local, local communities—your streets, your roads, your schools... something that should matter to so many people, that's really, in other ways, just absolutely boring, and giving them tools to plug into it.... That to me has all the opportunity in the world. (E. Morningstar, personal communication, May 11, 2007)

She relates a story about someone whose post criticized a town pedestrian walk sign. The local Alderman got on the site, responded to the concern, and they met with each other.

The publicity surrounding the launch was exciting, although Ms. Morningstar found it a bit "like the Wild West at first". New people were signing on daily and she sensed that "something's happening". One organization called to say they endorsed a piece of legislation and wanted their name added to the list, and complained when it had not appeared the next time they checked the site. The *Boston Globe* took the unusual step of linking to that site rather than the official Mass.gov/governor one. Mr. SteelFisher sees "a very interesting new world... [where] we can't be afraid to do something just because we're not sure where the path will be" (C. SteelFisher, personal communication, May 9, 2007).

DESCRIPTION OF WEBSITE CONTENT: FEATURED ISSUES, POLICIES AND WORKING GROUPS

The Governor's website has three major elements: a searchable issue comment blog, a featured policies section and 'working groups'. The homepage spotlights text and video messages, news and initiatives involving the Governor. It also has a button for contributing to 'Team Patrick', a De-

Figure 1. Page view of the issue archive and scorecard

valPatrick TV video link, and elsewhere on the site, explanations for using the site, creating an account, and tech support with contact information (see Figure 1). The original community event calendar had few posts and disappeared from the site after about three months, in July 2007.

Issues

From mid-April to early June 2007, the twelve issues garnering the most votes on the Governor's website remained the same, although several of the lowest ranking of the twelve changed places. A year later, two early frontrunners dropped off the list of top vote getters on the issue scorecard, DevalPatrick Gives Us a Voice and More Funding to Public Education. They were replaced by Citizens' Wetlands Appeals, first created July 2007 and ranked third by November of that year through April 2009, and It's Time to Close Fernald State School, first created August 2007, but dropping from tenth to twelfth place between February

2008 and April 2009. A new issue moved into the top tier, 8th place as of April 2009, The People's Right to Redress the SJC's Marriage Ruling, with 366 votes.

The number of users, votes cast and issues identified increased, between 19 and 22% over the six week period from mid-April to early June 2007. Half of the issues received no votes (152 or 26%) or only one vote (141 or 24%), although some of those replicate issue topics posted by others that did receive votes. (Individuals sometimes initiate a new post rather than vote and comment in support of existing issues, which they might have to scroll through the archive to find.) Two years later, more than half of the issues received no votes (37.5%) or only one vote (21%), a reflection of declining interest and activity more generally.

A sidebar on the homepage highlights three different featured issues each month, which include a page or two response posted by the Governor, and retrieves all citizen comments logged to date. The featured issues are not necessarily among the

Table 1. Comparison of website issues with poll of Massachusetts citizens

Issue	Governor's website	MA state poll*
Gay Marriage	19%	2%
Shared Parenting for children of divorced/never married parents	11%	
Chapter 70 (state aid to public K-12 schools)	7%	--
ORV (Off Road Vehicle) Use in State Parks	7%	--
Renewable Energy	5%	--
Gun Control	5%	--
Taxes	4%	15%
Education	3%	8%
Housing/Homelessness	2%	1%
Governor/His Credibility	2%	2%
Health Care	1%	13%
Illegal Immigration	1%	5%
Budget	>1%	19%
Economy/Jobs	>1%	11%
Crime	>1%	6%
Other	32%	7%
Don't know/Refused	--	12%

*Note: Conducted April 17, 2007 by 7News/Suffolk University; N = 400
Question: What is the most important issue facing Governor Patrick?

highest on the vote scorecard. For example, the continuously featured state park funding issue ranked 12th on the scorecard, polling short of 200 votes in June 2007, and ranked 9th in April 2009, polling 305 votes.

Visitors had 88 keywords they could use in June 2007 (118 in April 2009) to find issues of interest on which to comment or cast a vote of support. The person creating a new issue becomes its coordinator and may form a coalition with others who have common goals and want to pool their votes for the scorecard. Searching on the term 'coalition list' returns 50 entries in June 2007 and 129 entries by April 2009, although fully half from the latter have no related issues or votes from supporters associated with them. Coalitions facilitate connections among users to promote interaction (Foot and Schneider, 2006). Currently, supporters can email the coordinator,

but the coordinator cannot communicate with all of them about getting together or what they're going to do. Opt-in and opt-out rules are being developed so this functionality can be rolled out.

The issues receiving the most votes on the Governor's website differ from those identified as most important in a professional poll of Massachusetts citizens (see Table 1). Gay marriage leads the issues on the website, but is near the bottom in the list of important issues generated by the poll. The top two vote getters on the website represent highly charged family issues, suggesting visitors are more interested in expressing their opinions than using the site as a vehicle for organizing to influence legislation. In contrast, the professional poll identified the top issues as the budget, taxes, health care and the economy/jobs, which rank near the bottom on the website's issue scorecard.

Several of the issues that generated a large number of votes on the Governor's website represent specific state or local issues such as Chapter 70 state aid to public schools or a contract for corrections officers rather than broad, enduring questions of public policy such as taxes, education, health care, or crime. A specific or local focus typifies the plethora of issues receiving few votes, for example farm excise taxes, licensing for massage therapists, Attleboro Revitalization Project, Help Revere Beach, Perkins Braille & Talking Book Library for the Blind, Thatcher Road Bridge; others reflect the poster's personal agenda (support the arts) or a pet peeve (declare war on graffiti).

Featured Policies and Working Groups

The Governor's policies featured on the site in June 2007 and remaining into 2008 (property tax relief, education and jobs/economic development) correspond much more closely to the poll rankings than to the issue concerns voted by website visitors. He promotes these same issues in person at town hall style meeting events saying "You want property tax relief? Come and get it," and suggesting that the audience call or write state legislators as well as contact other voters with similar interests through his website. A fourth policy, Civic Engagement, appears in April 2009 to encourage community service, volunteerism and civic action via the Governor's new initiative Commonwealth Corps. Engaging citizen discussion of issues online is risky, burdensome and problematic, in large part because the politician can lose control of its content (Stromer-Galley, 2000). By avoiding citizen initiated issues and emphasizing his own legislative agenda and campaign promises, the Governor maintains control while seeking to leverage political dividends from the website's interactivity. The Governor's website position taking also reflects strategic framing of issues (Xenos and Foot, 2005).

The newest 'Governor's Working Groups' feature launched early in May 2007. The first of these addressed property tax over reliance, offering an overview of the issue, resource links to additional information and position papers (e.g. authored by Boston's Mayor), a list of organizational and individual endorsers (e.g., municipal associations, city councils, mayors, and private citizens), and an invitation to submit public testimony for posting to the website, and concluding with a plug for the Governor's legislative initiative The Municipal Partnership Act. In August 2007 the Governor created the second working group, The Grassroots Readiness Project, a call to support and advance state education reform for which he established a council that will develop a 10-year strategic plan. These calls to take action are the most explicit attempt to move beyond connecting users to mobilizing them in the pursuit of policy goals (Foot and Schneider, 2006). Citizens do not yet have the ability to email their state legislators directly from the site. By facilitating endorsements, personal advocacy and ultimately contacting, this feature will support multiple dimensions of mobilization that may, as a result, empower those using them.

REACTIONS FROM THE PUBLIC, PRESS AND POLITICIANS

Citizens' Feedback and Visits

Not surprisingly, citizens' postings about the website have been favorable: "DevalPatrick. com Gives Us a Voice" ranks tenth in the issues identified by website visitors, garnering 183 votes plus some individual entries on the same topic. Occasionally, a suggestion about how to improve the website or a question about a glitch encountered using the site appears. Site rules state that inflammatory or obscene content will be removed. Anonymous posts are not allowed: posters are urged to use their real names, which

Figure 2. Comparison of web traffic rankings of www.mass.gov with www.devalpatrick.com

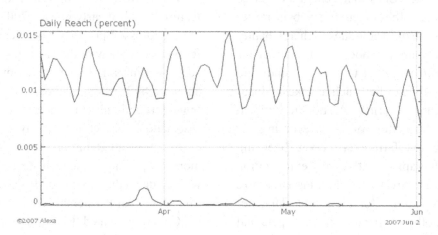

now appear next to comments as first and last initial plus the person's town.

Website traffic rankings are a different indicator of public response to the website. Alexa.com provides global usage patterns over a rolling three month period based on a combined daily measure of reach and unique page views for all sites on the Web. Its sample of millions of Alexa Toolbar users built for Windows, Macintosh and Linux includes Internet Explorer, Firefox and Mozilla browsers. Both the average reach and page views increased since the launch of the Governor's website at the end of March 2007. After ten weeks, its visitors represented .000125% of global Internet users, earning a U.S. traffic rank of 192,929 with average page views at 5.5. For perspective, visitors to the official Massachusetts state government website represented .0108% of users, earning a U.S. traffic rank of 1,672 with average page views at 3.8 (see Figure 2).

There were some notable surges in traffic to the Governor's website. The first occurred in the last week of March 2007 as launch of the new site generated publicity. (It is a redesign of his gubernatorial campaign website with the same url and host, the Deval Patrick Committee.) Controversy over the disclosure of registrants' home addresses and some unpublished phone numbers broke in the news media the following

week, and probably generated the second surge in traffic. The third week of April was notable for the letter posted to the site by the Governor's wife commenting on her treatment for depression and exhaustion and return to work, which was widely covered by Boston news outlets. The new "Working Groups" feature launched the first week of May, which may account for the next up tick in visitor interest. This preliminary mapping suggests that events and activities involving the website generate traffic primarily when they are reinforced by other media coverage.

Media Coverage

Local news media coverage of the website in the initial months after its launch consisted of three articles in the *Boston Globe* featuring the site and three others mentioning it in articles focused on the Governor's legislative agenda. A search produced no media coverage by the city's second major daily newspaper, the *Boston Herald*. WCVB-TV, Channel 5 Boston aired a story on the controversy over initial public access to voters' addresses and some unlisted phone numbers through the site. New England Cable Network (NECN) only mentioned the Governor's website in stories it aired about his wife's return to work and the letter she posted about that.

Blogs specializing in Massachusetts politics also devoted space to the website, at the time of its launch and the first week when the controversy erupted over voters' addresses and phone numbers. Neither the Massachusetts Democratic nor Republican Party blog has covered the website. BlueMassGroup lauded the site as a tool for participating more actively in government so citizens' voices are heard. In contrast, mASS backwards criticized the site as a vehicle to push the agenda of interest groups and the Republican minority, financed by political donations to the Governor's campaign committee, and ineptly managed (because of access to voters' addresses). Another, Civilities, focused on the limitations of the site and available software to support its purpose, concluding, "There's been enough experiments in online issue caucusing, but we need more successful ones before they are deployed on a large scale with grand expectations."

Politicians' Survey Responses

In June 2007, Massachusetts state legislators were invited to respond to a mailed survey about their reactions to the Governor's website. The response rate was 40 out of 197 or 20.3%. The large majority (62.5%) had never visited the Governor's website, although nearly half (47.2%) felt they would visit a few times. As a result, most had formed no opinion of it (69.2%) and felt it was unlikely they would post a comment to it (61.5%). In contrast, almost half (47.2%) felt it was generally a very good idea for public officials to use technology to communicate directly with constituents, with slightly lower percentages agreeing on its use for state issues (43.6%) and local issues (38.5%). This is consistent with their other positive responses about technology use, which rated email as a much better (30.8%) or somewhat better (30.8%) communication tool than U.S. mail, and revealed that the large majority (81.1%) had their own official campaign website in the last election.

A second survey was sent by email to public officials (mayors, city or town managers or administrators and councilors or selectmen) among the endorsers listed under the Working Group "Property Tax Over Reliance" in July 2007. Their response rate to five open-ended questions was 12 out of 49 or 24%. These public officials were unanimous in feeling that the website was a good, additional communication tool. At the same time, none of them had received any feedback from the public about their listing on the site as an endorser of "Property Tax Over Reliance". They had learned about the website through their personal connections to the Governor's campaign or through the Massachusetts Municipal Association. They became endorsers by virtue of their positions, for example by vote of the Board of Selectmen or in their role as City Councilors, and wanted to register concern about what they had experienced firsthand as a serious local problem.

Rather than the push back the Governor's committee worried about, state legislators and public officials at the local level had limited awareness of, personal involvement with, or public feedback about the website. Ignorance and indifference would be a more accurate characterization of their response (and of the low response rate overall) two months after its launch. Moreover, they were receptive, in principle, to this use of technology as a communications tool. Some embraced it cautiously as merely an additional vehicle or for targeted groups and purposes, while others enthusiastically welcomed the transparency and interactivity it brought to government and its relationship with citizens. Despite that openness, however, these local politicians were still more disposed to, and comfortable with, using traditional methods for connecting with each other and for organizing to advocate around issues of concern to them and in their communities. In sum, while the Governor is "pushing" the marketing of his website and its use as a communications tool, there is limited "pull" from recipients, either politicians or constituents. Until there is demand from them,

Figure 3. Increase in number of users and issues over time

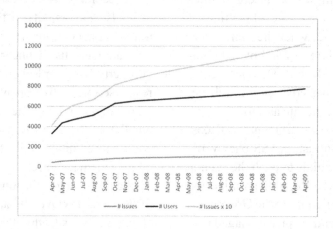

because it advances their own political purposes or reduces the costs of their political activism or participation, devalpatrick.com reverts to an instrument of the permanent campaign rather than advancing higher level e-participation goals.

A Two Year Retrospective on the Response

By all measures, devalpatrick.com has lost ground in subsequent months. By November 2008, a year and a half past the ten week mark, its visitors represented only .000045% of global Internet users, recording a much lower U.S. traffic ranking of 286,255, with average page views at only 2.4. Another six months later and two years after the launch, global reach fell to .000026% with a U.S. traffic rank of 1,010,085 and an average of 1.6 page views. The number of users as recorded on the site evidenced its largest growth in the first two months after launch, 33% from April to May. Over the next five months, the number of users grew an average of almost 10% per month, but thereafter fell to an average of only about 1.5% per month (see Figure 3). Their level of activity similarly diminishes over time. Tracking the number of issues generated by visitors to the site reveals the same pattern: following an initial surge of 32% from April to May, the average increase in

issues posted to the site drops to about 10% over the next five months, and thereafter tails off to an average growth rate of about 2% per month. This replicated pattern is evident in Figure 3, which depicts an additional trend line created by multiplying the actual number of issues per month by ten to adjust for the difference in scale between the numbers of issues and users.

These data underscore the difficulty of maintaining public interest in a website absent an extraordinary marketing effort or a specific event that generates significant media coverage. For example, in November 2008, opponents attempting to stall the Lantana land swap in Randolph, Massachusetts placed the issue on the Governor's website. They sent group members an e-mail asking them to visit the "Stop the Lantana Land Swap" page to let the governor know they did not want the Commonwealth to give away three acres of the Blue Hills Reservation to a private developer. In less than a week, the website received approximately 200 votes in favor of blocking the land swap; many also posted personal comments (*Boston Globe*, November 23, 2008). Apart from a letter to the editor posted on wickedlocal.com February 15, the Google News Archive logs no other stories for the search term "devalpatrick. com" in 2008. Local environmental groups cite the over 500 votes for "Citizens' Wetlands Appeals" and its third place ranking on the issue scorecard in November 2007 as evidence their issue is of concern to the general public (*Boston Globe*, November 23, 2008). It is one of only 20 news media stories logged that year.

FUTURE RESEARCH DIRECTIONS

The U.S. lags behind European countries in citizens' and politicians' use of e-participation tools. While devalpatrick.com represents one of the earliest and most extensive initiatives to date, like others of its genre, it has had difficulty sustaining interest and activity from citizens, the media and other politicians alike. The site may prove much more valuable as a campaign resource for the Governor's re-election campaign in 2010, which would be useful to investigate. A comparative study of other governors' personal websites would offer insights into what features and functionality they have in common that might suggest best practice, and provide additional information about their trajectory of success or failure. Interviews with these other site designers and producers would point to what set of factors motivates these politicians and how they perceive the challenges attached to creating and maintaining them. Do these differ from those for elected officials at lower levels of office?

The Obama Administration and its website recovery.gov may spawn and or invigorate a large number and variety of e-participation vehicles in the U.S. That site and its impact on others will be well worth watching and tracking over time. Despite the initial surge of attention generated after the launch of recovery.gov, a similar decline is in evidence two months later. It will be interesting to determine whether a high intensity promotional effort or newsworthy events turn that around or merely generate temporary bumps in attention and site traffic. This initiative might offer an interesting case study that could be compared with similar national level efforts in countries

such as Canada, the United Kingdom, or others associated with the European Commission's sixth framework programme. As the technology advances, new applications emerge, and access to it widens, researchers will want to measure and understand their impact on the behavior of both citizens and politicians.

CONCLUSION

The devalpatrick.com site reflects the major preoccupations associated with the permanent campaign: polling (issue scorecard), fundraising, and public posturing (featured policies). And the Governor is endeavoring to create and leverage his positive 'brand' to achieve legislative goals and, ultimately, re-election. The level of citizen engagement facilitated through his site is unique among U.S. elected public officials, and consistent with the themes of engagement and empowerment that he stressed throughout his campaign.

Such a strategy is not without risks. Cook (2002) finds that campaigning to promote public support for legislative initiatives brings very limited results. Moreover, he cautions that campaigning over the heads of the legislature is marginally successful at best, and engenders distrust and zero-sum politics at worst. Although the site developers expressed concern about a possible backlash from state legislators, our survey responses indicate that the larger problem is low level awareness and indifference. What may prove more important are long term gains in legitimacy, political capital and leverage. It will be well worth watching how these play out over the course of this experiment in e-participation.

The devalpatrick.com site makes bigger promises of high level e-participation goals than it is currently able to deliver, and there is no guarantee the public response will reach critical mass. Initially, site traffic grew, but over time it has diminished. The site provides informative resources on a variety of policy questions and a sampling, albeit a self-selected one, of public opinions about them. The site also supports a variety of features that allow visitors to interact with the Governor's team, such as posts and contributions, which constitute intermediate level involving. The two highest levels, connecting and mobilizing, however, are only partially implemented as yet. Visitors do not contact the Governor, state or local officials, other political organizations or the press directly from the site, nor do the issue postings constitute two-way communication. As the example of the town pedestrian sign shows, such interaction is not precluded; it simply is not an expedited or reliable outcome right now. The infrastructure to permit mobilizing activity through the website, though planned, must work through a variety of thorny problems from privacy concerns to logistics and scalability. That said, devalpatrick.com has laid the groundwork for groundbreaking e-democracy. The question moves from will others follow, to when?

ACKNOWLEDGMENT

The author wishes to acknowledge the assistance of Elizabeth Morningstar, Executive Director, Deval Patrick Committee and Charles SteelFisher, Director of New Media, Deval Patrick for Governor.

REFERENCES

Benoit, P. J., & Benoit, W. L. (2005). Criteria for evaluating political campaign webpages. *The Southern Communication Journal, 70*(3), 230–247.

Berntzen, L., Healy, M., Hahamis, P., Dunville, D., & Esteves, J. (2006, October). *Parliamentary Web Presence: A Comparative Review.* Paper presented at the 2nd International Conference on e-Government, Pittsburgh, PA.

Bimber, B., & Davis, R. (2003). *Campaigning online: The Internet in U.S. elections.* Oxford, UK: Oxford University Press.

Blumenthal, S. (1982). *The permanent campaign.* New York: Touchstone Books.

Conners, J. (2005, September). *Meetup, Blogs and Online Involvement: U.S. Senate Campaign Web Sites of 2004.* Paper presented at the 101st Annual Meeting of the American Political Science Association, Washington, D.C.

Cook, C. (2002). The contemporary presidency: The performance of the 'permanent campaign': George W. Bush's public presidency. *Presidential Studies Quarterly, 32*(4), 753–765. doi:10.1177/0360491802238707

Dunne, K. (2008). *The Value of Using Local Political Online Forums to Reverse Political Disengagement.* Unpublished doctoral dissertation, University of Surrey, United Kingdom. Retrieved April 30, 2009, from http://groups.dowire.org/groups/research/files/f/930-2008-10-31T173650Z/PhD.pdf.

Foot, K. A., & Schneider, S. M. (2006). *Web campaigning.* Cambridge, MA: MIT Press.

Franklin, B. (1994). *Packaging politics.* London: Edward Arnold.

Gibson, R. K., Margolis, M., Resnick, D., & Ward, S. J. (2003). Election campaigning on the WWW in the USA and UK: A comparative analysis. *Party Politics, 9*(1), 47–75. doi:10.1177/135406880391004

Gibson, R. K., & Ward, S. (2000). A proposed methodology for studying the function and effectiveness of party and candidate Web sites. *Social Science Computer Review, 18*(3), 301–319. doi:10.1177/089443930001800306

Gilchrist, V. J., & Williams, R. L. (1999). Key Informant Interviews. In Crabtree, B. F., & Miller, W. L. (Eds.), *Doing Qualitative Research* (2nd ed., pp. 71–88). London: Sage.

Gulati, G. J. (2003, August). *Campaigning for Congress on the World Wide Web and the implications for strong democracy.* Paper presented at the 99th Annual Meeting of the American Political Science Association, Philadelphia, Pennsylvania.

Kamarck, E. C. (2002). Political campaigning on the Internet: Business as usual? In Kamarck, E. C., & Nye, J. S. Jr., (Eds.), *governance.com: Democracy in the information age* (pp. 81–103). Washington, DC: Brookings Institution.

Klotz, R. J. (2007). Internet campaigning for grassroots and astroturf support. *Social Science Computer Review, 25*(1), 3–12. doi:10.1177/0894439306289105

Lusoli, W. (2005). Politics makes strange bedfellows. *The Harvard International Journal of Press/Politics, 10*(4), 71–97. doi:10.1177/1081180X05281029

Menefee-Libbey, D. (2001). The permanent campaign and its future. *Presidential Studies Quarterly, 31*(2), 383–384.

Needham, C. (2005). Brand Leaders: Clinton, Blair and the limitations of the permanent campaign. *Political Studies, 53*(2), 343–361. doi:10.1111/j.1467-9248.2005.00532.x

Ornstein, N., & Mann, T. (2000). *The permanent campaign and its future.* Washington, DC: American Enterprise Institute.

Phillips, F. (2006, November 8). *By bonding with voters, Patrick withstood attacks; Rejected advice to fight back.* The Boston Globe, p.B7.

Stromer-Galley, J. (2000). On-line interaction and why candidates avoid it. *The Journal of Communication, 50*(4), 111–132. doi:10.1111/j.1460-2466.2000.tb02865.x

West, D. M. (2005). *Digital government: Technology and public sector performance.* Princeton, NJ: Princeton University Press.

Williams, C. B., Aylesworth, A., & Chapman, K. J. (2002). The 2002 e-campaign for U.S. Senate. *Journal of Political Marketing, 1*(4), 39–63. doi:10.1300/J199v01n04_03

Williams, C. B., & Gulati, G. J. (2006, September). *The Evolution of Online Campaigning in Congressional Elections, 2000-2004.* Paper presented at the 102nd Annual Meeting of the American Political Science Association, Philadelphia, Pennsylvania.

Xenos, M. A., & Foot, K. A. (2005). Politics as usual or politics unusual? Position-taking and dialogue on campaign Web sites in the 2002 U.S. Elections. *The Journal of Communication, 55*(1), 169–185. doi:10.1111/j.1460-2466.2005.tb02665.x

KEY TERMS AND DEFINITIONS

E-Democracy (or digital, online or web-augmented democracy): The use of Information and Communication Technologies (ICT) by government actors and political groups to address and/or conduct public affairs.

E-Participation: The use of ICT to enable and strengthen citizen involvement in various aspects and processes of democratic governance.

Grassroots Political Campaign: Person to person activities undertaken at the local level to engage, organize and mobilize citizens around a political goal.

Issue Advocacy: Activities undertaken to influence the position or actions of public officials, citizens or other groups on a matter of public concern.

Issue Comment Blog: A section of a blog where readers can post their reactions to website content generated by its producer or other readers, and organized by topic or policy area.

Issue Scorecard: A tally of the votes received or supporters registered by a particular public policy topic that is generally rank ordered and displayed in descending order, from highest to lowest.

Online Decision-Making Processes and Organizing Tools: The use of ICT to elicit, tabulate and disseminate opinion on public policy proposals, decisions or actions through Internet hosted media and platforms.

Opt-In/Opt-Out Rules: Website users opt-in, or grant permission, to receive specific information or services, by providing their email address or other means of contacting. Opt-out requires users to remove themselves from a program that automatically sends them specific information or services by virtue of some other, related activity such as making a purchase or initiating an organizational membership.

The Permanent Campaign: A term coined by pollster and strategist Pat Caddell in 1977 to describe the blurring of the line between campaigning and governing. Its chief attributes are a preoccupation with polling, fund-raising, and public posturing.

Website Traffic Rankings: A combined measure of page views and users (unique visitors) compiled from diverse data sources and averaged over time to ascertain whether a site is gaining or losing popularity and how it compares with other sites. In the Alexa.com metric, a site that has a low rank or number is more popular than one with a high rank or number, assuming the difference is significantly large.

Chapter 11
UK E-Voting:
A Lost Opportunity for Participatory Democracy

Mark Liptrott
Edge Hill University, UK

ABSTRACT

This chapter evaluates the UK government strategy to promote electronic voting through the public policy process as an integral part of the e-government agenda to enhance participatory democracy. It argues that the formulation of the present policy is flawed as it lacks a diffusion strategy to enhance the likelihood of policy adoption. The electoral modernisation policy arose from concerns regarding the falling voter turnout at elections and is being introduced via local authorities through a series of voluntary pilot schemes. If issues influencing local authority pilot participation are not resolved e-voting may be permanently rejected by local elected representatives and so will not be available to citizens. This author identifies variables influencing pilot participation and suggests a revised public policy model incorporating selected diffusion concepts at the formulation stage of the linear policy process. The model is used to propose recommendations to enhance the likelihood of voluntary adoption of a policy introduced by central government for voluntary implementation by local government.

INTRODUCTION

The entymology of the word 'democracy' reflects its definition in Greek, 'demos' means people and 'kratia' means rule. Democracy is still evolving and one core point is whether it means popular power with the citizens engaged in self-regulation and rule, or whether it is a means to legitimate decision-making

DOI: 10.4018/978-1-61520-933-0.ch011

by representatives (Held, 1987). This divide serves to illustrate the different approaches to the idea of participation. One is regarding direct democracy where citizens have direct participation in governmental decision-making and the second where there is a separation of the people from their government by a system of representative democracy. The pluralist notion of encouraging citizen involvement found favour with participatory democrats who accepted the notion of checks on the representative body by making it regularly accountable to the community. In a modern democracy 'power' has come to mean the rule of the people which in reality means popular accountability and influence through representation and political parties (Parry and Moyser, 1994). To-days democracies reflect Weber's and Schumpeter's realist stances whereby candidates struggle for political office and voters can either accept the candidate's bid or reject it. The people choose their leaders then leave them to make decisions.

Voting is the "primary means by which most citizens contribute to collective decision-making in a democratic polity" but many citizens feel that the formal machinery of democracy no longer offers them the opportunity to influence government decisions (Birch and Watt, 2004, p64; RFT, 2006). The Rowntree Reform Trust (RFT) (2006) introduce the possibility of "quiet authoritarianism" where as a result of the failure of a large part of the population to engage in political activity, policy is made by a small clique and government is not held to account by the public, thereby general elections become "empty rituals." They also note with disquiet that democracy only exists because it offers the citizen a voice in matters which concern them and "when this collective voice is not being expressed efficiently democracy is threatened" (p35).

Political participation lies at the heart of democratic politics, and it has been suggested that through participation citizens learn to exercise the skills of democratic citizenship (Kelleher and Lowery, 2008). Despite the decline in the basic act of participation, voting, in this modern pluralist society there appears to be increased activism via pressure or interest groups resulting in citizens identifying with groups rather than the whole community (Hindeness, 2000). There is a danger that the members of these groups will forget that they are citizens of a wider society and so will not vote (RFT, 2006). This problem was recognised earlier by Held (1987) and Crick, (2002) who recommended addressing this issue by developing new models of participation, as public participation is the "mechanism of democratic government" (p54).

The policy of electoral modernisation is one of the ways the UK government hopes to encourage an increase in political participation. It is an integral component of the UK government's e-government agenda the objectives of which broadly mirror those from across the EU, particularly those agreed in the e-European Action Plans of 2002 and 2003 and the resolution on the Implementation of the e-Europe 2005 Action Plan (2003), to achieve an e-economy in Europe harnessing ICT to increase democratic participation, capable of a modernised service delivery based on customer needs (Pleace, 2008). As a requirement for modernising public administration, the UK government aimed to establish e-enabled service provision by 2005 which it hoped would stimulate participatory democracy by increasing voter numbers at subsequent elections (Electoral Commission, 2003; Nixon and Koutakou, 2008).

This chapter presents the argument that there are weaknesses in the formulation of the UK's electoral modernisation policy. The UK central government does not appreciate the need to incorporate diffusion concepts into the policy process to enhance policy design and thereby increase the likelihood of policy adoption. The argument is based on research into the pilots of e-voting which took place in 2003 and 2007. The UK government has chosen to implement e-voting through the public policy process with local government acting as the conduit through which to introduce the new voting methods. Local authorities are elected bodies, subordinate to the UK central government, administering local services in accordance with Parliamentary statutes (Wilson and Game, 2002). They can choose whether to participate in the e-voting trials and 2003 saw the largest pilot programme with 59, out of almost 400, authorities taking part. Fourteen of those trials included Internet voting (Electoral Commission, 2003). However, local authority enthusiasm for the new voting methods appears to have been waning as only 12 local authorities took part in the 2007 trials, 5 of which included the Internet (DCA, 2007). As the adoption of the new voting methods depends on local discretion, if local authorities continue to refuse to adopt e-voting it will be unavailable to the citizens.

The research adopted a case study approach underpinned by the realist paradigm which involves looking behind appearances to discover mechanisms which explain human behaviour (Robson, 2002). The enquiry reviewed the Election Officers' responses through the lens of the public policy process and Rogers' (2003) diffusion of innovations theory. Rogers' model was chosen, as it is a seminal work offering diffusion principles for both organisational and individual decision processes. Alternative models mainly offer concepts pertaining to the end-user which, for e-voting is the voter, they were not used in this study as this enquiry specifically targeted the pivotal local authorities positioned between central government and the citizens. Three theories from Rogers' framework were used to understand the reasons for the Election Officers' decision-making. The first was Rogers' innovation-decision process for organisations, the second was the innovation-decision process for the individual, and the third was the perceived attributes theory identifying five attributes the perceptions of which affect innovation adoption.

The methods of enquiry for the 2003 research consisted of a review of the normative literature, a series of semi-structured interviews with 6 Election Officers, 3 from the 14 authorities, which had included Internet voting in their pilot, and 3 from authorities which had declined participation in the pilot programme. Four confirmatory interviews were conducted, 2 with Election Officers of pilot authorities and 2 with Election Officers of non-pilot authorities. These were supplemented with further interviews, one with Turner, Chief Executive of the Association of Electoral Administrators (AEA) and the other with a member of the Electoral Modernisation Team within the Ministry of Justice (MoJ) at the Home Office who offered the government perspective. The Election Officers were assured of anonymity. The extended research in 2007 consisted of telephone interviews with Election Officers of seven of the fourteen authorities which had included the Internet in their 2003 pilots but had not joined any 2007 pilots.

The findings identified the drivers behind local authority decision-making as they considered an innovation introduced through the public policy process for voluntary implementation by local authorities and the results suggest that integration of the public policy model and the diffusion model would enhance policy adoption.

The structure of the chapter proceeds as follows; the next section outlines the rationale behind the UK government's introduction of e-voting briefly describing the central/local government relationship. The following section discusses variables influencing local authority decision-making in 2003 and 2007, and compares those variables with influential variables identified from prior research. The subsequent section relates the findings from 2003 and 2007 to Rogers' diffusion concepts to evaluate the UK government's diffusion approach. The penultimate section proposes a revised policy model incorporating diffusion concepts and suggests recommendations to enhance the likelihood of adoption of public policies introduced by central government for voluntary implementation by local government. The chapter concludes with a suggestion for future research based on the findings from this study.

BACKGROUND: THE RATIONALE FOR CHANGE

Voting is the one political action which is performed by the majority of people, however, turnouts in UK elections at every level is falling and "a democracy in which the public does not participate is in trouble" (ICAVM, 2002, p5). Falling turnouts are recognised as potential threats to democracy and such threats can trigger public policy formulation (Hogwood and Gunn, 1988;ICAVM, 2002). The government's consultation paper *Local Government: Local Democracy and Community Leadership* (1998) stated that the more people who vote, the greater the democratic legitimacy of the decisions taken by those who are elected, so participation in elections is crucial to the health of democracy. The turnout of 59.4% in the 2001 General election led to fears that future low turnouts could mean that the authorities have no real mandate (ICAVM, 2002). There was no significant improvement in the 2005 General Election with a turnout of 61.3% (Electoral Commission, 2005). In addition to the low turnouts at General Elections, turnouts at other elections have been very low. During the period 1990-1999 turnouts at local elections averaged 25% and the turnout for European Elections has never exceeded 40% (RFT, 2006). Concern had also been expressed in the Public Administration Select Committee (PASC) sixth report *Innovations in Citizen Participation in Government* (2001) which commented that it was "extraordinary that this collapse in electoral participation, put alongside other evidence on civic disengagement, has not been treated as a civic crisis demanding an appropriate response. Political life has simply continued as if nothing has happened" (para 4).

This disquiet resulted in the *Representation of the People Act* (2000), which established a framework for local authorities to take part in pilot schemes trialing new voting procedures (Fairweather and Rogerson, 2002). This legislation committed central government to the introduction of the new voting methods and Nick Raynesford, then a Minister in the Office of the Deputy Prime Minister, stated in 2003 "These innovations will help to make elections more relevant, straightforward and accessible for voters" (Electoral Commission, 2003, p1). Accordingly central government embarked upon a programme of piloting, testing then implementing a range of new voting procedures using new technology. Local authorities were, and still are, asked to volunteer to participate in the pilot programme, this discretion has no guarantee and can be withdrawn at any time.

VARIABLES AFFECTING PILOT PARTICIPATION

2003 Pilots-Drivers for Local Decision-Making

Findings from the interviews indicated that among many contextual and personal variables influencing the adoption of e-voting in 2003 there were two main drivers. The pilot authorities had their reasons for joining the trials and the non-pilot authorities had their reasons for not joining the trials.

The variable that most influenced the local authorities in this study not to join the 2003 e-voting pilots was the lack of resources. Central government only funds the electronic element of the pilot schemes, leaving the administrative aspects to be funded from local coffers. Election Officers of the authorities that refused pilot participation believed that to organise an e-election in conjunction with a traditional election required a revision of their working practices, an increase in the number of specialist staff and an appropriate increase in funding. They were not willing to commit their authorities to any extra expenditure as they considered that their authorities had higher priorities for local funds, as one officer explained

I would certainly like to join the pilot scheme but we must prioritise and I consider that public funds could be better spent. That said, if government allocated additional funds to allow us to recruit specialist, experienced staff and gave us all the funding to conduct all the elements in the trials, I would join in. Only being a small council we could not take it on board, we could not afford the possibility of having to partially fund a pilot.

Support for their views came from Turner who recognised that central government never fully funds anything, and from Election Officers of the authorities that joined the pilot scheme who believed that the increased workload, for smaller authorities, would be an inhibiting factor to their participation in the pilot programme. Central government appeared to have completely ignored past research which demonstrates that adequate funding is a prerequisite to provide the tools for the implementation of a policy programme (Birkland, 2005; Rose, 2005).

The variable exercising most influence on the Election Officers, who joined the 2003 pilots, was status. The participating authorities sought to achieve Beacon Status in Electoral Processes and so achieve recognition as an innovative authority. This elevated status ensured a high score during the Comprehensive Performance Review which, in turn for a little co-operation, resulted in an increase in funding and a decrease in central monitoring. The increase in status from participation in the pilots was not limited to the organisation; there were benefits for the individual Election Officers as they enhanced their reputations and their career prospects. Two of the Election Officers had established reputations as speakers at conferences and seminars to encourage the adoption of e-voting and one commented that "it has not done my career any harm."

This conclusion supports prior research which recognises the adoption decision may be based on self interest and that personnel within an organisation may concentrate on career advancement (Skopcol, 1993; Sorgaard, 2004). The member of the Electoral Modernisation Team at the Home Office maintained that there were no rewards for local authorities participating in e-voting but those Election Officers realised that participation in government initiatives, such as the e-voting pilot programme, brought tangible benefits for their authorities and themselves.

2007: Enthusiasm Waning

The main aim of the 2007 pilots was to test how voting at different times and in different locations could improve the voting process (Electoral Commission, 2007). Twelve local authorities out of 388 volunteered for the pilots and only 5 of those authorities tested Internet voting. The remaining 9 authorities which had trialed Internet voting in 2003 did not volunteer to take part. Seven Election Officers from those authorities were interviewed to establish reasons that authorities, which were once enthusiastic to join the pilot programme, had declined further pilot participation. Their responses showed that their decision regarding 2007 pilot participation was influenced by 3 variables. Firstly negative e-voting experiences during the 2003 pilots, secondly the impact of restructuring and finally the obligations imposed by central legislation.

There were 2 aspects of the 2003 e-voting experience that influenced against further participation in the pilots. The first centred on the amount of work involved in conducting an e-election in conjunction with a traditional election. These officers were not opposed to e-voting but considered that the negligible increase in voter numbers (below 6%) did not justify the extra workload and expenditure imposed on their authorities (Electoral Commission, 2003).

The second inhibiting aspect of the 2003 pilot focused on the issue of security. In 2003 these Election Officers had experienced breakdowns in the security of the software and there was a consensus that the contractors had not realised the obligations of electoral legislation. As one officer explained "the Internet at the polling stations stopped working and we had to rely on written registers and the contractors did not realise the timetables and rules which govern elections." Another officer told of problems with broadband as it became obvious it had been hacked and the databases could not communicate with each other. The solution was to revert to dial-up which slowed the voting process. At the count further techno-logical problems appeared. The digital key that allowed the officer to extract the data would not work. He then had to contact the contractor who had to extract the data and dictate the information to a typist to enter onto a spreadsheet. The officer concluded that the technology was not yet "ready for use" consequently "question marks could be raised against the election results". These fears confirmed Turner's assertion in the 2003 research, that there should be no e-voting until "there are copper-bottomed guarantees on security".

The 2nd variable influencing pilot participation in 2007 was the impact of restructuring. The impact of compulsory restructuring of local authorities appears to have had a cumulative effect. Since the Labour government came to power the emphasis has been on "modernisation" involving ongoing external and internal restructuring (Seldon, 2001, p122). The Election Officers of authorities preparing for major structural change, such as becoming a unitary authority, did not volunteer for the 2007 pilots as it was judged that staff were fully committed to organising the restructuring. One respondent was the sole remaining member of the election team following a complete staff change. He had then to recruit and train additional staff. Less radical change also impacted on the officers' receptivity to further change. An Election Officer in an authority, which had undergone manage-ment reorganisation, succinctly described pilot participation as "too much to cope with."

The 3rd variable concerned the increase in legislation and central directives. The Election Officers identified this variable as the greatest driver against pilot participation. They deplored the amount of changes imposed on local gov-ernment but reserved particular venom for the *Electoral Administration Act* (2006) which contained obligations that were judged to be too onerous to encourage participation in any new voting initiatives. The officers explained that in 2007 the legislation was new, and they cited the requirement to check postal voters identifiers as

the reason for the non-participation in the pilot scheme. One officer described this obligation as "very time consuming" as, despite the availability of software, at least 10% of the identifiers had to be checked by staff. He explained that 100% of identifiers needed to be checked and he would be held to account in case of any challenges dur-ing the counting of the votes. As a result it was believed that any authority with a large number of postal votes would not risk compromising the conduct of an election by volunteering to conduct a combined traditional and e-election.

The Diffusion of E-Voting

This section discusses the relationship of the e-voting policy to Rogers' diffusion principles. The discussion considers the initial stage of Rogers' (2003) innovation-decision process in organisa-tions, (agenda setting), then moves to the first three stages of the innovation-decision process for the individual, (knowledge, persuasion and decision), and finally to the perceived attributes theory. Local authorities fulfil the criteria for organisations (Schein, 2004) and as such pass through the initial stage of the innovation decision process for organisations, agenda setting. E-voting is then placed on the local authority agenda when each authority receives the e-mail inviting pilot participation. The officers and council members of the local authorities then act as individuals as they consider adoption through the innovation-decision process for individuals and as they are passing through this process they assess the innovation, in this case, e-voting, based on their perception of its attributes.

The Innovation: Decision Process for Organisations

Agenda Setting/Matching

Rogers (2003) argues that an organisation will adopt an innovation if the organisation believes there is a need for it. Local authorities in both phases of this research did not acknowledge a 'need' for e-voting. Evidence suggested that the initial decision to join the trials was borne out of enthusiasm for e-voting felt by the individual Election Officers.

The Innovation: Decision Process for the Individual

Knowledge and Persuasion

Rogers' (2003) model for the individual consists of a linear set of stages beginning with first knowledge of the innovation, followed by persuasion to adopt or reject it, usually influenced by peer pressure, before passing to the decision stage involving the formation of an attitude to the innovation based on its attributes, thence either to rejection or, implementation and confirmation.

Evidence from 2003 and 2007 suggests that central government had not appreciated central/local communication as a driver for policy adoption. The importance of communication with stakeholders is recognised by the OECD which is aware of the need for new approaches to engagement, to enhance commitment at all levels to new policies, and recommends that evaluative strategies should be used to revise policies (Macintosh, in OECD, 2003). Despite recommendations from the AEA and government researchers, Fairweather and Rogerson (2002), there was no campaign to impart knowledge of the nature or best practice of e-voting to local authorities or their members, neither was there a targeted campaign aimed at the less enthusiastic local authorities, when prior research has recommended that the most effective method of enhancing adoption of an innovation is to target those who are slow to adopt it (Pettigrew et al, 1994;Rogers, 2003).

In 2003 and 2007 the Election Officers considered that they had sufficient information from central government, and from formal and informal contacts with other local authority officers,

to enable them to decide on pilot participation. However, the pilot Election Officers believed that their constructive local evaluation assessments, submitted to the Electoral Commission within 3 months of a pilot scheme, had been ignored and the non-pilot authorities were not asked for their suggestions to modify the policy.

Prior research holds that both the actions of a Change Agent, working in conjunction with opinion leaders, and the influence of the mass media and near peers can encourage adoption (Rogers, 2003). In 2003 and 2007 the UK government's Change Agent (in 2003 the Office of the Deputy Prime Minister, in 2007 the Department for Constitutional Affairs, and later the Ministry of justice at the Home Office) made limited contact with potential adopters and the use of opinion leaders was non-existent. There was no evidence that the mass media influenced decision-making either in 2003 or 2007. Since so few local authorities joined the trials there is no evidence of peer pressure to encourage participation. Rather the formal and informal contacts between Election Officers were regarded as opportunities for mutual support where peer information appeared to present the negative aspects of e-voting administration.

Decision

Evidence suggests that prior to the 2003 pilots local councillors who did not understand the new technology had some concerns regarding public capacity and access to the new voting methods, confirming Downs' (1957) contention that politicians act in their own best interests and will not take risks which may affect their chances of re-election. In 2007 there appeared to be a greater understanding, by councillors, of the new technology. Nevertheless, in both 2003 and 2007, the assessments of e-voting by the key actors, the Election Officers, exercised most influence within local authorities. In their roles as gatekeepers, the officers either denied council members information or slanted their approach to the information in order to encourage council members to decide in accordance with the officers' wishes. Although there might have been occasions where the Election Officers were over ruled, this occurrence was rare.

Perceived Attributes

Rogers (2003) argues that the decision to adopt is based on the potential adopter's perception of the attributes of the innovation, particularly the relative advantage, complexity, compatibility, trialability and observability. The better the perception of the attributes, the greater the likelihood of innovation adoption.

Relative Advantage

Neither the Election Officers who had joined the pilot programme in 2003 and 2007, nor those who had not, held high opinions of the attributes of this innovation. They all recognised that e-voting had some advantages over conventional voting, such as electronic counting, and it was viewed as a natural progression in the use of everyday electronic transactions with the potential to provide an improved service for the public. Since nationally the majority of local authorities had not trialed e-voting, the disadvantages of the lack of resources would seem to have outweighed the advantages. Those local authorities that had trialed e-voting had not necessarily done so because they deemed e-voting to be an improvement in voting procedures but they had used e-voting to further their own ends which for them was the real advantage of the new voting methods.

Complexity

Both pilot and non-pilot Election Officers in 2003 and 2007 did not regard e-voting as complex. They were confident that by offering both e-voting and traditional methods of voting, citizens would not be discouraged from voting by the mechanism of casting a vote. However, there was a consensus that the administration of a parallel e-election and traditional election was complex and without the necessary resources e-voting would remain unattractive to the majority of Election Officers.

Compatibility

The compatibility construct is synonymous with trust and e-voting requires a substantial amount of trust to facilitate adoption (Carter and Belangers, 2005; Schaupp and Carter, 2005). Any new voting methods must be perceived as trustworthy if local government officers and council members are to adopt them and promote their usage to the public (ICAVM, 2002). The Election Officers did not regard e-voting as compatible with traditional voting both for reasons of administration, as outlined above, and for issues of security. Security issues did not appear to influence local decision making prior to the 2003 pilots, but problems experienced during the 2003 pilots had caused once enthusiastic Election Officers to reject further pilot participation in 2007.

Trialability

In offering pilot schemes of e-voting the UK central government had employed a recognised strategy to promote innovation adoption (Rogers, 2003). Nevertheless, it appeared to have altered its approach to the pilots, as in 2003 there was an open door inviting a more widespread use of technology than in previous years with a combination of 17 schemes offering the opportunity to vote using a variety of channels including the Internet, the telephone, text messaging and digital TV (Electoral Commission, 2003). Although at that time the government's wish to target certain e-voting methods meant that local authorities did not necessarily receive permission for the type of pilot they requested. Since 2003, the opportunity to test a wide range of new voting procedures appears to have diminished as central government

Figure 1. Public policy diffusion model (adapted from M. Liptrott, 8th European Conference of E Government, Lausanne, Switzerland, 2008)

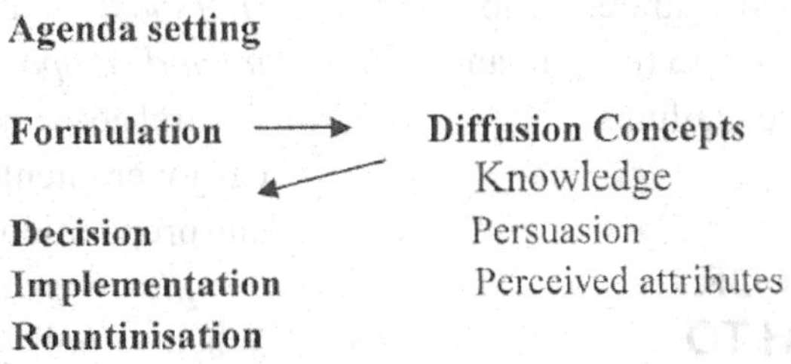

Agenda setting

Formulation $\longrightarrow$ Diffusion Concepts
Knowledge
Decision Persuasion
Implementation Perceived attributes
Routinisation

only allows targeted pilots to test certain aspects of e-voting (DCA, 2007). The inability to continue with certain types of pilot scheme militated against further pilot participation in 2007. There was a consensus that the Election Officers in both phases of the research wished to see an end to the trials and they considered that the government needed either to address the issues raised and introduce e-voting, or abandon it.

Observability

Local authorities reported that they considered the most observable features of e-voting to be the slight increase in voter turnout, and the complexity of simultaneously administering an e-election and traditional ballot, as discussed above.

E-voting has the potential to raise voter turnout but there was only slight increase in voter turnout during the 2003 pilot schemes, between 0-5% (Electoral Commission, 2003, p62). There are doubts whether any increase is sustainable as voters may regard e-voting as a novelty and revert to traditional voting methods after trying the new methods, or abstain from voting (Fairweather and Rogerson, 2002). The 2007 pilot did not appear to have an effect on turnout. The Electoral Commission's report (2007) on the e-voting pilot found that individuals who voted by electronic means would have voted anyway.

A Revised Public Policy Diffusion Model

The basis for this research is an understanding of the integration of the public policy model and the diffusion model. Local authorities became involved in the central government policy process to introduce e-voting at the implementation stage when they were asked to volunteer for the voting trials. This request was then placed on their policy process agenda and the issue of the diffusion of e-voting was only considered by central government at that point.

A New Model

The primary purpose of the proposed new model is to focus on the integration of a diffusion strategy into the design of a public policy at the formulation stage, rather than waiting until the policy implementation stage. Figure 1, shows a revised public policy diffusion model amalgamating selected diffusion concepts at the policy formulation stage.

The revised model of the policy process and diffusion principles proposes that Rogers' constructs of knowledge, persuasion and the attributes of an innovation should be considered during the formulation of a public policy. Careful consideration of these issues would ensure that public policies would be introduced in conjunction with a strategy to enhance adoption. The implementation and routinisation stages as seen in both the diffusion and policy models remain the same. Failure on behalf of central government to appreciate the need to devise an effective diffusion strategy prior to policy implementation is likely to result in an increase in the number of policy failures.

RECOMMENDATIONS FOR A REVISED APPROACH TO POLICY FORMULATION

This section offers advice to the UK government to enhance the likelihood of the voluntary adoption of a public policy introduced by central government for implementation by local government. These recommendations draw on the new public policy diffusion model in Figure 1, and the results of the research. The diffusion concepts addressed by the following recommendations are shown in brackets.

- A formal diffusion strategy should be incorporated into the design of each new policy. *(Knowledge, persuasion and decision)*
- During the formulation phase of a policy, central government should consult with local government regarding the content of the policy, the implementation strategy and the requirements of the local authorities to aid implementation. *(Agenda setting/matching and perceived attributes)*
- During the formulation stage of a policy designed for voluntary implementation, there should be an information strategy segmenting the target audience with increased promotional emphasis on those less likely to adopt. (*Knowledge, Persuasion*)
- Central government should employ opinion leaders to introduce and promote the policy to local government officers and members. *(Persuasion)*
- Central government should fully fund new initiatives including staff education

and training, the provision of specialist staff and administrative reorganisation. *(Persuasion, relative advantage, complexity and compatibility.)*
- Central government should consult with local government to agree realistic legislative and preparation timescales. *(Compatibility, complexity and observability)*
- When a policy is introduced through a pilot programme central government should devise a method of presenting the new policy in a non-threatening manner. For example, the introduction of e-voting could have been prefaced by allowing a local voting trial on a minor local matter. *(Trialability and observability)*
- When a new policy is introduced through a series of pilot schemes, a provisional target date should be proposed when the policy will either be revised or withdrawn. *(Observability and trialability)*
- Following the initial pilot scheme, central government should formulate and publish an outline of best practice. *(Knowledge and observability)*
- An effective evaluation process should establish reasons for compliance with the policy and reasons for non-compliance. Evaluative recommendations from local authorities should form the basis for policy additions or revisions. *(Knowledge, trialability and observability)*

CONCLUSION

The UK government appears to have adopted an incrementalist philosophy underpinned by "serial reconsideration" towards the introduction of electronic voting as a strategy to address falling voter turnouts at elections (Lindblom and Woodhouse, 1993, p29). There is not to be a sudden switch to the new procedures, elections are to offer multi-channels of voting in order that citizens can cast their vote using the medium which most suits them (Fairweather and Rogerson, 2002).

The policy to introduce e-voting may be based on false assumptions as policy makers may not conclusively be able to identify the "real" policy problem as there are myriad pressures on government and its challenge is how to respond (Lindblom and Woodhouse, 1993, p21; Macintosh, in OECD, 2003). Officials usually instigate new reforms at times of crisis (Birkland, 2005). The Public Administration Select Committee (2001) described the collapse in the number of voters as a crisis and noted that central government proposed e-voting as an attempt to reverse the fall in numbers of people casting their votes. However, much of the literature argues that the decline in voter numbers is not due to the voting methods but is due to public disengagement with conventional political activity. Fairweather and Rogerson (2002) note the public's dislike and mistrust of politicians describing the citizens' sense of political impotence as they consider that their vote will not make a difference to the outcome of an election. Further reinforcement of the view that citizens are not voting due to their disillusionment with political life comes in the report from the ICAVM (2002), recognising that within this particular political environment, improving voting methods will not increase the turnout at elections. The Rowntree Trust in its 2006 report *Power* says that the level of "alienation felt towards politicians, the main political parties and the key institutions of the political system is extremely high and widespread." They add that it is the system that the voters reject not the voting methods (p16).

Certain variables which influenced pilot participation in 2003 had less influence in 2007, while issues only identifiable during the 2003 elections influenced decision making in the subsequent years. Rewards for innovation are believed to be important when introducing changes into an organisation (Pettigrew at al, 1994). While rewards of an increase in organisational and personal status

influenced Election Officers' decision-making prior to the 2003 elections, those rewards appear to have had less impact in the later years. However, the risks to the integrity of the ballot experienced during the 2003 elections resonated through the years and proved to be a critical factor in local decision-making in 2007.

Policy makers fail to appreciate the difficulties in policy implementation and where implementation relies on agreements among a large number of participants the prospects for success are reduced (Hogwood and Gunn, 1988; Pressman and Wildavsky, 1984; Maddock, 2002). There are almost 400 local authorities and the introduction of e-voting into the English local government system relies on the cumulative adoption of the new methods of voting to ensure critical mass, but with so few local authorities willing to even try the new voting methods, it appears unlikely that the strategy of voluntary pilots will secure mass adoption. Central government's determination to continue with the pilots may be justified as so few local authorities have trialed e-voting that it is likely not all problems have been encountered.

Evidence suggests that the Election Officers exercise a large measure of influence over the decisions to join the pilot schemes and therein lies a paradox. The UK policy of e-voting is an integral component of the policy to modernise UK e-government processes to enhance participatory democracy by providing an increase in the number of channels through which to cast a vote. However, non-elected officials working within local democratic structures, and entrusted to oversee the diffusion of this policy, have largely acted to prevent its adoption.

Policy failure is linked to attempts to control discretion (Olsen and Manger, 1993). Overtly central government appears to promote decentralisation by promoting local authorities to become enabling authorities overseeing the implementation of this policy, but the opposite is actually happening. Ostensibly local authorities can autonomously decide whether to join the pilot schemes. However central government has attempted to covertly limit that discretion by the use of additional legislation and regulation targeting the type of e-voting pilot, directing resources to particular types of pilot and not providing sufficient funds for local authorities to adapt administrative systems.

The design of a public policy is closely linked to its implementation as decisions at the design phase influence the way in which a policy is implemented which in turn influences the outcomes of the policy (Birkland, 2005). Evidence suggests weaknesses in the design of the policy, as central government had not considered diffusion of this innovation as an integral part of the policy design. Support for this notion comes from the Electoral Commission in its report on the 2007 pilot scheme where it recommends a strategy to address issues of transparency, security and public trust, and sufficient time for planning e-voting pilots. Following this concern mirrored in the report from the Committee on Standards in Public Life (2007), the pilot programme has been suspended, although preparatory work will continue. The above model, Figure 1, illustrates the level of synchronisation required between the diffusion of innovations model and the public policy model to enhance policy adoption. Until central government accepts that there are government controlled mechanisms blocking the diffusion of e-voting, the policy will fail.

FUTURE RESEARCH DIRECTIONS

Future research would analyse the formulation and implementation strategies of a sample of new Acts of Parliament introducing public policies for voluntary implementation by local government. The enquiry would establish the extent to which the obligations within those Acts impact on local discretion and assess whether that influences the likelihood of voluntary policy adoption.

During this research Election Officers commented on the impact of the continuing flow of legislation and directives from central to local government. The consensus was that these initiatives were under-funded and placed additional stress on staff. New directives often limit local discretion and subvert local aims by providing a series of expensive hurdles that slow, or in some cases, thwart local government plans. The respondents cited the *Electoral Administration Act* (2006) as an example of unwarranted burdens imposed on Electoral teams.

This Act is based on recommendations from the Electoral Commission in their report of June 2003 entitled *Voting for Change*. The aim of the Act is to improve the administration of elections, to increase accessibility of voting, tighten security and minimise fraud (Electoral Commission, 2007). Among the many provisions that create new burdens for local councils are the establishment of a standardised electoral register creating access to a national registration database (LGA, 2005). Further provisions allow individuals to register to vote up to 11 days before an election, afford the ability for anonymous registrations for individuals who feel threatened, and provide a new duty for election officials to "encourage participation" by the public in the electoral process. This new duty requires the promotion of registration by an annual canvas to find out who is entitled to vote, sending a reminder form to each property that does not return the original form which is then followed by a letter and form to the occupier of any property who has not responded for 2 years. It is a requirement that visits be made to non-responding properties. The Electoral Commission has powers to set performance standards for maintaining electoral registers and delivery of elections and referendums. While the idea of performance standards to promote best practice garners support, the idea that the standards should include voter turnout is rejected as "this is largely beyond the direct influence of councils" (LGA, 2005, p2). In an effort to combat electoral fraud Election Officers will be required to collect and maintain a record of signatures and dates of birth of all postal voters and update the record every five years. It will be necessary to write to all postal voters requesting this information. Ultimately the Electoral Commission's goal is to ensure 100% of postal voting personal identifiers (signatures and dates of birth) are checked at each election but in the interim a minimum of 20% are to be verified (Electoral Commission, 2007).

The selection of provisions contained in this new Act, outlined above, demonstrates the type of increased burden on local authorities. They need to recruit and train additional staff to complete the administrative requirements of canvassing, personal visits and assembling and updating a database of personal identifiers. These examples indicate that local discretionary power is threatened, as local responsibility for compiling and maintaining the register of voters will be removed and the role of the Electoral Commission will evolve from guiding and promoting standards of good practice to that of an inspectorate.

The value of this future research lies in establishing the impact of central government legislation or directives on local operations and discretion, and the consequent impact on the central/local government relationship. If the research results confirm anecdotal evidence it may then be possible to recommend the revision or removal of some of these centrally derived initiatives thus restoring local discretion and strengthening the autonomy of local government.

REFERENCES

Birch, S., & Watt, B. (2004). Remote Electronic Voting: Free, Fair and Secret? [Oxford, UK: Blackwell Publishing.]. *The Political Quarterly*, 60–72. doi:10.1111/j.1467-923X.2004.00572.x

Birkland, T. (2005). *An Introduction to the Policy Process* (2nd ed.). New York: Sharpe.

Carter, L., & Belangers, F. (2004). The influences of perceived characteristics of innovating on e-government adoption. *Information Systems Journal*, *15*(1), 5–25. doi:10.1111/j.1365-2575.2005.00183.x

Crick, B. (2002). *Democracy: A Very Short Introduction*. Oxford, UK: Oxford Paperbacks.

Department of Constitutional Affairs (DCA). (2007). *Electoral Modernisation Pilots–Local Government Elections 3 May 2007 – Details of pilot initiatives*. London: DCA.

Electoral Commission. (2007). *Changes in England resulting from the Electoral Administration Act 2006*. London: Electoral Commission.

Electoral Commission. (2007). *Democracy Matters: Key Issues and Conclusions*. London: Electoral Commission.

Fairweather, B., & Rogerson, S. (2002). *Implementation of e-voting in the UK.-Technical Options Report*. London: DCA.

Held, D. (1987). *Models of Democracy*. Cambridge, UK: Blackwell.

Hill, M. (2005). *The Public Policy Process* (4th ed.). Harlow, UK: Pearson.

Hindeness, B. (2000). Representative Government and Participatory Democracy. In Vandenberg, A. (Ed.), *Citizenship and Democracy in a Global Era* (pp. 102–113). London: Macmillan Press.

Hogwood, B., & Gunn, L. (1988). *Policy Analysis for the Real World. Oxford, UK: Oxford University Press The Independent Commission Alternative Voting Methods (ICAVM) (2002). Elections in the 21st Century: from paper ballot to e-voting*. London: Electoral Reform Society.

Kamal, M. M. (2006). IT innovation adoption in the government sector: identifying the critical success factors. In. *Journal of Enterprise Information Management*, *19*(2), 192–222. doi:10.1108/17410390610645085

Kelleher, C., & Lowery, D. (2008). Central City Size, Metropolitan Institutions and Political Participation. *British Journal of Political Science*, *39*, 59–92. doi:10.1017/S0007123408000392

Lindblom, C., & Woodhouse, E. (1993). The Policy Making Process 3rd ed. Upper Saddle River, NJ: Prentice Hall Local Government Association (LGA) (2005). Electoral Administration Bill. London: Local Government Association

Macintosh, A. (2003) Using Information and Communication Technologies to Enhance Citizen Engagement in the Policy Process. In OECD (Ed) Promise and Problems of E-Democracy: Challenges of Online Citizens Engagement (pp. 19-140) Paris: OECD Publications

Maddock, S. (2002). Making modernization work: New narratives, change strategies and people management in the public sector. *International Journal of Public Sector Management*, *15*(1), 13–43. doi:10.1108/09513550210414578

Nixon, P., & Koutrakou. (2008). *Europe: Rebooting the system* London: Routledge

Olsen, M., & Marger, M. (1993). *Power in Modern Societies*. Oxford, UK: Westview Press.

Parry, G., & Moyser, G. (1994). More participation, more democracy. In Beetham, D. (Ed.), *Defining and Measuring Democracy* (pp. 44–62). London: Sage.

Pettigrew, A., Ferlie, E., & McKee, L. (1994). *Shaping Strategic Change*. London: Sage.

Pleace, N. (2008). E-government and the United Kingdom. In Nixon, P. & Koutrakou (eds) E-government in Europe: Rebooting the system. (pp. 34-56) London: Routledge

Pressman, J., & Wildavsky, A. (1984). *Implementation* (3rd ed.). London: University of Berkeley.

Public Administration Select Committee. (2001). *6th Report Innovations in Citizen Participation*. London: HMSO.

Robson, C. (2002). *Real World Research* (2nd ed.). Oxford, UK: Blackwell.

Rogers, E. (2003). *Diffusion of Innovations* (5th ed.). New York: Free Press.

Rose, R. (2005). *Learning from Comparative Public Policy*. London: Routledge.

Rowntree Charitable Trust and the Rowntree Reform Trust (RFT). (2006). *Power to the People: An independent enquiry into Britain's democracy*. London: The Power Inquiry.

Schaupp, L., & Carter, L. (2005). E-voting: from apathy to adoption. *The Journal of Enterprise Information Management*, *18*(5), 586–601. doi:10.1108/17410390510624025

Schein, E. (2004). *Organisational Culture and Leadership*. San Francisco: Wiley and Son.

Seldon, A. (2001). *The Blair Effect*. London: Little, Brown and Company.

Serour, M., & Henderson-Sellers, B. (2002). The Role of Organisational Culture on the Adoption and Diffusion of Software Engineering Process: An Empirical Study. In Bunker, D., Wilson. D., and Elliot, S. (Eds) The Adoption and Diffusion in an IT environment of critical change (pp. 76-89) Australia: Pearson

Skocpol, T. (1993). The Potential Autonomy of the State. In Olsen, M., & Marger, M. (Eds.), *Power in Modern Societies* (pp. 306–313). Oxford, UK: Westview Press.

Sorgaard, P. (2004). Co-ordination of e-government: Between politics and pragmatics. In Damsgaard, J., & Henriksen, H. (Eds.), *Networked Information Technologies Diffusion and Adoption*. London: Kluwer.

The Electoral Commission. (2003) *The Shape of Elections to come* London: Electoral Commission Electoral Commission (2005). *Election Results*. Retrieved November 30, from htpp://www.electoralcommission.org.uk/election-data

ADDITIONAL READING

Anderson, J. (2000). *Public Policy Making* (4th ed.). Washington, DC: Houghton Mifflin Co.

Bunker, D., Wilson, D., & Elliot, S. (2002). *The Adoption and Diffusion of IT in an Environment of Critical Change*. Australia: Pearson.

Candy, S. (2001). *Public Attitudes Towards the Implementation of Electronic Voting Qualitative Research Report*. London: BRMB Market Research.

Carter, L., & Belangers, F. (2004). The influences of perceived characteristics of innovating on e-government adoption. *Information Systems Journal*, *15*(1), 5–25. doi:10.1111/j.1365-2575.2005.00183.x

Coaffee, J., & Johnston, L. (2005). The management of local government modernization; Area decentralization and pragmatic localism. *International Journal of Public Sector Management*, *18*(2), 164–177. doi:10.1108/09513550510584982

Committee on Standards in Public Life. (2007). *Review of the Electoral Commission*. London: HMSO.

Dye, T. (2002). *Understanding Public Policy* (10th ed.). London: Prentice Hall.

Eason, K. (1998). *Informational Technology and Organisational Change*. London: Taylor Francis.

Electoral Commission. (2007). *Changes in England resulting from the Electoral Administration Act 2006*. London: Electoral Commission.

Gritalis, D. A. (2003). *Secure Electronic Voting*. Norwell, MA: Kluwer Academic Publishers.

Hedstrom, K. (2004). The Socio-political construction of Caresys in Damsgaard, J and Henriksen, H (Eds) Networked Information Technologies Diffusion and Adoption London: Kluwer.

Jeyaraj, A., Rottman, J., & Lacity, M. (2006). A review of the predictors, linkages and biases in IT innovation adoption research. *Journal of Information Technology*, *21*(1), 1–23. doi:10.1057/palgrave.jit.2000056

Kautz, K., & Larsen, E. (2000). Diffusion theory and practice: Disseminating quality management and software process improvement innovations. *Information Technology & People*, *13*(1), 11–26. doi:10.1108/09593840010312726

Kersting, N., & Baldersheim, H. (Eds.). (2004). *Electronic voting and democracy: A comparative analysis*. London: Palgrave. doi:10.1057/9780230523531

McMaster, T., & Wastell, D. (2005). Diffusion – or delusion? Challenging an IS research tradition. *Information and People*, *18*(4), 383–404. doi:10.1108/09593840510633851

Mustonen-Ollila, E., & Lyytinen, K. (2003). Why organisations adopt information system process innovations: a longitudinal study using Diffusion of Innovation theory. *Information Systems Journal*, *13*, 275–197. doi:10.1046/j.1365-2575.2003.00141.x

O'Callaghan, R. (1998). Technology Diffusion and Organisational Transformation: An Integrated Framework. In Larsen, T., & Maguire, E. (Eds.), *Information Systems Innovation and Diffusion* (pp. 390–410). Hershey, PA: Idea Group.

Rose, R. (1989). *Politics in England* (5th ed.). London: Macmillan Press.

Sobh, R., & Perry, C. (2006). Research design and data analysis in realism research. *Journal of Marketing*, *40*(11/12), 1194–1209. doi:10.1108/03090560610702777

Swan, J., Newell, S., & Robertson, M. (2000). The diffusion, design and social shaping of production management information systems in Europe. *Information Technology & People*, *13*(1), 27–45. doi:10.1108/09593840010312744

KEY TERMS AND DEFINITIONS

E-Voting: Voting by electronic means including digital TV, the Internet, telephone, kiosk (includes electronic vote counting).

Local Authorities: Subordinate agencies providing local government through which central government can organise service provision. Their autonomy derives from the members being elected by local people to represent the interests of the communities in which they live and the council is the legal embodiment of the local authority.

Electoral Commission: An independent body established by the UK Parliament to encourage public participation in, and raise awareness of, the democratic process, modernise electoral processes and regulate political parties.

Rogers' Diffusion of Innovations Theory: A meta-theory presenting a hypothesis to explain the reasons that some innovations are successful and others are not.

Public Policy Process: Conceptual model attempting to simplify the production of a public policy.

Association of Electoral Administrators: The Association was founded in 1987 as a professional body to represent the interests of electoral administrators in the United Kingdom. The Association now has over 1600 members.

Independent Commission on Alternative Voting Methods: An enquiry established by the Electoral Reform Society which campaigns for strengthening of democracy primarily through the reform of the voting system, to report on alternative electoral practices.

Chapter 12
Deliberation, Participation, and "Pockets" of E–Democracy

Michael K. Romano
Western Michigan University, USA

ABSTRACT

Over the past few decades, researchers have attempted to unravel the puzzle of whether or not democracy exists online. According to recent evaluations (Norris, 2001; Hindman, 2009), while we find that the 'Net may have the potential to help spread democracy through its open-endeddiscussions and mass appeal, it has deteriorated into an elite-level discourse due to what is commonly referred to as the "Long Tail" effect (Anderson, 2006) by researchers. This chapter reevaluates the popular theories of democracy online and calls into question the relevance of the question "does digital democracy exist?" Instead, I propose that digital democracy should be evaluated in terms of the sustainability of democratic tendencies within a given site, rather than its mere existence. I argue that scholars have jumped to the conclusion that the potential for democracy online has withered because they have focused too heavily on how a few key websites function to control the majority of traffic on the Web, and have not looked deeper into the infrastructure that is built within these websites and others to evaluate whether or not at a micro-level these sites act and public forums for the open deliberation of ideas and common questions. Instead of viewing democracy through a democratic lens based on liberal proceduralism, we should think of digital democracy existing in "pockets" – self-contained, community-based, democracy based on small, semi-autonomous, group dynamics.

INTRODUCTION

A fundamental inconsistency exists within today's society between the creation of new, interactive participatory spaces through information technology, on the one hand, and the decreased role of the individual as a general participant in governance on the other. The questions of whether digital democracy exists and if individuals, groups or policy makers can harness democratic values on the 'Net

DOI: 10.4018/978-1-61520-933-0.ch012

in order to empower and affect change in politics, both online and off, has generally been combined into one single question: Does democracy exist online? According to scholars, the advent of the Internet as a political medium for the mass public through the creation and implementation of new open, interactive, user-centered applications such as webblogging or "blogging" held great potential to strengthen both online and offline democracy through citizen participation in politics. This early argument for digital democracy was quelled, however, as scholars began to examine the Internet more thoroughly; often concluding that the Internet had not fulfilled any democratic promise but instead had become a forum for "new elites"- the popular blogger or the frequent forum poster.

Recent evaluations (Norris, 2001; Hindman, 2009) have concluded that if we view democracy on the Internet as being achieved through a framework of open deliberation available to users through such popular outlets such as blogging, then the current state of 'the 'Net' is lacking in respect to democratic principles; specifically, that the voices of individuals are equal in an online space, all having the same potential for being heard. According to these accounts, while we find that the Internet may have the potential to help spread democracy through its open-ended discussions and mass appeal, in reality it has deteriorated into an elite-level discourse due to what is commonly referred to in research as the "Long Tail" effect (Anderson, 2006), where a single site sees a disproportionate amount of web traffic in comparison to other like sites. However, such theories based solely on the readership of a particular user's blog or a particular website's proportion of web traffic have overlooked how the Internet works as a participatory forum for deliberation, where individuals come to hear and be heard using a particular website as their own public space to air comments on any given topic.

The question of digital democracy needs to be refocused. Instead of questioning whether or not democracy exists online as some inherent feature built into the Web's coding, the question should be rephrased into one of sustainability of democratic moments built around the sharing of common information. The question then should not be "does democracy exist" but rather "can democracy be sustained online?" Any given site on the Internet can now be designed so that it can allow for democratic tendencies - such as the free exchange of ideas and the freedom to speak openly without fear of punishment - to exist via the sharing of some common connection between individuals. But is this shared commonality sustainable for any prolonged period of time? Scholars have jumped to the conclusion that the potential for democracy online has withered because they have focused too heavily on the long tail effect and how a few key websites function to control the majority of traffic on the Web, and have not looked deeper into the infrastructure that is built within these websites and how individuals utilize this structure in order to build a democratic space. Instead of viewing the Internet through a democratic lens based on liberal proceduralism, where individuals who are presented with a number of alternative choices select only those alternatives that fall in line with their perspectives, we should instead question the sustainability of individual "pockets" of democracy – self-contained, community-based democracy based on small, semi-autonomous, group dynamics.

The purpose of this chapter is to lay the groundwork for a different conception of the role the Internet plays in modern society. I will begin by first outlining some of the major arguments and conceptions of democracy and how these conceptions function to define the democratic space online, along with giving some of the more potent arguments against such an idea. Afterward, I will expand beyond the literature by arguing that the question of "digital democracy" needs to be shifted from liberal proceduralist notions of whether or not democracy exists online, toward questioning sustainability of a democratic space once it has been created. Once this new theory of sustainability is established, some time will be taken to re-examine some of the more critical arguments against digital democracy discussed earlier in the chapter, in order to examine whether looking at the 'Net's democratic potential in terms of its sustainability affects what critics argue. What I find is that while the arguments of critics seem still valid at face value, if we think about digital democracy in terms of sustained "pockets" that ignite and extinguish depending on the potential power of democratic "moment", critic's arguments do not seem as damning as they once were. Finally, some time will be taken to focus on future research questions that can be asked about e-governance and citizenship once we refocus the definition of digital democracy away from the traditional notion of deliberative democracy that is utilized by liberal proceduralism toward the question of sustainability.

BACKGROUND

Since the 1980s, the theme of democratic theory and discourse has shifted away from the notion of participation in governance as the foundation of democracy toward a focus upon free and open deliberation in the public sphere (Hauptmann, 2001). According to Hauptmann (2001), the basic criticism of participatory democracy levied against leftist deliberative scholars was that participatory theory was, "unrealistic, both in its conception of modern societies and in its visions of their transformations" via political participation (Hauptmann, 2001: 399). Instead of focusing on transformations of society through participation in governance, deliberative democrats tended to focus more attention on how democracies could legitimately justify and implement decisions that were not based on unanimous consent. The question, then, for deliberative scholars was how can democracy be sustainable in a complex, diverse society such as the one's that exist in modern

society, where it is often improbable for a consensus to be reached on all actions or topics. Democratic sustainability then, for the purposes of this chapter will be defined as the ability of a given conglomeration of individuals (such as a group, party, or society) to maintain "good" democratic tendencies such as freedom of expression, equality of citizens and so forth as well as maintain their ability to be a part of the governing process over a prolonged period of time. I state "good" democratic tendencies here because when we discuss democracy, often times it is used as a guise to describe some normative notion of what we determine as "good" in a society, however not all democratic tendencies can be considered "good" for all given societies. A "good society", however, is often called a democratic society, and as such, its practices are good as well.

In applying this conception of democracy to governance, deliberative democrats often start their arguments, in one way or another, by stating that a rule of action (such as policies implemented by government) is only justifiable if those who are affected by the rule or action had a hand in making the decision. Loosely, this is what Habermas (1991) refers to as a "discourse ethic" (pg. 196-97). Habermas (1991) contends that in a competition of arguments, which we can define deliberation as being, "proponents and opponents engage in competition…in order to convince one another, that is, in order to reach a consensus" (pg. 160). The strong criterion of consensus put forth by Habermas is generally relaxed when examining modern, diverse societies, however. Restated with this relaxation of the consensus criterion then, actions in a deliberative democracy are based upon the majority agreement of what constitutes a public good – things deemed worthy or desireable in their attainment by most members of a society (Benhabib, 1996). This criterion for legitimating action, shared by most liberal proceduralist theories, is actualized in deliberative democracy through the open, free and fair sharing of information via communication and deliberation with other free and equal citizens in the public sphere. Decisions are made and legitimated via the rule of the majority, but there is an understanding in theories of deliberative democracy that those decisions are not set in stone and can be reexamined at a later time if necessary (Benhabib, 1996).

The problem with this sustainability criterion is that it is often the case that societies cannot maintain good democratic tendencies for a prolonged period of time. The sustainability criterion assumes that general interest in continuing these "good" democratic tendencies is an interest held by the individuals who make up a given group, however it is often the case, according to some, that high interest in democratic governance among the masses of a society is highly improbable. Robert Michels (1915), in his *Political Parties*, notes that any organization, regardless of how democratic or autocratic they may start out as, will eventually succumb to oligarchic rule, or develop oligarchic tendencies. This is what is commonly referred to as the "Iron Law of Oligarchy". One of the reason's Michels' points to for why this occurs is the passivity of mass society to govern themselves. As Michels' (1915) notes, "the majority is really delighted to find persons who will take the trouble to look after its affairs" (pg. 38). Something, or someone, must generally move the masses to action then, and for Michels that generally means some form of leadership by an elite group of individuals, who will make decisions for the masses.

Generally speaking, advances in communication technology, from the invention of the printing press and the postal service system to telegraphs and telephones, have all operated in some form in order expand the public sphere and the abilities of individuals and groups to communicate with one another, with the assumption being that greater communicative ability increases the ability to deliberate among diverse populations and thus sustain good democratic tendencies. When the Internet was just starting to grow into a commercial enterprise outside of the labs and

universities across the United States, it was the hope of deliberative scholars that the 'Net would, "expand the public sphere, broadening the range of ideas discussed and the number of citizens allowed to participate" in politics (Hindman, 2009: 7). This hope was not absurd, since the primary infrastructure of the Internet, the protocols, wires, computers and hardware as well as the constraints of the code that make up the different layers of the Internet, all act in order to create a sphere of communication between different nodes; whether those nodes are individuals, groups, organizations, or institutions that all act in concert with one another in modern society. On the Internet then, communication is key. More so than other forms of communication technology, the Internet has allowed individuals a fast, relatively easy way to participate and to open up lines of communication between individuals or groups with the institutions that make up their governments.

But this communication does not necessarily mean that the goal of deliberation on the Internet is consensus. At its inception, the Internet's main function was to share information. The ability to deliberate came only as new and differing ideas began to fill the space that the Internet had created. As the Internet expanded and its popularity grew, partly due to the invention and development of the World Wide Web (WWW)[1] created by English physicist Sir Timothy John Berners-Lee in the late 1980s, a more "user friendly" Internet began to take shape, creating a space for the expansion of the political voice of the average citizen. When Mosaic, the first popular graphical Web browser, was released by a group of college students at the University of Illinois in 1993, it changed the face of the Internet forever. According to Matthew Hindman (2009), Mosaic, which was commercialized as the Netscape browser soon after its release in 1993, "transformed [the Internet] from a haven for techies and academics into the fastest growing communication technology in history" (pg. 1). As more and more people began to "go online", many noted that the biggest promise the Internet had was in the realm of politics; where the Web could be utilized to give the people a voice in their government through their new found ability to speak with little to no editorial censorship as there is with newspapers and other "traditional medias". The 'Net also promised to give smaller fringe political groups and parties the ability to rise and gain support, leading supporters to state that the Internet has a "democratizing" affect on society (Powell, 2002; Trippi, 2005). The Supreme Court of the United States tended to agree with proponents of digital democracy as well. In *Reno vs. ACLU*, in which the Supreme Court struck down two major clauses of the Communications Decency Act of 1996, which attempted to regulate and define "obscenity" and "indecency" on the Internet, Justice John Paul Stevens, writing the opinion on behalf of the unanimous Court[2], noted the democratizing power that the Web had, stating:

Any person or organization with a computer connected to the Internet can "publish" information...

Through the use of chat rooms, any person with a phone line can become a town crier with a voice that resonates farther that it could from any soapbox. Through the use of Web pages, mail exploders, and newsgroups, the same individual can become a pamphleteer. As the District Court found, "the extent on the Internet is as diverse as human thought".

For many then, the democratic power of the Internet is solely its power to give a voice to the individual or group. As stated by John Perry-Barlow (1996), founding member of the Electronic Frontier Foundation (EFF) "We are creating a world where anyone, anywhere may express his or her beliefs, no matter how singular, without fear of being coerced into silence or conformity" (eff.org, 1996).

Political scholars (Hindman, 2009; Sunstein 2001; Davis 1999), however, have been more critical about the democratic power of the Internet. If participation in politics is understood to be meaningful primarily through deliberation in the public sphere as proceduralist and deliberative democrats argue (Rawls, 2005; Cohen, 1989; Gutmann and Thomas, 1996), then it follows that, as Sidney Verba, Kay Lehman Schlozman, and Henry Brady (1995) state in *Voice and Equality*, "meaningful democratic participation requires that the voices of citizens in politics be clear, loud, and equal" (pg. 509). In this respect, the Internet does not fulfill on its democratic promise. Parkinson (2006) notes that while we may be able to get more people to "sit at the same table" together through the use of information technology like the Internet it is not necessarily the case that individuals can deliberate together in the traditional sense. Deliberative sites on the Internet may allow individuals to talk with one another, in this regard, but critics argue that it is not so much that individuals are talking with one another but rather talking past one another. Cass Sunstein (2001) argues that perhaps they are not talking to each other at all, since the Internet has allowed individuals the almost unlimited ability to filter the information they receive. The Internet allows individuals so much freedom of choice in what they see, Sunstein (2001) argues, that the 'Net becomes polarizing; causing individuals to view only information that corresponds to their viewpoints without having interaction with an opposition view through "general interest intermediaries" – things such as traditional newspapers, magazines, and broadcasting (pg. 11).[3] With a general interest intermediary, individuals have a higher likelihood of interacting with the opposing viewpoint, but with increased power over choice and the ability of individuals to shape their news according to their own individual preference – what Sunstein imagines as the "Daily Me" style of news – the likelihood of reading the opposing view decreases dramatically or disappears entirely.

Sunstein is not alone in making this argument, however, as scholars such as Robert Putnam (2000) state concern that the Internet will produce was he terms "cyberbalkanization" (pg. 178) – the division of cyberspace into fragmentary, hostile factions over an issue or topic with no room for communication with each other and, in some cases, outright hostility to the "other". The fragmentation of individuals into non-interacting groups online causes the loudness digital political voices to be dampened tremendously. It is assumed that in a deliberative democracy, deliberation must occur between oppositional sides on an issue, with both sides able to come to the deliberation with a sense of understanding that the opposing viewpoint has a valid reason for being stated. The competition of ideas, held by deliberative democrats such as Habermas (1991)Benhabib (1996) and others as crucial to democratic practices is in danger of becoming obsolete on the Internet because digital open "public forums" do not exist, or are in danger of becoming extinct (Sunstein, 2001). On the Internet, democracy suffers, according to critics, because opposing views are keeping themselves separate from each other, loosing exposure to the "other" and causing public debate to become polarized and coarse. Meaningful deliberation, on the other hand, requires that individuals come to the deliberation with an open mind that is, a willingness to accept their viewpoint as perhaps incorrect and accept an alternative or at least a willingness to accept others viewpoints and opinions as valid, while not generally accepting them as truths (Benhabib, 1996; Rawls, 2005; Young, 1996). This feature is fundamentally lacking, according to critics, in most online deliberation since much of the "deliberation" that is occurring is occurring between like-minded niches of individuals with a similar viewpoints and agendas.

More recently, critics of digital democracy (Hindman, 2009) have also noted that the democracy on the Internet is highly unlikely since the structure of the Web and the search behavior of most online users follow what is called a "power law" distribution. A power law distribution, it should be understood, is a mathematical law applied to the Web that states that the, "probability of finding a Web site with a given number of pages, n, is proportional to $1/n^\beta$, where β is a number greater than or equal to 1" (Huberman, 2001). When applied to the Internet, the basic understanding of a power law is as follow: a few key Web sites – what I will refer to as "elite" Web sites – gain an overwhelming majority of the traffic online, while a majority of Web sites garner a smaller number of Web traffic by comparison. For researchers such as Hindman (2003, 2009) power law distributions reveal the inherent inequality of digital space since Web sites produced by elites are always at the top of search indexes provided by Google or Yahoo!, since they are the most heavily linked sites[4], leaving other Web sites with little or no traffic. This argument is sometimes also referred to as the "Long Tail" effect, since graphical representations of the effect are often highly skewed along the X-axis. As we will see a bit later, it is questionable just how strong the Long Tail's effect truly is, and it seems likely that political scholar's may have misinterpreted just what the effect of the Long Tail is on political discourse.

"Pockets" of Democracy

Does the Internet have a response to the critiques levied by political scholars? Is the 'Net non-democratic or suffering from democratic apathy? Do we need democracy online in the first place? In the previous section, I outlined some of the doubts raised by political scholars about the democratic integrity of the Internet. But what is digital democracy in the first place? And is it something that is actually desirable?

It is not uncommon for new technologies to be viewed as democratic. Previous research by Starr (2004) has shown that new communication technologies, from the printing press to the telephone, radio and soon have been seen as democratic by their very nature. However, the first thing we must not forget that the Internet, along with any other communicative device, is a tool. It is only as democratic or despotic as those who regulate it want it to be. Thus the "free, unregulated democratic Internet" of the United States, is not the same as the government controlled, regulated Internet of China or Singapore. There is no innate essence to the Internet that makes it prone toward "good" democratic tendencies, such as equality or freedom. I argue, with Lessig (1999), that cyberspace is a structure – something that has been constructed and as such something that can (and is) the product of regulation. That regulation can be strict and government controlled, as is the case with China's "Great Firewall", which censors and blocks certain websites from being viewed by browsers connected to China's proxy servers. Regulation can also be loosely controlled via the market, with little to no government regulation, such as the case in the United States, where independent Internet Service Providers (ISP) are often left with the responsibility to regulate the how the Internet can be utilized by users who access from within the United States. The difference between regulated and unregulated networks – such as the China or the United States respectively – is, "a matter of code – a difference in the software" (Lessig, 1999: 27).

How, then, should we understand democracy, in order to apply it to the Internet? While most scholars tend to believe that the best definition of democracy that can be applied to the Internet is the deliberative proceduralist definition put forth by authors such as Habermas (1991), Rawls (1971, 2005), Benhabib (1996), or Cohen (1989), in which, as stated earlier, actions of government are seen as valid and democratic if all those who are affected by the decision had a hand in choosing and deciding the outcome through a process of open deliberation, I contend that democracy can best be defined online using the definition put forth by Sheldon Wolin (1996), stating that:

Democracy is a project concerned with the political potentialities of ordinary citizens, that is, with their possibilities for becoming political beings through the self-discovery of common concerns and of modes of action for realizing them. (pg. 31)

It is important, first, to note what is meant here by the political. Wolin (1996) argues that the political is the, "idea that a free society composed of diversities can nonetheless enjoy moments of commonality when, through public deliberation, collective power is used to promote or protect the well-being of the collectivity" (pg. 31). Online, the individual can experience these moments of commonality not just in individual blogs that pop up and disappear every day, but also in the commentary left *by the readers* of a popular, or unpopular, blog, as well as the open, free discussion groups and bulletin boards provided by most common interest groups sponsored through Google.com and Yahoo!. Viewing democracy online using Wolin's definition allows us to better understand how and when democracy exists. "Digital democracy" is not something inherent, nor is it something written in some declaration; instead it is something that is discoverable and developed through the interaction of individuals in a virtual space. Democracy then is not the end in itself, the pedestal that we place the Internet on due to some innate power that it has to allow the individual to have a voice, as critics argue. Instead, the Internet is the *means* through which individuals can enter politics, that is, to become part of the political.

There are two important aspects that need to be examined with regard to the sustainability of digital democracy if we are to use Wolin's definition. First, democracy online should be considered fragmentary, in the sense that "democracy" does not exist in some totality of a system or within the infrastructure of the Web as it was designed when being developed in the universities across the United States. Democracy online is made up of momentary incidents of commonality that are found online between average citizens. These incidents of commonality can occur in many ways, from the simple creation of a common interest group online to the mutual online support of a political candidate. The Internet is not some bounded nation or finite space that can be boxed up and displayed and labeled "democratic" or not. If democratic tendencies are not found in one public site online, it does not necessarily mean that democracy does not exist altogether. Democracy is found in "pockets" online – fragmentary public forums where average citizens gather to discuss a particular topic at length and create cultures and patterns within a given topic or issue. These pockets of democracy are comprised of given communities, created around a central topic or idea in common, but at the same time comprised of differing viewpoints on the world. The pocket remains democratic, and indeed remains intact, only as long as the individuals within it maintain a remembrance of the "democratic moment" – the moment in which a group of individuals become a community around a given topic of discussion. The individual, in this case, is not the passive consumer of information as described by Hindman (2009), Sunstein (2001) and others who base their arguments of digital democracy on the *readership* of a particular weblog - the diaries and commentaries posted online commonly referred to as "blogs" – but instead sees the individual as also active "doers and actors" (Young, 1990: 37), interested in promoting, "many values of social justice in addition to fairness in the distribution of goods…expressing our experience, feelings, and perspective on social life in contexts where others can listen" (Young, 1990: 37). These critiques of digital democracy have focused their attention on the elites, and thus on the oligarchical nature of the Web in terms of how web traffic is divided. Democratic "pockets" however, has a place for the elites as well. "Elites" – the well educated, well informed blogger or forum poster, most often whom works within the industry they are commenting

on – supply the democratic moment that is so important to this fragmentary form of democracy. They are suppliers, important to the democratic process because they supply the starting point for deliberation among ordinary individuals. The individual does not have to just passively read what an elite has to say and absorb that information, as they have to do with newspapers or television in most cases. The individual now can talk back quickly and easily, often without strict editorial filters; they can openly express their opinion about what is said in a popular blog via the comments section that often follows any article or blog. It is here where democratic "pockets" exist - through open dialogues, conversations between individuals who are active and interested in a given topic. The dialogues exist continually, constantly in flux and never stagnant as long as those involved remember the democratic moment when they were brought together as a community.

There is a second, slightly less intuitive aspect of digital democracies sustainability. When defining digital democracy as a continuation of a democratic project concerned with the creation of commonality between individuals, we find that democracy rarely exists for very long online with regard to a single topic, issue, cause or other commonality, but at the same time exists almost constantly online with regard to the potentiality of democratic moments to appear. "Moments" of democracy, as described by Wolin (1996), are the times in which individuals discover common links between one another and form into self-governing groups around a given topic or cause. That is, the democratic moment is the realization of the political as defined by Wolin and used to describe democracy online. Democratic moments online are only sustained for as long as those individuals involved maintain the conversation. This can be a matter of days, weeks, months, or mere minutes depending on the topic. Sometimes, the moment can even set its own deadline for ending, such as online support for political candidates, which, generally speaking, ends after Election Day. What is important is that while the democratic moment might ignite and die out quickly on one site on the 'Net, it is recurring continually at all times as well. The democratic process is recreated in a process of renewal, when ordinary citizens create new cultural patterns of commonality on topics of interest. As stated before, the Internet is not some finite space with limits and boundaries, and as such the possibility for a democratic moment at any given point in time is infinite, while at the same time the possibility of a moment dying out is infinite as well.

Critiques of Digital Democracy and the Democratic Moment

Does thinking about democracy online in terms of sustainability of individual pockets do anything to affect the way in which we view digital democracy? Recall earlier it was stated that if politics is understood to be meaningful primarily through deliberation in the public sphere then as Verba, Schlozman and Brady (1995) point out, "meaningful democratic participation requires that the voices of citizens in politics be clear, loud, and equal" (pg. 509). Deliberative sites on the Internet may allow individuals to talk with one another but critics argue that most often it is not so much that individuals are talking with one another but rather talking past one another. Because of this, critics argue, digital voices are far from being loud, in regard to being easily found online so that voices can be heard, and as such, the term "digital democracy" is a bit of a misnomer. In this section I will first examine the argument that the digital voice of the average individual has the unique characteristic of being generally softer than those of "elites" online, and then analyze this arguments using the definition of democracy with regard to the sustainability of the democratic moment online discussed in the previous section. What I find is that while the initial arguments made by political scholars that loudness of digital voices is an issue that causes the Internet to seem less democratic

than proponents of cyber-democracy believe, if we reconsider the question to one focused on the idea of the sustainability of democratic moments online, we find that the voice of citizens on the Internet is louder than it might first appear.

Loudness of voice poses a fundamental problem online according to critics of digital democracy. The belief by proponents of digital democracy that individuals will be able to have loud voices that permeate throughout the public sphere has been argued to be a bit far-fetched. Richard Davis (1999) noted that the Internet will not be as revolutionary as futurists (proponents such as Perry-Barlow) led us to believe, arguing that, "existing dominate players are adapting to the Internet, and…the Internet is not an adequate tool for public political involvement" (pg. 168). Further backing up this argument, Hindman (2008) argues against the theory that political discourse on the Internet can have "trickle-up" affect as proponents believe. "When everybody has a modem, the people who end up getting read are not middle schoolers or a, as NBC News anchor Brian Williams imagines, 'guy named Vinny in an efficiency apartment in the Bronx who hasn't left the efficiency apartment in two years.' They are overwhelmingly educational, social, business, and technical elites" (Hindman, 2008: www.matthewhindman.com). This, Hindman describes, is due to what he refers to as "Googlearchy" on the Web – the phenomenon where a few heavily linked sites dominate the political information on the Web, even if users use different search engines in their hunt for information or even if they use no search engine at all. As Robert Iger, president of ABC-TV, notes about the Internet, "In a world in which there is massive choice, there's still going to be a need for someone to create order" (quoted from Davis, 1999: 169). The mass public online goes primarily to elites for their information, to news Web sites of major news outlets such as ABC-news, MSNBC, the New York Times and so on. In the literature on public opinion, scholars such as Zaller (1992) and Page and Shapiro (1992) draw a distinction between those who craft the news – those who write and disseminate information – and those who receive the news. This model, in communicative theory, is a one-way transmission model, where elites transfer knowledge to the masses, without engaging in conversation with the masses they are seeking to inform. This translates into what is referred to as the "Long Tail" (Anderson, 2006), where most Web traffic is situated on a few key sites where most individuals go to get their information; sites such as ABCNews.com, MSNBC.com or BBC.com. Thus, if political voice must be "loud" in the sense that it can be easily heard by the masses in order to be meaningful, than on the Internet most voices are meaningless, since the Web traffic to most small public sites online is disproportionately smaller than traffic to larger sites or the sites with more well known authors (Sunstein, 2001). The theory that more media choices will translate into a diversity of viewpoints being funneled into the public sphere, as well, as been debunked by critics as being highly unlikely; either because of the choices that users make in political information selection (Hindman 2009) or because the expansion of options of what to do when surfing the Web had led many users to overlook political information in favor of entertainment (Prior, 2005).

The mass public online goes primarily to elites for their information, to news Web sites of major news outlets such as ABC-news, MSNBC, the New York Times and so on. In the literature on public opinion, scholars such as Zaller (1992) and Page and Shapiro (1992) draw a distinction between those who craft the news – those who write and disseminate information – and those who receive the news. This model, in communicative theory, is a one-way transmission model, where elites transfer knowledge to the masses, without engaging in conversation with the masses they are seeking to inform. This notion of communication is the norm in the traditional broadcast era of radio, newspapers, and television, and is one

that researchers such as Hindman (2009) attribute to the Internet in their arguments that meaningful deliberation boils down to the readership of a particular blog or Web traffic to a particular website, however it does not accurately portray the existence of moments of democracy created by those readers or users who use elite websites in order to sustain and build conversations. One of the implicit characteristics of a deliberative democratic theory is that individuals who are taking part in deliberations are taking part in a conversation, that is, they are talking to one another. They give and receive information, and as long as this process continues the democratic moment is sustained. The communication model that best fits the description of communication on the Internet is not the traditional one-way media model, but rather a two-way communication model. In a two-way communication model, both sender and receiver (in this case, both the elite and the masses) are involved in dialogue with each other on a given topic; feeding off of each other and completing their knowledge of a given topic based upon what they learn from each other. Online, the dialogue occurs in two ways: either through a discussion board attached to a particular topic or issue, where individuals come together to discuss the complexity of an issue that they are interested in (among other things usually), or more simply, through the comments section, located conveniently underneath a majority of blogs on the Web. As such, elites do not just transmit the messages to the masses without repercussion, they are subject to critique and praise by those interested in what they have to say; the elites, in some cases, *become the democratic moment* around which a community is built. This is no better exemplified than during Presidential elections in the United States, particularly the 2004 primary race of Democrat Howard Dean and the major success of Democrat Barack Obama in 2008. Both candidates utilized the Web extensively in their campaigns, gaining major following and building large, broad based communities around their campaign messages.

But the elites, in this case either Howard Dean or Barack Obama, are not just the transmitter of the message, they are part of the community as well, changing and evolving their message as the dialogue continues. As Howard Dean, an avid blogger while on the campaign trail during the 2004 Presidential campaign noted in an interview with Wired! Magazine, when it came to the comments section of his Web site, "We listen. We pay attention. If I give a speech and the blog people don't like it, next time I change the speech…what we've given people is a way to shout back, and we listen, they don't even have to shout anymore" (Wired.com, 2004).

A final concern of digital democracy comes in the question posed by Sunstein (2001) on what to do about the unlimited power of the individual to filter their information. The argument about filtering is posed on the understanding that the individual is a singular identity. This is rooted in the proceduralist notion that human beings have specific preferences among a set of alternatives that can be ordered based upon the benefit to the individual in the singular. Action, in this case, is based upon individual preference. Sunstein's "Daily Me" is an unadulterated example of this individualism at work online, where the individual focuses all of his or her attention on a singular topic which they are interested in, closing off themselves to all other opinions or topics. Filtering, according to Sunstein, is unavoidable, it will occur no matter what medium we choose and will continue so long as human history continues. The problem, for Sunstein, is that on the Internet, which is a democratic space according to Sunstein, the individual has the ability to unlimitedly filter and choose what information they are interested in. "Only tyrannies force people to read or to watch" according to Sunstein (2001: pg. 11). However, the fragmented pockets of democracy online allow individuals the ability to fragment themselves as well. The ability to fragment one's identity entirely is primarily found on the Internet. This is what Lessig (1999) refers to as the ability of individuals

to "authenticate" him or herself online and offline (pg. 30-1). Offline – that is, in the "real world" in which we all exist – individuals are able to self-identify themselves to others quickly and easily. A quick glance at offline me will automatically assert certain facts about who I am without me having to identify them to others verbally: I am a male, relatively young, I am Caucasian and average of build. These traits identify me as an individual and I have, for the most part, no control over letting others see these identifiers.[5] Online, however, I have the ability to control any and all ways that I identify myself, to a point. The only identifier that I, as an individual, cannot control online is my affinity for a certain issue or topic. The individuals that I meet and converse with on a discussion forum about public policy regarding regulation on the Internet in the United States might not know that I am white; they might not know that I have brown hair; but they do know through my participation on such a forum that I support what is commonly referred to as "Net Neutrality." Similarly, the people I converse with on an online forum about cats may not know my stance on Net Neutrality, nor any of the identifiers mentioned above, but they do know that, as a member of a forum on cats, I either have a cat or love cats, or both. Just as the adage, made famous by *New Yorker* cartoonist Peter Steiner (1993) goes, "Online, no one knows you're a dog" (pg. 61). What people do know is your belief in a certain democratic moment, the creation of a community around the topic of Net Neutrality or cats. Individuals, as such, are not singular in their identities, and their ability to filter online is only as efficient as the groups and Web sites they choose to view and participate on. Other individuals on an online public forum may post whatever they wish, within reason and based upon the rules agreed upon by the community they are involved with. The simple addition of a section on "politics" on a given forum exposes the individual to potentially unwanted viewpoints and subjects on a given political topic that might be outside the traditional interest of a community (such as cats, or Net Neutrality). Filtering can still occur at this point – the individual can just choose not to read or participate in those posts about politics – but this is an ability that he or she has in the offline world just as much as the online one.

FUTURE RESEARCH DIRECTIONS

This chapter has been primarily focused on rebuilding the theory of digital democracy through a shift in focus in how we analyze the existence of "online democracy". It has been the argument of this chapter that the standard questioning of "does democracy exist on the Internet?" should be retooled and focused instead on the perhaps more suitable and answerable question of "How can we sustain the values of democracy online?" The purpose of this chapter has also been an attempt to outline some of the more substantial critiques the Internet's abilities to open up lines of deliberation between individuals in order to create a more democratic web. Future research then should start by refocusing theories of digital democracy with the understanding that a democratic Internet is a user-defined project in expanding the political and common potentialities between individuals. The project is one of community building; of finding a common thread that connects individuals who cannot, and perhaps will never, see each other face to face. The furthering of the democratic project online can focus on a number of different focal points found online. Specifically, we can question what the role of government regulation is on the democratic project? What is the role of the moderator – those individuals, groups or companies who develop, build, and maintain a given website – in the maintenance and control of the democratic moment and, more broadly, on the democratic project of a particular pocket of democracy online? What role does the individual play specifically in this process as well?

CONCLUSION

As I have stated multiple times throughout the course of this chapter, the Internet is not a solid constituted body or institution that can be fitted with a particular definition of democracy such as free and equal choice among alternatives by individuals with their own individual preferences. Instead, we should understand that democracy is a project, an attempt at finding common links with one another through the sharing of information and the open and free exchange of ideas. While this is not to say that the Internet is a "project in democracy" – as stated at the beginning of the chapter, the Internet is a tool, built by people and regulated to some degree by the government or by independent service providers – I do mean to say that the Internet does have limitless potential to be democratic. Democracy, both online and offline, is an ongoing cycle of development that is paved around a "democratic moment" – a time when new bonds of commonality are created amongst a group of like-minded individuals. Offline these moments are generally rare; they occur most potently with the forming of new nations, the signing of constitutions or the creation of new and lasting groups. Most often, these moments, in order to be considered significant, must exist for a prolonged amount of time before being extinguished and renewed through some new democratic act. Online, however, democratic moments exist almost infinitely, as new interest groups and communities are created constantly around given topics. These moments, unlike their offline counterparts, can exist for mere minutes, as individuals comment and deliberate with each other on blog posts and open forums, or can exist just as long as their offline counterparts, and individuals come back to the communities they've found and feel a common bond with, engaging in deliberations and sharing information with one another.

What this chapter has attempted to show is that the traditional ways of viewing digital democracy from the perspective that democracy is based on the ability of individuals to choose their information from a set of equally attainable alternatives does not accurately portray the democratic tendencies being utilized on the 'Net. Instead, digital democracy should be based upon the level of interaction and deliberation that actually occurs between individuals on a given site. The massive amounts of information that exists on the Internet makes it almost impossible for a single individual to visit every site on a given topic, and some sites are bound to give more information, better information, or more favorable information to individuals interested in any given number of topics. What is important is that when scrutinizing the 'Net we recall that no active site on the Internet has no traffic. Someone always listens, even if those who listen are close relatives or friends. The democratic moment that is made when individuals come together online continues so long as those individuals continue to use the site they have found online as a public forum, as a point of deliberation, and continue to participate in the deliberation. Once inanimate, individuals shift their attention to a new moment, a new community, which opens up new opportunities from exposure to ideas and information. The individual is never the passive recipient of information, as they were in traditional one-way communication models, but instead are active in the dialogue until the individual decides to silence him or herself, or the democratic moment is put out due to some set time frame or other factor.

REFERENCES

Anderson, C. (2006). *The Long Tail: Why the Future of Business is Selling Less of More*. New York: Hyperion Publishing.

Benhabib, S. (1996). Toward a Deliberative Model of Democratic Legitimacy. In Benhabib, S. (Ed.), *Democracy and Difference: Contesting the Boundaries of the Political* (pp. 67–94). Princeton, NJ: Princeton University Press.

Bimber, B. (2000). The Gender Gap on the Internet. *Social Science Quarterly, 81*, 868–876.

Cohen, J. (1989). Deliberation and Democratic Legitimacy. In Hamlin, A., & Pettit, P. (Eds.), *The Good Polity: Normative Analysis of the State* (pp. 17–34). Hoboken, NJ: Wiley-Blackwell Press.

Davis, R. (1999). *The Web of Politics: The Internet's Impact on the American Political System*. New York: Oxford University Press.

DiMaggio, P., Hargittai, E., Ceste, C., & Shafer, S. (2004). Digital Inequality: From Unequal Access to Differentiated Use. In Neckerman, K. (Ed.), *Social Inequality* (pp. 355–400). New York: Russell Sage Foundation.

Gutmann, A., & Thompson, D. (1996). *Democracy and Disagreement*. Cambridge, MA: Harvard University Press.

Habermas, J. (1991). *Moral Consciousness and Communicative Action. C. Lenhardt & S.W. Nicholsen (Trans.)*. Cambridge, MA: MIT Press.

Hauptmann, E. (2001). Can Less Be More?: Leftist Deliberative Democrats' Critique of Participatory Democracy. *Polity, 33*(3), 397–421. doi:10.2307/3235441

Hindman, M. (2008). *The Only Criterion for Membership Is a Modem*. Retrieved March 16th, 2009, from http://www.matthewhindman.com/index.php/2008070736/The-Myth-of-Digital-Democracy/-The-Only-Criterion-for-Membership-Is-a-Modem.html

Hindman, M. (2009). *The Myth of Digital Democracy*. Princeton, NJ: Princeton University Press.

Hindman, M., & Cukier, K. N. (in press). More News, Less Diversity. *The New York Times*.

Hindman, M., Tsioutsiouliklis, K., & Johnson, J. A. (2003). *Googlearchy: How a Few Heavily Linked Sites Dominate Politics Online*. Paper presented at the annual meeting of the Midwest Political Science Association. Chicago, IL.

Huberman, B. A. (2001). *The Laws of the Web: Patterns of Ecology of Information*. Cambridge, MA: MIT Press.

Lessig, L. (1999). *Code and Other Laws of Cyberspace*. New York: Basic Books.

Michels, R. (1915). *Political Parties: A Sociological Study of the Oligarchical Tendencies of Modern Democracy. Translated by Eden Paul and Cedar Paul*. New York: The Free Press.

Mossberger, K., Tolbert, C. J., & Stansbury, M. (2003). *Virtual Inequality: Beyond the Digital Divide*. Washington, DC: Georgetown University Press.

National Telecommunications and Information Administration (NTIA). (2000, February). *Falling Through the Net: Toward Digital Inclusion*. Report, Washington, DC: National Telecommunication and Information Administration.

National Telecommunications and Information Administration (NTIA). (2002, February). *A Nation Online: How Americans Are Expanding Their Use of the Internet*. Report, Washington, DC: National Telecommunication and Information Administration.

National Telecommunications and Information Administration (NTIA). (2002, September). *A Nation Online: Entering the Broadband Age*. Report, Washington, DC: National Telecommunication and Information Administration.

Nielsen, J. (2003). Diversity is Power for Specialized Sites. Retrieved March 4th, 2009, from http://www.useit.com/alertbox/20030616.html

Norris, P. (2001). *Digital Divide: Civic Engagement, Information Poverty, and the Internet in Democratic Societies*. New York: Cambridge University Press.

O'Gorman, K. (2007). Brian Williams Weighs in on New Medium. *We Want Media*. Retrieved March 16th, 2009, from http://journalism.nyu.edu/pubzone/wewantmedia/node/487

Page, B. I., & Shapiro, R. I. (1992). The Rational Public: Fifty Years of Trends in Americans' Policy Preferences. Chicago, I: University of Chicago Press.

Parkinson, J. (2006). *Deliberating in the Real World: Problems of Legitimacy in Deliberative Democracy*. New York: Oxford University Press.

Perry-Barlow, J. (1996). A Declaration of the Independence of Cyberspace. Retrieved March 16th, 2009, from http://www.eff.org/ ~barlow/Declaration-Final.html

Powell, M. K. (2002). *Remarks of the FCC Chairman at the Broadband Technology Summit*, U.S. Chamber of Commerce, Washington, D.C., April 30th. Retrieved March 9th, 2009, from http://www.fcc.gov/Speeches/Powell/2002/spmkp205.html

Prior, M. (2005). News vs. Entertainment: How Increasing Media Choice Widens Gaps in Political Knowledge and Turnout. *American Journal of Political Science*, *49*(3), 577–592. doi:10.1111/j.1540-5907.2005.00143.x

Putnam, R. (2000). *Bowling Alone: The Collapse and Revival of American Community*. New York: Simon and Schuster.

Rawls, J. (1971). *A Theory of Justice*. Cambridge, MA: Harvard University Press.

Rawls, J. (2005). *Political Liberalism*. New York: Columbia University Press.

Starr, P. (2004). *The Creation of the Media: Political Origins of Modern Communication*. New York: Basic Books.

Steiner, P. (1993, July 5). Online No One Knows You're a Dog (pp 61). *The New Yorker*.

Sunstein, C. (2001). *Republic.com*. Princeton, NJ: Princeton University Press.

Trippi, J. (2005). *The Revolution Will Not Be Televised: Democracy, the Internet, and the Overthrow of Everything*. New York: Regan Books.

US Supreme Court. (1997). Reno vs. ACLU. (U.S. 521). Washington, DC: U.S. Government Printing Office.

Verba, S., Schlozman, K., & Brady, H. (1995). *Voice and Equality*. Cambridge, MA: Harvard University Press.

Wilhelm, A. G. (2000). *Democracy in the Digital Age: Challenges to Political Life in Cyberspace*. London: Routledge.

Wolf, G. (2004). How the Internet Invented Howard Dean. *Wired! Magazine*. Retrieved April, 18th, 2008, from http://www.wired.com/wired/archive/12.01/dean.html

Wolin, S. (1996). Fugitive Democracy. In Benhabib, S. (Ed.), *Democracy and Difference: Contesting the Boundaries of the Political* (pp. 31–45). Princeton, NJ: Princeton University Press.

Wolin, S. (1996). What Revolutionary Action Means Today. In Mouffe, C. (Ed.), *Dimensions of Radical Democracy: Pluralism, Citizenship, Community* (pp. 240–253). Brooklyn, NY: Verso Press.

Young, I. M. (1990). *Justice and the Politics of Difference*. Princeton, NJ: Princeton University Press.

Young, I. M. (1996). Communication and the Other: Beyond Deliberative Democracy. In Benhabib, S. (Ed.), *Democracy and Difference: Contesting the Boundaries of the Political* (pp. 120–136). Princeton, NJ: Princeton University Press.

Zaller, J. (1992). *The Nature and Origins of Mass Opinion*. New York: Cambridge University Press.

ENDNOTES

[1] It should be noted that the World Wide Web (WWW) is a specific information layer which can be used on the Internet. It is only one of many different ways to share information over the Internet, and is not "the Internet" as it is commonly mistaken as being. Other information layers that can be utilized by the Internet are FTP protocols, used to transfer files and data from point to point, and SMTP protocols, most commonly used by email services to send mail across the Internet. My thanks to Jacinda Swanson for noting that this difference between WWW and the Internet should be pointed out directly, since the two terms are commonly confused and used in an interrelated manner.

[2] It should be noted that the court was unanimous in the decision but divided in their understanding on one of the statutes in question. Justice Sandra Day O'Connor, joined by Chief Justice William Rehnquist, wrote a concurring opinion with Justice Stevens.

[3] Note that Sunstein references these three items as "general interest intermediaries" in their *traditional* forms, not in the forms that we see online, or in the case of television, in the "post broadcast" age of extensive cable television.

4   This, as noted before, is the phenomenon of "Googlearchy" described by Hindman (2003).

5   I could presumably work out extensively, thus changing my body type to a particular identifier, however I do not have full control over what a "large" build is versus "small" etc.

Chapter 13
A Review of City Portals:
The Transformation of Service Provision under the Democratization of the Fourth Phase

Mark Deakin
Edinburgh Napier University, UK

ABSTRACT

This chapter reviews the development of portals by cities, their digital technologies and socially-inclusive platforms and sets out a simple four-phase model of e-government to describe their on-going transformation. It goes on to discuss e-government's recent transition from stage three to four, some of the post-transactional issues underlying their democratization of service provision and the participation of citizens in the consultations and deliberations this transformational process supports.

INTRODUCTION

As gateways to electronically-enhanced services, city portals provide online access to a growing number of e-government services. As such they have been successful in exploiting the opportunities technology offers to make local and regional government services available electronically, over the web. Today all larger and 'small-to-medium' sized cities have portals offering online access. As electronically-enhanced services they are seen as valuable alternatives to traditional modes of provision for the simple reason governments can now use digital technologies as socially-inclusive platforms.

DOI: 10.4018/978-1-61520-933-0.ch013

Socially-inclusive platforms with the digital technologies needed to deliver electronically-enhanced services over the web and as customized products capable of meeting everyone's requirements online, via multi-channel access.

City Portal

City portals are core to this modernization of government and have undergone four phases of development as part of the ongoing search for electronically-enhanced levels of service provision. These phases of development are as follows:

- websites providing information about available services;

- portals allowing the users of such websites to engage with the material hosted online and interact with it;
- platforms extending such online interaction into web-based transactions;
- web-based services allowing citizens to participate in this process of customization.

This chapter captures this fourfold classification of city portals and tracks their development from youthful experiments in tele-presence to mature exercises in the deployment of digital technologies. In doing so it focuses attention on the so-called fourth phase of this development and the deployment of digital technologies as socially-inclusive platforms. In particular on the digital technologies of socially-inclusive platforms whose post-transactional notion of e-government is open, transparent and accountable. Open, transparent and accountable with regards to the communitarian-based logic administrations are increasingly adopting to democratize decisions taken about future levels of service provision.

The Fourfold Classification

Over the past decade, it has become common to come across portals offering *information* about available services. Static text on relatively fixed sites, has, however, proven insufficiently engaging for those using such services, resulting in the call for providers to develop *interactive* services. Interactive services that are not only considered to be capable of underpinning *transactions*, but which are also seen as able to support a major step-change in the development of e-government. That is to say, able to support a 'step-up' from the transactional logic of existing developments and onto a stage which allows e-government to 'come of age' by way of online consultations and deliberations. Online consultations and deliberations that are constructive in building a platform through which all matters relating to future levels

of service provision can be subjected to a process of *democratization*.

In moving between these four phases of development, portals are said to undergo a process of *transformation* (Torres et.al, 2005; Werrakkody and Dhillon, 2009). The first three phases of these developments are often said to be influenced by 'New Public Management' (NPM) approaches to e-government, where the users of the services are generally treated as passive consumers. The fourth phase is, however, often represented as a major step-change in the development of e-government. For here we begin to witness the development of users not as passive consumers, or even customers, but more dynamically as 'active citizens'. As active citizens whose engagement in e-government is no longer exclusively transactional, but that now also includes their involvement as user communities participating in the online consultations and deliberations which support the democratization of service provision.

This transformation from simply putting government online (phase one and two) to e-government, can be illustrated by reference to the S-shaped learning curve developed by Davidson et.al (2005). Figure 1 represents this 'learning curve' and serves to highlight the level of maturity required to develop from one stage of service provision to another. It also serves to capture the process of development city portals have been subject to and track their progression from youthful experiments in tele-presence to mature exercises in e-government. Mature in the sense such exercises in e-government manage the deployment of digital technologies as socially-inclusive platforms (Deakin and Allwinkle, 2006, 2007)Socially-inclusive platforms that allow their user communities to actively participate in this transformation via the online consultations and deliberations which it makes possible (Deakin, Allwinkle and Campbell, 2006, 2007).

Figure 1. The e-government maturity model of city portals

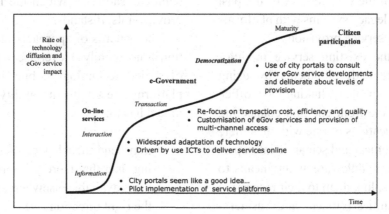

THE TRANSFORMATION

Representing the transformation of city portals as a shift from youthful experiments to mature deployments is useful because it not only captures the four phases of development, but the fact the progression from one to another is based on a changing user community whose platforms rest on an emerging set of modelling languages, enterprise architectures, organisational networks, integration frameworks, collaborations, protocol standards and core technological infrastructures. Importantly, such a representation also draws attention to what is all too often missed in such state-of-the-art accounts of e-government developments: the fact the community of practice underlying such digital technologies and socially-inclusive platforms are both fat and thin, personal and corporate, needing their organisational requirements to be met by accessing higher-levels of service provision.

State-of-the-art accounts of e-government developments: be they from representatives of the NPM models underpinning such transactional developments, or those supporting the communitarian logic of their transformation, tend to miss this because they divide the subject in two. In this instance into those of consumers, or customers under phases one, two and three of the respective e-government developments and to the citizens of phase four. The challenge here therefore, is not to leave them divided in this way, but find a platform capable of uniting them as part of a diverse user-community driving the transformation from one stage to another and as part of a step-wise logic.

THE PAST FIVE YEARS

This has been the challenge city portals have faced over the past five years: that of matching the diversity of user community expectations with the digital technologies which are needed for socially-inclusive platforms to meet the needs of their personal and corporate organisational requirements. Whether the post-transactional demands of this diverse user-community are being achieved through the push of digital technologies, or the socially-inclusive platforms of user-pull is the e-government question very much in hand. However, the most recent attempts made to match one with the other tend to follow a step-wise logic and develop this democratization as an exercise in the rational unified modelling of a service-orientated architecture. The logic of this exercise in modelling the service-orientated architecture of city platforms tends to develop by:

- setting out and agreeing a clear vision of the user community's expectations of the services offered;

- breaking with the silo mindset of the past by replacing legacy systems with platforms of integrated service provision;
- integrating the existing service modules with proto-type developments by using middleware capable of linking back office functions to the front end and connecting the communications of one with the other;
- using the technical and semantic interoperability of the middleware as the means to route services, link them to their respective user communities (citizens and businesses) and connect them to meet front-end expectations;
- exploiting such platforms as the means to migrate from legacy systems by way of and through the back office reorganisation needed for e-government to embark on the step change such a transformation requires;
- underpinning this democratization of service provision with the organisational learning needed and knowledge management systems required to support the institutionalization of the new working practices such a collaborative platform for the delivery of services demands.

Towards Digitally-Inclusive Platforms

Approaching the transformation in this way is useful because it allows for an analysis of the emerging community of practice by type of user and draws particular attention to citizens, businesses and both the leaders and officers of local and regional government as the organisations driving this enterprise. This is useful for the reason such an approach to the development of city portals throws light on the need for them to not only be supported by digital technologies, but underpinned by socially-inclusive platforms that are capable of embodying the diverse community of users they represent into the very constitution of the

democratisation on which the future of service provision itself stands.

The benefits of approaching the transformation as not merely an exercise in the development of digital technologies, but socially-inclusive platforms, rest with the ability such a unified model has to:

- transcend their legacy as websites providing data that merely informs users of services available elsewhere, pointing them in the right direction (Deakin et.al, 2006a);
- operate as gateways to those services that are available over the web and for users to access online courtesy of the middleware which allows the information needed to be routed from the back office and to front-end where it is required (Deakin, 2006b);
- match such needs and requirements on the basis of a platform that is socially-inclusive and technology which meets the expectations of a diverse user community, rather than other criteria exclusive to any one group and potentially divisive in nature (Deakin and Allwinkle, 2007; Lombardi, et.al, 2009);
- function as sites with the potential to be transformative by deploying the platform's socially-inclusive technology as a means of providing their user communities with higher levels of service provision. Higher levels of service provision that are based on core infrastructures and standards of interoperability which are enhanced through the ontology of natural language. Natural language that also increases the prospect of civic engagement through the deployment of semantic web technologies which themselves support organisational learning and the management of knowledge objects drawn from the digital libraries underlying the platform's middleware. Those digital libraries that underpin the use of geo-data

and visualisations which themselves work to support simulations of the environmental and economic developments forming the content of the high level services in question (Deakin, 2009).

Under this fourth phase of development the net is cast wide. This is because for the digital technologies to be socially-inclusive the platform has to be wide ranging and deep, personal, corporate, organisational, sector-based and thematic, set within government frameworks and on standards agreed between international agencies. That is within government frameworks and on standards agreed between international agencies which in turn allow platforms of this kind to exploit opportunities the internet provides for working collectively, sharing data, information and programmes between enterprises. That is between enterprises which cooperate with one another in strategic alliances. Strategic alliances that in turn work to actively promote the types of developments which lead to a 'mainstreaming' of 'phase four' city portals..

THE USER COMMUNITY AS A SOCIALLY-INCLUSIVE BODY

What all this does is reconstitute the user community as a socially-inclusive body deploying digital technologies as a means of underpinning the notion of active citizenship. As the agency of such change, this development of active citizenship is nothing less than significant. This is because sitting on the types of socially-inclusive developments outlined so far, the intelligence embedded in the city portals unlocks the hitherto hidden potential digital technologies have to mature as sites offering the safety and security needed to stand as platforms capable of transforming local and regional government. For under this scenario city portals are no longer merely sites providing data for informing 'visitors' about their administra-

tive territories, or directing them to the relevant pages where all of this can be accessed, browsed or acted upon as the basis of a transaction. This is because in their transformed state they do this and a great deal more and achieve this by offering a higher level of service provision. Higher in the sense they manage to use the socially-inclusive nature of the digital technologies upon which they stand as the very means to not only sustain service developments, but do this in the interests of good governance.

That is to say, in the interests of governance which is good in the sense such developments are not only open and transparent in the way they account for a diversity of user communities, but support this through their participation in the very consultations and deliberations integral to this democratisation of service provision.

From this it is evident city portals have a diverse community of users, whose data needs to be personalised and information customised, so users of the sites can actively browse, enquire, query, comment even challenge the content of the communications. This is because under these portals citizens have a long reach into service provision and delve deep into matters concerning the business of data supply and information exchange. So much so they now become a major driving force behind the fourth phase of portal developments and key to their future as websites.

The following offers an attempt to capture the significance of this development in the sense:

- their communications are now becoming more extensive;
- this longer reach is also based on a deeper engagement with the process of service provision;
- this more extensive, longer and deeper reach into the process of service provision itself develops as a typology of communications codified as:
  ○ citizen to citizen
  ○ citizen to government

- ○ government to citizen
- ○ citizen to business
- ○ business to business
- ○ business to government
- ○ government to citizen
- all these types of communication need to be joined-up, routed, channelled and proactively managed, as not only transactions but as cases in the management of a democratically-driven transformation. As cases where the services of previous phases are bundled together and configured to offer a higher level of provision.

CITIZENS AS A SOCIALLY-INCLUSIVE BODY UNDERPINNED BY DIGITAL TECHNOLOGIES

Here we see a typology of reciprocal communications, with users at the front-end underpinning citizen engagement and business supporting the back office's transformation of local and regional government. The complex organisational structure such communications demand in turn means city portals need to be n-tiered and x-tensive, allowing the notion of citizenship to come to the fore as a driving force behind a more user-centric change in the business of service provision. User centric change that is based on a socially-inclusive use of digital technologies and as a platform for citizens to browse material which is built, not so much on the transactional logic of 'event-based management', but the 'life cycle' of interests their user communities are founded on. This way citizens are treated as a socially-inclusive body underpinned by digital technologies designed to reciprocate such values through collaborative working (with business) and in distributed networks embedding the intelligence governing their development.

Citizens to the Fore

It is with this democratization of service provision that citizens come to the fore. Here where the developments undergo the transition from phase three to four and citizenship surfaces as a key agent of the change this introduces into the process of service provision. Current developments suggest the changes are two-fold. Firstly, the development of front-line services dealing with citizen enquiries as *customers*, capable of being dealt with through automated service responses and the use of avatars to complete transactions: the so-called 'call centre' approach to the transformation. Secondly, the development of the so-called 'post-transactional' services and those not seeing citizens as customers, but *partners* in the consultations and deliberations they, government and business alike enter into for the purposes of considering and subsequently agreeing future levels of provision.

While both responses are quite rightly seen as putting service provision on a new digital footing, it is noticeable such platforms serve different purposes and perhaps most importantly of all, the social and technical infrastructure upon which they are built provides the opportunity for the ecology of the emerging system to represent them as integral components of the transformation. This is important because with the former the benefits are mainly economic, to do with the efficiencies of process rationalisation and automation in particular. Under this logic the technical and semantic integration of the platform allows the services to be provided, not only at less expense and therefore with greater efficiency, but to a higher level of value because they can be accessed and delivered more effectively. With the latter the benefits are not just technical - to do with levels of cost savings, or semantic - about the value this adds - but social. Social in the sense these developments allow citizens to be included in (as oppose to excluded from) consultations about the said rationalisations and deliberations over matters of cost and value related to future levels of service provision. Levels of service provision that are in turn subject to public scrutiny, needing to be made accountable and transparent as part of the measures which underlie the consultation and deliberative requirements of this democratic transformation.

The Key Unlocking the Potential

The key to this democratization, however, rests with the technical and semantic infrastructure of city portals and whether their platforms are designed in such a way as to include the ecology of the system underpinning such developments and supporting their transformation. That eco-system which in many respects is unique: not only because this particular community of practice is asked to consider the environmental, economic and social qualities of the service provision which is being transformed, but for the reason the absence of the former (environmental) means any democratisation of the latter (economic and social) shall not be inclusive but remain exclusive.

If this is the case and the developments remain exclusive, then it can be said the system lacks the ecological-integrity demanded and any benefits of the transformation will not be environmental, only economic, or social. This in turn tending to signify the interoperability of the user community's infrastructure - the embedded intelligence everything rests on – is inadequately designed as an ecosystem. That is not designed as a (data management and information processing) system which is capable of standing as a platform strong enough to carry the full economic and social weight of the transformation.

For if we are to uncover the virtuous nature of an ecosystem in which all of this is made possible and as a development that in turn may be sustained, it shall be necessary for the user community to double back on itself and discover the point where the vested interests of government, business and citizens strategically align with one

another and coalesce around the transition from the notion of customers to that of partners. That is to say, double back on themselves and discover the point where the said interests align with one another and coalesce as equals around not just the efficiencies of competition for customers, but the co-operation and collaboration going on between citizens as user communities working in partnership with one another. That is within co-operative relations and collaborations in which the links between the economics of the business sector (as user communities) and connections this in turn has to the social body of citizens become tangible. Where, in particular, the economics of the business sector and social body of citizens become tangible as a community of practice. In particular, as a community of practice that is underpinned by technical and semantic standards which work together and offer a platform for organisations of this kind to support the *customisation of partnerships*. That customisation of partnerships which under the fourth phase is sufficiently inclusive – in this instance trans-active, consultative and deliberative enough - to be considered an integral part of the self-organizing enterprise this particular democratization of service provision does much to cultivate.

BENCHMARKING CITY PORTALS

From this it is evident there is a pressing need to benchmark city portals against the standards laid down for the democratization of service provision. This means measuring them against:

- state-of-the art surveys of recent city portal development across Europe, in America, the Middle East and Asia, in order to verify the baseline standards. Torres et.al (2005) provides a survey of recent developments across Europe. Huang (2007) offers a review of portals in North America (Hernández (2007) also evaluates the position in South America. Kaaya (2005) offers an assessment of the portal developments in Africa. Lianjie et.al (2005) also offer an analysis the transformation in Asia;

- a futures analysis of city portals, drawing on cutting-edge research and technical development projects, paying particular attention to leading regional and local examples;
- a classification of the portal's attributes by user community - citizens, business and government – and analysis of their development trajectory;
- assessment of the weight given to citizens as key drivers of change in this user-centric development;
- analysis of the way ahead for such user-centric portals in terms of key:
  ○ presentational challenges
  ○ multi-channel access needs
  ○ their enterprise architectures and underlying business models
  ○ the interoperability requirements of the aforesaid
  ○ the technical and semantic challenges underlying their operation within distributed systems of vertical and horizontal (front and back-office) integration
- use of the aforesaid survey, classification, assessment and analysis to characterise the transition to fourth phase city portals;
- examples of best practice in managing the transition towards such levels of service provision. In particular those demonstrating the ecosystems of the emerging platforms, their economic and social benefits;
- the:
  ○ personalisation of web-pages and site content
  ○ use of multi-channel access as a platform of communications supporting this development
  ○ call centre provision of front-line services

  ○ back-office use of e-learning platforms, knowledge management systems and digital libraries supporting post-transactional consultations and deliberations on service improvements
  ○ key environmental, economic and social applications developed to support the customisation of partnerships underlying this transformation
  ○ examples of attempts by local and regional government to mainstream this transformation and sustain the development as a process of civic renewal
- a reflection on the challenge the said developments pose for local and regional government in terms of the step changes their transformation of services demands from front and back-office operations;
- the solutions adopted to meet the said challenges;
- use of the above to set out the way ahead for local and regional government and possibilities which exist to accelerate the transition and align them with the targets for performance measurement laid down for such purposes.

CONCLUSION

As gateways to electronically-enhanced services, city portals provide online access to a growing number of e-government services and in taking this form they have been successful in exploiting the opportunities technology offers to make the content of local and regional government services available electronically, over the web. This success can be measured in terms of the fact all large and 'small-to-medium' sized cities have portals offering online access. Today they are seen as valuable alternatives to traditional modes of provision for the simple reason governments can now use digital technologies as socially-inclusive platforms for delivering services over the web and make them readily available online via multi-channel access.

Portals are core to this modernisation of government. Under the fourth phase of development, the service platform is wide ranging and deep, personal, corporate, organisational, sector-based and thematic, set within government frameworks and on standards agreed between international agencies. With this transformation it is citizens who come to the fore. For it is here where the developments undergo the transition from phase three to four and citizenship surfaces as a key agent of the change this introduces into the process of service provision.

Examinations of these developments suggest the changes are two-fold: firstly; the development of front-line services dealing with citizen enquiries as *customers*, capable of being dealt with through automated service responses and the use of avatars to complete transactions: the 'call centre' approach to the transformation. Secondly, through the development of so-called post-transactional services and those not seeing citizens as customers, but *partners* in the consultations and deliberations they, government and business alike enter into for the purposes of considering and subsequently agreeing future levels of provision.

This signifies that if left divided in this 'call centre', cum 'post-transactional manner', the interoperability of the user community's infrastructure may be inadequately designed to stand as a platform capable of carrying the full economic and social weight of the transformation. This being important to recognise because if we are to uncover the virtuous nature of the environment in which all this takes place and moreover how any such developments can be sustained, it shall be necessary for the user community in question to double back on itself and discover the point where the vested interests of government, business and citizens strategically align with one another and coalesce around the transition from the notion of customers to that of partners. Fortunately, proto-type portal developments recognise the

significance of these changes and need there is to base such transformations on digitally-inclusive platforms.

The findings of the research reviewed here offers a programme of work designed to meet this requirement and build upon the advances already made in this direction. It proposes this should be done by using the *type of review outlined in this chapter to benchmark the developments*. Furthermore, it proposes that any such exercise should itself be subject to *peer group review and take the opportunity which*

this provides to conduct a third party evaluation of the particular contribution such proto-types make, not only to the development of e-government, but democratization such a transformation of service provision also paves the way for.

REFERENCES

Davison, R., Wagner, C., & Ma, L. (2005). From government to e-government: a transition model. *Information Technology & People*, *18*(3), 280–299. doi:10.1108/09593840510615888

Deakin, M. (2009). The IntelCities Community of Practice: the eGov services model for socially-inclusive and participatory urban regeneration programmes. In Riddeck, C. (Ed.), *Research Strategies for eGovernment Service Adoption*. Hershey, PA: Idea Group Publishing.

Deakin, M., & Allwinkle, S. (2006). The IntelCities community of practice: the e-learning platform, knowledge management system and digital library for semantically-interoperable e-governance services. *International Journal of Knowledge. Culture and Change Management*, *6*(3), 155–162.

Deakin, M., & Allwinkle, S. (2007). Urban regeneration and sustainable communities: the role of networks, innovation and creativity in building successful partnerships. *Journal of Urban Technology*, *14*(1), 77–91. doi:10.1080/10630730701260118

Deakin, M., Allwinkle, S., & Campbell, F. (2006). The IntelCities e-Learning platform, knowledge management system and digital library for semantically rich e-governance services. *International Journal of Technology. Knowledge and Society*, *2*(8), 31–38.

Deakin, M., Allwinkle, S., & Campbell, F. (2007). The IntelCities Community of Practice: the eGov Services for Socially-inclusive and Participatory Urban Regeneration Programmes. In Cunningham, P. (Ed.), *Innovation and the Knowledge Economy: Issues, Applications and Case Studies*. Washington, DC: ISO Press.

Haung, Z. (2005). A comprehensive analysis of U.S. counties' e-Government portals: development status and functionalities. *European Journal of Information Systems*, *16*(2), 149–164. doi:10.1057/palgrave.ejis.3000675

Hernández, M. G. (2007). *Latin America Online: Cases, Successes and Pitfalls*. Hershey, PA: IRM Press.

Kaaya, J. (2005). Implementing e-Government Services in East Africa: Assessing Status through Content Analysis of Government Websites, *Electronic. Journal of E-Government, 2*, 139–154.

Lombardi, P., Cooper, I., Paskaleva, K., & Deakin, M. (2009). The challenge of designing user-centric e-services: European dimensions. In Reddick, C. G. (Ed.), *Research Strategies for eGovernment Service Adoption*. Hershey, PA: Idea Group Publishing.

Ma, L., Chung, J., & Thorson, S. (2005). E-government in China: Bringing economic development through administrative reform. *Government Information Quarterly, 22*(1), 20–37. doi:10.1016/j.giq.2004.10.001

Torres, L., Pina, V., & Acerete, B. (2005). E-government developments on delivering public services among EU cities. *Government Information Quarterly, 22*, 217–238. doi:10.1016/j.giq.2005.02.004

Torres, L., Pina, V., & Ryo, S. (2005). E-government and the transformation of public services in EU countries. *Online Information Review, 29*(5), 531–553. doi:10.1108/14684520510628918

Werrakkody, V., & Dhillon, G. (2009). From eGovernment to TGovernment. In Riddeck, C. (Ed.), *Research Strategies for eGovernment Service Adoption*. Hershey, PA: Idea Group Publishing.

Chapter 14
E–Government and the EU:
Democratisation through Technology?

Brian Lake
University of Limerick, Ireland

ABSTRACT

This chapter looks at the efficacy of The European Union's e-government initiatives in addressing a key problem of European integration – a lack of democratic legitimacy. Citizens of the European Union witnessed endemic corruption in the EU's governing institutions in the late 1990s. As part of a long-term project to ensure greater transparency and accessibility, the EU launched an e-government initiative, the "Information Society." This chapter addresses the unique challenges for e-government and citizen participation at the supranational level. In a polity such as the EU, concepts of citizenship and democracy take on new dimensions. Technology as a social process is examined, and its relationship with public policy explored. It is in this context that the effectiveness of the EU's e-government initiative is considered. As this chapter argues, the ability of e-government initiatives to increase citizen awareness does not necessarily correspond to an increase in democratic legitimacy.

INTRODUCTION

The European Union has a democracy problem. That there exists a problem is not in dispute. It is an immutable factor in almost any discussion of the European Union – a theme of constant debate. This discussion and debate culminated in the "Convention on the Future of Europe" - also referred to as the European Convention. The Convention is the

product of the Laeken Declaration of December 2001 on the Future of the European Union. The declaration summarises the problem succinctly:

...the European institutions must be brought closer to its citizens. Citizens undoubtedly support the Union's broad aims, but they do not always see a connection between those goals and the Union's everyday action. They want the European institutions to be less unwieldy and rigid, and above all, more efficient and open... ...More importantly

DOI: 10.4018/978-1-61520-933-0.ch014

however, they feel that deals are all too often cut out of their sight and they want better democratic scrutiny. (Communities, 2001b)

As the Convention declares in its mission statement, "the purpose of the Convention is to propose a new framework and structures for the European Union which are geared to changes in the world situation, the needs of the citizens of Europe and the future development of the European Union."[1] At present, the European Union claims to derive its legitimacy from the democratic values it projects, the aims it pursues and the instruments of governance it possesses. It freely admits that this is insufficient. The function of the Convention on the Future of Europe is a need to determine, "how we can increase the democratic legitimacy of the present institutions, a question which is valid for the three institutions [the Council of Ministers, the European Parliament, and the European Commission]." (Communities, 2001b).

As policy developers, these three executive institutions play a central role in the development of the European Union as a polity. They are responsible for the implementation of policy designed to promote the European Union's e-government initiative, the Information Society (IS). They are also responsible for the social management of technology, in cooperation with the member-states.

The history of the executive institutions of the EU is that of a bureaucratic elite, with a demonstrable leaning towards technocratic practices. (Hayward, 1995; Siedentop, 2000; Stirk, 1996; Teivainen, 2002; Young, 1984) If such a historical context is an appropriate one, then the democratising agenda of the Information Society faces significant obstacles. This is not necessarily a failure of Information Communication Technologies (ICTs) as an instrument for social change, but of the unique political infrastructure that characterises the EU.

In order to make a compelling case for this proposition, several steps are necessary. First, an overview of recent institutional history provides a context from which we can establish that the European governing institutions have been identified as elite-oriented and inward looking. Second, the importance of social participation in technology must be addressed. The ability of technology to shape the dialog between a governing body and a citizenry, or public sphere, is an important factor when considering the impact of ICTs on a political process. Third, a democratic 'yardstick' must be established. What constitutes the citizenry or public sphere of the EU? Does it differ from national publics? Based on these questions and their answers, at what point can the democratic potential of ICTs have been said to be realised? A reasonable indicator of success is a prerequisite to determining how effective the "Information Society" e-government initiative has been as a democratising influence.

The availability of public opinion statistics via the Eurobarometer series of public opinion analyses provides a clear measure that allows us to establish several vital points. First, that satisfaction with democracy in the EU is declining. Second, while awareness of institutions has risen, trust in them has not. Third, that access to communication technologies has increased sharply in the 1993-2008 period – coinciding with the establishment of e-government programmes at the EU level. Fourth and finally, that the Internet and electronic media are fast becoming the preferred methods of accessing information on the EU.

The compilation and comparison of these statistical measures allow us to draw some conclusions about the success of the Information Society e-government initiative as a means of democratising the EU. A primary goal of the Information Society has been achieved - greater access to and use of ICTs in bringing the EU closer to its citizens. While this goal has been met, the anticipated consequences of EU e-government policy have not resulted in democratisation. The opposite has occurred – as citizens learn more about the EU, they tend not to like what they see. E-government programmes have preformed their role of bringing the EU closer to the public. Increased awareness however, has not led to increased accountability or legitimacy. The question remaining is why this is the case.

Communication technologies have indeed changed public discourse, increasing both the volume and free flow of information. Their use as a component of the Information Society e-government initiative have made the inner workings of the EU more apparent. What communication technologies have been unable to do is change the structure of EU governance. Unlike a national government, executive institutions are not held to account for their actions. This is due to institutional structure and insufficient control by elected components of the executive. Public opinion surveys reflect a growing awareness of this state of affairs. Access via e-government portals and more information about the EU has correlated with a decline in trust, a rise in apathy, and a decline in support for EU membership.

BACKGROUND

Institutional Accountability and Behaviour in the 1990s

The lack of democratic legitimacy in the Commission as an institution became clearer as allegations of fiscal mismanagement grew in the 1980s and 1990s. The potential for such corruption arose not only from the secretive nature of Commission decision-making, but from its small size and budget. The small size of the Commission and its under-funding force it to contract out many administrative and policy tasks.

A lack of transparency in awarding these contracts brought the Commission into disrepute as such contracts became increasingly lucrative. The European Parliament capitalised on this opportunity to exercise what democratic oversight it could, seeking to gain sufficient power in the future to hold the Commission accountable (Hoskyns & Newman, 2000).

Concerns over fraud in the Common Agricultural Policy (CAP). grew in the 1980s, casting doubt on the management capabilities of the Commission. The Maastricht Treaty granted the Parliament the right to establish an ombudsman to receive complaints from citizens about poor administration practices in Community institutions. The EP also received the right to set up committees of inquiry to look into accusations of mismanagement and misuse of community law.

The ombudsman was one of the first gestures towards democratic accountability to citizens of the member-states. The ombudsman represents one of the only links between the European institutions and the public but depends on the EU becoming sufficiently transparent for its role to be meaningful (Hoskyns & Newman, 2000).

Concern over Commission budgetary practices led the Parliament's Committee on Budgetary Control to refuse to discharge the Community budget in 1998. It accused the Commission of arrogance for refusing to answer questions over apparent mismanagement. (Hoskyns & Newman, 2000) Unsure if this amounted to a censure of the Commission the Parliament adopted a resolution on financial management in January 1999. It laid the groundwork for the establishment of a special committee to investigate the Commission. The Commission president, Jaques Santer, agreed to the creation of the committee and to respond to its findings. As Neil Nugent states, "It was probably only because Santer agreed to the special committee to investigate the allegations of fraud, nepotism and mismanagement that the Commission avoided being censured" (Nugent, 2001, p. 54).

The lack of democratic accountability was highlighted by the committee as one of the major shortcoming of the Commission. It stated in its conclusions that,

The principles of openness, transparency and accountability are at the heart of democracy and are

the very instruments allowing it to function properly. Openness and transparency imply that the decision-making process, at all levels, is as accessible and accountable as possible to the general public. It means that the reasons for decisions taken, or not taken, are known and that those taking decisions assume responsibility for them and are ready to accept the personal consequences when such decisions are subsequently shown to have been wrong. (Communities, 1999, p. 9.3.3)

The democratic accountability of the Commission was stressed as being paramount. Although the role of the Commission as an instrument of policy creation had grown, it had remained bureaucratic and closed in nature. Worse, the members of the Commission had failed to exercise a sense of responsibility. By doing so they had diminished any democratic legitimacy that the Commissioners could claim. The Committee concluded its condemnation of Commission policy-making, saying of the Commissioners,

It is becoming difficult to find anyone who has even the slightest sense of responsibility. However, that sense of responsibility is essential. It must be demonstrated, first and foremost, by the Commissioners individually and the Commission as a body. The temptation to deprive the concept of responsibility of all substance is a dangerous one. That concept is the ultimate manifestation of democracy. (Communities, 1999, p. 9.4.25)

The Commission was accused of fraud, nepotism and mismanagement of its power. Meeting on the day the report was published, and with the awareness that censure was inevitable, the Santer Commission resigned (Nugent, 2001). The Commissioners still occupied their offices for the next six months however, in a caretaker capacity.[2] This was due to EP elections and the customary EU slowdown in August. This circumstance allowed some time for the governments of the member states to decide what to do about such a unique situation.

In the wake of the damage done to the credibility of the Commission it was decided that a new college of Commissioners would be appointed, with Romano Prodi, a former Italian Prime Minister, as Commission president. Prodi insisted from the outset of his tenure that significant changes in the structure of the Commission would be his first priority. Codes of conduct for the Commissioners were established. These codes also regulated how Commissioners could interact with service providers. Each new Commissioner was also obliged to commit to resign if the President of the Commission required them to do so.[3]

A portfolio for administrative reform was created, with a report due by early 2000 on the reform of the Commission. The white paper that resulted from the report recommended major organisational reforms, but no structural reforms that would increase the direct democratic accountability of the Commission.

The effects of these events leading up to and following elections to the EP in June 1999 were to bring the Commission under closer scrutiny from the European publics. This provided an indication of the strength of the emerging European public sphere. For the first time there was widespread condemnation of the Commission by the citizens of the Union. The resignation of the Commission was widely interpreted as a major victory for the European Parliament. While this detracted from the legitimacy of the Commission, it reinforced the legitimacy and accountability of the directly elected EP, which bore responsibility for disciplining the Commission on behalf of the European electorate. That the Commission could continue in its role despite censure demonstrated the significant gap between the nation-state and supranational perceptions of democratic accountability and demonstrates that despite efforts towards reform, the institutional structure of the Commission was not attuned to public opinion.

This separation between the dictates of public opinion and Commission practice provide an indication of the success of an initiative to make the

EU more transparent and accessible. The success of the EU Information Society may bring the operation of the EU executive institutions into clearer focus. But this does not mean that the functions themselves will change as a result of closer public scrutiny. The impact of technology itself must first be gauged. In doing so we can better understand the relationship between the tools of e-government initiatives and the EU, and determine the possible impact of communication technologies on the existing institutional structure.

Technology as a Social Process

On an epistemological level, the growth of technology into a process of society has led to a broader conceptualization and definition of technology (Fig, 1998). Technology is more than the tools, machines and other implements of society. It is the rational organisation of social behaviour to achieve a given goal. This approach to technology has received little attention in the EU. As a primarily economic association, the EU has not sought to concern itself with the social impacts of technology. Instead the focus has been on creating a receptive business environment for their introduction. Pausing to ask what technology is and what its growth means for the EU system of governance is a worthwhile endeavour.

When thinking about technology, its different usages should be considered. Technology can refer to a wide variety of things. It can be a body of technical knowledge, rules, and concepts. It can refer to the practice of technological professions such as the sciences, which includes attitudes, norms, and assumptions about its application. It can refer to the physical tools resulting from the practice of technological professions. It can refer to the organisation of the above into large-scale social systems of medical, military, transportation and other such institutions. Finally, technology can refer to the quality of life that results from the introduction of these technologies, or the character of social life that results from technological activity

(Fig, 1998). In the same context, the character of democracy in the governing European institutions can be viewed under the aforementioned quality of life that results from technological activity.

Discussions of technology are often confused because the participants are unclear as to the context it is used in. Critics of technology are often more concerned with the attitude of technology experts or the behaviour of institutions that use technology than they are about the technological knowledge or the implements of technology. This represents a focus on the content to the detriment of the medium. This distinction is rarely made. To oppose one approach of technology is often seen as opposing them all. As the engine of new proposals and initiatives, the European Commission is responsible for the development of the Information Society e-government initiative. It is Commission policy towards the Information Society that is questioned – rarely are the effects of the technologies themselves considered.

Societal Consequences of Technology

As Darin Barney argues, technology says something about what we are, or wish to be, and how we live together (Barney, 2000). Our relationship to technology is a complicated one. As we develop new technologies, they have the effect of altering our perceptions of the world around us.

The adoption of new communication technologies has changed perspectives on communication dramatically. The EU serves as a prime example of this change in its creation of GSM (Global System for Mobile Communications). GSM was created as a means of ensuring common communications standards throughout Europe – in effect, a mobile phone that worked anywhere from Limerick to Lesbos. As newspapers noted on the occasion of the 20th anniversary of GSM, "...the biggest problem was not in making the equipment or designing the protocols but getting countries and companies working together, not just in name but in spirit" ("Happy 20th birthday, GSM," 2007).

In 1990 there were eleven million GSM customers. This reached 281 million by the end of 2000. By June 2006, the GSM customer base grew to 2 billion (Livingston, 2006). By 2009, the size of the GSM market grew to 3.72 billion subscribers – an 89.4 per cent share of the global wireless telephony market (*GSM/3G Market Update*, 2009). The impact of policy towards something as innocuous as a mobile phone has proven to have a profound effect on how people perceive communication, and altered their expectations of the technology as well.

Martin Heidegger held that technology had a way of revealing truths about human nature. He also held that the cognitive framework or mental preconceptions underlying the aggressive development of technology concealed other ways of understanding human experience (Fig, 1998).

The rapid introduction of new technologies such as GSM makes it almost impossible to determine their impact. Langdon Winner makes a case that we lack our bearings in dealing with things technological. He argues that many of our conceptions of technology "…reveal a disorientation that borders on dissociation from reality" (Winner, 1978, p. 8). Winner illustrates the difference between the use of the word "technology" in the eighteenth and nineteenth centuries and his perspective on its use in the twentieth century. As understood by Winner, technology in the past spoke directly about tools, machines, factories and industry. It did not consider technology as a social phenomenon unto itself (1978). The idea of technology as something that had a social impact was not widespread. The tools were simply seen as reducing the complexity of a given task

The social interpretation of the word itself changed in the twentieth century. What sufficed in the past to describe a limited assortment of tools and industries has now exploded into an incredibly diverse collection of meanings. There exist tools, instruments, machines, organisations,

methods, techniques, systems and what Winner describes as "the totatility of these and other things in our experience" (Winner, 1978, p. 8). Winner in effect is arguing that human character has been altered through interaction with technology. The "tool-like" qualities of technology have been shed to become part of our humanity.

The idea of what constitutes technology has become more and more inclusive. The shift has been towards a definition that is vague, expansive and in the opinion of Winner, highly significant. Winner prefers the definition of technology adopted earlier by Jacques Ellul (Ellul refers to it as *la technique*). Technology is acknowledged as having begun with the machine, but has left the physical behind. For Ellul, technology is the ability of people to manipulate the tools available to them for the betterment of those they serve. As Ellul states, "Wherever there is research and application of new means as a criterion of efficiency, one can say there is a technology." (Ellul, 1980, p. 26). Technology is not an object in this case, but an ability.

Ellul provides an example of the integration of the technology of machinery into nineteenth century society. The needs of the machines were gradually balanced against the needs of the populace. From this perspective technology is the ability to inventory the needs of the machine and bring it into line with the population. As Ellul states, "The machine could not integrate itself into nineteenth century society, technique integrated it… Technique has enough of the mechanical in its nature to enable it to cope with the machine, but it surpasses and transcends the machine because it remains in close touch with the human order" (Ellul, 1964, p. 5).

In much the same way, the rise of communication technologies such as the mobile phone have not been due exclusively to the technology. The creation of infrastructure and investment in phone miniaturization technology were necessary to meet the technological demands of the project. Governmental regulatory regimes created an atmosphere of interoperability between potentially differing technologies. The mobile phone however, had to represent a significant improvement over existing technologies, be simple to use and meet the efficiency demands of the population. Otherwise, the technology would be abandoned. The needs of the technology were thus weighed against the needs of the population. This consideration of the balance between the objects of technology and their use is now new. It instead marks a shift towards the old root components of the word, in which the object and its use are given equal weight.

Ellul further reinforces the idea of technology as something more than the sum of its parts. Technology is not something as simple as a communications network or a computing device. The conception of technology in popular culture implies that it must have a physical presence. Technology as understood by Winner and Ellul is more of a social instrument than a physical object. Heidegger, Winner and Ellul argue that the idea of technology has altered how we think about new technologies. We interpret new technologies in the context of the old.

Social Participation in Technology

There are two fundamental misconceptions about technology. First, people tend to think of technology as hardware. Technological devices that we interact with physically such as mobile phones, televisions, cameras, and refrigerators define our experience of technology. What we forget is that people and their institutions must furnish instructions as to their use. Technology is a process of generating and exploiting knowledge so deeply engraved into our society that all its citizens are profoundly affected (Ellul, 1964).

Edward Wenk (1986) points out the second misconception. It arises because we forget that everyone is directly involved in technology. The engineer, the mechanic and the scientist are obvious examples of those who influence technology. All have a direct impact on the development of technology. But a great deal of influence lies in the hands of the bankers and investors who finance construction projects, policy makers and legislators who allocate resources and set standards for things such as water quality, weapons systems, or mass transit. The impact of citizens is felt as well in four different ways. They can be felt as consumers of technological products, as voters who determine the election of parties with a policy platform, as investors in technological enterprises, or as the victims of technological impacts on the environment.

As consumers, investors or victims, the EU citizen makes an impact on the use and regulation of technology. As voters however, they are barred from influencing the Commission and the Council of Ministers, only the latter of which has an indirect and fragmented connection to an electorate. While the European Parliament possesses the legitimacy conferred by direct elections, it lacks the ability to hold the other governing institutions accountable.

The full impact of technology in human affairs becomes apparent when we consider technology as a social process. Technology has altered risks to individuals and society as a whole. Technology has lengthened life spans and reduced infant mortality rates, but it has also introduced risks through pollution and overpopulation. It has allowed instant communication and swift transportation, bringing cultures into closer contact. This contact often leads to conflict – both ideologically and physically. In some cases, faith in technology becomes an ideology in and of itself (Dinerstein, 2009). Some cultures thrive on technology, while others struggle to cope with it.

On the institutional scale, technology acts as a mobilizing agent to concentrate wealth and power. In doing this, it plays a political role in every society. Technology can induce change in a society. The Internet has been used to encourage the free flow of information. But technology can also be used to maintain the status quo. Electronic surveillance can be used to suppress political dissent. Technology has a tendency to discriminate against the unrepresented and the disadvantaged, and to support the elitist establishment (Wenk, 1986). This is a common feature across all societies, whether they are developed or developing, pre-capitalist or capitalist, agrarian or socialist.

Because of the choices involved regarding beneficiaries, technology has become more political. A great deal of wealth and power may well be concentrated in the hands of an individual responsible for the distribution of a technology. As an example, a corporation controlling the software running on most computers in the world has tremendous leverage in influencing what information people can access, and how they perceive that technology. Whoever controls the development of such software has a great deal of power. Technology thus becomes political. At the same time the use of the Internet, electronic voting lists and TV campaigning has had the opposite affect – making politics more technological. As Wenk concludes, it is the impacts of technology that cannot be neutral (1986).

Decisions on technology are not exclusively the domain of the marketplace and inventors. Supplying the resources through which technologies are developed and used, regulating their use, and encouraging an atmosphere for development is a matter of public policy. Public policy is a political affair, decided by public officials. It is the non-elected creation of public policy that presents the subject of discussion in the case of the EU. Scientists and engineers do not decide on the expenditures to be invested in communications, or which weapons to develop – these are political decisions. Technology is inextricably bound to public policy. It cannot be considered in isolation, as it cannot exist without the resources allocated to its development and maintenance.

To speak of technology denotes action as well as description. It is a typical thing in society "to do" technology. It is a part of social, political and cultural life. The absence of technology is the exception rather than the rule. To gain a better understanding of the social impact of technology, Wenk proposes the idea of technology as an amplifier. Technology amplifies many aspects of human behaviour. Through computers, we amplify our minds and memories. Through the lever, the wheel and the bomb, we amplify our muscle (Wenk, 1986).

Technologies allow us to see things otherwise invisible, to hear things otherwise inaudible and to measure things otherwise undetectable. (Wenk, 1986) These are the more obvious amplifiers of technology. The social amplifiers of technology are less apparent. Technology can facilitate or threaten freedom. It promotes the economic machine yet creates disparities between those who have technology and those who do not. It expands the volume and complexity of networks of communication and expands human contact, yet increases the possibility of conflict. Technology increases the options available to decision makers, but at the same time increases both the risk and the cost of error.

Technology has a powerful influence on culture. But the reverse is also important. Culture has a powerful effect on technology. We define the social purposes to which it is directed, by determining the beneficiaries; by adopting tradeoffs; by determining the ethical course of action. A patent awarded exclusively for a drug can have a profound societal effect, in limiting its availability to those with the means to pay. (Wenk, 1986) Limiting environmental impacts through international treaties is another salient example of society both influencing technology and being influenced by technology.

As Wenk puts it, "the technologically laden future isn't what it used to be. But human nature is" (1986, p. 11). Human nature has been amplified by technology much in the same way as technology has magnified the social impacts. Technology has made both the positive and the negative potential of humanity more pronounced.

Given the ubiquity of technology and its powers to influence human affairs, there is a strong incentive to manage technology in a manner that leads to the most socially satisfactory outcome. Governments play an integral role in the development of these technologies, making public policy an important factor in the social management of technology. The application of public policy towards the use of ICTs though e-government initiatives is intended to manage technological development with a mind towards increasing democratic legitimacy. Before we can effectively evaluate the success of such efforts, it is first necessary to determine what 'democracy' means as used in this context. In doing so, we can determine what conditions are necessary for a process to be legitimately called 'democratic'.

Establishing a Measure of EU Democratisation

Democracy is a commonly used word, necessitating a clear idea of what goals are sought when striving for democratic outcomes. As David Held notes, "The history of the idea of democracy is curious; the history of democracies is puzzling" (1987, p. 1). That democracy is the proper choice for the EU is a common assertion. Regardless of ideological views, most political regimes aspire to democracy in some form or another. Democracy, "…seems to bestow an 'aura of legitimacy' on modern political life: rules, laws, policies and decisions appear justified and appropriate when they are 'democratic'" (1987, p. 1). The legitimacy accompanying democracy is thus a tempting goal for the executive institutions of the EU, or at least for those institutions who would benefit from it. The value of adopting norms of democratic behaviour lies in the legitimacy bestowed as a result.

To understand the value of democracy requires knowing something about its origins. 'Democracy' originates from the Greek word *demokratia*. Its root meanings are *demos*, or people, and *kratos,* or rule. Simply put, democracy is a form of government in which the people rule. Although

this appears to be an unambiguous concept, the details are more complicated (Held, 1987). First, establishing who 'the people' are and the role they are to play is a concern. Determining the conditions conducive to participation is also difficult, especially so in the case of the EU. Balancing the role of the citizen in the nation-state versus their role in the international environment of the EU is problematic, as there exists no precedent for achieving such a balance. The rights and obligations of the citizen in the governance of a state are clearly defined. Those rights and obligations have made a piecemeal transition to the international level. European citizenship has not been enhanced in the past decade, and falls short of the rights and privileges bestowed on members of nation-states. Although there is value attached to being an EU citizen, determining what identity accompanies EU citizenship is more difficult.

Second, the idea of rule is a complicated one. Determining how broadly or narrowly the scope of rule is to be applied is a difficulty, as well as what areas (law and order, relation between states, the private sphere) that rule applies to (Held, 1987). Determining what limits rule places on the citizen is also difficult. The freedom of citizens to dissent as well as their obligations under rule must be clear. Democracies must have a sense of when it is appropriate to use coercion against those inside and outside their political sphere. This is an especially difficult requirement for the European Union as it has limited powers of coercion, usually only applicable by the governments of its member-states.

The justification for democracy as a form of governance is that it achieves at a minimum some of what are considered fundamental values. These values are generally accepted and are given political creditability in their use by democratic institutions (Eriksen & Fossum., 2000). Although there is little common agreement on the range of democratic values, some stand out above others. Democracy, "…refers to a form of government in which citizens enjoy an equal ability to participate meaningfully in the decisions that closely affect their common lives as individuals in communities" (Barney, 2000, p. 22). It is the criteria of meaningful participation that is the root of the problem for the European Union.

The introduction of e-government initiatives via the EU's Information Society is one possible example where the medium of communication may encourage greater public participation in the governance of the EU. The EU is often perceived as an organisation based in distant Brussels, working behind closed doors. Allowing citizens to view information on EU activities regardless of location is an example of how the technological medium makes possible limited citizen observation of European governance. It does not provide a meaningful forum for full participation however.

Being a collective decision-making instrument, democracy places inherent limits on individual liberty. Democracy is not constituted wholly by freedom of consumer choice in a market or the freedom to do whatever one wants. As a means of compensating for these limits, the citizen is granted the ability to influence the outcome of policies developed to serve the common interest. This gathering together of private individuals to define the public practices of a community is one of the central aspects of a democracy. It is also one of the most noticeable absences in the EU.

Not all decisions made are necessarily in the interest of the community as a whole. The participation of self-interested groups contributes to decisions made that are binding on the public life of the community. The process by which these decisions are made however are required to allow participation in a meaningful way. Participation must be meaningful if the concept of liberty is to be preserved. The symbolic participation of a select minority is insufficient to meet the requirements of democratic governance.

The rule of a select minority is a key component of the democratic deficit of the European Union. Attempting to resolve this deficit within an intergovernmental framework seems an impracticable option. Yet a national federal framework at the EU level is unacceptable to the member-states. The EU has affirmed that it is founded on the, "…indivisible universal values of human dignity, freedom, equality and solidarity" (Communities, 2001a). Further, the Union also, "…places the individual at the heart of its activities, by establishing the citizenship of the Union and by creating an area of freedom, security and justice" (2001a). The EU has set itself a democratic imperative, resolving to involve the citizen in the democratisation of the EU.

Democratic Governance and the Public Sphere

A public sphere is the product of equality and liberty in a democracy. While the theoretical requirements of equality are rarely met in full, even their partial attainment can lead to the creation of a public sphere, also referred to as a 'public.' A public is the community which determines those interests that are relevant to it. As the conditions for democracy have not been fulfilled on a European-wide level, there exists instead a grouping of national publics. Each public can determine what interests are relevant to it, but there is little ability to coordinate on an international level.

In order for a public to exist at the European level, equality and liberty must be promoted through the promotion of political linkages. Such linkages involve an extension of party politics and public debate to the European level. In moving the forum of discussion to this level citizens can effectively choose the issues important to them and elect their leaders on a pan-European basis. (Smith & Wright, 1999).

There is what has been described as, "…a remoteness, opaqueness and inaccessibility in European governance." (Smith & Wright, 1999, p. 136). There is no single accountable public authority with the power to handle regulatory processes. If the public is to fulfil its agenda-setting function in a democracy, it is necessary for a public to be able to force a government to vacate its office. Although the members of the European Parliament are accountable to their electorate, its status as an autonomous governing body remains in question. It is the weaker link in the chain of governing institutions, unable to check fully the powers of the Council of Ministers.

This weakness stems from an inability to act on the behalf of the citizens it represents. Although elected to voice the views of the citizens, it lacks the authority to ensure those views are addressed. This implies that the power of citizenship in the EU is less that the power realised by citizenship in a nation state. Citizenship of the EU can be considered as being akin to membership in an organisation. Yet, components of nation-state citizenship are a part of EU citizenship. Much like the EU itself, the rights and obligations of the EU citizen remain difficult to enumerate.

In a polity such as the European Union, what constitutes the basis of membership is an important consideration. Every polity must establish a community of members to which its authority is effectively extended. Membership in a polity is not generally bound to a territory, like citizenship. When one identifies himself or herself as a citizen of a particular state, they are identifying a specific territory in which they are subject to laws. Citizens of the EU however, are not citizens of its other member-states. Yet they are citizens of the EU when they travel within it. This is part of the uniqueness of the EU as a democratic polity.

The EU has effectively blurred the line between membership and citizenship. There remain certain conventions of citizenship though that are undisputed. The first of these is that a democratic polity consists of its citizens only, who are the last and only source of sovereignty. The citizens of the EU are the last source of sovereignty, albeit indirectly. Citizen approval via referenda is required for major change in the structure of the EU – namely treaty revision. This does not address the operation of government, only its structure.

A second principle of citizenship is the acceptance of equality within the polity. Citizens must accept this value of democracy as the practical application of a political principle. It remains to the government to make democratic input possible, but the people must accept it as the status quo. Equality for the citizen remains an abstract and artificial principle, and does not necessarily extend to the economic and social realm.

The third principle of citizenship remains consistent with the values of democracy. The basis of citizenship is derived from the idea of the individual as a member of the public sphere. The liberty of the citizen allows for assertion of opinion through the electoral process, effectively influencing the operation of government. This inability to wield influence is one of the most significant obstacles to overcome if the EU is to resemble a democracy in its methods of operation.

A fourth principle concerns how the governing offices are constituted. A responsible government of representatives is made up of citizens. These citizens occupy time-limited 'offices' and effectively remain equal under the law.

These basic principles of citizenship are derived from T.H. Marshall's account of the components of citizenship; civil, political and social. Civil aspects of citizenship for Marshall consist of liberty, freedom of speech and the right to own property. The political refers to the right to participate in the decision-making process. Social rights encompass welfare, security and education (Marshall, 1965).

In light of this definition of citizenship the distinction between membership and citizenship in a polity such as the EU remains uncertain. Citizenship of a member-state automatically bestows EU citizenship. Citizenship of the EU is imprecise however. A clear set of rights and obligations are not conferred upon the citizen, and little extra outside national citizenship is granted that could not be achieved through treaty. EU citizenship, while having some of the substance and symbolism of member-state citizenship, is not of an equal

Figure 1. Perceptions of EU membership

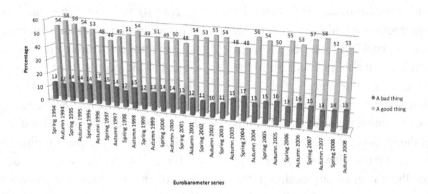

standing. Given this state of affairs, we can assert with some confidence that the conceptual basis for citizenship at the EU level differs from that of the nation-state. The implementation of e-government initiatives such as the Information Society intent on improving democratic legitimacy may thus result in outcomes not consistent with those outcomes anticipated at the nation-state level.

Democratic Accountability, the Information Society and Public Opinion

As illustrated in an overview of recent EU history, the executive institutions of the EU have been chastised for failing to meet minimum standards of democratic accountability. The European Commission has been accused of fraud and mismanagement. The European Parliament, despite efforts to constrain the Commission, has been hampered by an inability to quickly hold non-elected branches of the EU executive to account.

This lack of democratic oversight has not been ignored. The goals of the Information Society e-government initiative have emphasised bringing the public's of the EU closer to the Union – in other words, making it easier for them to be generally aware of the mechanisms of EU governance. (*Recommendations to the European Council*

Europe and the global information society, 1994) The goals in doing so are to increase social cohesion and improve the democratic legitimacy of the governing institutions. As an overview of Eurobarometer public opinion surveys over the past decade shows, the impact of the Information Society initiative has been a mixed one. While it has largely succeed as a means of bringing the EU closer to its public, improved awareness of governing institutions via e-government initiatives has not translated into demonstrable gains in trust – a benchmark for democratic legitimacy.

The ostensible purpose of e-government initiatives in the EU is to increase citizen awareness, and by extension increase the legitimacy of the governing institutions. But statistical trends over the past decade point to stagnant support for EU membership. These statistics cannot conclusively attribute this drop in support to any failure of e-government initiatives. They do indicate that in the decade since the Information Society was conceived and implemented, the EU has experienced a net decline in public support. It remains to be determined however, if the IS has mitigated an inevitable trend, or if the institutional structure of the EU has obstructed the ability of ICTs to promote democratisation.

Awareness of the governing institutions of the EU has increased markedly in the decade since

Figure 2. Trust in European Commission 1999-2008

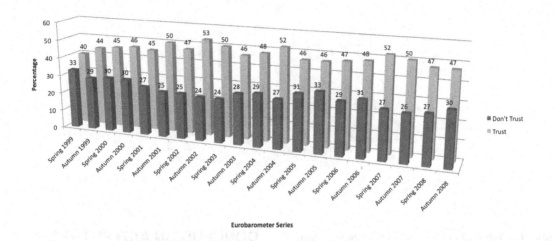

the inception of the IS. In 1993 only 18 per cent of respondents were familiar with the European Commission (*Eurobarometer 39*, 1993; *Eurobarometer 40*, 1993). Only 40 per cent were familiar with the European Parliament (*Eurobarometer 41*, 1994). By 2004 awareness had increased to 80 per cent and 92 per cent respectively (*Eurobarometer 61*, 2004). Widespread recognition of governing institutions had become the norm by 2004 to the point where this question was no longer asked, instead concentrating on issues of trust.

As access to information about the EU and its governing institutions has grown, trust has declined. This has coincided with an increase in access to communication technologies, a central goal of the Information Society e-government initiative. The non-elected governing institutions have suffered the greatest lost of trust. In 1993, 53 per cent of EU citizens tended to trust the European Commission. By early 1999 only 40 per cent indicated trust in the Commission (*Eurobarometer 52*, 1999). This low point coincided with the *de facto* censure of the Commission by the Parliament. By 2008 trust had rebounded to 47 per cent of EU citizens (*Eurobarometer 69*, 2008). The general trend however, has been consistently low level of

trust. Those indicating distrust in the Commission as a governing institution rose from 25 per cent in 1993 to 30 per cent in 2008 (*Eurobarometer 40*, 1993; *Eurobarometer 70*, 2008).

The European Parliament has retained greater public support. Trust in it as an institution has fluctuated from a low of 50 per cent in 1999 to a high of 57 per cent in 2001 (*Eurobarometer 56*, 2001). Yet over the decade since the inception of the information society initiative, trust in the Parliament as a governing institution has remained stagnant at 54 per cent (*Eurobarometer 70*, 2008). These numbers are indicative of an identifiable trend. Despite increased access to ICTs, a shift in preference towards ICTs to obtain information about the European Union, and a sense that the European Parliament is significantly more important to EU citizens than five years ago, there has been a net gain of zero per cent trust in the past ten years.

As outlined in this chapter, technology does play a vital role in the operations of a governing body. The use of technology either as the subject or an object of policy development has implications for popular public support. The goals of the EU Information Society have been openly eco-

Figure 3. Prefered Methods of Learning about the EU

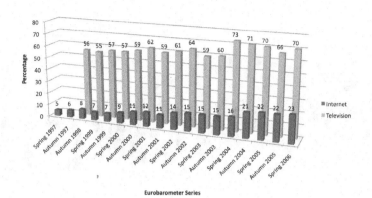

nomic, but have also sought to bring democratic legitimacy to the governing institutions of the EU. Increased legitimacy has not been the result.

Compilation and analysis of statistical data has indicated that the first decade of the EU Information Society e-government initiative has borne witness to two phenomenon: Increased access to communication technologies and a growing preference for their use as a means of learning more about the EU. In this respect, the primary goals of the Information Society strategy can judged a success. The IS has allowed its citizens to become more aware and attuned to EU policy development and institutional operation. The anticipated social consequences of this have not met with initial expectations.

Greater awareness of institutional operation has not coincided with increased democratic legitimacy, nor the accountability that accompanies it. Trust in governing institutions has decreased or stagnated. Support for EU membership has declined to under half of the EU population. Yet more people are aware of EU governing institutions than ever before. A decade of public opinion survey data allows us to clearly establish these points as fact. What such data cannot do is explain why trust has declined as awareness and access to communication technologies has risen.

CONCLUSION AND FUTURE RESEARCH DIRECTIONS

This chapter begins with two relatively noncontroversial propositions. First, the European Union suffers from a democratic deficit. It's unique historical development and intergovernmental origins have resulted in a supranational governance structure that lacks a direct accountability to citizens characteristic of national governments. Second, the e-government initiative known as the "Information Society" is anticipated as having positive consequences for institutional transparency and democratic legitimacy. While primarily a policy initiative based in economic terms, it also envisions using e-government tools to bring European publics closer to EU governing institutions. In effect, the Information Society intends to increase awareness of the workings of EU decision-making, and by extension, reinforce democratic legitimacy.

As this chapter asserts, such assumptions conflict with the idea of technology as a social process. Rather than seeing communication technologies as tools intended to solve a problem, a more nuanced view is required. Technologies can be thought of as organised social behaviour directed towards a certain goal. Such behaviours are not independent of the culture they are developed in. Cultural influences dictate how technologies are developed, and in return, the technologies shape cultural expectations as they become ubiquitous.

An initial investigation of public opinion trends over a decade provides some indications for further research. Promoting e-government initiatives and reducing national-level regulatory burdens within the EU has coincided with an increase in access to the Internet. It has also coincided with greater use of communication technologies to learn about the EU. In this respect, the economic policy underpinning the IS initiative has had positive social impacts. But the impact on democratic legitimacy remains unchanged.

Eurobarometer surveys indicate increased citizen awareness of EU institutions, and greater use of supplied e-government resources to learn about their operation. But trust in the non-elected governing institutions of the EU remains low. Future research should address how the governmental structure of the European Union differs from that of the nation-state. Citizens at the national level are able to act on the information they access via e-government services. At the supranational level no action is possible – the ballot box only applies to the weakest of the core governing institutions – the European Parliament. If improved access to information does not affect citizens' ability to affect political change, are the democratic possibilities of information technology negated? Greater examination of the EU's unique structure and ongoing development may shed light on this question.

REFERENCES

Barney, D. (2000). *Prometheus wired: the hope for democracy in the age of network technology.* Chicago: University of Chicago Press.

Communities, E. (1999, March 15). *First report on allegations regarding fraud, mismanagement and nepotism in the European Commission.* Committee of Independent Experts, EU.

Communities, E. (2001a). *Charter of Fundamental Rights of the European Union.* Retrieved (n.d.), from http://www.europarl.eu.int/charter/default_en.htm

Communities, E. (2001b). *Laeken Declaration on the Future of the European Union.* Retrieved October 13, 2005, from http://european-convention.eu.int/pdf/LKNEN.pdf

Dinerstein, J. (2009). Technology and Its Discontents: On the Verge of the Posthuman. *American Quarterly, 58*(3), 569–570. doi:10.1353/aq.2006.0056

Ellul, J. (1964). *The Technological Society.* New York: Vintage Books.

Ellul, J. (1980). *The Technological System.* New York: Continuum Publishing Cooperation.

Eriksen, E. O., & Fossum, J. E. (2000). *Democracy in the European Union: Integration through Deliberation?* London: Routledge.

(1993). *Eurobarometer 39.* Brussels: Commission of the European Communities.

(1993). *Eurobarometer 40.* Brussels: Commission of the European Communities.

(1994). *Eurobarometer 41.* Brussels: Commission of the European Communities.

(1999). *Eurobarometer 52.* Brussels: Commission of the European Communities.

(2001). *Eurobarometer 56.* Brussels: Commission of the European Communities.

(2004). *Eurobarometer 61.* Brussels: Commission of the European Communities.

(2008). *Eurobarometer 69.* Brussels: Commission of the European Communities.

(2008). *Eurobarometer 70*. Brussels: Commission of the European Communities.

GSM. 3G Market Update (2009). *Happy 20th birthday, GSM* (2007, 07 Sept, 2007). Retrieved July 28, 2009, from http://news.zdnet.co.uk/leader/0,1000002982,39289154,00.htm

Hayward, J. (1995). *The Crisis of Representation in Europe*. London: Frank Cass & Co. Ltd.

Held, D. (1987). *Models of Democracy*. Cambridge, UK: Polity Press.

Hoskyns, C., & Newman, M. (2000). *Democratizing the European Union: Issues for the twenty-first century*. Manchester, UK: Manchester University Press.

Livingston, V. (2006). *Two Billion GSM Customers Worldwide*. Retrieved July 29, 2009, from http://www.prnewswire.com/cgi-bin/stories.pl?ACCT=109&STORY=/www/story/06-13-2006/0004379206&EDATE=

Marshall, T. H. (1965). *Class, Citizenship and Social Development*. New York: Anchor Books.

Nugent, N. (2001). *The European Commission*. New York: Palgrave.

Siedentop, L. (2000). *Democracy in Europe*. London: Allen Lane.

Smith, D., & Wright, S. (1999). *Whose Europe? The turn towards Democracy*. Oxford, UK: Blackwell Publishers.

Stirk, P. M. (1996). *A History of European Integration Since 1914*. New York: Pinter.

Teivainen, T. (2002). *Enter Economism Exit Politics: Experts, economic policy and the damage to democracy*. London: Zed Books Ltd.

Wenk, E. J. (1986). *Tradeoffs: Imperatives of Choice in a high-tech world*. Baltimore: The John Hopkins University Press.

Winner, L. (1978). *Autonomous Technology: Technics-out-of-Control as a theme in Political Thought*. Cambridge, MA: The MIT Press.

Young, J. W. (1984). *Britain, France and the Unity of Europe 1945-1951*. Bath, UK: Leicester University Press.

ADDITIONAL READING

Anderson, S. S., & Eliassen, K. A. (1996). *The European Union: How Democratic Is It?* London: Sage Publications.

Beetham, D., & Lord, C. (1998). *Legitimacy and the European Union*. London: Longham.

Bell, D. (1973). *The Coming of Post-Industrial Society: A Venture in Social Forecasting*. New York: Basic Books Inc.

Bellamy, R., & Warleigh, A. (2001). *Citizenship and Goverance in the European Union*. London: Continuum.

Bijker, W. E., & Law, J. (1994). *Shaping Technology/Building Society: Studies in Sociotechnical Change*. Cambridge, MA: The MIT Press.

Castells, M. (1997). The Information Age: Economy, Society and Culture: *Vol. II. The Power of Identity*. Malden, MA: Blackwell Publishers Inc.

Castells, M. (2001). *The Internet Galaxy: Reflections on the Internet, Business, and Society*. Oxford, UK: Oxford University Press.

Coombes, D. (1970). Politics and Bureaucracy in the European Community: a Portrait of the Commission of the E.E.C. London: George Allen and Unwin ltd.

Deutsch, K. W. (1953). *Nationalism and Social Communication: An inquiry into the Foundations of Nationality*. New York: John Wiley & Sons Inc.

Dinerstein, J. (2009). Technology and Its Discontents: On the Verge of the Posthuman. *American Quarterly, 58*(3), 569–570. doi:10.1353/aq.2006.0056

Ellul, J. (1964). *The Technological Society*. New York: Vintage Books.

Gore, A. (1996). Basic principles for building an information society. *International Information Communication and Education, 15*(2).

Hickman, L. A. (1990). *Technology as a Human Affair*. New York: McGraw-Hill Publishing Company.

Innis, H. A. (1951). *The Bias of Communication*. Toronto, Canada: University of Toronto Press.

Ionescu, G. (1976). *The Political Thought of Saint-Simon London*. UK: Oxford University Press.

Kitschelt, H. (2000). Linkages Between Citizens and Politicians. *Democratic Polities, 33*(6), 845–880.

Kraft, M. E., & Vig, N. J. (1988). *Technology and Politics*. Durham, NC: Duke University Press.

McLuhan, M. (1962). *The Gutenberg Galaxy*. Toronto, Canada: University of Toronto Press.

Meisel, J. H. (1958). *The Myth of the Ruling Class: Gaetano Mosca and the Elite*. Michigan, USA: University of Michigan Press.

Norris, P. (2000). *A Virtuous Circle: Political Communication in Postindustrial Societies*. Cambridge, UK: Cambridge University Press. doi:10.1017/CBO9780511609343

Postman, N. (1992). *Technopoly: The Surrender of Culture to Technology*. New York: Alfred A. Knoff Inc.

Recommendations to the European Council Europe and the global information society (1994). *Recommendations to the European Council Europe and the global information society*. Retreived (n.d.), from http://www.rewi.hu-berlin.de/datenschutz/report.html#chap1

Rehn, O. (1999, November 9). *Transparency in practice: the Commission viewpoint*.Speech by Dr Olli Rehn, Head of Cabinet of Commissioner Erkki Liikanen Pronounced at Transparency Conference in the European Parliament. (Brussels, Retreived from (n.d.), http://www.euractiv.com/cgi-bin/eurb/cgint.exe/106704?1100=1&204&OIDN=500246

Reinhard, W. (1996). *Power Elites and State Building*. Oxford, UK: Oxford University Press.

Schumacher, E. F. (1975). *Small is Beautiful: Economics as if People Mattered*. New York: Harper & Row Publishers, Inc.

Schuurman, E. (1995). *Perspectives on Technology and Culture. Sioux Centre*. IA: Dordt College Press.

KEY TERMS AND DEFINITIONS

Information Society (IS): An economic policy initiative originating with the Bangemann Report of 1994 – a comprehensive plan by the European Commission for policy encompassing economic development, social cohesion and the development of an EU-wide policy to promote the use of Information Communication Technologies in Europe. Also referred to as eEurope or e-government. Information Society can be considered an umbrella term for all policy development concerning communication technologies in the EU.

Information Communications Technologies (ICTs): As computing and communication technologies converged in the 1980s, it became possible to offer computerised communication services over telecommunications equipment. These became known as Information Communication Technologies. It encompasses any type of information transfer facilitated by computer-based technology.

European Union: An economic and political union of 27 member-states (at the time of writing)

European Commission: Formally known as the Commission of the European Communities, The Commission is the executive branch of the European Union. The body is responsible for proposing legislation, implementing decisions, and enforcing directives.

European Parliament: European Parliament (EP) is the directly elected parliamentary institution of the European Union.

Council of Ministers: The principal decision-making institution of the European Union, represented by ministers of member-states. Formally known as The Council of the European Union, informally referred to as the Council of Ministers, or simply the Council.

Global Standard for Mobile Communications (GSM): A standard for mobile telephone communications first developed in 1982 by the European Conference of Postal and Telecommunications Administrations (CEPT) and adopted by the European Telecommunications Standards Institute (ETSI) in 1989. The most popular standard for mobile phones worldwide.

ENDNOTES

[1] http://european-convention.eu.int/

[2] Jacques Santer was the exception. He resigned and departed in June 1999, after being elected to the European Parliament in the summer elections.

[3] This measure was undertaken to avoid the dilemma of the previous Commission. Edith Cresson, a Commissioner central to fraud allegations, refused to resign. This eventually drew the entire Commission into the investigation, leading to a collective resignation.

Chapter 15
Evaluating Social Networking in Public Diplomacy

Hyunjin Seo
Syracuse University, USA

Stuart Thorson
Syracuse University, USA

ABSTRACT

While many e-government applications have focused on governments connecting with their citizens, recently social networking tools have begun to transform the practice of public diplomacy by permitting governments to build and maintain direct relationships with citizens of other countries. In this chapter, we describe several such initiatives undertaken by the U.S. Department of State (DOS). Our particular focus is on efforts aimed at South Korea. We present results from interviews with DOS officials responsible for technology-based relationship-focused public diplomacy as well as with U.S. Embassy officials tasked with managing one of these initiatives–Café USA–and South Korean participants in Café USA. The chapter concludes with a discussion of the implications of e-government applications that cross national boundaries for our understanding of citizenship and suggestions for further research aimed at evaluating the effects of e-government applications within public diplomacy.

INTRODUCTION

Since the development of the modern nation state, diplomacy has been a function largely reserved to national governments and their official representatives. However, the rise of international and transnational groups and organizations has resulted in non-state actors such as the United Nations or groups such as Greenpeace or ICANN playing roles that might earlier have been the sole purview of national governments. More recently, the availability of increasingly wide-scale and low-cost access to pervasive computing and communications networks has led to citizen involvement in activities traditionally reserved to government representatives (Castells, 2008).

Initially, this direct citizen involvement generally took the form of individuals (or organized groups of individuals) lobbying foreign policy bureaucracies of national governments for policy change. Now,

DOI: 10.4018/978-1-61520-933-0.ch015

though, we are beginning to see both national governments and non-governmental organizations using computer-based social networking tools such as Facebook, Twitter, and web chat rooms to greatly expand both the range of actors in what has been traditionally thought of as the diplomatic process *and* the kinds of interactions between these actors.

Moreover, social networking tools have begun to transform the practice of public diplomacy by permitting governments to build and maintain direct relationships with citizens of *other* countries. The stated goal of these new public diplomacy efforts is often to support understandings of policy decisions as well as (or even opposed to) convincing foreign nationals of the correctness of those decisions. Focusing on developing shared understandings even in the face of sharp policy disagreements helps to distinguish modern public diplomacy initiatives from mere propaganda.

In this chapter we report on social networking initiatives by the U.S. Department of State, with particular emphasis on initiatives in South Korea. South Korea is of special interest since it (i) is of considerable strategic importance to the United States and (ii) has a Confucian tradition that places emphasis on *relationships* as opposed to rigid *contract-based* understandings, and (iii) is one of the most wired countries in the world. Our interest here is two-fold. It is first to provide concrete examples of how a particular national government is beginning to directly engage citizens of other countries thus bypassing traditional filters and gatekeepers, such as the mass media. Second, it is to initiate serious discussion of impacts this changing architecture of diplomacy may have on the practice of foreign policy.

Our primary focus is on Café USA[1], an initiative by the U.S. Embassy in the South Korean capital, Seoul, to reach out to that country's citizens. Café USA is part of the Embassy's efforts to interact with the younger generation in South Korea, a substantial proportion of which are regarded to have anti-U.S. sentiments (Kim & Lim, 2007). This online community initiative, which will be described more fully below, represents an important example of networked public diplomacy, as it enables two-way communication between U.S. Embassy officials and South Korean citizens through the Internet. For this study, we interviewed U.S. State Department officials who have been in charge of the Embassy's public diplomacy as well as South Korean members of Café USA. Documentation and archival materials were used to corroborate findings from other sources (Yin, 2003).

Scope of Diplomacy Enlarged

A national government's diplomatic initiatives aimed directly at foreign citizens are often termed *public diplomacy*. Though it is increasingly difficult to separate domestic publics from foreign publics in this era of global interconnectedness, public diplomacy is aimed mainly at foreign publics (Nye, 2005; Tuch, 1990; Snow, 2007; USIA, 1987). Therefore, we define public diplomacy as governmental or nongovernmental activities that promote national interest through efforts to inform, engage, and influence foreign audiences. Such activities may, of course, reach the government's or organization's own citizens as well.

Public diplomacy has received growing attention from scholars and practitioners as public opinion in foreign countries has increasingly become recognized as being relevant to a country's diplomatic initiatives (Gilboa, 2008; Nye, 2005; Snow, 2007). Interest in public diplomacy has also been reinforced by an increased appreciation of *soft power* or *smart power* as a central element of international relations (Catto, 2001; Nye, 2005; Nye 2008). According to Nye, *soft power* refers to the power to get what you want through attraction rather than coercion. Empirical studies of international marketing show that country image plays an important role in consumer choice behavior (e.g., Nebebzahl & Jaffe, 1996; Parameswaran & Pisharodi, 2002). That is, products' country of origin provides consumers cues for their evaluations and purchase intentions of products. This, in turn, reinforces countries' willingness to invest resources in public diplomacy in order to improve their national image within global markets.

Edmund A. Gullion, former dean of the Fletcher School's Edward R. Murrow Center for Public Diplomacy, coined the term public diplomacy in 1965 describing it as:

Public diplomacy... deals with the influence of public attitudes on the formation and execution of foreign policies. It encompasses dimensions of international relations beyond traditional diplomacy; the cultivation by governments of public opinion in other countries; the interaction of private groups and interests in one country with those of another; the reporting of foreign affairs and its impact on policy; communication between those whose job is communication, as between diplomats and foreign correspondents; and the processes of inter-cultural communications.

In its early days, public diplomacy focused on government-initiated activities. Thus, scholars and practitioners confined use of the term to government actions (Tuch, 1990; U.S. Department of State, 1987). For example, Tuch (1990) said public diplomacy is "a government's process of communicating with foreign publics" to enhance their understanding of its nation's ideas, values, institutions, culture, and policies. However, initiatives from the private sector have increasingly gained in importance (Henrikson, 2006). That is, both academics and practitioners have recognized the importance of expanding both Track Two-style diplomacy involving discussions and negotiations at the nongovernmental level as well as cultural and scientific exchanges and collaborations between countries (Henrikson, 2006; Cull, 2008).

This enlarging of the scope of diplomacy has resulted from many interdependent factors including the growing number of global issue-based NGOs and global media. It also stems from an increasing sense that problems can no longer be neatly divided into those that are *domestic* and those that are *foreign*, as well as the spread of various forms of democracy resulting in a greater sense of political efficacy among many in the world.

Another force making public diplomacy ever more significant is the development of networked information technology (CSIS, 1998; Falconi, 2007). Thanks to transnational digital networks, countries are no longer linked solely by foreign ministers and traders but also directly by millions of individuals (Benkler, 2007; CSIS, 1998). This has facilitated the uncoordinated and often spontaneous connecting of activities of otherwise diverse groups and individuals around particular issues. Scholars have pointed out that information technology, in particular the Internet, is the "wild card" of public diplomacy in this network era, while traditional outlets such as state-sponsored broadcasting may be become less relevant (Burt & Robison, 1998; Fulton, 2002).

From an architectural perspective, this has led to a decentralization of many of the traditional functions of diplomacy. Whereas it used to be that what a person knew about international issues was almost entirely mediated by their national government and what the press chose to report, people in much of the world can now bypass both governments and traditional media to learn about international issues from multiple perspectives and, importantly, to dynamically create groups focused on those issues.

This creates tension. The rise of democracy means more and more citizens believe they have the right to hold their governments accountable for policies. At the same time, national governments, while still extremely important, have decreased capacity to centrally control the policy process. Citizens increasingly generate demands that democratic national governments can neither ignore nor fully satisfy.

As an example, the months long demonstrations in Seoul in 2008 were focused on limiting the importing of U.S. beef and went against a free trade diplomatic initiative agreed to by South Korean President Lee Myung-bak and then U.S. President George W. Bush. These demonstrations severely constrained the new Lee government's policy options. Moreover, the evidence is that these demonstrations were not centrally organized. Rather, as is so often the case in networked worlds, the protests were fueled by a combination of somewhat random events (such as good weather) conjoined with the ability to utilize traditional (e.g., television coverage) and new (e.g., Cyworld and SMS messaging) communication channels. Interestingly these new channels enable dynamic relationships which are not constrained to geographic proximity thus producing electronic small worlds within which people can cooperate at a distance. Moreover, these channels are interactive and permit development and maintenance of relationships that endure beyond the specific event that brought them into being. This example illustrates that, in the information age, the flow of information does not honor national boundaries. Koreans and Korean Americans living in the United States could support protests in Seoul and, at the same time, U.S. government messages could not be limited to only Korean (or U.S.) audiences. There have been important studies examining the increased use of online communication tools for global activism (Bennett, 2003a, 2003b, Rucht, 2004; Van Aelst & Walgrave, 2004), but little research has analyzed how these online media influence a government's relationships with foreign publics.

Social Networking, Public Diplomacy, and Relationships

U.S. public diplomacy in the past focused mainly on distributing information overseas through mass media, meetings with elites, and cultural events. Person-to-person exchange programs such as the Fulbright Program also played a role in U.S. public diplomacy (Snow, 2008).

In recent years, social networking has emerged as an increasingly significant component of public diplomacy within the U.S. Department of State. The DOS has its official blog, Dipnote[2], whose updates are posted to Twitter.[3] As of July 2009, more than 6,500 people are following Dipnote through Twitter. And, of course, Twitter is a social networking tool that does not limit the audience to particular geographic areas. For example, on 17 March 2009 followers of Dipnote received the tweet, "Reports that President Ravalomanana of Madagascar is seeking sanctuary at the U.S. Embassy in Antananarivo are FALSE." This message was of news interest to those following events in Madagascar from the United States as well as of practical political concern to citizens of Madagascar (who were reported to be using Twitter as a means of internal communication).

Another example of public diplomacy using social networking is the Democracy Challenge, a DOS-sponsored worldwide competition of short videos defining democracy. Contenders create videos that complete the phrase, "Democracy is…" More than 900 entries from 95 countries competed for six grand prizes in 2009. Described as "an effort to enhance the global dialogue on democracy,"[4] the Challenge project uses social networking tools. The delivery platform is YouTube[5] where contenders post videos. The DOS created a Facebook group[6] for the Challenge to increase global attention to the competition and to encourage global online voting to determine winners. All updates are posted to Twitter. Former Under Secretary of State for Public Diplomacy and Public Affairs James K. Glassman said:

The Challenge breaks fresh ground for the use of new media in public diplomacy. We in the State Department and our partners are not trying to define democracy for young people around the world. Rather, the Challenge asks participants to share their visions of what democracy means. If the Challenge can generate thought and debate about democracy, on the medium of choice for young people, we'll have achieved success.[7]

Democracy Challenge winners participate in screenings of their videos in Hollywood, New York, and Washington D.C., hosted by the Directors of Guild of America and the Motion Picture Association of America. The Challenge involves a unique partnership of democracy and youth organizations, the film and entertainment industry, academia, and the U.S. government.

These types of networked public diplomacy–public diplomacy based on online means of communication–offer important implications for *relationship management* between a country and its publics. The interactivity of Internet-based communication tools helps countries reach out through two-way symmetrical communication or dialogic relationships (Coombs, 2004; J. Grunig & Huang, 2000, Kent & Taylor, 1998). In fact, relationship building or relationship management has gained increasing attention from public relations scholars, given its demonstrated significance for an organization's success at achieving goals (Ledingham & Bruning, 1998, 2000). It is no less important for public diplomacy, the success of which often hinges on how a country builds and maintains relationships with foreign publics.

The relationship management function has taken on new significance in recent years as terrorist threats have resulted in U.S. embassies becoming citadels with little opportunity for informal interaction with local citizens. As Ambassador Donald Gregg put it, "The day when USIS [U.S. Information Service] had virtually open libraries is nothing but a fading memory."[8] In this context, networked public diplomacy provides an electronic bridge between the embassy and local citizens.

As mentioned above, social networking applications bring new actors into the diplomatic process and facilitate development and maintenance of relationships among these actors. Indeed this is perhaps the central feature of the emerging world of networked diplomacy. These new relationships, in turn, are affecting the very nature of diplomacy. This is especially obvious in the case of U.S. relations with countries such as South Korea where, as noted above, relationships are particularly important.

Our argument here follows from Richard Nisbett (2003) and Raymond Cohen's (1991) examination of cultural factors in international negotiations. In his book, *The Geography of Thought*, Nisbett advances and empirically tests a theory that East Asia and the West, heavily influenced by Confucian thought and Aristotelian thinking respectively, have acculturated people to two, somewhat distinct, modes of cognition. While Nisbett's data make it clear that these differences are not immutable (for example, East Asians living in the West take on characteristics of Western modes of thought), the case is quite compelling and measurable differences do seem to exist.

The United States and South Korea provide a case for the two cultures studied by Nisbett. Of special interest here is one such difference. That is that the typical East Asian ontology is heavily populated with relationships while the typical Western ontology is largely comprised of categories. Confucianism puts relationships at the center of a person's existence. A person's identity is constituted by one's duties and responsibilities to others. As a consequence, an overriding social objective is maintaining harmonious balance resulting from each person understanding, accepting, and fulfilling her/his roles in the set of relationships which, taken together, constitute the social order. Metaphorically, think of a Confucian state as a symphony orchestra wherein each musician understands, accepts, and fulfills her/his role and plays her/his instrument not to stand out but rather to contribute to the overall sound of the orchestra. Fundamental to understanding Korea is recognizing its history as a Confucian entity.

The United States, on the other hand, is a culture largely focused on science and control. From this perspective, the world is composed of objects and categories understood via empirical means and then controlled through the development of abstract theories. Contrary to the Korean case, an individual's identity stems not so much from his/her relationship to others but from her/his independence from others and ability to make choices in whatever way s/he chooses. The United States is, continuing the metaphor, a nation of rock stars where each musician strives to be differentiated from all others.

Cohen (1991) makes similar distinctions between Western and non-Western thinking in his analysis of negotiation styles in different cultures. Cohen said supreme values in individualism-oriented Western states are the development of individual personality, self-expression, and personal achievement. In non-Western states characterized by collectivism or interdependent ethos, an individual's identity and decisions are based on her/his relationship with other individuals or groups. Unlike Western states, non-Western states are "concerned less with abstract principles of absolute justice than with the requirements of continuing harmony" (p. 25). In their approaches to conflict resolution, people in non-Western states depend on "mechanisms of communal reconciliation" rather than formal processes, regulations, or law. In particular, Cohen suggests that negotiation styles of different countries can be placed along a continuum from individual-oriented approaches on one end to collective-oriented approaches on the other end. As a consequence of their distinct ontologies, U.S. and Korean negotiators have frequently been unable to develop empathetic understandings of each other's positions.

As we will demonstrate, this lack of understanding was a key motivator of the Café USA program. Below we present data from our preliminary evaluation of Café USA. Central among questions we will be investigating is the degree to which this initiative focuses on relationship building as opposed to contract-based understandings.

Café USA

The U.S. Embassy in Seoul has played a crucial role in dealing with political, security, economic, and cultural issues involving the two allies. While diplomatic relationships between the United States and Korea trace back to the late 1870s, U.S. roles in ending the Japanese colonial rule of Korea (1910-1945) and during and after the Korean War (1950-1953) have defined many aspects of current bilateral relations. The U.S. Embassy, located in the heart of downtown Seoul, embodies the modern history of U.S.-Korea relations. In particular, the presence of U.S. troops in South Korea has been a source of contention between the two countries (Kim & Lim, 2007).

In recent years, the U.S. Embassy has faced a series of massive rallies by South Korean activists on issues such as relocation of U.S. troops in South Korea and U.S. beef imports into South Korea (BBC, 2004, 2008). In response, it has made efforts to forge two-way communication with the South Korean public to better understand how South Koreans perceive U.S. policies concerning their country and to effectively explain U.S. positions (Hill, 2004). Café USA, the online community run by the U.S. Embassy, is part of the Embassy's effort to engage the South Korean public. In announcing the launch of the online community, then-U.S. Ambassador to South Korea Christopher Hill (2004) said:

As we live in a high-tech era, the Embassy must find new ways to reach out to people. I look forward to reading the views of the Korean public by reading the posts on Café USA and sharing my thoughts on Korea-U.S. relations with the Korean people. I know it is important for us to listen to Korean viewpoints, and I hope people will find Café USA a useful forum to express their views on Korean-American relations.

Café USA is hosted on a South Korean server (Daum) and includes multiple online chat groups as well as video and other news posted by the Embassy. Café USA also serves as a portal into the larger Embassy web presence where, for example, South Korean residents can inquire about visa procedures and schedule appointments for visa interviews. Thus Café USA encompasses both diplomatic services and relationship building. The study reported here focuses on the relationship side of Café USA. As of February 2010, Café USA had about 11,000 registered online members in Korea and abroad.

Café USA, with its interactive features, is more effective at building dialogic relationships with foreign publics, compared with other tools for one-way online communication, such as static web pages (Kent & Taylor, 1998). Café USA encourages dialogue and feedback from the South Korean public with features such as "Dialogue with current U.S. Ambassador Kathleen Stephens," "Discussion on Political/Security Issues," "Discussion on Economic/Trade Issues," "Other U.S.-Korea Issues," "Visa/Consular Affairs," "English Speakers," "Youth Discussion Group," and "This Week in American History."

RESEARCH QUESTIONS

The study poses the following research questions (RQs):

RQ1: *How does the U.S. Embassy use Café USA for relationship building and relationship management with the South Korean public?*

The first research question is intended to investigate the ways in which the U.S. Embassy in Seoul uses the online community to build and manage relationships with the South Korean public. Data gathered are used to explain major features and purposes of Café USA. This research question also deals with how U.S. officials value

their relationships with the South Korean public in their diplomatic activities.

RQ2: *How does the U.S. Embassy evaluate the role of Café USA for improving relationships with the South Korean public?*

The second research question is designed to study the Embassy's evaluation of its online initiative. It examines the Embassy's perception of whether or not Café USA has contributed to building its relationship with the South Korean public. In particular, this question will generate important information about how effectiveness of public diplomacy can be measured.

RQ3: *How do South Koreans perceive the role of Café USA in improving their relationships with the U.S. Embassy?*

The third research question involves the role of Café USA from the perspectives of its users. This question examines how South Korean online members of Café USA think of the U.S. Embassy's initiative and whether they perceive Café USA has helped improve their relationships with the Embassy (if they believe it has). It also asks whether the South Koreans think the U.S. Embassy's efforts have influenced their perceptions of the U.S. Embassy and the United States in general.

Data Collection Procedure

As suggested above, the use of computer social networking tools is a relatively recent phenomenon within the U.S. Department of State. Consequently, our primary interests in this study centered on how Korean members of Café USA and State Department officials perceived and evaluated Café USA and we focused on getting a sense of how our respondents thought about these issues. To provide provisional understandings of this, we utilized a case study approach (Café USA) and, within that case, did in-depth interviews with both Café USA members and U.S. diplomats. In a future study we intend to use the results of these interviews to design survey-based measures usable with larger samples. However, interview results reported here should be read as providing an indication of how respondents conceptualized the role of social networking within Café USA and not as quantitative estimates of the range of views of any larger population.

Three types of data collection procedures were used in this study: in-depth interviews, documentation, and archival material. The majority of the data were gathered from interviews with five U.S. diplomatic officials who are or have been in charge of public diplomacy in South Korea and South Korean members of Café USA. Findings from these interviews were corroborated by documentation and archival material. Documentation analysis was based on materials posted on the Café USA website and U.S. and South Korean news reports about the U.S. Embassy in Seoul and its Café USA project. In particular, we analyzed media coverage of the Embassy's efforts to build and maintain relationships with the South Korean public amid growing anti-U.S. sentiment in South Korea in recent years. As part of archival material analysis, we examined press releases, newsletters, and other government documents published by the U.S. Embassy in Seoul and the State Department.

Relationship Management (RQ1)

Former and current U.S. officials interviewed for this research emphasized that it is important for a country to engage in two-way communication with its publics in order to build and manage relationships with them. They noted that Café USA has contributed to building a relationship between the Embassy and the South Korean public by enhancing the Embassy's ability to engage in meaningful dialogue. In particular, three aspects of relationship management were identified through

the interviews: Mutuality, networking, and assurances of legitimacy (Hon & J. Grunig, 1999; Kent & Taylor, 1998; L. Grunig, et al., 2002).

Mutuality

The interviewees said Café USA engages in two-way symmetrical communication with the South Korean public, thus enhancing mutual understanding. The minister-counselor for public affairs at the U.S. Embassy in Seoul noted that Café USA is "a vehicle for constructive engagement" which is "mutual, respectful, and interactive." According to the chief of public affairs at the Embassy, Café USA allowed for continuing dialogue between the Embassy and South Korean members of the online community. That is, materials the Embassy posts to the Café USA website generate questions and discussions among members of the online community. Then the Embassy staffers respond accordingly, maintaining the dialogue via the online medium.

A former information specialist at the U.S. Embassy Seoul, who was directly involved in creating and managing Café USA, said the online community has changed the nature of communication between the Embassy and the South Korean public "from monologue to dialogue." In other words, with the help of Café USA and other forms of online communication tools, the Embassy has transformed its communication with the South Korean public from one-way speech to two-way dialogue.

A public diplomacy coordinator for Korea and Japan at the U.S. Department of State said Café USA, through its two-way communication, enhances mutual understanding between the Embassy and the South Korean public. The official, who worked at the U.S. Embassy in Seoul in the early 2000s, emphasized in particular the significance of listening to the entire dialogue. The diplomat added that the main task of public diplomacy officers is to inform foreign publics of the country's policies but not to necessarily change their opinions toward the United States. "Even if foreign audiences disagree with us, at least I want them to disagree with us for the right reason," the diplomat said. The official added that technologies available today offer more opportunities for public diplomacy officers to better listen to and inform foreign audiences.

A former U.S. ambassador to South Korea, who has been involved in U.S. public diplomacy in South Korea for decades, commended Café USA for its role in facilitating two-way communication between the Embassy and the South Korean public. The ambassador said, "I think Café USA is a very good technique to allow a wider variety of views to be heard and to be responded to by people inside the Embassy." He further indicated that this is an important change from the time when Embassy officials used to rely almost exclusively on press summaries to learn what the Koreans were thinking and respond occasionally.

Networking

The interviewees said Café USA is used by Embassy Seoul to expand and improve networking with the South Korean public. The minister-counselor explained that Café USA has helped the Embassy bring ordinary citizens into its official programs. Traditionally these programs involved only elite members of society like diplomats, CEOs, business leaders, lawmakers, and media representatives. The diplomat said the Embassy is constantly monitoring what types of new media South Koreans are interested in using to adjust features of Café USA to meet their interests. "We want to engage real people where they really are," he said.

In addition to online networking, Café USA enables offline networking between the Embassy and Café USA members. The minister-counselor said the Embassy regularly invites Café USA members to see a movie with Embassy officials and then exchange views face-to-face after the movie. "It was interesting to see who they are and hear their

stories. It started from a virtual program and we turned it into a real, live program," the diplomat said. He added that those offline meetings work to enhance mutual understanding between the Embassy and the South Korean public.

The public diplomacy coordinator emphasized the importance of governments expanding their base of contacts to the general public, especially since the influence of public opinion has increased with the development of Internet technology. The diplomat explained that "[e]lites are still very very important, but increasingly there is more emphasis put on working with younger audiences in particular." According to the former U.S. ambassador to Seoul, the U.S. Embassy in Seoul put more emphasis on interacting with the South Korean public in the wake of protests over the deaths of two South Korean school girls killed by U.S. servicemen in a road accident in 2002.

Café USA generates other networks through mainstream media that often covers ongoing discussions on the website. The minister-counselor said some programs on the online community have shown their "after-life" in media reports referring to Café USA's interviews with the U.S. ambassador or other posted materials. This expands the Embassy's outreach to and consequent relationship building with South Koreans who are not members of Café USA.

Assurances of Legitimacy

The Embassy uses Café USA to assure the South Korean public of its commitment to maintaining a relationship with them and taking their concerns seriously. According to the minister-counselor, one of the strategies of assurances is to encourage a sense of "one person at a time." He said the Embassy hopes that South Koreans will feel that the two sides are having one-on-one engagement through Café USA and other online means of communication. He explained that this is "the only way" that the Embassy can build and manage relationships with South Korean citizens.

Therefore, the Embassy actively posts materials to Café USA, emails relevant materials through the Embassy listserv, and tries to be responsive to questions or requests from South Korean citizens. He described this approach as the strategy of "the virtual last three feet."

I believe one of the most famous public diplomats, Edward R. Murrow famously said that the best diplomacy is conducted at the last three feet. That is, the really significant and meaningful public diplomacy that changes people's hearts and minds, takes place face-to-face. It takes one person talking to one person. It is me talking to you. We are at the virtual last three feet.

In order to demonstrate its commitment to maintaining relationships, the Embassy has continued to adjust its online communication tools to keep up with the trend of Internet use in South Korea. The minister-counselor said: "Here again, the question is what are people doing now?" He explained that such an effort could help the Embassy assure the public that it really cares about reaching out to them and listening to their opinion.

An information specialist at the Embassy, who works on Café USA, explained that "Café USA is a vehicle for engagement and it continues to evolve." For example, with growing interest in blogging, the Embassy has created a blog board for current (2010) U.S. Ambassador to South Korea Kathleen Stephens through which she shares personal stories and photos. This is especially relevant since Amb. Stephens is a former Peace Corps volunteer in Korea and speaks Korean. The public diplomacy coordinator stressed that it is necessary for foreign service officials to understand how the public in different societies use and adapt to technology in various ways.

Evaluating E-Diplomacy (RQ2)

The interviewees explained that the Embassy does not have systematic measures to evaluate Café USA. Both scholars and practitioners have acknowledged that few measurements have been developed in order to evaluate relationships, particularly long-term relationships, between an organization and its key publics (Hon & J. Grunig, 1999). However, Embassy officials have introduced some measures to assess the Café USA program.

Short-Term Measures

For short-term measures, Embassy Seoul has considered both the quantity and quality of the public's engagement with the online community. According to the minister-counselor, the Embassy has examined both whether the public engages in dialogue with the Embassy through Café USA and, if so, whether they do so in a meaningful way. He explained they want to know if "[W]e have a real discussion. In other words, do people just pop on out of curiosity or do they pop on because they are really interested in hearing about the United States?" For this reason, the Embassy has taken into account both the number of hits to the site and the number of messages posted by South Koreans. Messages without real substance are not counted in such evaluations. The Embassy also considers if and how the mainstream media cover discussions or materials on Café USA.

Longer-Term Measures

U.S. officials explained that the Embassy considers the level of both satisfaction and trust South Koreans feel with Café USA in evaluating the online community project. These two criteria are examples of some of the longer-term measures by which to evaluate the success of the relationship between an organization and its publics (Hon & J. Grunig, 1999; L. Grunig, et al., 2002). Satisfaction in the context of evaluating relationships refers to how favorably one party feels toward the other as positive expectations about the relationship are reinforced. Satisfaction can occur when the parties believe that the benefits outweigh the costs in their relationship and feel that the other party is taking positive steps to maintaining the relationship.

The minister-counselor said one way the Embassy judges whether Café USA is successful is by evaluating the satisfaction of their partners—ordinary South Korean citizens visiting the site. The public diplomacy coordinator also said public diplomacy officials consider from a general customer service point of view which factors might dissatisfy people. The U.S. officials said, however, the Embassy does not have concrete measures to evaluate how satisfied South Koreans are with Café USA other than anecdotal evidence.

The U.S. officials also emphasized that trust is another long-term criteria of evaluation. They explained that the Embassy hopes that two-way communication through Café USA will convey a sense of commitment and respect to South Korean people. The former information specialist at the Embassy said it is important that South Koreans feel that the Embassy cares about them and is "sincerely interested" in engaging them. The minister-counselor regarded Café USA as an important medium in forging friendships with ordinary South Koreans:

Café USA is a community, and the dialogue and the engagement is ongoing. It is like being friends. You are not with friends only when you are with them; They continue to be your friends and you continue to have engagement. You get together from time to time. We engage in dialogue, and the willingness to meet with one another continues beyond the just physical activities on Café USA.

Another important method for building trust is to reduce people's misunderstandings of U.S. positions on issues involving Korea. The minister-counselor said his dialogue with South Korean members of Café USA made him realize that some of their disagreements with the United States were due to misunderstandings of U.S. policies.

According to him, the Embassy would prefer the South Korean public to hate, love, or respect the United States based on facts and for right reasons. He explained that, "[t]he goal is coming to an understanding. We may never agree, but at least we understand one another."

Relationship Building from South Koreans' Perspective (RQ3)

We interviewed seven South Korean online members of Café USA to investigate their perceptions of Café USA in helping improve their relationships with the Embassy. Three of them were college students, and the others were businessman, office worker, and military officer. Four of them were in their 20s, two in their 30s, and one in his 40s. In regard to their relationships with the Embassy, they emphasized three aspects of relationships: communal mutuality, access, and trust (Hon & J. Grunig, 1999; L. Grunig, J. Grunig, & Dozier, 2002). Most of all, the South Koreans said it is important for the Embassy to make people like them feel respected and enjoy dealing with the Embassy in relationship building and management between the two sides.

Communal Mutuality

The South Korean online members of Café USA cited two-way communication as the most important contribution of the online community to their relationships with the Embassy. They said the online communication channels make them think the Embassy is attentive to what they say and regards their opinion as legitimate. A South Korean college student said:

In the past, I thought that the United States is unilateral and is not interested in public opinion of other countries. Café USA has helped me abolish such an image. I think the United States is trying to take into account what South Koreans think about U.S. policies related to South Korea.

Another South Korean member said the Embassy had often been regarded as heavy-handed but it has improved its image by directly interacting with South Koreans through new channels such as Café USA. Most of them mentioned web chatting with Embassy officials helped them understand the U.S. government's positions on Korea and other international issues. The Embassy has organized web chatting between Café USA members and the ambassador and other Embassy officials to discuss bilateral relations and issues of common concern. Korean staff at the Embassy translate U.S. officials' responses into Korean.

Access

The South Korean online members of Café USA cited increased access to the U.S. Embassy as one of the most important roles of the online community in their relationship with the Embassy. Most of all, they said the U.S. Embassy in Seoul had been perceived to be very closed in terms of sharing information and interacting with South Korean citizens. One of the Café USA members said, Café USA is an "easy access to the once enclosed U.S. organization." South Koreans said Café USA has helped them to get information about political, diplomatic, and economic issues relating to the United States.

A South Korean university student said that he was very impressed by the U.S. Embassy's efforts to be more accessible to South Koreans. He said this distinguishes the U.S. Embassy from the other embassies in Seoul. Therefore, he said he values his relationship with the U.S. Embassy more than the other embassies.

Trust

South Korean members were divided over whether their trust in the U.S. Embassy has improved after forging their relationship with the U.S. Embassy through Café USA. Some of them said they became more trustful of the Embassy, as they found its ef-

forts to open dialogue with South Korean citizens to be sincere. One of the Café USA members said, "I think the Embassy really wants to understand how South Koreans think about controversial bilateral issues, and I feel they really want to improve relationships with ordinary citizens in South Korea." He said he likes the User-Created Content section, a Café USA feature that enables South Koreans to contribute content that they made themselves.

Other South Koreans, however, said Café USA did not influence how much they trust the U.S. Embassy or the U.S. One said he believes it is a form of propaganda: "I think the Embassy made this to propagate a positive image of the United States, so Café USA does not affect my fundamental views of the United States." This impression stems partly from what South Koreans perceive as a lack of diverse views on Café USA. One of the South Korean interviewees said he gets the impression that most of Café USA members are those who already have favorable views toward the United States. He said: "What I found out about the views of the visitors (of Café USA) was that generally their views are favorable to the United States. Café USA is not the place where you can get diverse opinions."

One of the reasons of lack of diverse opinions may be that the Embassy maintains "walls" around the site. One needs to be a "full" member to post comments to Café USA. The Embassy decides on the full membership after having a member's brief introduction of his/herself and reasons for joining Café USA. Guests or associate members can write only to the section designed to have them request for full membership. According to the Embassy, it suspends membership of those who post "inappropriate" materials, such as spam, personal invectives, or commercials.

This creates the problem of "preaching to the choir." That is, Café USA is generally reaching only a limited audience comprised of those who may already have had favorable views of the United States.

Discussion

As discussed above, social networking tools like Café USA can help governments build and maintain relationships with publics in other countries. Café USA has evolved to become an important channel for the U.S. Embassy Seoul to institutionalize dialogic relationships with South Korean citizens. However, there are challenges and limitations in social media-based public diplomacy. One of the major difficulties a government faces in conducting public diplomacy is that such efforts often are viewed as mere propaganda. Consistent with this, our interviews with the South Korean members found evidence that some Café USA members saw the Embassy's online initiative as an effort to spread positive ideas and opinions of the United States. This reflects the misconception that the term public diplomacy is a euphemism for propaganda (Gilboa, 2000). While propaganda is one-sided dissemination of ideas and opinions that often contain deliberate lies or deceptions, public diplomacy is supposed to pursue honest, two-way dialogue with foreign publics (CSIS, 1998; Nye, 2005; Snow, 2007).

Public diplomacy agencies should make better use of online communication tools to engage in sincere talks with foreign publics. One way to approach this is to understand that complicated sign-up procedures and aggressive deleting of unwelcome messages quickly create a walled garden in which open discussion of contrasting viewpoints become extremely difficult. We suggest that reducing the barriers to participation together with very clear and objective rules about what constitutes an inappropriate post (off topic, inappropriate language, and so on) will result in increased participation and, most importantly, a sense that the communications efforts are *sincere*. This is a difficult lesson for traditional organizations such as corporations and governments to act on as they are much more comfortable when they control messages centrally. However, there is mounting evidence that social networking tools

work best in decentralized environments (and here Café USA's hosting on a non-government owned server is a significant step in the right direction) and that in such environments communities can and will develop and enforce standards of appropriate behavior.

It is also important to note that agencies should carefully consider country-specific factors in laying out online strategies for relationship management with foreign publics. Different countries show different patterns of Internet use, so organizations should be able to tailor their online communication tools to meet the interests of publics in the target country. In addition, core social and cultural values and beliefs should be well studied before launching online programs in order to demonstrate an organization's sincere commitment to building and managing relationships with the public.

SUGGESTIONS FOR FUTURE RESEARCH

Although this study contributes to the research and practice of relationship building in public diplomacy in a number of ways, it has several limitations that should be considered in future research. First, this study provides rich data on one government organization's networked public diplomacy, but would have benefited from comparative investigations of similar organizations. For example, it will be useful to explore how U.S. embassies in other countries use online means of communication to interact with publics in their host country. A cross-cultural study can also examine how diplomatic organizations of different countries use online media differently. Second, this study is a preliminary one. As such, the sample size was quite small and, on the Korea side, only included Café USA members. A more complete study would involve a much larger number of members as well as a sample of demographically similar non-members.

In spite of these very real limitations, it is interesting that our results are largely consistent with those produced by larger studies of private sector organizations. At the same time, it is important to note that embassies are in many ways quite dissimilar from corporations. Ultimately, embassies are accountable back to their central government and, at least in the case of liberal democracies, to the citizens who elected that government. That is, embassies are inherently political entities and this often intensifies difficulties of communication. For example, the value of openness often comes into conflict with national security demands for secrecy. The result is that communications intended sincerely may be overtaken by events well beyond embassy control.

Nonetheless, in our view it is the political nature of embassies that should make social networking tools particularly attractive since the rough and tumble worlds created within social networks are often ideal sites for demonstrating the complexity of communications and the importance of nuance in international affairs.

CONCLUSION

In this chapter we (i) introduced the notion of *public diplomacy*, (ii) argued that social networking tools are changing the ways in public diplomacy is practiced, (iii) provided examples of the U.S. Department of State's use of these tools, and (iv) offered an extended overview and preliminary evaluation of one such application—Café USA as implemented by the U.S. Embassy in South Korea.

This study produced several important findings. First, it demonstrated how public diplomacy using social networking helps institutionalize dialogic relationships between a government and foreign publics. This reduces Embassy's reliance on traditional intermediaries such as the mass media. Mutuality is at the heart of the dialogic relationship. In such a relationship, a government attentively listens to what foreign publics say, engaging and accommodating alternative viewpoints rather than speaking over them. This is one of the most important characteristics of networked public diplomacy, a major shift from one-way "megaphone diplomacy" (Fulton, 2002). As evidenced by quotes from Embassy officials, this sort of shift is a stated objective of Café USA.

Second, public diplomacy through online communication tools allows the Embassy to redefine and broaden its networking. While governments largely focused on elite foreign audiences in the past, social networking tools offer the opportunity to connect with a much broader range of foreign publics. This aspect of networking is crucial, given the increasing relevance of public opinion in foreign countries to a country's diplomatic initiatives (Gilboa, 2008; Nye, 2005).

Third, this study highlights the difficulties a government has in evaluating its public diplomacy initiatives. As previous studies point out, organizations typically lack measures to assess programs aimed at building relations with key constituencies (Hon & J. Grunig, 1999; L. Grunig, et al., 2002). We found that the Embassy relied on anecdotal evidences or short-term measures (e.g., the number of hits to its online tools) to evaluate such programs. Therefore, even though the Embassy emphasized relationship management with foreign publics, it lacks resources to develop specific measures to explore them.

By providing empirical data on how the U.S. Embassy uses social networking to help manage relationships with its foreign publics, this study advances research in relationship management in public diplomacy. This study also contributes to more general research on evaluations of an organization's programs aimed at building and managing relationships with key publics.

ACKNOWLEDGMENT

We thank The Henry Luce Foundation and The Korea Society for their cooperation and support of this research. Former U.S. Ambassador to South Korea Donald P. Gregg provided very helpful comments on an earlier draft of this chapter. In addition we acknowledge with gratitude the cooperation of diplomats at the U.S. Department of State in Washington and U.S. Embassy Seoul.

REFERENCES

BBC. (2004, January 19). *Roh backs US troops relocation*. Retrieved October 10, 2008, from http://news.bbc.co.uk/2/hi/asia-pacific/3408895.stm

BBC. (2008, June 10). *S. Koreans rally against U.S. beef*. Retrieved October 20, 2008, from http://news.bbc.co.uk/2/hi/asia-pacific/7445387.stm

Benkler, Y. (2006). *The Wealth of Networks: How Social Production Transforms Markets and Freedom*. New Haven, CT: Yale University Press.

Bennett, W. L. (2003a). Communicating global activism. *Information Communication and Society*, 6(2), 143–168. doi:10.1080/1369118032000093860

Bennett, W. L. (2003b). New media power: The Internet and global activism. In Couldry, N., & Curran, J. (Eds.), *Contesting Media Power*. New York: Rowman and Littlefield.

Broom, G. M., Casey, S., & Ritchey, J. (1997). Toward a concept and theory of organization-public relationships. *Journal of Public Relations Research*, 9, 83–98. doi:10.1207/s1532754xjprr0902_01

Burt, R., & Robison, O. (1998, October 9). *Reinventing Diplomacy in the Information Age*. CSIS Report.

Castells, M. (2008). The new public sphere: Global civil society, communication networks, and global governance. *The Annals of the American Academy of Political and Social Science, 616*, 78–93. doi:10.1177/0002716207311877

Catto, H. E. (2001 July 23). The end of diplomacy? *iMP Magazine*. Retrieved February 14, from http://www.cisp.org/imp/july_2001/07_01catto.htm

Cohen, R. (1991). *Negotiating across cultures: Communication obstacles in international diplomacy*. Washington, DC: United States Institute of Peace Press.

Coombs, W. T. (2004). Interpersonal communication and public relations. In Heath, R. L. (Ed.), *Handbook of Public Relations* (pp. 105–114). Thousand Oaks, CA: Sage Publications, Inc.

Cull, N. J. (2008). Public diplomacy: Taxonomies and histories. *The Annals of the American Academy of Political and Social Science, 616*, 31–54. doi:10.1177/0002716207311952

Falconi, T. M. (2007, February 28). *Enhancing Britain's global reputation: The perception of country identity in social media. A presentation to the Management School*. Retrieved March 14, 2007, from http://www.tonisblog.com/?p=153

Fulton, B. (1998, October 9). *Reinventing diplomacy in the information age*. Center for Strategic and International Studies (CSIS).

Fulton, B. (2002). *Net diplomacy I: Beyond foreign ministries*. U.S. Institute of Peace.

Gilboa, E. (2000). Mass communication and diplomacy: A theoretical framework. *Communication Theory, 10*(3), 275–309. doi:10.1111/j.1468-2885.2000.tb00193.x

Gilboa, E. (2008). Searching for a theory of public diplomacy. *The Annals of the American Academy of Political and Social Science, 616*(1), 55–77. doi:10.1177/0002716207312142

Grunig, J. E., & Huang, Y. H. (2000). From organizational effectiveness to relationship indicators: Antecedents of relationships, public relations strategies, and relationship outcomes. In Ledingham, J. A., & Bruning, S. D. (Eds.), *Public relations as relationship management: A relational approach to the study and practice of public relations* (pp. 23–53). Mahwah, NJ: Lawrence Erlbaum.

Grunig, L. A., Grunig, J. E., & Dozier, D. M. (2002). *Excellent public relations and effective organizations: a study of communication management in three countries.* Mahwah, NJ: Lawrence Erlbaum.

Henrikson, A. K. (2006). What can public diplomacy achieve? The Netherlands: Netherlands Institute of International Relations (Clingendael).

Hill, C. (2004, November 8). *U. S. Embassy launches Cafe USA.* Retrieved March 10, 2008, from http://seoul.usembassy.gov/caf_usa.html

Hon, L. C., & Grunig, J. E. (1999, November). *Guidelines for measuring relationships in public relations.* Gainesville, FL: The Institute for Public Relations, Commission on PR Measurement Evaluation.

Kent, M. L., & Taylor, M. (1998). Building dialogic relationships through the world wide web. *Public Relations Review, 24*(3), 321–334. doi:10.1016/S0363-8111(99)80143-X

Kim, S., & Lim, W. (2007). How to deal with South Korea. *The Washington Quarterly, 30*(2), 71–82. doi:10.1162/wash.2007.30.2.71

Ledingham, J. A., & Bruning, S. D. (1998). Relationship management in public relations: Dimensions of an organization-public relationship. *Public Relations Review, 24*(1), 55–65. doi:10.1016/S0363-8111(98)80020-9

Ledingham, J. A., & Bruning, S. D. (2000). A longitudinal study of organization-public relationship dimensions: Defining the role of communication in the practice of relationship management. In Ledingham, J. A., & Bruning, S. D. (Eds.), *Public relations as relationship management: A relational approach to the study and practice of public relations.* Mahwah, NJ: Lawrence Erlbaum.

Nebenzahl, I. D., & Jaffe, E. D. (1996). Measuring the joint effect of brand and country image in consumer evaluation of global products. *International Marketing Review, 13*(4), 5–22. doi:10.1108/02651339610127220

Nisbett, R. E. (2003). *The geography of thought.* New York: Free Press.

Nye, J. S. (2005). *Soft power: The means to success in world politics.* New York: Public Affairs.

Nye, J. S. (2008). Public diplomacy and soft power. *The Annals of the American Academy of Political and Social Science, 616*(1), 94–109. doi:10.1177/0002716207311699

Parameswaran, R., & Pisharodi, R. M. (2002). Assimilation effects in country image research. *International Marketing Review, 19*(3), 259–278. doi:10.1108/02651330210430695

Rucht, D. (2004). The quadruple 'A. In van de Donk, W., Loader, B. D., Nixon, P. G., & Rucht, D. (Eds.), *Cyberprotest: New Media, Citizens and Social Movements* (pp. 29–56). London: Routledge.

Snow, N. (2007). *The arrogance of American power: What U.S. leaders are doing wrong and why it's our duty to dissent.* Oxford, U.K.: Rowman & Littlefield Publishers.

Snow, N. (2008). International exchanges and the U.S. image. *The Annals of the American Academy of Political and Social Science, 616*(1), 198–222. doi:10.1177/0002716207311864

Tuch, H. N. (1990). *Communicating with the world: U.S. public diplomacy overseas*. New York: St. Martin's Press.

U.S. Department of State. (1987). *Dictionary of international relations terms*. Washington, DC: U.S. Department of State.

Van Aelst, P., & Walgrave, S. (2004). New media, new movement? The role of the internet in shaping the 'anti-globalization' movement. In van de Donk, W., Loader, B. D., Nixon, P. G., & Rucht, D. (Eds.), *Cyberprotest: New Media, Citizens and Social Movements* (pp. 97–122). London: Routledge.

Yin, R. K. (2003). *Case study research: Design and methods*. Thousand Oaks, CA: Sage.

ENDNOTES

[1] http://cafe.daum.net/usembassy

[2] blogs.state.gov

[3] twitter.com/dipnote

[4] Retrieved on 9 March 2009 from http://www.videochallenge.america.gov/release3.html

[5] www.youtube.com/democracychallenge

[6] http://www.facebook.com/pages/Democracy-Video-Challenge/47823853139

[7] Retrieved on 9 March 2009 from http://www.videochallenge.america.gov/release3.html

[8] The first author's interview with Ambassador Donald Gregg on 13 April 2009

Chapter 16
Online Activism and Computer Mediated Communications

Stephen Fariñas
Florida International University, USA

ABSTRACT

The use of the internet by radical activists is a significant and growing aspect of e-activism, but has received little attention in the e-participation literature. This chapter aims to fill this gap by examining the use of computer mediated communications by radical groups in promoting their causes. The intrinsic nature of radical movements is such that their ideas cannot be disseminated through the mainstream media. Radical activists communicate through alternative media, of which internet has emerged as a significant source to mobilize as well as to disseminate. We focus on the internet use by two groups of radical activists: environmentalist and anti-globalisation groups. Since these groups have a radical agenda, they use the internet to circumvent government censorship. Beyond this, however, their uses of CMC are quite distinctive. Environmental activists were among the first to use the web as organizing and mobilizing tools. They promote their agenda through alternative forms of media which can easily be made available over the internet, e.g. magazines, booklets, flyers, leaflets, videos, and radio broadcast. Environmental activists also engage in several forms of cyberactivism, e.g. hacktivism. They actively participate in the e-rulemaking process by working to change policy. Anti-globalisation groups, on the other hand, primarily use independent media centers (Indymedia) to promote their cause. Independent media centers are versatile enough to be quickly established during a protest, allowing activists to mobilize interested parties quickly. Activists have also made effective use of e-mail listservs and the internet. However, anti-globalisation groups participate very little in the e-rulemaking process. Rather, these groups ultimately aim to do away with government control and corporate hegemony.

DOI: 10.4018/978-1-61520-933-0.ch016

INTRODUCTION

The internet is emerging as an important means of mobilizing social movements. The internet provides a democratic forum for different movements to reach the maximum number of people in the shortest amount of time. In other words, organizations are able to reach their targeted audience in an efficient a manner as possible. Space and time are no longer obstacles. Even censorship ceases to be a major threat. The internet is but one part of a large repertoire of tools available for activists to use to further their campaigns. All of these tools fall under the umbrella of information technology (IT) or information communications technology (ICT). This paper concentrates on the use of computer mediated communications (CMC). This subset of ICT deals exclusively with communications effected via computers.

Computer mediated communications allows users, who would not otherwise have an opportunity, to have a voice in the rule-making process. Some users may not have the time, access, or inclination to participate in more traditional forms of civic engagement. CMC levels the playing field. It makes the democratic process more democratic. This holds especially true for members of the radical environmental and anti-globalisation movements. Members of these two groups often shun participation in more conventional means of effecting change in government decision making. The "organization" of these groups is non-hierarchical. Although referred to as a movement, members generally participate autonomously or in small groups. Participation in large groups tends to be reserved for protests and/or demonstrations. Participation at an individual level (or in small groups) necessarily limits the amount of information gathered, as well as mitigates the effects of any particular course of action. Online activism balances the scales.

Unlike mainstream activists and groups who choose to work with government because they believe in its legitimacy, radical activists work against government because they believe it to be illegitimate. CMC allows radical activists to remove themselves as much as possible from formal contact with government while still allowing the former to influence the latter. While not necessarily bringing about radical change, radical activists at least plant the seeds of thought/action to be later harvested by their mainstream counterparts (both those in and outside of government). Radicals serve as catalysts for political action – whether as movers and shakers themselves directly affecting government decision making or galvanizing more moderate activists to participate in e-democracy.

We have chosen to cover radical environmentalism and radical anti-globalisation separately for two reasons. First, their missions are unique. Although certain ideological aspects of each movement overlap (e.g. multi-national corporations adversely affecting the environment and society), each movement is distinctive enough to merit its own philosophy. Second, whereas radical environmentalists aim to change policy, radical anti-globalisation activists not only aim to change policy, they also aim to do away with government control and corporate hegemony. Both movements differ in their missions and their ultimate goals. However, they are both similar in their use of alternative media as an agent of social change. Through "engagement and organization of radical media" (Vatikiotis, 2005), participants have a direct, participative role in events as opposed to the passive one preferred by mainstream media.

The following sections will offer analyses into the use of the internet and other CMCs by the radical environmental and anti-globalisation movements and will show how these groups seek to stake their claim in the e-democracy landscape. Radical environmentalists are those activists who use tactics considered to be extreme in order to defend and protect what they see as a threatened environment. Tactics can include destruction of logging equipment, blocking logging roads by forming human chains, tree-sits, sabotaging construction projects which encroach on ecologically sensitive land, etc. Radical environmentalists have turned to CMC to augment real-world tactics. For example, where once alternative forms of media such as magazines, booklets, flyers, leaflets, videos, and radio broadcasts were once strictly a real-world product accessed only in physical form, activists have moved these forms of activism online. Notable campaigns using CMC as a primary tool have included Friends of the Earth (FoE) urging members to use e-mail to lobby politicians, and the McSpotlight campaign. The anti-globalisation term refers to groups and individuals who are against neo-liberal globalisation. The proper term, then, would be anti-neo-liberal globalisation (Jordan & Taylor, 2004). The movement is in favor of globalisation for reasons of, for example, cheaper, more accessible global communication. Opposition is directed towards the globalisation of economic neo-liberal policies benefitting corporations and being implemented by international institutions such as the World Bank, International Monetary Fund (IMF), World Trade Organization (WTO) and the Group of 8 (G8). Online tactics used by anti-globalisation activists have included Indymedia and electronic civil disobedience (ECD).

The chapter will begin with the area of environmental activism. This section will provide a background on the environmental movement as a whole. Then it will segue into the philosophy underpinning radical environmentalism. The following section will offer examples of how radical environmentalists have used CMC to participate in the e-rulemaking process. Anti-globalisation activism is the next area of analysis. This section begins with a brief overview of the Zapatistas. It is meant as an illustrative guide to the philosophy behind the anti-globalisation movement. The next two sections, *Activism* and *Hacktivism*, highlight the different methods activists have used to further their agendas. The chapter concludes with some closing remarks on the use of CMC by radical environmentalists and anti-globalisation activists.

MAIN FOCUS OF THE CHAPTER

Environmental Activism

Background

Concern for the environment did not become part of the American psyche until the late 19th century. It was during this time, under the leadership of Gifford Pinchot (during the presidency of Theodore Roosevelt), that conservation became federal policy. The focus of federal policy was the forested area in the West. This is considered the first wave of environmentalism. The second wave began after the Dust Bowl era of the 1930s and saw its peak during the administration of Franklin Roosevelt. World War II shifted the national focus away from conservation. The third wave of environmentalism began after the publication of *Silent Spring* by Rachel Carson in 1962 (List, 1993; Zelko, 2006). *Silent Spring* serves as a warning of the damage caused by the uncontrolled use of pesticides. It was a wake-up call that galvanized the populace into action, leading to the first Earth Day in 1970. Environmental protection laws began to be passed in the 1970s. Prior to the third wave, environmentalism was mainly an intellectual pursuit nestled in the realm of federal conservation policy. Interest waxed and waned until the anti-environmentalism of the Reagan administration rekindled interest in the environment. It was at this juncture that a notable schism formed between radical environmentalism and mainstream environmentalism. Clarion calls for militant defense of the environment were being sounded as far back as the late 1960s. It would take until the 1980s and 1990s for these calls to be heeded.

Rather than a mostly reactive approach to activism, environmentalists began taking a more proactive, radical approach using philosophy as a guide. It was during the 1980s and 1990s that philosophy began to play are more prominent role in the actions undertaken by environmental activists. Philosophy continues to play a prominent role. Indeed, actions are not undertaken unless they can be justified. The divide between mainstream environmentalism and radical environmentalism likewise became more prominent. Radical environmentalism refers to and describes the philosophy as well as the tactics used to implement the philosophy (List, 1993). "Radical" is taken to mean ideas and actions which are outside of what is socially accepted, i.e. mainstream. While people in the mainstream tend to use the term in a derisive manner, those within the radical environmental movement use it as a badge of honor. The philosophy has its underpinnings in deep ecology (Delicath, 1996). There is a tacit understanding in the radical environmental movement that in order for positive change to occur in the defense and preservation of the Earth, humans must move beyond an anthropocentric outlook toward a biocentric one. This is known as *deep ecology*. Anthropocentrism is rejected in favor of biospheric egalitarianism; there is no distinction made between humans and non-human animals (Muir & Veenendall, 1996), and between humans and the environment. Everything is connected. This idea was first described by Norwegian philosopher Arne Naess. There is some discrepancy in regards to the year in which deep ecology was first introduced. List (1993) and Scarce (2006) put the year at 1972, whereas Cramer (1998) and Taylor (1995) put the year at 1973. Naess defined deep ecology as "a normative, ecophilosophical movement that is inspired and fortified in part by our experience as humans in nature and in part by ecological knowledge" (Dunlap & Mertig, 1992). Under deep ecology, humans are not the "be all end all" but are a part of all that exists – everything in Nature possesses intrinsic value and worth (eco-centric view). The term *ecocentric* was developed to clarify any misunderstanding that *biocentric* refers only to living beings (Scarce, 2006). Both terms are used interchangeably. "Biocentric equality" is the second norm / value of deep ecology. The first is self-realization. Self-realization moves

beyond the self to include the environment and allows the natural world to flourish without excessive human intervention (Cramer, 1998; Scarce, 2006). The normative worldview espoused by deep ecology is in sharp contrast to the dominant view that everything in Nature is subordinate to human interests. As such, deep ecology fundamentally questions the prevailing consumer culture created by capitalism. Shallow ecology encompasses this anthropocentric outlook. In describing shallow ecology, Arne Naess states that humans fight against pollution and the depletion of resources out of "concern for the health and affluence of people in the developed countries" (List, 1993; Dunlap & Mertig, 1992).

Philosophy also influences the "structure" of the movement. The decentralized nature of the grassroots environmental movement draws its inspiration from and has its roots in the anarchist writings of Pyotr Kropotkin and Murray Bookchin (Castells, 1997). These anarchist writings have reinforced the counter-cultural undertones of grassroots, radical environmentalism. In this branch of the environmental movement, there is a dichotomous relationship between technology and saving the environment. On the one hand, technology is seen to have a disastrous effect on the planet, what Dartnell (2006) calls the "Frankenstein" model. On the other hand, technology has no doubt advanced the environmentalist cause. The trepidation regarding technology arises from three points: 1.) indiscriminate expansion of technology does indeed harm the environment; 2.) over-reliance on technology decreases the value of the human-to-nature relationship; and 3.) over reliance on technology decreases the value of the human-to-human relationship. However much unease there exists between environmentalism and technology, Castells (1997) argues that "environmentalism is a science-based movement." It is this relationship with science and technology that moved environmental awareness from the confines of high society to the grass roots. Prior to the emergence of the network society in the

1970s, ecological awareness was something of an intellectual trend associated with groups such as the Audubon Society. The goal was to influence people in positions of power so they in turn could either influence legislation or donate money to the cause, or both (Castells, 1997). The foci began to shift from intellectual discussion to a long-term outlook. The shift presaged a more nuanced conflict: conservation vs. preservation.

Activism

Environmental activists were among the first groups on the web and have also been at the forefront of using ICT as organizing and mobilizing tools, especially the internet (Castells, 1997; Pickerill, 2001; Pickerill, 2003), e.g. as in the case of a multi-national (Canada, Chile, United States) group of environmental organizations forming around Friends of the Earth, the Sierra Club, Greenpeace, Defenders of Wildlife, the Canadian Environmental Law Association, and other groups to protest the passing of NAFTA due to its lack of environmental regulations. The North America Free Trade Agreement (NAFTA) is also a point of contention for anti-globalisation groups. We will address this in the appropriate section. Environmental groups and individuals, particularly at the grass-roots level, do not usually have the resources that more well-heeled organizations possess. The internet offers a low-cost alternative capable of delivering the message without regards to distance and time. The advantage is obvious since traditional media focuses its attention on "resource-wealthy" groups (Klota, 2004). There is some controversy in the environmental activist ranks regarding damage to the environment as a result of computer use. However, computer users attempt to mitigate the damage caused by reusing computer components and using renewable energy sources rather than the power grid (Pickerill, 2001). Activists must weigh the damage caused by computer against the benefits gained. Computer mediated communication (CMC) can also be used to lobby adversaries, undertake informational campaigns, or as a channel for alternative media. "Forms of cyberactivism include the use of CMC to trigger campaigns and coordinate action, to distribute tactical information, in e-mail petitions, and for direct lobbying." (Pickerill, 2003) Five key ways in which CMC is used as a tactical tool are: lobbying using e-mail or online fax facilities; broadcasting live video, photograph, or text direct from real world protests; creating unofficial websites; using hacktivism and civil disobedience (Pickerill, 2003); and staging image events for mass-media dissemination (DeLuca, 1996).

Following are two examples of CMC use as a tactical tool. Friends of the Earth (FoE) has encouraged its members to lobby politicians using e-mail in place of letters and faxes. The idea here is that members can reach a larger audience in less time and at a fraction of the cost were they to use the United States Postal Service or faxes. McSpotlight made public the e-mail addresses of McDonald's executives in their campaign against the company. These were posted on the McSpotlight website; members were encouraged to e-mail McDonald's executives. The common thread between FoE and the McSpotlight campaign is time. An action is made more effective by timely and coordinated execution. The internet can also be used as a mobilization tool. Pickerill (2001) describes five ways in which the internet is used for mobilization: using the internet as a gateway to activism; using it to raise the profile of group campaigns; stimulating local activism; mobilizing online activism; and attracting participants to existing protests. Most people come into contact with many environmental issues through communication technology. Sometimes this is their only contact with the movement (DeLuca, 1996).

The internet also serves as a dialogic tool for activist organizations. Organizations must compete for, amongst other things, attention in order to remain viable. They must engage in a public relations campaign. The goal is to create a two-way channel of communication between the organization and the public where information and ideas are the currencies of choice. Taylor, Kent, and White (Fall 2001) conducted a study of 100 activist organizations to gauge the extent to which organizations were engaging their public in dialogue. The authors operationalized five principles: dialogic loops (incorporation of interactive features), ease of interface (the ease with which visitors navigate a site and find information), conservation of visitors (convincing visitors to stay on the site for an extended period of time), generation of return visits (encouraging multiple and repeated visits to the site), and providing information relevant to a variety of publics (usefulness of information to diverse population). Organization sites were selected from the EnviroLink Network website (http://www.envirolink.org). The authors found that activist organizations are not taking full advantage of the "dialogic capacity" of the internet. The implicit understanding is that activist organizations actually want to establish a dialogue with visitors. There is no mention of the organizations selected for study so it is impossible to determine their ideological leanings – mainstream or radical. These are the types of organizations that possess the resources, financial and otherwise, to maintain a more developed website. Radical organizations, on the other hand, participate in what We call "guerilla CMC activism". The intent of radical environmental organizations' online presence is to mobilize support. Websites act as a supplement to and a promoter of real-world direct action. Although dialogue may be desired, it is not an overriding concern.

Computer mediated communication (CMC) has aided activists in disseminating their message through alternative forms of media such as magazines, booklets, flyers, leaflets, videos, and radio broadcasts. The rationale behind utilizing alternative forms of media rests on mainstream media being owned by corporate interests (Pickerill, 2003). When a particular media outlet is owned by the very organization one is fighting against, it follows that said organization will suppress dissenting views and/or distort their true intentions. To a certain extent, radical environmental activists rely on mainstream media to reach a wider audience than would normally be reached through alternative sources. Alternative media generally only reaches a targeted audience and those who actively seek alternative sources of information. Mainstream media offers a conduit to the masses, however biased this conduit may be. Before the proliferation of computer mediated communication, alternative forms of media were limited to physical versions of the media, in the case of magazines, booklets, flyers, leaflets, and videos and depended on specialized distribution channels. Proliferation of CMC has enabled activists to reach a wider captive audience. Also enabling activists to reach a wide audience is creating events that garner media attention, makes people think, sparks debate, and promotes mobilization. This is based on the traditional French anarchist tactic of *l'action exemplair* (Castells, 1997). Although environmental activists have embraced the use of CMC and ECD, they have not disavowed the value and effectiveness of real world direct action. Real world direct action continues to be the preferred method of fighting for their cause; CMC and ECD are used as supplementary tactics. Yang (2003) makes this point by stating that one of the three ways the internet has helped the environmental movement is by being used as a tool to coordinate online and offline action. The other two reasons the internet has helped the movement are by enabling environmental activity with limited financial resources and in an oppressive political environment; and by allowing groups with websites to gain a presence and public visibility. A more nuanced benefit of the internet is in its contribution to the structure of grass roots environmental groups. Similar to the horizontal structure of networked groups described by Juris (January 2005), the populist image of the internet eliminates the need for a centralized governance structure. According to Pickerill (2001), decentralization "has made grassroots direct action networks a more permanent (and thus less transient) feature of the environmental movement." In order for the environmental movement to succeed as a whole, radical grassroots (underground and above ground) groups and mainstream groups must coalesce into a united front. Granted, there are vast philosophical differences between groups. The internet can bridge this divide.

Computer mediated communications and information communications technology have no doubt changed the relationship between citizens and government, especially in places such as China where government borders on the omniscient. This change is particularly noticeable in the area of environmental protection. Communist government attempts to silence activists completely and bring them under state and party control have been largely thwarted by the latter group (Mauch, Stoltzfus, & Weiner, 2006). Government and research centers have also embraced the internet. However, environmental sites surpass government and research center sites in quantity. Greener Beijing (http://www.grchina.org/greenerbeijing.htm) was launched in 1998 by Song Gang. Members, numbering 2,700, primarily work in maintaining the web site, although they do conduct environmental protection projects and organize environmental awareness activities. Online discussion forums have been used to by middle school students to begin a battery recycling program. Online activities have also focused on drawing national attention to the endangered Tibetan antelope. Green-Web (http://www.green-web.org/) was launched in 1999 by Gao Tian. The group's most aggressive campaign began in February 2002 and consisted of an online petition campaign to protect wetlands in Beijing, habitat of many species of birds. Green-Web's site is composed of a discussion forum, information center, electronic newsletter, topics specific to environmental protection, and links to other environmental websites. Han Hai Sha, *Boundless Ocean of Sand*, (http://www.desert.org.cn/) was

founded in 2002. Volunteers were recruited by group e-mails and electronic bulletin announcements appearing on the websites of Green-Web and Friends of Nature (Chinese environmental group). The group promotes awareness on desertification and mobilizes the community to act on important desertification issues. It relies on the internet to disseminate information and reach members (Yang, 2003).

Anti-Globalisation Activism

EZLN - Zapatistas

Use of the internet by anti-globalisation groups was brought to the fore by the EZLN (Ejército Zapatista de Liberación Nacional), otherwise known as the Zapatistas, in the early 1990s (Kahn & Kellner, 2004; Postmes & Brunsting, Fall 2002). Castells (1997) refers to the Zapatistas as the "first informational guerilla movement". The guerilla movement arose as a response to the marginalization of indigenous people in the face of ratification of NAFTA. The Zapatistas made their existence known on 01 January 2004 in the Mexican state of Chiapas. Their intention was to stage an armed uprising against the Mexican government. The Mexican army engaged the Zapatistas in an armed struggle lasting 12 days (Bob, 2005). The Zapatistas soon realized that they would better achieve their goals through building solidarity than through armed struggle. The EZLN harnessed the communicative powers of the internet to broadcast their struggle beyond Chiapas to the rest of Mexico and the world, and to form a sense of solidarity with other leftist groups worldwide. Thus was born the Transnational Zapatista Solidarity Network. Oleson (2005) outlines the history of the Transnational Zapatista Solidarity Network in five phases, beginning in January 1994 and ending February 2004. The movement continues to this day. Bob (2005) argues that the success of the Zapatistas is due in large part to the effective marketing of their cause and themselves, with a hefty reliance on computer mediated communication (CMC). This stands in contrast to the *Ejército Popular Revolucionario* (EPR) – Popular Revolutionary Army – which attacked six government installations during the months of August through September in 1996. Their grievances were similar to the EZLN. However, they failed to garner outside support because of poor marketing.

The impetus for the Zapatista entrance to the world stage was the pending ratification of NAFTA. The Zapatistas exemplify resistance to economic neo-liberal policies. Supporters of neo-liberal policies claim such policies lead to greater economic activity, which in turn lead to higher corporate profits. Increased profits would then lead to higher standards of living. Opponents of neo-liberalism see things differently. They claim that local cultures and economies are vanquished in the face of corporate greed. Subcomandante Marcos, leader of the EZLN, writes:

Neo-liberalism, the doctrine that makes it possible for stupidity and cynicism to govern in diverse parts of the earth, does not allow participation other than to hold on by disappearing. 'Die as a social group, as a culture, and above all as a resistance. Then you can be part of modernity,' say the great capitalists, from their seats of government, to the indigenous campesinos. These indigenous people with their rebellion, their defiance, and their resistance irritate the modernizing logic of neomercantilism. (Marcos, 2000, pp.280-282)

The Zapatistas exemplify opposition to anti-globalisation. They are used here as a case study to provide an illustrative background into the anti-globalisation movement. Their circumstances are indeed unique. However, their reasons for struggle are universal and can be applied to other anti-globalisation groups.

Activism

Anti-corporate globalisation movements belong to a class of movements known as computer-supported social movements, which is part of the larger computer-supported social networks (CSSN). These movements operate on local, regional, and global levels using the internet as their base. Activists move between online and offline activity. Since the World Trade Organization (WTO) protests in Seattle, Washington in December 1999 (otherwise known as the 'Battle for Seattle'), activists have increasingly used e-mail, Web pages, and open source software to plan actions and disseminate information (Juris, January 2005). Open source software is particularly problematic to governments and corporations because of its open and democratic nature. Open source software is not proprietary and that lends it to modification on an as-needed basis, making it an extremely valuable tool for anti-globalisation activists. Proprietary software (e.g. Microsoft) is controlled by the corporation owning the program. Its basic programming code cannot be modified. Open source software is as much a tactical tool as it is a statement of protest.

Use of personal computers connected to the internet has become the "hallmark of the movement's communication identity" (Sampedro, 2004). Activists have made particularly effective use of e-mail listservs and the internet. E-mail listservs are a low-cost option for organizing protests given their speed and geographic reach. Similarly, the internet has facilitated long-distance communications and, ironically, complemented face-to-face communications. Telephones, both landline and mobile, remain vital activist communications tools. Joseba from Indymedia - Barcelona illustrates how activists around the world used listservs to share a prominent news story, create an article based on this news, then translate the article into French, German, Italian, and Spanish, as well as adding photos to the text. Another example illustrates the combined use of e-mails and telephones. E-mails were being exchanged between MRG (Catalan Movement for Global Resistance) International and a Dutch collective during planning for a European Peoples Global Action (PGA) meeting. The phone was used to settle disagreements which were "impossible to solve without interactive communication." Activists have also used the internet to create Web pages during mobilizations. These have been used to provide information, resources, and contact lists; post documents and calls to action; and have sometimes hosted real-time discussion forums and IRCs (internet relay chat rooms) (Juris, January 2005).

In addition to facilitating communications, the internet has also facilitated networking amongst different anti-globalisation activists and organizations. The networks are characterized by rejection of capitalism and all forms of oppression, a call to direct action and civil disobedience, and an organizational philosophy based on decentralization and autonomy (Juris, January 2005). Decentralized and autonomous networks reflect the anarchist tenets behind the anti-corporate and anti-globalisation movements. Networking has also changed the structure of activist organizations. Leftist parties rely on hierarchical command structures to operate; they are hegemonic in nature. Organizations based on networking coordinate under an umbrella group composed of different, smaller groups structured horizontally versus the vertical structure of the leftist parties (Juris, January 2005). Groups organized around ideas instead of people allow for the indefinite continuation of the movement.

The anti-corporate globalisation movement relies on alternative media for information. Alternative media is defined as being constituted of independent sources of news and information beyond the corporate-controlled media (Juris, January 2005). Outlets are independently owned and operated, they express mainly dissident points of view, and they operate on a horizontal basis versus the hierarchical approach of the corporate-

controlled media (Meikle, 2002). Alternative media are increasingly becoming network-oriented and internet-based. The first IMC (independent media center), also known as Indymedia center, was established during the WTO protests in Seattle in 1999 by Australian programmer Mathew Arnison using open source software. Journalists reported from the streets as activists uploaded image, text, audio, and video files. Similar sites were subsequently created in Philadelphia, Portland, Vancouver, Boston, and Washington, D.C.; global locations include Prague, Barcelona, Amsterdam, Sao Paolo, and Buenos Aires. Indymedia centers are used especially by the more radical sectors. During the December 2001 protests against the EU (European Union) in Brussels, radical activists located their IMC in a squatted theater. Activists uploaded images and audio files, edited videos, and shared information. The ground floor of the theater was converted into Radio Bruxxel, featuring 24-hour programming (Juris, January 2005). The internet has allowed anti-globalisation groups to create counter-summit websites, websites providing counter-information, and weblogs (a la Indymedia – where the user is also the source of information) (Sampedro, 2004).

Live broadcasts during real world protests/ actions allow activists to reach supporters with news as it happens. Such was the case in London on 04 January 1999 during the occupation of Shell's headquarters. Despite being barricaded in the building without any power or access to telephone lines, environmental activists were able to use their mobile phones as modems to transmit digital photographs that had been uploaded to their laptops to supporters on the outside. In addition to transmitting information in real time, activists were able to stay one step ahead of the media. Video phones are widely available today, no doubt making transmission of video footage that much faster. Activists also uploaded their material to a website similar to Shell's thereby undermining the latter's site. This is known as *subvertising* and entails subverting a company's official website. Subverting an official website consists of hijacking a targeted site and using it for activists' purpose or creating a website similar to the official site and displaying activist material. McSpotlight made use of this tactic when it infiltrated McDonald's official site and created an online tour highlighting "inaccuracies and untruths". The McSpotlight website (http://www.mcspotlight.org) was launched in 1996 to offer support to the McLibel defendants who were being sued by McDonalds for distributing slanderous material (Pickerill, 2003). Campaigning against McDonalds is a cause that has been taken up by not only radical environmental and anti-globalisation groups, but also by animal liberation groups such as the Animal Liberation Front. Another similar tactic to the one used in the McSpotlight campaign is creating a site similar in appearance to the targeted official site and registering the site under a domain name similar or nearly identical to the official one. The British Field Sports Society is an organization promoting fox hunting. Having a presence online, the Society came under attack by activists. The official site was "BFS.com." Activists created a counter-site and registered it under the domain name of "BFS.org." Visitors arriving by mistake at the activist site were presented with information denouncing the British Field Sports Society (Pickerill, 2003). Other examples include the bearing by Indonesian government websites of the motto "Free East Timor" in 1998; in 1999, visitors to the Ku Klux Klan website (http://www.kkk.com) were redirected to the Southern Poverty Law Center site (http://www.hatewatch.org). All of the above are forms of hacktivism which serve to steal attention from the viewing public (Kreimer, November 2003) and redirecting it to activist issues.

Hacktivism

Hacktivism arose within the anti-globalisation movement at the end of the 20th century. Hacktivism is politically motivated hacking (Jordan,

2002) combining grassroots political protest with computer hacking (Jordan & Taylor, 2004). Hacking originally referred innovative use of technology, not just computers. As time progressed, however, hacking became associated with illicit and intrusive computer activity. Anti-authoritarian sentiment has always been present in hacking. The counter-cultural element emerged in response to the commodification/corporatisation of information and personal computers. It was at this point that hacking took an overtly political stance.

The year 1994 marks the founding of the Critical Arts Ensemble (CAE), an anti-globalisation group. The CAE's ideology is predicated upon the shift of information from a physical nature to an electronic nature. Information is a source of power. The more information one has, the greater the power one possesses. The power elite (e.g. state governments, corporations) have traditionally relied on physical manifestations of information as a source of power. With the shift of information to an online platform, power has shifted from the "real world" to the online realm. Thusly, resisters must shift the locus of their efforts from the streets to online. CAE even goes so far as to refer to the streets as "dead capital" (Jordan & Taylor 2004). Electronic civil disobedience (ECD) becomes the tactic of choice. Rather than preventing people from entering an establishment, as is done with traditional forms of civil disobedience, ECD aims to severely restrict, stop, or otherwise alter the flow of information.

Other examples of hacktivism include virtual sit-ins and denial-of-service attacks (Dartnell, 2006), e-mail bombing, website hacking, computer viruses, the disruption of databases, and computer break-ins. This takes protests out of the streets and turns it into electronic civil disobedience (ECD) (Pickerill, 2003). FloodNet was a program designed by the Electronic Disturbance Theater in the United States (Jordan, 2002; Kreimer, November 2003; Wray, 17 June 1998). The program allows activists to stage virtual sit-ins by making it possible for them to overwhelm an official website and block legitimate requests for information (Wray, 17 June 1998; Pickerill, 2003). In 1998, Electronic Disturbance Theater staged virtual sit-ins at the websites of Mexican President Ernesto Zedillo, the Pentagon, and the White House to protest the treatment of Zapatistas. One hundred thousand participants were able to register 600,000 hits per minute at the above-mentioned sites (Kreimer, November 2003). One particular sit-in took place on 29 Janaury 1998 from 6:00pm to 7:00pm. The sites targeted were those of Bolsa Mexicana de Valores, Grupo Financiero Bital, Grupo Financiero Bancomer, Banco de Mexico, and Banmex, all financial institutions. Participants were provided with website addresses and were instructed to visit each site. Once the sites were accessed, participants were to continuously click on the "reload" button in their web browser, allowing for a few seconds between clicks, for an hour. The objective was to slow down or even to shut down the sites by overloading the servers. Related to flooding the adversary's computer systems, e-mail bombs flood the recipient's e-mail inbox with thousands of messages simultaneously, effectively shutting down e-mail capabilities. Another example of ECD is the physical tampering of computers during office occupations. Tampering can range from something as simple as unplugging a computer from its power source to introducing viruses bearing activist messages into the computer (Kreimer, November 2003). Activists have been known to carry disks infected with viruses and downloading these onto the targeted computers (Pickerill 2003).

The aforementioned examples of hacktivism and ECD are referred to as mass virtual direct action, or MVDA. MVDA is meaningless unless a large number of people participate. Many people can participate, or one person can use a program to mimic the actions of many people. For example, the Electrohippie Collective, or ehippies, created a software program and embedded it in their webpage. Any user wishing to do so could then visit the website and download the program. The

program was developed to complement the street protests during the "Battle for Seattle" in 1999. The program continuously loaded pages from the World Trade Organization (WTO) website. If enough people downloaded and used the program, the WTO network could be affected. During the meeting, the network was halted twice and severely slowed down during much of the proceedings.

CONCLUSION

All of the above uses of the internet can be classified as "open", a category described by Meikle (2002) as being accessible to all, controlled by no one in particular, and with the capacity as a medium for change. The opposite is the "closed" system, described as controlled by corporations and largely limited to commercial use. There is no question – both categories exist today. The question is on the balance between the two. Activism online is alive and well. CMC, particularly the internet, has formed a symbiotic relationship with offline, real-world activism. Environmental and anti-corporate efforts are being challenged by business and government. One tactic of government repression is selective prosecution, whereby authorities selectively prosecute dissidents for crimes that would otherwise go unpunished (Kreimer, 2001). The internet has become a battle of wills. Means, i.e. financial resources, certainly play a role in this battle. Independent thought and perseverance will be the deciding factors in the outcome of control vs. free use.

An effective campaign is waged on different fronts. With the prevalence of global communication, spatial proximity all but ceases to become an issue in advancing a campaign. Personal computers (and other electronic media) are more available to more people than they were in the past. Any form of e-activism can be done at home. Not everyone is amenable to the idea of "taking it to the streets". A consistent theme throughout the literature has been that e-activism has served a complementary tactic to real-world activism. The Earth Liberation Front (ELF) and its counterpart organization in the animal liberation movement, the Animal Liberation Front (ALF), use the internet as a complement to their real-world direct actions. Once a direct action is completed, an anonymous communiqué is sent to the respective press office and is subsequently published online and, at times, in print media as well. Even these most radical of groups, considered domestic terrorists by the Federal Bureau of Investigation (FBI), are making prodigious use of CMC.

Actions by radical activists are labeled according to the "radicalism vs. terrorism" scale. On this scale, there is no gray area – a person is either considered a radical or a terrorist. The classification depends on the person making it. A radical activist or someone sympathetic to the radical cause will refer to actions as *radicalism*. Those opposed to radical ideology, e.g. government, corporations, and some mainstream activists, will refer to radical actions as *terrorism*. Use of such terms is a powerful tool alongside CMC. Radical online activism is not only a battle of technology; it is also a battle of words.

REFERENCES

Bob, C. (2005). *The marketing of rebellion: Insurgents, media, and international activism.* New York: Cambridge University Press.

Castells, M. (1997). *The power of identity* (*Vol. 2*). Oxford, UK: Blackwell Publishers.

Cramer, P. F. (1998). *Deep environmental politics: The role of radical environmentalism in crafting American environmental policy.* Westport, CT: Praeger.

Dartnell, M. Y. (2006). *Insurgency online: Web activism and global conflict.* Toronto, Canada: University of Toronto Press.

Delicath, J. W. (1996). In search of ecotopia: Radical environmentalism and the possibilities of utopian rhetorics. In Muir, S. A., & Veenendall, T. L. (Eds.), *Earthtalk: Communication empowerment for environmental action* (pp. 153–169). Westport, CT: Praeger.

DeLuca, K. (1996). Constituting nature anew through judgment: The possibilities of media. In Muir, S. A., & Veenendall, T. L. (Eds.), *Earthtalk: Communication empowerment for environmental action* (pp. 59–78). Westport, CT: Praeger.

Dunlap, R. E., & Mertig, A. G. (Eds.). (1992). *American environmentalism: The U.S. environmental movement, 1970 – 1990.* Philadelphia: Taylor and Francis.

EcoNet. (n.d.). *EcoNet.* Retrieved January 31, 2008, from http://www.jca.apc.org/~y-okada/igc/econet/

Jordan, T. (2002). *Activism! Direct action, hacktivism, and the future of society.* London: Reaktion Books Ltd.

Jordan, T., & Taylor, P. A. (2004). *Hacktivism and cyberwars: Rebels with a cause?* London: Routledge.

Juris, J. S. (2005, January). The new digital media and activist networking within anti–corporate globalization movements [Electronic version]. *The Annals of the American Academy of Political and Social Science, 597*, 189-208. Retrieved March 6, 2008, from http://ann.sagepub.com.ezproxy.fiu.edu/cgi/reprint/597/1/189

Kahn, R., & Kellner, D. (2004). New media and internet activism: From the Battle of Seattle to blogging [Electronic version]. *New Media & Society, 6*(1), 87-95. Retrieved January 14, 2009, from http://nms.sagepub.com.ezproxy.fiu.edu/cgi/reprint/6/1/87

Klota, R. J. (2004). *The politics of internet communication*. New York: Rowman & Littlefield Publishers, Inc.

Kreimer, S. F. (2001, November). Technologies of Protest: Insurgent Social Movements and the First Amendment in the Era of the Internet [Electronic version] [from http://www.jstor.org.ezproxy.fiu.edu]. *University of Pennsylvania Law Review*, *150*(1), 119–171. Retrieved March 6, 2008. doi:10.2307/3312914

List, P. C. (1993). *Radical environmentalism: Philosophy and tactics*. Belmont, CA: Wadsworth Publishing Company.

(2000). Marcos. InPonce de León, J. (Ed.), *Our word is our weapon: Selected writings Subcomandante Marcos* (pp. 280–282). London: Serpents Trails.

Mauch, C., Stoltzfus, N., & Weiner, D. R. (2006). *Shades of green: Environmental activism around the globe*. Boulder, CO: Rowman & Littlefield Publishers, Inc.

Meikle, G. (2002). *Future active: Media activism and the internet*. New York: Routledge.

Muir, S. A., & Veenendall, T. L. (1996). *Earthtalk: Communication empowerment for environmental action*. Westport, CT: Praeger.

Oleson, T. (2005). *International Zapatismo: The construction of solidarity in the age of globalization*. New York: Zed Books.

Pickerill, J. (2001). Environmental internet activism in Britain [Electronic version]. *Peace Review, 13*(3), 365-370. Retrieved January 14, 2009, from http://shockandawe.us/archives/Environment/5107877.pdf

Pickerill, J. (2003). *Cyberprotest: Environmental activism online*. Manchester, UK: Manchester University Press.

Postmes, T., & Brunsting, S. (2002). Collective action in the age of the internet [Electronic version] [from http://psy.ex.ac.uk/~tpostmes/PDF/PostmesBrunstingSSCoRe.pdf]. *Social Science Computer Review*, *20*(3), 290–301. Retrieved January 14, 2009.

Sampedro, V. (2004). The alternative movement and its media strategies. In Polet, F. (Ed.), *Globalizing resistance: The state of struggle* (pp. 243–257). London: Pluto Press.

Scarce, R. (2006). Eco-Warriors: Understanding the radical environmental movement (Updated ed.). Walnut Creek, CA: Left Coast Press.

Taylor, B. R. (1995). *Ecological resistance movements: The global emergence of radical and popular environmentalism*. Albany, NY: State University of New York Press.

The EnviroLink Network. (n.d.). *EnviroLink*. Retrieved January 31, 2008, from http://envirolink.org/

Vatikiotis, P. (2005). Communication theory and alternative media. *Westminster Papers in Communication and Culture*, *2*(1), 4–29.

Wray, S. (1998, June 17). *The Electronic Disturbance Theater and electronic civil disobedience*. Retrieved March 16, 2008, from http://www.thing.net/~rdom/ecd/EDTECD.html

Yang, G. (2003). Weaving a green web: The internet and environmental activism in China [Electronic version]. *China Environment Series, 6*, 89-93. Retrieved March 6, 2008, from http://wwics.si.edu/topics/pubs/greenweb.pdf

Zelko, F. (2006). The origins of postwar environmental protest in the United States. In Mauch, C., Stoltzfus, N., & Weiner, D. R. (Eds.), *Shades of green: Environmental activism around the globe* (pp. 13–40). Boulder, CO: Rowman & Littlefield Publishers, Inc.

ADDITIONAL READING

Hill, K. A., & Hughes, J. E. (1998). *Cyberpolitics: Citizen activism in the age of the internet*. Lanham, MD: Rowman & Littlefield Publishers, Inc.

McCaughey, M., & Ayers, M. D. (2003). *Cyber-activism: Online activism in theory and practice*. New York: Routledge.

North American Earth Liberation Front Press Office. (n.d.). Retrieved April 22, 2009, from http://www.elfpressoffice.org/main.html

Van de Donk, W., Loader, B. D., Nixon, P. G., & Rucht, D. (Eds.). (2004). *Cyberprotest: New media, citizens, and social movements*. London: Routledge.

Wapner, P. (1996). *Environmental activism and world civic politics*. Albany, NY: State University of New York Press.

Section 3
E–Governance

Chapter 17
Digital Cities:
Towards Connected Citizens and Governance

Leonidas Anthopoulos
TEI Larissa, Greece

Panos Fitsilis
TEI Larissa, Greece

ABSTRACT

The digital cities, from their online forms such as America-On-Line and Kyoto cases, to their ubiquitous forms such as Beijing, Hull (UK) and Trikala (Greece) cases, have achieved in simplifying citizen access to Local and Central Government services. Early digital cities succeed in delivering improved public services to citizens even with no digital skills, closing digital divide and establishing digital areas of trust in local communities. This chapter presents the evolution of the digital cities, from the web to the ubiquitous architecture, which can deliver multiple services to different target groups and can behave as a common "interface" between citizens and all kinds of public agencies. The chapter will focus on the latest digital city architecture, and on the experiences from the digital city of Trikala (Greece), in order to present how digital city impacts local attitudes regarding e-Government. Moreover, the chapter will attempt to evaluate digital city's progress and its performance concerning citizen contacts to e-Government.

INTRODUCTION

Multiple approaches have been given to the digital city: *digital environments collecting official and unofficial information from local communities* (Wang & Wu, 2001) *and delivering it to the public via web portals are called information cities* (Sairamesh, Lee, & Anania, 2004; Sproull & Patterson, 2004;

Widmayer, 1999); *networks of organizations, social groups and enterprises located in a city area are called digital cities.* These definitions were given by major case studies such as the America-On-Line, the Kyoto's and the Hull's etc., which are analyzed in this chapter in order to present the ubiquitous environment that is generated in many areas all over the world.

Although digital cities were initiated as information based platforms (web portals, databases,

DOI: 10.4018/978-1-61520-933-0.ch017

virtual reality applications etc.), they soon evolved to wide(metro)-area information systems (IS) that deliver different kinds of services to the local communities. Their infrastructures concern network equipment (fiber optic channels and wi-fi networks in the city area), service oriented information systems (e.g. e-Government IS, e-Democracy portals, public Agency web applications etc.), public access points (e.g. wireless hotspots, info kiosks etc.), and social service systems (e.g. intelligent transport systems, tele-care and tele-health networks etc.). These environments composed a recent digital city definition (Anthopoulos & Tsoukalas, 2005): *city-area infrastructures and applications aiming to cover local needs and support local community's everyday life.* This definition evolved to the ubiquitous city or U-city (Wikipedia, 2009): *a city or region with ubiquitous information technology. All information systems are linked, and virtually everything is linked to an information system through technologies such as wireless networking and RFID tags.*

Both recent digital city and U-city approaches face various challenges: the opportunity for the digital city to become a) a common interface for public transactions in the city area, b) an area-of-trust for the citizens where they can exchange opinions, they can support decision making and they can describe their real needs to the political leadership. These approaches can develop a "global e-Government environment" in city areas, where citizens can access both local and central public services. This global environment can be called "Metropolitan e-Government environment" and its main targets concern: a) the collection of local information, b) the use of local information for the sustainable development of the city and c) the continuous evaluation and improvement of the architecture, and of the quality of the offered services.

In the Background section of this chapter the evolution of the digital city from the web to its recent ubiquitous architecture is presented. We mainly focus on the latest architecture of the digital

city, in order to present how it affects social attitudes in local communities, concerning e-Government. We applied a recent evaluation framework –the Software Project Observatory Framework (SPoF)- (Fitsilis and Anthopoulos, 2008) in the digital city of Trikala (Greece), in order to investigate whether the Metropolitan e-Government environment can support the diffusion of the ICT and of the digital public transactions in a city area.

BACKGROUND

Since the early 90s different digital cities were implemented all over the world (Table 1). The first case was the *America-On-Line cities* (Wang and Wu, 2001), where web environments offered digital transactions and chatting options. America-On-Line simulated a city via grouping services according to civilian logic. The digital city of *Kyoto* (Japan) (Ishida, 2002; Ishida, Aurigiri & Yasuoka, 2001) and the digital city of *Amsterdam* (Lieshout, 2001) were web environments simulating the city and its local life (streets, enterprises, malls etc.). This version of the digital city offered virtual meeting rooms for specific common interests, inviting citizens to participate. These web approaches were evolved to virtual reality environments (Van den Besselaar & Beckers, 1998) operating beyond the physical boundaries of a city.

Some unique cases that exploit Information and Communication Technologies (ICT) for the social development were implemented: the *Copenhagen Base* (Van Bastelaer, 1998) was a public database containing useful local information. People could initially access the database via the Internet and via text-TV. Today the Copenhagen Base is open to people for data supply and entry. Moreover, the *Craigmillar* city of Scotland (Van Bastelaer, 1998) used the ICT to structure groups of citizens who shared knowledge and offered social services to the local community. In Craigmillar –an ex-industrial area-, citizens collaborated in order to handle local needs.

The "Smart City" (Partridge, 2004) refers to a city where the ICT strengthen the freedom of speech and the accessibility to public information and services. In the smart cities the habitants can participate in social events easy and cheap. The smart city approach was initially applied in the case of *Brisbane* (Australia) and supported the social participation and the close of the digital divide.

Table 1. Different digital city cases and approaches

City	Digital City	Short Description
America-On-Line	America-On-Line Cities	Virtual groups exchanging knowledge over the Internet.
Kyoto	Digital City of Kyoto	City simulation via web and virtual reality interfaces.
Amsterdam	Digital City of Amsterdam	- City simulation via web and virtual reality interfaces. - MAN - Interconnection with digital city of Antwerp
Copenhagen	Copenhagen Base	Public database covering local needs.
Craigmillar	Digital City of Craigmillar	Groups of citizens sharing knowledge and social services covering local needs
Brisbane	Smart City of Brisbane	- Decision making services. - Virtual groups sharing knowledge
Hull	Digital City of Hull	- MAN - Public portals offering local information and services.
Beijing	Digital City of Beijing	- Fiber optic and wireless broadband networks in the city. - Public services mainly oriented to the Olympic Games.
Antwerp	Digital City of Antwerp	- MAN - eDemocracy services - Portals offering public information - Interconnection with digital city of Amsterdam
Geneva	Geneva-MAN	- MAN - Interconnected market
Seoul	Seoul Broadband Metropolis	- Fiber optic network all over the city
New York	Mobile City of New York	Wireless broadband network covering the city area.
Eurocities	European city network	ICT usage and experience exchange for: - Social Participation - Local community evolution - Sustainable development
Smart Communities	Interconnected cities from even different continents	Cities interconnected with broadband networks.
Blacksbourg	Knowledge Democracy of Blacksbourg	Environment with knowledge concerning the ICT.
Knowledge based cities	Knowledge Based Cities in Portugal	- Regional network of interconnected cities - Groups sharing knowledge
Digital Geographies		Virtual teams of users sharing knowledge, who are located in even different countries
Trikala	Digital City of Trikala	- ICT addressing local needs - Multitier architecture - Global e-Government environment - The digital city consists a trusted third party for transactions and knowledge exchange
New Sondgo	U-city of New Sondgo	Ubiquitous information systems in city area
Osaka	U-city of Osaka	Ubiquitous information systems in city area

The cases of *Hull* (UK, www.hullcc.gov.uk) and of *Beijing* (China) (Sairamesh et. al., 2004) used fiber optic backbones installed in the city, which were called "Metropolitan Area Networks (MAN)". MAN offered broadband access to public information and services from local agencies, in order to simplify habitants' everyday life. However, Beijing digital city was implemented for the purposes of the Olympic Games of 2008, and initially offered related information and services. MAN was used in the case of the Digital Metropolis of *Antwerp* (Van Bastelaer, 1998), the first digital city in Belgium. The Antwerp city collaborated with the City of *Amsterdam*, having a MAN too, in order to interconnect their municipal agencies and offer common information and services to their local communities. This group of digital cities supported the diffusion of the ICT for the decision making by the municipal leadership. *Geneva* city (Van Bastelaer, 1998) on the other hand, used its MAN to interconnect the foreign enterprises that were located in the area. It then offered the MAN for public use, and constructed a digital market for all local businesses.

The *Seoul* city introduced the "Broadband Metropolis" notion, where the MAN was extended to interconnect the households and the local enterprises (Townsend, 2004). The last mile connection to the MAN is established with fiber optic channels (Fiber-to-the-Home, FTTH), composing a healthy competitive environment for telecommunication vendors, and an attractive field for private investments.

"Mobile cities" such as the *New York* (New York City Economic Development Corporation, 2005), installed wireless broadband networks in the city, which were accessible (free-of-charge) by the habitants. Both e-learning and e-Government services were offered from local or national organizations in the mobile cities.

The *Eurocities* (http://www.eurocities.org) is a European network of cities, which focus on the development of "an inclusive, prosperous and sustainable ICT environment operating in the area of a city". The participating cities exchange their experiences and they cooperate in the development of an open market and in the treatment of corruption in municipal agencies. The final product of the Eurocities initiative is the development of prototype digital city, covering local needs in Europe. A public portal called "the Demos" has been developed, containing information from all participants. Moreover, pilot projects are being implemented concerning e-democracy and decision making applications.

The World Foundation of Smart Communities (http://www.smartcommunities.org) is a nonprofit educational organization studying the development of "Smart Communities"; meaning "cities with broadband networks interconnecting their local resources with resources from other geographic areas". The Smart Community uses the ICT in order to improve living and working. Lots of cities from Singapore, Malaysia, Canada, Hong Kong, Spain, German, Ireland, Holland and Saudi Arabia, participate in the Smart Community network.

The Communities of the Future (http://www.communitiesofthefuture.org) is a nonprofit organization defining the digital city as "a knowledge democracy". This approach concerns the development of societies, where the novel privileges (privilege to access public information and services), risks (privacy and security) and challenges (social participation) based on the ICT, are analyzed and participation is encouraged. The Knowledge Democracy approach was applied in *Blacksbourg* (Australia) implementing the "Blacksbourg Electronic Village" (http://www.bev.net), where habitants with common interests (e.g. citizens, local administration, engineers) are grouped together, composing the "neighborhoods" entities.

In "knowledge based cities" (Mountihno & Heitor, 2003) the ICT support local democracy and local economy. This approach was applied in Portugal and uses broadband networks developed by telecommunication vendors connecting cities and local economies. Virtual organizations are structured in this network of cities, such as virtual organization for the municipalities, for the enterprises, for the citizens with common interests etc. The interconnected cities structure a regional virtual environment, where cities support each other's progress via the ICT.

The "digital geography" (Zook, Dodge, Aoyama & Townsend, 2004) is an approach that extends city physical boundaries and structures teams of interconnected citizens who share knowledge of common interest. The digital geography uses the Internet and the mobile networks to compose digital communities where knowledge is exchanged and where growth is supported. Emphasis is given to the development of Digital States in the same country, which are small-scale digital geographies. Digital geographies are graphically presented with communication zones in the same or in multiple geographic areas.

In *Trikala* (central Greece) a novel approach to the digital city was given (Anthopoulos & Tsoukalas, 2005), which extended the above cases and older ones (Moon, 2002): "the digital city is an ICT-based environment whose priorities concern a) the availability of digital means that support local needs and transactions, b) the transformation of the local community to a local information society, c) the direct and indirect, official and unofficial information collection, in order to support the sustainable development of the local community". The Trikala case is analyzed further in the next section, supporting the main focus of this chapter.

The cost minimization of broadband services, and the simplification of IS installation and maintenance resulted in further digital city cases. Moreover, the "cloud services" and the "ubiquitous computing" technologies offered by the big international ICT vendors, result in the evolution of the digital city to the "Ubiquitous City" (or U-city). The U-city architecture is being implemented in South Korea (e.g. New Songdo (Hyang-Sook, Byung-Sun. & Woong-Hee, 2007)) and Japan (e.g. Osaka (Osaka ICT Industry, 2008))

and delivers information anytime, anywhere to anybody, via interconnected information systems and ubiquitous ICT over the city. However, this novel ubiquitous approach is accompanied with the development of new urban spaces where the pervasive computing will be applied.

All of the above refer to either digital environments operating in the physical boundaries of a city or to environments that create virtual communities beyond the geographic area of a city. Although different priorities were given on each case, common ICT infrastructures are used (broadband networks and information systems) and virtual teams of citizens are structured. The analysis of the technologies combined in a digital or in a ubiquitous city is beyond the purposes of this chapter.

Most of the presented cases were initiated by the private sector (e.g. telecommunication vendors) or by individuals who have common interests, knowledge and needs. Exceptions concern the Beijing and the Craigmiller cases, where the digital city faced special needs, such the Olympic Games and the unemployment respectively. The evolution of the presented cases is based on the coordination of a big vendor or by a local university, meaning a "top-down" procedure (Anthopoulos, Siozos & Tsoukalas, 2007). An exception is the Greek Trikala case, where the digital city is growing with the participation of local stakeholders (local chamber, groups of citizens and enterprises) under the leadership of the municipality, meaning a "bottom-up" procedure (Anthopoulos, et. al, 2007).

Digital cities face common challenges, such as the encouragement of the social participation, and the economic and the sustainable growth of the local community. Today, all digital cities focus on the quality and on the variety of the information that they offer to their habitants (public content and services, private content, video-on-demand and other entertainment services, social networks etc.).

MAIN FOCUS OF THE CHAPTER

The previous sections of this chapter showed that various metropolitan ICT cases have been evolved the last two decades all over the world. Recent digital cities invest huge on ICT, installing dense fibre optic networks and complex information systems in the cities, while most cases were initiated by municipalities, by local universities and telecommunication vendors. Since digital cities are implemented all over the world, huge funding is spent for them, and they are still evolving with the use of ubiquitous technologies, they are considered as an important factor for the ICT and for the development of transactions between local governments and local communities. Furthermore, municipalities consider the digital cities as great opportunities for local capital growth and for social participation in local politics, while there is a lot of argument concerning their sustainability and growth (New Millennium Research Council, 2005).

Furthermore, the digital cities deliver e-Government customer oriented services, they simplify citizen access to central administrative procedures, and they maximize administrative efficiency, productivity and transparency (Duk Hee Lee, 2007) with system integration, and with both process and service redesign in local public administration. Additionally, according to (Anthopoulos & Tsoukalas, 2005) the digital city can be considered as a "global e-Government environment" that delivers all kinds of services -more than the administrative ones- to the local community, it interconnects virtual teams located in the city in order to deliver their needs and their opinions to the local administration, and it can predict future citizen needs. These points of view show that digital cities compose a prosperous environment for e-Government and e-Democracy.

This chapter aims to present how a digital city can work as a common e-Government environment for both local and central services, and how this behaviour can impact the local attitudes of

citizens concerning e-Government. In our study, we use the Trikala case study to present how it delivers public information and services to the local community. We used the development experiences, e-Trikala official publications and a local newspaper web portal to investigate how local attitudes were transformed since 2005 when the digital city began its operation. Then we applied the SPof evaluation framework in order to assess how well this digital city performs. The whole procedure is useful, since it presents a methodology for discovering and evaluating e-Government evolution and performance.

In Trikala, central Greece, local needs were prioritized with the "bottom-up" procedure, and they were grouped into the following axes of precedence (Anthopoulos & Tsoukalas, 2005):

- Local Economy and employment
- Improvement of everyday life concerning public transactions and transportation
- Education, vocational training and life-long learning
- Tourism and culture

On behalf of the municipality, a team of experts discovered funding and designed the necessary projects that could deal with the above axes of precedence. The set of projects delivered city-wide interconnected information systems and broadband networks, together with important public information and services. The logical architecture of the whole environment follows the multi-tier structure (LiQi, 2001), inspired by information cities (Sairamesh et al., 2004), (Sproull et al., 2004), (Widmayer, 1999), consisting of following layers (Figure 1):

- "Stakeholders layer", containing potential users of the digital city services: end-users (citizens, businesses, students), groups of end-users (local chamber, teams with common interests), servants who offer public and commercial services via the

Figure 1. The n-tier logical architecture of the digital city of Trikala

Stakeholders layer	
End users, groups of end-users, servants	
Service layer	
Web portals, engines, web services, geospatial services	
Business layer	
Enterprise Architecture, policies, operating rules	
Infrastructure layer	
MAN, metro Wi-Fi, information systems, phone centre, public access points	
Information layer	
Public, private, public/private data created and stored	

digital city (civil servants, public agencies, enterprises).

- "Service layer", including software applications that deliver public information and services to citizens and enterprises. The applications concern web portals, engines executing e-Government, e-Commerce and social (e.g. tele-care) services, web services transacting with other information systems (e.g. central e-Government systems, others located beyond city borders etc.), and geospatial services. This layer structures the *interface* between the habitants and the public administration (local and central ones). However, today no unique interface collecting all available services from digital city platforms exists, meaning that the digital city has not yet succeeded in its initial objectives. This web distribution of the digital city services can cause troubles to the habitants and can lead to information replication.

- "Business layer", which defines the policies, the operating rules and the Enterprise Architecture of the digital city. This layer declare how each system will be designed, installed and interconnected in the digital city, while it defines the "WHOs and HOWs" for each transaction delivered via the digital city. This layer extends the originally defined architecture by (Anthopoulos & Tsoukalas, 2005), it is introduced in this chapter and it infects all the other layers of the architecture.

- "Infrastructure layer", containing the local broadband networks (MAN and a metro Wi-Fi), an intelligent transport system, phone centre for public calls, and public access points in the city hall and in other public buildings. Concerning the broadband connectivity, both a MAN and a metro Wi-Fi are installed in the city today. The Wi-Fi is accessed by more than 2,000 registered users and it is based on more than 10 points of access. However, the MAN was implemented with European funding (under the Information Society Framework Programmes (www.infosoc.gr)), and it interconnects only public agencies today. No private organization can access the MAN, nor can FTTH connections extend it to the households and to the local enterprises.

- "Information layer", consisting of information and data that is produced and stored in the infrastructure layer. The information can be public, private or both public/private and the digital city can apply policies for security and privacy, in order to define who can access what resource and to protect sensitive information. Today, there is no common data repository in the digital city of Trikala. Each information system belongs to a unique organization, and the information that it is produced and hosted

Figure 2. The physical architecture of the digital city of Trikala

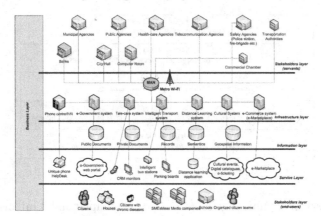

in each one, belongs to that organization. The digital city cannot apply common security and privacy rules to different information systems and can only observe transactions.

The e-Trikala physical architecture is presented in (Figure 2). The digital city environment interconnects all viable and ICT resources in the city and it can deliver information from everywhere to anyone, meaning that it formulates a ubiquitous city. This environment can behave as a *global e-Government environment* (Metropolitan e-Government environment), with the following characteristics:

- Each citizen has a unique identity in the digital city and he can be authorized once, with the use of the same credentials in order to access different resources.
- Further citizen certificates will not be required for service execution, since any necessary information will be retrieved "transparently" among the digital city systems.
- Authentication tools, local content and services can be available via a common web portal. Habitants use the digital city portal to access local commercial, public or social services.

- Each transaction is executed and monitored by the digital city infrastructures.
- The digital city can be evolved to an "intelligent e-Government environment", since it will be able to "predict" the execution of some public services by monitoring citizen needs (with the consent of the involved parties). For instance, a citizen application for residence movement could be accompanied by records update in tax-systems, by a new service triggering concerning the power Supply Company etc.
- The digital city is a virtual organization, consisting of various virtual teams (Godard, Saliou & Bignon, 2001). This virtual organization is used for knowledge sharing and exchange, and for decision making.

Although the e-Trikala case study was an ambitious approach, aiming to interconnect virtual with physical environments (Einmann & Paradiso, 2005), only a few of its primary targets have been achieved while they are reconsidered. In this section we present the divergences from e-Trikala initial targets, together with the reasons that lead to these differentiations.

After the completion of projects' design by the team of experts, the municipality structured an office responsible for the procurement and for the management of the projects. Projects have been procured and implemented from 2005. Today, project deliverables operate under pilot conditions, while the municipal office has been evolved to a municipal company, able to exploit project deliverables and knowledge. The municipal company is also responsible for deliverables operation, and for digital city monitoring, reviewing and evolution.

Concerning the *broadband access*, the initial objectives were that anyone (end-users and groups of end-users) could access the digital city via its broadband networks from everywhere. Today, the metro Wi-Fi covers the 2/3 of city area, and it is open to anyone in its range. Users can access the metro Wi-Fi free-of-charge with the combination of a username and password given to them upon registration. Registration follows the traditional procedure, which demands the physical presence of the user at the municipality, in order to fill-in and to submit an application form. On the other hand, the MAN is accessible only for public organizations, because Greek legislation does not permit private connections yet. It is expected that individuals and the private sector will be able to access the MAN by 2012. Until then, FTTH connections will not be able to extend the MAN, and habitants will access the digital city resources indirectly via the Internet or by phone. The broadband networks' operation is by now a municipal obligation, meaning that monitoring, maintenance and policy application is a difficult procedure that lacks compared to the private competition.

Concerning the *offered services* no one-stop portal for the digital city exists so far. On the contrary, each project delivered a different but interoperable portal, offering its custom services and information. The municipal company has installed a web portal for the digital city (www.e-trikala.gr), but the web services to the projects portals have not been implemented yet. The reason is that each project deliverable belongs to a different organization of the city, and even hosting on central public infrastructures in the digital city demands legal confirmation.

E-Government progress is weak in e-Trikala case. The digital city has achieved in miniature town hall behavior (Layne & Jungwoo, 2001), establishing "vertical connections among municipal agencies", and it offers four (4) services online. The same services are offered to the wider state region, beyond the city boundaries. Moreover, a call center offers helpdesk services to the citizens, concerning public transactions. Other digital public services are offered via the citizen service (KEP) offices (www.kep.gov.gr) and central public agencies, which are executed beyond digital city infrastructures.

However, e-Trikala case performs significantly well regarding social services: tele-care and e-health services are widely accepted by citizens with special needs, who have obtained digital devices from the municipality, in order to be monitored online by the local hospital, doctors and psychologists. Heart diseases are monitored effectively by the local hospital, with the use of an information system installed in the infrastructure layer. Health records are collected and transmitted online, and some privacy issues have to be investigated further. Additionally to tele-care and e-health services, the intelligent transport system performs satisfyingly in e-Trikala: the period of testing has passed and statistical analysis on traffic data has been performed. Today, "smart bus stations" located around the city, inform citizens about the estimated departure times of buses.

The rate of the digital city of Trikala regarding the *business layer* is not satisfactory. No Enterprise Architecture has been composed, either common standards or blueprints have been defined for the future ICT projects that will be designed and implemented in the city area. Moreover, security and privacy issues have not been analyzed and each information system follows independent policies and rules. The municipal leadership has emphasized in the implementation of the designed projects, and only recently the development of the municipal company is a strategic direction.

The digital city performs similarly in *information layer*: the infrastructures do not contain common storage repositories for the information created and used in the city, and each project has its own storage capacities. The reasons concern the possession of the data and the proper legal alignment for public data construction, storage, access and use.

All other public services (e.g. tax and other administrating services) are either offered directly via central systems to which citizens are obliged to access or they are executed with the traditional methods. It is expected that by 2012 a central web portal will operate as a one-stop-shop for public services coming from the inside or the outside of the digital city.

Since the ubiquitous architecture of a digital city can be considered as a Metropolitan e-Government environment, the evaluation of the quality of offered services and of the overall behavior of the global environment is necessary. Moreover, we expected that the existence of a digital city can affect citizen attitudes concerning e-Government, and we wanted to measure how do citizens evaluate the digital city progress and quality.

The assessment of quality of service is a complex procedure, and different observatories follow different evaluation methods. The World Bank (Kaufmann, Daniel, Kraay, Aart, Mastruzzi & Massimo, 2008) measures *citizen satisfaction* for instance, with the number of Public web portals offering most desirable public services in different countries. The United Nations on the other hand (United Nations, 2008), evaluate quality of service according to the number of stages of digital public services. National observatories in Europe (e.g. the Greek Information Society Observatory, www.observatory.gr) measure citizen satisfaction with the evaluation of political implications of e-Government.

Other approaches such as the ACSI (www. theacsi.org) use direct measurement methods performing surveys for customer satisfaction, while project management theory offers the SERVQUAL

instrument (Asubonteng, McCleary & Swan, 1996). Many e-Government evaluation models have been proposed to measure e-Government progress and citizen satisfaction (Van Der Westhuizen and Edmond, 2005; Corlane Barclay, 2008; Victor, Panikar and Kanhere, 2007) suggest different perspectives for e-Government evaluation. For the purposes of this chapter we will use the Software Project Observatory Framework (SPoF) (Fitsilis & Anthopoulos, 2008). The Framework consists of metrics that evaluate software projects, which are sufficient for our e-Trikala case, since citizens do not interact with infrastructures but with software: (a) project organization metrics that evaluate municipal and municipal company organization efficiency, (b) project processes metrics, which evaluate project process alignment and agility, (c) project results metrics, reflecting the installed software size and demanding infrastructure resources, (d) social-economics metrics, describing the software implications and e) citizen satisfaction indices, measuring service acceptance by the end-users.

In order to apply the SPoF in e-Trikala case, we used the experiences from the project design and implementation until 2005, in combination with project publications on official web portal (www.e-trikala.gr). The SPoF returns very interesting results (Table 2) concerning e-Trikala progress, confirming the progress findings presented in the previous section: initial budget was overcome by 6.7 percent; although the project demands 12 percent annual maintenance costs it is estimated that current infrastructures have an 8 year lifecycle. Project preparation and management demanded 2.23 percent over the initial budget. Municipal staff requires a training budget of 3.22 percent of the digital city budget, while only 2 from the 30 municipal officers hold project management skills. On the other hand, the municipality performs well concerning its consistency, since it is certified for management, and all 15 digital city projects had an average duration turnover ratio 0.125.

The digital city's software products deliver online only a 4.55 percentage of public services

(4 out of 88 registered services) and none of them demanded legislation update. Process alignment is low, due to the low ratio of service availability, while process agility performs well, having all available digital services interoperable amongst each other and with other national public services. However, interoperability is optional for current services, and they have not interconnected with

Table 2. SPoF index values concerning e-Trikala progress

Project Organization Metrics			Project processes metrics		
a. Direct cost indexes			a. Process alignment		
K01	Initial estimated budget for project	4.500.000,00 €	K31	Re-designed processes	4
K02	Final project cost	4.800.000,00 €	K32	Process digitization	16
K03	Cost for project preparation	35.000,00 €	K33	Hybrid Processes	0
K04	Cost for project management	72.000,00 €	K34	e-Service availability	4,55
K05	Investment estimated "lifecycle"	8	K35	Electronic procedure ratio	1.45
K06	Annual maintenance cost	576.000,00 €	K36	Processes with legal confirmation	0
b. Staff's skills			b. Process agility		
K11	Training programs cost	100.000,00 €	K41	Web services	4
K12	Executives' maturity	2	K42	Interoperable services	4
K13	Costs for personnel employment	45.000,00 €	K43	Software conformity	4
c. Organization's consistency					
K21	Project duration turnover	0.125	Social-economics metrics		
K22	Organization Certified	Yes	a. Social implications		
			K61	Service usage	412
Project results metrics			K62	Contribution to quality of life	3
K51	Discrete subsystems	32	K63	Time savings ratio	12,86
K52	Discrete modules	18	K64	Contribution to competitiveness	0
K53	Internal interfaces	22	b. Political implications		
K54	External interfaces	4	K71	Contribution to democracy	0
K55	Service size	4	c. Direct cost		
K56	Process size	0,0039	K81	Contribution to employment	9,5
K57	Transaction size	0,0014	K82	Operational cost savings	112,00 €
			K83	Personnel decrease	0
Citizen satisfaction			d. Indirect cost		
K101	Direct end-user satisfaction	87	K91	Personnel time savings	2
K102	Indirect end-user satisfaction	0	K92	Return of Investment	un-known
K103	Fully digitally execution	4			
K104	Semi-digitally execution	0			
K105	Public executives' satisfaction	unknown			
K106	Service reliability	0			
K107	Service complexity	3			
K108	Service consistency	1			

other services yet. Software project results have normal index values, and low resources (required bandwidth and capacity) are still required. The social-economic perspective of the SPoF gives very important results for the digital city progress: employment is kept steady in municipal organizations and new personnel opportunities are offered during project implementation. Moreover, the available public services provide cost and time savings in the municipal organizations, but they have not contributed to competitiveness and to democracy yet.

We also had to collect data concerning citizen satisfaction from digital city services and operational behavior. We conducted online surveys during the period March to April 2009 on a local newspaper portal (www.e-erevna.gr) in order to collect relative data. This newspaper is the most famous in Trikala, having a daily activity of more than 1,000 unique readers. Only registered users could join surveys and fill-in the questionnaire, while each user could participate once. A number of 109 registered readers participated in all of the surveys and the survey results are presented in (Table 3).

Some major questions -inspired from the ACSI investigations- were given online to the habitants. The first question concerned the familiarity of the habitants to the local online services, asking which of the services offered by the digital city they have applied for. The second question wanted to measure citizen satisfaction, and asked whether the citizen who had applied for a service would use it again. The third and the fourth questions targeted citizen attitudes on e-Government and e-Democracy: asked about an offered or a non-offered service that citizens would wish to be available in the digital city; the fourth question investigated whether citizens would participate in decision making methods, which are available in the digital city. The fifth question measured system's quality, asking whether the system kept citizen profile, whether response time was sufficient and whether the service result was 'clear'

to the citizen. Finally, the sixth question wanted to investigate web portal's quality, asking about user-friendliness, content straightforward, content transparency and actuality, and about service fulfillment and transparency. All answers gave the option of "I do not know" for cases that participants have never accessed a digital city service.

According to the survey data only 3.6 percent of the questioned citizens have accessed an e-Government service, while they all appeared willing to apply for public services online. *Residence change* is the most attractive e-Government service to the audience, while *metro Wi-Fi* and *online municipal council sessions* are the most popular digital city services. However, only the *e-Health* and *tele-care* social services perform well concerning citizen satisfaction, while all of the questioned citizens would apply for FTTH broadband connections. The audience appears informed concerning digital city services, and they all filled in the third question about future services: They all expect online availability (more services online), and mostly *urban services* and *online voting*. Surprisingly, 79.8 percent of the audience suggested (by filling in a free text field on the questionnaire) the online availability of the *municipal finances*, which can be explained as a social reluctance to the ways municipal administration handles public finances.

Additionally, citizens appear reluctant concerning e-Democracy performance in the digital city: only 19.3 percent have used phone complaints and helpdesk (Demosthenis helpdesk service), while 43.1 percent is willing to use phone services. Moreover, the investigated audience does not "trust" decision making contribution (answers of the 4th question), since 95.4 percent would participate in municipal council sessions, meaning that citizens believe that all decisions are taken politically by the council.

Finally, digital city systems perform well concerning their quality; online services keep citizen profile, most (75 percent) users transacted sufficiently and took clear results from the online

Table 3. Web survey results

		Residence change	Birth certificate	Marriage certificate	Hunting Permission			
1	Which of the digital city e-Government services have you accessed?	2	0	1	1			
	How well in a scale (0-100) would you evaluate the service?	90.5	unknown	80	80			
	Which of the digital city e-Government services would you apply for in the future?	55	12	31	11			
		Metro Wi-Fi	FTTH	Intelligent Transportation	Tele-care	e-Health	Municipal Call Center (Demosthenis)	Watching municipal council session online
2	Which of the digital city services have you accessed?	101	0	41	4	87	21	107
	Which of the digital city services would you apply for in the future?	18	109	7	96	109	47	109
		Municipal certificates	Urban services	Online complaints	Municipal finances	Decision making	Online voting	Mayor's Briefing
3	Which of the following digital services would you expect to be available online?	18	99	35	87	46	101	72
		Demosthenis HelpDesk	Web surveys	Requests For Comments on municipal proposals	Requests for proposals for a local issue	Online participation on council session		

Table 3. continued on following page

Table 3. continued

		Residence change	Birth certificate	Marriage certificate	Hunting Permission			
4	Which of the following decision making services would you access?	47	78	78	91	104		
		Stores citizen profile	Sufficient response time (<15 sec)	Clear service results				
5	Do the e-Government services offer the following options? (*for the citizens who have accessed the e-Government services*)	4	3	3				
		User friendliness (accessibility options, FAQs, online Help)	Content straightforward	Content transparency	Content actuality	Service fulfillment	Service transparency	
6	Which of the following options did you mention on e-Trikala web portal?	61	58	55	74	4	4	

services, while all (according to the results of the 6th question) appear satisfied from service fulfillment and transparency. On the other hand, citizens expect more from the e-Trikala web portal: 44 percent expect more from its friendliness, while almost 50 percent expects more accurate and transparent content.

CONCLUSION

Digital city environments have evolved since the early 90s when they first entered the digital era. Web sites and virtual reality applications transformed to smart and knowledge repositories, which began interacting with groups of citizens inside city boundaries. Then broadband networks and other intelligent technologies were applied over the city, resulting in current digital cities. However, South Korea shows digital city future, with the application of ubiquitous computing in metropolitan environments. In this chapter we presented how current digital cities can simplify e-Government transactions, and how they can support ICT diffusion and e-Democracy attitudes in a city: we called this environment "Metropolitan e-Government environment", where new challenges concerning e-Government arise.

The evaluation of the Metropolitan environment regarding quality of service and citizen satisfaction was a challenge for this chapter and we presented a procedure of collecting and evaluating data. We used the Software Project Observatory Framework (SPoF) as an evaluation model and some important results were extracted in e-Trikala case study. We mentioned the wide acceptance of the social services, as well as with the social willing for improvement and for service availability that we discovered in our investigation. The whole procedure can be applied in many similar cases, where citizen attitudes are affected by an e-Government system, and where citizen attitudes can influence further e-Government progress.

Policies and rules guiding metropolitan transactions will be investigated in future research. Moreover, our future research will focus on how the ubiquitous technologies will impact the habitants' attitudes, and on how local communities evaluate u-city performance. We will also consider social networks installed in future digital cities, and on how they affect decision making by the political leadership. We will investigate further the recent u-cities that are under development in various cases, together the continuous transformation of current digital cities in order to conclude and cover those issues.

REFERENCES

Anthopoulos, L., Siozos, P., & Tsoukalas, I. A. (2007, April). Applying Participatory Design and Collaboration in Digital Public Services for discovering and re-designing e-Government services. *Government Information Quarterly*, *24*(2), 353–376. doi:10.1016/j.giq.2006.07.018

Anthopoulos, L., & Tsoukalas, I. A. (2005) The implementation model of a digital city. The case study of the first digital city in Greece: e-Trikala. *Journal of e-Government* (Haworth Press, Inc., University of Southern California, Center for Digital Government), *2*(2). Retreived 2005, from http://www.haworthpress.com/web/JEG/ and http://www.egovjournal.com/

Asubonteng, P., McCleary, K. J., & Swan, J. E. (1996). SERVQUAL revisited: a critical review of service quality. *Journal of Services Marketing*, *10*(6), 62–81. doi:10.1108/08876049610148602

Duk, H. L. (2007). *E-Government and digital city in Korea*. Retrieved July, 2009, from http://217.116.28.251/deds/260907/dhee.pdf

Einmann, E., & Paradiso, M. (2004). When space shrinks - digital communities and ubiquitous society: Digital cities and urban life: A framework for international benchmarking. In *Proceedings of the Winter International Symposium on Information and Communication Technologies* (WISICT '04). ACM.

Fitsilis, P., & Anthopoulos, L. (2008) Introducing e-Government software project observatory. In *Proceedings of the Hanoi Forum on Information - Communication Technology (ICT)* Retrieved 2008, from http://www.hanoiforum.vnu.edu.vn

Godart, C., Saliou, H., & Bignon, J. C. (2001). Asynchronous Coordination of Virtual Teams in Creative Applications (co-design or co-engineering): Requirements and Design Criteria. In *Proceedings of the Information Technology for Virtual Enterprises (ITVE 2001) Workshop* (p. 135 – 142). IEEE.

Hyang-Sook, C., Byung-Sun, C., & Woong-Hee, P. (2007). Ubiquitous-City Business Strategies: The Case of South Korea. In *Proceedings of the Management of Engineering and Technology* (PICMET 2007), IEEE.

Ishida, T. (2002, July). Digital city Kyoto. *Communications of the ACM*, *45*(7). doi:10.1145/514236.514238

Ishida, T., Aurigiri, A., & Yasuoka, M. (2001). *World Digital Cities: Beyond Heterogeneity*. Retrieved April, 2005, from http://www.kid.rcast.u-tokyo.ac.jp

Kaufmann, D., & Kraay, A. Mastruzzi, & Massimo (2008, June 24). *Governance Matters VII: Aggregate and Individual Governance Indicators*, 1996-2007, World Bank Policy Research Working Paper No. 4654.Retrieved (n.d.), fromhttp://ssrn.com/abstract=1148386

Layne, K., & Jungwoo, L. (2001). Developing fully functional e-government: A four stage model. *Government Information Quarterly*, *18*, 122–136. doi:10.1016/S0740-624X(01)00066-1

Lieshout, V. (2001). Configuring the digital city of Amsterdam. *New Media & Technology*, *3*(1), 27–52.

LiQi. (2001). *Digital city-the 21 century's life style*. Beijing, China: CyberGIS Studio, Peking University, Institute of Remote Sensing & GIS. Retrieved April, 2005, from http://unpan1.un.org

Mountihno, J., & Heitor, M. (2003, September 18-19). Digital Cities and the challenges for a Knowledge-Based View of the Territory: evidence from Portugal. In *Proceedings of the Digital 3 Workshop "Local Information and Communication Infrastructures: experiences and challenges*, Amsterdam, The Netherlands.

New Millennium Research Council. (2005). *Not In The Public Interest – The Myth of Municipal Wi-Fi Networks*.Retrieved July, 2009, from http://www.broadbandcity.gr/content/modules/downloads/Not_In_The_Public_Interest_The_Myth_of_Municipal_WiFi_Networks_(New_Millenium_Research_Council).pdf

New York City Economic Development Corporation. (2005). *Telecommunications and Economic Development in New York City: A Plan of Action*. Retrieved April, 2005, from http://newyorkbiz.com/about_us/TelecomPlanMarch2005.pdf

Osaka, I. C. T. Industry (2008). *Ubiquitous City Osaka*. Online Publication. Retrieved April 28th, 2009, from http://www.ibpcosaka.or.jp/invest/e/environment/ict/ICT2007e.pdf

Partridge, H. (2004). Developing a Human Perspective to the Digital Divide in the Smart City. In *Proceedings of the "ALIA 2004, challenging ideas*, Queensland University of Tehcnology Brisbane, Australia.

Sairamesh, J., Lee, A., & Anania, L. (2004, February). Information Cities. *Communications of the ACM*, *47*(2).

Sproull, L., & Patterson, J. (2004, February). Making Information Cities Livable. *Communications of the ACM*, *49*(2).

Townsend, A. (2004, December 7). Seoul: Birth of a Broadband Metropolis. *Environment and Planning B*, *34*(3), 396–413.

United Nations. (2008). *UN E-Government Survey – From e-Government to Connected Government. United Nations*. Retrieved 2008, from http://unpan1.un.org/intradoc/ groups/public/documents/UN/UNPAN028607.pdf

Van Bastelaer, B. (1998, October 29-30) Digital Cities and transferability of results. In *Proceedings of the 4th EDC Conference on Digital Cities*, Salzburg, Germany (pp. 61-70).

Van den Besselaar & P., Beckers, D. (1998) Demographics and Sociographics of the digital city. In *Community Computing and Support Systems* (pp. 108-124), Berlin, Germany: Springer Verlag.

Wang, L., & Wu, H. (2001). *A Framework of Integrating digital city and Eco-city. School of Business, Hubei University, Wuhan, China*. Retrieved March, 2005, from www.hku.hk/cupem/asiagis/fall03/Full_Paper/Wang_Lu.pdf

Widmayer, P. (1999). Building Digital Metropolis: Chicago's Future Networks. *IT Professional*, *1*(4), 40–46. doi:10.1109/6294.781624

Wikipedia (2009). *The Definition of the Ubiquitous City*. Retrieved April 28th, 2009, from http://en.wikipedia.org/wiki/Ubiquitous_city

Zook, M., Dodge, M., Aoyama, Y., & Townsend, A. (2004). *"New Digital Geographies: Information, Communication and Place"*. *Geography and Technology*. The Netherlands: Kluwer Academic Publishers.

KEY TERMS AND DEFINITIONS

E-Government: The implementation and delivery of digital public services to citizens and enterprises.

E-Governance: The transformation of the public sector into a more efficient form, able to execute simplified public services, to minimize operation costs and to respond with means closer to the private sector.

Ubiquitous Computing: Ubiquitous computing names the third wave in computing, just now beginning. First were mainframes, each shared by lots of people. Now we are in the personal computing era, person and machine staring uneasily at each other across the desktop. Next comes ubiquitous computing, or the age of calm technology, when technology recedes into the background of our lives. Alan Kay of Apple calls this "Third Paradigm" computing. Mark Weiser is the father of ubiquitous computing (http://sandbox.xerox.com/ubicomp/).

Chapter 18
Explaining the Global Digital Divide:
The Impact of Public Policy Initiatives on E-Government Capacity and Reach Worldwide

Girish J. Gulati
Bentley University, USA

David J. Yates
Bentley University, USA

Anas Tawileh
Cardiff University, UK

ABSTRACT

The rapid development of information and communication technologies (ICTs) has created an environment for citizens to have greater access to their government and to make citizen-to-government contact more inclusive. Previous research does not provide a comprehensive explanation for variation in recent e-government initiatives and, in particular, the impact of national public policy initiatives that seek to expand access to ICTs. This chapter examines the global digital divide by analyzing the impact of national policies on the ITU's Digital Opportunity Index and the UN's Web Measure Index in 171 countries. A multivariate regression analysis shows that when controlling for economic, social and political development, there is greater capacity for e-governance in countries that have a regulatory authority for telecommunications, competition in telecommunication industries, and higher financial investment in technological development. The analysis also shows that none of the examined policy initiatives appear to affect the reach of ICTs within countries.

DOI: 10.4018/978-1-61520-933-0.ch018

INTRODUCTION

E-government refers to the use of information and communication technologies (ICTs) to provide and improve government services, transactions with constituents, and connections with other arms of government (Fang, 2002). In theory, the rapid development of information and communication technologies (ICTs) over the past 25 years should have created an environment for citizens across the globe to have greater access to their elected representatives and policy makers and to make citizen-to-government contact more inclusive. In practice, the realities of e-government are more complicated. For businesses and the middle class in many countries, the benefits of e-government include better access to public information and improved delivery of government services. For the less fortunate and more isolated members of society, e-government and advances in technology can help overcome the geographical, institutional, and social barriers to information and communication technologies. In the early stages of development, however, new technologies may reinforce or even widen existing economic, political and social inequalities between the haves and have-nots (Forestier, Grace & Kenny, 2002; Guillén & Suárez, 2005; van Dijk, 2005).

Concerns over an emerging "digital divide" between developed and developing countries also have captured the attention of researchers and policymakers and now is seen as significant a problem as the divide within national boundaries (*The Economist*, 2005; Hudson, 2006). Much of the previous research supports the view that technological advances mostly have created new or exacerbated existing inequalities between the information rich and poor, both within nations and between nations (Mossberger, Tolbert & Gilbert, 2006; van Dijk, 2005; Yates, McGonagle & Tawileh, 2008). Most of these studies, however, have tended to be either largely descriptive or qualitative case studies of a limited number of countries. While a few of these studies have at-tempted to provide comprehensive explanations for the global digital divide, almost all have been hindered by access to recent data for a large number of cases (Baliamoune-Lutz, 2003; Guillén & Suárez, 2005; Robison & Crenshaw, 2002; Zhao et al. 2007). None of the larger-N studies (Azari & Pick, 2009; Chinn & Fairlie, 2007; Fuchs, 2009; Kim, 2007; Norris, 2001; Pick & Azari, 2008; West, 2005), moreover, have assessed the impact of national public policy initiatives that encourage e-governance and expand access to ICTs and, as a result, mitigate the advantages enjoyed by the most affluent countries.

This chapter examines the global digital divide by analyzing the impact of national policy initiatives on the availability of e-government resources and the public's access to telecommunication products and services. After reviewing the findings from previous cross-national analyses and numerous case studies, we develop a series of testable hypotheses on the impact that national strategic planning, deregulation of the telecommunications industries, and financial investment in ICTs have on a nation's performance in developing e-government capabilities and in promoting opportunities for citizens to participate in the global information society (G-8, 2000; Porat, 1977). To test our hypotheses, we use multivariate regression analysis to estimate the effects of policy variables on the United Nations' Web Measure Index and the International Telecommunication Union's Digital Opportunity Index in 171 countries. We show that when controlling for measures of economic, social and political development, public policy initiatives at the national level have a strong, significant impact on the development of e-governance. These same policy initiatives have little or no impact on increasing the diffusion of ICTs, however. We conclude with a discussion of why policy initiatives have not always been able to bridge the digital divide and suggest alternatives to help lesser-developed countries increase access to technology for their citizens.

BACKGROUND

The potential for information and communication technologies (ICTs) to transform society and tackle development challenges has been the subject of considerable debate. Several researchers maintain that ICTs can play a significant role as a powerful enabler for nations, societies and individuals (Avgerou, 1998; Dutton & Peltu, 1996; Heeks, 2008; Schech, 2002). Some also suggest that ICTs can facilitate a more inclusive democratic discourse between citizens and their governments (Hague & Loader, 1999; Orihuela & Obi, 2007). These arguments, however, have been countered by others who question the potential for ICTs for development and argue that these technologies have largely reinforced, and sometimes widened, inequalities within and between countries. Fuchs (2009), Haywood (1998), Norris (2001) and West (2005), among others, report significant divisions in the use of ICTs along the lines of education, income, race, ethnicity, gender, language, age and disability.

The digital divide within national boundaries can be as significant as it is between developing and developed countries. For example, Meng and Li (2002) highlight the digital divide between the three main economic regions in China: eastern, central and western. They demonstrate a significant disparity in per capita ICT investment in these three regions. Other indicators in which they found high variability include penetration rates for telephones: 15.41 per 100 in the eastern region, 7.58 in the central and 5.53 in the western (1999), and Internet users: 0.56%, 0.14% and 0.18% for the same regions respectively.

Access to ICTs in Latin America has been shown to differ mainly based on income. ICTs are thus considered to be poor tools to promote equality (Forestier, Grace & Kenny, 2002). In fact, the high cost of access to ICTs in developing nations excludes the majority of the population from the information society. High ICT cost also exacerbates the income divide by adding layers of information inequality between those who can afford to pay for ICT services and those who cannot (Guillén & Suárez, 2005). Similar obstacles and challenges appear across the African continent. In Ghana and South Africa, for example, Fuchs & Horak (2008) describe how inherent divisions and inequalities due mainly to poverty and illiteracy have hindered the efforts to bridge the digital divide.

Inequalities in the access to ICTs (van Dijk, 2000) result from four main hurdles: (a) lack of basic skills and 'computer fear'; (b) no access to computers and networks; (c) insufficient user friendliness; (d) insufficient and unevenly distributed usage opportunities. Hence, policy makers need to understand the role of ICTs in relation to people's ability to participate in society in order to formulate and implement sound policies to promote equality and participation (Norris, 2001; Robison & Crenshaw, 2002; van Dijk, 2005).

Sreekumar (2007) goes further to suggest that ICTs can, in addition to reinforcing existing social divides, create new divides. His study of the cyber kiosks in rural India reveals "abysmally low" participation of among women and the underprivileged in ICT projects and initiatives. The question of inclusion, according to Sreekumar, needs to be addressed as "a matter of structure rather than choice.". This is particularly important as the Internet becomes the "the dominant domain of the public sphere as well as the site of governmental action and service delivery" (Sreekumar, 2007). Odame (2005) elaborates on the divisions across gender barriers and suggests that women's ability to utilize ICTs to improve their public sector participation is severely limited by income, education, mobility and religious constraints.

In an attempt to leverage the potential of ICTs for socio-economic development, many countries have crafted ICT strategies and formulated policies to increase the adoption of ICTs among their citizens and stimulate participation in public discourse. Few studies analyze the impact of national policies on addressing the digital divide.

Furthermore, many of these studies (Beilock & Dimitrova, 2003; Fuchs, 2009; Guillén & Suárez, 2005; Maitland & Bauer, 2001; Robison & Crenshaw, 2002; Volken, 2002; Zhao et al. 2007) focus primarily on Internet penetration as a measure of the digital divide. These studies show that competition to deliver telecommunication services lowers the cost of access to ICTs, and that higher income results in higher Internet usage. Guillén & Suárez (2005), for example, analyzed the impact of regulatory, political, and sociological variables on global Internet growth and concluded that "differences in Internet use are the result of an array of forces over which governments and multilateral organizations have varying degrees of influence." In particular, they found that privatization and deregulation of the telecommunications sector are policies that are highly effective in increasing Internet penetration.

Some studies find that the symptoms of a growing digital divide between the information haves and have-nots persist even in the face of aggressive policy initiatives. Fuchs & Horak's (2008) study of digital inequalities in South Africa found that market liberalization was unable to narrow the digital divide, mainly due to vast inequalities in income distribution and social, educational and skills barriers. Similarly in Ghana, liberalization of the telecommunications sector and capital investment by the public sector were unable to overcome inequalities in wealth and education.

The findings from past research suggest that national policy initiatives are instrumental in developing the information and communication technology sectors, which, in turn, have encouraged greater government responsiveness to the public through the use of technology and broadened the availability of ICT products and services. We hypothesize that

(H₁): National policy initiatives to promote information and communication technologies increase a nation's capacity for e-government.

Although the evidence in the case studies is somewhat mixed with respect to extending the reach of ICTs, we hypothesize that after controlling for wealth and other factors, that

(H₂): National policy initiatives to promote information and communication technologies increase a nation's diffusion of ICTs.

While previous research provides rich detail on the connection between technology policy and e-government capacity and reach, as well as the challenges to realizing these policy objectives, it is impossible to make any valid generalizations on the contribution that government policies have in bridging the digital divide relative to other factors. To date, there has not been any research that has used a large-scale, cross-national approach to assess the impact of national public policy initiatives that seek to expand access to ICTs. With data we present below, we test our two research hypotheses to develop a comprehensive understanding of the role of national policy initiatives in bridging the global digital divide.

IMPACT OF POLICY INITIATIVES ON E-GOVERNMENT CAPACITY AND REACH

Data and Methods

To test our hypotheses that policy initiatives contribute to explaining variation in e-government capacity and digital opportunity, we estimated two multivariate regression models that build on the models specified by Fuchs (2009), Kim (2007), Norris (2001) and West (2005) in their cross-national studies. While these large-scale, cross-national studies and the research described earlier in this chapter offer significant insight into the reasons behind low ICT usage and low Internet penetration, all of these studies have offered a narrow focus on access to ICTs as the primary measure of the digital divide. In their paper "From the 'digital divide' to 'digital inequality': Studying Internet use as penetration increases", DiMaggio & Hargittai (2001) argue for a shift in attention from the digital divide to *digital inequality*, where digital inequality refers "not just to differences in access, but also to inequality *among* persons with formal access to the Internet."

In keeping with this suggestion, we measure the digital divide in two complementary dimensions. First, our indicator for e-government capacity and dependent variable in the first model is the United Nations' Web Measure Index (WMI) for 2008, a subset of the broader E-Government Readiness Index. We did not use the full E-Government Readiness Index because many of its individual indicators measure telecommunication infrastructure and education levels, which would be redundant with independent variables that we intended to include in our models and that we discuss below. Constructed for 184 countries, the Web Measure Index measures the extent of e-government capacity by assessing the services and information available on a country's national government's Web sites. Values on this index can range from 0 to 1, with Denmark (1.0), Sweden (0.98) and the United States (0.95) exhibiting the highest scores, and the Central African Republic, Somalia, and Zambia exhibiting the lowest (0.0).[1]

Our indicator for diffusion of ICTs and dependent variable in the second model is the International Telecommunication Union's Digital Opportunity Index (DOI) for 2006/07. Constructed for 175 countries, the DOI measures digital opportunity by assessing the widespread availability of various telecommunication services and information technologies. Values on this index can range from 0 to 1, with South Korea exhibiting the highest score (0.80) and Chad, Guinea-Bissau, and Myanmar exhibiting the lowest (0.04).[2]

Our independent variables include four policy variables and three variables that have been found to be related to e-government capacity and diffusion of ICTs in previous studies.

Resources and Capacity

Previous cross-national studies of e-government capacity have assumed that countries with more wealth and an affluent population will be in a stronger position to spend more on technological development. In addition, people who have a higher level of education are more likely to favor a government that is more transparent and participatory and to demand more advanced information technology and telecommunication products and services (Fuchs, 2009; Norris, 2001; West 2005). Furthermore, more affluent and technologically-developed societies are more likely to make ICTs available to a mass audience (Bimber, 2003). The empirical evidence linking resources to e-government capacity and reach has not shown a consistent pattern, however. The absence of a clear, discernable pattern could be the result of analysts using different indicators for resources in their models or using indicators that capture only a small portion of the underlying concept (Norris, 2001; West, 2005).

We use the United Nations' Human Development Index (HDI) for 2008 to account for a nation's economic resources and human capacity. The HDI combines measures of a country's gross domestic product, living standards, literacy rates, and mortality rates into a single, more comprehensive indicator of a nation's resources and has been used extensively in cross-national studies of development (Lijphart, 1999). The HDI was computed for 176 countries, with scores ranging from 0.339 for Sierra Leone to 0.968 for Iceland.

Political Freedom and Structure

Societies that allow for peaceful transitions of power, widespread electoral participation, and checks on power also are more likely to demand that government use new means for providing transparency and citizen participation. Democratic governments also should be inclined to be more inclusive in an attempt to widen its electoral appeal. Moreover, societies that have a culture of encouraging political expression and facilitating communication between government and citizens are more likely to demand that their governments use technology to provide more transparency and avenues for participation (Dahl, 1989; Kim, 2007; Lijphart, 1999).

To account for the impact of the political structure and a culture of democratic politics, we included the Center for Systemic Peace's Polity 2 score for 2007. The Polity 2 score aggregates 11 indicators of institutionalized democracy and 11 indicators of institutionalized autocracy into a single measure of democratic government. These indicators assess the competitiveness of political participation in the country, the openness and competitiveness of executive recruitment, and constraints on the government's chief executive. Indicators for the extent of civil liberties and press freedom are not part of the Polity 2 score. Values on Polity 2 normally range from -10 to 10, with Qatar and Saudi Arabia obtaining scores of -10 and 23 countries obtaining scores of 10.[3] For political freedom, we standardized Freedom House's Press Freedom Index (a measure of the extent of the free flow of information) and Civil Liberties Index (a broad measure of the extent of free expression) and then averaged the two indices to construct a broader measure of political freedom. Iceland and Finland scored highest on this measure (1.35), while North Korea (-2.01) and Myanmar (-1.99) scored the lowest.[4]

National Regulatory Authority

A review of a number of case studies indicate that nations that have been most successful at developing information and communication technologies are those that have established an independent executive-level department or national-level agency responsible for promoting and managing the expansion of telecommunication products and services (Azari & Pick, 2009; Chinn & Fairlie, 2007; Hudson, 2006; ITU, 2007; Keniston &

Kumar, 2004; Pick & Azari, 2008; UN ESCAP, 2007). We should expect that establishment of these types of telecommunications regulatory bodies should also lead to modernization of ICTs within government including the electronic means of communicating with the public. Thus, countries with the presence of some sort of independent regulatory authority should be expected to score higher on the Web Measure Index than those countries that do not. With regards to diffusion of ICTs, however, we expect that in some countries the presence of a national regulatory authority, might be helpful, too new or powerless to have an impact, or even harmful.

(H_{1a}): A national telecommunications regulatory authority increases a nation's capacity for e-government.

(H_{2a}): A national telecommunications regulatory authority increases a nation's diffusion of ICTs.

Data indicating whether or not a country had a national regulatory authority for telecommunications in 2007 were obtained from the International Telecommunication Union's ICT Eye database. This variable was coded "1" if an authority was present in that year and "0" if it was not. In 2007, 76% of the countries had established a national regulatory authority for telecommunications.[5] Each country's score on the National Regulatory Agency variable and the other three policy variables are provided in the Appendix.

Competition in Telecommunication Industries

Previous research also reveals that nations with greater ICT development are those that have more competition for providing basic telecommunication services (Guillén & Suárez, 2005; Hudson, 2006; ITU, 2007; Keniston & Kumar 2004; World Bank, 2006). Many of these same studies and others highlight the decisions that governments made when the mobile telecommunications industry was in its infancy. Rather than control, subsidize, or try to actively promote competition in the development of this industry, many governments took a more laissez-faire approach to this industry and allowed the marketplace to allocate resources (Garrard, 1997; ITU, 2007; World Bank, 2006). Countries that have competitive, less-regulated telecommunication industries should have a higher score on the e-government index than those countries that have regulated or publicly-owned phone industries.

(H$_{1b}$): Competition in basic telecommunication services increases a nation's capacity for e-government.

(H$_{2b}$): Competition in basic telecommunication services increases digital opportunity for a nation's citizens.

(H$_{1c}$): Competition in mobile telecommunication services increases a nation's capacity for e-government.

(H$_{2c}$): Competition in mobile telecommunication services increases digital opportunity for a nation's citizens.

Data indicating the presence or absence of competition in the fixed-line and mobile telecommunication industries also were obtained from the International Telecommunication Union's ICT Eye database. Our indicator for fixed line competition was coded "1" if the ITU characterized the industry as fully competitive, "0.5" if the industry was characterized as partially competitive, and "0" if the industry was either publicly-owned or was a government-regulated monopoly. The same coding procedure was used to categorize the level of competition in the mobile telecommunications market.

Financial Investment

The case studies are clear that the information technology and telecommunication industries have flourished when the public sector has made direct financial investment in the relevant infrastructure and structural resources (Hudson, 2006; Servon, 2002). Private sector investment in the form of research and development spending also has been essential in developing these industries (Azari & Pick, 2009; Dutton & Peltu, 1996; Nixon & Koutrakou, 2007).

(H$_{1d}$): Higher financial investment in the ICT sector increases a nation's capacity for e-government.

(H$_{2d}$): Higher financial investment in the ICT sector increases a nation's diffusion of ICTs.

We reviewed a number of indicators in the World Bank's Work Development Indicators (WDI) database that could measure the financial resources that a nation invests in information technology and telecommunications. None of the indicators provided a comprehensive picture of investment, but focused on only a small segment of government and industry activity. To address this concern, we constructed an additive index of seven indicators of a nation's financial commitment to developing ICTs. These seven indicators are:

1. Telecommunications revenue (as a percentage of GDP);
2. Telecommunications investment (as a percentage of revenue);
3. Research & development spending (as a percentage of GDP);
4. ICT expenditures (as a percentage of GDP);
5. Computer, communications and other services (as a percentage of service exports);
6. High-technology exports (as a percentage of manufacturing exports); and
7. Natural log of international Internet bandwidth (bits per second per person).

Table 1. The impact of policy initiatives on e-government capacity: Multivariate regression analysis of the web measure Index.

	Unstandardized Coefficients		Standardized	
	B	Std. Error	Beta	Sig.
(Constant)	-0.332	0.068		0.000
Affluence (HDI)	0.717	0.077	0.552	0.000
Democracy (Polity 2)	0.004	0.002	0.149	0.006
Political freedom index	0.002	0.016	0.007	0.921
Policy variables				
National regulatory authority (1=present)	0.072	0.031	0.120	0.019
Competition in basic services (1=full)	0.095	0.028	0.184	0.001
Competition in mobile services (1=full)	0.070	0.035	0.101	0.046
Financial investment index	0.052	0.025	0.114	0.036

N = 173; Adjusted R Squared = 0.658; Std. Error of the Estimate = 0.134.

Of the nearly 240 variables available in the WDI database, we selected these seven because of their conceptual connection to investment in information or communication technology. Because most of the benefits of investment may not be realized until a few years into the future, we measure investment over a number of years by averaging the data available between 2000 and 2007. The average over this period also was used for practical reasons: the data were not reported every year for every country. Once averages were computed for each indicator, we standardized each average in the form of Z-scores and then computed the average score across the seven indicators for each country. An ICT investment score was able to be computed for 190 countries, with values ranging from 1.74 (Macedonia and Liechtenstein) to -1.81 (Liberia). The two countries with the highest scores had missing data on many other variables and, thus, were excluded from the analysis. Of the countries used in the analysis, the Philippines had the highest score, at 1.18.

Data Analysis and Findings

E-Government Capacity

The results of the regression analysis of the Web Measure Index (WMI) on four policy variables, the two political variables, and the Human Development Index are reported in Table 1. The independent variables together explain 65.8% of the variance in the WMI. This represents a substantial improvement over past cross-national studies that were limited in their access to valid data measuring core concepts and did not include policy variables in their models (Kim, 2007; Norris, 2001; West 2005).

The coefficients in the first row indicate that there is a strong connection between the affluence of a country and the availability of government information and services online. When holding all other variables constant, a 0.01 unit increase in a country's score on the HDI increases their score on the Web Measure Index by nearly 0.072 on the 0 to 1 scale. The coefficients are statistically significant at the .01 level and provide support for the widespread view that countries with higher levels of wealth, education, and other quality of life measures will be the most likely to provide its citizens with services online.

The second and third rows of data report the coefficients for political structure and political freedom. The coefficients for political structure indicate that countries that are the most democratic are the most likely to provide information and government services online. A one unit increase in a country's Polity 2 score increases a country's score on the WMI by 0.004 when controlling for all other variables. Unlike in Norris (2001) and West (2005), we find that the relationship between democracy and e-government capacity to be statistically significant, supporting the view that that democratic governments are more responsive to citizen' demands. In substantive terms, however, the impact of the *level* of democracy is somewhat small. On the -10 to 10 scale, the difference between a country who scored a 5 (e.g., Russia) on the Polity 2 score and a country who scored a 10 (e.g., the United States) would be only 0.02 on the WMI. Moreover, the difference between the United States and a country such as Saudi Arabia who scored on the bottom of the Polity 2 score would be only .08.

The coefficients for political freedom are not significant at any conventional level of statistical significance and indicate that e-government capacity is not a function of a more open or free society. This finding offers no evidence for the view that a culture of protecting political expression and facilitating communication between government and citizens encourage governments to use the Internet to provide more transparency and avenues for participation. Thus, while e-government seems to be a natural feature of democratic governments, a longstanding culture of political communication does not seem to affect whether that citizen-to-government communication should also take place online.

The coefficients in the next row indicate that countries that have a national regulatory authority for information technology and communication have a greater online presence than countries that do not have a nationwide agency. When holding all other variables constant, countries with a national

regulatory authority increase their score on the Web Measure Index by 0.07 on the 0 to 1 scale. The coefficients are statistically significant at the .05 level and provide support for our hypothesis (H_{1a}) that those countries that have a coordinated national strategy for developing ICTs will be more likely to provide their citizens with services online. Moreover, the regression results indicate that the effect of national strategy can be quite substantial. Estonia, for example, would drop from 12th to 21st in the rankings on the Web Measure Index, below the Czech Republic and in a tie with New Zealand. At the same time, the absence of a national authority in China may explain partially its 48th place ranking and why it has fewer e-government services than lesser-developed countries such as Bolivia and the Dominican Republic.

The fifth and sixth rows of data report the coefficients for competition in local services and competition in the mobile market. These coefficients indicate that countries that have open competition in these two telecommunication industries also have a greater online presence than countries that have a more regulated market. Countries with competition in their fixed line telecommunication industry increase their score on the Web Measure Index by almost 0.10 when controlling for all other variables. Competition in the mobile phone industry increases their score by 0.07. Both sets of coefficients provide support for our hypotheses (H_{1b} at the .01 level, and H_{1c} at the .05 level) that countries that have competition in their telecommunication industries will be more likely to provide e-government services. Privatization in both industries can create a highly favorable environment for government to develop online service delivery and communications with its citizens. The United Arab Emirates and Kuwait share similar economic, political, and social characteristics, but the UAE (0.72) scores much higher on the Web Measure Index than Kuwait (0.41). The findings here suggest that some of this difference can be attributed to competition in fixed-line and mobile services in the UAE and a closed market in these industries in Kuwait. Not only do service providers have a more efficient means of providing the infrastructure to connect citizens and their government, governments are able to purchase the appropriate products and services to implement e-government, and citizens have more choices in service providers.

The coefficients for ICT investment indicate that countries that devote more financial resources to developing and promoting information technology, telecommunications, and other communication industries also are more likely to develop an online presence for their governments. When controlling for the effects of all other variables, a one-unit increase in the indicator for ICT investment leads to an increase of 0.05 on the Web Measure Index. In other words, a country that invests the mean value on our index of financial investment would have a score 0.05 higher on the WMI than a country that invested one standard deviation below the mean. And a country that invested an amount equal to about one standard deviation above the mean would be 0.05 points higher on the e-government score than a country at the mean and more than 0.1 above a country that had invested an amount that was one standard deviation less than the mean. Singapore's score on our ICT investment index was about one standard deviation above the mean and score on the Web Measure Index was 0.61. India's score on the ICT investment scale was closer to the mean, 0.07, and score on the Web Index was 0.48. This analysis indicates that increased investment in ICTs could help India close the gap in e-government capacity with their regional neighbor (as suggested by H_{1d}).

Together, these four policy variables can increase a government's capacity to provide information and services electronically by a substantial margin. Establishing a national regulatory authority, allowing for competitive fixed-line and mobile telecommunication markets, and increasing investment in ICT development could raise a country's e-government capacity as measured by the Web Measure Index by almost 0.3. Past cross-national studies that have excluded policy variables from their models (Kim, 2007; Norris, 2001; West, 2005) have been able to provide only a limited explanation for variation in e-government capacity. While a country's affluence explains much of the reason that a nation rises to the top of the rankings for e-government capacity (and is the primary source of the global digital divide), it is the policy variables that seem to help explain variation within the group of wealthy countries. In addition, among nations that are not as affluent, well thought out policy initiatives can have a substantial effect on increasing that nation's e-government capabilities.

Information and Communication Technology Diffusion

The results of the regression analysis of the Digital Opportunity Index (DOI) on our four policy variables, two political variables, and the Human Development Index are reported in Table 2. The independent variables together explain 83.4% of the variance in the DOI. The coefficients in the first row of Table 2 indicate that there also is a strong connection between the affluence of a country and the opportunity for citizens to participate in the global information society. When holding all other variables constant, a 0.01 unit in a country's score on the HDI increases their score on the DOI by nearly 0.081 on the 0 to 1 scale. The coefficients are statistically significant at the .01 level and show that the benefits of technology are available to a larger portion of a country's population in countries with higher levels of affluence.

The second and third rows of data report the coefficients for political structure and political freedom. In contrast to what we found in the model of e-government capacity, the coefficients for political structure are not statistically significant and indicate that the inequities of the digital divide do not vary by the level of democracy in a country. Also unlike the e-government model, the

Table 2. The impact of policy initiatives on diffusion of ICTs: multivariate regression analysis of the digital opportunity index.

	Unstandardized Coefficients		Standardized	
	B	Std. Error	Beta	Sig.
(Constant)	-0.208	0.039		0.000
Affluence (HDI)	0.807	0.044	0.744	0.000
Democracy (Polity 2)	0.000	0.001	-0.015	0.688
Political freedom index	0.037	0.009	0.189	0.000
Policy variables				
National regulatory authority (1=present)	-0.022	0.018	-0.045	0.207
Competition in basic services (1=full)	0.031	0.016	0.073	0.062
Competition in mobile services (1=full)	0.033	0.020	0.057	0.105
Financial investment index	0.023	0.014	0.059	0.114

N = 171; Adjusted R Squared = 0.834; Std. Error of the Estimate = 0.077.

results for the digital opportunity model show that the diffusion of technology is more widespread in countries with more political freedom. Holding all other variables constant, a one unit increase in the political freedom index increases a country's score on the DOI by 0.037. This relationship is statistically significant at the .01 level, supporting the hypothesis that a longstanding commitment to civil liberties and political communication will lead to more widespread availability of communication technologies (Beilock & Dimitrova, 2003; Robison & Crenshaw, 2002). In substantive terms, however, the impact of the *level* of political freedom is quite small. Comparing Russia (-1.22) and the United States (1.18) again, the difference in scores on the political freedom index is quite substantial. Yet an absence of any difference on this index would reduce the difference between the two countries on the DOI by less than 0.09.

The coefficients in the next row of Table 2 indicate that a country's ranking on the DOI is not affected by the presence or absence of a national regulatory authority for telecommunications and, thus contradicts our hypothesis (H_{2a}) that it would increase the diffusion of technologies. While a national regulatory body seems to have been essential in helping government provide information

and services online, it has not been helpful in making the benefits of ICTs widely available. We suspect that the reason for this observation is that a national telecommunications regulatory body not only needs to be well established, but also be supporting helpful policy initiatives. Perhaps the most important policy initiative is competition in providing telecommunication services. However, many national regulatory authorities support privately-held or state-owned monopolies in the telecommunications industry.

The coefficients in the fifth and sixth rows indicate that a country's ranking on the Digital Opportunity Index also is not affected by the presence or absence of competition in basic telecommunication services or mobile telecommunication services. These observations contradict our hypotheses (H_{2b} and H_{2c}) that competition in these sectors would increase diffusion of ICTs. The results for mobile telecommunication services are particularly surprising since mobile communication is increasingly important in the developing world. There are now three times more mobile phone users than land-line phone users. Also, the capabilities of mobile communication devices increase and/or become more affordable every year. It is possible that this combination of trends explains why competition to provide fixed-line telecommunication services does not have a significant impact on a nation's digital opportunity, but it is unclear why competition to provide mobile services also does not have a significant impact.

The coefficients for ICT investment indicate that there is no relationship between the amount of financial resources that a country invests in developing and promoting ICTs and the widespread availability of ICTs. This finding contradicts the hypothesis (H_{2d}) that higher levels of investment in telecommunications infrastructure, products and services will increases the extent of technology diffusion in a country. As has been the case with the development of new information and communication technologies in the past, the first gains are made in infrastructure development and distribution to business and industry as well as the most affluent in society. As the production of products that rely on broadband and next-generation mobile technology increases and the demand in the commercial sectors slows, prices to consumers are likely to fall and make these products more widely available (Rogers, 1995). Thus, it may be that in most countries that have invested greatly in ICT development, demand for new ICTs has yet to reach a critical mass.

While policy variables were found to be essential in increasing a country's capacity to provide information and services on-line, these same policies had little or no effect in expanding opportunities for the public so that they could access electronic information and communication services. Rather, a country's affluence explains much of the reason that a nation rises to the top of the rankings for digital opportunity and is the primary resource for bridging the digital divide within a country. In addition to affluence, greater political freedom expands digital opportunity for a nation's citizens.

FUTURE RESEARCH DIRECTIONS

Using multivariate regression analysis, the results in this chapter show that when controlling for economic, social and political development, there is greater capacity for e-governance in countries that have a regulatory authority for telecommunications, competition in the telecommunication industries, and higher financial investment in technological development. The same policy initiatives, however, do not appear to have a significant impact on a country's diffusion of information and communication technologies.

The four policy variables we examine capture important policy initiatives; however, no set of policy variables is ever complete. We urge future researchers to expand the list of policy variables we use in this chapter. The ITU ICT databases include other policy variables that should be of theoretical interest to others. We encourage researchers to review the ITU data to use in their own work and maybe even to inspire new research questions. And of course, policymakers will continue to develop new initiatives to further modernize government services and address unequal access to technology and, thus, provide us with even more avenues for future research.

One possible area of future research may be to explore possible conditional relationships between digital opportunity and competition in basic services, competition in mobile services, and financial investment. The coefficients for basic services are significant at the .10 level and the coefficients for mobile services and ICT investment are significant at nearly the .10 level, .11 to be precise. While this likely means that there is no relationship between digital opportunity and these policy variables, it also is possible that there is a significant relationship under certain conditions or in certain types of countries.

Another possible area of research is to examine further the resources of the national regulatory authorities, their relationship with the private sector, and what these agencies actually do. Some of these agencies not only are granted considerable resources in terms of money and staff by their national governments, but also have a greater institutional presence, which allows them to have greater influence over telecommunications policy and regulation. Some agencies may be able to manage business investment decisions in a way that serves the public interest, while others are present to promote the interests of the industry.

Another possible area of future research is to consider additional (and alternative) outcome variables to determine the effectiveness of national public policy with respect to e-government capacity and reach. While we chose the Web Measure Index and the Digital Opportunity Index as dependent variables to model the capacity of e-governments and the diffusion of ICTs, respectively, Kim (2007) and West (2005, 2008) use a somewhat different methodology to rank countries in their level of e-government readiness. In addition, all of these e-government indices have several sub-components, allowing researchers to estimate the effect of policy variables separately for information, functionality and effectiveness. One might also want to go in a different direction by using these indices as independent variables in order to assess the impact that e-government has on increasing political participation and civic engagement as well as cultivating trust in and satisfaction with government.

CONCLUSION

The development of information and communication technologies (ICTs) has created an environment for citizens across the globe to have greater access to their elected representatives and policy makers and to make citizen-to-government contact more inclusive. Much of the previous research suggests that these technological advances have mostly exacerbated existing inequalities between developed and developing nations and created new inequalities within societies between the

information rich and poor. There seems to have been very little research, however, that provides comprehensive explanations for the global digital divide and, in particular, the impact of national public policy initiatives that seek to expand e-government capacity and access to ICTs. Most of these studies have tended to be either largely descriptive, qualitative case studies, or quantitative analyses that have had a narrow concept of ICTs. While a few studies have attempted to provide comprehensive explanations for the global digital divide, almost all have been hindered by access to recent data for a large number of cases. Our study is the first large-N study to assess the impact of national public policy initiatives on encouraging e-governance and expanding access to ICTs.

This chapter examined the global digital divide by analyzing the impact of national public policies on the UN's Web Measure Index and ITU's Digital Opportunity Index in 171 countries. Specifically, we developed a series of testable hypotheses on the impact that national strategic planning, competition in the telecommunication industries, and financial investment in ICTs have on a nation's performance in developing e-government capabilities and promoting opportunities for citizens to participate in the information society. We find that polices matter and, as a result, mitigate, to some extent, the advantages enjoyed by the most affluent countries. When controlling for economic, social and political development, there is greater capacity for e-governance in countries that have a regulatory authority for telecommunications, competition in the associated industries, and higher investment in technological development. The same policy initiatives, however, do not appear to have a significant impact on a country's diffusion of information and communication technologies. Instead, we find that diffusion of ICTs among citizens is mostly explained by a nation's affluence (or human development) and political freedom. Of the specific policy efforts examined, it is clear that enabling competition in the telecommunication industries has the greatest impact on the capacity of e-government and the diffusion of ICTs.

Yet, while we present strong evidence that policies matter, we also show that resources in terms of wealth, education and quality of life matter more for leveraging the benefits of e-government capacity and digital opportunity. Thus, we also show the limits that technology and policy have in addressing the digital divide, at least in the short-term. While our findings offer an important contribution to study of the relationship between technology, policy and inequality, we hope that it also will guide decision makers in capitals across the globe to take an active role both in developing the ICT sector, but also with the purpose of improving human development, which, in turn, may allow the current information and communication revolution to improve the lives of those who have yet to benefit.

REFERENCES

Avgerou, C. (1998). How can IT enable economic growth in developing countries? *Information Technology for Development, 8*(1), 15–28.

Azari, R., & Pick, J. B. (2009). Understanding global digital inequality: The impact of government, investment in business and technology, and socioeconomic factors on technology utilization. In *42nd Hawaii International Conference on System Sciences,* Waikoloa, Big Island, HI.

Baliamoune-Lutz, M. (2003). An analysis of the determinants and effects of ICT diffusion in developing countries. *Information Technology for Development, 10*(3), 151–169. doi:10.1002/itdj.1590100303

Beilock, R., & Dimitrova, D. V. (2003). An exploratory model of inter-country Internet diffusion. *Telecommunications Policy, 27*(3-4), 237–252. doi:10.1016/S0308-5961(02)00100-3

Bimber, B. (2003). *Information and American democracy: Technology in the evolution of political power*. New York: Oxford University Press. doi:10.1017/CBO9780511615573

Chinn, M. D., & Fairlie, R. W. (2007). The determinants of the global digital divide: A cross-country analysis of computer and Internet penetration. *Oxford Economic Papers, 59*(1), 16–44. doi:10.1093/oep/gpl024

Dahl, R. A. (1989). *Democracy and its critics*. New Haven, CT: Yale University Press.

DiMaggio, P., & Hargittai, E. (2001). *From the 'digital divide' to 'digital inequality': Studying Internet use as penetration increases*. Princeton University Center for Arts and Cultural Policy Studies, Working Paper Series number, 15.

Dutton, W. H., & Peltu, M. (1996). *Information and communication technologies: Visions and realities*. New York: Oxford University Press.

Fang, Z. (2002). E-government in digital era: Concept, practice, and development. *International Journal of the Computer, the Internet and Management, 10*(2), 1-22.

Forestier, E., Grace, J., & Kenny, C. (2002). Can information and communication technologies be pro-poor? *Telecommunications Policy, 26*(11), 623–646. doi:10.1016/S0308-5961(02)00061-7

Fuchs, C. (2009). The role of income inequality in a multivariate cross-national analysis of the digital divide. *Social Science Computer Review, 27*(1), 41–58. doi:10.1177/0894439308321628

Fuchs, C., & Horak, E. (2008). Africa and the digital divide. *Telematics and Informatics, 25*(2), 99–116. doi:10.1016/j.tele.2006.06.004

G-8. (2000). *Okinawa charter on global information society*. Retrieved April 27, 2009, from http://unpan1.un.org/intradoc/groups/public/documents/apcity/unpan002263.pdf.

Garrard, G. A. (1997). *Cellular communications: Worldwide market development*. Boston, MA: Artech House Publishers.

Guillén, M. F., & Suárez, S. L. (2001). Developing the Internet: Entrepreneurship and public policy in Ireland, Singapore, Argentina, and Spain. *Telecommunications Policy, 25*(5), 349–371. doi:10.1016/S0308-5961(01)00009-X

Guillén, M. F., & Suárez, S. L. (2005). Explaining the global digital divide: Economic, political and sociological drivers of cross-national Internet use. *Social Forces, 84*(2), 681–708. doi:10.1353/sof.2006.0015

Hague, B. N., & Loader, B. (1999). *Digital democracy: Discourse and decision making in the information age*. New York: Routledge.

Haywood, T. (1998). Global networks and the myth of equality: Trickle down or trickle away? In *Proceedings of Cyberspace Divide* (pp. 19–34). Equality, Agency and Policy in the Information Society.

Heeks, R. (2008). ICT4D 2.0: The next phase of applying ICT for international development. *IEEE Computer, 41*(6), 26–33.

Hudson, H. E. (2006). *From rural village to global village: Telecommunications for development in the information age*. London: Lawrence Erlbaum Associates.

ITU. (2007). World information society report 2007: Beyond WSIS. In *Proceedings of International Telecommunication Union Report*. Geneva, Switzerland: United Nations.

Keniston, K., & Kumar, D. (2004). *IT experience in India: Bridging the digital divide*. New Delhi, India: Sage Publications.

Kim, C.-K. (2007). A cross-national analysis of global e-government. *Public Organization Review, 7*(4), 317–329. doi:10.1007/s11115-007-0040-5

Lijphart, A. (1999). *Patterns of democracy: Government forms and performance in thirty-six countries*. New Haven, CT: Yale University Press.

Maitland, C. F., & Bauer, J. M. (2001). National level culture and global diffusion: The case of the Internet. In Culture, technology, communication: Towards an intercultural global village (pp. 87-128).

Meng, Q., & Li, M. (2002). New Economy and ICT development in China. *Information Economics and Policy, 14*(2), 275–295. doi:10.1016/S0167-6245(01)00070-1

Mossberger, K., Tolbert, C., & Gilbert, M. (2006). Race, place, and information technology. *Urban Affairs Review, 41*(5), 583–630. doi:10.1177/1078087405283511

Nixon, P. G., & Koutrakou, V. N. (Eds.). (2007). *E-government in Europe: Re-booting the state*. New York: Routledge.

Norris, P. (2001). *Digital divide: Civic engagement, information poverty, and the Internet worldwide*. New York: Cambridge University Press.

Odame, H. H. (2005). Gender and ICTs for development: Setting the context. In Gender and ICTs for Development: A Global Sourcebook (pp. 13-24).

Orihuela, L., & Obi, T. (2007). E-government and e-governance: Towards a clarification in the usage of both concepts. In E-governance: A Global Perspective on a New Paradigm (pp. 26-32).

Pick, J. B., & Azari, R. (2008). Global digital divide: Influence of socioeconomic, governmental, and accessibility factors on information technology. *Information Technology for Development, 14*(2), 91–115. doi:10.1002/itdj.20095

Porat, M. (1977). *The information economy*. Washington, DC: US Department of Commerce / Office of Telecommunications.

Robison, K. K., & Crenshaw, E. M. (2002). Post-industrial transformations and cyber-space: A cross-national analysis of Internet development. *Social Science Research, 31*(3), 334–363. doi:10.1016/S0049-089X(02)00004-2

Rogers, E. (1995). *Diffusion of innovations* (4th ed.). New York: Routledge.

Schech, S. (2002). Wired for change: The links between ICTs and development discourses. *Journal of International Development, 14*(1), 13–23. doi:10.1002/jid.870

Servon, L. J. (2002). *Bridging the digital divide: Technology, community, and public policy*. Malden, MA: Wiley-Blackwell. doi:10.1002/9780470773529

Sreekumar, T. T. (2007). Cyber kiosks and dilemmas of social inclusion in rural India. *Media Culture & Society, 29*(6), 869–889. doi:10.1177/0163443707081692

The real digital divide. (2005, March 12). The real digital divide; Technology and development. *The Economist.*

UN ESCAP. (2007). *Integration of information and communication technologies into national development plans for Central Asian states*. Bangkok, Thailand: United Nations.

van Dijk, J. (2000). Widening information gaps and policies of prevention. In Digital democracy: Issues of theory and practice, (pp. 166-183).

van Dijk, J. (2005). *The deepening divide: Inequality in the information society*. London, UK: Sage Publications.

Volken, T. (2002). Elements of trust: The cultural dimension of Internet diffusion revisited. *Electronic Journal of Sociology, 6*(4), 1–20.

West, D. M. (2005). *Digital government: Technology and public sector performance*. Princeton, NJ: Princeton University Press.

West, D. M. (2008). *Improving technology utilization in electronic government around the world*. Washington, DC: Brookings Institute.

World Bank. (2006). *Information and communications for development 2006: Global trends and policies*. Washington, DC: World Bank Publications.

Yates, D. J., McGonagle, T., & Tawileh, A. (2008). How open source software and wireless networks are transforming two cultures: An investigation in urban North America and rural Africa. *International Journal of Technology. Knowledge and Society, 4*(6), 145–157.

Zhao, H., Kim, S., Shu, T., & Du, J. (2007). Social institutional explanations of global Internet diffusion: A cross-country analysis. *Journal of Global Information Management, 15*(2), 28–55.

ADDITIONAL READING

Barber, B. R. (1998). Three scenarios for the future of technology and strong democracy. *Political Science Quarterly, 113*(4), 573–589. doi:10.2307/2658245

Best, S. J., & Krueger, B. S. (2005). Analyzing the representativeness of Internet political participation. *Political Behavior, 27*(2), 183–216. doi:10.1007/s11109-005-3242-y

Chadwick, A., & Howard, P. (Eds.). (2008). *Routledge handbook of Internet politics*. New York: Routledge.

Crandall, R. W. (2005). *Competition and chaos: U.S. telecommunications since the 1996 Telecom Act*. Washington, DC: Brookings Institution Press.

Farrell, G., & Isaacs, S. (2007). Survey of ICT and education in Africa: A summary report, based on 53 country surveys. Washington, DC: infoDev.

Fountain, J. E. (2001). *Building the virtual state: Information technology and institutional change.* Washington, DC: Brookings Institution Press.

Garson, G. D. (2006). *Public information technology and e-governance: Managing the virtual state.* Sudbury, MA: Jones & Bartlett Publishers.

Heeks, R., & Bailur, S. (2007). Analyzing e-government research: Perspectives, philosophies, theories, methods, and practice. *Government Information Quarterly, 24*(2), 243–265. doi:10.1016/j.giq.2006.06.005

Helbig, N., Ramón Gil-García, J., & Ferro, E. (2009). Understanding the complexity of electronic government: Implications from the digital divide literature. *Government Information Quarterly, 26*(1), 89–97. doi:10.1016/j.giq.2008.05.004

Hindman, M. (2008). *The myth of digital democracy.* Princeton, NJ: Princeton University Press.

ITU. (2009). *Measuring the information society: The ICT Development Index, International Telecommunication Union Report.* Geneva, Switzerland: United Nations.

Nuechterlein, J. E., & Weiser, P. J. (2007). *Digital crossroads: American telecommunications policy in the Internet age.* Cambridge, MA: MIT Press.

Sunstein, C. (2007). *Republic.com 2.0.* Princeton, NJ: Princeton University Press.

United Nations. (2003). *Building the information society: A global challenge in the new millennium.* Geneva, Switzerland: World Summit on the Information Society.

United Nations. (2005). *Tunis agenda for the information society.* Tunis, Tunisia: World Summit on the Information Society.

KEY TERMS AND DEFINITIONS

Digital Opportunity Index: The Digital Opportunity Index (DOI) is an index based on national ICT indicators. It is considered a valuable tool for benchmarking the most important indicators for measuring the diffusion of ICTs. The DOI is based on 11 ICT indicators, grouped in three clusters: opportunity, infrastructure and utilization. The DOI is a tool that governments, telecommunication operators, development agencies, researchers and others can use to measure the digital divide and compare ICT performance within and across countries. The DOI has been compiled for 181 countries for a period of three years from 2004-2006.

E-Government Readiness Index: The United Nations E-Government Readiness Index is a ranking of the countries of the world according to two primary indicators: i) the state of e-government readiness; and ii) the extent of e-participation. Constructing a model for the measurement of digital government services, the E-Government Readiness Index assesses the member states of the UN according to a quantitative composite index of e-government readiness based on website assessment (i.e., the Web Measure Index), telecommunication infrastructure, and human resource endowment.

Human Development Index: The United Nations Human Development Index (HDI) is an index used to rank countries by level of "human development." The HDI combines normalized measures of life expectancy, literacy, educational attainment, and GDP per capita. It is used as a standard means of measuring human development—a concept that refers to the process of widening the options of persons, giving them greater opportunities for education, health care, income, employment, etc.

Information and Communication Technologies: The term Information and Communication Technologies (ICTs) refers to the broad collection of information technologies and computer &

communication technologies used to communicate, process, store, and retrieve both data and information.

International Telecommunication Union: The International Telecommunication Union (ITU) is the United Nations agency responsible for global information and communication technology issues, and is a focal point for governments and the private sector in developing networks and services. Among its many activities, the ITU coordinates the shared use of the radio spectrum, promotes international cooperation in assigning satellite orbits, and establishes standards for communications systems.

Polity 2 Score: Polity 2 scores are widely used for their assessment of the degree of democracy and autocracy in the political structures of national regimes. The Polity 2 score for a nation state captures the regime authority spectrum on a 21-point scale ranging from -10 (hereditary monarchy) to +10 (consolidated democracy). Polity scores are maintained and published by the Center for Systemic Peace at George Mason University.

Web Measure Index: The e-government Web Measure Index (WMI) is based on a quantitative analysis of a nation's web presence and features. The primary web site assessed is the national portal or the official homepage of the government, along with the websites of five ministries (education, health, labor, social welfare and finance). Underlying the WMI is a five-stage model of progression of e-government sophistication: emerging presence, enhanced presence, interactive presence, transactional presence, and connected presence. The WMI has been compiled by the United Nations for more than 190 countries in select years between 2003 and 2008.

ENDNOTES

[1] Details on the methodology and the individual items used to construct the Web Measure Index, the broader E-Government Readiness, and a complete summary of the data are available at http://unpan1.un.org/intradoc/groups/public/documents/UN/UNPAN028607.pdf.

[2] Details on the methodology for constructing the Digital Opportunity Index and a complete summary of the data are available at http://www.itu.int/osg/spu/publications/worldinformationsociety/2007/.

[3] Countries "in transition" were assigned values of -66 (i.e., Afghanistan, Bosnia Herzegovina, and Iraq), -77 (i.e., Somalia), and -88 (i.e. Ivory Coast). Because of missing data on other variables, only Bosnia is included in our analysis. See http://www.systemicpeace.org/inscr/p4manualv2007.pdf for a complete description of the Polity scores, its component indicator, and access to the raw data.

[4] See http://www.freedomhouse.org/template.cfm?page=15 for the most recent *Freedom in the World* report and accompanying data. The data from the most recent *Freedom of the Press* survey is available at http://www.freedomhouse.org/template.cfm?page=362.

[5] Data can be accessed at http://www.itu.int/ITU-D/icteye/Default.aspx.

APPENDIX

E-Government Policy Variables for 195 Countries

	National Regulatory Agency	Competition in Basic Services	Competition in Mobile Services	Financial Investment in ICTs
Afghanistan	Present	Full Competition	Partial Competition	-0.211
Albania	Present	Full Competition	Partial Competition	-0.444
Algeria	Present	Partial Competition	Partial Competition	-0.595
Andorra	Absent	Monopoly	Monopoly	1.171
Angola	Present	Full Competition	Full Competition	0.085
Antigua & Barbuda	Absent	Monopoly	Full Competition	-0.007
Argentina	Present	Full Competition	Full Competition	-0.041
Armenia	Present	Monopoly	Partial Competition	-0.293
Australia	Present	Full Competition	Full Competition	0.238
Austria	Present	Full Competition	Partial Competition	0.334
Azerbaijan	Absent	Partial Competition	Partial Competition	-0.238
Bahamas	Present	Partial Competition	Monopoly	-0.259
Bahrain	Present	Full Competition	Partial Competition	-0.167
Bangladesh	Present	Full Competition	Full Competition	-0.377
Barbados	Present	Partial Competition	Partial Competition	0.437
Belarus	Absent	Full Competition	Full Competition	-0.243
Belgium	Present	Full Competition	Partial Competition	0.324
Belize	Present	Monopoly	Partial Competition	0.057
Benin	Present	Monopoly	Full Competition	-0.413
Bhutan	Present	Monopoly	Full Competition	-0.100
Bolivia	Present	Monopoly	Full Competition	-0.026
Bosnia Herzegovina	Present	Full Competition	Full Competition	0.219
Botswana	Present	Partial Competition	Partial Competition	-0.365
Brazil	Present	Full Competition	Full Competition	0.278
Brunei	Present	Partial Competition	Monopoly	-0.169
Bulgaria	Present	Partial Competition	Partial Competition	0.182
Burkina Faso	Present	Monopoly	Full Competition	-0.145
Burundi	Present	Full Competition	Full Competition	-0.495
Cambodia	Absent	Partial Competition	Partial Competition	-0.943
Cameroon	Present	Monopoly	Full Competition	-0.099
Canada	Present	Full Competition	Full Competition	0.426
Cape Verde	Present	Partial Competition	Partial Competition	-0.068
Central African Republic	Present	Monopoly	Full Competition	-1.186
Chad	Present	Monopoly	Partial Competition	-1.793
Chile	Present	Partial Competition	Full Competition	-0.020
China	Absent	Partial Competition	Partial Competition	0.409

Colombia	Present	Monopoly	Full Competition	0.158
Comoros	Absent	Monopoly	Monopoly	-0.059
Congo	Absent	Full Competition	Full Competition	-0.250
Congo, Democratic Republic	Present	Full Competition	Full Competition	-0.509
Costa Rica	Present	Monopoly	Monopoly	0.399
Croatia	Present	Full Competition	Full Competition	0.128
Cuba	Absent	Monopoly	Monopoly	-0.188
Cyprus	Present	Full Competition	Full Competition	0.034
Czech Republic	Present	Full Competition	Partial Competition	0.372
Denmark	Present	Full Competition	Partial Competition	0.501
Djibouti	Absent	Monopoly	Partial Competition	-0.140
Dominica	Absent	Monopoly	Monopoly	0.924
Dominican Republic	Present	Full Competition	Full Competition	1.032
East Timor	Absent	Monopoly	Partial Competition	not available
Ecuador	Present	Full Competition	Full Competition	-0.335
Egypt	Present	Monopoly	Full Competition	-0.232
El Salvador	Present	Full Competition	Full Competition	-0.112
Equatorial Guinea	Absent	Full Competition	Full Competition	-0.842
Eritrea	Present	Monopoly	Partial Competition	-0.336
Estonia	Present	Full Competition	Partial Competition	0.344
Ethiopia	Present	Monopoly	Monopoly	-0.468
Fiji	Absent	Monopoly	Monopoly	-0.139
Finland	Present	Full Competition	Full Competition	0.737
France	Present	Full Competition	Full Competition	0.353
Gabon	Present	Monopoly	Full Competition	-0.203
Gambia	Present	Partial Competition	Full Competition	-0.136
Georgia	Present	Full Competition	Full Competition	0.316
Germany	Present	Full Competition	Full Competition	0.431
Ghana	Present	Partial Competition	Partial Competition	-0.469
Greece	Present	Full Competition	Partial Competition	-0.177
Grenada	Present	Partial Competition	Full Competition	0.737
Guatemala	Present	Full Competition	Full Competition	-0.348
Guinea	Present	Partial Competition	Partial Competition	-0.520
Guinea-Bissau	Present	Monopoly	Partial Competition	-0.624
Guyana	Present	Monopoly	Partial Competition	0.776
Haiti	Present	Partial Competition	Partial Competition	-0.595
Honduras	Present	Monopoly	Monopoly	-0.165
Hungary	Present	Full Competition	Partial Competition	0.553
Iceland	Present	Full Competition	Full Competition	0.253
India	Present	Full Competition	Full Competition	0.074
Indonesia	Present	Partial Competition	Full Competition	-0.383
Iran	Present	Partial Competition	Partial Competition	-0.334

Iraq	Absent	Monopoly	Partial Competition	not available
Ireland	Present	Full Competition	Full Competition	0.678
Israel	Absent	Monopoly	Full Competition	0.779
Italy	Present	Full Competition	Full Competition	0.131
Ivory Coast	Present	Partial Competition	Partial Competition	0.331
Jamaica	Present	Full Competition	Partial Competition	0.384
Japan	Absent	Full Competition	Full Competition	0.626
Jordan	Present	Full Competition	Full Competition	0.383
Kazakhstan	Absent	Full Competition	Partial Competition	-0.362
Kenya	Present	Full Competition	Partial Competition	-0.038
Kiribati	Present	Partial Competition	Partial Competition	0.781
Korea, North	Absent	Monopoly	Partial Competition	not available
Korea, South	Present	Full Competition	Full Competition	0.634
Kosovo	Absent	Monopoly	Partial Competition	-1.334
Kuwait	Absent	Monopoly	Monopoly	-0.419
Kyrgyzstan	Present	Full Competition	Full Competition	-0.177
Laos	Present	Partial Competition	Partial Competition	-0.489
Latvia	Present	Full Competition	Full Competition	0.032
Lebanon	Present	Monopoly	Monopoly	0.520
Lesotho	Present	Full Competition	Full Competition	-0.344
Liberia	Present	Monopoly	Partial Competition	-1.808
Libya	Absent	Monopoly	Monopoly	-0.883
Liechtenstein	Present	Full Competition	Partial Competition	1.413
Lithuania	Present	Full Competition	Partial Competition	-0.072
Luxembourg	Present	Full Competition	Full Competition	0.147
Macedonia	Present	Monopoly	Full Competition	1.742
Madagascar	Present	Partial Competition	Partial Competition	0.097
Malawi	Present	Monopoly	Full Competition	-0.915
Malaysia	Present	Full Competition	Full Competition	0.751
Maldives	Present	Monopoly	Partial Competition	0.133
Mali	Present	Partial Competition	Partial Competition	-0.241
Malta	Present	Full Competition	Full Competition	0.969
Marshall Islands	Absent	Monopoly	Partial Competition	0.226
Mauritania	Present	Full Competition	Full Competition	0.919
Mauritius	Present	Full Competition	Full Competition	-0.155
Mexico	Present	Full Competition	Full Competition	-0.232
Micronesia	Absent	Monopoly	Full Competition	-0.154
Moldova	Present	Full Competition	Full Competition	0.408
Monaco	Absent	Monopoly	Monopoly	not available
Mongolia	Present	Full Competition	Full Competition	-0.407
Montenegro	Present	Full Competition	Full Competition	not available
Morocco	Present	Full Competition	Full Competition	0.054

Mozambique	Present	Monopoly	Full Competition	-0.266
Myanmar	Absent	Monopoly	Monopoly	-0.584
Namibia	Present	Monopoly	Partial Competition	-0.482
Nauru	Absent	Monopoly	Partial Competition	-1.334
Nepal	Present	Partial Competition	Partial Competition	-0.527
Netherlands	Present	Full Competition	Full Competition	0.788
New Zealand	Present	Full Competition	Full Competition	0.161
Nicaragua	Present	Full Competition	Full Competition	-0.584
Niger	Present	Monopoly	Full Competition	-0.541
Nigeria	Present	Partial Competition	Partial Competition	-0.163
Norway	Present	Full Competition	Full Competition	0.523
Oman	Present	Monopoly	Partial Competition	-0.217
Pakistan	Present	Full Competition	Full Competition	-0.302
Palau	Absent	Monopoly	Partial Competition	0.538
Panama	Present	Full Competition	Partial Competition	-0.059
Papua New Guinea	Present	Monopoly	Monopoly	0.978
Paraguay	Present	Monopoly	Full Competition	0.313
Peru	Present	Full Competition	Full Competition	-0.330
Philippines	Present	Full Competition	Full Competition	1.178
Poland	Present	Full Competition	Full Competition	-0.102
Portugal	Present	Full Competition	Full Competition	0.058
Qatar	Present	Partial Competition	Partial Competition	-0.202
Romania	Present	Full Competition	Full Competition	0.160
Russian Federation	Absent	Partial Competition	Full Competition	-0.170
Rwanda	Present	Partial Competition	Partial Competition	-0.581
Samoa	Present	Monopoly	Partial Competition	-0.183
San Marino	Absent	Monopoly	Full Competition	0.351
São Tomé and Príncipe	Present	Monopoly	Monopoly	0.077
Saudi Arabia	Present	Full Competition	Full Competition	0.294
Senegal	Present	Full Competition	Full Competition	0.429
Serbia	Present	Partial Competition	Full Competition	-0.019
Seychelles	Absent	Monopoly	Partial Competition	0.052
Sierra Leone	Present	Monopoly	Full Competition	-0.387
Singapore	Present	Full Competition	Full Competition	0.985
Slovakia	Present	Full Competition	Full Competition	0.203
Slovenia	Present	Full Competition	Full Competition	0.014
Solomon Islands	Absent	Monopoly	Partial Competition	0.422
Somalia	Absent	Full Competition	Partial Competition	-1.707
South Africa	Present	Full Competition	Partial Competition	0.128
Spain	Present	Full Competition	Full Competition	0.102
Sri Lanka	Present	Monopoly	Partial Competition	-0.357
St. Kitts & Nevis	Absent	Monopoly	Partial Competition	-0.399

St. Lucia	Present	Monopoly	Full Competition	-0.309
St. Vincent & the Grenadines	Present	Full Competition	Full Competition	0.627
Sudan	Present	Partial Competition	Partial Competition	-0.225
Suriname	Present	Monopoly	Partial Competition	0.277
Swaziland	Absent	Monopoly	Monopoly	0.044
Sweden	Present	Full Competition	Full Competition	0.727
Switzerland	Present	Full Competition	Full Competition	0.640
Syria	Absent	Monopoly	Partial Competition	-0.507
Taiwan	Absent	Monopoly	Partial Competition	-1.334
Tajikistan	Absent	Monopoly	Partial Competition	-0.107
Tanzania	Present	Monopoly	Full Competition	-0.860
Thailand	Present	Full Competition	Full Competition	0.110
Togo	Present	Partial Competition	Partial Competition	0.118
Tonga	Absent	Partial Competition	Partial Competition	-0.153
Trinidad & Tobago	Present	Full Competition	Partial Competition	-0.225
Tunisia	Present	Monopoly	Full Competition	-0.141
Turkey	Present	Monopoly	Full Competition	-0.172
Turkmenistan	Absent	Full Competition	Full Competition	-0.809
Tuvalu	Absent	Monopoly	Partial Competition	-1.334
Uganda	Present	Full Competition	Full Competition	-0.326
Ukraine	Present	Full Competition	Partial Competition	-0.007
United Arab Emirates	Present	Partial Competition	Partial Competition	-0.168
United Kingdom	Present	Full Competition	Full Competition	0.793
United States	Present	Full Competition	Full Competition	0.702
Uruguay	Present	Monopoly	Full Competition	-0.205
Uzbekistan	Absent	Partial Competition	Full Competition	-0.517
Vanuatu	Present	Partial Competition	Full Competition	-0.355
Vatican City	Absent	Monopoly	Partial Competition	-1.334
Venezuela	Present	Full Competition	Full Competition	-0.345
Vietnam	Absent	Full Competition	Full Competition	0.211
Yemen	Absent	Monopoly	Full Competition	-0.393
Zambia	Present	Monopoly	Full Competition	-0.726
Zimbabwe	Present	Full Competition	Full Competition	-0.196

Chapter 19
Helping to Bridge the Digital Divide with Free Software and Services

Jason G. Caudill
Carson-Newman College, USA

ABSTRACT

The growing importance of digital media in citizens' participation in government is a major issue in obtaining government services, elections and campaigning in the 21ˢᵗ century. In order to participate in the consumption and creation of online media, citizens must have access to, and knowledge of, appropriate technology resources. There exists a gap between those who have access to technology and those who do not A gap commonly referred to as the digital divide. While there are many different aspects to the digital divide one of them is access to the software necessary to participate in digital media. A potential solution to the software component of the digital divide is the use of open source software and free online services. Implementing these solutions can play a part in narrowing the digital divide and producing better informed citizens more capable of participating in the modern electoral process.

INTRODUCTION

Recent national elections in the United States have shown that new media, the use of Internet resources, is playing a critical role in the campaigns and elections of government officials. Personal networking technologies, Web 2.0, and the online presence of many people from all walks of life are influencing the modern electoral process. This places a new, and critical, importance on information literacy and information access.

In addition to electoral activities, citizens' interaction with government at all levels is becoming more dependent on technology access. Across the United States and the world governments are moving to online electronic services for basic service provision in order to both save money and provide easier, faster access to citizens. While this move is making services easier to access online it may also make those same services more difficult to access

DOI: 10.4018/978-1-61520-933-0.ch019

via traditional means like the telephone or face to face communication in an office.

The problem connected to this ever-growing online presence of government officials and government services is that not everyone has access to the technology. The difference between technology haves and technology have-nots in society is generally referred to as the digital divide. While there are many different perspectives on the cause of the divide, and many different potential solutions for solving the different problems, this chapter is focused on the technical component of the digital divide and how to solve the problem of individuals not being able to afford software and other services to be active participants in new media.

BACKGROUND

New Technology, New Divisions

As technology becomes a more and more ingrained part of the world's society technology's importance to individuals becomes more and more significant. Increased access to technology expands an individual's opportunities for education and for staying informed and actively involved in the affairs of their community, their country, and the world. Unfortunately, even with the expansive availability of technology in many developed countries today, including the United States, there are still many people who do not have regular access to technology.

The commonly observed difference in lifestyle and community participation between people with access to technology, the technology "haves", and people without access to technology, the technology "have-nots", is real. This difference is referred to as the digital divide, the difference in opportunity and activity seen between the technology haves and technology have-nots. While the digital divide can be easily defined as a difference between owning or having access to

technology versus not having such access, the implications go far beyond simple possession of modern amenities.

Technology have-nots, those on the negative side of the digital divide, lack more than just hardware and software. These are people who lack access to the leading edge of communication and education. The implications of the digital divide to political participation may rest on the concept that, "Traditional democratic theory is predicated on citizens in a democracy being interested and participating in politics, knowledgeable about how government works and aware of alternate solutions to problems of public policy, and voting consistent with a set of values or principles" (Shelley, Thrane, & Shulman, 2006, p. 8). The increasing use of technology to disseminate political and electoral information means that the digital divide can, in part, negatively impact citizens' knowledge and political participation.

The dissemination of information, the active discussion of issues, is at the core of modern technology in politics. Access to this information is what the digital divide is really about in the political arena and the information itself, the way in which it is accessed and used, is new. To completely understand the importance of technology access for engaged citizens the format and content of new media must be understood.

New media may be broadly defined as media that is, "…fluid, individualized connectivity, a medium to distribute and control freedom" (Chun & Keenan, 2006, p. 1). In terms of specific technologies, new media can include blogs, social networking sites, virtual worlds, and more traditional technologies such as personal web sites and online distribution of digital media (Caudill & Noles, 2009). As a new and still developing category of technology, the definition of new media is still evolving. Basically, the term speaks to a culture of connectivity and the ability for individual voices to reach broad audiences virtually instantaneously.

As a single, but powerful, example of this phenomenon, while writing this chapter the author's hometown was struck by a tornado outbreak. While the mainstream media was still struggling to get detailed reports out, individuals had already posted video to the web from multiple locations in the city documenting not only the aftermath of the storm, but also multiple perspectives of the actual tornado touchdowns. Information was available almost instantaneously, and this occurred in the aftermath of the worst storms on record for that area, in a city where main roads were closed and power outages were rampant.

Admittedly, tornado outbreaks are a vastly different phenomenon from political activity, but the power and pervasiveness of new media reach across the categories. The principles involved are very similar. Whether the topic is a natural disaster or a political one, news of the event can reach a world audience almost before the event is over thanks to new media. New media, particularly Web 2.0 applications adopted by government agencies, can give users of these technologies greater opportunities for contributing to government processes and services (Osimo, 2008). While this close, fast-paced connection to the community can be a valuable asset, it can also be a very dangerous threat to politicians and others who find their mistakes or miscues spread throughout the world.

Natural disasters are, however, an excellent example of the requirement for governments to provide services to their citizens. Following a natural disaster there are many services, ranging from reports of power outages to requests for disaster recovery funding, which require citizens to file forms and communicate with the government. In more normal times citizens also need this kind of access to government services for everything from driver's license renewals to property tax payments. Regardless of the situation, citizen access to electronic government services can be an important part of online government participation.

The movement of government services to online provision is much more than a convenience for citizens; it also has the potential to impact the overall fiscal health of a government organization. When properly implemented an online system can, over time, be much more cost-effective to operate than a more traditional service model. Face to face interaction at an office and also traditional mail interactions both have relatively high costs associated with them and can generate a large percentage of wasted funds.

There will likely never be a complete elimination of face to face interaction between citizens and their government, nor should there be. Traditional models of face to face service, however, can be inefficient and wasteful. Under today's tight budgets and difficult political climate there may not be justification for staffing offices all day, Monday through Friday, to serve citizens when for much of that time employees are left idle. Already many government offices are working reduced hours in face to face support roles in order to reduce the money spent on such operations. One of the ways that appropriate levels of service are being maintained in such situations is the use of online service provision.

Much like the face to face service provision government services via postal mail are also facing budgetary restrictions. On the surface postal mail appears to be more cost-effective than face to face service but the savings may vary by use. The materials required to deal in postal mail, plus the postage charges and the labor hours involved in handling the paper documents all contribute to what can be a relatively high cost operation. Compounding the issues of postal mail is the growing movement towards green operations for government; paper waste is not a positive part of green operations.

As with information about elections, access to electronic government services is limited to those who have access to the appropriate technology resources. Those without access to computers, network connections, and appropriate software for working with online services are left with no option other than the decreasing access to face to face or postal mail government services. The net effect is that those on the have-not side of the digital divide are disconnected from government on multiple levels; they enjoy full access to neither the electoral process nor government services.

Technical Tools to Address the Digital Divide

Both the digital divide and new media are inherently technical issues; they depend on digital technology for their very existence. It is therefore reasonable that in order to provide citizens with access to new media, thus bridging the digital divide, technical solutions will have to be used. Open source software and freeware are two different, but related, alternative solutions that can be beneficial to helping people access new media.

Open source software and new media have a natural connection. New media is media created and distributed by networks of everyday people, not professional news producers or filmmakers whose profession is media, but people with an interest, or even a passion, for creating media. Open source software, similarly, is software created and distributed by people who are passionate about programming and sharing their products with others. The communities, the motivations, between the two practices are similar.

Open source software may be best known for being free. The most widespread form of distribution for open source software is under the GNU General Public License (GPL). GPL promotes four primary freedoms for software users:

1. "the freedom to use the software for any purpose,
2. the freedom to change the software to suit your needs,
3. the freedom to share the software with your friends and neighbors, and

4. the freedom to share the changes you make." (Smith, 2008).

The zero cost of open source software is certainly an important factor in people's adoption of the software. The real value of the open source movement, however, and what makes open source software a viable product, is the nature of its development and use. Regardless of cost, even at a cost of nothing, people will not use software that fails to reliably function or to perform the functions that are needed. From the government perspective, this can be seen in the four most common justifications for the use of open source software; cost, open standards, security, and benefit to the community (Fitzgerald and Suzor, 2005). With such benefits in mind, governments have "…begun to document the benefits open standards can bring to their citizens and business constituents" (Simon, 2005, p 228).

The open source community is the key to what makes open source software such a powerful part of the information technology world. The real power behind open source software is the independent programming community that supports it (Dorman, 2005). Point 2 from the GPL, "the freedom to change the software to suit your needs," is a key to producing quality programs. Much like new media, open source software benefits from a multitude of inputs. The free cost of use and robust development behind open source software has seen its inclusion in major projects seeking to bridge the digital divide, such as the One Laptop Per Child (OLPC) project (Malakooty, 2007).

Many open source programs will be initially created by just one or a few programmers. Once they complete their initial work and begin to distribute the program, however, the open source community begins to play a part in what happens with the software. When the program is first completed it will likely be released to a limited audience for testing, what is usually called a beta test. Part of what makes open source software open source is that not only are the programs free, but the source code, the actual language behind the program, is also available. Beta testers will have access to this code along with the program itself.

Beta testers are often other programmers or software users with a unique interest in a certain type of application. These users test the first edition of an open source program and, as they use the software and discover problems, document and discuss the problems that they find. Sometimes these problems are solved by the programmers who originally wrote the software, but sometimes other programmers who are working as beta testers discover problems and then write solutions to them and forward those solutions to the original programmers. Without access to the program's source code this type of involvement would not be possible.

After beta testing has been completed the final version of the software for distribution will be made available to regular users. Even at this point, however, the open source community will continue to work towards improvement of the program. Partly, this may consist of fixing problems that come to light after beta testing is complete, or it may involve adding new functionality to the program that users identify as being useful.

Over the life of an open source program this cycle will repeat itself with each new release of the program. Beta testing will occur with each new edition and users will continue to identify new features that they would like to see added to the program. Through this community effort open source programs will not only grow and develop, but in many cases they will do so at a faster pace than commercial programs.

Open source software does offer many great advantages, but the open source projects do not provide universal coverage of technology categories. Other software, distributed as freeware, can help to fill in the spaces left open by open source efforts. While different, freeware does share many commonalities with open source software and the two technologies can combine to create excellent opportunities for digital divide solutions.

Freeware is also software that does not charge people to acquire or use the product, but it is a different distribution than the GPL. Users have the opportunity to download, install, and use freeware without any charge, but they do not get access to the source code. This means that freeware programs have a smaller number of contributors than open source programs and may be less developed and advance at a slower pace. This is not always the case, as some freeware programs are very well developed and supported, but the difference is worth noting.

One of the other differences between freeware and open source software may be in the user's freedom to distribute the software. Under the GPL, users can freely distribute the software to others, as long as they do not charge for the product. Some freeware allows for this, but some requires the permission of the software creator to distribute. While this is not an issue for individual users, it may cause problems for organizations that want to provide software to others.

Free services are a different, but related category. At their core, free services include a free software component; even fully online services have software to make them function. Many free online services are accessible and provide functionality for users with just a username and password. While most of these services are completely online, some may require users to download and install a free local application on their computer to work with the online component.

Like open source software, the focus on freeware and free services is more than just being free of cost. While the free cost is important, the freeware applications and free services which are worth using are those that work reliably. For many applications, the combination of open source software, freeware, and free services can provide a highly useful set of tools to users without any cash investment into software.

MAIN FOCUS OF THE CHAPTER

Issues, Controversies, Problems

New Media and New Politics

The presidential elections of 2008 were probably the most media intensive, in terms of both traditional and new media, of any political campaigns in history. Even so, the interaction of new media and politics did not begin here. How many times have people seen Howard Dean's campaign-ending yee-haw yell on stage during his primary run for 2004? Admittedly, the mainstream media covered this as well, but the gaffe blossomed as an online video hit. Before this occurrence, however, Dean played a much more important role in establishing the value of online campaigning. Using the power of the Internet in politics, "By the end of 2003, Dean had gone from being an unknown candidate with very few financial resources to the leader in the race and the most successful primary fund-raiser in the history of the Democratic party" (Anstead and Chadwick, 2008, p. 60). In 2008 two Obama campaign staffers made national news for posing in what would certainly qualify as an inappropriate manner with a life-size cardboard cutout of Hilary Clinton. The media acquired the photos, not from rival campaign workers, but from the guilty parties' own Facebook page.

Examples like those above may be the first to come to mind when a discussion turns to new media and politics. Admittedly, those examples are memorable, and for many they are entertaining as well. The lesson to be learned here, however, is not in the funny anecdotes connected to new media's role in politics, but the breadth of coverage and power of influence of this new media.

New media works from both sides of political campaigns. Campaigns produce and distribute their materials using the same digital media resources that are used by their media-savvy constituents. Campaign web sites, Youtube videos, Facebook and MySpace profiles, and Twitter accounts are all tools that are being used to spread campaign messages.

Concurrently, media users frequent the same sites, not only to view the content but to create and post their own. Comments are left about media posted by campaigns, hit counts lead people to the most popular items, and users exchange and discuss their own media creations. Over time communities develop and for a lucky few, like Obamagirl from the 2008 elections, even fame develops on the new media distribution sites.

These new communities can develop literally overnight and influence large groups of voters. Throughout the history of politics, access of voters to information has been a defining factor in the political system. One of the reasons for the original electoral college in the United States, the body of voters who actually cast ballots directly for the presidency, was to allow a smaller number of people, who could be reached with information about the candidates, to make an informed decision. Over time the number of people who could be informed about the candidates increased. Newspapers, railroad tours, and the telegraph were nineteenth century innovations that helped move towards a more educated electorate, and in the twentieth century technology expanded to provide American citizens with common access, first to radio, and then to television.

At every step, politicians were forced to pay more attention to what they said, how they said it, and with the advent of television even how they looked when they said what they had to say. Franklin Roosevelt was able to achieve a new unity with the American people through the radio with his fireside chats. Just a couple of decades later, Richard Nixon may have lost his bid for the presidency because of his ghostly appearance in a televised debate against rival John F. Kennedy. In these famous cases and others the voting public's opinion about a candidate or office-holder had a very real impact on both the individual politician and also the political landscape. Thorburn and Jenkins (2003) address the Roosevelt and

Nixon-Kennedy events as, "These events were important, in part, because they enabled candidates to address directly a significant portion of the electorate" (p. 2).

Today, in a significant shift from past media connections to politics, politicians no longer have control over the timing or release of all of the campaign's media. Thorburn and Jenkins (2003) contrast today's environment with that of the first fireside chats and televised debates as "The current diversification of communication channels…is politically important because it expands the range of voices that can be heard in a national debate, ensuring that no one voice can speak with unquestioned authority" (p. 2). While news coverage has had the ability to film virtually every minute of a candidate's or office holder's day for many years, even that coverage was limited by time available on nightly news shows and other limitations. New media is different. Anything captured by anybody can be quickly and easily posted from virtually anywhere thanks to widely available technologies like 3G mobile broadband. There are virtually no censorship limits and an unlimited amount of time in which to broadcast.

The first elections of the twenty-first century have seen new media leap to the forefront of political campaigning. In the span of just eight years, from the 2000 to the 2008 elections new media went from a relatively small component of campaigning to a major consideration. MySpace, Facebook, Twitter, and YouTube became a primary means through which to disseminate information to voters and the community. In a surprising shift of focus, mainstream traditional media outlets actually started to cover what was happening in the new media as supplemental news to the campaigns. In less than a decade Internet media moved from a new technology to a major focus across segments of society.

The importance of this shift to the everyday citizen is that they now have the opportunity to actively participate in political media. Their voice can be heard across the world and they can gather information from that same wide world. Providing as many people as possible with access to this new media can play a role in better informing the electorate and advancing the political process.

The Problem with the Digital Divide

On the surface, the absence of computers and network connections in people's homes or communities may appear to be a simple matter of socio-economics. Often, in fact, levels of computer ownership and network access are closely correlated to a community's income, with lower-income communities showing much lower overall numbers of technology ownership and access. The connection of the digital divide to political activity, however, goes much deeper and is much more serious than a simple question of income.

Because new media has become such an ingrained part of the electoral process it is increasingly important for voters to have access to the information disseminated through new media outlets. Outside of elections, citizens also need computer access to take advantage of online government services. Beyond this, people need the ability to participate in the dialog that takes place in the arena of new media. To do either of these things, access or create information, voters need the technical tools with which to participate.

The digital divide can take many forms. Sometimes a household is without any type of computer at all. Sometimes a household may have a computer but be lacking either any network access at all or the broadband access necessary to view online video and other media-intensive, high-bandwidth new media objects. Also, an individual may have the ability to use computer hardware and network access through a public library or other source, only to find that the available source is lacking some necessary software.

The other component of the digital divide is not necessarily an issue of access, but that of ability. The best computer systems, software, and network connections available are of no use to someone who lacks the ability to use a computer (Selwyn, 2004). If technology is available, but training is not, then the individual is left with just as little opportunity for new media access as someone in the other part of the digital divide who lacks the technology.

Often, these two components of the digital divide are seen together. People who lack access to technology may also never have the opportunity to learn how to use technology. Sometimes community initiatives will exist to provide computers, or provide training, but a person may not be able to get both the training and the computers. Obviously, the digital divide is a complex problem. This is not an issue that is solvable by simply investing large sums of money to computer giveaway programs or similar initiatives.

Regardless of what form the digital divide takes, the effect is the same; a lack of access and lack of opportunity to fully engage in government services and the modern electoral process. In relation to the political process, this is the key problem created by the digital divide. A healthy democracy depends on an informed citizenry, and rarely in history has denying a portion of the population access to information proved to have positive results.

Bridging the Digital Divide

Bridging the digital divide, closing the gap between the technology haves and technology have-nots, can be an understandably complex task. There are so many different parts of the problem, and so many possible combinations of the different potential parts, that a single solution is probably not possible. What is possible, however, is to address the different component problems of the digital divide as individual problems to be solved independently.

Issues of technology ownership are probably the easiest digital divide problems to solve. If a person is disconnected from new media simply because they can not afford a computer and a net-

work connection then there are easily implemented solutions. The most immediate that may come to mind is to just buy computers and give network access to people in their homes. While definitely a solution, this may not be fiscally feasible.

If placing computers and network access in individual homes is beyond the reach of an organization working to bridge the digital divide, there are other options. Libraries or community centers can be used as central locations for just a few computers, and one shared network connection, to serve many people. While there are certainly other options for providing technology access to people, these are two of the most apparent, and most common, solutions to the problem.

Individuals who lack the necessary training to take advantage of technology are a different issue. Just investing money or physical resources into this problem will not resolve it. Time, and skilled instruction or well-designed instructional materials, must be invested to move people from a position where they may literally not know how to turn a computer on, to a position where they can actively engage in the new media society as consumers and participants. This presents a unique instructional design problem for those attempting to rectify the situation, but again, there are training program solutions available to do so.

Of course, the real world very rarely provides simple, single-issue problems, nor do simple, single-issue solutions often work. Fortunately, the combination of solutions to single issues can, properly managed, be built into an overall solution. While it is beyond the scope of any single chapter, or perhaps even any entire book, to address the issue in its entirety, there are technical solutions that can solve, or compliment other solutions to, these troubling issues.

Solutions and Recommendations

Advantages of Open Source Software

Software is the driving force behind consumer technology. While there may be a certain amount of chicken-and-egg discussion regarding whether software or hardware are the more important factors, a practical case can be made for the importance of software. Today, and for many years leading up to today, hardware capacity far surpasses that of software. The average home computer today is capable of much more processing power than what is required by the average user. Admittedly, some home users who are heavily engaged in computer gaming or media creation and editing will actually use all of the processing power on their computers, but there is simply no need for that level of power to support word processing, budgeting, or Internet use, the common activities of most home computer users.

Because of software's critical importance to computing overall this chapter focuses on software solutions to help bridge the digital divide. Admittedly, there are other solutions to other issues that are also important, but the open source solution is one that can be easily understood and easily implemented. In addressing the issues of the digital divide there are some different aspects of the problem that can be simultaneously addressed through the adoption of open source software. Obviously, free software solutions can help solve the problem of access to software, but there are other advantages to going to an open source solution.

Many open source programs have the advantage of what is called multi-platform compatibility. This just means that the software is available in versions for the Windows, Mac, and Linux operating systems. This can be important for a digital divide bridging process working with many different people or different locations. By choosing open source software packages that can be used with any of the popular operating systems a single set of applications can be distributed to multiple locations while maintaining consistency across sites.

Consistency is a very important part of any software distribution project. When the same software is used across locations or across users, the support component of the project is easier to configure and easier to administrate. Additionally, designing training for the users of the software is also easier when all users need to learn the same programs.

The work of the open source software development community as it relates to programming has already been explained. The development community also takes part in other activities, including discussion board activity and instructional design. While these are separate activities, both produce the result of giving open source software users a connection to the open source community and assurances that they are not left alone to learn or manage their software.

Users of open source software are not alone. Popular open source programs have very active online discussion forums. These forums are populated by people new to the software, everyday users, and even programmers who are actively involved in the development and problem resolution for the program. These forums are the primary location for discussions and exchanges of information from all categories of open source software users.

As explained earlier, one of the strengths of open source software is the speed with which it is improved or repaired. The discussion forums associated with each program are a major component of this development speed. Granted, the programming community behind open source software actually does the work, but it is these forums where much of the information originates. As users ask questions, post complaints, or just engage in discussion, expert users and programmers can gain direction for where to direct their efforts. For example, multiple questions about the same error might lead a programmer to diagnose and fix a problem with the software. Also, if many people are seen to want the program to perform some specific function that it is not capable of, a programmer might write an extension or a plug-in to improve the software to meet user demands.

While these advantages are important to the development and maintenance of the software, they also contribute to solving the problem of user education. Open source software forums are a wonderful resource through which new users can ask questions and receive sometimes very detailed instructions about how to use the software and how to perform specific tasks. This online community can be a very non-threatening place for new users to find not only information, but also support and encouragement.

Beyond the simple exchange of forum messages, new users can also benefit from the efforts of open source software supporters who have an interest in creating instructional media. While programmers contribute to open source software by programming, there are instructional designers and other technical experts who devote their time to creating user guides and even animated tutorials to show new users how to perform anything from very basic to very advanced functions with a particular piece of open source software. The availability of online training for open source software answers a previously identified demand of technology have-nots to receive training where they are and at times of their own choosing (Shelley, Thrane, & Shulman, 2006).

Useful Open Source Programs

There is simply no way to highlight every open source software project, and if there was there likely would be new efforts initiated from the time the writing stopped to the time the work got into print. What can be done, however, is to present some of the most popular open source programs from the most popular categories to give projects utilizing open source software a place to begin. Office suites, web browsers, and e-mail clients are

all programs that relate to basic technology access. Photo editors, audio editors, and other multimedia tools are more advanced components of digital media. Ultimately, web page creation software enables a user to create entirely new material for presentation on the Internet. All of these categories of software have open source alternatives that can enhance technology access and help to bridge the digital divide.

The office suite, most commonly a word processor, spreadsheet, and presentation program, possibly with other programs as well, may be the software most frequently purchased by the average user. Preparing text documents, making presentations, or doing tabulation and calculation tasks are all activities that can contribute to helping someone understand issues and create media that allows them to take a more active role in the political process. Often, however, an office suite is not included with a new computer. Many times a short-period trial subscription to an office suite is available, but to retain the use of the software the user has to pay a full license fee after a set period of time or after a set number of launches. Once this trial period is over, a user may be left without an office suite. Not only does this absence of software prevent the user from creating their own documents, but it prevents them from opening documents that they obtain online or have sent to them.

One of the most popular open source software programs available is OpenOffice. Created and maintained by Sun Microsystems, OpenOffice defines itself as "…the leading open-source office software suite for word-processing, spreadsheets, presentations, graphics, databases, and more" (OpenOffice.org). OpenOffice is available in twenty-nine languages and is compatible with Windows, Mac, and Linux operating systems (OS). While not every language is available on every OS, the flexibility and inclusivity of the program makes it an excellent candidate for bridging the digital divide.

A theme that will be seen with many other open source solutions, as is demonstrated by

OpenOffice, is that accessibility can work in concert with availability. The option of acquiring software configured to work on multiple OS's and using multiple languages makes open source applications ideal for bridging the digital divide. In a multi-lingual area a single type of software could be used for individuals from a broad variety of backgrounds.

One function that many users perform with a basic office suite is the task of desktop publishing. Producing flyers, newsletters, and other print distributions of information is a long-established component of grassroots political action and information dissemination. For those who have tried to use a word processor to do this, it becomes quickly apparent that while possible, a word processor is not the ideal tool for desktop publishing. While an advanced commercial office suite may include a desktop publishing application, many do not. The open source solution to desktop publishing is a program called Scribus.

Scribus is a fully featured desktop publishing program. The program can give users excellent functionality for their own use at home but also includes advanced features that allow for the creation of documents that can be printed at professional publishing outlets. With one software program it is thus possible to bring desktop publishing to everyone from home users to organizations. Scribus is available for Windows, Mac, and Linux OS's and also supports many different languages.

Of course, new media communication goes far beyond the digital creation of traditional documents. The heart of new media is on the Internet. With that in mind there are excellent open source tools available for working online.

A very popular and very powerful browser, Mozilla's Firefox, is an open source program. Admittedly, it is rare to find an OS that does not include a web browser of some kind at no additional cost to the user, but because of its functionality Firefox is worth examining as an open source solution. The power of the open source programming community and that community's ability to

expand and improve open source applications, may not be better demonstrated anywhere else than in Firefox.

As a browser Firefox is a very powerful tool. Tabbed browsing, user-customizable security and privacy settings, and master passwords are all part of the main Firefox package. The real power of Firefox, however, comes from the myriad add-ons that are available. Add-ons are simply additional programs that can be installed as part of a user's Firefox installation. At the time of this writing the Firefox add-ons available on the Mozilla site totaled 4,745. The add-ons cover a virtually limitless span of functions; from the very useful to what might be considered the very unusual, but properly selected and applied they have the power to transform Firefox from a basic browser into a central hub for information collection and cataloguing for all of a user's interests.

Communication being a primary consideration for new media users, Mozilla also offers a high-quality e-mail client, Thunderbird. Thunderbird is capable of supporting multiple e-mail accounts in multiple formats, including Google's product Gmail, which will be discussed in the next section about free services. Like Firefox, Thunderbird has a wide variety of add-ons to expand its functionality, a count of 1,074 at the time of this writing. Both Thunderbird and Firefox are available for Windows, Linux, and Mac OS's and support many different languages.

Moving forward in the interaction with new media users may shift from simply consuming and sharing online media to creating their own. Like many commercial media applications, commercial programs for the visual design and creation of web pages, often referred to as what you see is what you get (WYSIWYG – pronounced wiz-ee-wig) editors, can be expensive to purchase.

Kompozer is an open source WYSIWYG that provides users with a range of functionalities from the very basic to the more detailed and complex. Kompozer features its own, integrated file transfer protocol (FTP) server for managing website files on a server, along with built-in functionality for creating web forms and using cascading style sheets (CSS) in the creation of websites. For the even more advanced user Kompozer provides an HTML editor so that pages can be created or edited in a programming interface, working directly with the code for the website instead of the graphical interface. Kompozer is available for Windows, Mac, and Linux.

When creating web pages and websites, images can be powerful support for the text on the pages. To create or edit digital images software is needed. While many office suites and even OS's themselves will include elementary digital image editing software this is rarely sufficient for producing a quality final product. There are many open source programs connected to digital imagery and four of them will be covered here. Others exist for specific purposes, but the four presented here should provide a good overview of open source software's capacity for supporting digital imagery.

To create high-quality, original digital images an appropriate drawing program is needed. In technical terms, programs of this type are termed vector graphics programs. An open source vector graphics program is Inkscape. Inkscape provides beginning users with tools to create basic digital graphics but is also capable of performing advanced, professional-quality work. Inkscape is available for the Windows, Mac, and Linux OS's.

In addition to creating original digital images new media participants often have the need to work with digital photographs. A set of three open source applications can provide digital photographers with a full range of digital photo production and editing tools. From the first time the pictures are taken out of the camera to having the images ready to post online there is a sequence of technical tasks that need to be performed. Often, these tasks can be accomplished with a single piece of software, but by adopting specialty tools the work can be done more quickly, more efficiently, and at times with a higher quality.

When a collection of digital photos first come out of a digital camera users may be faced with a bewildering array of images from which to choose. These images may also need to be edited to improve their appearance, using basic digital editing tools such as adjusting the brightness and contrast of the image or cropping an image to remove parts of the photo that are not needed or that detract from the main subject of the photo. At this stage it is also helpful to make decisions about which photos will be retained for use and which will not undergo further editing. These first steps in selecting and editing digital photos can be best accomplished using a relatively new category of software called photography workflow software.

One of the well-developed open source solutions for photo workflow is a program called RawTherapee. RawTherapee allows users to import a folder of images, which is more efficient than working with images individually. Once imported, images can undergo basic editing and can also be ranked by the user from zero to five stars. The photos can be sorted by rank, which makes it very easy for a user to quickly pull up only their best images for further editing. After the editing is complete, images can be processed, the file formats can be converted, and the new images can be saved as a batch. These batch operations make the process much faster for the user and avoid the difficult and time-consuming steps of converting and saving images one at a time. RawTherapee is available for Windows and Linux OS's.

The next step in the photo workflow process is to do more detailed editing of the digital photos. For editing functions that go beyond the basic functions found in RawTherapee, The GNU Image Manipulation Program, commonly called The GIMP, can be used. The GIMP provides a wide range of image editing tools, ranging from the basics that can be performed in RawTherapee to advanced filters and scripts that can completely change the appearance of an image. The full spectrum of editing tools available in The GIMP is beyond what can be discussed here, but its ability to perform advanced editing functions and save files in a variety of formats is very important to its inclusion in an open source software suite to address issues of the digital divide. The GIMP is available for Windows, Mac, and Linux OS's.

After editing, there is a final step that is often overlooked by many users who work with digital images for the Internet. With some education, this can be overcome and there is an open source program to provide a solution. Today's digital cameras capture images at such high resolutions that the files that come out of the camera are far too large to be displayed on a computer screen at full resolution. Coupled with this is the fact that such high-resolution images also have very large file sizes, which use large amounts of server space for a website and also slow the loading of the web page on which they are displayed. Consequently, users often need to resize photos before uploading them to the Internet or trying to transmit them via e-mail.

Images can be resized in an image editor, but only one at a time. A resizing program allows users to take a batch of images and convert all of them to a different size and even to a different file type if that is necessary. PIXresizer is a free, although not strictly open source, program that provides resizing for batches of digital photos. PIXresizer is only available for Windows, but there are likely equivalent programs that can be found for other operating systems.

Free Services

Complimenting open source and free software programs are free online services that can enhance the user's interaction with new media. Much of the new media movement revolves around online services that provide users with the opportunity to view, post, and comment on media. There are a wide range of these services, but their free nature, combined with freely available software solutions, can greatly enhance the user experience with online media and, by extension, be a tool in bridging the digital divide.

At a basic level, there are social networking resources available to users at no charge. These sites are a growing component of political activity, as political campaigns and even political officials already in office are maintaining an active online presence in these social networking communities. Facebook, Twitter, and MySpace are the largest and best-known of these sites, and they offer similar opportunities for users to network with one another and actively participate in groups connected to politicians or specific political or social causes.

While originally these sites were intended for social purposes and, for MySpace and Facebook in particular, the domain of high school and college students, their influence has grown far beyond what was likely envisioned by their creators. The sites are open to all for free membership and are being utilized not only to exchange information and media in the cyber world, but to organize events and actions in the real world. This phenomenon is an example of how bridging the digital divide, providing ubiquitous technology access to all, can actually serve to bring people together and spur action in the real, physical world to accomplish real-world results.

Another component of free services are those that provide technology access to individuals at no cost. Google is likely the most advanced purveyor of these services to date, although there are others offering similar services. Website creation and hosting, e-mail accounts, photo galleries, and more can all be accessed and administrated at no cost to the user through Google and other providers. No longer does a user have to pay for an internet service provider (ISP) in order to have a secure, fully-featured e-mail account, nor do they need a hosting service to post a secure, stable website. These services are now available for free.

One of the very real advantages to these free services is that the online services are accessible from any computer with a network connection. In bridging the digital divide this can be very important. It may not be possible for an organization to provide computers and network access to all of the individuals they wish to serve. In this event, the organization may be able to provide a few computers with network access to a library or community center that is accessible by the people who need to step across the digital divide. By using free online services these individuals will have the opportunity to access their media and other tools from any networked location.

As an extension of this there are free service alternatives available to some of the open source software packages presented earlier. Google Docs provides fully online software for word processing, presentation preparation, and spreadsheet work. These services include online storage for documents and the ability to collaborate online with other users. While not as fully featured as traditional software packages, these free online services can assist users who must, through necessity, work on public computers instead of their own.

Complimentary Hardware Savings through Open Source Software

As discussed already, there is more than one dimension to the digital divide. While software is very important, it is admittedly useless without hardware on which to operate. Fortunately, software and free service solutions to the digital divide can, in part, help to solve the hardware component of the digital divide.

If open source software is taken to another level, that of open source operating systems, the hardware necessary to operate an advanced software suite becomes much more affordable. Linux, the open source OS of choice, is much less resource-intensive for hardware than competing commercial OS's. By using Linux, older, less expensive, or even freely donated, computers can be excellent hardware. If hardware can be easily and inexpensively acquired, then that hardware can be fully outfitted with open source software and, for a minimum financial investment, users

can be equipped with the technology they need to bridge the digital divide.

FUTURE RESEARCH DIRECTIONS

There are many opportunities for future research in applying open source software to bridge the digital divide. Documented testing of a large-scale project to deploy computers and open source software to disadvantaged users would be the first step in establishing a body of academic research in this field. Documentation of how the hardware was acquired, which operating systems and software were installed, and how these resources were distributed would be the first step in such a project, and could comprise a major research effort in and of itself. Technical issues, along with those of logistics and personnel management could be key components of such a study.

Following the collection and disbursement of resources, training would be another valuable study. Required resources, methods for assessing training needs of the subject population, and optimal delivery methods and instructional techniques to deliver the training would all be topics of interest. This training study could be the second component of a multi-study series on bridging the digital divide with open source software.

After resources have been distributed and users have been trained in the resources' use it will be critical to assess the impact of the program. A study focusing on changes in subjects' behavior in relation to political participation and engagement in new media would address this issue. In order to be successful, this would need to be a long-term study, with initial assessment of subjects taking place prior to the distribution of technology resources to establish a baseline. Subsequent studies after the distribution of the technology resources, then after the training, and also at periodic intervals beyond the end of the disbursement and training programs would be necessary to establish if there was real, long-term change in behavior and political participation as a result of the initiative to bridge the digital divide. Subject selection, control groups, and establishment of correlations between cause and effect regarding political activity and new media engagement would also be necessary components of this study.

There are doubtless many more opportunities for study in the use of open source software to bridge the digital divide. The studies proposed here, particularly the assessment phase, could be composed of multiple smaller studies. The future of research in this field is rich and the potential outcomes of the new knowledge generated from such research are virtually limitless.

CONCLUSION

The digital divide and the role of technology in modern government are large, broad-ranging issues. By recognizing the existence of these issues professionals in government, technology, education, and other fields can work together to mediate or eliminate the barriers that exist today. These issues are not those of technology or those of government, but rather they are issues about people and people's rights and needs to access and interact with their government. As the world moves more and more into digital means of communication those who are without access to such means are further and further disconnected from the help that they need.

The digital divide is a serious issue for the modern, technical society. While greater dissemination of information and more opportunities for political participation are achieved through the proper application of technology and new media these new advantages create new problems for those who lack access to technology resources. To complete the vision of ubiquitous inclusion in the political process the digital divide must be bridged and those without access to technology must be provided for and properly trained. The doing of this is not an act of charity, nor is

recognition of the problem any type of pity for those who are less advantaged. On the contrary, solving this problem and expanding participation in the political process speaks to the very soul of a republic; that the government is by the people, for the people, and of the people.

REFERENCES

Anstead, N., & Chadwick, A. (2008). Parties, election campaigning, and the Internet: Toward a comparative institutional approach. In Chaswick, A., & Howard, P. (Eds.), *The Routledge Handbook of Internet Politics*. New York: Routledge.

Caudill, J., & Noles, L. (2009). *New Media Education with Online Tools*. In *Proceedings of the Instructional Technology Conference at MTSU*.

Chun, W., & Keenan, T. (2006). *New media, old media*. New York: Routledge.

Dorman, D. (2005, January). The Coming Revolution in Library Software. In *Proceedings of the ALA Midwinter Conference*.

Fitzgerald, B., & Suzor, N. (2005). Legal Issues for the Use of Free and Open Source Software in Government. *Melbourne University Law Review*, *29*(2), 412–447.

Malakooty, N. (2007). *Closing the Digital Divide? The $100 PC and Other Projects for Developing Countries*. Irvine, CA: Personal Computing Industry Center.

Osimo, D. (2008). *Web 2.0 in Government. Why and How? JRC Scientific and Technical Reports*. Luxembourg: Institute for Prospective Technological Studies.

Selwyn, N. (2004). Reconsidering political and popular understandings of the digital divide. *New Media & Society*, *6*(3), 341–362. doi:10.1177/1461444804042519

Shelley, M., Thrane, L., & Shulman, S. (2006). Lost in cyberspace: barriers to bridging the digital divide in cyberspace. *International Journal of Internet and Enterprise Management, 4*(3), 228–243. doi:10.1504/IJIEM.2006.010916

Simon, K. (2005). The value of open standards and open-source software in government environments. *IBM Systems Journal, 44*(2), 227–238.

Smith, B. (2008). A Quick Guide to GPLv3. Retrieved April 10, 2009, from http://www.gnu.org/licenses/quick-guide-gplv3.html

Thorburn, D., & Jenkins, H. (2003). The Digital Revolution, the Informed Citizen, and the Culture of Democracy. In Thorburn, D., & Jenkins, H. (Eds.), *Democracy and New Media*. Cambridge, MA: MIT Press.

ADDITIONAL READING

Alexander, J. (1999). Networked communities: Citizen governance in the information age. In Moore, G., Whitt, J., Kleniewski, N., & Rabrenovic, G. (Eds.), *Research in Politics and Society* (pp. 271–289). Stamford, CT: JAI.

Bell, P., & Reddy, P. (2004) *Rural areas and the Internet: Rural Americans Internet use has grown but they continue to lag behind others*. Retrieved (n.d.), from http://www.pewtrusts.org/news_room_detail.aspx?id=17062

Bimber, B. (2001). Information and political engagement in America: The search for effects of information technology at the individual level. *Political Research Quarterly, 54*(1), 53–67.

Castells, M. (1996) The Information Age: Economy, Society and Culture. Volume I – the Riseof the Network Society. Oxford, UK: Blackwell.

Castells, M. (1997) The Information Age: Economy, Society and Culture. Volume II – the Power of Identity. Oxford, UK: Blackwell.

Castells, M. (1998). The Information Age: Economy, Society and Culture.: *Vol. III. End of Millenium*. Oxford, UK: Blackwell.

Castells, M. (1999) An Introduction to the Information Age. In H. Mackay and T. O'Sullivan (eds) The Media Reader: Continuity and Transformation (pp. 398–410). London: Sage.

Clement, A., & Shade, L. R. (2000) The access rainbow: Conceptualizing universal access to the information/communications infrastructure. In M. Gurstein (ed.) Community Infomatics: Enabling Communities with Information and Communications Technologies. Herhsey, PA: Idea Group Publishing.

Coleman, S., & Hall, N. (2001). *E-Campaigning and Beyond. Cyberspace Odyssey*. London: Hansard Society.

Devine, K. (2001). Bridging the Digital Divide. *Scientist (Philadelphia, Pa.), 15*(1), 28.

Graf, J., & Reeher, G. (2006). *Small Donors and Online Giving: A Study of Donors to the 2004 Presidential Campaigns*. Washington, DC: Institute for Politics, Democracy and the Internet, George Washington University.

Hindman, M. (2005). The Real Lessons of Howard Dean: Reflections on the First Digital Campaign. *Perspectives on Politics, 3*(1), 121–128. doi:10.1017/S1537592705050115

Jurich, S. (2000). The Information Revolution and the Digital Divide: a Review of Literature. *TechKnowLogia, 2*(1), 42–44.

Katz, J., Rice, R., & Aspden, P. (2001). The Internet 1995–2000: Access, Civic Involvement and Social Interaction. *The American Behavioral Scientist, 45*(3), 405–419.

Kluver, R., & Jankowski, N. J. (2007). *The Internet and National Elections: A Comparative Study of Web Campaigning*. London: Routledge.

Kohut, A. E. (2008). *Social Networking and Online Videos Take Off: Internet's broader role in campaign 2008*. T. P. R. Center, The PEW research center.

Lenhart, A., Horrigan, J., Rainie, L., Allen, K., Boyce, A., Madden, M., & O'Grady, E. (2003). *The Ever-Shifting Internet Population: A New Look at Internet Access and the Digital Divide*. Pew Internet & American Life Project.

Loges, W., & Jung, J. (2001). Exploring the Digital Divide: Internet Connectedness and Age. *Communication Research, 28*(4), 536–562. doi:10.1177/009365001028004007

Murdock, G. (2002). Debating Digital Divides. *European Journal of Communication, 17*(3), 385–390. doi:10.1177/0267323102017003695

Norris, P. (2001). *Digital Divide: Civic Engagement, Information Poverty and the Internet Worldwide*. Cambridge, UK: Cambridge University Press.

Parker, E. (2000). Closing the Digital Divide in Rural America. *Telecommunications Policy, 24*(4), 281–290. doi:10.1016/S0308-5961(00)00018-5

Servon, L., & Nelson, M. (2001). Community Technology Centres: Narrowing the Digital Divide in Low-income, Urban Communities. *Journal of Urban Affairs, 23*(3–4), 279–290. doi:10.1111/0735-2166.00089

Strover, S. (2003). Remapping the Digital Divide. *The Information Society, 19*, 275–277. doi:10.1080/01972240309481

Warschauer, M. (2004). *Technology and Social Inclusion: Rethinking the Digital Divide*. Cambridge, UK: MIT Press.

Wilhelm, A. (2000). *Democracy in the Digital Age*. London: Routledge.

Wilhelm, A. (2002). The Digital Divide. *The Information Society, 18*(4), 415–416. doi:10.1080/01972240290108212

Wilson, K., Wallin, J., & Reiser, C. (2003). Social stratification and the digital divide. *Social Science Computer Review, 21*(2), 133–143. doi:10.1177/0894439303021002001

Chapter 20
Citizen Consultation from Above and Below:
The Australian Perspective

Axel Bruns
Queensland University of Technology, Australia

Jason Wilson
University of Wollongong, Australia

ABSTRACT

Citizen engagement and e-government initiatives in Australia remain somewhat underdeveloped, not least for a number of fundamental structural reasons. Fledgling initiatives can be divided into a number of broad categories, including top-down government consultation through blogs and similar experimental online sites operated by government departments; bottom-up NGO-driven watchdog initiatives such as GetUp!'s Project Democracy site, modelled on projects established in the UK; and a variety of more or less successful attempts by politicians (and their media handlers) to utilise social networking tools to connect with constituents while bypassing the mainstream media. This chapter explores these initiatives, and discusses the varying levels of success which they have found to date.

INTRODUCTION[1]

In Australia, a range of state and Federal Government services have been provided online for some time, but attempts to achieve a more direct form of online consultation between citizen and governments, or even to establish a strong presence of politicians and parties online, remain relatively new. In part, this can be attributed to the comparatively slow take-up by Australians of advanced broadband services, which continue to be both slower and

more expensive than comparable services in other developed nations (Green & Bruns, 2007/2009). The 2007 federal election and its aftermath have created a new emphasis on online political information and e-government services, however. During the election itself, the conservative Coalition government, its successful Labor challengers, and several minor parties utilised popular social media sites such as *YouTube* and *Facebook* alongside their own party Websites to galvanise support and promote their policy platforms (Bruns, 2008). Further, the newly elected Labor government's restructure of relevant government departments to form the new Depart-

DOI: 10.4018/978-1-61520-933-0.ch020

ment of Broadband, Communication, and the Digital Economy (DBCDE) provided a clear indication of its policy intentions in this area; these have been underlined further by its 2009 announcement of an A\$43 billion nation-building project for the development of a fibre-to-the-home high-speed National Broadband Network (NBN).

Improved e-government services that aim to provide a better platform for citizen consultation are an obvious and necessary part of these developments. But governments confront a dilemma when implementing such services. Sluggish, inept, or half-hearted deployment of citizen consultation facilities leaves governments vulnerable to criticism from their constituents, and such criticism can be severely damaging to the public perception of governments if it reaches a large audience through viral transmission in online social media. In Australia, for example, it can be argued that the suboptimal utilisation of *YouTube* by the 2007 Coalition election campaign, and the user-generated material parodying it, further cemented the public image of then-Prime Minister John Howard as 'out of touch' (Bruns, Wilson, and Saunders, 2007). A speedy rollout of consultation facilities, by contrast, has the potential to generate more citizen participation than government staffers are able to engage with in a meaningful way, leading to similarly vocal criticism of citizen consultation projects as no more than PR exercises which have no real impact on policy decisions. Even a well-managed introduction of consultation facilities for example in specific areas of government responsibility may lead to disgruntled responses from users who would like to see their areas of interest treated as priorities.

Even when enthusiasm for e-government consultation is generally high among those most concerned with such initiatives, then, regardless of how that deployment is conducted, it is likely to disappoint a substantial section of that community because there is no clear consensus about how and where such consultation facilities should be deployed either at the citizen or at the government level, and no clear understanding of the appropriate processes for such deployment exists in either group.

In the Australian context, this dilemma was evident during a recent trial of a government consultation blog by the DBCDE, which we discuss below. The problems experienced by this blogging trial point to fundamental, systemic limitations to the feasibility of a government-led deployment of citizen consultation facilities, especially where no clear understanding of how to utilise such facilities is shared between politicians, public servants, and citizens. An alternative to the top-down approach is the development of citizen consultation sites from the bottom up, by individuals and third-sector organisations: such sites provide in the first place a space for the formation of (ideally, non-partisan) communities of interest debating current policy challenges amongst themselves, with reference to the statements of relevant political actors; additionally, they offer an opportunity for the government of the day to tap into their collective knowledge and interest in policy development to draw out input for and responses to proposed policy initiatives. Australian political advocacy group GetUp!'s *Project Democracy*, which aims to generate debate on current political issues with reference to the parliamentary Hansard transcripts, provides a useful example for one such third-party space, and we examine it in a second case study below.[2] A third model builds on more individualised initiatives by political actors to engage with their constituencies through utilising social networking services, personal blogs, and similar online tools. Here, too, success and failure remain close companions, and the fate of such initiatives depends crucially on striking an appropriate balance between top-down information transmission and bottom-up receptivity to input from the citizenry. Those politicians who do use these services successfully for consultative purposes may be gesturing towards a new mode of political communication. This possibility is discussed in the third case study below.

The Limitations of Top-Down Consultation

In late 2008, the Australian federal government's Department of Broadband, Communication, and the Digital Economy (DBCDE) launched its *Digital Economy* consultation blog. This move was suggested and foreshadowed in a number of earlier publications dating back even to the previous conservative federal government led by Prime Minister John Howard. In particular, a 2008 report by the Australian Government Information Management Office (AGIMO) had already pondered the "development of a government online consultation web space that includes blogs, online discussion forums and details of public consultations." It reported that

Respondents said they would be more likely to participate in government consultations if:

- the discussion topic were relevant to their personal circumstances;
- they had the opportunity to nominate the topics for discussion;
- discussion forums included the participation of Government officials;
- a range of registration options were available;
- the site was well designed, easy to find and use;
- participants were free to express their opinion without censorship; and
- it were unbiased in its operation. (AGIMO 2008: 2)

Such considerations were furthered in a post by Finance Minister Lindsay Tanner in a post to his 'blog' (in reality, an online op-ed column) on the Website of major Melbourne newspaper *The Age*, which similarly raised "a number of questions" that "need to be thought through":

Should we set up our own blogs or just pop up on blogs that are already operating?

How much leeway should we give public servants to express opinions on behalf of the government?

Should we have public servants blogging as informed private citizens or official representatives of government?

How much additional resources should be provided to fund government participation?

Should our blogging focus on specific areas of government activity?

These questions involve genuine dilemmas. To be worth the time and effort, government blogging will need to be genuine, relevant and meaningful. (Tanner, 2008a)

Some such questions were eventually answered in practice by the 8 December 2008 launch of the DBCDE *Digital Economy* blog, published as a special section on the DBCDE Website and introduced by a guest post by Tanner even though his colleague Senator Stephen Conroy is the Minister responsible for the Department. The post described *Digital Economy* as "the first of what will be several consultations taking place over the next six months, supplementing existing policy development processes", and noted that

While the primary aim of this blog is to get your feedback on aspects of the digital economy, we also want to use this opportunity to explore the mechanics of government blogging and hear your thoughts on how we should interact with you online. (Tanner, 2008b)

The launch of the blog came at a difficult time for the still relatively new government Department. Much of the public attention directed at it in preceding weeks had focussed on one of two key policy decisions: first, Minister Conroy's controversial support for the introduction of a mandatory Internet filter designed to prevent Australian Internet users from accessing 'undesirable' content, which had been heavily criticised by users and industry organisations from both a civil liberties and a technical feasibility perspective, and second, the Department's protracted battle with the formerly government-owned, ex-monopolist communications provider Telstra over DBCDE's exclusion of Telstra from the tendering process for the project to build the next generation of Australia's broadband network. (Public sentiment ran strongly against the 'cleanfeed' Internet filter, but was mainly in favour of Telstra's exclusion from the tendering process as this was seen to increase market competition and bring down broadband prices.)

As a result of such public preoccupations, a majority of comments on the initial *Digital Economy* blog posts dealt mainly with those two hot-button issues rather than engaging with the substance of those posts themselves. In just over ten days, Minister Tanner's opening post alone generated more than 750 on-site comments, mostly attacking the 'cleanfeed' filter or demanding swift progress on deploying next-generation broadband access. In other words, while as far as community involvement and consultation is concerned, the DBCDE blog can be seen as a success, the disregard of citizen respondents for the blog posts' topics themselves must be seen as a significant problem. If the point of the government blog is to engage in a kind of crowdsourcing, harvesting some of the better ideas put forward by commenters on the blog as input for its policy development processes, and perhaps also to harness satisfied participants as virtual marketers for the government's policies, then the blog failed to achieve its purpose.

This failure is neither simply the fault of citizen commenters (for responding in ways other than those intended and invited by the government) nor of government staffers (for attempting to avoid currently heavily debated topics in favour of the somewhat more diffuse "digital economy" theme) – rather, the failure is systemic and points to both sites speaking past one another, at cross purposes; as such, it provides a useful and instructive example for the problems which can arise from top-down citizen consultation efforts even where (as in the present case) we may assume that they were well-intentioned.

Although citizens were perhaps not using the blog in the way its creators had intended it to be used, the blog was as good a space as any to air their obvious grievances – precisely because this blog was the first of its kind, there were precious few other spaces online where so direct a feedback mechanism to the relevant minister and his staff was available. Perhaps DBCDE staff should simply have tackled key issues head-on, and should have posted articles about the Internet filter and the Telstra tender to their blog so that those articles could have acted as clearinghouses for all those comments, allowing the discussion around other posts to be detached from that topic: "if you want to harangue us for the filter proposal, here's your chance – just please leave the other posts alone."

Indeed, a post titled "We hear you…" on 12 December – four days after the *Digital Economy* blog's launch – promised as much:

in responding to the many comments on the blog to date (over 900 to date), there are a lot of comments related to the issue of ISP filtering. As we indicated in our introductory page, we plan to blog about this issue and respond to many of the issues you've already raised in the comments in an upcoming post and welcome anyone who has anything new to add to topic to respond to that thread. (DBCDE, 2008)

(That follow-up post, authored by Minister Conroy, was published another ten days later, on 22 December 2008; Conroy, 2008.)

But even if had been possible to quarantine all discussion about the Internet filter and the trouble with Telstra into dedicated posts, the underlying problem for the DBCDE blog is its inherent exposure as a – indeed, the only – high-profile government blog (with social media spreading the news, it achieved this profile even without any particularly substantial promotion for the blog). At issue here is the fact that there are significant and possibly immutable upper limits to the form of two-way community consultation represented by the 'government blog' format: as Clay Shirky has described it,

communities have strong upper limits on size, while audiences can grow arbitrarily large. Put another way, the larger a group held together by communication grows, the more it must become like an audience — largely disconnected and held together by communication traveling from center to edge — because increasing the number of people in a group weakens communal connection. (2002, n.pag.)

Contrary to communities, however, audiences (in Shirky's definition) are unable to engage in meaningful citizen consultation. Thus, by immediately attracting a sizeable number of commenters in its first days of operation – by virtue of its being an official government blog – the *Digital Economy* blog never had a chance to move through the phase in which those social structures establish themselves that are so crucial to the effective functioning of user communities *as* communities. What was (necessarily) missing from the DBCDE blog was the presence of a community with a sense of purpose and direction, a community which may have restrained its urge to engage in complaints about the 'cleanfeed' filter, repeated *ad nauseam*, and (assuming genuine participation by the other side) could have moved on to a more fruitful discussion aimed at finding a mutually acceptable compromise.

An established community can be relied upon to do a substantial deal of self-management and self-policing – ensuring that comments remain on-topic, that participants exercise a modicum of civility, and that newcomers are effectively socialised into the established environment; though supporting technologies have changed from mailing-lists and newsgroups to Web-based environments and social media, the basic principles for such community processes are well established (see e.g. the seminal work in Baym, 2000). But such communities are best grown organically, from a relatively small group of initial participants, as is evident in Australia's best-known political blogs; while – *pace* Shirky – with the right technological support structures in place some communities are able to grow very large (a site like *Slashdot*, for example, has managed to attract well over half a million users to its community spaces; see Bruns, 2005), it is very difficult indeed to retro-fit this sense of community into an existing site, even one as young as the DBCDE blog.

One question arising from this is whether future government blogs should have a more carefully phased roll-out. They may also be able to learn from the experience of sites like *Slashdot*, and to introduce more of the advanced community self-management and (ironically in this context) self-filtering functionality that exists there. This could involve peer-rating mechanisms allowing the community itself to highlight the best and hide the worst of what its commenters are saying, and perhaps even a contributor 'karma' system to reward consistently insightful and constructive contributors. Over time, this will help the community develop a sense of itself, and will curb instances of blind anti-government vitriol; additionally, it could also point DBCDE staff towards insightful voices in the community to be recruited for focus groups and other citizen consultation processes beyond the blog itself.

However, such technological support mechanisms do little to address the more fundamental problem that an official, top-down government blog must necessarily exist in a precarious, exposed position which may attract deliberate disruption from oppositional and lobby groups or may at the very least generate sustained criticism from interested respondents who are not necessarily at all intent on engaging in any form of constructive consultation processes. This is true even for blogs which – unlike *Digital Economy* – are not amongst the very first attempts by a sitting government to explore the use of online platforms for citizen consultation.

For this reason, it is also important for governments to explore alternative solutions to soliciting citizen responses through their own sites. In the context of the *Digital Economy* blog, for example, there already exist a number of very well-established Australian online communities which deal with a number of topics that fall within the purview of the Department. Rather than (or in addition to) inviting interested citizens to come and give feedback through the DBCDE blog, therefore, government staff may also need to engage directly and openly in such spaces. They could explore the views of the Australian Internet user community regarding the planned National Broadband Network, for example, by going to *Whirlpool.net.au*, the country's pre-eminent user-led Website for broadband discussion and advice; the *Whirlpool* community is at least as much a self-selecting group of interested stakeholders as is the DBCDE blog readership, and could contribute substantial expertise to the consultation process. Crowdsourcing policy ideas, in other words, can happen just as well by going out to meet the crowd where it is already gathered as it can by building a space where crowds may come to gather.

The Bottom-Up Alternative: Political Informatics

Indeed, the further development of spaces for citizen engagement may well be driven at least as much by the non-government sector as it is by government initiatives themselves. One area of particular interest in this context are new technologies and practices which offer customised

parliamentary information as a tool for political engagement and action and allow for a community-driven transition from political communication to *political informatics*. Such services radically disintermediate the flow of political, and specifically parliamentary news to the public. They work with officially published parliamentary records to offer customisable streams of political information, and are aimed at encouraging candidate monitoring, direct engagement with political representatives, and activism. They use the affordances of contemporary information technologies to enable the parsing, publication and syndication of specific information streams, but they are ultimately motivated by an evident dissatisfaction with the professional performance of politicians and journalists, and a desire to build social capital and public engagement with political institutions. One of the authors was involved in the construction of such a project – *Project Democracy* – on behalf of the Australian online political activist organisation GetUp!, and this practice-based experience provides a unique insight into the affordances and constraints of these technologies of political informatics.

Theories of political communication in contemporary democracies have tended to emphasise its mass-mediated nature. On the whole, the selection and presentation of information in mass-mediated democracies is the responsibility of professional journalists working within established media institutions. Politicians and political institutions attempt to manage aspects of their narratives and selections – moderating, supplementing or countering them by withholding, releasing or 'spinning' information, and at the end of this process, more or less critical news audiences derive information from and base their political choices, activism and decisions on the stream of industrially-produced news.

But there has been, in recent years, an erosion in public faith both in journalism and in political institutions. The current so-called 'crisis' in journalism is many-faceted (see Flew and Wilson, forthcoming): it consists, among other elements, of a growing disconnect between journalists and the communities they traditionally serve, perceptions of a deleterious corporate influence on reporting, the 'source capture' of journalists by political actors, the decline in quality with a crisis in the business model of commercial journalism, and industrial journalism's failure to anticipate and assimilate the impacts of technologies of self-publication, content sharing and syndication. There is, simultaneously, a crisis of faith in the efficacy and responsiveness of democratic political institutions, and a cynicism about the motivations and performance of individual politicians. The latter phenomenon has been considered from a range of perspectives in political science and related fields, but work by researchers like Stephen Coleman (see e.g. Coleman, 2005) shows how the immediacy of online communications technologies has exacerbated perceptions that politicians and political institutions are 'out of touch', and remote from voters and their concerns.

This loss of faith in political institutions and the mediators of political communication feeds into user-led initiatives engaged in the tracking, filtering, and criticism of the mainstream media's work (including especially the practices commonly described as citizen journalism and political blogging), but it has also led to efforts to disintermediate the flow of political information by giving the public new, more direct forms of access to information that technically is already on the public record, but available only in comparatively arcane, non-user-friendly formats. This particularly includes the records of parliamentary proceedings: in recent years, a number of international and Australian initiatives have focussed on developing tools which enable citizens to receive customised information feeds about such proceedings, to track the specific contributions of their various representatives to parliamentary debate, and to directly engage with these representatives to provide feedback on their activities. Rather than being driven by the parliamentary

information services which produce the records themselves, such efforts have been carried out mainly in the third sector; they cut out the 'middle man' of parliamentary journalism, and give users the tools to customise their information diet and focus their activism strategically on specific issues and representatives.

The longest-established and most prominent e-democracy initiative in political informatics is the UK-based *TheyWorkForYou.com*. The project's name implies its commitment to re-establishing a more direct relationship between citizens and their parliamentary representatives, and the site is a project of MySociety, an organisation that is itself operated by the charity UK Citizens Online Democracy. This initiative was founded by Tom Steinberg in 2003, and in 2004 developed *TheyWorkForYou* as an open-source e-democracy tool. Steinberg founded the charity after reading his flatmate James Crabtree's manifesto article, "Civic Hacking: A New Agenda for e-Democracy." In this, Crabtree defines an ethic for e-democracy projects which goes beyond offering a veneer of consultativeness for the ailing model of disengaged representative democracy:

This should become the ethic of e-democracy: mutual-aid and self-help among citizens, helping to overcome civic problems. It would encourage a market in application development. It would encourage self-reliance, or community-reliance, rather than reliance on the state.

Such a system would be about helping people to help themselves. It would create electronic spaces in which the communicative power of the internet can be used to help citizens help each other overcome life's challenges. Most importantly, by making useful applications, it would help make participatory democracy seem useful too. (Crabtree, 2003)

TheyWorkForYou is just one project among many from MySociety – others include services for e-petitioning, emailing MPs, monitoring electoral pledges, and *FixMyStreet*, which encourages people to put pressure on their local authorities to improve basic amenities. All of these services represent attempts to enact this ethic of citizen empowerment.

TheyWorkForYou works toward this goal by providing a politically-neutral space in which citizens can monitor, track, and contact their representatives, and access information about the workings of the parliament as a whole. The site allows its users to find individual representatives in the UK, Scottish, Northern Irish and Welsh assemblies, by postcode or from an alphabetical list. On the pages tracking individual representatives, citizens are able to view speech transcripts, voting records, declared interests, and contact details, and there are off-site links to biographies, electoral records and further contact information. Citizens can also sign up to receive email alerts whenever particular representatives speak in parliament. These speaking records are made available through parsing the electronic publication of the UK parliamentary record, the Hansard, which is also presented as a chronological stream of debates. This way, users can also track specific issues of interest.

Since its launch in 2004, the site has had significant uptake. It had 2 million unique visitors in 2007 (MySociety, 2009), and it has had a measurable effect on the conduct of parliamentary representatives; *inter alia*, it has forced the UK Government to explicitly licence Hansard, where no previous licence existed. Indeed, *TheyWorkForYou*'s presence in public debate has triggered claims that some representatives have been asking frivolous questions in parliament just to boost their activity metrics on the site; at the very least, this indicates parliamentarians' awareness of the site's efficacy in communicating the level of their political performance to the public. In response, the Leader of the House of Commons, Jack Straw, has claimed that the site's quantitative emphasis distorted the public's picture of parliamentary

work, but again, it is also significant in the first place that the service has itself become a subject of parliamentary debate.

TheyWorkForYou's open-source parsing software was adapted for the first and most significant effort at political informatics in the Australian context, OpenAustralia. OpenAustralia is a volunteer-run organisation whose very small staff – including Matthew Landauer and Kat Symanski – have worked in their spare time to reproduce many of *TheyWorkForYou*'s features for the Australian political context. Subtle differences between the Australian and British parliamentary systems have meant that some aspects of the service play out differently; for example, Australia's comparatively strict party discipline means that precious few dissenting votes are recorded among parliamentarians in the major parties. The fact that Australia's upper house, the Senate, is elected on a state-by-state basis also changes how and why users would monitor their representatives. On the whole, however, the project aimed for a faithful translation of the *TheyWorkForYou* model to the Australian context.

In September 2008, Australian online campaigning organization GetUp! launched the site under the title *Project Democracy*. GetUp! had been established on the model of organizations like MoveOn in the United States, using online campaigning techniques to encourage progressive activism outside of traditional political organisations. Among its successes as a campaigning organisation were contributions to the repatriation of Australian Guantanamo Bay detainee David Hicks and a national apology to indigenous Australians. Alongside such specific campaigning initiatives, the organisation had wanted to establish an e-democracy initiative on the model of *TheyWorkForYou*, but which could also be harnessed for more activist purposes. The swearing-in of a new Senate, which ended the Coalition's domination of that house during its time in government, provided a new opportunity to generate public pressure on individual senators to act on GetUp!'s chief areas of campaigning activity – including climate change policy, indigenous rights, and constitutional reform. *Project Democracy*, then, was an effort to utilise the affordances of political informatics services as a component of online campaigning.

GetUp! were able to build on the work of *TheyWorkForYou* and OpenAustralia in creating *Project Democracy* as a site that not only parsed parliamentary information and allowed the tracking of individual senators, but which also allowed the aggregation of relevant news from a range of additional sources. The site was launched in September 2008, as the new Senate elected in November 2007 reconvened. *Project Democracy*'s adaptation of open-source parliamentary parsing technology was embedded in a service which also offered users the capacity to contribute blog posts and commentary on parliamentary events, thereby providing the foundations for active and direct citizen engagement beyond a mere tracking of parliamentary activity. Additionally, mainstream news was filtered into a number of streams, published to the site, which focussed on individual representatives, States, and areas of specific policy interest; these custom feeds were created using feed and syndication tools like *Google Reader* and *Yahoo! Pipes*. The site also had built-in visual tools, including interactive maps of the floor of the Senate and Australia, so that users could find representatives by state, and according to where they sit on the parliament floor. Finally, weekly updates to users also offered campaigning information, summaries of media coverage, and news of upcoming parliamentary developments alongside parliamentary news.

Some challenges were shared by OpenAustralia and *Project Democracy* in accessing parliamentary information. In particular, a serious problem arose when the Australian Parliamentary Service changed the way it published Hansard online. By changing its publishing format to a searchable online record rather than a straight "shovelware" Web publication of the written record, the APS rendered the parsing technology obsolete. Although helpful and open to negotiation with NGOs, the APS made it clear that such organizations were not its priority when deciding how parliamentary information would be published and presented online. In effect, however, the APS ended up replicating part of the functionality of these existing services while making it impossible for them to continue without extensive further development work. These difficulties are still being negotiated by both organisations, and they point to the need for more liaison and collaboration between community-based and official e-democracy initiatives.

The story of sites such as *TheyWorkForYou* and *Project Democracy* provides an insight into how user-led, innovative extra-governmental e-democracy initiatives are being transmitted internationally, and how they can extend the affordances of their services in the process; they make use of open-source technology, and allow their own replication in different contexts. Such sites offer citizens a new opportunity to develop and maintain their specific political interests, track parliamentary debate related to relevant topics, and engage in focussed campaigning activities. Importantly, they do perhaps make parliaments and representatives seem less remote, and in doing so, they represent innovative third-sector solutions to the problem of political disengagement: in a sense, these are services which the state could not offer, but ought to be responsive to.

Such projects, then, provide an important bottom-up alternative or complement to the top-down, government-led attempts at citizen engagement through departmental blogging and similar initiatives which we have discussed above: as user-led initiatives emerging gradually from independent groups and organisations, they need not struggle nearly as much with the problem of developing sustainable community structures in the face of intense public exposure, but indeed are likely to gain wider public attention only as a direct result of attracting a critical mass of community participation. At the same time, however, they necessarily struggle much more with the challenge of attracting broad participation by mainstream political actors, for whom venturing out into such community spaces outside the control of government or party agencies is fraught with potential danger or embarrassment – and especially where they are supported by activist agencies, such sites also struggle to establish themselves as impartial and honest brokers of citizen engagement and consultation with political actors, even more so than journalistic or governmental citizen participation initiatives do.

Finally, such bottom-up initiatives also mainly address a specific clientele. To highlight this is less a direct criticism than a commentary on their structural dissimilarities with mass-mediated political coverage: although they deal with national institutions, such sites structurally fragment the attention of users along sub-national and single-issue lines. As they disintermediate the news reportage function of journalism, they are unable to narrativise the broader trajectory of political events – unless, as in *Project Democracy*, they offer users an opportunity to reintermediate the political process by contributing their own summarising coverage through blogs and other ongoing commentary (that is, by engaging in a form of citizen journalism). Thus, political informatics sites (if considered in isolation) may make it more difficult for those who are not already committed to tracking political news in some depth through other media to form a holistic view of continuing political debates. And for those not predisposed to seek out such additional political information and commentary, they lack the capacity for summary and compression that mainstream news media exhibit. (See Prior, 2006, for a discussion of the constraints of the post-broadcast, high-choice media environment.)

All in all, however, such services do constitute invaluable tools for activists, the politically committed, and not least also journalists looking for focussed streams of political information. Instead of relying on the selections made by the professional caste of journalists in the news industry, users can now make their own choices, and pursue their own priorities more closely – and where sites such as *Project Democracy* also add commentary and discussion functionality, they provide an important platform for citizen consultation which builds on parliamentary debate and thereby extends it to, or connects it with, parallel debates taking place within the citizenry. What remains missing from the picture, however, are more systematic attempts by governments and politicians to interact with these extra-parliamentary debates and draw useful ideas emerging from them back into the parliamentary and governmental components of the political process.

Connecting Top-Down and Bottom-Up through Social Media

User-driven, NGO-led initiatives are one way in which political communication has been disintermediated. Another is the growing practice of politicians communicating more directly with constituents (and non-constituents) using social media technologies. Like any category of social media users, depending on their communication strategies politicians can be more or less successful in adapting these technologies to their own purposes.

The 2008 US elections marked perhaps a watershed in online campaigning, and the Obama ticket in particular were innovative in campaigning in online spaces. Obama's campaign communication strategy not only provided innovative features on campaign Websites, which generated a much larger groundswell of donations and volunteers than the McCain campaign could manage, but it also branched out into the skilful use of existing social networking technologies. Obama's success was also abetted by skilful new media campaigners like MoveOn.org. Although not the first politician to experiment with these techniques, Obama's success has perhaps vindicated the strategy of working around media institutions to talk directly to voters, utilising viral and social campaigning techniques.

Less spectacularly, and beyond the campaign moment, individual politicians are "lifestreaming" to services like *Facebook* and *Twitter*, and experimenting with more direct forms of political communication and e-democracy. There are several potential advantages that politicians can derive from achieving such disintermediation by using social media and consequently creating more direct links with potential voters. Not only are politicians able to pass messages directly to voters who have chosen to follow or friend them in social media environments, but they are also able to determine constituents' concerns more directly, without these being co-opted by the agendas of media outlets campaigning in favour of their own preferred outcomes. Such use of social media by politicians therefore combines elements of top-down and bottom-up engagement by attempting to implement a more or less tightly managed citizen communication strategy in an inherently user-led environment outside the control of government or party. This places participating politicians in a potentially precarious situation in which possible threats are also evident. The trade-off for a more immediate form of citizen engagement is that in order to measure up to social media's demand for communicative authenticity, politicians must relinquish some measure of "message control" and prepare themselves for constituents demanding to talk back more directly to their representatives.

From the social media styles of Australian politicians, it is possible to nominate three styles of social media use, with differing degrees of effectiveness. The first group are 'managers', who attempt to carry over strategies of message control from the mass media and thus fail to address the affordances and requirements of social media. Australian politicians like Prime Minister Kevin Rudd and Opposition Treasury Spokesman Joe Hockey use their *Facebook* profiles as little more than a channel for pushing straightforwardly

political messages, for example; in Rudd's case, his *Facebook* and *Twitter* presences appear to be curated by someone other than himself, and in that sense they are little more than another arm of a media management effort which is otherwise carried out via broadcast media appearances and press releases. By absenting themselves from the upkeep of their social media presence, and by using these services in this way, such politicians treat social media as just another top-down, one-to-many channel, and in doing so may generate substantial resentment amongst existing social media users who expect politicians entering their online spaces to act according to their rules. Given that Rudd's own 2007 election campaign was innovative in its employment of online strategies, it is perhaps disappointing that the Prime Minister's office is forsaking social media's opportunities for a more extensive dialogue. (At the time of writing in mid-July 2009, Rudd has also launched an official "PM's Blog"; with one entry posted to date, and no direct responses by the PM to reader comments as yet, it is too early to assess the communication style of this initiative. See Rudd, 2009.)

A second group of social media users can be called "e-democrats". Although these politicians use their social media presence primarily to advertise their political activities and messages, they involve themselves personally in the social media environment, and take time to engage with other social media users, thus making use of some of the affordances of social media and responding to the unwritten rules of such environments. Malcolm Turnbull, Australia's Liberal opposition leader, uses his *Facebook* and *Twitter* profiles primarily to diarise his engagements and activities, but it is evident that he usually makes his own updates, and he is known to engage in dialogue with other users on these sites. In doing so, Turnbull is able to make more immediate personal connections with users which would not be possible in the broadcast environment, and lends a valuable aura of authenticity to his own presence. Nonetheless, the mix of top-down and bottom-up communication attempted here also risks providing a little of both worlds but satisfying nobody: users who wish for more extended bottom-up influence on policy development processes may come away disappointed if communication between citizens and politicians remains at a generic level, while politicians and party organisations hoping to profit from an increased access to the citizenry may be frustrated by the dilution of their messages in the absence of broadcast-style distribution processes.

Finally, a third group whom we might call "social politicians" may be pointing the way to a new kind of public sphere by using social media to expose a more mundane, quotidian self. Political actors in this group appear to have recognised that social media are not the best channel for retailing exclusively political messages, and that by personally investing in the versions of community found within social media environments, they are engaging with social media communities on their own terms. Understanding that environments like *Facebook* are where people engage in identity self-construction that blends their political, professional and personal selves leads to forms of engagement that contribute to an inclusive, extensive post-broadcast public sphere. This public sphere is not inherently political, and politicians participating here do so in the first place as citizens themselves, rather than as politicians; rather than attempting to establish a precarious top-down communicative stance in a bottom-up environment, they are in effect joining the 'bottom', the general citizenry, and from this draw additional legitimacy and a greater immunity against accusations of being 'just another politician'.

In the Australian context, one politician who has made interesting steps in this direction is Tasmanian State Premier David Bartlett. Bartlett's updates, photos, and his use of *Facebook* applications do not speak of a consultant-driven approach to social media; instead, we get the sense that he, like other users, is there because he enjoys being part of a networked community. His contributions

tend towards the personal and the everyday: what he reveals is often prosaic ("David wore the blue tie with red dots today") or idiosyncratic ("David is gearing up for the Hot Rods") – but it has the priceless patina of authenticity.

It may be that highly managed and polished media personae are artefacts of mass-mediated politics. For better or worse, many scholars and commentators argue that that period is passing away. Users of social media expect a much more conversational and unaffected style of political communication. There is palpable frustration on services like *Twitter* and *Facebook* when politicians will not engage in the dialogue that many users take to be the key function these spaces afford. As the media landscape changes, and more citizens become more engaged in online social networks, older methods of political communication and media management will start to have less purchase. Politicians struggling to import older methods of message management into new platforms might look to examples such as Bartlett's for an example of how to best exploit the affordances of social media: be yourself.

That said, such social media models of politics are far from unproblematic in their own right. One danger – and it is a danger – is that politicians may be elected because based on their social media profiles they appear to be 'nice people' rather than necessarily effective and knowledgeable at conducting the business of government. Another, especially for newly-elected politicians, is that the constraints of the political environment may mean that private persona and public actions of the politician are notably disjointed. For all the connections with the citizenry at the bottom – the fundament – of the political system that social media-savvy politicians may have built up, doubtlessly this would leave their social media 'friends' disenchanted and may even lead to a community-organised and virally transmitted backlash that could create substantial damage. It is possible that the fact that the existing political system has forced politicians to become a distinct professional class also limits their ability to portray themselves as 'normal' people in social media environments.

CONCLUSION

In discussing these various top-down, bottom-up, and mixed-mode efforts at building connections between governments, individual politicians and citizens, we are faced with initiatives and practices that are in their formative, even experimental stages. The precise motivations and starting-points for these efforts at disintermediated or reintermediated styles of political communication differ, and so do their perceived successes.

The DBCDE blog represents a qualified first step in the government's wider strategy for engaging with the community online, on the government's own terms. In spite of its limited success to date, and the temptation (not least for the public servants operating the site) to categorise the initiative as an unproductive dead end, it is also important to understand this effort as an experiment, necessarily carrying a potential of failure; on this basis, one can only hope that the righteous frustration currently being expressed at some of the Department's recent policy proposals does not in turn frustrate these (ultimately very welcome) attempts to develop new approaches to citizen consultation. After all, as untried as government consultation blogs are at the federal level in Australia, so too are citizens unused to being able to engage with their government in this way. Evidently, both sides still have a lot to learn about the other: in particular, perhaps, to manage – and to communicate – their expectations of such initiatives. While there are natural limits to top-down initiatives for citizen consultation (linked especially to the size and structure of the communities they are likely to attract), it is likely that they do have a role to play – especially perhaps for specific consultative projects away from the mainstream of public debate.

Similarly, with NGO-driven e-democracy intitiatives there is a necessity for a greater dialogue with government agencies, parliamentary representatives, third-sector service providers and users. At present, these bottom-up projects are able to generate a more open, community-driven form of citizen engagement, but their independent status also limits their reach both horizontally (they are largely preaching to the converted, attracting mainly only those citizens who are already strongly politically engaged) and vertically (the ideas developed and expressed by their constituencies generally fail to penetrate the corridors of power to a consistent, reliable, and sufficient extent). This is true especially if such initiatives are suspected by politicians or citizens of political bias in favour of particular activist goals.

However, if governments do come to recognise third-sector initiatives as a possible solution to the difficulties posed by in-house e-democracy initiatives (perhaps as replacements, but also as complements), and if NGOs can fulfil their aim of using these tools to facilitate more extensive political engagement amongst a greater cross-section of the citizenry, we may see the outlines of a new relationship between the state, citizens and the public sphere. A special role in this process may be able to be played by trusted third parties which are seen by all participants as neutral non-combatants: such parties may include especially the public broadcasters, which are increasingly positioning themselves as providers of (online and broadcast) spaces for citizen-politician interaction, but possibly also the university sector or widely trusted non-government organisations.

Finally, the question remains open whether another group of trusted neutral parties also includes the social media sites themselves – some of which may today be seen as assuming a position as universal service providers, thereby playing a quasi-neutral role that nonetheless conflicts with their obvious commercial interests. To what extent can a *Twitter* or *Facebook*, or one of their successors, provide the space for insightful political consultation with citizens on current political issues? Politicians using such social networking services may be pointing the way to a more dramatic reorganisation of political communication, especially when they become genuine and enthusiastic participants in a peer-to-peer, post-broadcast communications environment. Here, too, there is still a substantial learning curve ahead for them as well as their constituents, as both sides learn how best to apply these technologies to the purpose of enhancing political engagement, increasing the responsiveness of political actors and institutions, and thus improving citizen consultation.

Alternatively, perhaps a genuine use of such technologies for political communication would require any clear division into 'citizens' and 'politicians' to disappear, as the heterarchical structure of social media erodes distinctions between 'bottom' and 'top'. The engagement between politicians and citizens as peers which could result from this levelling may be desirable on the on hand, but on the other hand it is also possible that the realities of representative democracy inevitably require the presence of a distinct political class. If so, social media provide no inherently new answers, and what we are likely to see there is simply another iteration of the ongoing struggle to develop effective combinations between top-down and bottom-up models of citizen consultation.

REFERENCES

Australian Government Information Management Office (AGIMO). (2008, June) *Consulting with Government – Online*. Retrieved March 6, 2009, from http://www.finance.gov.au/publications/consulting-with-government-online/docs/AGIMO_ConsultGov.pdf

Baym, N. K. (2000). Tune. In *Log On: Soaps, Fandom, and Online Community*. Thousand Oaks, CA: Sage.

Bruns, A. (2005). *Gatewatching: Collaborative Online News Production*. New York: Peter Lang.

Bruns, A. (2008, March 26-28) *Citizen Journalism in the 2007 Australian Federal Election*. Paper presented at the AMIC 2008 conference: Convergence, Citizen Journalism, and Social Change, Brisbane. Retrieved March 6, 2009, from http://snurb.info/files/Citizen%20Journalism%20in%20the%202007%20Australian%20Federal%20Election.pdf

Bruns, A., Wilson, J., & Saunders, B. (2007, November 16) *Election Flops on YouTube*. Retrieved July 24, 2009, from http://www.abc.net.au/news/stories/2007/11/16/2093120.htm

Coleman, S. (2005). The Lonely Citizen: Indirect representation in an age of networks. *Political Communication, 22*(2), 197–214. doi:10.1080/10584600590933197

Conroy, S. (2008, December 22) Minister Conroy on: Promoting a Civil and Confident Society Online. Retrieved March 6, 2009, from http://www.dbcde.gov.au/communications_for_business/industry_development/digital_economy/future_directions_blog/topics/civil_and_confident_society_online

Crabtree, J. (2003) Civic Hacking: A New Agenda for E-Democracy *Open Democracy*. Retrieved May 1, 2009, from http://www.opendemocracy.net/debates/article-8-85-1025.jsp

Department of Broadband. Communications, and the Digital Economy (DBCDE). (2008, December 12) *"We Hear You..."* Retrieved March 6,2009, from http://www.dbcde.gov.au/communications_for_business/industry_development/digital_economy/future_directions_blog/topics/we_hear_you Flew, T., & Wilson, J. (Forthcoming) Journalism as Social Networking: The Australian youdecide2007 Project and the 2007 Federal Election. *Journalism: Theory and Practice*.

Green, L., & Bruns, A. (2007). au: Australia. In Felix Librero and Patricia B. Arinto. (Eds.) Digital Review of Asia Pacific Montréal: Sage.

MySociety. (2009) *TheyWorkForYou*. Retrieved July 18, 2009, from http://www.mysociety.org/projects/theyworkforyou/

Prior, M. (2007). *Post-Broadcast Democracy: How Media Choice Increases Inequality in Political Involvement and Polarizes Elections*. New York: Cambridge University Press.

Rudd, K. (2009) PM's Blog. *Prime Minister of Australia*. Retrieved July 24, 2009, from http://pm.gov.au/PM_Connect/PMs_Blog

Shirky, C. (2002, April 6). Communities, Audiences, and Scale. *Clay Shirky's Writings about the Internet: Economics & Culture, Media & Community, Open Source*. Retrieved February 24, 2007, from http://shirky.com/writings/community_scale.html

Tanner, L. (2008a, September 2) The Government Gets Blogging. *The Age*. Retrieved March 6, 2009, from http://blogs.theage.com.au/business/lindsaytanner/2008/09/02/thegovernment.html

Tanner, L. (2008b, December 8) Minister Tanner's Welcome. *Digital Economy*. Retrieved March 6, 2009, fromhttp://www.dbcde.gov.au/communications_for_business/industry_development/digital_economy/future_directions_blog/topics/minister_tanners_welcome

ENDNOTES

[1]   A version of this chapter was presented at the Conference on Electronic Democracy, Vienna, 7-8 Sep. 2009.

[2]   One of the authors of this chapter, Jason Wilson, was involved in developing *Project Democracy* during his time as GetUp!'s Director of e-Democracy.

Chapter 21
E–Government in Brazil:
Reinforcing Dominant Institutions or Reducing Citizenship?

José Rodrigues Filho
Universidade Federal da Paraíba, Brazil

ABSTRACT

Despite the popularity of, and blossoming research on the use of, information and communication technologies (ICTs) in the information society, especially in terms of e-government and e-democracy, little research has been conducted to answer questions related to the effects of ICTs on citizenship, which is said to be at risk. It is claimed that the political science research in modern democracy has narrowed citizenship down to voting, turning democracy into something to be experienced at election time only and not between elections. We need a very clear understanding of the opportunities brought by new technologies and the dangers and risks regarding the realization of citizenship and civil rights. If it is true that ICT has done little to change our democracy, and if it in itself does not guarantee the realization of the rights of the citizens, research work must be developed in order to better analyze the relationship between ICT and citizenship. Because this kind of research is almost non-existent, even in the developed world, this paper attempts to see whether e-government projects in Brazil are designed in ways which reflect our best understanding of freedom, social justice, addressing the sources of inequalities, alienation, and injustice.

INTRODUCTION

In the 1990s, in both the developed and developing countries, there was an emphasis on citizens' orientation regarding information technology policy. However, with new reform strategies employed

in the public sector through the rhetoric of New Public Management, based on techniques from private management models as part of the global terminology of good management, it soon became clear that citizens' orientation implies that citizens acquire the role of consumers or clients – recipients dependent on benefits provided by the welfare state. This dependency is evident when people are

DOI: 10.4018/978-1-61520-933-0.ch021

considered to be the consuming rather than the "contributing" part of society. To turn the citizens into clients or consumers seems to be a kind of erosion of citizenship.

The discourse on citizens' orientation became widespread after it was suggested that it was possible to design government structures with the focus on the citizens as consumers (Osborne & Gaebler, 1992, p. 90). Again, this appeared at a time when there was "considerable evidence to support a pessimistic analysis of the prospects of active citizenship in modern society" (Turner, 2001, p. 189).

It is argued that, while information and communication technologies (ICTs) have the potential to improve the democratic process, expand citizenship, and empower the people, they also have the ability to perpetuate or exacerbate existing inequalities and other divides. With regard to the gap in access to ICTs, some authors have stated that "the information revolution could paradoxically become a cause of even greater inequality and worsening poverty" among developing countries (McNamara & O'Brien, 2000). In addition, there have been comments about the dangers of digital opportunities, with authors pointing out that the "unequal diffusion of technology is likely to reinforce economic and social inequalities leading to a further weakening of social bonds and cultural cohesion" (United Nations Public Administration Network (UNPAN), 2005, p. 3).

In consequence, the debate on e-government initiatives is most often polarized between those who over-emphasize the negative aspects of ICT (the skeptical or "business as usual" view), on the one hand, and those who argue enthusiastically that ICT will enhance the democratic process (the optimistic or utopian view) on the other. Due to the importance of citizenship, we need a very clear understanding of the opportunities brought by new technologies and their dangers and risks regarding the realization of citizenship and civil rights.

Unfortunately there has been little research attempting to show the relationship between information technology and citizenship, even in the developed world. The reason might be too simple – the economic view of democracy and politics in some dominant democracies seems to continue to defend a very narrow concept of citizenship. In developing countries the situation is the worst, because the official propaganda in favor of some technologies as civic tools, along with most debates, has emphasized the condition of the technology without being clear about the concept of citizens' information society. If it is true that ICT has done little to change our democracy, and it in itself does not guarantee the realization of the rights of the citizens, research must be done in order to better analyze the relationship between ICT and citizenship.

Thus, there is a need for more empirical research surrounding citizenship and new technologies and not just theoretical discussions. It is known that most e-government initiatives both in developed and developing countries aim at promoting the use of ICTs that try to import successful experiences from e-commerce into e-government in order to improve the efficiency of government bureaucracies, traditionally seen as inefficient and resistant to organizational change.

Consequently, the concept of e-government, in many cases, is seen as a "set of market-driven reforms" in line with the narrow discourse of the New Public Management (NPM) rationale initiated in the early 1980s (Dunleavy & Hood, 1994; Hood, 1995) in the areas of financial management in the public sector, e-procurement, e-health, e-voting, and in tax control. These are solutions to well-structured problems that have worked all over the world as initiatives framed more towards controlling the lives of citizens than offering them some benefits in terms of (for example) the provision of information, focusing on a lean government team putting "your tax dollars" to work more efficiently in the delivery of a few services such as the renewal of a driver's license and submission of a tax declaration.

An attempt is made in this study to approach the topic of e-government from the point of view of Brazilian citizenship, looking at the impact of e-government tools such as e-voting and e-health on the realization of citizenship, and to see whether these projects in Brazil are designed in ways which reflect our best understanding of freedom and social justice, addressing the sources of inequalities, alienation, and injustice.

ICTS AND CITIZENSHIP

It is recognized that the concept of citizenship has changed and is still changing. For that reason, there are numerous and conflicting interpretations of the concept of citizenship, although it is commonly understood in terms of a framework of rights and obligations (Janoski, 1998). In many countries, for instance, there are some core political rights and obligations normally associated with citizenship – voting, deliberation or participation in the political process, and the access or right to the provision of information. So, what is the best way to improve citizenship and the political practices envisaged in these core political rights and obligations?

Thus, the concept of citizenship is varied and has changed throughout history, posing challenges to the information and technological societies. The diverse understandings of the term citizenship require a broad range of philosophical, sociological, and political theories for its discussions and debate. In a less narrow view, citizenships consist of a set of legal rights, protections, and duties between government and individual members of society. In a broad sense, citizenship represents a framework of universal political, civil, social, and participation rights. According to Janoski (1998), citizenship comprises active and passive rights and obligations: "Citizenship is passive and active membership of individuals in a nation-state with certain universalistic rights and obligations at a specified level of equality" (Janoski, 1998, p. 9). In short, there is no universal definition of citizenship, and it is considered as a contested concept with multiple definitions. Citizenship is "a peculiar and slippery concept with a long history" (Riley, 1992, p. 180).

When dealing with the concept of citizenship it is worth mentioning the two different traditions in the current debate on citizenship: the liberal tradition and the republican tradition. The liberal tradition characterizes politics as a "market" and as private in nature, maintaining that citizens act on the basis of self-interest (Holford & Edirisingha, 2000, p. 7). Corporate citizenship and consumer citizenship are based on the liberal tradition which considers that the term "citizen" has been transferred to market actors.

For Wiklund (2005, p. 719) in the liberal tradition the "conception of politics is found in most 20th-century liberal models of democracy, such as the elitist model of democracy developed by Joseph Schumpeter (1976), [...] the economic model of democracy developed by Anthony Downs (1957) and the pluralist model of democracy developed by Robert A. Dahl (1956)".

On the other hand, the republican (or communitarian) tradition considers politics as public in nature and not as a "market". "Political actors are not conceived as consumers, but as participants in public discussion. Politics is understood to be an open and public activity, distinct from the isolated and private choices of self-interested actors" (Wiklund, 2005, p. 704). According to the literature, rights and duties form the base for the substance of citizenship, with the liberal tradition focusing on citizens' rights, while the republican tradition can be characterized by its emphasis on duties.

In the information society, the internet and other technological artifacts and systems are considered as both means and objects of citizenship, appearing as if by magic to improve the practice of citizenship in the technological society. However, these "technologies are also used as means of anti-citizenship, by various state and commercial entities that employ digital networks for purposes of surveillance of censorship" (Barney, 2006, p. 2), making the idea of information technology as a means of citizenship extend far beyond the internet. "Technology is power in modern societies, a greater power in many domains than the political system itself" (Feenberg, 1999, p. 131).

Unfortunately most of the academic work produced so far does not seem to worry about the relationship between ICT and citizenship, with few people taking the matter seriously. For Winner (2005, p. 1) "much of this disinterest stems from a long standing euphoria about technological advance that precludes serious reflection about whether the arrival of a new technological device or system will truly be beneficial to political freedom and democratic governance". In this case, people endorse information technology enthusiastically, and "criticisms of any serious kind or requests for wider debate about policy options in technology are often regarded as negative and obstructive" (Winner, 2005, p. 2).

The expansion of ICTs requires an understanding of not only the opportunities created by new technologies but also the risks regarding the realization of citizenship and civil rights. Therefore, ICT and citizenship should not be separated, because ICT in itself does not guarantee the realization of the rights of the citizen. Despite the determinist view and the expanding literature favoring the use of ICTs in the information society, it is recognized that citizenship is at risk. The problem is that the conditions of technology is emphasized, but it is not fully clear what exactly is meant by the concept of a citizens' information society. Many initiatives are necessary to turn computers and the internet into tools for civic participation. If, in the developed world, it is found that "mere presence of favorable conditions for making ICT a civic tool are not enough" (Olsson, 2006, p.618), in developing countries the situation is too complex.

In the last two decades, the formalistic and dominant conception of citizenship, based on the liberal political philosophy, has been challenged, and new concepts of citizenship are been formulated in the wake of changes in economy, technology, politics, environment, culture, and many other contradictory social processes that are occurring in our society – locally, regionally, and globally. This paper will shortly describe how the liberal democratic perspective on citizenship can be criticized from an ecological, cultural, and technological point of view.

Cultural Citizenship

Cultural citizenship is considered as a term that is "emerging from the problematization of traditional citizenship models (Pawley, 2008, p. 594). It is said that the influential political science has narrowed citizenship down to voting, while "culturally inclined scholars have taken up citizenship in terms of community building and bonding" (Hermes, 2006, p. 301). As result of this, cultural citizenship is an ongoing process of *collective* and *constructive* learning, and not as a status that can be achieved or denied, or merely a list of rights and obligations (Ong, 1996; Stevenson, 2003; Delanty, 2007). It is stated that "Cultural citizenship aims to promote conversation where previously there was silence, suspicion, fragmentation or the voices of the powerful" (Stevenson, 2003, p. 152). In short, cultural citizenship is a dialectical process "contending that there is no system to overthrow and no revolutionary strategy adequate to these aims" (Stevenson, 2003, p. 153). It is a "contested desire" that must be continually practiced and negotiated.

Ecological Citizenship

Ecological citizenship, also referred to as "environmental" or "green citizenship", has emerged in academic debates promoting ecological values. Again, ecological citizenship tries to explore the limitations of existing forms of citizenship, linking ecology with social justice. It has been mentioned that ecological citizenship obliges us to rethink the traditional and liberal concepts of citizenship, taking us beyond those traditions. "If ecological citizenship is to make any sense, then, it has to do so outside the realm of activity most normally associated with contemporary citizenship: the nation state" (Dobson, 2003).

Technological Citizenship

It has been argued that the proliferation of ICT has given rise to an intense debate and a growing literature on technological citizenship in the information society, addressing topics ranging from e-democracy, e-voting, and the digital divide to electronic surveillance and the virtual public sphere. As result of this, it has been mentioned that a "number of influential approaches to technological citizenship have emerged out of the rapidly expanding literature" on these topics, although most of them focus "on the use of ICTs as tools to renew or enrich existing democratic practices and institutions" (Longford, 2005, p. 2).

For some authors there is a need for a critical and reflexive technological citizenship in order to enhance the democratization of democracy, which requires a kind of civic culture. For Longford (2005), our understanding of citizenship in the digital technology era "must transcend preoccupations with the digital divide, electronic voting and the like, to interrogate the terms of technological citizenship as they are encoded in cyberspace" (p. 2). Because in this era of digital technology, "citizenship norms, rights, obligations and practices are *encoded* in the design and structure of our increasingly digital surroundings" (p. 2), technological citizenship should be explored "in terms of the ways in which the Internet and the World Wide Web regulate and *govern* users", as citizens, in a quite invisible and opaque way (p. 2).

Therefore, due to the *politics of code* in this digital era, it is stated that an adequate conception of technological citizenship must include the politicization of code, which should not only be the province of hackers, into the internet. According to Longford (2005), "Genuine technological citizenship in the digital era entails a critical awareness of how code constitutes the conditions of possibility for different norms, models, and practices of online citizenship", along with the colonization of cyberspace by commercial, proprietary forms of code. As a result, he introduces another way of thinking about technological citizenship in the digital technology era, which is referred to as the problem of citizenship and code.

With the colonization of cyberspace by proprietary code, "the cybercitizen is being subtly reconfigured, *by design*, from an active subject of communication and creation into a passive consumer of on-line commercial products and entertainment" (Longford, 2005, p. 8). Therefore, in a representative or "thin democracy", where citizenship is limited to voting and the ordinary citizen lives privately as a consumer or as a marginalized client, the norm is the privatization of politics, passivity, and cynicism, because "market forces will not put the technology to creative and democratic uses but only to commercial uses" (Barber, 2001).

Within the last 10 years, in both developed and developing countries, neo-liberal market policies of privatization and deregulation have radically restructured many social institutions. As a result, in the communication sector, the access to communication that used to be a social good has slowly been redefined as a market good. Thus, in the Marshallian framework of citizenship, what was before considered a social right now has shifted to a private or market good. In this case, citizenship was reduced when it no longer supported a greater social welfare.

Unfortunately, in many cases, what are behind the discussions to increase the access to the internet are the interests of big corporations fighting for bigger slices of the market. In the United States, Wang (2008) has emphasized the need to consider information as a social right, urging "for a recon-sideration of internet access as a social right" (p. 3). In this appeal, Wang (2008) has mentioned that now, under "a needs-based rationale, the bridge of the digital divide is based on needs, not rights. In the light of neo-liberalism's influence on policy decisions, "access to services that were once considered a social right for all, become a privilege for some" (Wang, 2008, p. 24).

It is recognized that social rights are distributed unevenly across the population in all countries. In Brazil, where access to the internet is a privilege for around 10% of the population, it hard to think that market forces will bridge the digital divide or gaps in access. If the cost of making a phone call or surfing the internet in Brazil is one of the highest in the world, the current approach to add more computers to close the digital gap rather than eliminate it should be rejected, because it does not address the social, economic, political, and cultural factors that contribute to today's inequalities.

In this paper the challenge is to analyze the relationship between ICTs and citizenship, by considering the politics of code – in which norms, rights, and obligations are encoded in the structure of ICTs along with internet access as a private or market good and not as a social right – and the high cost of its use – severe digital and social inequal-ity – despite the potential of the ICT infrastructure which, it is claimed, is accessed by those who are already empowered in the political system.

E-GOVERNMENT IN BRAZIL

Though a developing country, Brazil has jumped into the top ten ICT countries, and public IT sec-tor spending is also increasing at a high rate. ICT spending in Latin America has also increased at a compound average rate of 13 percent between 1992 and 1999. With this rate, Latin American ICT growth in spending was almost twice that of North America and Western Europe between

1998 and 1999 (12.7 percent versus 7.3 percent and 5.7 percent, respectively). This information supports the argument that, although the base for ICT remains in the developed countries, the "hot market" for ICT is elsewhere, especially in the so-called BRIC countries (Brazil, Russia, India, and China) where there are high-growth technol-ogy markets.

Despite high investments in e-government ini-tiatives in Brazil, it is amazing that there has been relatively little research analyzing not only how public sector spending is done but also whether new ICTs are evaluated in a timely fashion. Most of what is known is reported by government agencies, but with very narrow insights into the political, social, and socio-technical problems involving the design, use, and implementation of information technology in the public sector (e-government). It is known that most e-government initiatives both in developed and developing countries aim at pro-moting the use of ICTs that try to import successful experiences from e-commerce into e-government in order to improve the efficiency of government bureaucracies, traditionally seen as inefficient and resistant to organizational change.

Consequently, the concept of e-government, in many cases, is seen as a "set of market-driven reforms" in line with the narrow discourse of the NPM rationale initiated in the early 1980s (Dunleavy & Hood, 1994; Hood, 1995) in the areas of financial management in the public sec-tor, e-procurement, e-voting, e-health, and in tax control. These are solutions to well-structured problems that have worked all over the world as initiatives framed more towards controlling the lives of citizens than offering them some benefits in terms of (for example) the provision of information, focusing on a lean government team putting "your tax dollars" to work more ef-ficiently in the delivery of a few services such as the renewal of a driver's license and submission of a tax declaration.

It is stated in the literature that ICTs are the means of increasing centralized control and surveillance within organizations (O'Loughlin, 2001; Elmer, 2003). In the case of Brazil, it has been mentioned that e-government has reinforced and increased governmental control over the lower bureaucracy, but this control does not reach the areas in which there are high public resource transactions, where the political elite, legislators, and the high bureaucracy still maintain power (Sanchez, 2003). This means that ICTs reinforce organizations and their control, but at the high organizational level this control does not work.

Therefore, many initiatives of the Brazilian digital government involved the creation and promotion of websites in an infrastructure oriented towards marketing the e-government project to the public. At the moment there are many online transactions between the government and citizens, such as online forms, employment recruitment, and the submission of tax declarations: every citizen who pays income tax has to submit his tax declaration via the internet. In short, the government in Brazil, as in many other countries, is following a "services-first-and-democracy-later" approach to e-government, as digital citizen interaction and participation is in its patchy, poor, and very early stages (Rodrigues Filho & Santos Junior, 2009).

In this work some preoccupations have been raised with regard to the so-called "digital opportunities", especially because inequalities exist not because people are deprived of access to e-government. There are many questions to be answered about the design, use, and implementation of ICT in Brazil. How democratic is e-government? How do digital opportunities reinforce some institutions without reducing traditional inequalities? Are digital opportunities empowering the people in Brazil? Is e-health in Brazil for the poor or against the poor? What does e-voting means for democracy? What services do citizens want and why? What do people want first – for their basic needs to be attended to or to have access to IT? Do people want services in electronic format when their basic needs are not met in the non-electronic format?

Some critiques have been made of e-government in Brazil in terms of the way that this seductive expression is used to reduce the extent of governing in the provision of services to the population. The question raised is: how to govern electronically if the community is not electronic? Nogueira Filho (2001), for instance, recognizes the benefits of online services to the population but is cautious about the imposition of the logic in the citizen/state relationship that can transform the former into a well-pleased customer, not worried enough to participate actively in government.

Similar critical comments have been made in the developed world. In a study involving the United States, Britain, and the European Union initiatives of e-government, Chadwick & May found that "the potential of the internet has been marginalized" due to the dominance of "an executive 'managerial' model of interaction at the expense of 'consultative' and 'participatory' possibilities" (2003, p.271). On the other hand, Alexander has mentioned that "e-government initiatives can serve to increase the democratic deficit in Canada" (2005, p.80) due to its emphasis on the technological and administrative dimensions.

Consequently, the discussion of e-government needs a deep theoretical formulation, and a deeper analysis of electronic services cannot be provided by the existing explanatory framework, which does not consider that every community or nation has its own specificities. It is believed that empirical comparative studies might be a great contribution for theoretical formulations. It seems to be hard to combine an approach very much based on market-driven forces (e-government) that suits existing political and bureaucratic elites with a real process of democratization (e-democracy). In other words, can the state provide services to please the citizens without democratic engagements?

In visiting one of the major e-government sites in Brazil (www.governoeletronico.gov.br/), it can be seen that in its guidelines the Brazilian government's policy towards e-government has abandoned the neo-liberal view, so far adopted, which considered the citizen as a client and user of public services. Instead, the citizenship view is emphasized and there is an effort to incorporate collective rights, social control, and participation promotion. This view, it is said, is the attempt to attend to citizens' needs and demands, taking into consideration universal principles, equality, and equity in the provision of services and information. In this case, the Brazilian government's rhetoric is that e-government is been developed in such a way to orient it towards citizens.. This implies that the information society is to be built from the point of view of local people and local knowledge. However, as it is now, e-government in Brazil is an isolated sector for technical professionals, because the wider society is absent in the politico-organizational architecture of e-government (Marcondes & Jardim, 2003).

As was questioned before, how can we think in terms of equality and equity in the distribution of social goods that were redefined as market goods? How can we think in an information society that is not built under the theory of the social shaping of technology? A well-documented example of information society development under citizens' orientation occurred in North Karelia, Finland, in the attempt to turn away from technological determinism. Despite having been part of everyday rhetoric, it is stated that nowadays "the original meaning of citizens' orientation has faded down", and in "the discourse of technology policy-makers citizens' orientation does not mean any more people's own action" (Turva-Hongisto & Talsi, 2006, p. 4). For these authors, people are no longer independent agents, but goals of outside actions. "Instead of being the starting point of development citizens are nowadays end-users who have only the role of consumer and client" (Turva-Hongisto & Talsi, 2006, p. 4).

There are many e-government initiatives in Brazil, especially at the national and state government level, but the discussion here is limited to the federal or national government. This study

tries to cover two ICTs projects in Brazil: e-voting and the National Health Card – e-Health. Some research work about these two projects has been mentioned in the literature (Rodrigues Filho & Gomes, 2008; Rodrigues Filho & Gomes, 2009). It is worth mentioning that these tools are included in the typologies and definitions of e-government as the use of information and communication technology and online services to the citizen (Michel, 2005), and as an approach for the improvement of public administrations, mentioned "as the principal indicators for measuring the quality of democracy" (Amoretti, 2007, p. 341).

Because data on information technology expenditure in Brazil are not easily provided by the government, a quite laborious amount of work was done in this study in order to compile data from the national budgets from 2001 to 2005. Thus, data on expenditures in ICT initiatives such as e-health and e-voting were gathered from national budgets, in addition to data on other social programs from budgets and official documents.

E-Health in Brazil

Over the past few years the use of emerging information technology such as electronic health records, digital radiology, telemedicine, and the health care smart card, has become the key for the delivery and management of health care services. The rapid propagation of these technologies in the health sector, with the potential to favor management and exchange of relevant data, may improve medical decision-making considerably, but this proliferation also creates many challenges and much disappointment.

The implementation of new IT-based tools in the developed world is almost always done under the supposition that there is a need to improve the quality of services already available in traditional, non-electronic formats, making them guaranteed to everyone. In other words, the services already exist, and there are hopes that their provision can be improved by the utilization of information technology tools. This is not always the case in developing countries where services in most cases are unavailable and, consequently, not guaranteed to everyone. While in the former case there are of course examples of success and failure in the application of information technology, in the latter investments in IT are made, but it is hard to talk about technology success. Failure is almost self-evident, as is the case with the National Health Card in Brazil.

In February 2000, the Brazilian health card, or the National Health Card, as it is called, was introduced in Brazil. The initial plan was to introduce the health card in 44 municipalities in 10 Brazilian States, most of them situated in the richer areas of the country. As in some other countries, one of the main objectives of the National Health Card was to simplify and to process reimbursement claims. This identification card, which holds the patient's number and name, not only allows the patient to have access to medical care in any part of the country but can facilitate data integration stored on an electronic record. In 2006, the government was planning to register more people and to distribute 50 million cards.

The implementation of the National Health Card therefore required a quite sophisticated infrastructure of hardware and software able to read the card and to give electronic access to patient information. In short, with the implementation of the card, it was possible to create a national central database, with data from patients treated at the local level, facilitating data sharing and integration. For this reason, investments in the National Health Card have been increasing considerably over the years, requiring an infrastructure in terms of software, hardware, and networks systems that should continue to be enhanced. However, due to resource limitation and the lack of access to health care, it is expected that the chances of the National Health Card system working reliably remain remote.

Table 1 shows that, in addition, the introduction of e-health in Brazil may have contributed

to reducing expenditures in other important social programs. While expenditures made by the Ministry of Health increased over the years with the implementation of the National Health Card (Smart Card), expenditures in other social programs decreased. During the last few years, the Ministry of Health has been spending more money on the health card than on clinical and biomedical research by national institutes. The same has happened in terms of research into tropical medicine, tuberculosis, oncological cancer prevention, and other endemic diseases. The constant changes in accounts classification in the national budget make it difficult to follow an historical expenditure analysis.

No doubt, the Health Card may be a very important instrument for the electronic patient record, facilitating the storage and exchange of health care information among medical professionals and health care institutions to the benefit of the patient. However, it is mentioned that in the United Kingdom, for instance, the project to create a National Electronic Patient Record (EPR) in the National Health Service (NHS), the world's largest IT program, is beset by worries, cost overruns, and critics urging Britons to boycott it.

Recently, a group of academics representative of several medical organizations expressed their concerns about the security of information on the care records systems. According to the national doctors' newssheet, "Doctors have spoken out against the controversial £12.4bn NHS IT system that is over budget and behind schedule", claiming that patient confidentiality is being put at risk by the system (The Register, 2006). Writing in the British Medical Journal, a number of doctors have also said that it is unwise to put the medical records of the entire population on one computer (The Register, 2006). Furthermore, *The Guardian* noted that Ross Anderson, Professor of Security Engineering at Cambridge University, has said: 'If enough people boycott having centralized NHS records, with a bit of luck the service will be abandoned" (The Guardian, 2006).

Table 1. Expenditures on e-voting and e-health vs. other social programs

| EXPENDITURE NATURE | 2001 | 2002 | 2003 | Values in US$ millions | |
				2004	2005
ELECTORAL JUSTICE (ELECTRONIC VOTING)	25,235.4	71,346.7	1,641.5	64,375.3	7,742.3
IMPLEMENTATION OF THE NATIONAL HEALTH CARD	16,538.9	22,156.5	13,403.5	23,491.4	30,810.2
ONCOLOGICAL CANCER PREVENTION/ TREATMENT	10,587.9	9,756.6	9,278.0	N/A	N/A
POPULATION VACCINATION	14,430.6	9,617.7	5,152.0	2,664.6	3,080.4
ADOLESCENT SOCIAL RE-INSERTION IN CONFLICTS WITH THE LAW	7,024	7,725	4,472.2	2,961.7	4,633.4

Source: SIAFI/TCU

Conversion of the Brazilian currency, real (R$), into US$: the Annual Average was calculated based on the daily official rate as registered by the Brazilian Central Bank. 2001 = 2.3522; 2002 = 2.9285; 2003 = 3.0715; 2004 = 2.9257; 2005 = 2.4341.

As a result, there are many factors which confirm that the National Health Card is not a public health priority, partly because of insufficient knowledge about the goals and functions of this system – and almost complete lack of knowledge on how it should work. and the lack of participation of the medical professions in its development. This is a top-down project based on the tool approach to technology, oriented towards corporate actor interests and health care administration rather than health care needs. Therefore, it seems that e-health in Brazil means less care for the poor, and, for the purposes of improving citizenship, it is necessary to attend to people's basic health care needs, because this is what they need most, not to have a nice smart card in their pockets.

E-Voting in Brazil

Brazil was the first country in the world to conduct a large scale election using e-voting machines, in which more than 100 million people voted electronically. But what does it mean for democracy to conduct an electronic election involving millions of poor people, most of them living under the poverty line and forced to vote compulsorily? Is the high investment in e-voting technologies designed for the benefit of millions of illiterate voters?

Does e-voting aggregate any other information to voters? Does it help the voter to think better and formulate his decision to vote? Is e-voting affordable and a demand-driven option, or is it simply an external supply fashion? What are the risks of e-voting to democracy? Why is e-voting not used fully in more traditional democracies? Can more fragile, less mature democracies be reinforced and advanced with the adoption of e-voting systems? Will e-voting empower the ordinary people? Are voters treated as clients or citizens in this process or are they just being used by corporate actors driven by hunger for profits? Does e-voting avoid vote buying?

These questions need to be answered in a broad sense. Unfortunately the space here does not offer this opportunity. It seems that for the Electoral Justice in Brazil, responsible for election administration, the great merit of voting machines is that voters know the election results just a few hours after its end. Not surprisingly, over the years there has been intense marketing propaganda created by the Electoral Justice about the use and security of the e-voting technology in Brazil.

However, some specialists in computer security believe that such machines are more vulnerable to tampering than any other form of voting system, and claims about fraud in the e-voting system in

Brazil have intensified over the years since the introduction of this technology. Some Brazilian experts have mentioned the lack of security in e-voting machines stating that, with them, the Electoral Justice has opened the doors for new and sophisticated types of fraud, much more serious than the traditional ones (Maneschy, 2000), once the ballot's verification has become private and the Electoral Justice the owner of the ballot boxes (Rezende, 2002). Despite many reports in the developed world mentioning the lack of security and risks of e-voting machines (The Caltech/MIT Project, 2001; Kohno, Stubblefield, Rubin, Wallach., 2003; The Brennan Center, 2006) and the emergent consensus that the existing technology does not attend sufficiently to the principles of computer security, members of the Electoral Justice in Brazil, who are lawyers and not technical experts, are insistently arguing that e-voting machines are secure enough, even though they are made by the same company that makes them for other countries where they are severely criticized due to their lack of security.

Table 1 shows that, in the years in which elections are held, expenditures on e-voting are quite high. These are expenditures related just to teleprocessing, data processing, and equipment and software maintenance. When the administration staff salaries are included, the costs of an electronic election are quite high. In recent years, it is quite disappointing to see that the introduction of e-voting in Brazil has occurred concurrently with trends for shutting down schools for the poor, degrading the provision of health care, and lowering the salaries of school teachers.

The motivation to use e-voting technology in the developed world is to increase turnouts, due to the discrediting of politicians and political parties in the eyes of voters. Additionally, it has been mentioned that the kind of electoral reforms proposed in many countries to make it easier for registered voters to cast their ballots tends to benefit politicians and their parties with perverse consequences towards political engagement (Berinsky, 2005).

In Brazil, many electoral reforms have been approved over the last few years, but with none of them aiming at improving political engagement. Although we do not know about the true relationship between e-voting technology and turnout, during the last election turnouts decreased in the Parliamentary election in Brazil. A decrease in turnout may be a reduction in citizenship, but its relationship with e-voting technology is not clear. In many countries there is some political participation at election time, but people need democracy between elections and not only at election time. People want to participate in the decision-making process between elections, and this is not always the case. It is here that the use of ICTs may help voters to have a better engagement in the political process. In the case of Brazil, voters need government "of, by, and for the people".

It is know that corruption in elections in Brazil and in many other countries is not an abstract thing. It is a crude and disgraceful reality. Since the year 2000, the NGO named Transparência Brasil has carried out surveys about vote buying in Brazil. According to Transparência Brasil (2006), the Electoral Justice in the country is responsible for neglecting the problem of vote buying. It is very strange that the Electoral Justice is very much in favor of the e-voting technology system used in Brazil and is enable to enforce the law to combat vote buying. Is there a need for e-voting technology for the election of corrupted politicians? Vote buying by itself is a sign of reduced citizenship (Rodrigues Filho, 2008).

So, e-voting in Brazil has not stopped vote buying, which is increasing, and in 2006 it was two times higher than in the previous elections. What is surprising is that vote buying is higher among persons with secondary or higher education than voters with only primary education or below. It is expected that the poorer the voters, the more vulnerable they are to offers. The surveys from Transparência Brasil (2006) have showed that this is not true. More offers were made to the poorer citizens, but vote buying is registered among the wealthier classes. In order to give an idea of the magnitude of the problem of vote buying in Brazil, in 2006 it was found that about 8% of voters were asked to sell their votes for money (Transparência Brasil, 2006). Considering the numbers of voters in 2006, this corresponds to about 8.3 million voters and represents more than the population in some European countries and some Brazilian states.

An electoral reform or a new technology may have a positive impact on democracy and citizenship, if developed and implemented from below and not using the top-down model of politics. Unfortunately the economic view of democracy and politics in some countries is enough to separate technology from citizenship, merely reproducing the traditional and dominant forces by which power is exercised.

CONCLUSION

Modern democracy has narrowed citizenship and reduced it down to the right to vote in elections, turning democracy into something to be experienced at elections time and not between elections. Turning the citizens into clients or consumers is a kind of erosion of citizenship, and this is evident when people are considered the "consuming" rather than the "contributing" part of society.

In this work an attempt was made to show that, while e-voting technology does not seem to be a democratic tool for civic and effective participation, e-health seems to be oriented towards corporate actor interests and health care administration rather than basic health care needs. What people need is access to the most basic primary health services and not a nice smart card. For the poor population, it is more worth spending money on health services than on a technology that has not been proved to offer them better health care. Furthermore, some electoral reforms may have perverse consequences for citizenship and democracy. Making it easier for all citizens to vote does not necessarily mean improvements

in democracy and citizenship, especially when a top-down political tool is designed in ways that bring more power to the political elite.

There is no doubt that e-voting facilitates the work of the Electoral Justice in Brazil when a few hours after an election the names of those elected can be announced. This brings prestige to the Electoral Justice, whose power is reinforced by e-voting technology. Over the last ten years there has been a massive official propaganda in Brazil about e-voting and its security, in addition to training and demonstrations on how to vote electronically. As a consequence, the majority of the Brazilian society trusts our e-voting system and its security. In this situation, it is quite hard to comment against the fabricated trust of e-voting technology in the country.

In spite of this, it seems that democracy in Brazil is at risk: women's representation in the Brazilian parliament has decreased; politicians become richer after they are elected; our representatives in Parliament are getting richer than their predecessors; turnouts decreased in the last election, and vote buying increased substantially. The Brazilian press is always commenting about corruption in the Brazilian Parliament and on the sophisticated criminal organization and structure geared towards buying votes. So, what is e-voting for when money seems to be choking our democracy to death?

If people care about citizenship, the time is appropriate for a debate about the relationship between many e-government and e-democracy initiatives in Brazil and citizenship. This debate should reflect on our best understanding of freedom and social justice, addressing the source of inequality and injustice, and the future of our democracy. We cannot survive without the help of technology, but we cannot let the market works and express our politics in a passive way.

Some ICTs projects in Brazil, like e-voting and e-health initiatives, merely reproduce traditional and dominant forms in which power is exercised. These are top-down tools that exacerbate inequality, alienation, and exclusion, but do not awaken the "consciousness of how men are deceived in a permanent way" (Moraes, 2007, p.1).

REFERENCES

Alexander, C. (2005). Northern exposure: Assessing citizenship, democracy and the great Canadian e-government expedition. *Technikfolgenabschatzung – Theorie und Praxis, 2*, 80-87.

Amoretti, F. (2007). International Organizations ICTs Policies: E-Democracy and E-Government for Political Development. *Review of Policy Research, 24*(4), 331–344. doi:10.1111/j.1541-1338.2007.00286.x

Barber, B. R. (n.d.). *The ambigous effects of digital technology on democracy in a globalizing world*. Retrieved May 18, 2009, from http://www.wissensgesellschaft.org/themen/demokratie/democratic.pdf

Barney, D. (2006). Teaching technology: A question of citizenship. Retrieved May 5, 2009, from: media.mcgill.ca/files/Darin_Barney_Teaching_Technology.pdf

Berinsky, A. (2005). The perverse consequences of electoral reform in the United States. *American Politics Research, 33*(4), 471–491. doi:10.1177/1532673X04269419

Chadwick, A., & May, C. (2003). Interaction between states and citizens in the age of the internet: "e-Government" in the United States, Britain and the European Union. *Governance, 16*(2), 271–300. doi:10.1111/1468-0491.00216

Dahl, R. A. (1956). *A preface to democratic theory*. Chicago, IL: University of Chicago Press.

Delanty, G. (2007). *Citizenship as a Learning Process: Disciplinary Citizenship versus Cultural Citizenship*. Retrieved May 15, 2009, from http://eurozine.com/pdf/2007-06-30-delanty-en.pdf

Dobson, A. (2003, November 27-28). *Ecological citizenship. An ESRC seminar series. Seminar 1: The shape of environmental citizenship: Theory and practice*. Retrieved May 15, 2009, from: http://www.ncl.ac.uk/environmentalcitizenship/papers/Dobson%20EcolCit.doc

Downs, A. (1957). *An economic theory of democracy*. New York: Harper.

Dunleavy, P., & Hood, C. (1994). From old public administration to new public management. *Public Money and Management, 14*(3), 9–16.

Elmer, G. (2003). A diagram of panoptic surveillance. *New Media & Society, 5*(2), 231–247. doi:10.1177/1461444803005002005

Feenberg, A. (1999). *Questioning technology*. London: Routledge.

Hermes, J. (2006). Citizenship in the age of the internet. *European Journal of Communication, 21*(3), 295–309. doi:10.1177/0267323106066634

Holford, H., & Edirisingha, P. (2000). *Citizenship and governance education in Europe: A critical review of the literature. University of Surrey*. UK: School of Educational Studies.

Hood, C. (1995). The new public management in the 1980s: Variations on a theme. *Accounting, Organizations and Society, 20*(2/3), 93–109. doi:10.1016/0361-3682(93)E0001-W

Janoski, T. (1998). *Citizenship and civil society*. Cambridge, UK: Cambridge University Press.

Kohno, T., & Stubblefield, A. Rubin, A., & Wallach, D. S. (2003). Analysis of the electronic voting system (Technical Report TR-2003). Johns Hopkins Information Security Institute.

Longford, G. (2005). Pedagogies of digital citizenship and the politics of code. *Techné: Research in Philosophy and Technology, 9*(1), 1–25.

Maneschy, O. (2002). *Burla Eletrônica*. Rio de Janeiro, Brazil: Fundação Alberto Pasqualini.

Marcondes, C. H., & Jardim, J. M. (2003). Políticas de informação governamental: A construção do governo eletrônico na administração federal do Brasil. *DataGramaZero - Revista de Ciência da Informação, 4*(2).

McNamara, K., & O'Brien, R. (2000, January 1). *Access to information and communication for sustainable development opportunities and challenges for international community -Recommendations of the access working group.* GKP II Conference, Global Knowledge Partenership Secretariat. Kuala Lumpur, Malaysia.

Michel, H. (2005). e-Administration, e-Government, e-Governance and the learning city: A typology of citizenship management using ICTs. *The Electronic Journal of E-Government, 3*(4), 213–218.

Moraes, R. A. (2007, March). Is a new critical language in the education still possible today? Osford Mini-Conference, Retrieved May 20, 2009, from http://construct.haifa.ac.il/~ilangz/oxford2007/Almeida%20Moraes.pdf

Nogueira Filho, D. (2001). Governo eletrônico. SECOP - Seminário Nacional de Informática Publica, 29. *Anais eletrônicos.* Retrieved May 12, 2009, from: http://www.abep.sp.gov.br/Download 29secopSP/governo

O'Loughlin, B. (2001). The political implications of digital innovations: Trade-offs of democracy and liberty in the developed world. *Information Communication and Society, 4*(4), 595–614. doi:10.1080/13691180110097021

Olsson, T. (2006). Appropriating civic information and communication technology: A critical study of Swedish ICT policy visions. *New Media & Society, 18*(4), 611–627. doi:10.1177/1461444806065659

Ong, A. (1996). Cultural citizenship as subject-making: Immigrants negotiate racial and cultural boundaries in the United States. *Current Anthropology, 37*, 737–762. doi:10.1086/204560

Osborne, D., & Gaebler, T. (1992). *Reinventing government.* Reading, MA: Addison-Wesley Publishing Company.

Pawley, L. (2008). Cultural citizenship. *Social Compass, 2*(2), 593–608.

Rezende, P. A. D. (2002). *Voto Eletrônico Amplia Chances de Fraude.* Folha de São Paulo.

Riley, D. (1992). Citizenship and the welfare state. In Allan, J., Braham, P., & Lewis, P. (Eds.), *Political and economic forms of modernity.* Cambridge: Polity Press.

Rodrigues Filho, J. (2008). E-Voting in Brazil – Reinforcing institutions while diminishing citizenship. 3rd International Conference, Gesellschaft für Informatik and E-Voting. August 6-, Bregenz, Austria.

Rodrigues Filho, J., & Gomes, N. P. (2008). E-Voting in Brazil – Exacerbating alienation and the digital divide. In Santap, S. M. (Ed.), *E-Democracy – Concepts and Practice.* Hyderabad, India: IFCAI Books.

Rodrigues Filho, J., & Santos Junior, J. R. (2009). Local e-government in Brazil – Poor interaction and local politics as usual. In Reddick, C. G. (Ed.), *Handbook of research on strategies for local e-government adoption and implementation – comparative studies.* Hershey, PA: IGI Global.

Sanchez, O. A. (2003). O poder burocrático e o controle da informação. Lua nova. *Revista de Cultura e Política, 58*, 89–119.

Schumpeter, J. (1976). *Capitalism, socialism and democracy.* New York: Harper.

Stevenson, N. (2003). *Cultural citizenship: Cosmopolitan questions*. Maidenhead, UK: Open University Press.

The Brennan Center of the NYU School of Law. (2006). *Brennan Center Report*. New York: NYU.

The Caltech/MIT Voting Technology Project. (2001). Residual votes attributable to technology – An assessment of the reliability of existing voting equipment. http://www.hss.caltech.edu/~voting/CalTech_MIT_Report_Version2.pdf. (Accessed: 15.05.2009).

The Guardian. (2006). *Ministers to put patients' details on central database despite objections*. Retrieved July 28, 2008, from http://society.guardian.co.uk/e-public/story/0,1937301,00.html

The Register. (2006). *Doctors attack the NHS IT system*. Retrieved July 28, 2008, from: http://www.theregister.co.uk/2006/07/19/patient_confidentiality_risk/

Transparência Brasil. (2006). *Compra de votos nas eleições de 2006, Corrupção e desempenho administrativo*. São Paulo. Retrieved May 16, 2009, from http://www.transparencia.org.br/docs/compravotos2006.pdf

Turner, B. S. (2001). The erosion of citizenship. *The British Journal of Sociology, 52*(2), 189–209. doi:10.1080/00071310120044944

Tuuva-Hongisto, S., & Talsi, N. (2006, March 15-17). *Citizens in fragmented technology policy*. International ProACT conference. Tampere, Finland.

United Nations Public Administration Network (UNPAN). (2005). *UN global e-government readiness report – From e-government to e-inclusion. Division for Public Administration and Development Management. Department of Economic and Social Affairs*. New York: United Nations.

Wang, T. (2008, September 4-6). *Internet access as a social right: Implications for social citizenship*. Annual academic conference of the International Sociological Association's research committee on poverty, social welfare and social policy (RC19). Stockholm, Sweeden.

Wiklund, H. (2005). A Habermasian analysis of the deliberative democratic potential of ICT-enabled services in Swedish municipalities. *New Media & Society, 7*(5), 701–723. doi:10.1177/1461444805056013

Winner, L. (2005). Technological euphoria and contemporary citizenship. *Techné: Research in Philosophy and Technology, 9*(1), 1–8.

KEY TERMS AND DEFINITIONS

Citizenship: Defined as an ongoing process and not merely as a list of rights and obligations.

E-Government: Defined as the use of information and communication technology in public administration combined with organizational change in order to improve public services and democratic processes (Europe's Information Society, 2003).

E-Health: The use of information technology in the health sector.

E-Voting: The use of voting machines to accelerated vote counting.

Health Card: An identification card that facilitates data integration stored on an electronic record for a national central database.

Technological Citizenship: Use of ICT to enhance the democratization of democracy and to see how technology influences democracy, and existing democratic practices, considering that the World Wide Web regulate and govern users, as citizens, in a quite invisible and opaque way (Longford, 2005, p. 2).

Thin Democracy: Defined as a representative democracy where citizenship is limited to voting and the ordinary citizen lives privately as a consumer or as a marginalized client.

Chapter 22
"Potential" Barriers to E–Government Implementation in Developing Countries

Marvine Hamner
George Washington University, USA

Doaa Taha
Independent Consultant, USA

Salah Brahimi
Grey Matter International Ltd, USA

ABSTRACT

Developing countries interested in initiating E-Government will confront a number of issues and challenges in this endeavor. These issues and challenges often manifest themselves as "potential" barriers to implementation including: the lack of infrastructure; sustainability; culture; knowledge, skills, abilities, and attitudes; and, privacy and security. However, as this article shows many of these will not be "real" barriers. This article also presents a number of solutions and recommendations for the potential barriers discussed. Furthermore, research has found that local customization of E-Government will be crucial in developing countries; and, that privacy and security issues do not appear to be as big a concern as may be thought. The intent of this article is to outline the issues and challenges (potential barriers) for E-Government implementation and discuss potential solutions to these barriers, in order to generate a dialogue to establish a solid, technological and social foundation for E-Government.

INTRODUCTION

E-Government can be viewed as a complex mix of and tension between: social inclusion and political engagement; management of change and innovation; and, standardization and integration of information technology. It includes legal, ethical and political responsibilities (Tassabehji, 2007; Srivastava, 2007; Grant, 2005a; Teicher, 2002). The overall intention of E-Government initiatives is to increase the efficacy, i.e. both the efficiency <u>and</u> effectiveness, of government. To achieve this, countries have been developing and implementing E-Government in a variety of forms for several years (Zambrano,

DOI: 10.4018/978-1-61520-933-0.ch022

2008). However, because it is still a relatively new application of information technology rigorous quantitative research on E-Government covers a broad and somewhat disjointed range of topic areas (Grant, 2005a) and often results in conflicting conclusions. Beyond research, the success of E-Government systems in use has been questioned (Akesson, 2008; Ebbers, 2008; Lovelock, 2002). Even an exact definition of E-Government has not yet been agreed to. Within this article,

E-Government is the term used to refer to a "system" that facilitates interaction between citizens and government via an information and communication technology. Interactions range from accessing government services to increased and enhanced citizen participation in government.

This definition can be applied to virtually every E-Government effort that has been completed, is underway or is being planned. Both the "supply-side" and the "demand-side" of E-Government are embodied in the "system," in which supply-side interactions are provided by the government and demand-side interactions are used by citizens. E-Government efforts can be small or large, narrowly targeted or very broad, simple or complex. On one hand, government efforts to provide citizens with easier, faster and less costly access to specific transactions such as renewing licenses through E-Government have been largely successful. This is consistent with citizens' expectations that electronic transactions with their government should mirror the availability and ease of other types of electronic transactions such as E-Commerce or E-Business (Tassabehji, 2007). On the other hand, E-Government efforts with regard to their overall impact are less clear. An exact meaning of the "intention to increase and/or enhance citizen participation" in government, and how that intention can be implemented through E-Government does not yet exist. For example, pseudo governmental agencies such as NGO's (non-governmental organizations) are publishing proposed activities on their websites and encouraging citizens to contact their governmental representatives to support these activities. Is this the intention when governments talk about increasing and/or enhancing citizen participation through E-Government?

Whether in developed or developing countries, citizens and their government have a relationship even in abstention. The 2002 Annual Global Accenture Study estimated that 80% of the world's population lives in developing countries (Chen, 2006). Unfortunately, in developing countries many citizens live in remote areas that are very long distances from government locations. These areas can also be very difficult to get to and/or from. E-Government provides needed access to governmental information and services for citizens in such areas. Further, many E-Government systems now encompass a broad range of information and communication technologies (ICT). For example, telephones and fax machines as well as the Internet and wireless devices such as palm pilots can all be used to conduct transactions with governmental agencies (Singh, 2008). These transactions range from determining where to go to procure various licenses to actually purchasing those licenses. But there are additional needs that can be met through the ICT provided by E-Government initiatives. In fact, within developing countries there is a relationship between ICT initiatives, e.g. a relationship between providing E-Government and bridging the digital divide (Helbig, 2009) that spans access to and the use of technology. By satisfying citizens' need to access government, E-Government could supply the technology required for many other social initiatives and strategies for growth.

For E-Government to be successfully implemented in developing countries a number of issues and challenges will have to be addressed first (Evans, 2005; Ndou, 2004). This article focuses on these issues and challenges as they are manifested in "potential" barriers to implementing E-Government. These barriers are labeled as "potential" because they may not present as much of a "real" barrier as has been perceived. These potential barriers include: infrastructure; privacy and security; sustainability; culture; and, knowledge, skills abilities and attitudes. This article also includes a number of ways to reduce the risk of costly failures, e.g. by considering and developing a broad national strategy that includes: all phases of E-Government; potential barriers to E-Government; and, their probable solutions.

BACKGROUND

Although the number of E-Government systems in use has been rapidly growing, many still consider research about E-Government to be "embryonic" (Grant, 2005a). In fact, there is as much chance that research results will be contradictory as there is for consistent results with prior research. In 2003 the United Nations Report, *UN Global E-Government Survey 2003*, discussed three "pre-requisites" for E-Government that span the entire range of research topics: "a minimum threshold level of technological infrastructure, human capital and E-Connectivity" (UN Survey, 2003). In terms of "E-Connectivity," by 2005 the UN found that "the total number of countries online" had risen to 179 out of 191 member states, or 94%. That "steady progress in ICT diffusion, human capital development and Member States' E-Government websites" meant that "the world average E-Government readiness had risen to 0.4267" (UN Report, 2005). However, even developed countries implement E-Government at very different rates with very different intentions. Implementers in Italy, Japan, the Netherlands, and South Africa have been described as "cautious" (Chen, 2006) while others are known as leaders in implementing E-Government, e.g. Australia (Teicher, 2002). This can be viewed in direct contrast to the fact that only roughly 3.4% of the population of Bangladesh has a telephone (UNCTAD, 2002; Palmer, 2002). This illustrates the diversity between countries and that the gap

between those who have access to and use technology and those who do not, the "digital divide," continues to widen despite global initiatives.

Given the broad range of issues and challenges to E-Government, to capture all the details in a holistic manner requires first taking a reductionist's point of view. At the top level E-Government can be broken down into its supply-side and its demand-side. Very simply stated, E-Government's supply-side encompasses ICT challenges and issues as well as government's strategy and intentions, e.g. government's strategy with regard to what services are to be provided and what level of citizen interaction is desired. Similarly, E-Government's demand-side encompasses citizen's needs and wants. Further reducing the supply-side and demand-side to their next levels begins to reveal the scope of complexity of E-Government. For example, challenges and issues for ICT include designing, developing and implementing infrastructure in remote and/or difficult to access regions, but also in regions with very low population densities. For companies involved in building infrastructure, it can be as difficult to make a "business case" to invest in building infrastructure in an area with a very low population density as it is to make the case for building infrastructure in a very remote area. On the demand-side, citizens, particularly those in remote areas, may need E-Government to enable any number of transactions but the lack of development of "human capital" may erect a seemingly insurmountable barrier. With regard to research, given this complexity it is easy to see why research efforts have covered a very broad range of topics and often yield apparently conflicting or contradictory results. With regard to implementing E-Government, the UN has evaluated a countries E-Government readiness by applying the "Web Measure Index, the Telecommunication Infrastructure Index and the Human Capital Index" (UN Report, 2005). Examples of the E-Government readiness in 2008 for a few developed and developing countries is given in Table 1.

Table 1. 2008 e-government readiness

Rank	Country	E-Gov Readiness
1	Sweden	0.9157
2	Denmark	0.9134
3	Norway	0.8921
4	United States	0.8644
7	Canada	0.8172
8	Australia	0.8108
10	United Kingdom	0.7872
37	Mexico	0.5893
65	China	0.5017
72	Bolivia	0.4867
90	Georgia	0.4598
91	Vietnam	0.4558
99	Guatemala	0.4283
103	Armenia	0.4182
108	Iran	0.4067
119	Syria	0.3614
131	Pakistan	0.3160
140	Morocco	0.2944
152	Mozambique	0.2559
156	Laos	0.2383
165	Haiti	0.2097
178	Sierra Leone	0.1463
....	Marshall Islands*	....
....	Somalia*	....

Notes: *Not yet online. (UN, 2008)

Even though most developed countries are using E-Government in some way and many developing countries demonstrate E-Government readiness, what do we really know about E-Government today? Some concern has been voiced that research has focused too heavily on the supply-side (Reddick, 2005). This is because it is easy to ascertain what government services are available electronically. Reports of advances in ICT are also easy to obtain. And, with the advances in ICT as well as in E-Commerce, it is easy for governments to be successful in providing specific transactions electronically. Increases in infrastructure, the number of Internet users, and literacy rates can also

be measured. But assessing progress in realizing the "full benefit" of E-Government is much more difficult, if only because what the "full benefit" is has never been defined. It is widely accepted that the "full benefit" of E-Government will vary widely and depend on local customization of E-Government (Zambrano, 2008).

Why is this important? Why is it important to have and sustain E-Government in developing countries? Virtually all research has found a direct and undeniable link between ICT, government and citizens' well-being (Trkman, 2009; Siau, 2006). It is important for citizens to have access to their government, in both their personal and in their

Table 2. Country facts for a few random developed and developing countries

Country	per capita GNI (US$)	Internet subscribers**	Telephony subscribers*.**
Canada	39,420	520	1,080
United States	46,040	630	1,228
Australia	35,960	698	1,470
United Kingdom	42,740	474	1,615
Norway	76,450	735	1,489
Somalia	not reported	11	73
Mozambique	320	not reported	<10
Haiti	480	70	64
Kyrgyz Republic	490	54	191
Laos	500	5	126

Notes: *Some have more than one telephone/telephone line.
**per 1,000 citizens.

professional lives. For example, in their personal lives citizens may want or need licenses such as a marriage license or to file a land registration. To start a business they may need a business license. To expand their professional life they may need additional licenses, or to file a tax return, or get additional education or training. In this regard E-Government can be a large part of people's lives. And, E-Government begins to play a direct role in developing countries where the access to government is hindered by the remoteness of a citizen's location or the sheer difficulty of surmounting physical barriers such as mountains, rivers, etc. In such places E-Government may be the only way of ensuring citizens' timely and consistent access to government.

Country Classifications

No one, single definition exists for the term "developing countries." In general, definitions of the terms "developing countries," "newly industrialized countries," and "developed countries" rest on an economic distinction about the material quality of life. In very broad terms a developing country is one with a "low level of material well being" (World Bank, 2009a). The differences

between countries include: a countries history, culture and economic status; knowledge, skills and abilities of citizens particularly those employed in governmental organizations; access to and use of technology; and, available technology and infrastructure. Relevant data on developed and developing countries from the World Bank (http://geo.worldbank.org/ 2009) and CIA World Factbook (https://www.cia.gov/library/publications/the-world-factbook/geos/mz.html 2009) include, but are not limited to: (See Table 2).

Gross national income (GNI) per capita reported is based on nominal values of the 2007 gross national income and calculated according to the Atlas Method (UN Statistical Manual, 2009). The developed countries included in Table 2 all have sufficient capital and the knowledge, skills and ability to develop the infrastructure, technology and systems required to implement E-Government. The developing countries in Table 2 simply do not have the capital (resources), the knowledge, skills and ability, or the technology and infrastructure to undertake an E-Government initiative by themselves.

Today, an "intermediate" category of countries exists, i.e. those countries that are considered "newly industrialized." "Newly industrialized country" (NIC) is a classification that includes socioeconomic attributes such as: strong leadership, greater freedom and rights, an open market economy where private enterprise enjoys international free-trade, and an industrial-base with a strong manufacturing sector (Fogel, 2009; Hoskisson, 2000; Young, 1993). Countries typically designated a NIC include South Africa, Mexico, Brazil, China, Egypt, India, Indonesia, Malaysia, the Philippines, Russia, Thailand, and Turkey. An alternative classification, i.e. "Emerging Market," is used for countries exhibiting "rapid industrialization" (Hoskisson, 2000). There will obviously be quite a bit of overlap in the countries included in these two classifications. Countries typically designated an "Emerging Markets" include: Argentina, Brazil, Chile, China, Columbia, Egypt, Hungary, India, Indonesia, Malaysia, Mexico, Morocco, Pakistan, Peru, the Philippines, Poland, Russia, South Africa, Taiwan, Thailand, and Turkey. Interestingly many of the countries designated as a NIC or Emerging Market have had relatively high socioeconomic conditions. For example, many of these countries have had a relatively strong manufacturing sector and correspondingly a relatively high per capita GDP. In addition, these countries have had relatively well developed educational systems. These socioeconomic attributes will play an important role in ICT initiatives including E-Government.

Sustainability

There are many reasons for implementing E-Government in developing countries. The primary reason is still that E-Government may be the best (and sometimes the only) way for people in remote areas, or areas that are physically difficult to access, to access their government and its services. In these areas the need for E-Government is often balanced against other needs such as basic human needs (water, food and shelter), healthcare, education, and so on. Although technology appears to be poised to make an enormous and potentially

simultaneous impact on many of these needs in the near future, there will still be issues and challenges not the least of which will be sustainability; economic sustainability, environmental sustainability, and social sustainability (Pade, Mallinson and Sewry; 2008; Prahalad and Hammond, 2002; Vergnes, 2001). Sustainability is often thought of in terms of a potential barrier to E-Government implementation. Conversely, E-Government could be thought of as a means of social and economic sustainability. Issues and challenges that affect sustainability, particularly those that impact citizens' access to government have been studied in detail (Dethier, 2009).

In the past, economics have often had a negative impact on technology or technology-based initiatives introduced in developing countries. Even if supply and demand has been present many efforts were not sustainable because they were unable to generate sufficient revenue due to very low levels of income, very low population density, etc. Challenges like these have provided the motivation to consider "bundling" ICT initiatives in order to integrate multiple funding sources to maximize the support available. This is not a new concept. Oliver (1975) reported that an economist at the World Bank, Paul Rosenstein-Rodan was first to espouse bundling projects together in his the "Big Push" theory (Oliver, 1975). Integrating support for multiple technology based efforts may be the only way to show a sufficient return on investment in a business case that includes economic sustainability (Heeks, 2001).

Factors Affecting E-Government and Strategies for E-Government

Research by Kim (2007) demonstrated that determinants of E-Government performance include economic wealth, education, urbanization, civil liberties, government effectiveness and the interaction between Internet usage and economic wealth. Other research reported government effectiveness referred to quality, competence, credibility and independence (Kaufman et al, 2003). Unless a foundation for the professional delivery of government services (quality) exists E-Government will not perform well regardless of the technology available (Kim, 2007). In addition, greater civil liberties were found to contribute directly to E-Government performance. Kim says that, "Unless civil liberties are widely permitted, e-government would not perform beyond a billboard as one-way communication with the public..." (Kim, 2007).

Heeks (2003) found that more than one-third of all E-Government implementations in developing countries are "total failures," more than half are at least "partial failures," whereas only about one-seventh can be considered successes. Al-Fakhri (2008) developed a list of issues that would need to be addressed for E-Government to become effective in Saudi Arabia. In addition to the technical factors reported, non-technical factors were cited as more pervasive and had the ability to make a bigger impact on the failure of E-Government in Saudi Arabia including: the current structure of government agencies; current government regulations; resistance to change particularly by senior managers in governmental agencies; and, resistance to change by governmental employees. In addition, security and the lack of trust were cited as enormous barriers to E-Government implementation, as was the dominance of the English language (Al-Fakhri, 2008).

Heeks (2002) evaluated the differences in E-Government initiatives between developing and developed countries including information, technology, processes, objectives and values, staffing and skills, management systems and structures, and other resources. These are very similar to the differences examined by Chen et al (Chen, 2006). Chen et al developed a framework that considers factors affecting a national E-Government infrastructure. These factors include: network access; networked learning; networked economy; network policy; and, culture and society. When countries, e.g. the United States and China, are

compared using this framework it was found that it may be completely inappropriate for developing countries to consider using E-Government initiatives in developed countries as prototypes for their own initiatives. Considerations of each country's strategic intentions are an important part of any E-Government initiative.

A Phased Approach to E-Government Implementation

The broad range of factors and strategies affecting E-Government has motivated many researchers to propose a phased approach to implementation (Lau, 2008; Layne, 2001). This article supports that position with local customization in each phase. A phased approach typically begins with a "Transactional Phase." Government agencies may have websites that "broadcast" information prior to the transactional phase, a "Phase 0." However, a static website without any intention of further development and interaction with citizens falls outside the definition of E-Government. Within the transactional phase citizens are able to complete a variety of electronic transactions with various government agencies, e.g. renewing their driver's license. The next phase, the "Engagement Phase," enables citizens to complete electronic transactions plus receive information from and communicate electronically with various government agencies and officials. The last phase, the "Participatory Phase," includes all the actions and interactions of the first two phases plus citizens are able to participate in their government, in ways strategically established by their government.

On the government's side, the "Transactional Phase" enables government agencies to streamline routine transactions resulting in increased efficiency and reduction of costs. In order to maximize these effects, barriers between government agencies will need to be reduced or eliminated (Grant, 2002). The "Engagement Phase" with direct communication between citizens and their government officials is intended to result in more effective government. Direct communication with government officials is also intended to increase the transparency of government agencies. This is instrumental in building trust and higher levels of citizen participation. The "Participatory Phase" enables strategic public administration by government. For example, this phase may allow citizens to customize their interaction with government including creating a "profile" within which "one click" can complete all their normal transactions and produce information about and from their specific government representatives. Moreover, if citizens move they should only have to modify their address in their profile to update all their transactions with all government agencies. Where appropriate, this phase can enable enhanced public administration such as Constituent Relationship Management (CRM) through a combination of outreach and increased exposure of government officials to their constituent citizens.

Taking the phased approach has the benefit of incorporating time into the initiative, time for building the required ICT infrastructure, beginning programs to educate or train citizens and government employees while developing the overall E-Government strategy. Relying on similarities to E-Commerce transactions, beginning at the "Transactional Phase" allows citizens and government agencies to succeed in their initial E-Government implementation. Recognizing and celebrating successes, small or large, is an important part of managing government (public) agencies. Implementation of the "Transactional Phase" can begin without major changes in the operation of government agencies, i.e. the same transactions are completed albeit through an electronic process. As E-Government evolves, reducing or eliminating barriers between government agencies can proceed in parallel with or after the "Transaction Phase" has been implemented.

ISSUES AND CHALLENGES FOR E-GOVERNMENT: POTENTIAL BARRIERS TO IMPLEMENTATION

There are a number of issues and challenges that developing countries will have to address prior to successfully implementing E-Government. The reason these issues or challenges are presented as potential barriers is because they may be more easily overcome or may not create as severe an impact as is currently perceived. These issues and challenges include: the lack of infrastructure; sustainability; culture; the knowledge, skills, abilities and attitudes of citizens and government employees; and, privacy and security. The Introduction above presents the background for these potential barriers. This section presents each of these potential barriers in the context of E-Government. Then solutions and recommendations are provided.

A Lack of Infrastructure: The "Traditional" View

The "traditional" view maintains that the lack of infrastructure is an enormous barrier to the implementation of E-Government. The *Report on the World Summit on the Information Society Stocktaking* highlights the over 1,700 activities have been reported that involve "capacity building" in terms of providing the necessary, corresponding "supply" of technology (ITU, 2008). Counter to the diffusion of traditional infrastructure, the United Nations Development Programme reported in "Delivering on the Global Partnership for Achieving the Millennium Development Goals" that over 77% of the population in developing countries now are able to receive a mobile cellular telephone signal (up from 46% in 2001) and 54% of the population in the Sub-Saharan Africa (up from 28%) (MDG Gap Task Force, 2008). Table 3 below lists data for mobile telephone penetration from a random sampling of developing and developed countries for the top ten countries

Table 3. Developing and developed countries' data sorted by mobile telephone penetration (per 1000's population)

	Population	per capita GDP	Literacy rate (%)	Fixed Telephony Penetration (per 1000)	Mobile Telephony Penetration (per 1000)	Internet Penetration (per 1000)
Top Ten Countries						
Spain	4.04E+07	30,100	98.0	428.6	2075.2	195.1
Israel	6.50E+06	25,800	97.0	462.4	1292.8	292.1
Czech Republic	1.02E+07	24,400	99.0	314.8	1188.7	342.4
Russia	1.41E+08	14,700	100.0	283.6	1061.0	181.7
Germany	8.24E+07	34,200	99.0	658.0	1023.4	468.6
Qatar	9.07E+05	80,900	89.0	251.6	1013.9	319.5
United Kingdom	6.08E+07	35,100	99.0	542.0	1005.3	618.7
Hungary	9.93E+06	19,500	99.0	337.3	1003.4	352.4
Kuwait	2.60E+06	39,300	93.3	196.5	976.6	314.5
Australia	2.06E+07	37,500	99.0	482.5	959.2	742.7
Bottom Ten Countries						
Syria	1.93E+07	4,500	73.6	68.0	0.0	3.1
Proposed Palestinian State	4.02E+06	600		23.8	0.0	14.9
Laos	6.68E+06	2,100	53.0	3.7	0.7	1.5
Pakistan	1.68E+08	2,600	49.9	17.1	0.9	7.2
Libya	6.17E+06	12,300	83.0	81.0	3.2	3.2
Tunisia	1.03E+07	7,500	74.3	63.6	4.9	38.9
Ukraine	4.63E+07	6,900	100.0	204.1	5.1	16.2
Oman	3.31E+06	24,000	81.4	60.7	18.1	36.3
Thailand	6.51E+07	7,900	96.0	86.1	47.6	18.4
Cambodia	1.42E+07	1,800	73.6	4.5	74.6	2.9

Developed countries are shaded light gray.

(highest penetration) and the bottom ten countries (lowest penetration) (infoplease, 2009). It is interesting to note that the list of top ten countries in terms of mobile telephone penetration include as many developing countries as it does developed countries.

While access to cellular telephone signals helps with many types of communications, e.g. public healthcare messages, it does not remove the real barriers to achieving the broadband ac-cess that is required for E-Government (Singh, 2008). Internet penetration in developed countries has largely followed patterns of "traditional" infrastructure, specifically power distribution and fixed telephone penetration. The lack of this "traditional" infrastructure is readily apparent in many developing countries, e.g. 30% of people in developing countries still do not have access to electricity. It has been said that broadband connectivity to the Internet is not currently possible without building the required infrastructure (MDG Gap Task Force, 2008). Development of the infrastructure required to support overall growth has been widely recognized as the single biggest challenge facing the deployment of E-Government and is being discussed in terms of national agendas and public-private partnerships. Even so it is difficult to imagine installing the kinds of power distribution grids in developing countries that already exist in developed countries. This is an area where new technologies could "leap frog" existing technology, providing the functionality of infrastructure without undergoing massive projects to actually build it.

Sustainability of E-Government

In large part the "sustainability" of E-Government requires determining how sufficient funding can be generated to the meet ongoing expenses. This can be done by developing either a cost-benefit analysis or a business model. In the cost-benefit analysis, costs are usually straight forward. However, funding for ongoing operations is not always clear and rarely accounted for. A business model approach is preferred over a cost-benefit analysis because in addition to benefits and costs the associated pro-forma financial statements include all (anticipated) expenses and revenue (funding) over time. Janssen developed a business model for E-Government based on public service networks from the field of E-Commerce. From this research Janssen concluded that the public service network that formed the foundation for each of the business models created new and different sets of issues and challenges within each model. No single business model appeared to comprehensively address all the issues and challenges that could arise from a single service offering through E-Government (Janssen, 2007) – from a research perspective. However, from a practical perspective a business model for E-Government can be made.

The Presence of Many Cultures

Culture is a very important part of our lives. Culture takes many forms; religious, political, organizational, group (e.g. tribal). Culture even plays a role in economics (e.g. class or caste systems) and more. No technology will be successful if its designers do not consider the impact of culture. Tenets of usability engineering that promote customization of E-Government will be crucial in addressing the diversity of culture. Even if there were a single solution, over time local requirements for E-Government would change, e.g. consider the changing cultural impacts of the democratic political system over time in the United States alone. Although the fundamental democratic principals do not change, the way those principals are applied is constantly changing. These changes directly impact the required functionality and operation of E-Government. This means that designers must create an interactive system that is sufficiently flexible to adapt to whatever changes may be coming.

Knowledge, Skills, Abilities and Attitudes

E-Government often has a gap between what citizens want and what government wants. Sometimes this gap is due to a genuine difference in goals and objectives; and, sometimes it is simply due to differences in knowledge, skills, abilities and attitudes (Ebbers, 2008). In 2005 Al-Fakhri et al (2008) began evaluating the status of the E-Government implementation in Saudi Arabia. Al-Fakhri (2008) found that although 88% of survey respondents indicated they had computers, only 18% said that the Internet was used for government tasks. Half of the survey respondents reported that their agencies do not have Internet connections. Roughly an equal number of respondents said they knew a Saudi E-Government portal existed as those who said they did not know. With regard to awareness about the E-Government implemen-

Table 4. Privacy and security challenges to citizens' adoption of e-government

Rank	Challenge
1	Security of Records and Information
2	Privacy of Records and Information
3	Security of Electronic Transactions
4	Potential for Identity Theft
5	Secure Government Technology (infrastructure, hardware, software, systems, etc.)
6	Secure Citizen Technology

tation, more than half of all survey respondents did not know whether or not their agency had a timeframe for E-Government implementation. Thirty-three percent of respondents indicated that they did not have an opportunity to participate in their agency's plan for E-Government implementation and an additional thirty-five percent did not know if they could have participated or not. Al-Fakhri (2008) found that the greatest challenges included the lack of knowledge about E-Government both in Saudi society and by government employees along with a lack of trust by government employees in their ability to complete their tasks online. This was confirmed by survey data acquired from experts who indicated that knowledge about E-Government would be one of the greatest challenges to its acceptance by managers. Experts also believe that another large challenge to overcome will be the resistance to change by government employees. This may be partly the result a generally negative attitude, principally due to a fear of consequences (e.g. lost records and lost social connections) and the belief that E-Government would ultimately result in the elimination of jobs.

Privacy and Security

Privacy and security are critical areas of concern within government agencies that are addressed through actual, typically technological, measures (Saltzer, 1984). Research has identified a "gap" between the level of privacy and security perceived by citizens and the actual privacy and security provided by government agencies (Tassabehji, 2007). This gap exacerbates a "lack of trust" by citizens. Even worse, many people are not aware of or do not understand security features already in place at their government's agencies. This further leads to a generally negative perception of E-Technologies overall, i.e. a perception based on "security fears," so that with regard to E-Government transactions over 60% of those polled in Europe were unlikely to use E-Government (Cremonini, 2003). For interactive systems, there are both technological and social aspects to privacy and security. Within the domains of usability engineering and HCI, security refers to risks, particularly those risks associated with information technology and how effective the technology is in detecting, responding to and protecting a system from those risks. Privacy deals with the control of or risk of losing control of access to information and/or individuals. Table 4 below lists and ranks what experts believe are the primary privacy and security challenges to citizens' adoption of E-Government.

Based on the definitions above, privacy and security are "social products" (Dourish, 2006). In the past, development of privacy and security technologies has frequently focused on system administrators and fallen short of end-user requirements, many of which are embedded in social systems. A study by Whitten and Tygar (1999) found that end-users' lack of understanding of security software directly resulted in insecure information practices (Whitten, 1999). Systems for which technological solutions addressing privacy and security were added on "after the fact" were almost never completely successful. Privacy and security must be integral parts of an interactive system's operations and as such cannot be pasted on the top of such systems after-the-fact (Dourish, 2006). According to Wenger (1998) information practices are the social way we manage information including sharing and withholding information, how we interpret acts of managing information, and how we strategically deploy the management of information. Interactive systems designed with these premises in mind include privacy and security as an integral part of the system, not as add-ons, visualize system activity and integrate the configuration with expected actions. This type of design transparently places value on privacy and security helping build trust by end-users, e.g. citizens (Dourish, 2006).

To understand the concept of trust, researchers have developed many models, including a dynamic multi-level, hierarchical development model of trust (Tassabehji, 2007). Using these models researchers found that building trust requires conveying sufficient information so that individuals develop a positive perception, in this case with regard to the government agency's protection of their privacy and security of their electronic transactions. It was also found that the factors that affect the process of building trust in E-Government are very similar to those that affect building trust in E-Commerce, with the addition of some sociopolitical factors (Tassabehji, 2007). Cremonini et al (2003) found that trust involves three components: 1) an accepted way of informing users of the current level of security; 2) fulfillment of the promise to deliver acceptable levels of privacy and security; and, 3) technological quality and professionalism.

In 2000 the International Organization for Standardization (ISO) released the first ISO standard for information security, ISO 17799. This standard was based almost entirely on the British standard BS 7799. These standards divided the discipline of information security into domains wherein there are sub-topics and control objectives. ISO 17799 has some 123 detailed control objectives within 34 topic areas (Lineman, 2005). ISO 17799 was revised in 2005 to include 257 control measures within 133 control objectives. Clearly, the typical citizen will not want to study and understand this level of detail about security in order to complete an electronic transaction via E-Government. Tassabehji et al (2007) proposed an automated agent for citizens that will explore a government agency's website and return current levels of privacy and security to citizens in a way that is easy to understand so that they can make an informed decision to use E-Government. It could return the level of security in "fuzzy" terms like "High" or "Low" (Tassabehji, 2007). Interactive systems built with "information practice" in mind, that enable citizens to assess levels of privacy and security, will inherently build trust based Cremonini's three components.

SOLUTIONS AND RECOMMENDATIONS

There are many issues and challenges for developing countries to consider as they think about implementing E-Government. This article has presented a few of the potential (primary) ones: the lack of infrastructure; sustainability; culture; the knowledge, skills, abilities and attitudes of citizens and government employees; and, privacy and security. There are also many potential solutions to these issues and challenges, e.g. new strategies and approaches as well as new technologies. Bundling ICT initiatives, what is frequently referred to today as building synergy, in a way that takes advantages of multiple funding sources and different technologies available is recommend to build sustainability; economic, technical, environmental, etc. (Heeks, 2001). Once a business plan has been completed that demonstrates the required sustainability for investment, the next step is to determine the best way to achieve the goals of the bundled initiatives.

Country data included in this article are taken from a random sample of eleven developed and 43 NIC, emerging market, and developing countries around the world, or 28% of the 191 member countries of the United Nations. Table 5 lists all the countries included in the random sample. These country data include per capita GDP, reported literacy rates, fixed telephone penetration, mobile telephone penetration and Internet penetration. Differences in these data lead to real differences in demographics, technological levels of readiness, etc. and therefore differences in technological priorities. Figure 1 lists the top twenty countries of the random sample in descending order of per capita GDP, in descending order by reported literacy rate, by fixed telephone penetration (per 1000 population), by mobile telephone penetration (per 1000 population), and by Internet penetration (per 1000 population). The top twenty countries, per capita GDP, fixed telephone and Internet penetration, are striking in their similarities, i.e. the developed countries included in the top ten countries on the list. The top twenty countries sorted by reported mobile telephone penetration is strikingly different. This list illustrates that in developing countries where "traditional" infrastructure does not exist, the deployment and use of newer technology (in this case mobile telephone technology) is much more widespread. Equally striking is the fact that the top ten countries per capita GDP, fixed telephone and to a large extent Internet penetration primarily include developed countries. It is assumed that the level of Internet penetration exists in these countries because of the diffusion of the Internet along fixed telephone lines. However, the list of top ten countries with the highest reported literacy rates does not correlate well with the countries having the highest per capita GDP or the highest levels of Internet penetration, as is also shown in Figure 1.

Given different technological priorities, if more funding for new technology was available this might alter the development trajectory of technologies such as 4G WiMAX. In fact, 4G development might alter one of the fundamental assumptions of this article. That is, this article has assumed that mobile technology cannot support the broadband applications required for E-Government (Singh, 2008). However, Ahmadi (2009) reports that in the near future (2011+) mobile WiMAX may be able to support more IP-based services and applications than ever. Other articles written in the 2008-2009 timeframe (Tran, 2008; Kang, 2008) indicate that this may or may not be feasible. And, technical challenges aside the question of technological sustainability of 4G has already been questioned. On July 24, 2009, Broadband News & Mobile Broadband News reported that a United Kingdom wide roll-out of this technology is unlikely. The reason is that this technology, (4G)WiMAX broadband, is in competition with the longer-term evolution of current 3G technology. Unless something changes, WiMAX broadband is not likely to survive. With regard to power generation, many technological gains have been made (Moharil, 2009; Phuangpornpitak, 2007; Lewis, 2007). But, it is still not clear what technology may be best for developing countries or how that technology might be fully developed (Steinmueller, 2001).

The question for developing countries is which technology will best (overall) support their ICT initiatives. If the best technology for developing countries is not the same as for developed countries will the impact of the combined market in developing countries be capable of altering the direction of technology for developed countries? Perhaps. In addition, many developing countries (NIC and emerging markets) have high literacy rates which will only make it easier to introduce and diffuse new technologies, adding more weight to the business case for developing new technologies. Consider that the prospect of adding only 10% of the population in India and China to the Internet would increase the number of users by more than 100 million (Rose, 2005). It is not clear

Table 5. Countries included in random sample

People's Democratic Republic of Algeria	Kingdom of Saudi Arabia	Republic of Kazakhstan	Bolivarian Republic of Venequela
Kingdom of Bahrain	Syrian Arab Republic	Lao People's Democratic Republic	United States of America
Republic of Djibouti	Tunisian Republic	Malaysia	Kingdom of Sweden
Arab Republic of Egypt	United Arab Emirates	United Mexican States	Canada
Islamic Republic of Iran	Republic of Yemen	Mongolia	Commonwealth of Australia
Republic of Iraq	Islamic Republic of Afghanistan	Federal Republic of Nigeria	United Kingdom of Great Britain and Northern Ireland
The Hashemite Kingdom of Jordan	Argentine Republic	Islamic Republic of Pakistan	Federal Republic of Germany
State of Kuwait	Barbados	Republic of the Philippines	Japan
Republic of Lebanon	Republic of Bolivia	Republic of Poland	French Republic
Great Socialist People's Libyan Arab Jamahiriya	Bosnia and Herzegovina	Russian Federation	Kingdom of Spain
Kingdom of Morocco	Federative Republic of Brazil	Kingdom of Thailand	State of Israel
Sultanate of Oman	Kingdom of Cambodia	Republic of Turkey	Republic of South Africa
West Bank and Gaza Strip	People's Republic of China	Republic of Hungary	
State of Qatar	Czech Republic	Ukraine	

Figure 1. Comparison of countries by literacy rate, fixed telephone penetration, mobile telephone penetration, and internet penetration

Rank in Descending Order by per capita GDP	Country	Rank in Descending Order by Literacy Rate (%)	Country	Rank in Descending Order by Fixed Telephony Penetration	Country	Rank in Descending Order by Mobile Telephone Penetration	Country	Rank in Descending Order by Internet Penetration	Country
1	Qatar	1	Ukraine	1	Sweden	1	Spain	1	Australia
2	United States	2	Russia	2	Germany	2	Israel	2	Japan
3	Sweden	3	Poland	3	United States	3	Czech Republic	3	Sweden
4	Kuwait	4	Mongolia	4	France	4	Russia	4	United Kingdom
5	Canada	5	Kazakhstan	5	Canada	5	Germany	5	United States
6	Australia	6	Hungary	6	United Kingdom	6	Qatar	6	Barbados
7	UAE	7	Czech Republic	7	Australia	7	United Kingdom	7	Canada
8	United Kingdom	8	France	8	Barbados	8	Hungary	8	Germany
9	Germany	9	Japan	9	Israel	9	Kuwait	9	France
10	Japan	10	Germany	10	Japan	10	Australia	10	Hungary
11	France	11	United Kingdom	11	Spain	11	Poland	11	Czech Republic
12	Spain	12	Australia	12	UAE	12	Bahrain	12	UAE
13	Israel	13	Canada	13	Hungary	13	Japan	13	Qatar
14	Czech Republic	14	Sweden	14	Iran	14	Argentina	14	Kuwait
15	Oman	15	United States	15	Czech Republic	15	France	15	Israel
16	Saudi Arabia	16	Spain	16	Poland	16	Barbados	16	Poland
17	Bahrain	17	Argentina	17	Russia	17	Jordan	17	Iran
18	Hungary	18	Barbados	18	Turkey	18	Algeria	18	Malaysia
19	Barbados	19	Israel	19	Bahrain	19	Mexico	19	Bahrain
20	Poland	20	Bosnia and Herzegovina	20	China	20	Kazakhstan	20	Argentina

Developed countries are shaded in light gray.

that support for development of different new technologies via developing countries will help the case for developed countries. On the other hand, given the potential market it will certainly not hinder it.

A note of caution should be conveyed about literacy rates and the many definitions of literacy. That is, there is no standard definition of literacy (Mancebo, 2005). Even in developed countries literacy can be an issue (UNESCO, 2006). Consider the United States of America (US) where the literacy rate in 2008 was estimated to be 99.0%. This literacy rate is determined by measuring the number of people who can read words equivalent to those learned in the first four years of an elementary (primary) education. A study by the US government released in 1993 reported that at that time 21-23% of adult US citizens were not "able to locate information in text" (US DOEd, 2002). An additional 50 million people, or 25-28% of US citizens were considered to be in the next-least literate group. A follow-on study by the same group of researchers found no significant difference in US adult literacy by 2006 (US DOEd, 2006).

In 2001, the National Literacy Mission – India (2009) reported that by its definition the literacy rate in India ranged from just over 90% to roughly 47% depending on the state, and in total averaged 60%. Today, UNESCO (2008) defines literacy as:

Literacy is the ability to identify, understand, interpret, create, communicate and compute using printed and written materials associated with varying contexts. Literacy involves a continuum of learning in enabling individuals to achieve his or her goals, develop his or her knowledge and potentials, and participate fully in the community and wider society. (UNESCO, 2008)

This discussion about the different view on literacy is intended to remind that the method by which data is defined, acquired and analyzed, must be considered when the data are used to make comparisons between countries. However, by all accounts NIC and emerging market countries have relatively high literacy rates, perhaps higher than the literacy rates in developed countries like the US. In other developing countries, it is very likely that the same ICT used for E-Government could support distance learning, e.g. programs that promote literacy.

Table 6 compares the per capita GDP for the top twenty countries and the bottom twenty countries included in the random sample. Based on all the data in this article it appears that the biggest barrier for NIC and emerging market countries will be funding, i.e. capital to invest in new technologies. There is no doubt that literacy is still a major concern in many developing countries. In these developing countries it appears that ICT investment should be integrated into larger national strategies that provide a convergent solution across social issues and challenges. Such a solution will be better and more sustainable.

One last recommendation is that attention be paid to lessons learned from other E-Government initiatives (Jaeger, 2003). It is important to understand what has been successful, in the context of what is desired, in order to continue being successful. Many prior E-Government initiatives have not been considered successes, even in developed countries. Still there are lessons to be learned and best practices to be developed. For example, governmental agencies that have tried to implement various types of ICT without adequate training for employees typically find that the technology is under-utilized. E-Similarly government initiatives that have not included user (citizen) input have resulted in systems that citizens do not use. No one article can include every lesson, every piece of information available; however, *Benchmarking E-Government: A Global Perspective* (Ronaghan, 2002) includes many system architecture and policy best practices.

Table 6. Comparison of vountries with the highest and the lowest per capita GDP

Rank in Descending (Highest) Order by per capita GDP	Country	per capita GDP	Rank in Ascending (Lowest) Order by per capita GDP	Country	per capita GDP
1	Qatar	80,900	1	Proposed Palestinian State	600
2	United States	45,800	2	Afghanistan	800
3	Sweden	41,100	3	Djibouti	1,000
4	Kuwait	39,300	4	Cambodia	1,800
5	Canada	38,400	5	Nigeria	2,000
6	Australia	37,500	6	Laos	2,100
7	UAE	37,300	7	Yemen	2,300
8	United Kingdom	35,100	8	Pakistan	2,600
9	Germany	34,200	9	Mongolia	3,200
10	Japan	33,600	10	Philippines	3,400
11	France	33,200	11	Iraq	3,600
12	Spain	30,100	12	Bolivia	4,000
13	Israel	25,800	13	Morocco	4,100
14	Czech Republic	24,400	14	Syria	4,500
15	Oman	24,000	15	Jordan	4,700
16	Saudi Arabia	23,200	16	China	5,300
17	Bahrain	20,500	17	Egypt	5,500
18	Hungary	19,500	18	Ukraine	6,900
19	Barbados	17,400	19	Bosnia and Herzegovina	7,000
20	Poland	16,300	20	Tunisia	7,500

Developed countries are highlighted in light gray.

SUMMARY AND CONCLUSION

This article has focused on issues and challenges for E-Government that must be resolved before implementation. When all the information about these issues and challenges has been considered it is recognized that their solutions will depend on local customization. The fundamental question is, "Of all the information known about E-Government, all the ICT and infrastructure available, all the monetary and human capital available, and knowledge of the nation's strategies, what needs to happen to make E-Government a reality here and now?" The answer to this question will be different in virtually every locality around the world. Interestingly, develop-ing technologies and societal shifts may directly impact whether these issues and challenges present real barriers – or not. For example, NIC, emerging market and developing countries appear to accept new technology more readily than developed countries regardless of whether the literacy rate is high or low. This may at least in part be due to the way culture has evolved in developed countries that have depended on the existence of traditional infrastructure. And, although E-Government mod-els used in developed countries cannot be directly applied to E-Government initiatives in developing countries there are still many lessons learned to take advantage of. Lessons learned are often turned into best practices that can be applied.

REFERENCES

Akesson, M., Skalen, P., & Edvardsson, B. (2008). E-government and service orientation: gaps between theory and practice. *International Journal of Public Sector Management, 21*(1), 74–92. doi:10.1108/09513550810846122

Al-Fakhri, M., Cropf, R., Higgs, G., & Kelly, P. (2008). E-Government in Saudi Arabia: Between Promise and Reality. *International Journal of Electronic Government Research, 4*(2), 59–82.

Al-Gahtani, S. (2004). Computer Technology Acceptance Success Factors in Saudi Arabia: An Exploratory Study. *Journal of Global Information Technology Management, 7*(1), 5–29.

Chen, Y., Chen, H., Huang, W., & Ching, R. (2006). E-Government Strategies in Developed and Developing Countries: An Implementation Framework and Case Study. *Journal of Global Information Management, 14*(1), 23–46.

Cherp, A., George, C., & Kirkpatrick, C. (2004). A methodology for assessing national sustainable development strategies. *Environment and Planning. C, Government & Policy, 22*, 913–926. doi:10.1068/c0310j

Cremonini, L., & Valeri, L. (2003). *Benchmarking Security and Trust in Europe and the U.S.* Santa Monica, CA: RAND.

Dethier, J. (2009). *World Bank Policy Research: A Historical Overview.* The World Bank, Development Economics, Operations and Strategy Department. doi:10.1596/1813-9450-5000

Dourish, P., & Anderson, K. (2006). Collective Information Practice: Exploring Privacy and Security as Social and Cultural Phenomena. *Human-Computer Interaction, 21*(3), 319–342. doi:10.1207/s15327051hci2103_2

Ebbers, W. E., Pieterson, W. J., & Noordman, H. N. (2008). Electronic Government: Rethinking channel management strategies. *Government Information Quarterly, 25*, 181–201. doi:10.1016/j.giq.2006.11.003

Evans, D., & Yen, D. C. (2005). E-government: An analysis for implementation: Framework for understanding cultural and social impact. *Government Information Quarterly, 22*, 354–373. doi:10.1016/j.giq.2005.05.007

Fogel, R. W. (2009). *The Impact of the Asian Miracle on the Theory of Economic Growth.* (NBER Working Paper No. 14967). Cambridge, MA: National Bureau of Economic Research.

Franklin, B. (1736). Poor Richard's Almanack. Philadelphia, PA: New Printing-Office near the Market (Yale University Library).

George, C. (2006). *The Government of Sustainable Development, Impact Assessment Research Centre* (Working Paper Series No. 18). Manchester M13 9QH, UK: University of Manchester, Institute for Development Policy and Management.

Grant, G. (2005a). Realizing the Promise of Electronic Government. *Journal of Global Information Management, 13*(1), Editorial Preface i-iv.

Grant, G. (2005b). Developing a Generic Framework for E-Government. *Journal of Global Information Management, 13*(1), 1–30.

Grant, J. (2002). Towards an e-future. *Australian CPA, 72*(9), 38–41.

Heeks, R. (2001). *Understanding e-Governance for Development (Paper No. 11). Manchester M13 9QH.* UK: University of Manchester, Institute for Development Policy and Management.

Heeks, R. (2002). Information Systems and Developing Countries: Failure, Success, and Local Improvisations. *The Information Society, 18*(2), 101–112. doi:10.1080/01972240290075039

Heeks, R. (2003). *Most eGovnerment-for-Development Projects Fail: How Can Risks be Reduced? (Paper No. 14). Manchester M13 9QH.* UK: University of Manchester, Institute for Development Policy and Management.

Helbig, N. (2009). Understanding the complexity of electronic government: Implications from the digital divide literature. *Government Information Quarterly, 26,* 89–97. doi:10.1016/j.giq.2008.05.004

Hoskisson, R. E., Eden, L., Lau, C. M., & Wright, M. (2000). Strategy in emerging economies. *Academy of Management Journal, 43*(3), 249–267. doi:10.2307/1556394

infoplease. (2009) *Countries of the World.* Retrieved March/April 2009, from http://www.infoplease.com/countries.html

ITU. (2008). *Report on the World Summit on the Information Society Stocktaking.* Retrieved (n.d.), from http://www.itu.int/wsis/stocktaking/index.html

Jaeger, P. T., & Thompson, K. M. (2003). E-government around the world: Lessons, challenges, and future directions. *Government Information Quarterly, 20,* 389–394. doi:10.1016/j.giq.2003.08.001

Janssen, M., & Kuk, G. (2007). E-Government Business Models for Public Service Networks. *International Journal of Electronic Government Research, 3*(3), 54–71.

Kaufman, D., Kraay, A., & Mastruzzi, M. (2003). Governance Matters III: Governance Indicators for 1996-2002. Retrieved February 12, 2009, from http://www-wds.worldbank.org/external/default/WDSContentServer/WDSP/IB/2003/08/23/000094946_03081404010948/Rendered/PDF/multi0page.pdf

Kim, C. (2007). A Cross-national Analysis of Global E-government. *Public Organization Review, 7*(4), 317–329. doi:10.1007/s11115-007-0040-5

Lau, T. Y., Aboulhoson, M., Lin, C., & Atkin, D. (2008). Adoption of e-government in three Latin American countries: Argentina, Brazil and Mexico. *Telecommunications Policy, 32,* 88–100. doi:10.1016/j.telpol.2007.07.007

Layne, K., & Lee, J. (2001). Developing fully functional E-government: A four stage model. *Government Information Quarterly, 18,* 122–136. doi:10.1016/S0740-624X(01)00066-1

Lewis, J. (2007). Technology acquisition and innovation in the developing world: Wind turbine development in China and India. *Studies in Comparative International Development, 42*(3-4), 208–232. doi:10.1007/s12116-007-9012-6

Lineman, D. (2005). [– *Security Policy Implications for Business.* Houston, TX: Information Shield.]. *The New ISO, 17799,* 2005.

Lovelock, P., & Ure, J. (2002). E-Government in China. In Zhang, J., & Woesler, M. (Eds.), *China's Digital Dream: The Impact of the Internet on the Chinese Society.* Bochum, Germany: The University Press Bochum.

MDG Gap Task Force. (2008). *Delivering on the Global Partnership for Achieving the Millennium Development Goals.* New York: The United Nations.

Mimicopoulos, M. (2004). *E-government funding activities and strategies.* New York: Department of Economic and Social Affairs, Division for Public Administration and Development Management, The United Nations.

Moharil, R., & Kulkarni, P. (2009). A case study of solar photovoltaic power system at Sagardeep Island, India. *Renewable & Sustainable Energy Reviews, 13*(3), 673–681. doi:10.1016/j.rser.2007.11.016

Ndou, V. (2004). E-Government for Developing Countries: Opportunities and Challenges. *The Electronic Journal on Information Systems in Developing Countries, 18*(1), 1–24.

NLM. (n.d.). *National Literacy Mission – India.* Retrieved July 29, 2009, from http://nlm.nic.in/unesco_nlm.htm

Oliver, R. W. (1975). *International Economic Cooperation and the World Bank.* London: Macmillan.

Pade, C., Mallinson, B., & Sewry, D. (2008). An Elaboration of Critical Success Factors for Rural ICT Project Sustainability in Developing Countries: Exploring the DWESA Case. *JITCAR, 10*(4), 32–55.

Palmer, I. (2002). State of the world: e-Government implementation. Available from *Faulkner Information Services.* Retrieved from http://www.faulkner.com/products/faulknerlibrary/00018297.htm

Phuangpornpitak, N., & Kumar, S. (2007). PV hybrid systems for rural electrification in Thailand. *Renewable & Sustainable Energy Reviews, 11*(7), 1530–1543. doi:10.1016/j.rser.2005.11.008

Prahalad, C. K., & Hammond, A. (2002). *Serving the World's Poor, Profitably.* Harvard, MA: Harvard Business Review.

Reddick, C. (2005). Citizen interaction with e-government: From the streets to servers? *Government Information Quarterly, 22*, 38–57. doi:10.1016/j.giq.2004.10.003

Report, U. N. (2005). Global E-Government Readiness Report 2005: From E-Government to E-Inclusion. New York: Department of Economic and Social Affairs, Division for Public Administration and Development Management, the United Nations.

Ronaghan, S. (2002). Benchmarking E-government: A Global Perspective. New York: Division for Public Economics and Public Administration, the United Nations.

Rose, R. (2005). A Global Diffusion Model of e-Governance. *Journal of Public Policy, 25*(1), 5–27. doi:10.1017/S0143814X05000279

Saltzer, J. H., Reed, D. P., & Clark, D. D. (1984). End-To-End Arguments in System Design. *ACM Transactions on Computer Systems, 2*(4), 277–288. doi:10.1145/357401.357402

Sein, M. K., & Harindranath, G. (2004). Conceptualizing the ICT Artifact: Toward Understanding the Role of ICT in National Development. *The Information Society, 20*, 15–24. doi:10.1080/01972240490269942

Siau, K., & Long, Y. (2006). Using Social Development Lenses to Understand E-Government Development. *Journal of Global Information Management, 14*(1), 47–62.

Singh, A. K., & Sahu, R. (2008). Integrating Internet, telephones, and call centers for delivering better quality e-governance to all citizens. *Government Information Quarterly, 25*, 477–490. doi:10.1016/j.giq.2007.01.001

Srivastava, S. C., & Teo, T. S. H. (2007). E-Government Payoffs: Evidence from Cross-Country Data. *Journal of Global Information Management, 15*(4), 20–40.

Statistical Manual, U. N. (2009). *Statistical Manual.* Retrieved April 30, 2009, from http://go.worldbank.org/USGWXVXW40

Steinmueller, W. (2001). ICTs and the possibilities for leapfrogging by developing countries. *International Labour Review, 140*(2), 193–210. doi:10.1111/j.1564-913X.2001.tb00220.x

Survey, U. N. (2003). U.N. Global E-government Survey 2003. New York: Department of Economic and Social Affairs and the Civic Research Group, the United Nations.

Tassabehji, R., Elliman, T., & Mellor, J. (2007). Generating Citizen Trust in E-Government Security: Challenging Perceptions. *International Journal of Cases on Electronic Commerce, 3*(3), 1–17.

Teicher, J., Hughes, O., & Dow, N. (2002). E-government: a new route to public sector quality. *Managing Service Quality, 12*(6), 384–393. doi:10.1108/09604520210451867

Trkman, P., & Turk, T. (2009). A conceptual model for the development of broadband and e-government. *Government Information Quarterly, 26*, 416–424. doi:10.1016/j.giq.2008.11.005

U.N. (2008). UN E-Government Survey 2008: From E-Government to Connected Governance. New York: Department of Economic and Social Affairs, Division for Public Administration and Development Management, the United Nations.

UNCTAD. (2002). Least developed countries at a glance. New York: the Information Communication Technology Task Force, the United Nations.

UNESCO. (2006). *Literacy for Life*. UNESCO Publishing.

UNESCO. (2008). *International Literacy Statistics: A Review of Concepts, Methodology and Current Data*. UNESCO Institute of Statistics.

UNESCO. (2009). *Literacy.* Retrieved July 29, 2009, from http://www.unesco.org/en/literacy

U.S. Dept of Ed. (2002). Adult Literacy in America GPO No. 065-000-00588-3. Washington, DC: Education Information Branch, Office of Educational Research and Improvement, U.S. Department of Education.

Vergnes, B. (2001). Information technology and sustainability. *The OECD Observer. Organisation for Economic Co-Operation and Development, 226/227*, 16–17.

Wenger, E. (1998). *Communities of practice: Learning, meaning, and identity*. Cambridge, UK: Cambridge University Press.

Whitten, A., & Tygar, J. (1999). Why Johnny Can't Encrypt. In the *Proceedings of the 8th USENIX Security Symposium* (pp 169-184). Washington, DC.

World Bank. (2009). *World Bank*. Retrieved July 25, 2009, from http://web.worldbank.org/WBSITE/EXTERNAL/DATASTATISTICS/0,contentMDK:20420458~menuPK:64133156~pagePK:64133150~piPK:64133175~theSitePK:239419,00.html

Young, A. (1993). *Lessons from the East Asian NICS: A Contrarian View*. NBER Working Paper No. 4482. Cambridge, MA: National Bureau of Economic Research.

Zambrano, R. (2008). E-Governance and Development: Service Delivery to Empower the Poor. *International Journal of Electronic Government Research, 4*(2), 1–11.

Chapter 23
Ontology Driven E-Government

Peter Salhofer
FH Joanneum, Austria

Bernd Stadlhofer
FH Joanneum, Austria

Gerald Tretter
FH Joanneum, Austria

ABSTRACT

Expectations of citizens concerning the quality of electronically available public services are steadily increasing. Thus more and more of these services are fully transactional (Layne und Lee, 2001) and offer tight integration of electronic access and underlying processes. Whereas this leads to better results in the terms of time, convenience and correctness, software systems become more complex and development effort rises as well. On the other hand, in the field of software engineering there exist several recommendations and approaches to reduce development time and increase the degree of software re-use. Some of these recommendations are known for decades (McIlroy, 1968). One approach that tries to tackle this problem at the very beginning of the development circle is Model Driven Architecture (MDA) (Miller et al, 2001). The core idea behind MDA is the creation of a comprehensive system model that is based on several abstraction levels (OMG, 2002). These different modeling layers as well as a set of transformations between them allow for the automatic generation of most of the code needed. Whereas typically UML 2, which is also based on the same multi-layer modeling approach, is used to create the required abstract descriptions, there already exist some efforts to extend MDA to semantic web technologies as well (OMG, 2006). This chapter describes an approach to apply an MDA-like methodology, which is entirely based on a semantic model to the e-Government domain. The goals are to ease access to e-Government services, provide a new level of user experience and of course to reduce the implementation and maintenance effort while significantly improving the overall quality of service.

DOI: 10.4018/978-1-61520-933-0.ch023

WHAT IS AN ONTOLOGY?

Ontologies are the basic elements of semantic systems since they describe the semantic aspects of any given domain. There are numerous definitions of the term ontology available. One that is very frequently cited, is the one by Thomas Gruber:

"An **ontology** *is an explicit specification of a conceptualization" (Gruber, 1995, p. 908)*

By citing (Genesereth and Nilson 1987) he also explains, that any approach of representing knowledge has to be based on conceptualisation, which in turn is a collection of "objects, concepts, and other entities that are assumed to exist in some area of interest and the relationships that hold among them". This makes a conceptualisation a simplified and abstract representation of the part of the world that should be modelled. All needed elements are explicitly specified by means of a representational vocabulary, thus leading to the more precise definition:

"In such an ontology, definitions associate the names of entities in the universe of discourse (e.g., classes, relations, functions, or other objects) with human-readable text describing what the names mean, and formal axioms that constrain the interpretation and well-formed use of these terms. Formally, an ontology is the statement of a logical theory." (Gruber, 1995, p. 909)

In a more recent article Gruber refines this definition and provides slightly different explanations depending on the context in which an ontology is used. For the context of computer and information sciences his definition is:

"...an ontology defines a set of representational primitives with which to model a domain of knowledge or discourse. The representational primitives are typically classes (or sets), attributes (or properties), and relationships (or relations among class members). The definitions of the representational primitives include information about their meaning and constraints on their logically consistent application." (Gruber, 2007)

In this article Gruber also argues, that the most important reason why ontologies are considered to be at the "semantic" level rather than at the "logical" level is their expressive power when it comes to logical constraints. This expressiveness comes close to first-order logic.

A similar but rather pragmatic definition can be found in (Hendler, 2001, p. 30):

"I define ontology as a set of knowledge terms, including the vocabulary, the semantic interconnections, and some simple rules of inference and logic for some particular topic"

A more formal definition, however, can be found in (Ehrig, Haase, Stojanovic, 2004):

Definition: An *ontology with datatypes* is a structure

$$O := (C, T, \leq_C, R, A, \sigma_R, \sigma_A, \leq_R, \leq_A, I, V, \iota_C, \iota_T, \iota_R, \iota_A)$$ consisting of

- six disjoint sets C, T, R, A, I and V called concepts, datatypes, relations, attributes, instances and data values,
- partial orders $\leq_C$ on C called concept hierarchy or taxonomy and $\leq_T$ on T called type hierarchy,
- functions $\sigma_R: R \rightarrow C^2$ called relation signature and $\sigma_A: A \rightarrow C \times T$ called attribute signature,
- partial orders $\leq_R$ on R called relation hierarchy and $\leq_A$ on A called attribute hierarchy, respectively,
- a function $\iota_C: C \rightarrow 2^I$ called concept instantiation,
- a function $\iota_T: T \rightarrow 2^V$ called datatype instantiation,
- a function $\iota_R: R \rightarrow 2^{I \times I}$ called relation instantiation,

- a function ι_A: $A \rightarrow 2^{I \times V}$ called attribute instantiation.

Here is a short example that will point out the meaning of the different elements used in this definition. Assume there is a simple ontology $O_{driving} = (C, T, \leq_C, R, A, \sigma_R, \sigma_A, \leq_R, \leq_A, I, V, \iota_C, \iota_T, \iota_R, \iota_A)$ that models certain aspects in the field of individual mobility where:

C={Thing, Person, Car, Driver, Drivinglicense}, T={String, Date},

$\leq_C$={(Thing, Person), (Thing, Car), (Thing, Drivinglicense), (Person, Driver)},

R={hasOwner,belongsTo}, A={hasName, hasExpirationDate},

σ_R={(hasOwner,(Car, Person)), (belongsTo,(Drivinglicense,Person))},

σ_A={(hasName,(Person,String)), (hasExpiration Date,(Drivinglicense,Date))},

$\leq_R$={}, $\leq_A$={}, I={JohnFoo, BMW320, CarDrivingLicense4711},

V={"John Foo", 31-12-2015},

ι_C={(Person, {JohnFoo}), (Car, {BMW320}), (DrivingLicense,{CarDrivingLicense4711})},

ι_T={(String,{"John Foo"}), (Date, {31-12-2015})},

ι_R={(hasOwner,{(BMW320, JohnFoo)}), (belongsTo, {(CarDrivingLicense4711, John-Foo)})}

ι_A={(hasName,{(JohnFoo, "John Foo")}),

(hasExpirationDate, {(CarDrivingLicense4711, 31-12-2005)})}

This formal definition covers most of the aspects that are mentioned in the other definitions above. There are classes, attributes, relationships among them and a vocabulary. The mapping between attributes and classes as well as the instantiation methods impose some constraints on the model that restrict the creation of valid elements.

Selection of a Semantic Framework

Currently there exist several competing semantic description and modeling frameworks that have been submitted as recommendations to the World Wide Web Consortium (W3C). Among these submissions are OWL-S (Martin et al., 2005) and WSMO (Fensel et al., 2007) that can both be used to describe semantic web services. To decide which of these frameworks is best apt to be the basis of the envisaged approach, evaluation prototypes based on both semantic frameworks were created and evaluated. Eventually a decision in favor of WSMO was made. Although there exists a comprehensive comparison between the two frameworks in question (Bruijn et al., 2005; Polleres et al., 2004), some of the facts that have influenced our decision will be pointed out in short.

A major difference between OWL-S and WMSO is the modeling language used by each. OWL-S uses OWL (W3C, 2004), which in turn is a semantic extension of RDF (add reference here) and uses XML as its notation. WSMO uses the Web Service Modeling Language (WSML) (Bruijn et al., 2006), which is a domain specific language based on the Meta Object Facility (MOF) (OMG, 2002). MOF is a framework for creating models based on meta-model that in turn are based on meta-meta-models and is the conceptual basis of UML 2 as well as MDA. Since the basic idea of Ontology Driven E-Government is the utilization of MDA concepts together with semantic modeling techniques to generate an e-Government solution that is based on a semantic model of the system.

Figure 1. Listing 1: A simple example modeled with OWL

```
<owl:Class rdf:ID="Person">
  <rdfs:label>Person</rdfs:label>
</owl:Class>

<owl:ObjectProperty rdf:ID="hasParent">
  <rdfs
:domain rdf:resource="#Person" />
  <rdfs:range rdf:resource="#Person" />
</owl:ObjectProperty>

<owl:ObjectProperty rdf:ID="hasName">
  <rdfs:domain rdf:resource="#Person" />
  <rdfs:range rdf:resource="http://www.w3c.org/2001/XMLSchema#string" />
</owl:ObjectProperty>

<owl:Restriction>
  <owl:onProperty rdf:resource="hasParent" />
  <owl:maxCardinality rdf:datatype="xsd:nonNegativeInteger">2</owl:maxCardinality>
  <owl:minCardinality rdf:datatype="xsd:nonNegativeInteger">2</owl:minCardinality>
</owl:Restriction>
```

Although the fact, that WSML is based on MOF was not decisive, it seems to be natural to use a framework that utilizes some of the MDA basic technologies. The important point in this context is that a semantic modeling framework needs to be expressive, powerful enough to cover all necessary system requirements and constraints and yet as simple as possible.

Figure 1(Listing 1) and Figure 2 (Listing 2) describe the same facts about a particular part of the world. Every person has one attribute, which is the person's name and has exactly two parents who are persons as well. Although this example might seem to be too simple and not directly related to the problem domain in question, it perfectly demonstrates the differences in compactness and readability. WSML shows some quite obvious advantages in this field compared to OWL. One of the consequences of the more compact notation is that models can be easily created and reviewed even without the use of sophisticated editors or tools. This is an important advantage in a systems engineering context. Beside the compact and expressive notation there exists a WSML variant called WSML-Flight that incorporates a description logic programming facility based on frame-logic (Kifer et al. 1995). Whereas typically semantic frameworks reflect non-monotonic logical systems and therefore are based on the open-world assumption (Alferes, Pereira, and Przymusinski 1996), WSML favors the closed-world assumption. In a systems engineering context this makes it much easier to model classical constraints that have to be met to prove the plausibility and correctness of a particular state.

Figure 2. Listing 2: The same example as shown in Listing 1 modeled with WSML

```
Concept Person
        hasName ofType (0 1) _string
        hasParent ofType (2 2) Person
```

Ontology Modelling Guidelines

Semantic methodologies and language frameworks offer a wide range of capabilities. Thus the question is whether there are any guidelines or best practices that will lead to their efficient use. Thomas Gruber (Gruber, 1995) therefore recommends the following design criteria that should be considered:

1. **Clarity:** An ontology should clearly define the intended meaning of its concepts and also include natural language documentation. Wherever possible, axioms should be used to express definitions. The motivation for the definition of a particular concept should have no impact on the definition itself, thus allowing the use of this concept in other contexts as well.
2. **Coherence:** An ontology should only allow for inferences that are consistent with the definition. This also applies to the natural language documentation. Any sentence derived from axioms must not contradict the definition or examples given in the documentation
3. **Extendibility:** An ontology should offer the conceptual foundation for a range of uses beyond the ones it was originally defined for. This should allow for extension and specialisation of this ontology without a need to revise existing definitions.
4. **Minimal encoding bias:** The notation used to define an ontology should have no influence on the resulting definitions. I.e., the convenience of notation or implementation should not drive the design.
5. **Minimal ontological commitment:** An ontology should be based on a minimum number of claims about the world being modelled and only define those terms that are essential for the given domain. This should allow other parties to specialise and instantiate the ontology as needed.

Most of these recommendations can be achieved by using a layered approach to ontology modeling. This means that there are several layers of abstraction allowing for efficient re-use of concepts as well as for the necessary domain specific specializations by extending, adapting or redefining concept defined in higher layers. Technically this is accomplished by defining different ontologies identified by different namespaces. More specific ontologies import the more abstract ones and add necessary attributes and concepts as well as additional axioms.

GEA-PA: A Candidate Meta-Model

The Governance Enterprise Architecture (GEA) (Peristeras and Tarabanis, 2006) provides reusable top-level models for the overall e-Government domain. GEA is the result of a business driven approach to create a reference ontology for the e-Government domain. Even it suggests the use of semantic web services (SWS) the GEA model itself is technology neutral (although there exists a WSMO implementation of GEA described in X. Wang et al. (2007). According to this model the interaction between citizens and public administrations (PA) is split into two major parts: planning/informative and execution/performative part.

The planning part consists of all activities and steps that need to be taken to provide citizens with all the information necessary to effectively identify, find and use public administration services. This is to answer the "Why, What, Who, Where and How questions" (Peristeras and Tarabanis, 2006). The planning part is split into the following three activities:

- **Mapping needs-to-services:** This step tries to bridge the gap between the different points of view of citizens and public agencies. Whereas citizens are typically driven by a particular need or desire, public organizations' concentrate on services. Thus there is an obvious need to map citizens'

Figure 3. GEA-PA service model (Adapted from Wang, 2007)

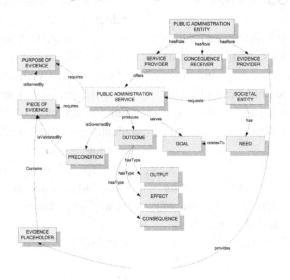

needs to (a set) of PA services that might serve these needs. This is the basis for allowing citizens to identify services that are most appropriate for their particular situation in a need-centric fashion.

- **Service discovery:** After a citizen's need was translated into a service that is needed within the previous step, this service can now be located. To facilitate this, GEA proposes a so called Central Public Administration Service Directory (CPASD) that holds necessary information to answer the *What*, *Who* and *Where* questions

- **Service exploration:** Within this phase citizens are provided with information from the actual service provider about the *When* and the *How*. This includes all necessary preconditions.

Like the planning part, the execution part is split into three phases as well:

- **Information gathering:** All information that is needed as input to the selected service is gathered. GEA refers to this type of information as *evidence*

- **Information checking:** Evidence provided is checked against the business rules of the service. This might happen in a single step but could also become relatively complex including conditional checks based on the input provided.

- **Providing Output:** This step provides proper communication about the consequences and effects of the service used. This includes information to other agencies that have to be notified about these effects.

GEA Object Model for Service Provisioning

This model is based on in-depth analyses of the e-Government domain and is intended to be a conceptual basis for a reference ontology in the field of PA services. An overview of the key concepts can be seen in Figure 3.

There are actually two different entities participating in the service provision model. *Social Entities* who are for example citizens or companies and *Governance Entities*. According to their assignment *Governance Entities* are split into two different types: *Political Entities* who *define Public Administration Services* (not explicitly shown in Figure 3) and *Public Administration Entities* who might play different *roles* in service provisioning. These *roles* are:

- **Service Provider:** Offers a Public Administration Service to Social Entities
- **Consequence Receiver:** A Public Administration Entity that needs to be informed about the outcome of a public service. E.g.: If a family with children moves into a new community the school authority needs to be informed after registration to make sure that the children will attend school.
- **Evidence Provider:** A Public Administration Entity that provides certain Piece of Evidence that is needed as input for the Public Administration Service.

Pieces of Evidence are facts and are typically contained in so called *Evidence Placeholders*. An *Evidence Provider* is typically a document that contains information about the fact. In the GEA object model exists a many-to-many relation between these concepts, stating that a *Piece of Evidence* can be contained in several *Evidence Placeholders* and also that an *Evidence Placeholder* can contain several *Pieces of Evidence*. E.g.: A typical *Piece Of Evidence* could be the date of birth of the applicant. This information could be proven by several different *Evidence Providers* such as passport, personal identity card, certificate of birth and so on.

Pieces of Evidence are checked against a service's *Preconditions* which represent some of the service's business rules. These preconditions have to be met to be eligible for service utilization. E.g.: To apply for a place in a Kindergarten the date of birth of the child (*Piece of Evidence*) has to be within a certain range (*Precondition*).

Every *Public* Administration Service results in some kind of output. The output is of one of the following types:

- **Output:** In the GEA object model the output is defined as the documented decision of the *Service Provider*. This information is typically sent to the Social Entity as an administrative document/decision.
- **Effect:** In semantic web services an effect describes the change of the state of the world whenever the service is executed successfully (E.g. an instance of person is transformed into an instance of driver if an application for a driving license was approved). In the GEA object model the *Effect* is the actual right or obligation (permit, punishment, certificate, ...) the Social Entity is entitled with. An *Effect* only exists if the service ends successfully (the *Social Entities* request was not rejected prematurely).
- **Consequence:** This type represents information that is forwarded to other interested parties.

In order to support the needs-to-service mapping step of the planning/informative part, the GEA object model contains *two* important concepts that allow linking *Social Entities* to *Public Administration Services*. These two concepts are *Need* and *Goal*. Need describes the citizen-centric view of the PA domain. Citizens have certain needs in particular situations (e.g. to build a house). A Goal describes the service-centric view of PA domain, which includes the outcome of PA services that might contribute to serve citizens' needs (e.g. acquiring a building permit). Mapping need to goals and therewith linking the citizen view to the PA view allows for user-friendly service discovery. Most of the ideas of GEA-PA have been incorporated in the meta-model of Ontology Driven E-Government, although some modifications have been necessary.

Creating Ontologies

To demonstrate the capabilities of this ontology driven approach to e-Government a prototype was built in cooperation with a large municipality. Support was limited to all procedures in the building and construction domain (e.g. application for a building permit), since this domain was considered to be probably the most complex one within the municipality. Thus, the rational was that by proving the concept in this field it should be demonstrated that this new approach could be applied to other less complex fields without major problems as well.

The very first step in creating a new ontology is to identify needed concepts and the relationships between them. Possible sources of information are legal regulations that apply to the domain in question as well as existing application forms and domain experts. Although there already exist some approaches for automatically identifying and extracting concepts from law texts (Biagioli et al. 2005; Schweighofer et al., 2001) in this project the analysis was conducted manually. Therefore all relevant terms that were used in the construction law (such as builder, building, public sewage, ...) were extracted an modeled as concepts in the ontology. In a next step, relationships between the identified concepts were established. Since the construction law sometimes refers to more generic terms such as *building*, in a different context more specific terms such as *residential house* were used. As a result, a taxonomy of concepts was created. According to Gruber's recommendations described above, concepts of different levels of abstraction where arranged in different ontologies and wherever possible, already existing ontologies were re-used (e.g. since a builder is either a physical person or a legal entity, an existing ontology describing these elements was imported and re-used).

Beside the taxonomy of concepts, restrictions imposed by the construction law were modeled as axioms, thus logically constraining the set of valid constructs within the ontology.

Goal-Oriented E-Government

The Government Enterprise Architecture for Public Administrations (GEA-PA) already contains the notion of *goal* and *need* to theoretically enable the identification of public services that are necessary or at least seem to be most appropriate for a particular situation that is described by a citizen's need. However, the use of goals to identify candidate services in not unique to GEA-PA but is used by every framework supporting the creation and utilization of semantic web services. In this context, a goal description is used to identify available service on the Internet that might be used to solve a given problem. Generally the following phases have to by passed through to use a semantic web service (Leitner 2003):

- **Goal discovery phase:** In this phase the actual goal of the user has to be correctly formulated using semantic notations.
- **Semantic web service discovery phase:** A set of semantic web services that might fulfill the goal is retrieved.
- **Service selection phase:** The web service that will actually be executed is selected from the set of retrieved services

An essential point is the formulation of the actual goal. This is non-trivial since the goal has to reflect the citizen's need but also has to be expressed in a semantic notation, bridging the gap between natural language and semantic technologies. Additionally there is some complexity arising from the domain as well since underlying regulations might be rather comprehensive and make numerous distinctions based on a given situation. For example, the construction law that applies to the prototype in question knows the following three procedures that might need to be used whenever something is built:

- *building development requiring a building permit:* In this case you have to apply for a building permit which will trigger a fairly complex process

- *notifiable building development:* In this case you have to notify the responsible authority providing detailed information about the project. The building authority can prohibit the project within six weeks. Otherwise permission is granted
- *building development not requiring a building permit:* In this case you just have to inform the responsible public agency about the fact that the construction work will start together with some basic information about the project.

Everything amounts to the question which of these services is needed in a particular situation that is in turn characterized by the citizen's goal. Such a goal could be expressed such as this:

"I want to build a garage."

The system should now decide which of the available services is needed to get permission to build a garage. However, this question can't be ambiguously answered yet, since the construction law distinguishes between different garages according to their size. Bigger garages (in respect to the number and type of vehicles) are considered to be "building development requiring a building permit" whereas smaller garages are treated as "notifiable building development". To actually decide which of these services is the appropriate one, more information about the garage is needed. If the goal is eventually formulated as

"I want to build a garage for three cars."

Goal Templates

More generally the decision in the situation described above could also be expressed using a relatively simple first-order logic axiom:

$$\exists x,y \begin{pmatrix} isSmallGarage(x) \wedge \big(isNewProject(y) \vee isRetrofittingProject(y) \big) \\ \rightarrow reqNotificationService(x,y) \end{pmatrix}$$

Which means, if there is a situation described by two variables x and y and x is considered to be a small garage whereas y is either representing a new build or retrofitting project than this combination of x and y requires the notification building development procedure. The variables used in the axiom represent concepts in the ontology and the predicates (e.g. *isSmallGarage*) prove certain assertions about them.

By allowing multiple of these rules with an arbitrary number of variables it becomes obvious that all possible situations can be modeled. This however leads to the following two questions:

- How can we refine a given goal such as "I want to build a garage" which is not specific enough to make an unambiguous decision to a more specific one such as "I want to build a garage for three cars"?
- How can we extract the variables needed to make a decision from a given goal?

One possible answer to this question is the use of so called goal templates. The basic idea is the formulation of a generic text template that is able to represent all facts that are needed to make decisions in the context of a given domain. The goal template used for building and construction services is:

"I want to {y}{x}."

Curly brackets represent placeholders for variables. These placeholders have to be initialized with appropriate concepts from the ontologies. This leads to goal templates such as:

"I want to {erect|retrofit|extend|tear down}{a construction}."

Figure 4. Part of the ontology showing garages

Variable y is initialized with the concept *BuildingProjectType* and variable x is initialized with the concept *Construction*, which is the most abstract super-type of everything that can be built. To select a service based on goal templates all concepts that appear within the template need to be refined (specialized). This means that every concept needs to be replaced by a more specific one (e.g. *Construction* is replaced by *SmallGarage*) that still is of the same type as the original concept (e.g. *SmallGarage is_a Construction*). Figure 4 shows the part of the ontology that represents the different types of garages. There are three types of garages (small, medium and big garages). Every garage is a *Building* but also a *VehicleParking-Place* that are both in turn a *Construction*. Thus the specification of the appropriate concept can also be performed recursively in several steps (e.g. replacing *Construction* with *Building* and then *Building* with *Garage* and so on). The exact semantics of this graph will be described in more detail in the next section.

Specialization and Classification

As shown in the previous section, the selection of a particular service or a set of needed services can be expressed using first-order logic axioms. Whereas the variables used in such rules represent concepts that are related to goal templates, the actual predicates (e.g. isSmallGarage(x)) are defined by the type of a given variable as it is derived from the concept tree using specialization an classification. Before the mechanism behind specialization and classification is explained it is necessary to create a sound theoretic background.

As already mentioned, an ontology is defined as (Ehrig, Haase, Stojanovic, 2004):

$$O_T := \left(C, T, \leq_C, \leq_T, R, A, \sigma_A, \sigma_R, \leq_R, \leq_A \right)$$

Consisting of a set of concepts C aligned in a hierarchy $\leq_C$, a set of Relations R with $\leq_R$, the siganture $\sigma_R : A \to C \times T$, a set of datatypes T with $\leq_T$, a set of attributes A with $\leq_A$, the signature $\sigma_A : A \to C \times T$.

Figure 5. Web dialog to further specify the current concept

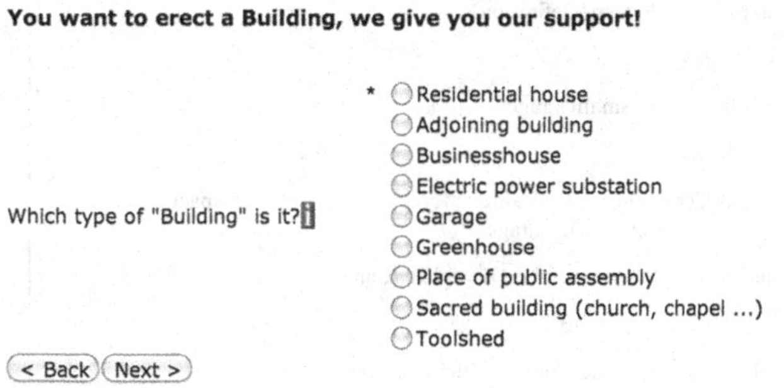

You want to erect a Building, we give you our support!

* ○ Residential house
○ Adjoining building
○ Businesshouse
○ Electric power substation
Which type of "Building" is it? ○ Garage
○ Greenhouse
○ Place of public assembly
○ Sacred building (church, chapel ...)
○ Toolshed

(< Back)(Next >)

A similar definition of an ontology not including data types can be found in (Bloehdorn et al, 2005). The *is_a* relationship between two classes is defined as follows:

$$c_1 \leq_C c_2 \big| c_1, c_2 \in C \Rightarrow c_1 \text{ is subconcept of } c_2$$

Defining a function *attr(c)*

$$attr(c) : C \rightarrow A$$

that returns the set *a* of attributes such that every element of *a* and the concept *c* are member of σ_A for some data type, the following statements also hold true:

$$c_1 \leq_C c_2 \big| c_1, c_2 \in C \Rightarrow attr(c_2) \subseteq attr(c_1)$$

This means that all sub-concepts contain all the attributes of all their super-concepts but might also posses additional attributes. Since a concept might also have several direct super-concepts, the following statement has to be true:

$$c_1 \leq_C c_2 \wedge c_1 \leq_C c_3 \big| c_1, c_2, c_3 \in C, c_2 \neq c_3 \wedge \neg \left(c_2 \leq_C c_3 \vee c_3 \leq_C c_2 \right)$$
$$\Rightarrow \left(attr(c_2) \cup attr(c_3) \right) \subseteq attr(c_1)$$

Sub-concepts are also called specializations of their super-concepts since they are more specific. In our ontology model, however, we use two different types of sub-concepts:

- **Specialization:** In this case, the sub-concept is a more concrete or specific concept than its super-concepts, thus it represents a new type of concept on its own.
- **Classification:** In this case, sub-concepts are used to categorize the instances of their direct super-concepts. The different sub-concepts reflect the categories relevant for specific public administration services.

As mentioned previously, concepts are used as variables in goal templates. These variables are then used to identify the appropriate service or a set of services and therefore have to be specific enough to perform this decision. Per definition, this means that every variable used within a particular goal that is based on a goal template is only allowed to contain non-abstract concepts before it can be considered for service selection. All leafs in the graph of concepts are supposed to be non-abstract whereas all nodes that appear on the right side of the σ_C relation and therefore have sub-concepts are abstract. Since a goal reflects what the user wants to achieve, specialization has to be performed by the user. Therefore currently a simple web-dialog is used that asks the user to further specify a given concept by selecting one

Figure 6. Listing 3: A sample axiom defining a SmallGarage

```
axiom SmallGarageDefinition1

definedBy

?x memberOf SmallGarage

impliedBy

?x[forVehicleType hasValue ?vehicleType, vehicleCapacity hasValue
?capacity] memberOf Garage

and (?vehicleType memberOf vehicle#Car

    and ?capacity < 3

or ?vehicleType memberOf vehicle#Motorcycle

    and ?capacity < 6).
```

of the known direct sub-concepts (see Figure 5). With every step the user adds additional information about the actual thing that plays a role in the goal and comes closer to one of the leafs in the tree of concepts.

Considering the garage example and the concept tree shown in Figure 4, the last step would be to decide whether the garage that should be built is a small, medium or big one. In a conventional application therefore extensive descriptions would be offered allowing the user to find out what is considered to be small, medium or big. Semantic technologies, however, are extremely good in performing automatic classification. Since the three mentioned subtypes of garages simply represent different classes rather than new types of concepts, a semantic reasoner can perform this last step as well. All it takes is a set of axioms that allows the reasoner to decide which kind of garage we are actually dealing with.

Figure 6 (Listing 3) shows the axiomatic definition of a small garage. The axiom defines that every instance of the concept *Garage* also is an instance of concept *SmallGarage* if the capacity of the garage doesn't contain more than three cars or more than six motor cycles. However, to actually decide whether a given garage is a small garage, some information about the garage is needed. Therefore, the application checks for relevant axioms and variables used within them (e.g. vehicleCapacity). After the set of all relevant variables, which are actually attributes of the concept in question, was identified, a dialog is dynamically created to ask the user for the lacking information (see Figure 7). After this information is provided the reasoner will classify the given garage and the correct service is determined as described in the next section.

Figure 7. Dialog with all fields needed for automatic classification

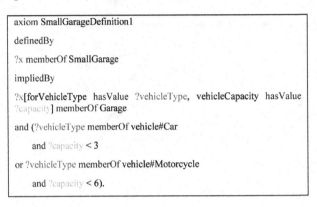

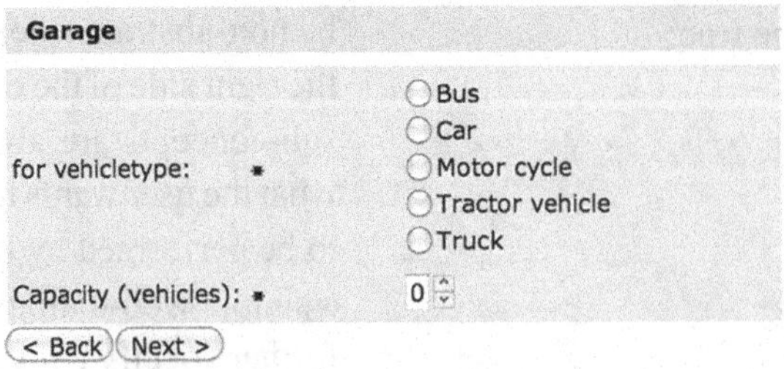

Figure 8. Goal-Service relationship

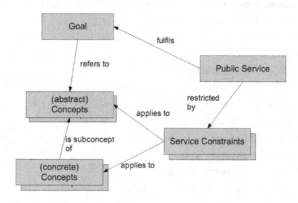

The Service Discovery Algorithm

Once the concrete goal is defined, the matching service or set of services has to be identified. The meta model therefore defines a way to link services to goals or, more precisely, to goal templates. Thus every public service that is modeled in the ontology refers to a goal (see Figure 8). In the case of the construction approval process used as the prototype domain for the approach presented, several *Public Services* are available which fulfill the goal *"I want to {erect|retrofit|extend|tear down}{a construction}"*. To uniquely identify one of these services or the set of necessary services, all abstract concepts in the goal template have to be replaced by non-abstract ones to express a concrete goal. Thus the combination of the actual construction and construction project makes it possible to identify the accurate service(s) for the given situation. By the use of so-called *Service Constraints* any complex scenario can be modeled. For example: if a big building is retrofitted, a building permit is required. However, if the work does not affect the exterior view a more convenient and faster building announcement will do.

The entire algorithm represents the following function:

$$findServices(g,c) : G[\times C]^n \to C^i$$
where g is a goal and c is a possibly empty set of concepts; the result is a set of required services

This can be accomplished by performing the following steps:

1. Start with an abstract goal template
2. For each concept the goal template refers to, go down the concept hierarchy till a leaf is reached (by use of specialization and classification)
3. Lookup the matching services

Semantic Forms

The basic idea of the approach presented here is to enable the generation of a fully operational electronic public service entirely based on a semantic model. Supporting citizens in identifying services that will help them to achieve their goals is only one part. Ontologies can also be used to

Figure 9. Listing 4: Concept describing inputs to building permit application

```
concept BuildingPermitApplicationRequest subConceptOf ConstructionServiceRequest
nonFunctionalProperties
    dc#description hasValue "concept representing input to building permit service"
endNonFunctionalProperties
    applicant ofType (1 *) personData#Person
    delegate ofType (0 1) personData#PhysicalPerson
    projectType ofType (1 1) ConstructionProject
    construction ofType (1 1) Construction
    buildingLocation ofType (1 1) BuildingLocation
    sitePlan ofType (1 1) segofUtil#File
    floorPlan ofType (1 1) segofUtil#File
    constructionViews ofType (1 1) segofUtil#File
...
```

access and utilize e-Government services, since they contain a comprehensive description of available public services. As shown in section "GEA-PA – A Candidate Meta-Model" this description contains necessary preconditions that have to be met as well as information that has to be provided in order to invoke a service (e.g. *Piece Of Evidence*, see Figure 3). This allows an application that is based on semantic models to check which information is expected by the service and also whether restricting preconditions are met. If the model is complete and contains a semantic description of all elements that are input to the

service, this description can be used to gather any expected data from the citizen.

Figure 9 (Listing 4) shows the WSML concept representing the required input to a building permit service. It says that an application must include at least one applicant, at most one delegate or mediator, a project type, the construction itself, the building location as well as miscellaneous blueprints and drafts. Since the ontology contains information about all the types that are used (e.g. it knows about the attributes that make up a physical person, such as name, address and so forth), a dynamically created user dialog can be used to ask

Figure 10. Example of a dynamically generated form

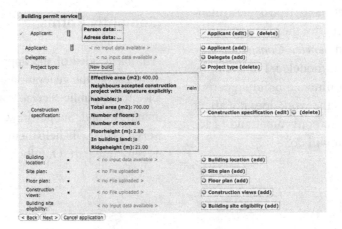

Figure 11. Conceptual overview of ontology driven e-government

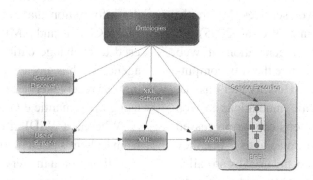

for the necessary information (see Figure 10). It is also possible to use abstract concepts as required input elements (such as *Person* which is either a physical person or a legal entity). In this case the specialization and classification mechanism described in the previous section is used first to identify the intended non-abstract concept, than values for the attributes of the selected concept have to be provided by the citizen.

This interactive ontology driven approach offers numerous advantages compared to conventional electronic forms:

- Once there exists a semantic model for a certain domain no forms have to be designed anymore.
- By structuring ontologies (e.g. by grouping all concepts concerning personal data within a separate ontology and introducing different levels of abstractions) concepts can easily be reused.
- Semantically enabled forms always know the context they are running in. For example, the form "knows" that the current construction represents a garage instead of an oil furnace. Thus, only the relevant attributes for describing a garage are rendered.
- The ontology contains numerous logical constraints and rules (axioms). These rules are permanently checked during form

completion. Therefore, the consistency of the gathered input data is guaranteed and data quality is tremendously increased.

The resulting form data is converted into XML that complies with the EDIAKT II Standard (Freitter, Gradwohl and Denner, 2006), which is an electronic interchange format for sharing files between different public agencies. As a consequence, the resulting request can be sent to any agency that is in charge of the selected service, making different responsibilities absolutely transparent to the citizen. This also allows this solution to become a single entry point to all public services. If, for example, a desire involves several services offered by different agencies, all of these services could be requested and the resulting files would be automatically dispatched to the administrative units in charge.

Service Implementation

So far service identification and service access based on semantic models and technologies were discussed. This section recommends an approach to extend the use of semantic models to even support the generation of executable semantic web services including the definition and execution of business processes. The suggested approach is not implemented in the prototype yet, nevertheless it can be considered as outlook to a future version of the system.

Typically, semantic web services (McIlraith, Son and Zeng, 2001; Burstein et al, 2005) are considered to be the next generation of web services and will revolutionize the way computers are used (Berners-Lee, Hendler and Lassila, 2001). By adding semantic annotations to web services, service descriptions can be processed and logically interpreted by machines so that they can be automatically found and used by so called computer agents. There exist several frameworks that aim at the implementation of semantic web services. Among them are OWL-S based and WSMO based implementations (Shafiq et al, 2007). While semantic web services are usually used to add annotations to already existing services, Ontology Driven E-Government is based on the idea to create the semantic model first and to use the resulting ontologies as domain model that forms the basis for the generation of an application or service. A schematic overview of this approach is shown in Figure 11.

Public services can be offered as web services. In the simplest case such a web service provides one single method that accepts an application and starts a process. In more complex cases that may rely on synchronous interaction, the web service might consist of several operations. Web services are defined by so-called WSDL (Web Service Descriptions Language) files. These files cover the description of the web service's functionality (offered operations, used data types, etc.) as well as the description of how and where its operations can be executed. Arguments and return types of operations are expressed as XML-schema types. Since the ontology already contains a comprehensive description of the public service it can be used to generate a WSDL file. Therefore service input has to be converted into XML. This involves the transformation of concept definitions into XML-schema and the transformation of instances (data provided by citizens) into XML according to the appropriate schema types. The latter step is already

integrated in the prototype since it uses EDIAKT II (Freitter, Gradwohl and Denner, 2006) to store the information that was gathered by the user. EDIAKT II is and XML format that is typically used to exchange entire files between different agencies. Thus any system that supports this format can receive service requests that were created using the semantic e-Government system.

Whereas a WSDL file describes a web service from a client's point of view it does not make any assertions about the service implementation. One way to implement a web service is to create a process defined in Web Services Business Process Execution Language (WS-BPEL) (OASIS 2007). BPEL allows for composing processes of web service operations and typical process control structures. Since a BPEL process itself is also exposed as web service operation it is straight forward to compose processes out of other sub-processes. To allow the creation of BPEL processes from ontologies it is necessary that all functional building blocks (activities used in the process) are also modeled as semantic services. This will eventually lead to a set of basic functions (e.g. retrieve a file from the document management system, approve a document, …).

To manage all needed services and BPEL processes an appropriate infrastructure is needed. Therefore the use of an Enterprise Service Bus (ESB) is recommended since it provides all the required functionality (Bernstein and Haas, 2008). Using this technology, all aspects of electronically provided public service's can be kept in a semantic model that is used to operationalise the service. This includes client side aspects such as service discovery and service utilization but also the back office process that is needed to provide a particular service.

CONCLUSION

The presented approach to develop e-Government services is solely based on semantic descriptions.

This semantic model can be used to support citizens that want to find a service, which will help them to achieve a particular goal. This significantly empowers citizens since they do no longer depend on domain experts but can use this system to find services they are eligible for. Beyond service discovery the model also allows to directly access a service by providing all needed information. The guided information gathering process offers an entirely new user experience since it only covers relevant information and plausibility and consistency are checked immediately. By extending the already existing prototype to back office processes as well, all aspects of an electronic service could be generated. This would significantly reduce development time and maintenance effort. Changes in requirements only need to be covered in the model whereas the actual software immediately adapts to the changes. Therefore this approach is suited to define a new paradigm in the field of e-Government.

REFERENCES

W3C (2004). *OWL Web Ontology Language Overview.*Retrieved June 30, 2009, from http://www.w3.org/TR/owl-features/

Alferes J. J., Pereira L. M., & Przymusinski T. C. (1996). Strong and Explicit Negation In Non-Monotonic Reasoning and Logic Programming, *JELIA '96, 1126* of LNAI.

Berners-Lee, T., Hendler, J., & Lassila, O. (2001). The Semantic Web - A new form of Web content that is meaningful to computers will unleash a revolution of new possibilities. *Scientific American, 284*(5), 34–43. doi:10.1038/scientificamerican0501-34

Bernstein, P. A., & Haas, L. M. (2008, September). Information integration in the enterprise. *Communications of the ACM, 51*(9), 72–79. doi:10.1145/1378727.1378745

Biagioli, C., Francesconi, E., Passerini, A., Montemagni, S., & Soria, C. (2005). Automatic semantics extraction in law documents. In *Proceedings of the 10th international Conference on Artificial intelligence and Law* (pp. 133-140), ACM.

Bruijn, J. D., Lara, R., Polleres, A., & Fensel, D. (2005). OWL DL vs. OWL Flight: Conceptual Modeling and Reasoning for the Semantic Web. In *Proceedings of the WWW '05: 14th international conference on World Wide Web*, ACM

Bruijn, J. D., Lausen, H., Polleres, A., & Fensel, D. (2006). The Web Service Modeling Language WSML: An Overview, *The Semantic Web: Research and Applications* [Springer.]. *Lecture Notes in Computer Science, 4011*, 590–604. doi:10.1007/11762256_43

Burstein, M., Bussler, C., Finin, T., Huhns, M. N., Paolucci, M., & Sheth, A. P. (2005). A semantic Web services architecture. *IEEE Internet Computing, 9*(5), 72–81. doi:10.1109/MIC.2005.96

Ehrig, M., Haase, P., Hefke, M., & Stojanovic, N. (2004). Similarity for ontology – a comprehensive framework. In *Workshop Enterprise Modelling and Ontology*. Ingredients for Interoperability.

Fensel, D., Lausen, H., Polleres, A., Bruijn, J. D., Stollberg, M., Roman, D., & Domingue, J. (2007). *Enabling Semantic Web Services: The Web Service Modeling Ontology*. Secausus, NJ: Springer.

Freitter, M., Gradwohl, N., & Denner, R. (2006). Empfehlung für das XML-Schema zu EDI-AKT II, V. 1.2.0 (German). Retrieved June 30, 2009, from http://www.ag.bka.gv.at/index.php/Portal:Ediakt

Genesereth, M. R., & Nilsson, N. J. (1987). *Logical Foundations of Artificial Intelligence*. Palo Alto, CA: Morgan Kaufmann Publishers Inc.

Gruber, T. R. (1995). Toward principles for the design of ontologies used for knowledge sharing. *International Journal of Human-Computer Studies*, *43*(5-6), 907–928. doi:10.1006/ijhc.1995.1081

Gruber, T. R. (2007). *Ontology*. Retrieved June 30, 2009, from http://tomgruber.org/writing/ontology-definition-2007.htm

Hendler, J. (2001, March). Agents and the Semantic Web. *IEEE Intelligent Systems*, *16*(2), 30–37. doi:10.1109/5254.920597

Kifer, M., Lausen, G., & Wu, J. (1995). Logical foundations of object-oriented and frame-based languages. [JACM]. *Journal of the ACM*, *42*, 741–843. doi:10.1145/210332.210335

Krummenacher, L. & Strang (2006). On the Modelling of Context-Rules with WSML. Workshop on Contexts & Ontologies: Theory, Practice and Applications. at *ECAI'06, Riva del Garda, Italy, 28. August 2006*.

Layne, K., & Lee, J. (2001). Developing Full Functional E-government: A Four Stage Model. *Government Information Quarterly*, *18*(2), 122–136. doi:10.1016/S0740-624X(01)00066-1

Leitner, C. (2003). *eGovernment in Europe: The State of Affairs*. Retrieved June 30, 2009, from www.eipa.eu/files/repository/product/20070214113429_egoveu.pdf

Martin, D., Paolucci, M., McIlraith, S., Burstein, M., McDermott, D., McGuinness, D., et al. (2005). Bringing Semantics to Web Services: The OWL-S Approach. In *Proceedings of the 1st International Workshop on Semantic Web Services and Web Process Composition* (pp.22-42). New York: Springer.

McIlraith, S. A., Son, T. C., & Zeng, H. (2001). Semantic Web services. *IEEE Intelligent Systems*, *16*(2), 46–53. doi:10.1109/5254.920599

McIlroy. M. D. (1968, October 7-11). Mass Produced Software Components. In P. Naur and B. Randell (Eds.), Software Engineering, Report on a conference sponsored by the NATO Science Committee, Garmisch, Germany (pp. 138-155). Brussels, Belgium: Scientific Affairs Division, NATO.

Miller, C., Mukerji, J., Burt, C., Dsouza, D., Duddy, K., & El Kaim, W. (2001). *Model Driven Architecture (MDA). Document number ormsc/2001-07-01. Architecture Board ORMSC, OMG*. New York: Springer.

OASIS. (2007). *Web Services Business Process Execution Language Version 2.0*. Retrieved June 30, 2009, from http://docs.oasis-open.org/wsbpel/2.0/OS/wsbpel-v2.0-OS.html

OMG. (2002). *Meta Object Facility (MOF) Specification*. Retrieved June 30, 2009, from http://www.omg.org/docs/formal/02-04-03.pdf

OMG. (2006). *Ontology Definition Metamodel, OMG Adopted Specification*. Berlin: Springer.

Peristeras, T. (2006). Reengineering Public Administration through Semantic Technologies and a Reference Domain Ontology. In *Proceedings of the AAAI Spring Symposium Semantic Web Meets e-Government*, Menlo Park, CA: AAAI Press.

Polleres, A., Lara, R., & Roman, D. (2004). *D4.2v01 Formal Comparison WSMO/OWL-S, DERI*. Retrieved June 30, 2009, from http://www.wsmo.org/2004/d4/d4.2/v0.1/20040315/

Schweighofer, E., Rauber, A., & Dittenbach, M. (2001). Automatic text representation, classification and labeling in European law. In *Proceedings of the 8th international conference on Artificial intelligence and law* (pp. 78-87). New York: ACM.

Shafiq, O., Moran, M., Cimpian, E., Mocan, A., Zaremba, M., & Fensel, D. (2007, May 13-19). Investigating Semantic Web Service Execution Environments: A Comparison between WSMX and OWL-S Tools. In *Proceedings of the Second international Conference on internet and Web Applications and Services ICIW.*, Washington, DC: IEEE Computer Society.

St., Haase, B., Sure, P., & Voelker, Y. (2005). *J. D.6.6.1 Report on the integration of ML, HLT and OM.* Retrieved June 30, 2009, from http://www.sti-innsbruck.at/fileadmin/documents/deliverables/Sekt/sekt-d-6-6-1-Int._ML__HLT__OM.pdf

Wang, X., Vitvar, T., Peristeras, V., Mocan, A., Goudos, S., & Tarabanis, K. (2007) WSMO-PA: Formal Specification of Public Administration Service Model on Semantic Web Service Ontology. In*Proceedings of the 40th Hawaii International Conference on System Sciences, HICSS,* (pp. 1-10)

Chapter 24
Virtual Neighborhoods and E-Government:
A Case Study Comparison

Rebecca Moody
Erasmus University Rotterdam, The Netherlands

Dennis de Kool
Center for Public Innovation, The Netherlands

Victor Bekkers
Erasmus University Rotterdam, The Netherlands

ABSTRACT

In this chapter the potential of GIS oriented neighborhood websites in the Netherlands will be researched. This new way of location based e-government will be analyzed by conducting four case studies in which neighborhood websites hold a central position. Relevant questions include to what degree these websites improve service delivery on the side of the government and to what degree the position of citizens is strengthened and whether they are pleased with the website and with the results. Attention will be paid to critical factors for success when designing the website but also while implementing the website and when the website is running. This will be done in terms of service delivery, closing of the gap between government and citizens and the strength of the position of citizens. Finally, we will answer the question on how GIS oriented neighborhood websites can be implemented so they have the highest potential by citizen satisfaction.

INTRODUCTION

The gap between citizens and government has been a subject of discussion in many countries as well as in the Netherlands for a while. The Dutch government feels it has to do something about this (perceived) gap, its legitimacy is at stake. Ways to diminish the gap between government and citizens and to regain trust from citizens are the improvement of electronic service delivery and an increase in citizen participation. Here we deal with an improved personalization towards location instead of towards citizens. Two developments have come together. First we see the neighborhood becomes an increasingly important frame of reference for the government. This can

DOI: 10.4018/978-1-61520-933-0.ch024

be demonstrated by more neighborhood based initiatives from local governments and from the plan 'krachtige wijken' (powerful neighborhoods) by Dutch government. Second Geographical Information Systems (GIS) play an increasingly important role. This is demonstrated for example by the emergence of Google Earth. Therefore it is not surprising that on neighborhood level experiments with GIS-oriented websites become more and more common. The potential of these initiatives can mostly be found in stimulating location based ways of service delivery and participation. Put differently, we are dealing with an improvement of service delivery by the government to citizens and an increase in participation by citizens in their neighborhood with the possibilities offered by modern information and communication technology (ICT). According to the report from the commission of municipal service delivery (Commissie Jorritsma) and the action plan 'Andere Overheid' (Different Government) the Dutch government should deliver its services to citizens more efficiently and effectively.

The goal of this chapter is to describe and analyze the degree in which these GIS oriented neighborhood websites improve service delivery by governments to citizens and whether they indeed strengthen participation. An electronic government becomes visible which we will term location based e-government'. It must be noted that the field of virtual neighborhoods and e-government is far larger as will be discussed here. For the sake of briefness only those issues will be covered which allow us to compare case studies in a way an answer to the main question can be given.

The central question in the chapter then will be: "To which degree do GIS oriented neighborhood websites improve service delivery by the government and strengthen participation by citizens?" In section 2 we will deal with the reason the neighborhood is an important frame of reference for the government. After that we will discuss the potential of GIS. In the fourth section the theoretical framework will be the central point of focus, which we will use to analyze the case studies. These case studies will be elaborated on in section 5. Finally we will draw some conclusions.

It must be noted that the field of virtual neighborhoods and e-government is far larger as will be discussed here. For the sake of briefness only those issues will be covered which allow us to compare case studies in a way an answer to the main question can be given.

THE NEIGHBORHOOD THROUGH THE LOOKING GLASS

The neighborhood is becoming an increasingly important frame of reference for Dutch government policy. (WRR, 2005) First the neighborhood is the place where societal problems and challenges become visible. The plan 'krachtige wijken' demonstrates a renewed focus on the neighborhood within the broad frame of the larger cities. Also local governments increasingly make policy based on neighborhoods.

Second the neighborhood is the living environment of citizens. Social en physical qualities of a neighborhood are of influence on the involvement of citizens and the degree of integration in society and their attitude towards the government. Therefore the importance of the neighborhood is mostly termed by social cohesion. (WRR, 2005) A diminishing social cohesion would contribute to an increase in anonymity, displacements, insecurity, well-being and trust from citizens towards the government. A possible answer to these problems could be found in a strengthening of small-scale connections in which people interact daily and in which their interaction with the government regarding day-to-day politics is given meaning. Citizens are able to be actively involved in these matters but often lack the motivation to do so. (WRR, 2005) The largest challenge here is to make sure citizens on neighborhood level have a 'feeling of belonging', 'active participation' and 'co decision'. Citizens, in several ways have the opportunity to organize themselves and participate actively to change or strengthen their neighborhood, in order to influence local policy on their neighborhood.

GIS can be an important instrument to give way to new manners of improving relations between citizens and government and to make new ways of service delivery and participation possible. Additionally GIS can play an important role in strengthening social cohesion in neighborhoods by visualizing on maps what is going on.

GEOGRAPHICAL INFORMATION SYSTEMS

Geographical Information Systems (GIS) are computerized systems for the purpose of saving, analyzing and demonstrating data on the basis of a geographical component. (Grothe, 1999) GIS are said to have several qualities and effects. (Bekkers & Moody, 2006; Bregt, 1999; Carver, 2001; Greene, 2003; Heywood et al. 2002; Pollard, 2000)

Firstly one of the qualities of GIS is the possibility to calculate large data sets. Based on these calculations cost-benefit analysis can be made easily. An example is the study of probable future landscape sites made by GIS.

A second quality is the possibility to link different data sets to one another. This can make sure that new information and new insights become visible. By integrating and visualizing different data sets it becomes possible to form an integral policy. Additionally GIS can strengthen the problem solving capabilities of the government, by for example linking information on social benefits with water use or type of car owned, in this way detecting fraud. (www.rcf.nl)

Third GIS can visualize problems and effects. Supported by multimedia applications and 3D techniques policy plans and results can be visualized for a large public. Social participation can be stimulated by using this quality, which can result in an increase in the quality of decision making. A clear example here is the Virtuocity project in the city of Helmond. This quality makes GIS different from other forms of ICT, where the mentioned qualities count for most forms of ICT, the visualizing function makes GIS different. GIS holds the function to visualize large sets of data making them accessible to nonexperts.

When looking at these qualities GIS can function in several ways. First GIS can support policy making and decision making, in for example spatial planning.

When communicating on policy results GIS can help in accounting for this policy, this can be done in the form of legitimizing policy. An example that will be discussed in more detail in section 5.3 is www.hoeveiligismijnwijk.nl

A third potential function of GIS is learning. Because GIS can visualize large data sets and is able to link data sets to one another, actors can learn new insights and can be able to fathom reality.

Fourth GIS can be used to monitor policy; By being on top of relevant developments it becomes possible to predict future developments. This is done for example for spatial developments. An example is the Monitor Nota Ruimte, that monitors spatial developments in the Netherlands. (De Kool, 2008)

Finally GIS can be used to increase transparency in policy making, this both in making a policy problem itself transparent but also by making effects of a decision transparent.

In the next section our theoretical framework will be elaborated on, based on this framework the cases will be analyzed.

THEORETICAL FRAMEWORK

In this chapter the central question deals with to what degree GIS oriented neighborhood websites improves service delivery by the government and strengthens participation by citizens. In order to

Table 1. Characteristics neighborhood

Motivation	- why do actors want a website? - why do actors want to participate on the website?
Problem perception	- what is the problem according to citizens? - how do they hope to solve the problem?
Added value	- does the website contribute to solving the problem? - how so?

analyze this, four case studies have been conducted by the means of two linkages. First the linkage between problem and solution and second the linkage between functionality and goal. We assume that actors in any problem negotiate with one another and have to choose between different alternatives in order to come to a policy solution. The two linkages determine the outcome of the process and therefore the success of the website. This interaction then is influenced by the characteristics of the neighborhood as well as the characteristics of the website. Both characteristics in turn influence the interaction between actors and as such the outcome.

The Linkage Problem: Solution

The success of the neighborhood website is first dependent on the linkage between the problem and the solution. This means the problem, as perceived by the actors, must be linked to the solution. The question here naturally is whether the perceived problem is solved by the solution the neighborhood website offers. Several actors interact in this process. On neighborhood level interaction takes place between actors in the neighborhood, the government and possibly other groups. After negotiation they come up with an outcome. This outcome should be the solution for the original problem.

The solution is thus the outcome of this interaction. The problem however is more difficult to define. What is important here are the characteristics of the neighborhood. These characteristics deal with whom the (potential) users are and what they

expert from their neighborhood website. This deals with citizens themselves and their judgment on the way in which the government deals with service delivery. Furthermore the characteristics deal with the motivation of the actors in the neighborhood to use or participate in the neighborhood website. The problem lies with the perception of citizens, what they perceive to be the problem constitutes for the problem. Also the perception of the added value of the website is important. Citizens need to feel the website will contribute to the solution to the experienced problem. (See Table 1)

The actors in the neighborhood then interact with others and will try to push their problem definition, and their preferred solution, forward. Finally after negotiation between all actors a solution is established. When this solution proves to be the solution for the defined problem then the linkage is successful and then one of the criteria for success for the website is obtained. In the case the problem is not solved by the solution than the linkage between problem and solution has failed and the success of the website cannot be optimal.

The Linkage Functionality: Goals

Secondly the success of the website is dependent on the linkage between functionality and goals. This does not only deal with the goal of the website itself but also with the degree to which the functionality of this goal.

The functionality of the website here is not regarded as given; the website is made by designers based on what other actors have asked them.

Table 2. Characteristics website

Accessibility	- readability? - user-friendliness?
Transparency	- completeness? - reliability?
Feedback	- which possibilities for participation does the website offer? - which patterns of interaction does the website establish?
GIS	- what is the added value of GIS? - how does GIS serve the goal?

These actors have had a large impact in how the website will look and what the possibilities on the website are. In order to research the functionality of websites there are a number of characteristics to be considered.

First accessibility is important. Here we deal with the readability and degree of user-friendliness of the website. It is important for citizens to understand the information displayed. Also a logical navigation and layout are important for this. Additionally it is important that website are easy to access, pass words, log-ins and plug-ins can make the website less accessible, especially for citizens with few technological skills or older computers. The criterion to measure the level of accessibility is a subjective one. Interviews and feedback on the website itself (when possible) demonstrate how accessible the website is in the views of citizens. This perception of citizens is the criterion used to measure accessibility.

A second characteristic is the transparency of the website. This firstly deals with completeness. It is important that the government communicates to citizens in a way that is as open and as nuanced as possible and does not withhold important information. Additionally the quality is important. The information must be up to date, relevant and reliable. As for the first characteristic, the level of transparency is measured by reactions of citizens, as found in interviews and feedback on the website. Therefore the level of transparency measured is a subjective measure.

A third characteristic is feedback. Here we deal with the potential possibilities for participation offered by the website, and the actual patterns of interaction the website establishes. The question here is whether the website indeed adds to interaction between citizens and government.

Finally we deal with the role of GIS in the design of the website. This because GIS can increase the functionality of the website, in terms of transparency, but also in ways to visualize and clarify information better than traditional forms of presentation. (See Table 2)

In terms of negotiations this means the design of the website is one of the matters on which actors can exert influence. This interaction in negotiations can lead to a certain design for a website. When the site is designed, the site can still be adapted at the moment actors protest or put forward new wishes.

When we look at the linkage between functionality and goal we see that the possibilities on the website must serve the goal in order to make a successful linkage. The goal is defined as the goal the actors who took the initiative to establish the website perceived it. It must be noted here that this is not the same as the problem perception. Where the problem deals with the perception of a problem for citizens in general, the goal refers to the goal as defined by those who initiated the website.

When the linkage between functionality of the website and the goal is made, the website fills one of the criteria of success. When the way the website functions does not meet the goal the success of the website will decrease.

Summarizing it can be said that a neighborhood website must meet two criteria to be successful, first the successful linking of problem and solution and second the successful linking of functionality and goal.

CASE STUDIES

In this section we will demonstrate by analyzing four cases how GIS can offer a contribution to a neighborhood oriented, electronic government. The selection of the case studies is based on the innovative character of the neighborhood websites. In all four cases these websites where the first in their kind. Additionally a distinction is made between top-down initiatives and bottom up initiatives, two cases are based on a top-down initiative and two on a bottom up initiative. Finally in the case selection variety in sectors of policy is taken into account.

In this way the four cases can offer a more broad view of neighborhood websites. Since these websites are not policy sector specific, a better insight can be given in the value of these sites. By a comparison of these websites this insight can be nuanced.

For the following research we have analyzed relevant documents, interviewed involved actors and analyzed the website in dept. In this way, by using several different methods of research (triangulation) the reliability of the research will be improved.

Neighborhood Oriented Service Delivery: Google Earth in Voorst

Through Google Earth the municipality of Voorst has established a way of service delivery by which citizens, through the internet, can view information on building permits, track and trace the ap-

pliance of their own permit, request information and add information themselves. For citizens it is now possible to go online by using their own internet connection and obtain the information they seek on their neighborhood as offered by the municipality. Furthermore citizens can now in an easy way request permits and obtain other services from their local government. In order to make the application more interactive citizens are able to add information themselves, they can add pictures through Google Earth and they are able to provide for written information on their neighborhood. This enables citizens to request information easily, from their own home instead of having to go to the city hall. Also this enables citizens to actively participate in their neighborhood by making pictures or other information visible on the internet for all their neighbors. This could not only result in the service delivered to citizens improving but also in a higher degree of coherence of the neighborhood itself.

Linkage Problem: Solution

Motivation

The launch of this plan fits the report of the Commission Jorritsma and has as a goal to help citizens to obtain geographical information on their neighborhood but also to request information through the internet.

Problem Perception

The goal of giving citizens information on their neighborhood is based on the idea to improve service delivery through the internet. Citizens should be able to obtain the information from the local government in an easy way. The municipality of Voorst does not only hope in this way to account for a better service delivery and flow of information but also to account for citizens being more involved in their neighborhood.

Added Value

After the launch of the program it is to be seen that citizens make use of the problem fairly much. On average a hundred people visit the website each day. Most popular are the building permits in the neighborhood, contact information and publications by the government. Also personal information is favorite, the status of ones own permit and information on the taxation of ones property is visited frequently. Research shows that citizens are happy with the speed and the easy way in which they can obtain information. The municipality of Voorst is satisfied with the relief in pressure this is at the physical desk for these matters. Citizens are also able to put information on the site, for example pictures, the popularity of this is low. To do this someone must log-in and a lot people do not want to do this. The municipality will have to, in order to make the website function properly in the future, moderate the site more intensively.

In the case we see hat problem and solution are linked rather successful. The problem is solved by the website and it turns out that citizens often use the application. All involved actors are satisfied with the application. The problem that should have been solved, namely participation of citizens causing a larger coherence in the neighborhood, through pictures and messages placed by citizens on the website seems to be a less successful linkage. Here the match between problem and solution is not made.

Linkage Functionality: Goal

Accessibility

The accessibility of the website is very large. By using an existing application as Google Earth, the way the website was to be used was clear. The user-friendliness of Google Earth had been tested already and where necessary adapted. The website is very readable, unnecessary jargon is avoided. However, citizens need to log in and this causes some resistance from citizens and causes the website to be less accessible.

Transparency

The website is transparent to a very large degree. It is clear what one can find and which service is offered. Even though there are still services which are not offered through the internet it becomes clear on the website what is possible.

Feedback

The website does not provide for an interactive forum. Citizens are able to put information on the site themselves but communication between citizens and government is not to be found other than information and service delivery. There is thus no possibility for feedback.

GIS Component

By using Google Earth it becomes possible for citizens to see in the blink of an eye what is all happening in their neighborhood. The visualization of this enlarges the user-friendliness and makes the website clear to citizens. A map is often easier to understand than a table of graph.

When we look at the linkage between functionality and goals of the website we see that this linkage is partly successful. The accessibility and the transparency of the website are large. But the obligation to log in lessens this accessibility. For feedback the linkage is not made very well, possibilities for this are not present. The GIS component does add in large portions to the functionality of the website. The linkage, because the lessened accessibility and the lack of feedback options, is not very successful.

Neighborhood Participation: Virtuocity in Helmond

In Helmond a GIS application was used as well, Virtuocity, in which citizens could walk, in 3-d images, though the inner city of Helmond. The inner cities of Helmond was to be restructured, instead of showing citizens a sketch or a maquette, the citizens of Helmond were offered a virtual walk through the new city. In this way they can see the planned reconstructions. Citizens can access Virtuocity through their own internet connection and choose an avatar. With this avatar one can walk around the neighborhood and see all the new plans the same way as when playing a computer game. Additionally there is a forum on which citizens can communicate with the local government and chat sessions with aldermen are organized. Virtuocity has accounted for not only increased communication between citizens and government but also, according to both a better quality of communication. Furthermore citizens felt involved in their own neighborhood, as interviews with citizens have demonstrated, and they were far more able to understand what the restructuring plans entailed.

Linkage Problem: Solution

Motivation

The launch of this application is part of the program "kenniswijk" (knowledge neighborhood). In this program the Ministry of Economical Affairs tries to create the possibility to let citizens participate in innovative projects in terms of ICT. The municipality of Helmond hopes with Virtuocity to inform citizens but also to consult them regarding the future of the city. The municipality also hopes the application will make sure that citizens feel more involved with their city.

Problem Perception

The goals of Virtuocity are numerous. First there is the goal of informing citizens on reconstructions in Helmond. Second there is a goal to make sure communication is open between citizens and government, through the chat and the forum. Finally the municipality also wants to hear citizens' opinions.

Added Value

Virtuocity is an application that is visited very frequently, around forty people visit the site a day. Also the chat sessions are visited frequently. It turns out that Virtuocity facilitates the communication with citizens, makes sure plans are in the open. This also because these plans can be easily visualized so it is clear what they entail. Based on the conducted interviews it can be concluded that citizens feel involved and taken seriously, this accounts for an increase in participation. According to the municipality of Helmond Virtuocity made sure that communication with citizens improved substantially.

In Helmond we see a successful linkage between problem and solution, the problem perception came from government as well as citizens and the solution, as a result of the interaction, proved to be satisfactory for all actors.

Linkage Functionality and Goal

Accessibility

The website is very accessible and registering is not necessary. However, it is so that a program has to be downloaded in order to use Virtuocity. This proved not to account for any problems. Before Virtuocity was launched the municipality of Helmond first installed a test panel to test the accessibility and the user-friendliness. Based on this several adjustment have been made.

Transparency

The website is fairly transparent. It is clear to citizens what the building plans are. This is very easy to be seen in the 3-d virtual world created by Virtuocity. On the forum it is also stated when these building plans will take place. Within the application there is also the possibility for citizens to receive extra information.

Feedback

The amount and possibility of feedback between citizens and government is very large. On the forum and on the chat all plans are discussed and citizens can react. Citizens can ask questions or voice criticism. The municipality of Helmond is much disciplined to react quickly to questions and remarks. Actual interaction clearly takes place to great satisfaction of government as well as citizens.

GIS Component

Virtuocity presents the new Helmond as a virtual world this has the advantage for citizens that plans are not visualized as 'flat maps'. A sketch by an architect is often difficult to understand for citizens, by walking through their own neighborhood and to see how it will look is much more appealing.

In Helmond the linkage between functionality and goal is very successful. Transparency and accessibility are present to a large degree. Feedback is apparent and the GIS component adds to the functionality. The functionality and the goal match each other almost completely.

Neighborhood Monitoring: Crimes in the Region Haaglanden

In April 2006 the police department Haaglanden launched the website www.hoeveiligismijnwijk. nl. On this website citizens can view eleven of the most frequent crimes committed within the region a neighborhood, namely car theft, intimidation, mugging, theft of mopeds, theft from cars, theft from companies, theft from houses, theft of bikes, ill-treatment, shoplifting and pick-pocketing. The viewers of the website can select the crimes-categories, the period in which the crimes took place and the municipality, district or neighborhood in which these crimes have been committed. Special software has been developed to show the data on geographical maps. By comparing current numbers with past data it is also possible to get insight in trends in crime. Besides crimes figures the website provides viewers also with information to prevent crimes. The idea behind this is that prevention measures will reduce the number of crimes within the region Haaglanden. In terms of e-government and service delivery the applications made sure the citizens were able to view the amount and the type of crime in their surrounding in a comprehensible way. Furthermore the hope existed that by demonstrating this to citizens they would be more willing to report crime.

Linkage Problem: Solution

Motivation

The launch of the website is part of a large campaign by the police department 'Haaglanden'. With this campaign the police hope to actively inform citizens and societal organization on the developments regarding criminal facts, unsafety and the results made by the police. The essential goal is to make the region safer.

Problem Perception

An important goal of the website is providing for a realistic image of local safety. In this way the website serves as a communication instrument to inform citizens on the results the police have made. Additionally a goal is the increase of involvement of citizens in the neighborhood. With the website therefore, the police hopes to urge citizens to look critically at problems in their own neighborhood. The idea is that well-informed citizens attribute to a safer environment. The increase of the reporting of crimes is also a sub-goal of the website.

Added Value

Citizens, as the results out of interviews show, are very keen on visiting the website. Also in parliament the initiative of the policy department Haaglanden has been noticed. The Minister of Internal Affairs proved to appreciate the initiative. In other police departments several steps have been taken to implement a similar website.

In this case we see that the linkage between solution and problem not completely matches. In the area of information provision the linkage proves to be a large success, citizens visit the website and are informed on the safety issues in their neighborhood. The active involvement of citizens in the safety of their neighborhood has, up till now, not been apparent.

Linkage Functionality and Goals

Accessibility

In terms of readability of the website unnecessary jargon is not used and the different crimes are explained. The layout of the website is very basic, the structure is logical.

The user-friendliness of the website is large. One does not need to log on or register which makes the website accessible. Next to crime statistics the website also provides for useful tips for the prevention of crime.

Transparency

The question can be posed whether the website provides for a complete view of reality. One must keep in mind the site is based on reported crimes. The police department acknowledges

that numbers can be misleading. If there is little parking space in an area, it is no more than fair that less cars will be stolen than in an area with lots of parked cars.

Feedback

Since the website presents crimes reported by citizens, according to the police department, the website in itself feeds this back to citizens. Citizens were also asked to give their opinion on the website and among those who do prizes can be won.

The website does not contain an interactive forum. Still the police departments views the website as an important portal by which citizens can contact the police.

GIS Component

With specially designed software the information on reported crimes is made available on geographical maps. The maps contain the numbers on eleven of the most frequent crimes. By using the map citizens in one blink of an eye can obtain a complete image of these crimes in their neighborhood.

The police department Haaglanden demonstrates a rather high success in the linkage between functionality and goals. The accessibility of the website is high and since there is no need to register the website is easy to use. The transparency however is not optimal. This because not all information is known and the published information cannot be interpreted properly without additional data on the circumstances. Feedback is not very much present and this is even strengthened by the lack of a forum on the website. Since this is not a goal of the website this does not account for a problem in the linkage between functionality and goals. The GIS component proves to add to the functionality of the website because of its visualizing function.

Neighbors Against Airport Hindrance

On June 24th 2003 the Platform Vlieghinder Regio Castricum (PVRC) (Platform for airport hindrance in the area of Castricum) was established. An important incentive for the start of this initiative by citizens was the use of a new airport runway, the so-called "Polderbaan" by the airport of Schiphol. This, according to citizens, had led to a large increase in noise nuisance. An important goal behind this association is to reduce the noise nuisance around the airport of Schiphol by providing the airport authorities and governments with grounded data. This data is real-life gathered by noise-measurement equipment around the airport and shown on a live 'radar' on the website www. vlieghinder.nl. Citizens have used this website to make sure that the government is aware of the actual noise hindrance caused by the new runway. They have used the website to mobilize and make sure that adequate information was given to their neighbors on the noise but also to the government. In terms of e-government and neighborhood coherence the hope existed the government would support citizens of the affected neighborhood to reduce their discomfort.

Linkage Problem and Solution

Motivation

The goal of the PVRC is decreasing the noise nuisance caused by Schiphol airport. The mission of this group is defending the interests of the citizens living in the area. To reach its goal the PVRC wants to use publicity and that is why they have started their website.

Problem Perception

There are several goals linked to the website. First the PVRC wants to decrease the noise nuisance and wants to decrease the information gap on the side of citizens. The PVRC also feels that legislation has done them wrong. The law claims there is a norm for the amount of noise allowed for areas next to the airport. But this norm does not apply to the areas of Castricum, Limmen, Heemskerk and parts of Beverwijk because these areas are located too far from the airport.

Added Value

The PVRC on the website voices its opinion that the government will not inform them on the noise nuisance. Because of this the PVRC actively tries to inform citizens themselves. Additionally the PVC is an interest group for citizens who try to influence political decision making. At present the PVRC is seen as a legitimate partner in negotiations.

For the case of the PVRC the linkage between problem and solution is practically a hundred percent successful. The goal of informing citizens proves to be a success but also being taken seriously in negotiations has been successful.

Linkage Functionality and Goal

Accessibility

The website is very readable, no jargon is used. The structure of the website can be improved, it must be said that the website is still being developed and runs on the employment of volunteers. The user-friendliness of the website is large and there is no need for registration.

Transparency

Informing citizens and government is the most important goal of the website, since the PVRC supposes that citizens have a lack of information compared to the airport. The website contains a lot of information among which background information, radar maps and flight routes. With the help of this information the PVRC can base there complaints on noise nuisance. The presentation of this information is not optimal.

Feedback

On the website interested citizens are urged to register and become a member. A cooperation with 18 citizens groups in the region is also established. According to the starters of the website the possibility for citizens to react is one of the key factors for success of the website. There are also meetings between members.

GIS component

The PVRC together with the Stichting Geluidsnet (Association Noise net) designed a system in which one can look at the actual flights by Google Earth. According to the starters of the website the combination of GIS, real-time measurements and internet account for one of the key success factors for the website.

The PVRC shows a very good linkage between problem and solution. The accessibility of the website is large, the transparency is also large even though the presentation of the information is not optimal. Also the feedback seems to be very functional. Citizens can respond and do so, an interactive website is granted. Also the GIS component proves to add to the goal.

CONCLUSION

Coming back to the main question we can conclude the following.

Linkages

When looking at the four case studies we can see that all case studies have different goals but also different groups of actors interacting with one another. As a criterion for success we stated that a website must meet a successful linkage between a perceived problem and solution and a successful linkage between functionality and goal.

Per case study we can se that in Voorst problem and solution match fairly well, the problem regarding public service delivery seems to be solved by the website, but the linkage between the problem of increasing coherence in the neighborhood and the solution for this cannot be found. In Helmond a very successful linkage can be found between the problem and the solution. The website matches the problem. In the police department Haaglanden we can see that the linkage between problem and solution is less than optimal, where the linkage is successful in providing information, it is less successful in involving citizens. In the case of PVRC the linkage between problem and solution is completely successful.

Looking at the linkage between functionality and goal we can see in the case of Voorst the linkage is not successful, feedback and transparency stay behind, even though the GIS component does highly add to the functionality of the website. In Helmond this linkage is successful, feedback and transparency are present and the GIS component adds highly to the functionality. Police department Haaglanden shows us a reasonable degree of success, transparency and feedback are less than optimal but the GIS component adds to the functionality of the website. Finally the PVRC demonstrates a very successful linkage between functionality and goal. (See Table 3)

Regarding the linkage between problem and solution we can see here that in all four cases there is success to a fair degree. It seems that the websites in which citizens have had a larger impact are more successful in this linkage (Helmond and PVRC) than the websites that are completely developed and influenced by the government. This can be explained by the idea that citizens account for the definition of the problem perception. When they have a more say so they also can influence a possible solution. We also see that the website where citizen involvement is high the score is higher. When citizens obtain the possibility to, within ones own problem perception, contribute

Table 3.

	Voorst	Helmond	Police department Haaglanden	PVRC
Motivation	+	+	+	+
Problem perception	+	+	+	+
Added Value	+/-	++	+/-	++
Linkage problem – solution	+/-	++	+/-	++
Accessibility	-	++	++	+
Transparency	+	+	--	++
Feedback	--	++	-	++
GIS component	++	++	++	++
Linkage functionality – goal.	-	++	+/-	++

to a solution, the added value of this solution will be higher.

The linkage between functionality and goal seems more difficult to achieve. In terms of accessibility we see that this is fairly easy, except when one has to register to enter the website. The transparency of the website seems to be fairly successful as well, a problem only seems to occur in the more complex matters in which a large amount of variables have to be taken into account (police department Haaglanden) Feedback proves to be a problem though, especially in websites where citizens had little involvement and impact, here it proves to be difficult to motivate citizens to become actively involved. The websites in which citizens had a large impact in design score significantly higher on the point of feedback. The GIS component proves in all cases to add to the functionality of the site and in this way adds to realizing the goal. GIS can make a website more clear, making sure citizens can see all the information in one blink of an eye, in a way easy to understand.

In the linkage between functionality and goal it seems that the website in which citizens had a large impact have a more successful linkage. This can be explained by the idea that in these websites citizens have had impact in the design of the website; making sure functionality is granted and serves the purpose.

Key Success Factors

Looking at both linkages we can conclude that in the cases of Helmond and PVRC both linkages are successful, and in the cases of police department Haaglanden and Voorst both linkages are less successful. Five key success factors can be derived from this.

First the influence of citizens on the process. It seems to be the case that when citizens have a large impact on the construction of a solution as well as the on the building of the functionality of the website, the website itself is more successful in both linkages.

Second a key success factor is the user-friendliness of GIS oriented neighborhood websites. The user-friendliness of the studied websites are is high. Furthermore it turns out that an obligation to register causes resistance among citizens

A third key success factor is the use of open source systems, so functionalities can be added and the application can be developed further.

Fourth the interactive content of the website is important. It is important that feedback can be given and the website is adequately moderated.

The fifth key success factor deals with reliability and completeness of information. A website providing this will be more successful than a website that does not.

Regarding the success of the studied websites we can conclude that a website in which citizens have a large impact on the problem perception and on the solution for this problem, have a larger degree of success than websites where this is not the case. This because feedback is not possible in the latter but also because the added value of the website increases when citizens can actively contribute in developing a solution for a problem. Accessibility turns out to be something that can be easily achieved, as well as transparency, especially when existing software is used, which is already tested for user-friendliness. Matters demanding a more complex explanation seem to be less successful for a neighborhood website, since these matters are very difficult to be presented in a transparent way. The GIS component in neighborhood websites proves to add to the success of the website to a very high degree, this because of the qualities of GIS. Because of which it becomes possible to view all information in the blink of an eye and present this information in a way understandable to many.

REFERENCES

Bekkers, V. J. J. M. (2001). De mythen van de elektronische overheid. Over retoriek en realiteit *Bestuurswetenschappen, 4.* 277-295.

Bekkers, V. J. J. M., & Homburg, V. M. F. (2005). *The information ecology of E-government: E-government as institutional and technological innovation in public administration.* Amsterdam: IOS Press.

Bekkers, V. J. J. M., & Moody, R. (2006). Geographical Information Systems and the policy formulation process: the emergence of a reversed mixed scanning mode? In Bekkers, V. J. J. (Ed.), *M Duivenboden, van H. & Thaens, M. (2006) Information and communication technology and public innovation: assessing the ICT-driven modernization of public administration.* Amsterdam: IOS Press.

Bregt, A. K. (1999). *Net werk in de Geo-informatiekunde.* Wageningen, The Netherlands: Universiteit Wageningen.

Carver, S. (2001). *Participation and Geographical Information: a position paper, Position paper ESF-NSF workshop Access to Geographic Information and participatory approaches using Geographic Information.* Italy: Spoleto.

Greene, R. W. (2003). *GIS in public policy: using geographic information for more effective government.* Redlands, CA: ESRI Press.

Grothe, M. (1999). *Keuze voor ruimte, ruimte voor keuze: de ontwikkeling van GIS-applicaties voor locatieplanning; een objectgeoriënteerde analyse.* Amsterdam: Vrije Universiteit.

Grothe, M., Nijkamp, P., & Scholten, H. J. (1996). Monitoring residental quality for the elderly using a geographical information system. *International Planning Studies, 1*(2), 199–215. doi:10.1080/13563479608721652

Heywood, I., Cornelius S., &. Carver, S (2002). *Geographical Information Systems,* London: Pearson-Prentice.

Kingston, R., Carver, S., Evans, A., & Turton, I. (2000). Web-based public participation geographical information systems: an aid to local environmental decision-making. *Computers, Environment and Urban Systems, 24*(2), 109–125. doi:10.1016/S0198-9715(99)00049-6

Kool, D. de, in cooperation with Bekkers, V. J. J. M. (2008). *Monitoring in kaart: een studie naar de doorwerking van op GIS gebaseerde beleidsinformatie in het leerproces van organisaties die een rol spelen bij de uitvoering van beleid,* Rotterdam Center for Public Innovation.

Natuurplanbureau, M. (2005). *Ruimtelijke Beelden: visualisatie van een veranderd Nederland in 2030.* The Netherlands: Bilthoven.

Pollard, P. (2000). Geographical Information Services: A UK perspective on the development of interorganisational information services. *Information Infrastructure and Policy, 6*(4), 185–195.

voor Regeringsbeleid. W. R. (2005). Vertrouwen in de buurt. Amsterdam: University Press.

Compilation of References

(1993). *Eurobarometer 39*. Brussels: Commission of the European Communities.

(1993). *Eurobarometer 40*. Brussels: Commission of the European Communities.

(1994). *Eurobarometer 41*. Brussels: Commission of the European Communities.

(1999). *Eurobarometer 52*. Brussels: Commission of the European Communities.

(2000). *Communication from the Commission to the Council, the European Parliament, the Economic and Social Committee and the Committee of the regions - Social Policy Agenda. In28.6.2000, COM(2000) 379 final, Commission of the European Community*. Brussels: CEC.

(2000). Marcos. InPonce de León, J. (Ed.), *Our word is our weapon: Selected writings Subcomandante Marcos* (pp. 280–282). London: Serpents Trails.

(2001). *Eurobarometer 56*. Brussels: Commission of the European Communities.

(2004). *Eurobarometer 61*. Brussels: Commission of the European Communities.

(2008). *Eurobarometer 69*. Brussels: Commission of the European Communities.

(2008). *Eurobarometer 70*. Brussels: Commission of the European Communities.

(n.d.). *Efile Express*. Retrieved April 29, 2009, from http://www.efile-express.com/

ACRC. (2009). *A report on civil petition operation assessment of 2008* [in Korean]. Seoul, Korea: Anti-Corruption & Civil Rights Commission.

Activegovernment. *Government Online Payments*. Retrieved April 30, 2009, from http://www.activegovernment.com/government-online-payments.htm

Adolfsson Jörby, S. (2000). Local agenda 21 in practice– A Swedish example. *Sustainable Development, 8*(4), 201–214. doi:10.1002/1099-1719(200011)8:4<201::AID-SD147>3.0.CO;2-0

Adolfsson Jörby, S. (2002). Local agenda 21 in four Swedish municipalities: A tool towards sustainability. *Journal of Environmental Planning and Management, 45*(2), 219–229. doi:10.1080/09640560220116314

Aguilar, L. F. (2003). *La hechura de las políticas*. México: Porrúa.

Aguilar, L. F. (2003). *Problemas públicos y agenda de gobierno*. México: Porrúa.

Aguilera, C. (2007). Participación Ciudadana en el Gobierno de Bachelet: Consejos Asesores Presidenciales. *América Latina Hoy, 46*, 119–143.

Ahituv, N., & Raban, Y. (2008). *Policy Recommendations for Improving E-Government use among low Socio-Economic Status Groups*. E-Government For Low Socio-Economic Status Groups (Elost). Retrieved July 25, 2009, from http://www.elost.org/ahituv.pdf

Akesson, M., Skalen, P., & Edvardsson, B. (2008). E-government and service orientation: gaps between theory and practice. *International Journal of Public Sector Management, 21*(1), 74–92. doi:10.1108/09513550810846122

Alexander, C. (2005). Northern exposure: Assessing citizenship, democracy and the great Canadian e-government expedition. *Technikfolgenabschatzung – Theorie und Praxis, 2*, 80-87.

Al-Fakhri, M., Cropf, R., Higgs, G., & Kelly, P. (2008). E-Government in Saudi Arabia: Between Promise and Reality. *International Journal of Electronic Government Research, 4*(2), 59–82.

Alferes J. J., Pereira L. M., & Przymusinski T. C. (1996). Strong and Explicit Negation In Non-Monotonic Reasoning and Logic Programming, *JELIA '96, 1126* of LNAI.

Al-Gahtani, S. (2004). Computer Technology Acceptance Success Factors in Saudi Arabia: An Exploratory Study. *Journal of Global Information Technology Management, 7*(1), 5–29.

Allee, V., & Schwabe, O. (2009). Measuring the Impact of Research Networks in the EU: Value Networks and Intellectual Capital Formation. Online version of Paper for *European Conference on Intellectual Capital Haarlem*, The Netherlands. Retrieved April 28, 2009, from http://www.vernaallee.com/value_networks/AlleeSchwabe-ResearchNetworks.pdf.

Alvarez, R., & Hall, T. (2004). *Point, Clic, and Vote: The future of Internet voting*. Washington, DC: Brookings Institution Press.

Alverez, R. M., & Nagler, J. (2001). The Likely Consequences of Internet Voting for Political Representation. *Loyola of Los Angeles Law Review, 34*, 1115–1152.

Amoretti, F. (2006). E-Government Regimes. In Anttiroiko, A., & Malkia, M. (Eds.), *Encyclopedia of Digital Government* (pp. 580–587). Hershey, PA: IGI Global.

Amoretti, F. (2007). International Organizations ICTs Policies: E-Democracy and E-Government for Political Development. *Review of Policy Research, 24*(4). doi:10.1111/j.1541-1338.2007.00286.x

Anderson, C. (2006). *The Long Tail: Why the Future of Business is Selling Less of More*. New York: Hyperion Publishing.

Anderson, J., Schwager, P., & Kerns, R. (2006). The Drivers for Acceptance of Tablet PCs by Faculty in a College of Business. *Journal of Information Systems Education, 17*, 429–440.

Anstead, N., & Chadwick, A. (2008). Parties, election campaigning, and the Internet: Toward a comparative institutional approach. In Chaswick, A., & Howard, P. (Eds.), *The Routledge Handbook of Internet Politics*. New York: Routledge.

Anthopoulos, L., & Tsoukalas, I. A. (2005) The implementation model of a digital city. The case study of the first digital city in Greece: e-Trikala. *Journal of e-Government* (Haworth Press, Inc., University of Southern California, Center for Digital Government), *2*(2). Retreived 2005, from http://www.haworthpress.com/web/JEG/ and http://www.egovjournal.com/

Anthopoulos, L., Siozos, P., & Tsoukalas, I. A. (2007, April). Applying Participatory Design and Collaboration in Digital Public Services for discovering and re-designing e-Government services. *Government Information Quarterly, 24*(2), 353–376. doi:10.1016/j.giq.2006.07.018

Anttiroiko, A. (2004). Towards citizen-centered local e-government-The case of the city of Tempere. In Khosrow-Pour, M. (Ed.), *Annals of Cases on Information Technology* (Vol. 6, pp. 371–385). Hershey, PA: Idea Group Publishing.

Arabianranta (2004). *Arabianranta* Retrieved April 28, 2009, from http://www.helsinkivirtualvillage.fi/Resource.phx/adc/inenglish.htx

Araya, E., & Barría, D. (2008). Modernización del Estado y Gobierno Electrónico en Chile, 1994-2006. *Buen Gobierno, 5*, 80–103.

Arendt, H. (2003). *La condición humana*. Barcelona, Spain: Paidós.

Armijo, M. (2002). Modernización Administrativa y de la Gestión Pública en Chile. In Tomassini, L., & Armijo, M. (Eds.), *Reforma y Modernización del Estado. Experiencias y Desafíos* (pp. 267–297). Santiago: LOM.

Arnstein, S. R. (1969). A ladder of citizen participation. *Journal of the American Planning Association. American Planning Association, 35*(4), 216–224. doi:10.1080/01944366908977225

Asubonteng, P., McCleary, K. J., & Swan, J. E. (1996). SERVQUAL revisited: a critical review of service quality. *Journal of Services Marketing, 10*(6), 62–81. doi:10.1108/08876049610148602

Atkinson, R. D., & Andes, S. (2008). *2008 State New Economy.* Information technology and innovation foundation. Retrieved April 30, 2009, from http://www.itif.org/files/2008_state_new_economy_index.pdf

Australian Government Information Management Office (AGIMO). (2008, June) *Consulting with Government – Online.* Retrieved March 6, 2009, from http://www.finance.gov.au/publications/consulting-with-government-online/docs/AGIMO_ConsultGov.pdf

Avgerou, C. (1998). How can IT enable economic growth in developing countries? *Information Technology for Development, 8*(1), 15–28.

Azari, R., & Pick, J. B. (2009). Understanding global digital inequality: The impact of government, investment in business and technology, and socioeconomic factors on technology utilization. In *42nd Hawaii International Conference on System Sciences*, Waikoloa, Big Island, HI.

Bajjaly, S. T. (1999). Managing Emerging Information Systems in the Public Sector. *Public Productivity & Management Review, 23*(1).

Baliamoune-Lutz, M. (2003). An analysis of the determinants and effects of ICT diffusion in developing countries. *Information Technology for Development, 10*(3), 151–169. doi:10.1002/itdj.1590100303

Baltimore Regional Transportation Board (BRTB). (2003). Vision 2030. *Final Rep.* Baltimore Metropolitan Council. Retrieved September 27, 2008 from http://baltometro.org/vision2030.org.html

Barber, B. (1984). *Strong democracy: Participatory politics for a new age.* Berkeley, CA: University of California Press.

Barber, B. R. (n.d.). *The ambigous effects of digital technology on democracy in a globalizing world.* Retrieved May 18, 2009, from http://www.wissensgesellschaft.org/themen/demokratie/democratic.pdf

Bargh, J. A., & Mckeanna, K. Y. (2004). The Internet and social life. *Annual Review of Psychology, 55,* 573–590. doi:10.1146/annurev.psych.55.090902.141922

Barney, D. (2000). *Prometheus wired: the hope for democracy in the age of network technology.* Chicago: University of Chicago Press.

Barney, D. (2006). Teaching technology: A question of citizenship. Retrieved May 5, 2009, from: media.mcgill.ca/files/Darin_Barney_Teaching_Technology.pdf

Barrati Esteve, J., Castella-Roca, J., Domingo-Ferrer, J., & Reniui Vilamala, J. (2007). Internet voting. In Anttiroiko, A., & Malkia, M. (Eds.), *Encyclopedia of Digital Government* (pp. 1125–1129). Hershey, PA: Idea Group Inc.

Barrett, B., & Usui, M. (2002). Local agenda 21 in Japan: Transforming local environmental governance. *Local Environment, 7*(1), 49–67. doi:10.1080/13549830220115411

Barry, B. (1970). *Sociologists, Economists and Democracy.* Chicago: University of Chicago.

Bauerlein, M. (2008). *The dumbest generation.* New York: Tarcher Penguin.

Baumgartner, J., & Francia, P. L. (2008). *Conventional wisdom and American elections: Exploding myths, exploring misconceptions.* Lanham, MD: Rowman & Littlefield.

Baym, N. K. (2000). Tune. In *Log On: Soaps, Fandom, and Online Community.* Thousand Oaks, CA: Sage.

BBC. (2004, January 19). *Roh backs US troops relocation.* Retrieved October 10, 2008, from http://news.bbc.co.uk/2/hi/asia-pacific/3408895.stm

BBC. (2008, June 10). *S. Koreans rally against U.S. beef.* Retrieved October 20, 2008, from http://news.bbc.co.uk/2/hi/asia-pacific/7445387.stm

Becker, T. (2007). Teledemocracy. In Anttiroiko, A., & Malkia, M. (Eds.), *Encyclopedia of Digital Government* (pp. 1519–1523). Hershey, PA: Idea Group Inc.

Beerepoot, M., & Sunikka, M. (2005). The contribution of the EC energy certificate in improving sustainability of the housing stock. *Environment and Planning B, 32*(1), 21–31. doi:10.1068/b3118

Beilock, R., & Dimitrova, D. V. (2003). An exploratory model of inter-country Internet diffusion. *Telecommunications Policy, 27*(3-4), 237–252. doi:10.1016/S0308-5961(02)00100-3

Bekkers, V. J. J. M. (2001). De mythen van de elektronische overheid. Over retoriek en realiteit *Bestuurswetenschappen, 4.* 277-295.

Bekkers, V. J. J. M., & Homburg, V. M. F. (2005). *The information ecology of E-government: E-government as institutional and technological innovation in public administration.* Amsterdam: IOS Press.

Bekkers, V. J. J. M., & Moody, R. (2006). Geographical Information Systems and the policy formulation process: the emergence of a reversed mixed scanning mode? In Bekkers, V. J. J. (Ed.), *M Duivenboden, van H. & Thaens, M. (2006) Information and communication technology and public innovation: assessing the ICT-driven modernization of public administration.* Amsterdam: IOS Press.

Bell, D. (1976). *The coming of post-industrial society: a venture in social forecasting.* New York: Basic Books.

Bellamy, C., & Taylor, J. (1998). *Governing in the information age.* Buckingham, UK: Open University Press.

Benhabib, S. (1996). Toward a Deliberative Model of Democratic Legitimacy. In Benhabib, S. (Ed.), *Democracy and Difference: Contesting the Boundaries of the Political* (pp. 67–94). Princeton, NJ: Princeton University Press.

Benkler, Y. (2006). *The Wealth of Networks: How Social Production Transforms Markets and Freedom.* New Haven, CT: Yale University Press.

Bennett, W. L. (2003a). Communicating global activism. *Information Communication and Society, 6*(2), 143–168. doi:10.1080/1369118032000093860

Bennett, W. L. (2003b). New media power: The Internet and global activism. In Couldry, N., & Curran, J. (Eds.), *Contesting Media Power.* New York: Rowman and Littlefield.

Benoit, P. J., & Benoit, W. L. (2005). Criteria for evaluating political campaign webpages. *The Southern Communication Journal, 70*(3), 230–247.

Berinsky, A. (2005). The perverse consequences of electoral reform in the United States. *American Politics Research, 33*(4), 471–491. doi:10.1177/1532673X04269419

Berners-Lee, T., Hendler, J., & Lassila, O. (2001). The Semantic Web - A new form of Web content that is meaningful to computers will unleash a revolution of new possibilities. *Scientific American, 284*(5), 34–43. doi:10.1038/scientificamerican0501-34

Bernstein, P. A., & Haas, L. M. (2008, September). Information integration in the enterprise. *Communications of the ACM, 51*(9), 72–79. doi:10.1145/1378727.1378745

Berntzen, L., & Winsvold, M. (2005). Web-based tools for policy evaluation en M. Böhlen, J. Gamper, W. Polasek & M. A. Wimmer (Eds.) *E-Government: Towards Electronic Democracy.* Italia: International Conference, TCGOV2005.

Berntzen, L., Healy, M., Hahamis, P., Dunville, D., & Esteves, J. (2006, October). *Parliamentary Web Presence: A Comparative Review.* Paper presented at the 2nd International Conference on e-Government, Pittsburgh, PA.

Berry, J. M. (2005). Nonprofits and Civic Engagement. *Public Administration Review, 65*(5), 568–578. doi:10.1111/j.1540-6210.2005.00484.x

Bevir, M., Rhodes, R. A. W., & Weller, P. (2003). Comparative Governance; Prospects and Lessons. *Public Administration, 81*(1), 191–210. doi:10.1111/1467-9299.00342

Biagioli, C., Francesconi, E., Passerini, A., Montemagni, S., & Soria, C. (2005). Automatic semantics extraction in law documents. In *Proceedings of the 10th international Conference on Artificial intelligence and Law* (pp. 133-140), ACM.

Bimber, B. (2000). The Gender Gap on the Internet. *Social Science Quarterly, 81*, 868–876.

Bimber, B. (2003). *Information and American democracy: Technology in the evolution of political power.* New York: Oxford University Press. doi:10.1017/CBO9780511615573

Bimber, B., & Davis, R. (2003). *Campaigning online: The Internet in U.S. elections.* Oxford, UK: Oxford University Press.

Bingham, L. B., Nabatchi, T., & O'Leary, R. (2005). The New Governance: Practices and Processes for Stakeholder and Citizen Participation in the Work of Government. *Public Administration Review, 65*(5), 547–558. doi:10.1111/j.1540-6210.2005.00482.x

Birch, S., & Watt, B. (2004). *Remote Electronic Voting: Free, Fair and Secret? The Political Quarterly Publishing Co. Ltd.* London: Sage Publications.

Birch, S., & Watt, B. (2004). Remote Electronic Voting: Free, Fair and Secret? [Oxford, UK:Blackwell Publishing.]. *The Political Quarterly, 60*–72. doi:10.1111/j.1467-923X.2004.00572.x

Birkland, T. (2005). *An Introduction to the Policy Process* (2nd ed.). New York: Sharpe.

Bishop, M., & Wagner, D. (2007). Risks of E-Voting. *Communications of the ACM, 50*, 120. doi:10.1145/1297797.1297827

Blumenthal, S. (1982). *The permanent campaign.* New York: Touchstone Books.

Blumler, J. G., & Coleman, S. (2001). *Realising Democracy Online: A Civic Commons in Cyberspace.* IPPR/Citizens Online.

Blumler, J. G., & Katz, E. (1974). *The uses of mass communications: Current perspectives on gratifications research.* Beverly Hills, CA: Sage.

Bob, C. (2005). *The marketing of rebellion: Insurgents, media, and international activism.* New York: Cambridge University Press.

Bolgherini, S. (2007). The Technology Trap and the Role of Political and Cultural Variables: A Critical Analysis of the E-Government Policies. *Review of Policy Research. 24*(3). The Policy Studies Organization.

Bonney, N. (2004). Local democracy renewed? *The Political Quarterly Publishing., 75*(1), 43–51.

Booth, W., Colomb, G., & Williams, J. (2003). *The craft of research.* Chicago: The University of Chicago Press.

Box, R. C., Marshall, G. S., Reed, B. J., & Reed, C. M. (2001). New public management and substantive democracy. *Public Administration Review, 61*(5), 608–615. doi:10.1111/0033-3352.00131

Boyte, H. C. (2005). Reframing Democracy: Governance, Civic Agency, and Politics. *Public Administration Review, 65*(5), 536–546. doi:10.1111/j.1540-6210.2005.00481.x

Brandon, P., & Lombardi, P. (2005). *Evaluation of sustainable development in the built environment.* Oxford, UK: Blackwell.

Bregt, A. K. (1999). *Netwerk in de Geo-informatiekunde.* Wageningen, The Netherlands: Universiteit Wageningen.

Bretschneider, S. (2003). Information Technology, E-Government, and Institutional Change. *Public Administration Review, 63*(6). doi:10.1111/1540-6210.00337

Broom, G. M., Casey, S., & Ritchey, J. (1997). Toward a concept and theory of organization-public relationships. *Journal of Public Relations Research, 9*, 83–98. doi:10.1207/s1532754xjprr0902_01

Brown, D. (2005). Electronic government and public administration. *International Review of Administrative Sciences, 71*(2), 241–254. doi:10.1177/0020852305053883

Brown, M. M. (2001). The Benefits and Costs of Information Technology Innovations: An Empirical Assessment of a Local Government Agency. *Public Performance & Management Review, 24*, No. (4). Sage Publications.

Browning, G. (1996). *Electronic Democracy: using the Internet to influence American Politics*. Wilton, CT: Pemberton Press.

Bruijn, J. D., Lara, R., Polleres, A., & Fensel, D. (2005). OWL DL vs. OWL Flight: Conceptual Modeling and Reasoning for the Semantic Web. In *Proceedings of the WWW '05: 14th international conference on World Wide Web*, ACM

Bruijn, J. D., Lausen, H., Polleres, A., & Fensel, D. (2006). The Web Service Modeling Language WSML: An Overview, *The Semantic Web: Research and Applications* [Springer.]. *Lecture Notes in Computer Science, 4011*, 590–604. doi:10.1007/11762256_43

Bruns, A. (2005). *Gatewatching: Collaborative Online News Production*. New York: Peter Lang.

Bruns, A. (2008, March 26-28) *Citizen Journalism in the 2007 Australian Federal Election*. Paper presented at the AMIC 2008 conference: Convergence, Citizen Journalism, and Social Change, Brisbane. Retrieved March 6, 2009, from http://snurb.info/files/Citizen%20 Journalism%20in%20the%202007%20Australian%20 Federal%20Election.pdf

Bruns, A., Wilson, J., & Saunders, B. (2007, November 16) *Election Flops on YouTube*. Retrieved July 24, 2009, from http://www.abc.net.au/news/stories/2007/11/16/2093120. htm

Burns, J. (1979). *Connections: Ways to discover and realize community potentials*. New York: McGraw Hill.

Burstein, M., Bussler, C., Finin, T., Huhns, M. N., Paolucci, M., & Sheth, A. P. (2005). A semantic Web services architecture. *IEEE Internet Computing, 9*(5), 72–81. doi:10.1109/MIC.2005.96

Burt, R., & Robison, O. (1998, October 9). *Reinventing Diplomacy in the Information Age*. CSIS Report.

Calderón, E., & Cazés, D. (1994). *Tecnología ciudadana para la democracia*. México: UNAM.

Calista, D. J., & Melitski, J. (2007). *Digital Collaboration: Clarifying the Roles of E-Government and E-Governance*. Paper presented at the American Society of Public Administration.

Callahan, K. (2007). *Elements of effective governance: Measurement, accountability and participation*. Boca Raton, FL: CRC Press.

Cap Gemini. (2004). *Online Availability of Public Services: How is Europe Progressing*. Retrieved April 28, 2009, from http://www.capgemini.com/news/2003/0206egov. shtml

Carr, V. H., Jr. (n.d.). *Technology Adoption and Diffusion*. Retreived March 15, 2009, http://tlc.nlm.nih.gov/ resources/publications/sourcebook/adoptiondiffusion. html

Carter, L., & Belanger, F. (2005). The Utilization of E-government Services: Citizen Trust, Innovation and Acceptance Factors. *Information Systems Journal, 15*, 5–25. doi:10.1111/j.1365-2575.2005.00183.x

Carter, L., & Belangers, F. (2004). The influences of perceived characteristics of innovating on e-government adoption. *Information Systems Journal, 15*(1), 5–25. doi:10.1111/j.1365-2575.2005.00183.x

Carver, S. (2001). *Participation and Geographical Information: a position paper, Position paper ESF-NSF workshop Access to Geographic Information and participatory approaches using Geographic Information*. Italy: Spoleto.

Carver, S., Evans, A., Kingston, R. & Thurston, R. (2001). Public participation, GIS and cyberdemocracy: Evaluating on-line spatial decision support systems. *Environment and Planning*, B, *28*(6) 907-921.

Castells, M. (1996). *The Rise of the Network Society, The Information Age: Economy, Society and Culture (Vol. I)*. Oxford, UK: Blackwell.

Castells, M. (1997). *The power of identity (Vol. 2)*. Oxford, UK: Blackwell Publishers.

Castells, M. (2001). *La Galaxia Internet*. Madrid: Plaza y Janés.

Castells, M. (2008). The new public sphere: Global civil society, communication networks, and global governance. *The Annals of the American Academy of Political and Social Science, 616*, 78–93. doi:10.1177/0002716207311877

Cates, C. (1979). Beyond muddling: Creativity. *Public Administration Review, 39*(6), 527–532. doi:10.2307/976179

Catto, H. E. (2001July 23). The end of diplomacy? *iMP Magazine*. Retrieved February 14, from http://www.cisp. org/imp/july_2001/07_01catto.htm

Caudill, J., & Noles, L. (2009). *New Media Education with Online Tools*. In *Proceedings of the Instructional Technology Conference at MTSU*.

Chadwick, A. (2003). Bringing e-democracy back in: Why it matters for future research on e-governance. *Social Science Computer Review, 21*(11), 443–455. doi:10.1177/0894439303256372

Chadwick, A., & May, C. (2003). Interaction between states and citizens in the age of internet: E-government in the United States, Britain and European Union. *Governance, 16*(2), 271–300. doi:10.1111/1468-0491.00216

Chaffee, S. H., Ward, L. S., & Tipton, L. P. (1970). Mass communication and political socialization. *The Journalism Quarterly, 47*, 647–659.

Chappelet, J., & Kilchenmann, P. (2005). Interactive Tools for e-Democracy: Examples from Switzerland en Böhlen, M., Gamper, J., Polasek, W., & Wimmer, M. A. (Eds.) *E-Government: Towards Electronic Democracy*. Italia: International Conference, TCGOV2005.

Chen, D., Lin, T., Huang, T., Lee, C., & Hiaso, N. (2009). Experimental e-deliberation in Taiwan: A comparison of online and face-to-face citizens' conferences in Beitou, Taipei. In Reddick, C. C. (Ed.), *Handbook of Research on Strategies for Local E-Government and Implementation: Comparative Studies* (pp. 323–347). Hershey, PA: IGI Global.

Chen, Y., Chen, H., Huang, W., & Ching, R. (2006). E-Government Strategies in Developed and Developing Countries: An Implementation Framework and Case Study. *Journal of Global Information Management, 14*(1), 23–46.

Cherp, A., George, C., & Kirkpatrick, C. (2004). A methodology for assessing national sustainable development strategies. *Environment and Planning. C, Government & Policy, 22*, 913–926. doi:10.1068/c0310j

Chinn, M. D., & Fairlie, R. W. (2007). The determinants of the global digital divide: A cross-country analysis of computer and Internet penetration. *Oxford Economic Papers, 59*(1), 16–44. doi:10.1093/oep/gpl024

Chun, W., & Keenan, T. (2006). *New media, old media*. New York: Routledge.

Chutimaskul, W., & Funilkul, S. (2004). The Framework of e-Democracy Development en Traunmüller, Roland, *Electronic Government: Third International Conference, EGOV2004*. España: Springer.

Coe, A., Paquet, G., & Roy, J. (2001). E-Governance and Smart Communities: A Social Learning Challenge. *Social Science Computer Review, 19*(1), 80–93. doi:10.1177/089443930101900107

Cogan, A., Sharpe, S., & Hertzberg, J. (1986). Citizen participation. In So, F. S., Hand, I., & Madowell, B. D. (Eds.), *The Practice of State and Regional Planning. Municipal Management Series*. Chicago: American Planning Association.

Coglianese, C. (2004). E-Rulemaking: Information Technology and the Regulatory Process. *Administrative Law Review, 56*, 353–402.

Cohen, J. (1989). Deliberation and Democratic Legitimacy. In Hamlin, A., & Pettit, P. (Eds.), *The Good Polity: Normative Analysis of the State* (pp. 17–34). Hoboken, NJ: Wiley-Blackwell Press.

Cohen, R. (1991). *Negotiating across cultures: Communication obstacles in international diplomacy*. Washington, DC: United States Institute of Peace Press.

Coleman, R., Lieber, P., Mendelson, A. L., & Kurpius, D. D. (2008). Public life and the internet: If you build a better website, will citizens become engaged? *New Media & Society, 10*, 179–201. doi:10.1177/1461444807086474

Coleman, S. (2001). *2001: A Cyber Space Oddysey- the Internet in the UK Election*. London: Hansard Society.

Coleman, S. (2005). The Lonely Citizen: Indirect representation in an age of networks. *Political Communication, 22*(2), 197–214. doi:10.1080/10584600590933197

Coleman, S., & Gøtze, J. (2001). *Bowling Together: Online Public Engagement in Policy Deliberation*. London: Hansard Society.

Communities, E. (1999, March 15). *First report on allegations regarding fraud, mismanagement and nepotism in the European Commission.* Committee of Independent Experts, EU.

Communities, E. (2001a). *Charter of Fundamental Rights of the European Union.* Retreived (n.d.), from http://www.europarl.eu.int/charter/default_en.htm

Communities, E. (2001b). *Laeken Declaration on the Future of the European Union*. Retrieved October 13, 2005, from http://european-convention.eu.int/pdf/LKNEN.pdf

Conners, J. (2005, September). *Meetup, Blogs and Online Involvement: U.S. Senate Campaign Web Sites of 2004.* Paper presented at the 101st Annual Meeting of the American Political Science Association, Washington, D.C.

Conroy, M. M., & Evans-Cowley, J. (2004). Informing and interacting: The use of e-government for citizen participation in planning. *Journal of E-Government, 1*(3).

Conroy, S. (2008, December 22) Minister Conroy on: Promoting a Civil and Confident Society Online. Retrieved March 6, 2009, from http://www.dbcde.gov.au/communications_for_business/industry_development/digital_economy/future_directions_blog/topics/civil_and_confident_society_online

Cook, C. (2002). The contemporary presidency: The performance of the 'permanent campaign': George W. Bush's public presidency. *Presidential Studies Quarterly, 32*(4), 753–765. doi:10.1177/0360491802238707

Coombs, W. T. (2004). Interpersonal communication and public relations. In Heath, R. L. (Ed.), *Handbook of Public Relations* (pp. 105–114). Thousand Oaks, CA: Sage Publications, Inc.

Cooper, I., Hamilton, A., & Bentivegna, V. (2005). Sustainable Urban Development: Networked Communities, Virtual Communities and the Production of Knowledge. In Curwell, S., Deakin, M., & Symes, M. (Eds.), *Sustainable Urban Development: the Framework, Protocols and Environmental Assessment Methods* (Vol. 1, pp. 211–231). London: Routledge.

Cooper, P. J. (1998). *Public Administration for the twenty-first century*. New York: Harcourt Brace & Company.

Cooper, T. L. (2005). Civic Engagement in the Twenty-First Century: Toward a Scholarly and Practical Agenda. *Public Administration Review, 65*(5), 534–535. doi:10.1111/j.1540-6210.2005.00480.x

Crabtree, J. (2003) Civic Hacking: A New Agenda for E-Democracy *Open Democracy*. Retrieved May 1, 2009, from http://www.opendemocracy.net/debates/article-8-85-1025.jsp

Craig, W., Weiner, H., & Harris, T. (2002). *Community empowerment, public participation and Geographic Information Science*. New York: Taylor & Frances.

Cramer, P. F. (1998). *Deep environmental politics: The role of radical environmentalism in crafting American environmental policy*. Westport, CT: Praeger.

Creighton, J. L. (2005). *The public participation handbook: Making better decisions through citizen involvement*. San Francisco: Jossey-Bass.

Cremonini, L., & Valeri, L. (2003). *Benchmarking Security and Trust in Europe and the U.S.* Santa Monica, CA: RAND.

Crick, B. (2002). *Democracy: A Very Short Introduction*. Oxford, UK: Oxford Paperbacks.

Crosby, N., Kelly, J. M., & Schaefer, P. (1986). Citizen panels: A new approach to citizen participation. *Public Administration Review, 46*(2), 170–178. doi:10.2307/976169

Cull, N. J. (2008). Public diplomacy: Taxonomies and histories. *The Annals of the American Academy of Political and Social Science, 616*, 31–54. doi:10.1177/0002716207311952

Cunill, N. (1997). *Repensando lo Público a Través de la Sociedad. Nuevas Formas de Gestión Pública y Representación Social.* Caracas: Nueva Sociedad.

Cunill, N. (2004). *Balance de la participación ciudadana en las políticas sociales. Propuesta de un marco analítico en Ziccardi, A. (Coord.) Participación ciudadana y políticas sociales en el ámbito local.* México: UNAM-IIS.

Curry, T. (2008, November 7). Young voters not essential to Obama win. *MSNBC.Com.*Retrieved January 9, 2009, from http://www.msnbc.msn.com/id/27582147/.

Curwell, S., Deakin, M., Cooper, I., Paskaleva-Shapira, K., Ravetz, J., & Babicki, D. (2005). Citizens'expectations of information cities: implications for urban planning and design. *Building Research and Information, 33*(1), 55–66. doi:10.1080/0961321042000329422

Dahl, R. A. (1956). *A preface to democratic theory.* Chicago, IL: University of Chicago Press.

Dahl, R. A. (1989). *Democracy and its critics.* New Haven, CT: Yale University Press.

Danziger, J. N., & Andersen, K. V. (2002). The Impacts of Information Technology on Public Administration: An Analysis of Empirical Research from the 'Golden Age' of Transformation. *International Journal of Public Administration, 25*(5), 591. doi:10.1081/PAD-120003292

Dartnell, M. Y. (2006). *Insurgency online: Web activism and global conflict.* Toronto, Canada: University of Toronto Press.

Davidoff, P. (1973). Advocacy and pluralism in planning. In Faludi, A. (Ed.), *A reader in planning theory* (pp. 277–296). Oxford, UK: Pergamon.

Davis, R. (1999). *The Web of Politics: The Internet's Impact on the American Political System.* New York: Oxford University Press.

Davis, R. (2005). *Politics online: Blogs, chat rooms, and discussion groups in American democracy.* New York: Routledge.

Davison, R., Wagner, C., & Ma, L. (2005). From government to e-government: a transition model. *Information Technology & People, 18*(3), 280–299. doi:10.1108/09593840510615888

Deakin, M. (2009). The IntelCities Community of Practice: the eGov services model for socially-inclusive and participatory urban regeneration programmes. In Riddeck, C. (Ed.), *Research Strategies for eGovernment Service Adoption.* Hershey, PA: Idea Group Publishing.

Deakin, M., & Allwinkle, S. (2006). The IntelCities community of practice: the e-learning platform, knowledge management system and digital library for semantically-interoperable e-governance services. *International Journal of Knowledge. Culture and Change Management, 6*(3), 155–162.

Deakin, M., & Allwinkle, S. (2007). Urban regeneration and sustainable communities: the role of networks, innovation and creativity in building successful partnerships. *Journal of Urban Technology, 14*(1), 77–91. doi:10.1080/10630730701260118

Deakin, M., Allwinkle, S., & Campbell, F. (2006). The IntelCities e-Learning platform, knowledge management system and digital library for semantically rich e-governance services. *International Journal of Technology. Knowledge and Society, 2*(8), 31–38.

Deakin, M., Allwinkle, S., & Campbell, F. (2007). The IntelCities Community of Practice: the eGov Services for Socially-inclusive and Participatory Urban Regeneration Programmes. In Cunningham, P. (Ed.), *Innovation and the Knowledge Economy: Issues, Applications and Case Studies.* Washington, DC: ISO Press.

Deakin, M., Huovila, P., Rao, S., Sunikka, M., & Vreeker, R. (2002). The assessment of sustainable urban development. *Building Research and Information, 30*(2), 95–108. doi:10.1080/096132102753436477

Delamaza, G. (2009 in press). Participation and Mestizaje of State-Civil Society in Chile. In Silva, P., & Cleuren, H. (Eds.), *Widening Democracy. Citizens and Participatory Schemes in Brazil and Chile.* Leiden: Brill.

Delanty, G. (2007). *Citizenship as a Learning Process: Disciplinary Citizenship versus Cultural Citizenship.* Retrieved May 15, 2009, from http://eurozine.com/pdf/2007-06-30-delanty-en.pdf

Delicath, J. W. (1996). In search of ecotopia: Radical environmentalism and the possibilities of utopian rhetorics. In Muir, S. A., & Veenendall, T. L. (Eds.), *Earthtalk: Communication empowerment for environmental action* (pp. 153–169). Westport, CT: Praeger.

Delli Carpini, M. X., & Keeter, S. (1996). *What Americans know about politics and why it matters.* New Haven, CT: Yale University.

DeLuca, K. (1996). Constituting nature anew through judgment: The possibilities of media. In Muir, S. A., & Veenendall, T. L. (Eds.), *Earthtalk: Communication empowerment for environmental action* (pp. 59–78). Westport, CT: Praeger.

Department of Broadband. Communications, and the Digital Economy (DBCDE). (2008, December 12) *"We Hear You..."* Retrieved March 6, 2009, from http://www.dbcde.gov.au/communications_for_business/industry_development/digital_economy/future_directions_blog/topics/we_hear_you Flew, T., & Wilson, J. (Forthcoming) Journalism as Social Networking: The Australian youdecide2007 Project and the 2007 Federal Election. *Journalism: Theory and Practice.*

Department of Constitutional Affairs (DCA). (2007). *Electoral Modernisation Pilots–Local Government Elections 3 May 2007 – Details of pilot initiatives.* London: DCA.

DeSario, J., & Langton, S. (Eds.). (1987). *Citizen participation in public decision making.* New York: Greenwood Press.

Dethier, J. (2009). *World Bank Policy Research: A Historical Overview.* The World Bank, Development Economics, Operations and Strategy Department. doi:10.1596/1813-9450-5000

Dill, D., Schneier, B., & Simons, B. (2003). Voting and Technology: Who Gets to Count Your Vote? *Communications of the ACM, 46,* 29–31. doi:10.1145/859670.859692

DiMaggio, P., & Hargittai, E. (2001). *From the 'digital divide' to 'digital inequality': Studying Internet use as penetration increases.* Princeton University Center for Arts and Cultural Policy Studies, Working Paper Series number, 15.

DiMaggio, P., Hargittai, E., Ceste, C., & Shafer, S. (2004). Digital Inequality: From Unequal Access to Differentiated Use. In Neckerman, K. (Ed.), *Social Inequality* (pp. 355–400). New York: Russell Sage Foundation.

Dinerstein, J. (2009). Technology and Its Discontents: On the Verge of the Posthuman. *American Quarterly, 58*(3), 569–570. doi:10.1353/aq.2006.0056

Dobson, A. (2003, November 27-28). *Ecological citizenship. An ESRC seminar series. Seminar 1: The shape of environmental citizenship: Theory and practice.* Retrieved May 15, 2009, from: http://www.ncl.ac.uk/environmentalcitizenship/papers/Dobson%20EcolCit.doc

Dorman, D. (2005, January). The Coming Revolution in Library Software. In *Proceedings of the ALA Midwinter Conference.*

Dorothy, N., & Pollak, M. (1981). *The Atom Besieged.* Cambridge, MA: MIT Press.

Douglas, S. J. (1987). *Inventing American broadcasting, 1899-1922.* Baltimore: Johns Hopkins University.

Dourish, P., & Anderson, K. (2006). Collective Information Practice: Exploring Privacy and Security as Social and Cultural Phenomena. *Human-Computer Interaction, 21*(3), 319–342. doi:10.1207/s15327051hci2103_2

Downs, A. (1957). *An economic theory of democracy.* New York: Harper.

Drew, D., & Weaver, D. (2006). Voter learning in the 2004 presidential election: did the media matter? *Journalism & Mass Communication Quarterly, 83,* 25–42.

Drummond, W. J., & French, S. P. (2008). The future of GIS. *Journal of the American Planning Association. American Planning Association, 74*(2), 161–176. doi:10.1080/01944360801982146

Duk, H. L. (2007). *E-Government and digital city in Korea*. Retrieved July, 2009, from http://217.116.28.251/deds/260907/dhee.pdf

Dulio, D. A., Goff, D. L., & Thurber, J. A. (1999). Untangled Web: Internet use during the 1998 election.(World Wide Web). *PS: Political Science & Politics, 32*(1).

Dunlap, R. E., & Mertig, A. G. (Eds.). (1992). *American environmentalism: The U.S. environmental movement, 1970 – 1990*. Philadelphia: Taylor and Francis.

Dunleavy, P., & Hood, C. (1994). From old public administration to new public management. *Public Money and Management, 14*(3), 9–16.

Dunleay, P. (2006). New Public Management is Dead–Long Live Digital-Era Governance. *Journal of Public Administration: Research and Theory, 16*(3), 467–494. doi:10.1093/jopart/mui057

Dunlop, T. (2008). Online Voting: Reducing Voter Impediments. *Policy Studies Journal: the Journal of the Policy Studies Organization, 36*, 685–686.

Dunne, K. (2008). *The Value of Using Local Political Online Forums to Reverse Political Disengagement*. Unpublished doctoral dissertation, University of Surrey, United Kingdom. Retrieved April 30, 2009, from http://groups.dowire.org/groups/research/files/f/930-2008-10-31T173650Z/PhD.pdf.

Dutton, W. H., & Peltu, M. (1996). *Information and communication technologies: Visions and realities*. New York: Oxford University Press.

Ebbers, W. E., Pieterson, W. J., & Noordman, H. N. (2008). Electronic Government: Rethinking channel management strategies. *Government Information Quarterly, 25*, 181–201. doi:10.1016/j.giq.2006.11.003

EcoNet. (n.d.). *EcoNet*. Retrieved January 31, 2008, from http://www.jca.apc.org/~y-okada/igc/econet/

EEA. (2007). *European Environment Agency. Halting the loss of biodiversity by 2010: proposal for a first set of indicators to monitor progress in Europe (Technical Report, 11)*. Copenhagen, Denmark: European Environment Agency.

Ehrig, M., Haase, P., Hefke, M., & Stojanovic, N. (2004). Similarity for ontology – a comprehensive framework. In *Workshop Enterprise Modelling and Ontology. Ingredients for Interoperability*.

Eifert, M., & Püschel, J. O. (2004). *National Electronic Government: Comparing governance structures in multi-layer administrations*. London: Routledge.

Einmann, E., & Paradiso, M. (2004). When space shrinks - digital communities and ubiquitous society: Digital cities and urban life: A framework for international benchmarking. In *Proceedings of the Winter International Symposium on Information and Communication Technologies* (WISICT '04). ACM.

Electoral Commission. (2007). *Changes in England resulting from the Electoral Administration Act 2006*. London: Electoral Commission.

Electoral Commission. (2007). *Democracy Matters: Key Issues and Conclusions*. London: Electoral Commission.

Ellul, J. (1964). *The Technological Society*. New York: Vintage Books.

Ellul, J. (1980). *The Technological System*. New York: Continuum Publishing Cooperation.

Elmer, G. (2003). A diagram of panoptic surveillance. *New Media & Society, 5*(2), 231–247. doi:10.1177/1461444803005002005

Emrealp, S. (2005). *Yerel gündem 21 uygulamalarına yönelik kolaylaştırıcı bilgiler el kitabı*. İstanbul, Turkey: IULA-EMME.

Environs Australia. (1999). *Our community our future: A guide to local agenda 21*. Canberra: Commonwealth of Australia.

Envision Utah. (2003). *The history of envision Utah*. Retrieved September 27, 2008 from http://content.lib.utah.edu/FHWA/image/1423.pdf

E-Participate. (2006). *The eParticipation Trans-European Network for Democratic Renewal & Citizen*

Engagement. Retrieved March 23, 2008, from www.eparticipate.eu

Eriksen, E. O., & Fossum, J. E. (2000). *Democracy in the European Union: Integration through Deliberation?* London: Routledge.

Espinoza, V. (2009in press). Citizens' Involvement and Social Policies in Chile: Patronage or Participation? In Silva, P., & Cleuren, H. (Eds.), *Widening Democracy. Citizens and Participatory Schemes in Brazil and Chile*. Leiden: Brill.

Estrategia Digital Executive Secretary. (2008). *Plan de Desarrollo Digital, 2008-2010*. Retrieved (n.d.), from http://www.estrategiadigital.gob.cl/files/Plan%20de%20Acci%C3%B3n%20Digital%202008-2010.pdf

Etxebarria, C., Barrutia, J. M., & Aguado, I. (2004). Local agenda 21: progress in Spain. *European Urban and Regional Studies, 11*(3), 273–281. doi:10.1177/0969776404041490

Etzioni, A. (1967). Mixed-scanning: A third approach to decision-making. *Public Administration Review, 27*(Dec), 385–392. doi:10.2307/973394

European Commission. (1998). Public sector information: A key resource for Europe. *Green Paper on Public Sector Information in the Information Society*, COM 585.

Eurostat. (2007). *Measuring progress towards a more sustainable Europe. 2007 monitoring report of the EU sustainable development strategy*. Luxembourg: Office for Official Publications of the European Communities. Retrieved April 12, 2008, from http://epp.eurostat.ec.europa.eu/cache/ITY_OFFPUB/KS-77-07-115/EN/KS-77-07-115-EN.PDF

Evans, D., & Yen, D. C. (2005). E-government: An analysis for implementation: Framework for understanding cultural and social impact. *Government Information Quarterly, 22*, 354–373. doi:10.1016/j.giq.2005.05.007

Evans, D., & Yen, D. C. (2006). E-Government: Evolving relationship of citizens and government, domestic, and international development. *Government Information Quarterly, 23*(2), 207–235. doi:10.1016/j.giq.2005.11.004

Eveland, W. P. Jr, & Scheufele, D. A. (2000). Connecting news media use with gaps in knowledge and participation. *Political Communication, 17*, 215–237. doi:10.1080/105846000414250

Fairweather, B., & Rogerson, S. (2002). *Implementation of e-voting in the UK.-Technical Options Report*. London: DCA.

Falconi, T. M. (2007, February 28). *Enhancing Britain's global reputation: The perception of country identity in social media. A presentation to the Management School*. Retrieved March 14, 2007, from http://www.tonisblog.com/?p=153

Fang, Z. (2002). E-government in digital era: Concept, practice, and development. *International Journal of the Computer, the Internet and Management, 10*(2), 1-22.

Federal Highway Administration and Federal Transit Administration (1996). Public involvement technique for transportation decision-making. *Publication No. FHWA-PD-96-031 HEP -30/9-96/(4M)QE*, USDoT. Washington, DC.

Federation of Tax Administrators. *States with*. Retrieved April 30, 2009, from http://www.taxadmin.org/fta/link/internet.html

Feenberg, A. (1999). *Questioning technology*. London: Routledge.

Feichtinger, J., & Pregernig, M. (2005). Imagined citizens and participation: Local agenda 21 in two communities in Sweden and Austria. *Local Environment, 10*(3), 229–242. doi:10.1080/13549830500075503

Fensel, D., Lausen, H., Polleres, A., Bruijn, J. D., Stollberg, M., Roman, D., & Domingue, J. (2007). *Enabling Semantic Web Services: The Web Service Modeling Ontology*. Secausus, NJ: Springer.

Fernandez, R., Fernández-Collado, F., & Baptista, P. (2006). *Metodología de la investigación*. México: McGraw-Hill.

Ferro, E., Helbig, N., & Gil-García, J. R. (2006). The Digital Divide Metaphor: Understanding Paths to IT Literacy. *NCDG Working Paper* No. 07-001. Cambridge MA: MIT Press.

Fitsilis, P., & Anthopoulos, L. (2008) Introducing e-Government software project observatory. In *Proceedings of the Hanoi Forum on Information - Communication Technology (ICT)* Retrieved 2008, from http://www.hanoiforum.vnu.edu.vn

Fitzgerald, B., & Suzor, N. (2005). Legal Issues for the Use of Free and Open Source Software in Government. *Melbourne University Law Review, 29*(2), 412–447.

Flanigan, W. H., & Zingale, N. H. (2006). *Political Behavior of the American Electorate* (11th ed.). Washington, DC: CQ Press.

Flyvbjerg, B. (1998). Empowering civil society: Habermas, Foucault and the question of conflict. In Douglas, M., & Friedman, J. (Eds.), *Cities for citizens* (pp. 185–211). Sussex, UK: Wiley.

Fogel, R. W. (2009). *The Impact of the Asian Miracle on the Theory of Economic Growth*. (NBER Working Paper No. 14967). Cambridge, MA: National Bureau of Economic Research.

Fontana, A., & Frey, J. (2000). The interview: from neutral stance to political involvement en Denzin, Norman y Lincoln, Yvonna S. (Eds.) Handbook of Qualitative Research. Thousand Oaks, CA: Sage Publications.

Foot, K. A., & Schneider, S. M. (2006). *Web campaigning*. Cambridge, MA: MIT Press.

Forester, J. (1993). *Planning in the face of power*. Berkeley, CA: University of California Press.

Forestier, E., Grace, J., & Kenny, C. (2002). Can information and communication technologies be pro-poor? *Telecommunications Policy, 26*(11), 623–646. doi:10.1016/S0308-5961(02)00061-7

Forman, C., Ghose, A., & Goldfarb, A. (2007, September). *Competition Between Local and Electronic Markets: How the Benefit of Buying Online Depends on Where You Live*. Net institute working paper no. 06-15. Retreived (n.d.), from http://ssrn.com/abstract=941175

Fountain, J. (2006). Challenges to Organizational Change: Multi-Level Integrated Information Structures (MIIS). *NCDG Working Paper* No. 06-001 Cambridge, MA: MIT Press.

Fountain, J. E. (2001). *Building the Virtual State. Information Technology and Institutional Change*. Washington, DC: Brookings Institution Press.

Fountain, J. E. (2009). Bureaucratic Reform and E-Government in the United Status: An Institutional Perspective. In Chadwick, A., & Howard, P. N. (Eds.), *Routledge Handbook of Internet Politics* (pp. 99–113). New York: Routledge.

Fountain, J. E., & Osorio-Urzua, C. A. (2001). Public Sector: Early stage of a deep transformation. In R. E. Litan & A. M. Rivlin (Eds.), *The economic payoff from the internet revolution* (pp. 235-268). Washington, DC: Brookings Institution Press. Freedom of Information Act (United States). *Wikipedia, the free encyclopedia* Retrieved April 1, 2008, from http://en.wikipedia.org/wiki/Freedom_of_Information_Act_%28United_States%29

Franklin, B. (1736). Poor Richard's Almanack. Philadelphia, PA: New Printing-Office near the Market (Yale University Library).

Franklin, B. (1994). *Packaging politics*. London: Edward Arnold.

Freitter, M., Gradwohl, N., & Denner, R. (2006). Empfehlung für das XML-Schema zu EDIAKT II, V. 1.2.0 (German). Retrieved June 30, 2009, from http://www.ag.bka.gv.at/index.php/Portal:Ediakt

French, S. P., & Skiles, A. E. (1996). Organizational structures for GIS Implementation. In M. J. Salling (Ed.). *URISA '96 Conference Proceedings* (pp.280-293). Salt Lake City, Utah.

Fuchs, C. (2009). The role of income inequality in a multivariate cross-national analysis of the digital divide. *Social Science Computer Review, 27*(1), 41–58. doi:10.1177/0894439308321628

Fuchs, C., & Horak, E. (2008). Africa and the digital divide. *Telematics and Informatics, 25*(2), 99–116. doi:10.1016/j.tele.2006.06.004

Fulton, B. (1998, October 9). *Reinventing diplomacy in the information age*. Center for Strategic and International Studies (CSIS).

Fulton, B. (2002). *Net diplomacy I: Beyond foreign ministries*. U.S. Institute of Peace.

G-8. (2000). *Okinawa charter on global information society*. Retrieved April 27, 2009, from http://unpan1.un.org/intradoc/groups/public/documents/apcity/unpan002263.pdf.

Gan, L. (1999). Implementation of agenda 21 in China: Institutions and obstacles. *Environmental Politics, 8*(1), 318–327.

Garcia-Sanchez, I. M., & Prado-Lorenzo, J. M. (2008). Determinant factors in the degree of implementation of local agenda 21 in the European Union. *Sustainable Development, 16*(1), 17–34. doi:10.1002/sd.334

Garrard, G. A. (1997). *Cellular communications: Worldwide market development*. Boston, MA: Artech House Publishers.

Garson, G. D. (1999). *Information technology and computer applications in public administration: Issues and trends*. Hershey, PA: Idea Group Publishing.

GartnerGroup. (2007). *What does Web 2.0 mean to Government?* Heeks, R., & Bailur, S. (2007). Analyzing e-government research: Perspectives, philosophies, theories, methods, and practice. *Government Information Quarterly, 24*(2), 243–265.

Gefen, D., Rose, G., Warkentin, M., & Pavlou, P. (2005). Cultural Diversity and Trust in IT Adoption. *Journal of Global Information Management, 13*, 54–79.

Genesereth, M. R., & Nilsson, N. J. (1987). *Logical Foundations of Artificial Intelligence*. Palo Alto, CA: Morgan Kaufmann Publishers Inc.

George, C. (2006). *The Government of Sustainable Development, Impact Assessment Research Centre* (Working Paper Series No. 18). Manchester M13 9QH, UK: University of Manchester, Institute for Development Policy and Management.

Gibson, R. K., & Ward, S. (2000). A proposed methodology for studying the function and effectiveness of party and candidate Web sites. *Social Science Computer Review, 18*(3), 301–319. doi:10.1177/089443930001800306

Gibson, R. K., Margolis, M., Resnick, D., & Ward, S. J. (2003). Election campaigning on the WWW in the USA and UK: A comparative analysis. *Party Politics, 9*(1), 47–75. doi:10.1177/135406880391004

Gibson, R. K., Römmele, A., & Ward, S. J. (2004). *Electronic democracy: Mobilisation, organisation and participation via new ICTs*. London: Routledge.

Gilboa, E. (2000). Mass communication and diplomacy: A theoretical framework. *Communication Theory, 10*(3), 275–309. doi:10.1111/j.1468-2885.2000.tb00193.x

Gilboa, E. (2008). Searching for a theory of public diplomacy. *The Annals of the American Academy of Political and Social Science, 616*(1), 55–77. doi:10.1177/0002716207312142

Gilchrist, V. J., & Williams, R. L. (1999). Key Informant Interviews. In Crabtree, B. F., & Miller, W. L. (Eds.), *Doing Qualitative Research* (2nd ed., pp. 71–88). London: Sage.

Gil-García, J. R. & Martínez-Moyano. (2007). Understanding the evolution of e-government: The evolution of systems of rues on public sector dynamics. *Government Information Quarterly, 24*, 266–290. doi:10.1016/j.giq.2006.04.005

Gil-García, J. R. (2005). *Enacting State Websites: A Mixed Method Study Exploring E-Government Success in Multi-Organizational Settings*. Nelson A. Rockefeller College of Public Affairs and Policy. University at Albany.

Gil-García, J. R., & Helbig, N. (2007). *Exploring E-Government Benefits and Success Factors. Encyclopedia of Digital Government* (Vol. 2). Hershey, PA: Idea Group Reference.

Gil-García, J. R., & Luna-Reyes, L. (2006). *Encyclopedia of E-Commerce, E-Government, and Mobile Commerce*. Hershey, PA: IDEA Group Reference.

Gil-García, J. R., & Luna-Reyes, L. (2007). *Modelo Multi-Dimensional de Medición del Gobierno Electrónico para América Latina y el Caribe. CEPAL-Colección Documentos de Proyectos.* Publicación de las Naciones Unidas.

Gil-García, J. R., & Pardo, T. (2005). E-Government Success Factors: Mapping Practical Tools to Theoretical Foundations. *Government Information Quarterly, 22*(2), 187–216. doi:10.1016/j.giq.2005.02.001

Godart, C., Saliou, H., & Bignon, J. C. (2001). Asynchronous Coordination of Virtual Teams in Creative Applications (co-design or co-engineering): Requirements and Design Criteria. In *Proceedings of the Information Technology for Virtual Enterprises (ITVE 2001) Workshop* (p. 135 – 142). IEEE.

González, R. (2005). Identidad y Actitudes Políticas en Jóvenes Universitarios: El Desencanto de los que no se Identifican Políticamente. *Revista de Ciencia Política, XXV*(2), 65–90.

Goodspeed, R. (2008). *The Internet as a participation tool.* Retrieved July 6, 2008 from http://goodspeedupdate.com/citizen-participation-and-the-internet-in-urban-planning

Government, H. M. (2002). *In the service of democracy: A consultation paper on a policy for electronic democracy.* London: Office of the e-Envoy.

Graber, D. A. (2001). *Processing politics.* Chicago, IL: University of Chicago.

Grant, G. (2005a). Realizing the Promise of Electronic Government. *Journal of Global Information Management, 13*(1), Editorial Preface i-iv.

Grant, G. (2005b). Developing a Generic Framework for E-Government. *Journal of Global Information Management, 13*(1), 1–30.

Grant, J. (2002). Towards an e-future. *Australian CPA, 72*(9), 38–41.

Green, L., & Bruns, A. (2007). au: Australia. InFelix Librero and Patricia B. Arinto. (Eds.) Digital Review of Asia Pacific Montréal: Sage.

Greene, R. W. (2003). *GIS in public policy: using geographic information for more effective government.* Redlands, CA: ESRI Press.

Grochowalska, J. (1998). The implementation of agenda 21 in Poland. *European Environment, 8*(3), 79–85. doi:10.1002/(SICI)1099-0976(199805/06)8:3<79::AID-EET156>3.0.CO;2-F

Grönlund, A. (2004). State of the art in e-Gov research: A survey, en Traunmüller, R. (Ed.) *Electronic Government: Third International Conference,* EGOV2004. España: Springer.

Gronlund, A. (Ed.). (2002). *Electronic government: Design, applications and management.* Hershey, PA: Idea Group Publishing.

Gross, T. (2002). E-democracy and community networks: Political visions, technological opportunities and social reality. In Gronlund, A. (Ed.), *Electronic government: Design, applications and management* (pp. 249–266). Hershey, PA: Idea Group Publishing.

Grothe, M. (1999). *Keuze voor ruimte, ruimte voor keuze: de ontwikkeling van GIS-applicaties voor locatieplanning; een objectgeoriënteerde analyse.* Amsterdam: Vrije Universiteit.

Grothe, M., Nijkamp, P., & Scholten, H. J. (1996). Monitoring residental quality for the elderly using a geographical information system. *International Planning Studies, 1*(2), 199–215. doi:10.1080/13563479608721652

Gruber, T. R. (1995). Toward principles for the design of ontologies used for knowledge sharing. *International Journal of Human-Computer Studies, 43*(5-6), 907–928. doi:10.1006/ijhc.1995.1081

Gruber, T. R. (2007). *Ontology.* Retrieved June 30, 2009, from http://tomgruber.org/writing/ontology-definition-2007.htm

Grunig, J. E., & Huang, Y. H. (2000). From organizational effectiveness to relationship indicators: Antecedents of relationships, public relations strategies, and relationship outcomes. In Ledingham, J. A., & Bruning, S. D. (Eds.), *Public relations as relationship management: A relation-*

al approach to the study and practice of public relations (pp. 23–53). Mahwah, NJ: Lawrence Erlbaum.

Grunig, L. A., Grunig, J. E., & Dozier, D. M. (2002). *Excellent public relations and effective organizations: a study of communication management in three countries.* Mahwah, NJ: Lawrence Erlbaum.

GSM. 3G Market Update (2009). *Happy 20th birthday, GSM* (2007, 07 Sept, 2007). Retrieved July 28, 2009, from http://news.zdnet.co.uk/leader/0,1000002982,39289154,00.htm

Guillén, M. F., & Suárez, S. L. (2001). Developing the Internet: Entrepreneurship and public policy in Ireland, Singapore, Argentina, and Spain. *Telecommunications Policy,25*(5),349–371. doi:10.1016/S0308-5961(01)00009-X

Guillén, M. F., & Suárez, S. L. (2005). Explaining the global digital divide: Economic, political and sociological drivers of cross-national Internet use. *Social Forces, 84*(2), 681–708. doi:10.1353/sof.2006.0015

Gulati, G. J. (2003, August). *Campaigning for Congress on the World Wide Web and the implications for strong democracy.* Paper presented at the 99th Annual Meeting of the American Political Science Association, Philadelphia, Pennsylvania.

Gutmann, A., & Thompson, D. (1996). *Democracy and Disagreement.* Cambridge, MA: Harvard University Press.

H&R Block Online. *H&R Block.* Retrieved April 29, 2009, from http://www.hrblock.com/taxes/products/product.jsp?productid=31

Habermas, J. (1987). The theory of communicative action: *Vol. 2. Lifeworld and system.* Cambridge, UK: Polity Press.

Habermas, J. (1991). *Moral Consciousness and Communicative Action. C. Lenhardt & S.W. Nicholsen (Trans.).* Cambridge, MA: MIT Press.

Hague, B. N., & Loader, B. (1999). *Digital democracy: Discourse and decision making in the information age.* New York: Routledge.

Hargittai, E., Di Maggio, P., Neuman, W. R., & Robinson, J. P. (2001). The social implications of the Internet. *Annual Review of Sociology, 27*, 307–336. doi:10.1146/annurev.soc.27.1.307

Harto de Vera, F. (2006). Tipologías y Modelos de Democracia Electrónica. *Revista de Internet. Derecho y Política, 2*, 32–44.

Haung, Z. (2005). A comprehensive analysis of U.S. counties' e-Government portals: development status and functionalities. *European Journal of Information Systems, 16*(2), 149–164. doi:10.1057/palgrave.ejis.3000675

Hauptmann, E. (2001). Can Less Be More?: Leftist Deliberative Democrats' Critique of Participatory Democracy. *Polity, 33*(3), 397–421. doi:10.2307/3235441

Hayward, J. (1995). *The Crisis of Representation in Europe.* London: Frank Cass & Co. Ltd.

Haywood, T. (1998). Global networks and the myth of equality: Trickle down or trickle away? In *Proceedings of Cyberspace Divide* (pp. 19–34). Equality, Agency and Policy in the Information Society.

Heeks, R. (1999). *Reinventing government in the information age: international practice in IT-enabled public sector reform.* London: Routledge.

Heeks, R. (2001). *Reinventing government in the information age: International practice in IT-enabled public sector reform.* London: Routledge.

Heeks, R. (2001). *Understanding e-Governance for Development (Paper No. 11). Manchester M13 9QH.* UK: University of Manchester, Institute for Development Policy and Management.

Heeks, R. (2002). Information Systems and Developing Countries: Failure, Success, and Local Improvisations. *The Information Society, 18*(2), 101–112. doi:10.1080/01972240290075039

Heeks, R. (2003). *Most eGovnerment-for-Development Projects Fail: How Can Risks be Reduced? (Paper No. 14). Manchester M13 9QH.* UK: University of Manchester, Institute for Development Policy and Management.

Heeks, R. (2008). ICT4D 2.0: The next phase of applying ICT for international development. *IEEE Computer, 41*(6), 26–33.

Helbig, N. (2009). Understanding the complexity of electronic government: Implications from the digital divide literature. *Government Information Quarterly, 26*, 89–97. doi:10.1016/j.giq.2008.05.004

Held, D. (1987). *Models of Democracy*. Cambridge, UK: Blackwell.

Held, D. (1987). *Models of Democracy*. Cambridge, UK: Polity Press.

Hendler, J. (2001, March). Agents and the Semantic Web. *IEEE Intelligent Systems, 16*(2), 30–37. doi:10.1109/5254.920597

Henrikson, A. K. (2006). What can public diplomacy achieve? The Netherlands: Netherlands Institute of International Relations (Clingendael).

Henry, S. (2003). Can Remote Internet Voting Increase Turnout? *Aslib Proceedings, 55*, 193–203. doi:10.1108/00012530310486557

Hermes, J. (2006). Citizenship in the age of the internet. *European Journal of Communication, 21*(3), 295–309. doi:10.1177/0267323106066634

Hernández, M. G. (2007). *Latin America Online: Cases, Successes and Pitfalls*. Hershey, PA: IRM Press.

Heywood, I., Cornelius S., &. Carver, S (2002). *Geographical Information Systems*, London: Pearson-Prentice.

Hill, C. (2004, November 8). *U. S. Embassy launches Cafe USA*. Retrieved March 10, 2008, from http://seoul.usembassy.gov/caf_usa.html

Hill, M. (2005). *The Public Policy Process* (4th ed.). Harlow, UK: Pearson.

Hillier, J. (2000). Going round the back? Complex networks and informal action in local planning processes. *Environment & Planning A, 32*, 33–54. doi:10.1068/a321

Hillier, J. (2002). *Shadows of power: An allegory of prudence in land-use planning*. London, UK: Routledge.

Hindeness, B. (2000). Representative Government and Participatory Democracy. In Vandenberg, A. (Ed.), *Citizenship and Democracy in a Global Era* (pp. 102–113). London: Macmillan Press.

Hindman, M. (2008). *The Only Criterion for Membership Is a Modem*. Retrieved March 16th, 2009, from http://www.matthewhindman.com/index.php/2008070736/The-Myth-of-Digital-Democracy/-The-Only-Criterion-for-Membership-Is-a-Modem.html

Hindman, M. (2009). *The Myth of Digital Democracy*. Princeton, NJ: Princeton University Press.

Hindman, M., & Cukier, K. N. (in press). More News, Less Diversity. *The New York Times*.

Hindman, M., Tsioutsiouliklis, K., & Johnson, J. A. (2003). *Googlearchy: How a Few Heavily Linked Sites Dominate Politics Online*. Paper presented at the annual meeting of the Midwest Political Science Association. Chicago, IL.

Hogwood, B., & Gunn, L. (1988). *Policy Analysis for the Real World. Oxford, UK: Oxford University Press The Independent Commission Alternative Voting Methods (ICAVM) (2002). Elections in the 21st Century: from paper ballot to e-voting*. London: Electoral Reform Society.

Holden, S. H. (2007). *A model for Adaptation: from the IRS e-file*. IBM center for the business of government. Retrieved June 26, 2009, from http://www.businessofgovernment.org/pdfs/management07.pdf

Holden, S., Norris, D. & Fletcher, P. (2003). Electronic Government at the Local Level: progress to date and future issues. *Public Performance and Management Review. 26*(4).

Holford, H., & Edirisingha, P. (2000). *Citizenship and governance education in Europe: A critical review of the literature. University of Surrey*. UK: School of Educational Studies.

Hon, L. C., & Grunig, J. E. (1999, November). *Guidelines for measuring relationships in public relations*. Gainesville, FL: The Institute for Public Relations, Commission on PR Measurement Evaluation.

Hood, C. (1995). The new public management in the 1980s: Variations on a theme. *Accounting, Organizations and Society, 20*(2/3), 93–109. doi:10.1016/0361-3682(93)E0001-W

Horrigan, J. B. (2008). *Home broadband 2008*. Pew internet & American life project. Retrieved May 4, 2009 from http://www.pewinternet.org/~/media//files/reports/2008/pip_broadband_2008.pdf

Hoskisson, R. E., Eden, L., Lau, C. M., & Wright, M. (2000). Strategy in emerging economies. *Academy of Management Journal, 43*(3), 249–267. doi:10.2307/1556394

Hoskyns, C., & Newman, M. (2000). *Democratizing the European Union: Issues for the twenty-first century*. Manchester, UK: Manchester University Press.

Howard, T. L. J., & Gaborit, N. (2007). Using virtual environment technology to improve public participation in urban planning process. *Journal of Urban Planning and Development, 133*(4), 233–241. doi:10.1061/(ASCE)0733-9488(2007)133:4(233)

Huang, W., Siau, K., & Wei, K. K. (2005). *Electronic government strategies and implementation*. Hershey, PA: Idea Group Publishing.

Huberman, B. A. (2001). *The Laws of the Web: Patterns of Ecology of Information*. Cambridge, MA: MIT Press.

Hudson, H. E. (2006). *From rural village to global village: Telecommunications for development in the information age*. London: Lawrence Erlbaum Associates.

Hudson-Smith, A., Batty, E. S., & Batty, S. (2003). Online participation: The Woodberry down experiment. *CASA Working Paper 60*. London: CASA.

Huovila, P. (2005, September) *e-Inclusion and e/m-Participation in IntelCities*. Presented at the IntelCities Conference, Rome. IntelCities – *Intelligent Cities project* (N°: IST.2002-507860) EU VI Framework, Information

Society Technologies. Retrieved October 12, 2007, from http://www.intelcitiesproject.com

Hyang-Sook, C., Byung-Sun, C., & Woong-Hee, P. (2007). Ubiquitous-City Business Strategies: The Case of South Korea. In *Proceedings of the Management of Engineering and Technology* (PICMET 2007), IEEE.

Illinois Department of Revenue. *Illinois Department of Revenue*. Retrieved April 29, 2009, from http://tax.illinois.gov/

Illinois Secretary of State. *Cyberdriveillinois*. Retrieved April 29, 2009, from http://www.cyberdriveillinois.com/

In.gov. (n.d.). *BMV: home*. retrieved April 29, 2009, from http://www.in.gov/bmv/

In.gov. (n.d.). *Indiana Department of Revenue i-file*. Retrieved April 29, 2009, from https://secure.in.gov/apps/dor/ifile/2008/

In.gov. (n.d.). *Indiana department of revenue: filing statistics*. Retrieved May 5, 2009, from http://www.in.gov/dor/3648.htm

Indiana Department of Commerce and Indiana Economic Council (2003). *Connections in an information age: indiana at work and home*. Retrieved January 27, 2008, from www.in.gov/legislative/igareports/agency/reports/econdev01.pdf

infoplease. (2009) *Countries of the World*. Retrieved March/April 2009, from http://www.infoplease.com/countries.html

Innes, J. E. (1996). Planning through consensus building: A new view of the comprehensive planning ideal. *Journal of the American Planning Association. American Planning Association, 62*(4), 460–472. doi:10.1080/01944369608975712

Innes, J. E. (1998). Information in communicative planning. *Journal of the American Planning Association. American Planning Association, 64*(11), 52–63. doi:10.1080/01944369808975956

Intelcity (2003) - *Towards Intelligent Sustainable Cities Roadmap,* (N°: IST-2001-37373) EU V Framework, Information Society Technologies. Retrieved January 12, 2009, from http://www.scri.salford.ac.uk/intelcity/

Interior Ministry (Chile). (2008). *Agenda de Modernización del Estado.* Retreived July 31, 2009, from http://www.modernizacion.gov.cl/filesapp/Presentacion%20Agenda%20Modernizacion.pdf

Internal revenue service (2008). *Advancing e-file study phase 1 report -- executive summary: achieving the 80% e-file goal requires partnering with stakeholders on new approaches to motivate paper filers.* Case number 08-1063, document number 0206.0209. Retrieved June 23, 2009, from http://www.irs.gov/pub/irs-utl/irs_advancing_e-file_study_phase_1_executive_summary_vl_3.pdf

Internal Revenue Service. *Online Services.* Retrieved April 29, 2009, from http://www.irs.gov/efile/article/0,id=151880,00.html?portlet=4

International Association for Public Participation. (2007). *IPA2 spectrum of public participation.* Retrieved March 10, 2009, from http://www.iap2.org/associations/4748/files/spectrum.pdf

Irvin, R. A., & Stansbury, J. (2004). Citizen participation in decision making: Is it worth the effort? *Public Administration Review, 64*(1), 55–65. doi:10.1111/j.1540-6210.2004.00346.x

Ishida, T. (2002, July). Digital city Kyoto. *Communications of the ACM, 45*(7). doi:10.1145/514236.514238

Ishida, T., Aurigiri, A., & Yasuoka, M. (2001). *World Digital Cities: Beyond Heterogeneity.* Retrieved April, 2005, from http://www.kid.rcast.u-tokyo.ac.jp

ITU. (2007). World information society report 2007: Beyond WSIS. In *Proceedings of International Telecommunication Union Report.* Geneva, Switzerland: United Nations.

ITU. (2008). *Report on the World Summit on the Information Society Stocktaking.* Retrieved (n.d.), from http://www.itu.int/wsis/stocktaking/index.html

Jaeger, P. T. (2005). Deliberative democracy and the conceptual foundations of electronic government. *Government Information Quarterly, 22*(4), 702–719. doi:10.1016/j.giq.2006.01.012

Jaeger, P. T., & Thompson, K. M. (2003). E-government around the world: Lessons, challenges, and future directions. *Government Information Quarterly, 20,* 389–394. doi:10.1016/j.giq.2003.08.001

Jamieson, A., Shin, H., & Day, J. (2002). *Voting and Registration in the Election of November 2000.* Washington, DC: US Census Bureau.

Janoski, T. (1998). *Citizenship and civil society.* Cambridge, UK: Cambridge University Press.

Janssen, M., & Kuk, G. (2007). E-Government Business Models for Public Service Networks. *International Journal of Electronic Government Research, 3*(3), 54–71.

Jefferson, D., Rubin, A., Simons, B., & Wagner, D. (2004). Analyzing Internet Voting Security. *Communications of the ACM, 47,* 59–64. doi:10.1145/1022594.1022624

Jensen, M., & Venkatesh, A. (2007). Government websites and political engagement: Facilitating Citizen entry into the policy process. In B. Thossen (Ed.). *Schriftenreihe Informatic:* Vol. 23. *Towards Electronic Democracy Conference Proceedings* (pp. 55-65). Linz, Austria: Trauner Verlag.

Johnson, T. J., & Kaye, B. K. (2003). A boost or bust for democracy? How the web influenced political attitudes and behaviors in the 1996 and 2000 presidential elections. *The Harvard International Journal of Press/Politics, 8*(3), 9–34. doi:10.1177/1081180X03008003002

Jones, S., & Fox, S. (2009). Generations online in 2009. *Pew Internet & American Life Project,* January 28, 2009. Retrieved February 12, 2009, from http://www.pewinternet.org/PPF/r/275/report_display.asp

Jordan, T. (2002). *Activism! Direct action, hacktivism, and the future of society.* London: Reaktion Books Ltd.

Jordan, T., & Taylor, P. A. (2004). *Hacktivism and cyberwars: Rebels with a cause?* London: Routledge.

Juris, J. S. (2005, January). The new digital media and activist networking within anti–corporate globalization movements [Electronic version]. *The Annals of the American Academy of Political and Social Science, 597*, 189-208. Retrieved March 6, 2008, from http://ann.sagepub.com.ezproxy.fiu.edu/cgi/reprint/597/1/189

Kaaya, J. (2005). Implementing e-Government Services in East Africa: Assessing Status through Content Analysis of Government Websites, *Electronic. Journal of E-Government, 2*, 139–154.

Kahn, R., & Kellner, D. (2004). New media and internet activism: From the Battle of Seattle to blogging [Electronic version]. *New Media & Society, 6*(1), 87-95. Retrieved January 14, 2009, from http://nms.sagepub.com.ezproxy.fiu.edu/cgi/reprint/6/1/87

Kakabadse, A., Kakabadse, N., & Kouzmin, A. (2003). Reinventing the democratic governance project through information technology? A growing agenda for debate. *Public Administration Review, 63*(1), 44–60. doi:10.1111/1540-6210.00263

Kamal, M. M. (2006). IT innovation adoption in the government sector: identifying the critical success factors. In. *Journal of Enterprise Information Management, 19*(2), 192–222. doi:10.1108/17410390610645085

Kamarck, E. C. (2002). Political campaigning on the Internet: Business as usual? In Kamarck, E. C., & Nye, J. S. Jr., (Eds.), *governance.com: Democracy in the information age* (pp. 81–103). Washington, DC: Brookings Institution.

Kampen, J., & Snijkers, K. (2003). E-democracy: A critical evaluation of the ultimate e-dream. *Social Science Computer Review, 21*(11), 491–496. doi:10.1177/0894439303256095

Kathi, P. C., & Cooper, T. L. (2005). Democratizing the Administrative State: Connecting Neighborhood Councils and City Agencies. *Public Administration Review, 65*(5), 559–567. doi:10.1111/j.1540-6210.2005.00483.x

Kaufman, D., Kraay, A., & Mastruzzi, M. (2003). Governance Matters III: Governance Indicators for 1996-2002. Retrieved February 12, 2009, from http://www-wds.

worldbank.org/external/default/WDSContentServer/WDSP/IB/2003/08/23/000094946_03081404010948/Rendered/PDF/multi0page.pdf

Kaufmann, D., & Kraay, A. Mastruzzi, & Massimo (2008, June 24). *Governance Matters VII: Aggregate and Individual Governance Indicators*, 1996-2007, World Bank Policy Research Working Paper No. 4654.Retrieved (n.d.), fromhttp://ssrn.com/abstract=1148386

Kelleher, C., & Lowery, D. (2008). Central City Size, Metropolitan Institutions and Political Participation. *British Journal of Political Science, 39*, 59–92. doi:10.1017/S0007123408000392

Keniston, K., & Kumar, D. (2004). *IT experience in India: Bridging the digital divide*. New Delhi, India: Sage Publications.

Kenski, K., & Stroud, N. J. (2006). Connections between internet use and political efficacy, knowledge, and participation. *Journal of Broadcasting & Electronic Media, 50*, 173–192. doi:10.1207/s15506878jobem5002_1

Kent, M. L., & Taylor, M. (1998). Building dialogic relationships through the world wide web. *Public Relations Review, 24*(3), 321–334. doi:10.1016/S0363-8111(99)80143-X

Kentucky.gov. *Home.* Retrieved April 29, 2009, from http://kentucky.gov/pages/home.aspx

Kentucky: Department of Revenue. *Individual Information.* Retrieved April 29, 2009, from http://revenue.ky.gov/individual/

Kifer, M., Lausen, G., & Wu, J. (1995). Logical foundations of object-oriented and frame-based languages. [JACM]. *Journal of the ACM, 42*, 741–843. doi:10.1145/210332.210335

Kim, C. (2007). A Cross-national Analysis of Global E-government. *Public Organization Review, 7*(4), 317–329. doi:10.1007/s11115-007-0040-5

Kim, C.-K. (2007). A cross-national analysis of global e-government. *Public Organization Review, 7*(4), 317–329. doi:10.1007/s11115-007-0040-5

Kim, H., & Nevo, S. (2008). Development and Application of a Framework for Evaluating Multimode Voting Risks. *Internet Research, 18,* 121–125. doi:10.1108/10662240810849621

Kim, H.-J., Lee, J., & Kim, S. (2008). Making the Connection between Local Electronic-Government Development Stages and Collaboration Strategy: A Case Study of Gangnam District, Seoul, Korea. *International Journal of Electronic Government Research, 4*(3), 36–56.

Kim, P. (2004, 14-18 July 2004). *Development of Democratic e-Governance in Cyberspace and Shaping e-governance for Quality of Life.* Paper presented at the 26th International Congress of Administrative Sciences, Seoul, Korea.

Kim, S., & Lim, W. (2007). How to deal with South Korea. *The Washington Quarterly, 30*(2), 71–82. doi:10.1162/wash.2007.30.2.71

Kinder, T. (2002). Vote early, vote often? Tele-democracy in European cities. *Public Administration, 83*(3), 557–582. doi:10.1111/1467-9299.00318

King, C. S., Feltey, K. M., & Susel, B. O. (1998). The question of participation: Toward authentic public participation in public administration. *Public Administration Review, 58*(4), 317–326. doi:10.2307/977561

Kingdon, J. (2003). *Agendas, Alternatives and Public Policies.* New York: Logman.

Kingston, R. (2006). *The role of participatory e-planning in the new English local planning system.* Retrieved May 13, 2009, from http://www.ppgis.manchester.ac.uk/downloads/e-Planning_LDFs.pdf

Kingston, R. (2007). Public participation in local policy decision-making: The role of web-based mapping. *The Cartographic Journal, 44*(2), 138–144. doi:10.1179/000870407X213459

Kingston, R., Carver, S., Evans, A., & Turton, I. (2000). Web-based public participation geographical information systems: an aid to local environmental decision-making. *Computers, Environment and Urban Systems, 24*(2), 109–125. doi:10.1016/S0198-9715(99)00049-6

Klinckenberg, F., & Sunikka, M. (2006). *Better buildings through energy efficiency: A roadmap for Europe.* Brussels, Belgium: Eurima.

Klota, R. J. (2004). *The politics of internet communication.* New York: Rowman & Littlefield Publishers, Inc.

Klotz, R. (2004). *The politics of Interne communication.* Lanham, MD: Rowman & Littlefield.

Klotz, R. J. (2007). Internet campaigning for grassroots and astroturf support. *Social Science Computer Review, 25*(1), 3–12. doi:10.1177/0894439306289105

Kohno, T., & Stubblefield, A. Rubin, A.,&Wallach, D. S. (2003). Analysis of the electronic voting system (Technical Report TR-2003). Johns Hopkins Information Security Institute.

Kool, D. de, in cooperation with Bekkers, V. J. J. M. (2008). *Monitoring in kaart: een studie naar de doorwerking van op GIS gebaseerde beleidsinformatie in het leerproces van organisaties die een rol spelen bij de uitvoering van beleid,* Rotterdam Center for Public Innovation.

Kreimer, S. F. (2001, November). Technologies of Protest: Insurgent Social Movements and the First Amendment in the Era of the Internet [Electronic version] [from http://www.jstor.org.ezproxy.fiu.edu]. *University of Pennsylvania Law Review, 150*(1), 119–171. Retrieved March 6, 2008. doi:10.2307/3312914

Kröll, H. (2000). El método de los estudios de caso, en Tarrés, Ma. Luisa (ed.) Escuchar, observar y comprender: sobre la investigación cualitativa en la investigación social. México: Porrúa: COLMEX/FLACSO.

Krueger, B. S. (2002). Assessing the potential of Internet political participation in the United States: a resource approach. *American Politics Research, 30,* 476–498. doi:10.1177/1532673X02030005002

Krummenacher, L. & Strang (2006). On the Modelling of Context-Rules with WSML. Workshop on Contexts & Ontologies: Theory, Practice and Applications. at *E-CAI'06, Riva del Garda, Italy, 28. August 2006.*

Kurzman, J. S. (2000). The politics of representation: Social work lessons from the advocacy planning movement. Advocates Forum, *6*(1).

Kweit, M. G., & Kweit, R. W. (1981). *Implementing citizen participation in a bureaucratic Society*. New York: Praeger.

Lahti, P., Kangasoja, J., & Huovila, P. (2006). *Electronic and Mobile Participation in City Planning and Management. Experiences from IntelCities – an Integrated Project of the Sixth Framework Programme of the European Union. Cases Helsinki, Tampere, Garðabær/Reykjavik and Frankfurt*. Picaset Oy, Helsinki, Finland. Retrieved July 29, 2009, from http://www.hel2.fi/tietokeskus/julkaisut/pdf/Intelcity.pdf.

Lang, R. (1986). Achieving integration in resource planning. In Lang, R. (Ed.), *Integrated Approaches to Resource Planning and Management*. Calgary, Canada: The University of Calgary Press.

Lau, T. Y., Aboulhoson, M., Lin, C., & Atkin, D. (2008). Adoption of e-government in three Latin American countries: Argentina, Brazil and Mexico. *Telecommunications Policy, 32*, 88–100. doi:10.1016/j.telpol.2007.07.007

Lawrence, J. (2008). Young voters poised to flex voting muscle. *USA Today*, May 6, 2008. Retrieved January 23, 2009, from http://www.usatoday.com/news/politics/election2008/2008-05-05-young-voters_N.htm

Layne, K., & Jungwoo, L. (2001). Developing fully functional e-government: A four stage model. *Government Information Quarterly, 18*, 122–136. doi:10.1016/S0740-624X(01)00066-1

Layne, K., & Lee, J. (2001). Developing Full Functional E-government: A Four Stage Model. *Government Information Quarterly, 18*(2), 122–136. doi:10.1016/S0740-624X(01)00066-1

Layne, K., & Lee, J. (2001). Developing fully functional E-government: A four stage model. *Government Information Quarterly, 18*, 122–136. doi:10.1016/S0740-624X(01)00066-1

Ledingham, J. A., & Bruning, S. D. (1998). Relationship management in public relations: Dimensions of an organization-public relationship. *Public Relations Review, 24*(1), 55–65. doi:10.1016/S0363-8111(98)80020-9

Ledingham, J. A., & Bruning, S. D. (2000). A longitudinal study of organization-public relationship dimensions: Defining the role of communication in the practice of relationship management. In Ledingham, J. A., & Bruning, S. D. (Eds.), *Public relations as relationship management: A relational approach to the study and practice of public relations*. Mahwah, NJ: Lawrence Erlbaum.

Leitner, C. (2003). *eGovernment in Europe: The State of Affairs*. Retrieved June 30, 2009, from www.eipa.eu/files/repository/product/20070214113429_egoveu.pdf

Lemp, J. D., Zhou, B., Kockelman, K. M., & Parmenter, B. M. (2008). Visioning versus Modeling: Analyzing the Land-Use-Transportation Futures of Urban Regions. *Journal of Urban Planning and Development, 34*(9), 97–107. doi:10.1061/(ASCE)0733-9488(2008)134:3(97)

Lenhart, A. (2009). *Adults and social network websites*. January 14, 2009. Retrieved February 19, 2009, from http://www.pewinternet.org/PPF/r/527/press_coverageitem.asp

Lessig, L. (1999). *Code and Other Laws of Cyberspace*. New York: Basic Books.

Leung, H. J. (2003). *Land use planning made plain* (2nd ed.). Toronto, Canada: University of Toronto Press.

Lewis, J. (2007). Technology acquisition and innovation in the developing world: Wind turbine development in China and India. *Studies in Comparative International Development, 42*(3-4), 208–232. doi:10.1007/s12116-007-9012-6

Lieshout, V. (2001). Configuring the digital city of Amsterdam. *New Media & Technology, 3*(1), 27–52.

Ligthart, F. A. T. M., Verhoog, S. M., & Gilijamse, W. (2000). Lange termijn energievisie op Parkstad, Amsterdam: Petten (ECN)

Lijphart, A. (1999). *Patterns of democracy: Government forms and performance in thirty-six countries*. New Haven, CT: Yale University Press.

Lin, N. (2001). *Social capital: A theory of social structure and action*. Cambridge, UK: Cambridge University Press.

Lin, N., Cook, K. S., & Burt, R. S. (2001). *Social capital: Theory and research*. New York: Aldine de Gruyter.

Lindblom, C. E. (1965). *The intelligence of democracy*. New York: The Free Press of New York.

Lindblom, C., & Woodhouse, E. (1993). The Policy Making Process 3rd ed. Upper Saddle River, NJ: Prentice Hall Local Government Association (LGA) (2005). Electoral Administration Bill. London: Local Government Association

Lindstrom, A., & Gronholm, B. (2002). *Progress and trends in local agenda 21 work within UBC Cities: Union of the Baltic Cities local agenda 21 survey 2001*. Turku: Abo University and Union of the Baltic Cities.

Lineman, D. (2005). [– *Security Policy Implications for Business*. Houston, TX: Information Shield.]. *The New ISO, 17799*, 2005.

Linster, M. (2003). *Environment Indicators. Development, Measurement and Use*. Paris: OECD.

Lippert, S., & Ojumu, E. (2008). Thinking Outside of the Ballot Box: Examining Public Trust in E-Voting Technology. *Journal of Organizational and End User Computing, 20*, 57–81.

LiQi. (2001). *Digital city-the 21 century's life style*. Beijing, China: CyberGIS Studio, Peking University, Institute of Remote Sensing & GIS. Retrieved April, 2005, from http://unpan1.un.org

List, P. C. (1993). *Radical environmentalism: Philosophy and tactics*. Belmont, CA: Wadsworth Publishing Company.

Livingston, V. (2006). *Two Billion GSM Customers Worldwide*. Retrieved July 29, 2009, from http://www.prnewswire.com/cgi-bin/stories.pl?ACCT=109&STORY=/www/story/06-13-2006/0004379206&EDATE=

Lombardi, P., & Cooper, I. (2007). eDomus vs eAgora: the Italian case and implications for the EU 2010 strategy. In P. Cunningham, & M. Cunningham (eds), Expanding the Knowledge Economy: Issues, Applications, Case Studies vol. 1 (pp. 344-351). Amsterdam: IOS Press

Lombardi, P., Cooper, I., Paskaleva, K., & Deakin, M. (2009). The challenge of designing user-centric e-services: European dimensions. In Reddick, C. G. (Ed.), *Research Strategies for eGovernment Service Adoption*. Hershey, PA: Idea Group Publishing.

Longford, G. (2005). Pedagogies of digital citizenship and the politics of code. *Techné: Research in Philosophy and Technology, 9*(1), 1–25.

Lorentsen, L. G. (2008). *Key environmental indicators*. Paris: OECD.

Lovelock, P., & Ure, J. (2002). E-Government in China. In Zhang, J., & Woesler, M. (Eds.), *China's Digital Dream: The Impact of the Internet on the Chinese Society*. Bochum, Germany: The University Press Bochum.

Luna-Reyes, L., Hernández García, J. M., & Gil-García, J. R. (2009). Hacia un Modelo de los Determinantes de Éxito de los Portales de Gobierno Estatal en México. *Gestión y Política Pública, XVIII*(2), 307–340.

Lusoli, W. (2005). Politics makes strange bedfellows. *The Harvard International Journal of Press/Politics, 10*(4), 71–97. doi:10.1177/1081180X05281029

Ma, L., Chung, J., & Thorson, S. (2005). E-government in China: Bringing economic development through administrative reform. *Government Information Quarterly, 22*(1), 20–37. doi:10.1016/j.giq.2004.10.001

Macintosh, A. (2002). e-Democracy: Citizen engagement and evaluation. In S. Friedrichs, T. Hart & O. Schmidt (Eds.), Balanced EGovernment:Connecting Efficient Administration and Responsive Democracy. Germany: Bertlesman Foundation.

Macintosh, A. (2003) Using Information and Communication Technologies to Enhance Citizen Engagement in the Policy Process. In OECD (Ed) Promise and Problems of E-Democracy:Challenges of Online Citizens Engagement (pp. 19-140) Paris: OECD Publications

Macintosh, A. (2004). *Characterizing e-participation in policy-making*. Retrieved March 5, 2009, from csdl2.computer.org/comp/proceedings/hicss/2004/2056/05/205650117a.pdf

Macintosh, A. (2004, January 4-5). Characterizing E-Participation in Policy-Making. Paper presented at the *37th Hawai International Conference on System Science 2004*, University of Hawai'i at Manoa, Manoa, HI.

Macintosh, A. (2006). eParticipation in Policy-making: the research and the challenges. In P. Cunningham & M. Cunningham (Eds.), Exploiting the Knowledge Economy: Issues, Applications and Case Studies (pp. 364-369) Amsterdam, The Netherlands: IOS press.

Macintosh, A., & Whyte, A. (2006). *Evaluating how eParticipation changes local democracy.* Paper presented at the eGovernment Workshop 2006, eGov06, London, UK.

Macintosh, A., & Whyte, A. (2008). Towards an Evaluation Framework for eParticipation, *Transforming Government People. Process and Policy, 2*, 16–26.

Macintosh, A., Davenport, E., Malina, A., & Whyte, A. (2002). Technology to support participatory democracy. In Gronlund, A. (Ed.), *Electronic government: Design, application and management* (pp. 226–248). Hershey, PA: Idea Publishing Group.

Macintosh, A., Malina, A., & Whyte, A. (2002). Designing e-democracy for Scotland. *Communications: The European Journal of Communications, 27*, 261–278.

Macintosh, A., McKay-Hubbard, A., & Shell, D. (2005b). Using Weblogs to Support Local Democracy, en Böhlen, Gamper, Polasek & Wimmer (Eds.) *E-Government: Towards Electronic Democracy.* Italia: International Conference, TCGOV2005.

Macintosh, A., Whyte, A., & Renton, A. (2005a). *From the Top Down: An evaluation of e-Democracy Activities Initiated by Councils and Government. Local e-Democracy National Project.* Bristol, UK: Bristol City Council.

Maddock, S. (2002). Making modernization work: New narratives, change strategies and people management in the public sector. *International Journal of Public Sector Management, 15*(1), 13–43. doi:10.1108/09513550210414578

Mahrer, H., & Krimmer, R. (2005). Towards the enhancement of e-democracy: identifying the notion of the 'middle man paradox'. *Information Systems Journal, 15*, 27–42. doi:10.1111/j.1365-2575.2005.00184.x

Maitland, C. F., & Bauer, J. M. (2001). National level culture and global diffusion: The case of the Internet. In Culture, technology, communication: Towards an intercultural global village (pp. 87-128).

Malakooty, N. (2007). *Closing the Digital Divide? The $100 PC and Other Projects for Developing Countries.* Irvine, CA: Personal Computing Industry Center.

Malloy, D. (2008). Candidates facing up to youth on the Internet. *Pittsburgh Post Gazette*, February 1, 2008. Retrieved January 23, 2009, from http://www.post-gazette.com/pg/08032/853990-176.stm.

Maneschy, O. (2002). *Burla Eletrônica.* Rio de Janeiro, Brazil: Fundação Alberto Pasqualini.

Mannheim, K. (1940). *Man and society in an age of reconstruction.* New York: Harcourt, Brace & World.

Manoharan, T. (2003). *Collaborative virtual environment for planning development control in cities.* PhD Thesis. Heriot-Watt University, UK.

Mantysalo, R. (2000). *Land-use planning as inter-organizational learning.* Acta Universitatis Ouluersis Technica, C 155, Oulu. Retrieved, August 25, 2003, from http://herkules.oulu.fi/isbn9514258444/

Marcondes, C. H., & Jardim, J. M. (2003). Políticas de informação governamental: A construção do governo eletrônico na administração federal do Brasil. *DataGramaZero - Revista de Ciência da Informação, 4*(2).

Margain, J. (2001). e-México: la estrategia del gobierno. *Política Digital, 1*, 48–51.

Margetts, H. (2005). Virtual Organizations. In Ferlie, E., Lynn, L. E. Jr, & Pollitt, C. (Eds.), *The Oxford Handbook of Public Management* (pp. 305–325). Oxford, UK: Oxford University Press.

Margetts, H. (2007). Electronic Government. A Revolution in Public Administration? In B. G., Peters. & J.

Pierre (Eds.) The Handbook of Public Administration (pp. 234-244). London: Sage.

Margetts, H. (2009). Public Management Change and E-Government: The Emergence of Digital-Era-Governance. In Chadwick, A., & Howard, P. N. (Eds.), *Routledge Handbook of Internet Politics* (pp. 114–127). New York: Routledge.

Margolis, M., & Resnick, D. (2000). *Politics as usual: The cyberspace "revolution"*. Thousand Oaks, CA: Sage Publications.

Maricopa Association of Government (MAG). (2000). *Valley vision 2025*. Retrieved, January 24 2008 from, http://www.mag.maricopa.gov/archive/vv2025/

Márquez, M. (2006). Una gran oportunidad para la democracia. *Política Digital., 27,* 56–57.

Marshall, T. H. (1965). *Class, Citizenship and Social Development*. New York: Anchor Books.

Martin, B., Stewart, D., & Hillison, J. (2001). Computer Anxiety Levels of Virginia Extension Personnel. *Journal of Extension, 39.*

Martin, D., Paolucci, M., McIlraith, S., Burstein, M., McDermott, D., McGuinness, D., et al. (2005). Bringing Semantics to Web Services: The OWL-S Approach. In *Proceedings of the 1st International Workshop on Semantic Web Services and Web Process Composition* (pp.22-42). New York: Springer.

Masters, Z., Macintosh, A., & Smith, E. (2004). Young People and e-Democracy: Creating a culture of participation, en Traunmüller, R. *Electronic Government: Third International Conference, EGOV2004.* España: Springer.

Mauch, C., Stoltzfus, N., & Weiner, D. R. (2006). *Shades of green: Environmental activism around the globe*. Boulder, CO: Rowman & Littlefield Publishers, Inc.

McGuirk, P. M. (2001). Situating communicative planning theory: Context, power and knowledge. *Environment & Planning A, 33,* 195–217. doi:10.1068/a3355

McIlraith, S. A., Son, T. C., & Zeng, H. (2001). Semantic Web services. *IEEE Intelligent Systems, 16*(2), 46–53. doi:10.1109/5254.920599

McIlroy. M. D. (1968, October 7-11). Mass Produced Software Components. In P. Naur and B. Randell (Eds.), Software Engineering, Report on a conference sponsored by the NATO Science Committee, Garmisch, Germany (pp. 138-155). Brussels, Belgium: Scientific Affairs Division, NATO.

McNamara, K., & O'Brien, R. (2000, January 1). *Access to information and communication for sustainable development opportunities and challenges for international community -Recommendations of the access working group.* GKP II Conference, Global Knowledge Partenership Secretariat. Kuala Lumpur, Malaysia.

McQuail, D. (1997). *Audience analysis*. London: Sage.

MDG Gap Task Force. (2008). *Delivering on the Global Partnership for Achieving the Millennium Development Goals*. New York: The United Nations.

Medaglia, R. (2007). The Challenged Identity of a Field: The State of the Art of eParticipation Research. *Information Polity, 12*(3), 169–181.

Meijer, A. (2006). ICTs and Political Accountability: An assessment of the impact digitization in government on political accountability in Connecticut, Massachusetts and New York State. *National Center for Digital Government Working Paper* No. 06-002. USA.

Meijer, F., Itard, L., & Sunikka-Blank, M. (2009). Comparing European residential building stocks: performance, renovation and policy opportunities. *Building Research and Information, 37*(5), 533–551. doi:10.1080/09613210903189376

Meikle, G. (2002). *Future active: Media activism and the internet*. New York: Routledge.

Menefee-Libbey, D. (2001). The permanent campaign and its future. *Presidential Studies Quarterly, 31*(2), 383–384.

Meng, Q., & Li, M. (2002). New Economy and ICT development in China. *Information Economics and Policy, 14*(2), 275–295. doi:10.1016/S0167-6245(01)00070-1

Michel, H. (2005). e-Administration, e-Government, e-Governance and the learning city: A typology of citizenship management using ICTs. *The Electronic Journal of E-Government, 3*(4), 213–218.

Michels, R. (1915). *Political Parties: A Sociological Study of the Oligarchical Tendencies of Modern Democracy. Translated by Eden Paul and Cedar Paul.* New York: The Free Press.

Millard, J. (2008). *E-participation recommendations: first version.* Retrieved March 5, 2009, from www.european-eparticipation.eu

Miller, C., Mukerji, J., Burt, C., Dsouza, D., Duddy, K., & El Kaim, W. (2001). *Model Driven Architecture (MDA). Document number ormsc/2001-07-01. Architecture Board ORMSC, OMG.* New York: Springer.

Mimicopoulos, M. (2004). *E-government funding activities and strategies.* New York: Department of Economic and Social Affairs, Division for Public Administration and Development Management, The United Nations.

Mindich, D. T. Z. (2005). *Tuned out.* Oxford, UK: Oxford University.

Moharil, R., & Kulkarni, P. (2009). A case study of solar photovoltaic power system at Sagardeep Island, India. *Renewable & Sustainable Energy Reviews, 13*(3), 673–681. doi:10.1016/j.rser.2007.11.016

Montecinos, E. (2008). Los Incentivos de la Descentralización en la Gestión Municipal Chilena. Gestión Política sin Participación Democrática. *Estado, Gobierno, Gestión Pública. Revista Chilena de Administración Pública, 12*, 105–123.

Moraes, R. A. (2007, March). Is a new critical language in the education still possible today? Osford Mini-Conference, Retrieved May 20, 2009, from http://construct.haifa.ac.il/~ilangz/oxford2007/Almeida%20Moraes.pdf

Morgan, D. (1997). *Focus Groups as Qualitative Research.* New York: Sage Publications.

Mossberger, K., Tolbert, C. J., & Stansbury, M. (2003). *Virtual Inequality: Beyond the Digital Divide.* Washington, DC: Georgetown University Press.

Mossberger, K., Tolbert, C., & Gilbert, M. (2006). Race, place, and information technology. *Urban Affairs Review, 41*(5), 583–630. doi:10.1177/1078087405283511

Mountihno, J., & Heitor, M. (2003, September 18-19). Digital Cities and the challenges for a Knowledge-Based View of the Territory: evidence from Portugal. In *Proceedings of the Digital 3 Workshop "Local Information and Communication Infrastructures: experiences and challenges*, Amsterdam, The Netherlands.

Moynihan, D. (2004). Building Secure Elections: E-Voting, Security, and Systems Theory. *Public Administration Review, 64*, 515–529. doi:10.1111/j.1540-6210.2004.00400.x

Moynihan, D. P. (2003). Normative and instrumental perspectives on public participation. *American Review of Public Administration, 33*(2), 164–188. doi:10.1177/0275074003251379

Moynihan, D. P. (2007). E-voting in United States. In Anttiroiko, A., & Malkia, M. (Eds.), *Encyclopedia of digital government* (pp. 797–802). Hershey, PA: Idea Group Inc.

MPAS. (2008). *Annual Report on Information Disclosure in 2007* [in Korean]. Seoul, Korea: Ministry of Public Administration and Security.

Muir, S. A., & Veenendall, T. L. (1996). *Earthtalk: Communication empowerment for environmental action.* Westport, CT: Praeger.

Murray, G. (2005). Democracy in the Information Age. *Australian Journal of Public Administration, 65*(2).

Musso, J., Weare, C., & Hale, M. (2000). Designing Web Technologies for Local Governance Reform: Good Management or Good Democracy? *Political Communication, 17*(1), 1–19. doi:10.1080/105846000198486

mvl.ky.gov. *Registration renewal requirements.* Retrieved April 29, 2009 from http://mvl.ky.gov/mvlweb/requirementpage.jsp

MySociety. (2009) *TheyWorkForYou.* Retrieved July 18, 2009, from http://www.mysociety.org/projects/theyworkforyou/

Naciones Unidas. (2005). *Global e-government readiness report 200: from e-government to e-inclusion.* Retreived (n.d.), from www.unpan.org/egovernment5.asp

National Telecommunications and Information Administration (NTIA). (2000, February). *Falling Through the Net: Toward Digital Inclusion.* Report, Washington, DC: National Telecommunication and Information Administration.

National Telecommunications and Information Administration (NTIA). (2002, February). *A Nation Online: How Americans Are Expanding Their Use of the Internet.* Report, Washington, DC: National Telecommunication and Information Administration.

National Telecommunications and Information Administration (NTIA). (2002, September). *A Nation Online: Entering the Broadband Age.* Report, Washington, DC: National Telecommunication and Information Administration.

Natuurplanbureau, M. (2005). *Ruimtelijke Beelden: visualisatie van een veranderd Nederland in 2030.* The Netherlands: Bilthoven.

Navia, P. (2009 in press). Top-Down and Bottom-Up Democracy in Chile under Bachelet. In Silva, P., & Cleuren, H. (Eds.), *Widening Democracy. Citizens and Participatory Schemes in Brazil and Chile.* Leiden, The Netherlands: Brill.

Ndou, V. (2004). E-Government for Developing Countries: Opportunities and Challenges. *The Electronic Journal on Information Systems in Developing Countries, 18*(1), 1–24.

Nebenzahl, I. D., & Jaffe, E. D. (1996). Measuring the joint effect of brand and country image in consumer evaluation of global products. *International Marketing Review, 13*(4), 5–22. doi:10.1108/02651339610127220

Nedovic'-Budic', Z., Kan, R. G., JohnsTon, D. M., Sparks, R. E. & White, D. C. (2006). CommunityViz-based prototype model for assessing development impacts in a naturalized floodplain-EmiquonViz. *Journal of Urban Planning and Development, 132*(4), 201–210. doi:10.1061/(ASCE)0733-9488(2006)132:4(201)

Needham, C. (2004). The citizen as a consumer: E-government in the United Kingdom and United States. In Gibson, R. (Eds.), *Electronic democracy: Mobilization, organization, and participation via new ICTs* (pp. 43–69). New York: Routledge.

Needham, C. (2005). Brand Leaders: Clinton, Blair and the limitations of the permanent campaign. *Political Studies, 53*(2), 343–361. doi:10.1111/j.1467-9248.2005.00532.x

Negroponte, N. (1995). *Being digital* (1st ed.). New York: Knopf.

Neskey Roadmap. (2003). *New partnerships for Sustainable development in the Knowledge Economy.* Retrieved April 22, 2009, from www.vernaallee.com/value_networks/Neskey_Exec_Summary.pdf

Netchaeva, I. (2002). E-Government and E-Democracy: A comparison of the opportunities in the North and South. *The International Journal for Communication Studies, 64,* 467–477.

New Millennium Research Council. (2005). *Not In The Public Interest – The Myth of Municipal Wi-Fi Networks.* Retrieved July, 2009, from http://www.broadbandcity.gr/content/modules/downloads/Not_In_The_Public_Interest_The_Myth_of_Municipal_WiFi_Networks_(New_Millenium_Research_Council).pdf

New York City Economic Development Corporation. (2005). *Telecommunications and Economic Development in New York City: A Plan of Action.* Retrieved April, 2005, from http://newyorkbiz.com/about_us/Telecom-PlanMarch2005.pdf

Newton, K. (1999). Mass media effects: Mobilization or media malaise? *British Journal of Political Science, 29,* 577–599. doi:10.1017/S0007123499000289

Nic incorporated. *Nic incorporated.* Retrieved April 30, 2009, from http://www.nicusa.com/html/index.html

Nie, N., & Verba, S. (1972). *Participation in America: Political Democracy and Social Equality.* New York: Harper and Row.

Nie, N., Verba, S., & Kim, J.-O. (1978). *Participation and Political Equality: A Cross-National Comparison.* Cambridge, MA: Cambridge University Press.

Nielsen, J. (2003). Diversity is Power for Specialized Sites. Retrieved March 4th, 2009, from http://www.useit.com/alertbox/20030616.html

Nisbett, R. E. (2003). *The geography of thought.* New York: Free Press.

Nixon, P. G., & Koutrakou, V. N. (Eds.). (2007). *E-government in Europe: Re-booting the state.* New York: Routledge.

Nixon, P., & Koutrakou. (2008). *Europe: Rebooting the system* London: Routledge

NLM. (n.d.). *National Literacy Mission – India.* Retrieved July 29, 2009, from http://nlm.nic.in/unesco_nlm.htm

Nogueira Filho, D. (2001). Governo eletrônico. SECOP - Seminário Nacional de Informática Publica, 29. *Anais eletrônicos.* Retrieved May 12, 2009, from: http://www.abep.sp.gov.br/Download 29secopSP/governo

Nonnecke, B., & Preece, J. (2000). *Lurker demographics: Counting the silent.* Paper presented at the Proceedings of CHI 2000. Hague, TheNetherlands.

Norris, D., Fletcher, P., & Holden, S. (2001). *Is your local government plugged in? Highlights of the 2000 electronic government survey.* Washington, DC: International City/Council Management Association.

Norris, P. (2000). *A virtuous circle: Political communications in post-industrial societies.* Cambridge, UK: Cambridge University.

Norris, P. (2001). *Digital Divide: Civic Engagement, Information Poverty, and the Internet in Democratic Societies.* New York: Cambridge University Press.

Norris, P. (2001). *Digital divide: Civic engagement, information poverty, and the Internet worldwide.* Cambridge, UK: Cambridge University.

Nugent, N. (2001). *The European Commission.* New York: Palgrave.

Nugent, S. (2002). *Digital Democracy in Ireland.* Dublin, Ireland: Seminar Presentation on Trinity College.

Nye, J. S. (2005). *Soft power: The means to success in world politics.* New York: Public Affairs.

Nye, J. S. (2008). Public diplomacy and soft power. *The Annals of the American Academy of Political and Social Science, 616*(1), 94–109. doi:10.1177/0002716207311699

O'Gorman, K. (2007). Brian Williams Weighs in on New Medium. *We Want Media.* Retrieved March 16th, 2009, from http://journalism.nyu.edu/pubzone/wewantmedia/node/487

O'Leary, R., Gerald, C., & Bingham, L. B. (2006). Introduction to the Symposium on Collaborative Public Management. *Public Administration Review, Supplement to Volume 66*(6), 6-9.

O'Loughlin, B. (2001). The political implications of digital innovations: Trade-offs of democracy and liberty in the developed world. *Information Communication and Society, 4*(4), 595–614. doi:10.1080/13691180110097021

O'Toole, K. (2009). Australia local government and e-governance: from administration to citizen participation? In *M. Khesrow-Pour, E-government diffusion, policy and impact: Advanced issues and practices* (pp. 174–184). Hershey, PA: IGI Global.

OASIS. (2007). *Web Services Business Process Execution Language Version 2.0.* Retrieved June 30, 2009, from http://docs.oasis-open.org/wsbpel/2.0/OS/wsbpel-v2.0-OS.html

Odame, H. H. (2005). Gender and ICTs for development: Setting the context. In Gender and ICTs for Development: A Global Sourcebook (pp. 13-24).

OECD (Organisation for Economic Cooperation and Development). (2001). *Citizens as partners: OECD handbook on information, consultation and public participation in policy making.* Paris: OECD.

OECD (Organisation for Economic Cooperation and Development). (2003). *Promise and problems of e-democracy: Challenges of online citizen engagement.* Paris: OCED.

OECD. (2003a). *Promise and Problems of E-democracy: Challenges of Online Citizen Engagement*. Washington, DC: OECD Publishing.

OECD. (2003b). *The e-Government Imperative. OECD e-Government Studies*. Washington, DC: OECD Publishing.

OECD. (2005a). *Evaluating public participation in policy making*. Washington, DC: OECD Publishing.

OECD. (2005b). *OECD Government Studies: México*. Washington, DC: OECD Publishing.

OECD. (2005c). e-Government for Better Government. OECD e-Government Studies. Washington DC: OECD Publishing.

OECD. (2005d). Governance of Innovation Systems.: *Vol. 3. Case Studies in Cross-Sectorial Policies*. Washington, DC: OECD Publishing.

OECD. (2007). *Participative Web and User-created Content*. Washington, DC: OECD Publishing.

Official payments corporation. *Official payments corporation*. Retrieved April 30, 2009, from https://www.officialpayments.com/index.jsp

Ohio Bureau of Motor Vehicles. *BMV.* Retrieved April 29, 2009, from https://www.oplates.com/

Ohio.gov. *Department of Taxation*. Retrieved April 29, 2009 from http://www.tax.ohio.gov/index.stm

Oleson, T. (2005). *International Zapatismo: The construction of solidarity in the age of globalization*. New York: Zed Books.

Oliver, R. W. (1975). *International Economic Cooperation and the World Bank*. London: Macmillan.

Olsen, M., & Marger, M. (1993). *Power in Modern Societies*. Oxford, UK: Westview Press.

Olsson, A. (2004). Electronic Democracy and Power, en Traunmüller, R. (Ed) *Electronic Government: Third International Conference, EGOV2004*. España: Springer.

Olsson, T. (2006). Appropriating civic information and communication technology: A critical study of Swedish ICT policy visions. *New Media & Society, 18*(4), 611–627. doi:10.1177/1461444806065659

OMG. (2002). *Meta Object Facility (MOF) Specification*. Retrieved June 30, 2009, from http://www.omg.org/docs/formal/02-04-03.pdf

OMG. (2006). *Ontology Definition Metamodel, OMG Adopted Specification*. Berlin: Springer.

Ong, A. (1996). Cultural citizenship as subject-making: Immigrants negotiate racial and cultural boundaries in the United States. *Current Anthropology, 37*, 737–762. doi:10.1086/204560

Online Taxes. *Olt* Retrieved April 29, 2009 from http://www.olt.com/main/home/default.asp

Oravec, J. (2005). Preventing E-Voting Hazards: The Role of Information Professionals. *Journal of Organizational and End User Computing, 17*, 1–4.

Orihuela, L., & Obi, T. (2007). E-government and e-governance: Towards a clarification in the usage of both concepts. In E-governance: A Global Perspective on a New Paradigm (pp. 26-32).

Ornstein, N., & Mann, T. (2000). *The permanent campaign and its future*. Washington, DC: American Enterprise Institute.

Orrego, C., & Araya, R. (2002). *Internet en Chile: Oportunidad para la Participación Ciudadana. Temas de Desarrollo Humano Sustentable Documento 7*. Santiago, Chile: PNUD.

Osaka, I. C. T. Industry (2008). *Ubiquitous City Osaka*. Online Publication. Retrieved April 28th, 2009, from http://www.ibpcosaka.or.jp/invest/e/environment/ict/ICT2007e.pdf

Osborne, D., & Gaebler, T. (1992). *Reinventing government*. Reading, MA: Addison-Wesley Publishing Company.

Oseguera, J. (2003). Democracia y tecnología. *Política Digital, 10*, 58–59.

Osimo, D. (2008). *Web 2.0 in Government. Why and How? JRC Scientific and Technical Reports.* Luxembourg: Institute for Prospective Technological Studies.

Pade, C., Mallinson, B., & Sewry, D. (2008). An Elaboration of Critical Success Factors for Rural ICT Project Sustainability in Developing Countries: Exploring the DWESA Case. *JITCAR, 10*(4), 32–55.

Page, B. I., & Shapiro, R. I. (1992). The Rational Public: Fifty Years of Trends in Americans' Policy Preferences. Chicago, I: University of Chicago Press.

Palmer, I. (2002). State of the world: e-Government implementation. Available from *Faulkner Information Services*. Retrieved from http://www.faulkner.com/products/faulknerlibrary/00018297.htm

Panopoluou, E., Tambouris, E., & Tarabanis, K. (2009). Eparticipation initiatives: How is Europe progressing? European Journal of ePractice, 7(March), 1-12.

Parameswaran, R., & Pisharodi, R. M. (2002). Assimilation effects in country image research. *International Marketing Review, 19*(3), 259–278. doi:10.1108/02651330210430695

Pardo, T., & Kumar, T. (2007). Interorganizational Information Integration: A Key Enabler for Digital Government. *Government Information Quarterly, 24*(4), 691–715. doi:10.1016/j.giq.2007.08.004

Parent, M., Vandebeek, C. A., & Gemino, A. C. (2005). Building Citizen Trust Through E-government. *Government Information Quarterly, 22*(4), 720–736. doi:10.1016/j.giq.2005.10.001

Parkinson, J. (2006). *Deliberating in the Real World: Problems of Legitimacy in Deliberative Democracy.* New York: Oxford University Press.

Parry, G., & Moyser, G. (1994). More participation, more democracy. In Beetham, D. (Ed.), *Defining and Measuring Democracy* (pp. 44–62). London: Sage.

PARSOL. (2004). *E-Planning and e-regulation by local authorities for local authorities.* Retrieved May 15, 2009, from http://www.planningportal.gov.uk/wps/portal/search?scope=204&langid=0

Partridge, H. (2004). Developing a Human Perspective to the Digital Divide in the Smart City. In *Proceedings of the "ALIA 2004, challenging ideas,* Queensland University of Tehcnology Brisbane, Australia.

Pasek, J., Kenski, K., Romer, D., & Jamieson, K. Hall. (2006). America's youth and community engagement: how use of mass media is related to civic activity and political awareness in 14- to 22- year-olds. *Communication Research, 33,* 115–135. doi:10.1177/0093650206287073

Patton, D., & Worthington, I. (1996). Developing local agenda 21: A case study of five local authorities in the UK. *Sustainable Development, 4*(1), 36–41. doi:10.1002/(SICI)1099-1719(199603)4:1<36::AID-SD32>3.0.CO;2-C

Pawley, L. (2008). Cultural citizenship. *Social Compass, 2*(2), 593–608.

Peristeras, T. (2006). Reengineering Public Administration through Semantic Technologies and a Reference Domain Ontology. In *Proceedings of the AAAI Spring Symposium Semantic Web Meets e-Government,* Menlo Park, CA: AAAI Press.

Perry-Barlow, J. (1996). A Declaration of the Independence of Cyberspace. Retrieved March 16th, 2009, from http://www.eff.org/ ~barlow/Declaration-Final.html

Pettigrew, A., Ferlie, E., & McKee, L. (1994). *Shaping Strategic Change.* London: Sage.

PEW Internet & American Life Project. (2006) *Total Online Activities Report.* Retrieved October 23, 2007, from http://www.pewinternet.org/trend/asp.

Pew Research Center. (2006). The cell phone challenge to survey research. Retrieved May 15, 2006, from http://people-press.org/reports/display.php3?ReportID=276

Pew Research Center. (2008). Internet's broader role in campaign 2008: Social networking and online videos take off. Retrieved May 11, 2008, from http://people-press.org/report/384/internets-broader-role-in-campaign-2008

Phillips, F. (2006, November 8). *By bonding with voters, Patrick withstood attacks; Rejected advice to fight back.* The Boston Globe, p.B7.

Phuangpornpitak, N., & Kumar, S. (2007). PV hybrid systems for rural electrification in Thailand. *Renew-*

able & Sustainable Energy Reviews, 11(7), 1530–1543. doi:10.1016/j.rser.2005.11.008

Pick, J. B., & Azari, R. (2008). Global digital divide: Influence of socioeconomic, governmental, and accessibility factors on information technology. *Information Technology for Development, 14*(2), 91–115. doi:10.1002/itdj.20095

Pickerill, J. (2001). Environmental internet activism in Britain [Electronic version]. *Peace Review, 13*(3), 365-370. Retrieved January 14, 2009, from http://shockandawe.us/archives/Environment/5107877.pdf

Pickerill, J. (2003). *Cyberprotest: Environmental activism online*. Manchester, UK: Manchester University Press.

Pieters, W., & Kiniry, J. (2005). Internet Voting Not Impossible. *Communications of the ACM, 48*, 12.

Pleace, N. (2008). E-government and the United Kingdom. In Nixon, P. & Koutrakou (eds) E-government in Europe:Rebooting the system. (pp. 34-56) London: Routledge

Polantz, P. (2008, April 21). Digital campaigns attract young voters. *CBS News*. Retrieved January 23, 2009, from http://www.cbsnews.com/stories /2008/04/21/politics/uwire/main4033484.shtml

Political attitudes in the 1996 and 2000 presidential elections. *Harvard Journal of Press/ Politics, 8*, 9-34.

Pollard, P. (2000). Geographical Information Services: A UK perspective on the development of interorganisational information services. *Information Infrastructure and Policy, 6*(4), 185–195.

Polleres, A., Lara, R., & Roman, D. (2004). *D4.2v01 Formal Comparison WSMO/OWL-S, DERI*. Retrieved June 30, 2009, from http://www.wsmo.org/2004/d4/d4.2/v0.1/20040315/

Porat, M. (1977). *The information economy*. Washington, DC: US Department of Commerce / Office of Telecommunications.

Portney, K. (2005). Civic Engagement and Sustainable Cities in the United States. *Public Administration Review, 65*(5), 579–591. doi:10.1111/j.1540-6210.2005.00485.x

Postmes, T., & Brunsting, S. (2002). Collective action in the age of the internet [Electronic version] [from http://psy.ex.ac.uk/~tpostmes/PDF/PostmesBrunstingSSCoRe.pdf]. *Social Science Computer Review, 20*(3), 290–301. Retrieved January 14, 2009.

Powell, M. K. (2002). *Remarks of the FCC Chairman at the Broadband Technology Summit*, U.S. Chamber of Commerce, Washington, D.C., April 30th. Retrieved March 9th, 2009, from http://www.fcc.gov/Speeches/Powell/2002/spmkp205.html

Prahalad, C. K., & Hammond, A. (2002). *Serving the World's Poor, Profitably*. Harvard, MA: Harvard Business Review.

Pratchett, L. (1999). New technologies and the modernization of local government: An analysis of biases and constraints. *Public Administration, 7*(4), 731–750. doi:10.1111/1467-9299.00177

Pressman, J., & Wildavsky, A. (1984). *Implementation* (3rd ed.). London: University of Berkeley.

Prieto-Martin, P. (2005). *Virtual environments for citizen participation*. Retrieved December 15, 2008, from, http://www.e-participa.org/en/files/e_Participa.VirtualEnvironmentsForCitizenParticipation.doc.

Prior, M. (2005). News vs. Entertainment: How Increasing Media Choice Widens Gaps in Political Knowledge and Turnout. *American Journal of Political Science, 49*(3), 577–592. doi:10.1111/j.1540-5907.2005.00143.x

Prior, M. (2007). *Post-Broadcast Democracy: How Media Choice Increases Inequality in Political Involvement and Polarizes Elections*. New York: Cambridge University Press.

Public Administration Select Committee. (2001). *6th Report Innovations in Citizen Participation*. London: HMSO.

Putnam, R. (1993). *Making democracy work*. Princeton, NJ: Princeton University Press.

Putnam, R. D. (2000). *Bowling alone: The collapse and revival of American community*. New York: Simon & Schuster.

Putnam, R. D. (2002). *Democracies in flux: The evolution of social capital in contemporary society.* Oxford, UK: Oxford University Press.

Rabotnikof, N. (2005). *En busca de un lugar común.* México: UNAM.

Rallings, C., & Thrasher, M. (2007). The Turnout "Gap" and the Costs of Voting. *Public Choice, 131,* 333–344. doi:10.1007/s11127-006-9118-9

Ramadan-Mamata, M., Lerberghe, F., & Best. (2005). *European eDemocracy Award Report.* Brussels, Belgium: POLITECH Institute.

Ramírez, A. (2001). *Modernización de la Gestión Pública. El caso Chileno (1994-2000). Estudio de Caso 58.* Santiago: Departamento de Ingeniería Industrial, Universidad de Chile.

Ranerup, A. (1999). Internet-enabled applications for local government democratization: Contradictions of the Swedish experience, en Heeks, R. (Ed.) Reinventing Government in the Information Age. London: Rutledge.

Rawls, J. (1971). *A Theory of Justice.* Cambridge, MA: Harvard University Press.

Rawls, J. (2005). *Political Liberalism.* New York: Columbia University Press.

Rech, A. (2005). E-Citizen: Why Waiting for e-Governments? en Böhlen, Gamper, Polasek & Wimmer (Eds.) *E-Government: Towards Electronic Democracy.* International Conference, TCGOV2005. Italia: Springer.

Reddick, C. (2005). Citizen interaction with e-government: From the streets to servers? *Government Information Quarterly, 22,* 38–57. doi:10.1016/j.giq.2004.10.003

Report, U. N. (2005). Global E-Government Readiness Report 2005: From E-Government to E-Inclusion. New York: Department of Economic and Social Affairs, Division for Public Administration and Development Management, the United Nations.

Rezende, P. A. D. (2002). *Voto Eletrônico Amplia Chances de Fraude.* Folha de São Paulo.

Riley, D. (1992). Citizenship and the welfare state. In Allan, J., Braham, P., & Lewis, P. (Eds.), *Political and economic forms of modernity.* Cambridge: Polity Press.

Riley, T. B. (2003). *E-Government vs. E-Governance: Examining the Differences in a Changing Public Sector Climate (No. 4).* Ottawa, Canada: Common Wealth Centre for E-Governance.

Rivera, E. (2003). *Nueva Economía, Gobierno Electrónico y Reforma del Estado.* Santiago, Chile: Universitaria.

Rivera, E. (2006). Un problema de innovación institucional. *Política Digital, 27,* 60–61.

Rivera, J. (2001). e-gobierno: ¿estrategia política o tecnológica? *Política Digital, 1,* 24–29.

Roberts, A. S. (2000). Less Government, More Secrecy: Reinvention and the Weakening Law. *Public Administration Review, 60*(4), 308–320. doi:10.1111/0033-3352.00093

Roberts, N. (2004). Public deliberation in an age of direct citizen participation. *American Review of Public Administration, 34*(1), 315–353. doi:10.1177/0275074004269288

Robins, M. D., Simonsen, B., & Feldman, B. (2008). Citizens and resource allocation: Improving decision making with interactive web-based citizen participation. *Public Administration Review, 68*(3), 564–575. doi:10.1111/j.1540-6210.2008.00891.x

Robison, K. K., & Crenshaw, E. M. (2002). Post-industrial transformations and cyber-space: A cross-national analysis of Internet development. *Social Science Research, 31*(3), 334–363. doi:10.1016/S0049-089X(02)00004-2

Robson, C. (2002). *Real World Research* (2nd ed.). Oxford, UK: Blackwell.

Rocheleau, B. (2003). Politics, Accountability and Governmental Information Systems en Garson, D. (ed.), Public Information Technology: Policy and Management Issues. Hershey, PA: Idea Group Publishing.

Rodrigues Filho, J. (2008). E-Voting in Brazil – Reinforcing institutions while diminishing citizenship. 3rd International Conference, Gesellschaft für Informatik and E-Voting. August 6-, Bregenz, Austria.

Rodrigues Filho, J., & Gomes, N. P. (2008). E-Voting in Brazil – Exacerbating alienation and the digital divide. In Santap, S. M. (Ed.), *E-Democracy – Concepts and Practice*. Hyderabad, India: IFCAI Books.

Rodrigues Filho, J., & Santos Junior, J. R. (2009). Local e-government in Brazil – Poor interaction and local politics as usual. In Reddick, C. G. (Ed.), *Handbook of research on strategies for local e-government adoption and implementation – comparative studies*. Hershey, PA: IGI Global.

Roeder, S. Poppenborg, Michaelis, Märker, & Salz. (2005). Public Budget Dialogue: An innovative approach to e-Participation, en Böhlen, Gamper, Polasek & Wimmer (Eds.) *E-Government: Towards Electronic Democracy*. International Conference, TCGOV2005. Italia: Springer.

Rogers, E. (1995). *Diffusion of innovations* (4th ed.). New York: Routledge.

Rogers, E. (2003). *Diffusion of Innovations* (5th ed.). New York: Free Press.

Ronaghan, S. (2002). Benchmarking E-government: A Global Perspective. New York: Division for Public Economics and Public Administration, the United Nations.

Rose, J., Grönlund, A., & Andersen, K. (2007). Introduction. In Advic, Anders et al (Eds.) Understanding eParticipation. Contemporary PhD eParticipation Research in Europe (pp. 1-15).Without city: Demo-Net.

Rose, R. (2005). A Global Diffusion Model of e-Governance. *Journal of Public Policy*, 25(1), 5–27. doi:10.1017/S0143814X05000279

Rose, R. (2005). *Learning from Comparative Public Policy*. London: Routledge.

Rowntree Charitable Trust and the Rowntree Reform Trust (RFT). (2006). *Power to the People: An independent enquiry into Britain's democracy*. London: The Power Inquiry.

Rucht, D. (2004). The quadruple 'A. In van de Donk, W., Loader, B. D., Nixon, P. G., & Rucht, D. (Eds.), *Cyberprotest: New Media, Citizens and Social Movements* (pp. 29–56). London: Routledge.

Rudd, K. (2009) PM's Blog. *Prime Minister of Australia*. Retrieved July 24, 2009, from http://pm.gov.au/PM_Connect/PMs_Blog

Sacramento Area Council of Governments (SACOG) and Valley Vision. (2005). *Sacramento region blue print: Preferred blueprint alternative*. Retrieved, March 17, 2008, from http://www.sacregionblueprint.org/sacregionblueprint/

Sæbo, Ø., & Nilsen, H. (2004). The support for different democracy models by the use of a web-based discussion board, en Traunmüller, R. (ed.) *Electronic Government: Third International Conference, EGOV2004*. España: Springer.

Sager, T. (1990). *Communicate or calculate*. Stockholm: NORDPLAN.

Sager, T. (1994). Communicative planning theory. Avebury,UK: Aldershot.

Sairamesh, J., Lee, A., & Anania, L. (2004, February). Information Cities. *Communications of the ACM*, 47(2).

Salamon, L. M., & Elliott, O. V. (2002). *The tools of government: A guide to the new governance*. Oxford, UK: Oxford University Press.

Saltzer, J. H., Reed, D. P., & Clark, D. D. (1984). End-To-End Arguments in System Design. *ACM Transactions on Computer Systems*, 2(4), 277–288. doi:10.1145/357401.357402

Saltzstein, A. L. (2003). *Governing American urban areas*. Belmont, CA: Wadsworth Thomson Learning.

Sampedro, V. (2004). The alternative movement and its media strategies. In Polet, F. (Ed.), *Globalizing resistance: The state of struggle* (pp. 243–257). London: Pluto Press.

Sanchez, O. A. (2003). O poder burocrático e o controle da informação. Lua nova. *Revista de Cultura e Política*, 58, 89–119.

Sanoff, H. (2000). *Community participation methods in design and planning*. New York: John Wiley & Sons, Inc.

Saward, M. (2000). *Democratic Innovation: Deliberation, representation and association*. London: Routledge.

Scarce, R. (2006). Eco-Warriors: Understanding the radical environmental movement (Updated ed.). Walnut Creek, CA: Left Coast Press.

Schaupp, L., & Carter, L. (2005). E-voting: From Apathy to Adoption. *Journal of Enterprise Information Management, 18*, 586–601. doi:10.1108/17410390510624025

Schech, S. (2002). Wired for change: The links between ICTs and development discourses. *Journal of International Development, 14*(1), 13–23. doi:10.1002/jid.870

Schein, E. (2004). *Organisational Culture and Leadership*. San Francisco: Wiley and Son.

Schumpeter, J. (1976). *Capitalism, socialism and democracy*. New York: Harper.

Schweighofer, E., Rauber, A., & Dittenbach, M. (2001). Automatic text representation, classification and labeling in European law. In *Proceedings of the 8th international conference on Artificial intelligence and law* (pp. 78-87). New York: ACM.

Schwester, R. (2009). Examining the barriers to e-government adoption. *Electronic Journal of e-government, 7*(1), 113-122. Retrieved July 25, 2009, from http://www.ejeg.com/volume-7/vol7-iss1/schwester.pdf

Scott, J. (2006). "E" the people: Do U.S. Municipal Government Web Sites Support Public Involvement? *Public Administration Review, 66*(3), 341–353. doi:10.1111/j.1540-6210.2006.00593.x

Scott, J. K. (2006). "E" the People: Do U.S. Municipal Government Web Sites Support Public Involvement? *Public Administration Review, 66*(3), 341–353. doi:10.1111/j.1540-6210.2006.00593.x

Scully, D. (2004). (Manuscript submitted for publication). E-democracy [Institute of Technology Tallaght. Irlanda.]. *Evolution; International Journal of Organic Evolution*.

Sears, D. O. (1983). The persistence of early political predispositions: The roles of attitude object and life stage. In Wheeler, L., & Shaver, P. (Eds.), *Review of personality and social psychology* (*Vol. 4*, pp. 79–116). Beverly Hills, CA: Sage.

Sears, D. O. (1986). College sophomores in the laboratory: influence of a narrow data base on social psychologys view of human nature. *Journal of Personality and Social Psychology, 51*, 515–530. doi:10.1037/0022-3514.51.3.515

Seeger, C. J. (2004). *VaSS Builder: A customizable Internet tool for community planning and design participation*. Retrieved May 11, 2009, from http://www.kolleg.loel.hs-anhalt.de/studiengaenge/mla/mla_fl/conf/pdf/conf2004/41_seeger-c.pdf

SEGPRES (Secretaría General de la Presidencia). (2006a). *Reforma del Estado en Chile: 2000-2006*. Santiago, Chile: SEGPRES.

SEGPRES (Secretaría General de la Presidencia). (2006b). *Gobierno Electrónico en Chile. El Estado del Arte II*. Santiago, Chile: SEGPRES.

Seifert, J. W. (2003). *A primer on e-government: sectors, stages, opportunities and challenges of online governance. Congressional research service*. Retrieved April 24, 2009, from http://www.fas.org/sgp/crs/rl31057.pdf

Sein, M. K., & Harindranath, G. (2004). Conceptualizing the ICT Artifact: Toward Understanding the Role of ICT in National Development. *The Information Society, 20*, 15–24. doi:10.1080/01972240490269942

Seldon, A. (2001). *The Blair Effect*. London: Little, Brown and Company.

Selwyn, N. (2004). Reconsidering political and popular understandings of the digital divide. *New Media & Society, 6*(3), 341–362. doi:10.1177/1461444804042519

Selznick, P. (1949). *TVA and the grass roots; a study in the sociology of formal organization*. Berkeley, CA: Univ. of California Press.

Serour, M., & Henderson-Sellers, B. (2002). The Role of Organisational Culture on the Adoption and Diffusion of Software Engineering Process: An Empirical Study. In

Bunker, D., Wilson. D., and Elliot, S. (Eds) The Adoption and Diffusion in an IT environment of critical change (pp. 76-89) Australia: Pearson

Servon, L. J. (2002). *Bridging the digital divide: Technology, community, and public policy.* Malden, MA: Wiley-Blackwell. doi:10.1002/9780470773529

Setälä, M., & Grönlund, K. (2006). Parliamentary Websites: Theoretical and Comparative Perspectives. *Information Polity, 11*(2), 149–162.

Shafiq, O., Moran, M., Cimpian, E., Mocan, A., Zaremba, M., & Fensel, D. (2007, May 13-19). Investigating Semantic Web Service Execution Environments: A Comparison between WSMX and OWL-S Tools. In *Proceedings of the Second international Conference on internet and Web Applications and Services ICIW.*, Washington, DC: IEEE Computer Society.

Shah, D. V., Cho, J., Eveland, W. P. Jr, & Kwak, N. (2005). Information and expression in a digital age: modeling internet effects on civic participation. *Communication Research, 32*, 531–565. doi:10.1177/0093650205279209

Shelley, M., Thrane, L., & Shulman, S. (2006). Lost in cyberspace: barriers to bridging the digital divide in cyberspace. *International Journal of Internet and Enterprise Management, 4*(3), 228–243. doi:10.1504/IJIEM.2006.010916

Shiffer, M. J. (1992). Towards a collaborative planning system. *Environment and Planning B, 19*(6), 709–722. doi:10.1068/b190709

Shirky, C. (2002, April 6). Communities, Audiences, and Scale. *Clay Shirky's Writings about the Internet: Economics & Culture, Media & Community, Open Source.* Retrieved February 24, 2007, from http://shirky.com/writings/community_scale.html

Shulman, S. W. (2005). eRulemaking: Issues in Current Research and Practice. *International Journal of Public Administration, 28*, 621–641. doi:10.1081/PAD-200064221

Siau, K., & Long, Y. (2006). Using Social Development Lenses to Understand E-Government Development. *Journal of Global Information Management, 14*(1), 47–62.

Sieber, R. (2006). Public participation geographic information systems: A literature review and framework. *Annals of the American Association of Geographers, 96*(3), 491–507. doi:10.1111/j.1467-8306.2006.00702.x

Siedentop, L. (2000). *Democracy in Europe.* London: Allen Lane.

Silva, P. (2004). Doing Politics in a Depoliticised Society: Social Change and Political Deactivation in Chile. *Bulletin of Latin American Research, 23*(1), 63–78. doi:10.1111/j.1470-9856.2004.00096.x

Silva, P., & Cleuren, H. (2009 in press). Assessing Participatory Democracy in Brazil and Chile: An Introduction. In Silva, P., & Cleuren, H. (Eds.), *Widening Democracy. Citizens and Participatory Schemes in Brazil and Chile.* Leiden, The Netherlands: Brill.

Simkins, C. (2008, September 18). Young voters divided over whether they will vote in U S presidential election. *Voice of America.* Retrieved January 23, 2009, from http://www.voanews.com/english/archive/2008-09/2008-09-18-voa27.cfm

Simon, K. (2005). The value of open standards and open-source software in government environments. *IBM Systems Journal, 44*(2), 227–238.

Singh, A. K., & Sahu, R. (2008). Integrating Internet, telephones, and call centers for delivering better quality e-governance to all citizens. *Government Information Quarterly, 25*, 477–490. doi:10.1016/j.giq.2007.01.001

Skocpol, T. (1993). The Potential Autonomy of the State. In Olsen, M., & Marger, M. (Eds.), *Power in Modern Societies* (pp. 306–313). Oxford, UK: Westview Press.

Smith, B. (2008). A Quick Guide to GPLv3. Retrieved April 10, 2009, from http://www.gnu.org/licenses/quickguide-gplv3.html

Smith, D., & Wright, S. (1999). *Whose Europe? The turn towards Democracy.* Oxford, UK: Blackwell Publishers.

Smith, G. (2000). Toward deliberative Institutions, en Saward, M. (ed.) Democratic Innovation. London: Routledge.

Snellen, I. (2002). Electronic governance: Implications for citizens, politicians and public servants. *International Review of Administrative Sciences, 68*(2), 183–198. doi:10.1177/0020852302682002

Snellen, I. (2005). E-Government: A Challenge for Public Management. In Ferlie, E., Lynn, L. E. Jr, & Pollitt, C. (Eds.), *The Oxford Handbook of Public Management* (pp. 398–421). Oxford, UK: Oxford University Press.

Snellen, I. T. M. (2002). Electronic governance: implications for citizens, politicians and public servants. *International Review of Administrative Sciences, 68*(2), 183–198. doi:10.1177/0020852302682002

Snow, N. (2007). *The arrogance of American power: What U.S. leaders are doing wrong and why it's our duty to dissent*. Oxford, U.K.: Rowman & Littlefield Publishers.

Snow, N. (2008). International exchanges and the U.S. image. *The Annals of the American Academy of Political and Social Science, 616*(1), 198–222. doi:10.1177/0002716207311864

Som - State of Michigan. (n.d.). *Som*. Retrieved April 29, 2009, from http://www.michigan.gov/

Sorgaard, P. (2004). Co-ordination of e-government: Between politics and pragmatics. In Damsgaard, J., & Henriksen, H. (Eds.), *Networked Information Technologies Diffusion and Adoption*. London: Kluwer.

Sotelo, A. (2006). *México: un gobierno digital en expansión*. México: Abraham Sotelo.

Southern California Association of Governments [SCAG]. (2004). *Southern California compass: Growth Vision Report*. Retrieved September 28, 2008, from http://www.socalcompass.org//about/index.html

Sproull, L., & Patterson, J. (2004, February). Making Information Cities Livable. *Communications of the ACM, 49*(2).

Sreekumar, T. T. (2007). Cyber kiosks and dilemmas of social inclusion in rural India. *Media Culture & Society, 29*(6), 869–889. doi:10.1177/0163443707081692

Srivastava, S. C., & Teo, T. S. H. (2007). E-Government Payoffs: Evidence from Cross-Country Data. *Journal of Global Information Management, 15*(4), 20–40.

St., Haase, B., Sure, P., & Voelker, Y. (2005). *J. D.6.6.1 Report on the integration of ML, HLT and OM*. Retrieved June 30, 2009, from http://www.sti-innsbruck.at/fileadmin/documents/deliverables/Sekt/sekt-d-6-6-1-Int._ML__HLT__OM.pdf

Starr, P. (2004). *The Creation of the Media: Political Origins of Modern Communication*. New York: Basic Books.

State of Michigan Department of Treasury. (n.d.). *Michigan taxes*. Retrieved April 29, 2009, from http://www.michigan.gov/taxes

State of Michigan Secretary of State. (n.d.). *License plate registration renewals*. Retrieved April 29, 2009 from http://www.michigan.gov/sos/0,1607,7-127-1640_14837-133039--,00.html. (n.d.). *Taxact*. Retrieved April 29, 2009, from https://www.taxactonline.com/

Statistical Manual, U. N. (2009). *Statistical Manual*. Retrieved April 30, 2009, from http://go.worldbank.org/USGWXVXW40

Steiner, P. (1993, July 5). Online No One Knows You're a Dog (pp 61). *The New Yorker*.

Steinmann, R., Krek, A., & Blaschke, T. (2004). Analysis of online GIS participatory applications with respect to the differences between the U.S. and Europe. *Paper Published in the Proceedings of Urban Data Management Symposium*, Chioggia, Italy.

Steinmueller, W. (2001). ICTs and the possibilities for leapfrogging by developing countries. *International Labour Review, 140*(2), 193–210. doi:10.1111/j.1564-913X.2001.tb00220.x

Stevenson, N. (2003). *Cultural citizenship: Cosmopolitan questions*. Maidenhead, UK: Open University Press.

Stirk, P. M. (1996). *A History of European Integration Since 1914*. New York: Pinter.

Stromer-Galley, J. (2000). On-line interaction and why candidates avoid it. *The Journal of Communication, 50*(4), 111–132. doi:10.1111/j.1460-2466.2000.tb02865.x

Sunikka, M. (2006). *Policies for improving energy efficiency if the European Housing Stock*. Amsterdam: IOS Press.

Sunstein, C. (2001). *Republic.com*. Princeton, NJ: Princeton University Press.

Survey, U. N. (2003). U.N. Global E-government Survey 2003. New York: Department of Economic and Social Affairs and the Civic Research Group, the United Nations.

Susskind, L., & Cruikshank, J. (1987). *Breaking the impasse: Consensual approaches to resolving public disputes*. New York: Basic Books.

Takao, Y. (2004). Democratic Renewal by 'Digital' Local Government in Japan. *Pacific Affairs, 77*(2), 237–262.

Talen, E. (2000). Bottom-up GIS: A new a tool for individual and group expression in participatory planning. *Journal of the American Planning Association. American Planning Association, 66*(3), 491–807.

Tanner, J. (2005). *Estonians Cast Online Ballots in World's First Nationwide Internet Election*, The Associated Press. Retreived (n.d.), from http://www.abcnews.go.com/Technology/wireStory?id=1213426

Tanner, L. (2008a, September 2) The Government Gets Blogging. *The Age*. Retrieved March 6, 2009, from http://blogs.theage.com.au/business/lindsaytanner/2008/09/02/thegovernment.html

Tanner, L. (2008b, December 8) Minister Tanner's Welcome. *Digital Economy*. Retrieved March 6, 2009, from http://www.dbcde.gov.au/communications_for_business/industry_development/digital_economy/future_directions_blog/topics/minister_tanners_welcome

Tassabehji, R., Elliman, T., & Mellor, J. (2007). Generating Citizen Trust in E-Government Security: Challenging Perceptions. *International Journal of Cases on Electronic Commerce, 3*(3), 1–17.

Taxslayer.com. (n.d.). *Taxslayer*. Retrieved April 29, 2009, from http://www.taxslayer.com/

Taylor, A. J., & Burt, T. E. (2001). Pluralising tele-democracy: Not-for profits in the democratic polity. In Prins, J. E. J. (Ed.), *Designing e-government* (pp. 29–39). Hague, The Netherlands: Kluwer Law International.

Taylor, B. R. (1995). *Ecological resistance movements: The global emergence of radical and popular environmentalism*. Albany, NY: State University of New York Press.

Teicher, J., Hughes, O., & Dow, N. (2002). E-government: a new route to public sector quality. *Managing Service Quality, 12*(6), 384–393. doi:10.1108/09604520210451867

Teivainen, T. (2002). *Enter Economism Exit Politics: Experts, economic policy and the damage to democracy*. London: Zed Books Ltd.

The Brennan Center of the NYU School of Law. (2006). *Brennan Center Report*. New York: NYU.

The Caltech/MIT Voting Technology Project. (2001). Residual votes attributable to technology – An assessment of the reliability of existing voting equipment. http://www.hss.caltech.edu/~voting/CalTech_MIT_Report_Version2.pdf. (Accessed: 15.05.2009).

The Electoral Commission. (2003) *The Shape of Elections to come* London: Electoral Commission Electoral Commission (2005). *Election Results*. Retrieved November 30, from htpp://www.electoralcommission.org.uk/election-data

The EnviroLink Network. (n.d.). *EnviroLink*. Retrieved January 31, 2008, from http://envirolink.org/

The Global e-policy and e-governance institute & Rutgers University e-governance institute. (2003). *Assessing websites and measuring e-government index among 100 world cities*. Study sponsored by division of public administration and development, department of economic and social affairs, United Nations.

The Global e-policy and e-governance institute & Rutgers University e-governance institute. (2005). *Assessing websites and measuring e-government index among*

100 world cities. Study sponsored by division of public administration and development, department of economic and social affairs, United Nations.

The Guardian. (2006). *Ministers to put patients' details on central database despite objections*. Retrieved July 28, 2008, from http://society.guardian.co.uk/e-public/story/0,1937301,00.html

The real digital divide. (2005, March 12). The real digital divide; Technology and development. *The Economist.*

The Register. (2006). *Doctors attack the NHS IT system.* Retrieved July 28, 2008, from: http://www.theregister.co.uk/2006/07/19/patient_confidentiality_risk/

Therivel, R. (2004). *Sustainable Urban Environment – Metrics, Models and Toolkits: Analysis of sustainability/social tools*, Oxford, North Hinksey Lane. Retrieved (n.d.), from http://download.sue-mot.org/soctooleval.pdf

Thomas, J. (1995). *Public Participation in public decisions*. San Francisco: Jossey-Bass Publishers.

Thomas, J. C. (1990). Public Involvement in Public Management: Adapting and Testing a Borrowed Theory. *Public Administration Review, 50*(4), 435–445. doi:10.2307/977079

Thomas, J. C. (1993). Public Involvement and Government Effectiveness: A Decision-Making Model for Public Managers. *Administration & Society, 24*(4), 444–469. doi:10.1177/009539979302400402

Thomas, J. C. (1995). *Public Participation in Public Decisions: New Skills and Strategies for Public Managers.* New York: Jossey-Bass.

Thomas, J. C., & Streib, G. (2003). The new face of government: citizen-initiated contacts in the era of e-government. *Journal of Public Administration Research & Theory: J-PART, 13*(1), 83 (19).

Thorburn, D., & Jenkins, H. (2003). The Digital Revolution, the Informed Citizen, and the Culture of Democracy. In Thorburn, D., & Jenkins, H. (Eds.), *Democracy and New Media*. Cambridge, MA: MIT Press.

Toffler, A. (1980). *The third wave* (1st ed.). New York: Morrow.

Tolbert, C. J., & McNeal, R. S. (2003). Unraveling the effects of the Internet on political participation. *Political Research Quarterly, 56*, 175–185.

Toledo Llancaqueo, V. (2007). Prima Ratio. Movilización Mapuche y Política Penal. Los Marcos de la Política Indígena en Chile 1990-2007. *OSAL, VIII*(22), 253–293.

Torres, L., Pina, V., & Acerete, B. (2005). E-government developments on delivering public services among EU cities. *Government Information Quarterly, 22*, 217–238. doi:10.1016/j.giq.2005.02.004

Torres, L., Pina, V., & Ryo, S. (2005). E-government and the transformation of public services in EU countries. *Online Information Review, 29*(5), 531–553. doi:10.1108/14684520510628918

Townsend, A. (2004, December 7). Seoul: Birth of a Broadband Metropolis. *Environment and Planning B, 34*(3), 396–413.

Transparência Brasil. (2006). *Compra de votos nas eleições de 2006, Corrupção e desempenho administrativo*. São Paulo. Retrieved May 16, 2009, from http://www.transparencia.org.br/docs/compravotos2006.pdf

Trippi, J. (2004). *The revolution will not be televised: Democracy, the Internet, and the overthrow of everything.* New York: HaperCollins.

Trippi, J. (2005). *The Revolution Will Not Be Televised: Democracy, the Internet, and the Overthrow of Everything.* New York: Regan Books.

Trkman, P., & Turk, T. (2009). A conceptual model for the development of broadband and e-government. *Government Information Quarterly, 26*, 416–424. doi:10.1016/j.giq.2008.11.005

Tuch, H. N. (1990). *Communicating with the world: U.S. public diplomacy overseas.* New York: St. Martin's Press.

Tulloch, D. L., & Shapiro, T. (2003). The intersection of data access and public participation: Impacting GIS users' success? *URISA Journal, 15*(2), 55–60.

Turbotax online. (n.d.). *Turbotax*. Retrieved April 29, 2009, from http://turbotax.intuit.com/

Turner, B. S. (2001). The erosion of citizenship. *The British Journal of Sociology, 52*(2), 189–209. doi:10.1080/00071310120044944

Tuuva-Hongisto, S., & Talsi, N. (2006, March 15-17). *Citizens in fragmented technology policy.* International ProACT conference. Tampere, Finland.

U.N. (2008). UN E-Government Survey 2008: From E-Government to Connected Governance. New York: Department of Economic and Social Affairs, Division for Public Administration and Development Management, the United Nations.

U.S. Department of State. (1987). *Dictionary of international relations terms.* Washington, DC: U.S. Department of State.

U.S. Dept of Ed. (2002). Adult Literacy in America GPO No. 065-000-00588-3. Washington, DC: Education Information Branch, Office of Educational Research and Improvement, U.S. Department of Education.

UN (United Nations). (2003). *World Public Sector Report 2003. E-Government at the Crossroads.* New York: United Nations.

UN (United Nations). (2005). *Global E-Government Readiness Report 2005. From E-Government to E-Inclusion.* New York: United Nations.

UN (United Nations). (2008). *2008 Global E-government Readiness Report. From E-Government to Connected Governance.* New York: United Nations.

UN ESCAP. (2007). *Integration of information and communication technologies into national development plans for Central Asian states.* Bangkok, Thailand: United Nations.

UNCTAD. (2002). Least developed countries at a glance. New York: the Information Communication Technology Task Force, the United Nations.

UNESCO. (2006). *Literacy for Life.* UNESCO Publishing.

UNESCO. (2008). *International Literacy Statistics: A Review of Concepts, Methodology and Current Data.* UNESCO Institute of Statistics.

UNESCO. (2009). *Literacy.* Retrieved July 29, 2009, from http://www.unesco.org/en/literacy

United Nation. (2007). *Indicators of Sustainable Development: Guidelines and Methodologies.* New York: United Nations publications. Retrieved July 28, 2009, from http://www.un.org/esa/sustdev/natlinfo/indicators/guidelines.pdf

United Nations Public Administration Network (UNPAN). (2005). *UN global e-government readiness report – From e-government to e-inclusion. Division for Public Administration and Development Management. Department of Economic and Social Affairs.* New York: United Nations.

United Nations. (2008). *UN E-Government Survey – From e-Government to Connected Government. United Nations.* Retrieved 2008, from http://unpan1.un.org/intradoc/groups/public/documents/UN/UNPAN028607.pdf

US Supreme Court. (1997). Reno vs. ACLU. (U.S. 521). Washington, DC: U.S. Government Printing Office.

Van Aelst, P., & Walgrave, S. (2004). New media, new movement? The role of the internet in shaping the 'anti-globalization' movement. In van de Donk, W., Loader, B. D., Nixon, P. G., & Rucht, D. (Eds.), *Cyberprotest: New Media, Citizens and Social Movements* (pp. 97–122). London: Routledge.

Van Aerschot, L., Kunz, J., Haglund, E., et al. (2007). *Cross-cultural analysis on barriers and incentives for lsgs' use of e-government.* e-government for low socio-economic status groups (elost). Retrieved July 25, 2009 from http://www.elost.org/d5-2.pdf

Van Bastelaer, B. (1998, October 29-30) Digital Cities and transferability of results. In *Proceedings of the 4th EDC Conference on Digital Cities,* Salzburg, Germany (pp. 61-70).

Van den Besselaar & P., Beckers, D. (1998) Demographics and Sociographics of the digital city. In *Community Computing and Support Systems* (pp. 108-124), Berlin, Germany: Springer Verlag.

Van der Graft, P., & Svensson, J. (2006). Explaining e-Democracy Development. *Information Policy, 11*, 123.

van Dijk, J. (2000). Widening information gaps and policies of prevention. In Digital democracy: Issues of theory and practice, (pp. 166-183).

van Dijk, J. (2005). *The deepening divide: Inequality in the information society*. London, UK: Sage Publications.

Van Raaij, F., & Verhallen, T. (1983). A behavioral model of residential energy use. *Journal of Economic Psychology, 3*(1), 39–63. doi:10.1016/0167-4870(83)90057-0

Vatikiotis, P. (2005). Communication theory and alternative media. *Westminster Papers in Communication and Culture, 2*(1), 4–29.

Venkatesh, V., Morris, M., Davis, G., & Davis, F. (2003). User Acceptance of Information Technology: Toward a Unified View. *Management Information Systems Quarterly, 27*, 425–478.

Verba, S., Schlozman, K., & Brady, H. (1995). *Voice and Equality*. Cambridge, MA: Harvard University Press.

Vergnes, B. (2001). Information technology and sustainability. *The OECD Observer. Organisation for Economic Co-Operation and Development, 226/227*, 16–17.

Volken, T. (2002). Elements of trust: The cultural dimension of Internet diffusion revisited. *Electronic Journal of Sociology, 6*(4), 1–20.

Vonk, G., Geertman, S., & Schot, R. (2005). Bottlenecks blocking the widespread usage of planning support systems. *Environment & Planning A, 37*(5), 909–924. doi:10.1068/a3712

voor Regeringsbeleid. W. R. (2005). Vertrouwen in de buurt. Amsterdam: University Press.

W3C (2004). *OWL Web Ontology Language Overview*. Retrieved June 30, 2009, from http://www.w3.org/TR/owl-features/

Wang, L., & Wu, H. (2001). *A Framework of Integrating digital city and Eco-city. School of Business, Hubei University, Wuhan, China*. Retrieved March, 2005, from www.hku.hk/cupem/asiagis/fall03/Full_Paper/Wang_Lu.pdf

Wang, S., Archer, N., & Zheng, W. (2006). An Exploratory Study of Electronic Marketplace Adoption: A Multiple Perspective View. *Electronic Markets, 16*, 337. doi:10.1080/10196780600999775

Wang, T. (2008, September 4-6). *Internet access as a social right: Implications for social citizenship*. Annual academic conference of the International Sociological Association's research committee on poverty, social welfare and social policy (RC19). Stockholm, Sweeden.

Wang, X., Vitvar, T., Peristeras, V., Mocan, A., Goudos, S., & Tarabanis, K. (2007) WSMO-PA: Formal Specification of Public Administration Service Model on Semantic Web Service Ontology. In *Proceedings of the 40th Hawaii International Conference on System Sciences, HICSS*, (pp. 1-10)

Warnecke, L., Beattie, J., Cheryl, K., Lyday, W., & French, S. (1998). *Geographic information technology in cities and counties: A nationwide assessment*. Washington, DC: American Forests.

Warschauer, M. (2003). *Technology and social inclusión: Rethinking the digital divide*. Cambridge, MA: MIT Press.

Wattenberg, M. P. (2007). *Is voting for young people?* New York: Pearson Longman.

Weber, L. M., Loumakis, A., & Bergman, J. (2003). Who participates and why?: an analysis of citizens on the Internet and the mass public. *Social Science Computer Review, 21*, 26–42. doi:10.1177/0894439302238969

Webler, T., & O'Renn, O. (1995). A Brief Primer on Public Participation: Philosophy and Practice. In *Fairness and competence in citizen participation: evaluating models for environmental discourse*. Boston: Kluwer Academic.

Weeks, E. C. (2000). The Practice of Deliberative Democracy: Results from Four Large-Scale Trials. *Public Administration Review, 60*(4), 360–372. doi:10.1111/0033-3352.00098

Wei Phang, C., & Kankanhalli, A. (2007). Promoting citizen participation via digital government. In Anttiroiko, A., & Malkia, M. (Eds.), *Encyclopedia of Digital Government* (pp. 1352–1357). Hershey, PA: Idea Group Inc.

Weisenmiller, M. (2008, February 13). Election outcome may hinge on youth vote. *IPS: Inter Press Service*. Retrieved January 23, 2009, from http://www.ipsnews.net/news.asp?idnews=41190

Welch, E. W., & Pandey, S. K. (2007). E-Government and Bureaucracy: Toward a Better Understanding of Intranet Implementation and Its Effect on Red Tape. *Journal of Public Administration: Research and Theory, 17*(3), 379–404. doi:10.1093/jopart/mul013

Wenger, E. (1998). *Communities of practice: Learning, meaning, and identity.* Cambridge, UK: Cambridge University Press.

Wenk, E. J. (1986). *Tradeoffs: Imperatives of Choice in a high-tech world.* Baltimore: The John Hopkins University Press.

Werrakkody, V., & Dhillon, G. (2009). From eGovernment to TGovernment. In Riddeck, C. (Ed.), *Research Strategies for eGovernment Service Adoption.* Hershey, PA: Idea Group Publishing.

West, D. M. (2005) *State and Federal government in the United States, Providence, RI: Center for Public Policy, Brown University.* Retrieved September 30, 2006, from http://www.insidepolitics.org/egovt05us.pdf

West, D. M. (2005). *Digital government: Technology and public sector performance.* Princeton, NJ: Princeton University Press.

West, D. M. (2008). *Improving technology utilization in electronic government around the world.* Washington, DC: Brookings Institute.

West, D. M. (2008). *State and federal electronic government in the united states.* Washingtong, DC: The Brookings Institution.

Whitten, A., & Tygar, J. (1999). Why Johnny Can't Encrypt. In the *Proceedings of the 8th USENIX Security Symposium* (pp 169-184). Washington, DC.

Widmayer, P. (1999). Building Digital Metropolis: Chicago's Future Networks. *IT Professional, 1*(4), 40–46. doi:10.1109/6294.781624

Wikipedia (2009). *The Definition of the Ubiquitous City.* Retrieved April 28th, 2009, from http://en.wikipedia.org/wiki/Ubiquitous_city

Wiklund, H. (2005). A Habermasian analysis of the deliberative democratic potential of ICT-enabled services in Swedish municipalities. *New Media & Society, 7*(5), 701–723. doi:10.1177/1461444805056013

Wild, A., & Marshall, R. (1999). Participatory practice in the context of local agenda 21: A case study evaluation of experience in three English local authorities. *Sustainable Development, 7*(3), 151–162. doi:10.1002/(SICI)1099-1719(199908)7:3<151::AID-SD111>3.0.CO;2-0

Wilhelm, A. G. (2000). *Democracy in the Digital Age: Challenges to Political Life in Cyberspace.* London: Routledge.

Williams, C. B., & Gulati, G. J. (2006, September). *The Evolution of Online Campaigning in Congressional Elections, 2000-2004.* Paper presented at the 102nd Annual Meeting of the American Political Science Association, Philadelphia, Pennsylvania.

Williams, C. B., Aylesworth, A., & Chapman, K. J. (2002). The 2002 e-campaign for U.S. Senate. *Journal of Political Marketing, 1*(4), 39–63. doi:10.1300/J199v01n04_03

Winner, L. (1978). *Autonomous Technology: Technics-out-of-Control as a theme in Political Thought.* Cambridge, MA: The MIT Press.

Winner, L. (2005). Technological euphoria and contemporary citizenship. *Techné: Research in Philosophy and Technology, 9*(1), 1–8.

Wolf, G. (2004). How the Internet Invented Howard Dean. *Wired! Magazine*. Retrieved April, 18th, 2008, from http://www.wired.com/wired/archive/12.01/dean.html

Wolin, S. (1996). Fugitive Democracy. In Benhabib, S. (Ed.), *Democracy and Difference: Contesting the Boundaries of the Political* (pp. 31–45). Princeton, NJ: Princeton University Press.

Wolin, S. (1996). What Revolutionary Action Means Today. In Mouffe, C. (Ed.), *Dimensions of Radical Democracy: Pluralism, Citizenship, Community* (pp. 240–253). Brooklyn, NY: Verso Press.

Wong, W., & Welch, E. (2004). Does E-Government promote accountability? A Comparative analysis of website openness and government accountability, en *Governance: An International Journal of Policy, Administrations and Institutions, 17*, No. (2).

World Bank. (2006). *Information and communications for development 2006: Global trends and policies.* Washington, DC: World Bank Publications.

World Bank. (2009). *World Bank*. Retrieved July 25, 2009, from http://web.worldbank.org/WBSITE/EXTERNAL/DATASTATISTICS/0,contentMDK:20420458~menuPK:64133156~pagePK:64133150~piPK:64133175~theSitePK:239419,00.html

Wray, S. (1998, June 17). *The Electronic Disturbance Theater and electronic civil disobedience.* Retrieved March 16, 2008, from http://www.thing.net/~rdom/ecd/EDTECD.html

Wulz, F. (1986). The concept of participation. *Design Studies, 7*(3), 153–162. doi:10.1016/0142-694X(86)90052-9

Wyld, D. C. (2007). *The Blogging Revolution: Government in the Age of Web 2.0.* Washington, DC: IBM Center for The Business of Government.

Xenakis, A., & Macintosh, A. (2004). Levels of Difficulty in Introducing e-Voting, en Traunmüller, R. (Ed.) *Electronic Government: Third International Conference, EGOV2004.* España: Springer.

Xenakis, A., & Macintosh, A. (2008). A Framework for the Analysis of Procedural Security of the e-Electoral Process. *International Journal of Public Administration, 31*, 711. doi:10.1080/01900690701690759

Xenos, M. A., & Foot, K. A. (2005). Politics as usual or politics unusual? Position-taking and dialogue on campaign Web sites in the 2002 U.S. Elections. *The Journal of Communication, 55*(1), 169–185. doi:10.1111/j.1460-2466.2005.tb02665.x

Xenos, M. A., & Moy, P. (2007). Direct and differential effects of the Internet on political and civic engagement. *The Journal of Communication, 57*, 704–718.

Yaakup, A. B., Abu Bakar, Y., & Sulaiman, S. (2004, May 10-12). Web-based GIS for collaborative planning and public participation toward better governance. In *Proceedings of the 7th International seminar on GIS for Developing Countries.* Johor Bahru

Yang, G. (2003). Weaving a green web: The internet and environmental activism in China [Electronic version]. *China Environment Series, 6*, 89-93. Retrieved March 6, 2008, from http://wwics.si.edu/topics/pubs/greenweb.pdf

Yao, Y., & Murphy, L. (2007). Remote electronic voting systems: An exploration of voters' perceptions and intention to use. *European Journal of Information Systems, 16*(2), 106–120. doi:10.1057/palgrave.ejis.3000672

Yates, D. J., McGonagle, T., & Tawileh, A. (2008). How open source software and wireless networks are transforming two cultures: An investigation in urban North America and rural Africa. *International Journal of Technology. Knowledge and Society, 4*(6), 145–157.

Yifachel, O. (1999). Planning theory at a crossroad: The third Oxford Conference. *Journal of Planning Education and Research, 18*(3), 267–270. doi:10.1177/0739456X9901800308

Yin, R. K. (2003). *Case study research: Design and methods.* Thousand Oaks, CA: Sage.

Young, A. (1993). *Lessons from the East Asian NICS: A Contrarian View.* NBER Working Paper No. 4482. Cambridge, MA: National Bureau of Economic Research.

Young, I. M. (1990). *Justice and the Politics of Difference*. Princeton, NJ: Princeton University Press.

Young, I. M. (1996). Communication and the Other: Beyond Deliberative Democracy. In Benhabib, S. (Ed.), *Democracy and Difference: Contesting the Boundaries of the Political* (pp. 120–136). Princeton, NJ: Princeton University Press.

Young, J. W. (1984). *Britain, France and the Unity of Europe 1945-1951*. Bath, UK: Leicester University Press.

Zaller, J. (1992). *The Nature and Origins of Mass Opinion*. New York: Cambridge University Press.

Zambrano, R. (2008). E-Governance and Development: Service Delivery to Empower the Poor. *International Journal of Electronic Government Research, 4*(2), 1–11.

Zelko, F. (2006). The origins of postwar environmental protest in the United States. In Mauch, C., Stoltzfus, N., & Weiner, D. R. (Eds.), *Shades of green: Environmental activism around the globe* (pp. 13–40). Boulder, CO: Rowman & Littlefield Publishers, Inc.

Zhao, H., Kim, S., Shu, T., & Du, J. (2007). Social institutional explanations of global Internet diffusion: A cross-country analysis. *Journal of Global Information Management, 15*(2), 28–55.

Ziccardi, A. (2004a). *Claves para el análisis de la participación ciudadana y las políticas sociales en el espacio local, en Ziccardi, A. (Coord.) Participación ciudadana y políticas sociales en el ámbito local*. México: UNAM-IIS.

Ziccardi, A. (2004b). *Espacios e instrumentos de participación ciudadana para las políticas sociales del ámbito local, en Ziccardi, A. (Coord.) Participación ciudadana y políticas sociales en el ámbito local*. México: UNAM-IIS.

Zook, M., Dodge, M., Aoyama, Y., & Townsend, A. (2004). *"New Digital Geographies: Information, Communication and Place". Geography and Technology*. The Netherlands: Kluwer Academic Publishers.

About the Contributors

Christopher G. Reddick is an associate professor and chair of the Department of Public Administration at the University of Texas at San Antonio. Reddick's research and teaching interests are in public administration and e-government. Reddick recently edited and authored two books—*Handbook of Research on Strategies for Local E-Government Adoption and Implementation: Comparative Studies, and Homeland Security Preparedness and Information Systems: Strategies for Managing Public Policy.*

* * *

Dr. Stephen K. Aikins is a faculty member in the Department of Government and International Affairs. He holds graduate degrees in Public Administration, Information Systems Management and Business Administration. He is a Certified Public Accountant, a Certified Information Systems Auditor and a Certified Business Manager. He has published in the areas of information security and e-government. His research interests include risk management policy, government auditing and public economics.

Jason Allen is a Finance Officer serving in the Army currently stationed in Germany. He has served one tour in Afghanistan as a financial advisor to the Afghan National Police. He has a Bachelor of Science degree in Management Information Systems from Southern Illinois University - Edwardsville and a Master's of Business Administration from Arizona State University. At some point in the future he would like to attain a Doctorate, Juris Doctorate, or Master of Laws and teach at a college or university or practice law. His hobbies include staying active by playing soccer and golf, and outdoor activities such as camping, hiking, and traveling.

Dr Leonidas Anthopoulos studied computer science at Aristotle University of Thessaloniki, Greece. At his previous job positions, as an Expert Counselor at the Hellenic Ministry of Foreign Affairs in e-Government and e-Diplomacy areas, as an IT researcher and manager at the Research Committee of the Aristotle University of Thessaloniki (Greece), Municipality of Trikala (Greece), Administration of Secondary Education of Trikala (Greece) and Information Society S.A. (Greece), he designed and supervised multiple major IT projects. Currently, Dr Leonidas Anthopoulos is an Assistant Professor at the Project Management Department of the Technological Education Institute of Larissa, School of Business and Economics, Project Management Department (Greece). He is the author of several articles published on prestigious scientific journals, books and international conferences. His research interests concern, among others, e-Government, Enterprise Architecture, Social Networks, etc. He is also a member of evaluator committees for the Greek General Secretariat of R&D and for the Greek Information Society.

Diego Barría is a PhD Researcher at the Department of Latin American Studies of Leiden University, where he is writing a dissertation on public sector change in Chile, between 1880 and 1931. He previously has published on topics such as e-government in Chile, Union participation in policy-making processes in Latin America, and administrative reforms in historical perspective. E-Mail: barriatraverso@vtr.net

Dr. Jody C Baumgartner is an assistant professor of political science at East Carolina University. He received his Ph.D. in political science from Miami University in 1998, specializing in the study of campaigns and elections. He has several books to his credit, including *Modern Presidential Electioneering: An Organizational and Comparative Approach* (Praeger, 2000); *Checking Executive Power* (Praeger, 2003), co-edited with Naoko Kada; *The American Vice Presidency Reconsidered* (Praeger, 2006); *Conventional Wisdom and American Elections: Exploding Myths, Exploring Misconceptions* (Rowman & Littlefield, 2007), written with Peter Francia; and, *Laughing Matters: Humor and American Politics in the Media Age* (Routeledge, 2007), co-edited with Jonathan Morris. He has also written or collaborated on two dozen articles and book chapters on political humor, the vice presidency, and other subjects.

Prof. Dr. V.J.J.M. Bekkers (1963) is professor of public administration at Erasmus University Rotterdam. He holds the chair on the empirical study of public policy and public policy processes. He is also academic director of the Center of Public Innovation. Furthermore he is research director of the department of public administration. .He studied political science and public administration at Nijmegen University where he has got his degree with honors (1987). He obtained his Ph.D. from Tilburg University. His research interests are related to the introduction and use of new information and communication technologies in the policy processes within public administration and the innovation challenges which emerge in its slipstream.

Douglas B. Bock is a Professor in the Computer Management and Information Systems department at Southern Illinois University Edwardsville. He received his B.S. in Management, MBA, and Ph.D. in the Management of Information Systems from Indiana University. His teaching responsibilities include database administration and .NET programming. His primary research emphasis is in the area of data modeling, software metrics, and system implementation issues. His most recent textbooks, Oracle SQL and SQL for SQL Server are both published by Pearson Education/Prentice-Hall. He has published and presented over 60 articles in various information systems journals and conferences. He is a Microsoft Certified Solution Developer for .NET technology.

Salah Brahimi, Grey Matter International Ltd, will be a keynote speaker at the upcoming Gulf Petroleum Association annual conference. In addition, he is often invited to speak in the area of Emergency Management and Preparedness, particularly with regard to the economic impact of incidents and business continuity. Mr. Brahimi has also just received a mandate from SABIC (Saudi Arabia's Government backed petrochemicals giant) to advise on restructuring its massive private equity acquisitions special situations portfolios and to advise on foreign currency transactional policies. In January he served as the advisor to the Saudi G-20 preparatory Committee on the global financial crisis and has been involve in these issues from his time at the World Bank.

Axel Bruns is a Chief Investigator in the ARC Centre of Excellence for Creative Industries and Innovation (CCi) and an Associate Professor in the Creative Industries Faculty at Queensland University of Technology in Brisbane, Australia. He is the author of *Blogs, Wikipedia, Second Life and Beyond: From Production to Produsage* (2008) and *Gatewatching: Collaborative Online News Production* (2005), and the editor of *Uses of Blogs* with Joanne Jacobs (2006; all released by Peter Lang, New York). He blogs about user-led content creation at produsage.org, contributes to the gatewatching.org group blog on citizen journalism and e-democracy with Jason Wilson and Barry Saunders, and more information on his research can be found on his Website at snurb.info. Bruns is General Editor of *M/C – Media and Culture* (www.media-culture.org.au).

Jason G. Caudill holds a bachelor's degree in Business, an MBA, and a PhD in Instructional Technology from the University of Tennessee. Jason currently serves as an Assistant Professor of Business Administration at Carson-Newman College, where he teaches in the areas of Management Information Systems and Management. Jason's primary research interests are in the application of technology for online learning, the management of technology, and open source software. Jason holds memberships in multiple honor societies, including The Honor Society of Phi Kappa Phi and Sigma Xi, the Scientific Research Society. Outside of work Jason enjoys the outdoors, woodworking, and college football and basketball.

Hee Jung Cho is a research fellow at the Social Science Research, Sogang University. She received Ph. D. in political science from Sogang University and worked as an e-voting policy making team member of the National Election Commission of Korea. She conducts research in the areas of political use of technology and network democracy such as e-voting and e-campaign. She is a member of the Korean Political Science Association. She has published information technology and politics related articles in several venues including *Korean Political Science Review*.

Ms. Isabel A. Cole, M.I.S., is a librarian and document specialist who has worked at the Internet Public Library and the Indiana State Library, as well as the Software Patent Institute. Her Master's degree concentration was Library Science, which included study of referencing and cataloging. Her Master of Information Science degree is from the University of Michigan.

Dr. Roland J. Cole, J. D., Ph.D, is a lawyer and policy analyst who has worked for several think tanks and several law firms and taught in Schools of Public Policy, Business, and Law at three major universities – the University of Washington, the University of Michigan, and Indiana University. He was the co-founder and first president of the international Association of Personal Computer User Groups and was for many years the Executive Director of the Software Patent Institute. He also serves as Director of Technology Policy for the Sagamore Institute for Policy Research and a subcontractor to Thomas P. Miller & Associates. His degrees are from Harvard University.

Mark Deakin is Director of the Centre for Learning Communities, Reader and Teaching Fellow in the School of Engineering & the Built Environment, Edinburgh Napier University. His research is inter-disciplinary, cutting across academic, scientific and technical boundaries, working thematically to uncover what ICT-related actions contribute to sustainable urban development. This work has involved him developing ICT-related policies mapping out the social needs and informational requirements of urban sustainability and eGovernance challenges the digitisation of communication technologies pose.

Dennis de Kool has studied public administration at the Erasmus University Rotterdam in the Netherlands. He finished his PhD thesis in 2007. His thesis was focused on the impacts of monitors on intergovernmental relationships. Currently he is working as a researcher at the Center for Public Innovation. One of his recent research activities is a study about the impacts of GIS-based monitors on learning processes within public organizations.

Thomas Doellman was a student at Southern Illinois University Edwardsville at the time of this research. He completed his B.S., major in Computer Management Information Systems from the School of Business. He is currently completing graduate studies at the University of Florida in Gainesville, Florida.

Stephen Fariñas is a student at Florida International University studying for his Ph.D. in Public Management. His dissertation research will focus on creating a hybrid housing model by combining components from ecovillages and community land trusts (CLTs). The idea is to combine the environmental and social sustainability of ecovillages with the affordability and social sustainability of CLTs to create truly sustainable and affordable housing. Further research will be conducted in two areas. The first area will focus on which governance structure(s) will function best in this new hybrid housing model. The second area will focus on the impact of community residents on local housing and land policy.

José Rodrigues Filho is an associate professor of Management Information Systems at the Universidade Federal da Paraíba, Brazil. He was Takemi Fellow at Harvard University and completed his postdoctoral studies at the Johns Hopkins University (School of Public Health). He completed his doctoral studies at the University of Manchester, England. He was visiting professor at Acadia University and Dalhousie University (Canada), and associate professor at the Universidade Federal de Pernambuco, Brazil. His areas of interests include management information systems, specially, health information, nursing information and hospital information systems, in addition to e-government and e-voting.

Prof. Panos Fitsilis studied computer engineering at Patras University, Greece. He received his PhD (1995) in Software Engineering. He worked, as software engineer and as business unit manager at large software development companies, and he was responsible for the development, deployment and operation of a number of prestigious IT systems for European Commission. Since 2003 he has been Professor at Technological Education Institute of Larissa, School of Business and Economics, Project Management Department. Currently, Prof. Panos Fitsilis is Head of Project Management Department and Deputy Director at Technological Research Center of Thessalia, Greece. He is the author of three books and author of many articles published on scientific journals and magazines. Further, he was member of the development team of Hellenic Standard on managerial capability of public organization, ELOT -1429. His research interests include: Project Management, Software Engineering, e-Government Systems, Business Process Reengineering, etc.

J. Ramon Gil-Garcia is an Assistant Professor in the Department of Public Administration and the Director of the Data Center for Applied Research in Social Sciences at *Centro de Investigación y Docencia Económicas (CIDE)* in Mexico City. Currently, he is a Research Fellow at the Center for Technology in Government, University at Albany, State University of New York (SUNY) and a Faculty Affiliate at the National Center for Digital Government, University of Massachusetts Amherst. Dr. Gil-

Garcia is the author or co-author of articles in prestigious academic journals such as *The International Public Management Journal, Government Information Quarterly, Journal of the American Society for Information Science and Technology*, and *European Journal of Information Systems*, among others. His research interests include collaborative electronic government, inter-organizational information integration, adoption and implementation of emergent technologies, digital divide policies, new public management, public policy evaluation, and multi-method research approaches.

Girish J. "Jeff" Gulati is an Assistant Professor of Political Science at Bentley University who earned his Ph.D. from the University of Virginia. Dr. Gulati's research areas are telecommunications policy, e-government, political communication & the news media, campaigns & elections, and representation in theory and practice. Additionally he has designed studies assessing higher education programs and policies, election polls, and surveys for non-profits, interest groups and local governments. His recent work on new media and e-government has appeared in *Harvard International Journal of Press/Politics, Social Science Computer Review, Politicking Online, The Year of Obama* and other various academic journals, edited volumes, and conference proceedings. Dr. Gulati also serves on the editorial boards of the *Journal of Information Technology & Politics* and *Journal of Political Marketing*.

Marvine Hamner is an Assistant Professor at George Washington University in Washington, DC, USA. Dr. Hamner is also a co-founder of a women-owned small business, LeaTech LLC. Dr. Hamner has over 20 years experience working and managing a variety of projects from research grants to multi-million dollar commercial programs and holds patents in the U.S. as well as several other countries. Dr. Hamner is an Associate Editor for the *Journal of Homeland Security and Emergency Management*. In addition, she reviews manuscripts for the Institute of Physics, *Measurement Science and Technology Journal, Computers and Industrial Engineering*, as well as *Personality and Individual Differences*. Dr. Hamner is currently an Associate Fellow with the American Institute of Aeronautics and Astronautics and a member of the International Association of Emergency Managers. She is a member of the MIT Club of Washington, the Women's Business Center in Washington, D.C., and the Philosophical Society of D.C.

Pekka Huovila is a Chief Research Scientist at VTT Technical Research Centre of Finland. His research interests focus on performance and sustainability of the built environment and decision support tools for the sustainable knowledge society. Pekka has contributed to number of international research projects to public and private clients, such as Perfection, SURE, CREDIT, ManuBuild, Stand-Inn, IW-LORB, Value4Network, Asia Pro Eco, Intelcities, Mosaic, Tissue, PeBBu, Intelcity, Neskey, Roadcon, CRISP and Bequest. He acts also as a Visiting Professor at the University of Salford, UK.

Sungsoo Hwang is an assistant professor at the Department of Public Administration, Yeungnam University in Daegu, Korea. He formerly taught at the Grand Valley State University, MI, USA. He received his Ph.D. in public affairs from the University of Pittsburgh and worked as a project team member for the Pittsburgh Neighborhood and Community Information System. He conducts research in the areas of collaborative governance with an emphasis on utilizing information technology such as Geographical Information Systems. He is a member of International Working Group on Online Consultation and Public Policy Making, funded by National Science Foundation. He has published information technology related articles in several venues including *Government Information Quarterly*.

Jennifer Kurtz, MBA, a technology and economic development consultant currently focused on information security and privacy, led Indiana's statewide broadband infrastructure initiative as Indiana's eCommerce Director. The *Indiana Interconnect* report and conference highlighted opportunities for improving Indiana's technology-based economic development capacity, showcased community success stories, and influenced improved broadband deployment in Indiana. She also wrote the Governor's Technology Roundtable report and served on the 2003/2004 eGov Task Force that helped Indiana achieve a #4 ranking for eGov services. In addition, she built and managed the telecommunications infrastructure for Delco Remy International and has held appointments at Purdue and Ball State Universities.

Brian Lake is a PhD researcher in the department of Computer Science and Information Systems at the University of Limerick, Ireland. A political science graduate of Memorial University of Newfoundland, Canada, Brian also holds a Masters by Research in Politics from Acadia University, Nova Scotia, Canada, specialising in democratisation and e-government. He currently serves as a learning technologist for universities in the United Kingdom, investigating the social impact of learning technologies. His research interests include the politics of free software in European Union decision-making – operationalised via "open source" software communities as political institutions. As a method of applying this interest practically, Brian undertakes qualitative text-analysis within a framework of critical discourse theory.

Mark Liptrott is a University Lecturer in Information Systems within the Business School at Edge Hill University and his research has focussed on the public policy process and the diffusion of e-voting in the UK. Mark has been a regular contributor to the Electronic Journal of E-Government and presented for the last three years at the European Conference of E Government. His research has been published in various journals including the UK Government Computing News Magazine. He is an associate editor for the Journal of Information Technology and Citizenship and reviews for a number of other journals. In 2009 he was an invited speaker at the International Conference on e-Government and e-Governance, in Ankara, Turkey.

Patrizia Lombardi* is a leading expert in the use of environmental assessment methods and an established figure in the field of evaluating sustainable development for over 20 years. She has coordinated or served as lead partner in several Pan-European Projects on urban sustainability and Information Technologies, including EU BEQUEST, INTELCITY Roadmap, IP INTELCITIES, S.U.R.Pr.I.S.E. Interreg III C, ISAAC and PERFECTION. She has published widely in the field and was co-author of the book 'Evaluating Sustainable Development in the Built Environment' which is being issued to the Universities of the G8 countries at their Summit in Turin in May 2009.

Fernando Gonzalez Miranda is an Adviser to the Secretary of Administration at *Universidad Autónoma del Estado de México (UAEM)* in the city of Toluca, State of México. He is also working for the Organization and Administrative Development Direction in the same institution. He has a Masters degree on Public Administration and Policy from *Centro de Investigación y Docencia Económicas (CIDE)*. His research interests include democratic electronic government, digital divide policies, governance, and policy networks.

Rebecca Moody has studied political science at the University of Leiden in the Netherlands. Currently she is working at the Erasmus University in Rotterdam on her PhD thesis on the influence of Geographical Information Systems on agenda-setting and policy design. Additionally she has participated in a project dealing with micro mobilization by traditional and new media.

Eduardo Araya Moreno is Professor at the Faculty of Economics and Management Sciences of the University of Valparaíso, Chile. He is currently writing a PhD dissertation on ICT using by political parties in Chile, Costa Rica and Uruguay. He has published papers on State features in the Informational Society, features of personnel training programs in topics related to e-government, and e-government in Chile. E-Mail: edarmo@yahoo.com

Bekir Parlak is a professor in the Department of Public Administration at the University of Uludag in Turkey. He received his Ph. D. degree in Province Administration and Local Governments from the University of Cumhuriyet. His research interests are e-government, local e-government, theory of democracy, administrative history. He teaches courses on Public Administration, Local Governments, Governance and E-Government, Comparative Government Systems, Personnel Management, Modern Management Techniques, Administrative Reforms in Turkey and Turkish Administrative History.

Anne Powell is an Associate Professor in the Computer Management and Information Systems department at Southern Illinois University Edwardsville. She received both her MBA and Ph.D. in the Management of Information Systems from Indiana University. She has ten years corporate experience that includes work as a Systems Engineer for EDS Corporation and as programmer, systems analyst and business analyst for American United Life Insurance Company in Indianapolis. Her primary teaching responsibilities are the Systems Analysis and Design course series. Her research specializations include virtual teams and the impact of new technology on individuals, teams, and organizations. Her work has been presented at numerous conferences and has been published in numerous Information Systems academic journals.

Michael Romano is currently a doctoral student in the Department of Political Science at Western Michigan University. His current research interests focus on the expanding role of the media in politics, focusing specifically on how changes in information technology affected campaigns and elections. He also is interested how we learn political values from and how our political values are reflected in popular culture. Tentatively his dissertation will focus on the online/offline dichotomy of political participation during campaigns and how these two types of participation overlap.

Peter Salhofer is holding a professorship in computer science at FH JOANNEUM, University of Applied Sciences, Graz, Austria. Before he joined FH JOANNEUM he was working for the municipality of the City of Graz where he was responsible for the introduction of New Public Management methods as well as for other modernization projects. His main research interests currently lie in the adaption and integration of semantic technologies into system engineering practices with a strong connection to e-Government. He is the author of several publications in this field and also managed several software development projects aiming at improved Government-to-Citizen interaction.

Zahid Sobaci received his Ph.D. in public administration at Uludag University. He is currently a research assistant at Department of Public Administration, Uludag University. Zahid Sobaci has published several articles. His research topics include administrative reform, e-government, new public management.

Hyunjin Seo is a Ph.D. candidate and adjunct professor at the S.I. Newhouse School of Public Communications, Syracuse University. Seo holds an M.A. in journalism from the University of Missouri-Columbia. Her research interests include international communications, public diplomacy, public relations, and new media. Her research and writing has generated top paper awards at international conferences and has been published in international journals such as *Asian Journal of Communication*, *International Journal of Public Opinion Research*, and *Public Relations Review*. Her dissertation that aims to establish and test a theory explaining how national image is formed in the era of information technology and social networking. Seo has worked as both a journalist and a public relations consultant in the U.S. and South Korea. She was a diplomatic correspondent for a leading English-language newspaper in South Korea and has assisted U.S. and Korea-based nongovernmental organizations with their public relations campaigns.

Bernd Stadlhofer is a research assistant for software engineering, databases and information systems at FH JOANNEUM, University of Applied Sciences, Graz, Austria. His main research interests currently lie in the adaption and integration of semantic technologies into system engineering practices with a strong connection to e-Government. He participated in several publications in this field.

Dr Minna Sunikka-Blank is a registered architect and a Lecturer at the Department of Architecture in the University of Cambridge and Fellow in Architecture at Churchill College in Cambridge. Her research focuses on improving policies for energy efficiency in the European housing stock. She has worked on Environmental Impact Assessment, the management of environmental properties in real estate management, sustainable energy supply in urban renewal projects and comparative policy analysis in Finland, the UK and in the Netherlands and published several books and research articles on the subject.

Dr. Doaa Taha is an independent consultant in Washington, DC in the areas of Business Management and Emergency Management. Dr. Taha earned her doctorate through George Washington University's Institute for Crisis, Disaster and Risk Management. Her research in Emergency Management is highly regarded. She has several articles on Emergency Management in the area of Business Continuity and Continuity of Operations.

Anas Tawileh is a researcher and consultant for Information and Communication Technology for Development (ICT4D). Anas worked on many projects to bring technology to developing countries and has designed, developed and delivered several training and capacity building programs and workshops. He is currently working as consultant for the International Development Research Centre's ICT4D project in the Middle East. His experience also includes more than seven years of working with international organizations including the European Commission, the Open Society Institute and the Association for Progressive Communications.

Stuart Thorson is professor of international relations and political science and is the Donald P. and Margaret Curry Gregg Professor at the Maxwell School of Syracuse University. Thorson has co-edited two books on conflict resolution and published over 40 articles and book chapters about foreign policy, decision-making, computer modeling, and democratic theory. His current research interests are the uses of information technology in support of governance and the role of science in diplomacy. Thorson directs the Maxwell School's integrated information technology research collaboration with Kim Chaek University of Technology (Democratic People's Republic of Korea) and is co-director of Syracuse University's Regional Scholars and Leaders Seminar initiative. He is a founding member of the National Committee on North Korea (U.S.), a co-founder of the U.S. - DPRK Scientific Engagement Consortium, and a board member of the Korea Society.

Gerald Tretter is a research assistant for software engineering, databases and information systems at FH JOANNEUM, University of Applied Sciences, Graz, Austria. His main research interests currently lie in the adaption and integration of semantic technologies into system engineering practices with a strong connection to e-Government. He participated in several publications in this field.

Christine B. Williams, a Professor of Government in the Global Studies Department at Bentley University, received her M.A. and Ph.D. degrees from Indiana University. Dr. Williams currently serves as the managing editor, North America for the *Journal of Political Marketing*, as Associate Editor and on the senior Editorial Board of the *Journal of Information Technology andPolitics* and on the International Advisory Board of the *International Journal of E-Politics*. Her research area is political communication, with emphasis on new and emerging technologies. Dr. Williams is a member of a National Science Foundation funded project team studying design issues for public safety response management systems. Her work has appeared in academic journals, trade and professional association publications, as well as news media outlets worldwide

Jason Wilson is a Lecturer in Digital Communications in the School of Social Sciences, Media and Communication at the University of Wollongong, Australia. His research interests include digital game cultures, citizen journalism and the online public sphere, mobile media and new media history. He has previously held academic appointments at the University of Bedfordshire (UK) and in the Creative Industries Faculty at Queensland University of Technology. Along with his record as a researcher, Jason has experience as a new media practitioner. He was the project manager and chief editor of YouDecide2007, a citizen journalism service run during the 2007 Federal Election. He was also E-Democracy Director at online campaigning organisation GetUp!, where he project-managed the Project Democracy service.

David Yates is an Assistant Professor of Computer Information Systems at Bentley University. David's research areas include computer networking, data communications, sensor networks, embedded systems, operating systems, and computer architecture. Before joining Bentley, David held research and academic positions at the University of Massachusetts and Boston University. His work has been published and presented at international symposiums and conferences, and appeared in refereed journals. In the corporate arena, he was a co-founder and vice president of software development at InfoLibria – a startup that grew to become a leading provider of hardware and software for building content distribution and delivery networks before it was acquired. With various colleagues, he holds several U.S.

patents for processes and systems related to computer networking, content management, and mobile computing. He holds a PhD and MSc from the University of Massachusetts. He also holds a BSc from Tufts University.

Index